Not All Diamonds and Rosé

Not All Diamonds and Rosé

The Inside Story of the Real Housewives
from the People Who Lived It

 DAVE QUINN

Andy Cohen Books
Henry Holt and Company
New York

Andy Cohen Books
Henry Holt and Company
Publishers since 1866
120 Broadway
New York, New York 10271
www.henryholt.com

Andy Cohen Books® and ▮ ® are registered trademarks of Macmillan Publishing
Group, LLC.

Library of Congress Cataloging-in-Publication data is available.

ISBN: 9781250765789

Our books may be purchased in bulk for promotional, educational, or business use.
Please contact your local bookseller or the Macmillan Corporate and Premium
Sales Department at (800) 221-7945, extension 5442, or by e-mail at
MacmillanSpecialMarkets@macmillan.com.

First Edition 2021

Designed by Meryl Sussman Levavi

Printed in the United States of America

10 9 8 7 6 5 4 3 2 1

When you haven't forgiven those who've hurt you, you turn back against your future. When you do forgive, you start walking forward.

—*Tyler Perry*

Say it, forget it. Write it, regret it.

—*Dorinda Medley*

Contents

But Now We Said It:
A Who's Who of Cast, Network Executives, and Production
xi

Part I
"Meet the Wives"
The Real Housewives of Orange County
1

Part II
"Bite of the Apple"
The Real Housewives of New York City
101

Part III
"Just Peachy"
The Real Housewives of Atlanta
171

Part IV
"Flipping the Table"
The Real Housewives of New Jersey
225

Part V
"Capitol Wives"
The Real Housewives of D.C.
303

Part VI
"Shine of a Diamond"
The Real Housewives of Beverly Hills
309

Part VII
"Ocean Views"
The Real Housewives of Miami
375

Part VIII
"Chesapeake Babes"
The Real Housewives of Potomac
391

Part IX
"Cowgirl Country"
The Real Housewives of Dallas
423

The Tagline Catalog
451

Author's Note
467

Acknowledgments
469

Photograph Credits
471

But Now We Said It

A Who's Who of Cast, Network Executives, and Production

Cast

Mary Schmidt Amons: Housewife, *Real Housewives of D.C.*

Teresa Aprea: Housewife, *Real Housewives of New Jersey* (Season 6)

Taylor Armstrong: Housewife, *Real Housewives of Beverly Hills* (Seasons 1–3)

Jennifer Aydin: Housewife, *Real Housewives of New Jersey* (Season 9–Present)

Cynthia Bailey: Housewife, *Real Housewives of Atlanta* (Season 3–Present)

Cindy Barshop: Housewife, *Real Housewives of New York City* (Season 4)

Chris Bassett: Househusband, *Real Housewives of Potomac* (Season 3–Present)

Shannon Storms Beador: Housewife, *Real Housewives of Orange County* (Season 9–Present)

Garcelle Beauvais: Housewife, *Real Housewives of Beverly Hills* (Season 10–Present)

Alexis Bellino: Housewife, *Real Housewives of Orange County* (Seasons 5–8)

Greg Bennett: Guest, *Real Housewives of New Jersey*

Kelly Killoren Bensimon: Housewife, *Real Housewives of New York City* (Seasons 2–4)

Lea Black: Housewife, *Real Housewives of Miami* (Seasons 1–3)

Kary Brittingham: Housewife, *Real Housewives of Dallas* (Season 4–Present)

Gizelle Bryant: Housewife, *Real Housewives of Potomac* (Season 1–Present)

Kandi Burruss: Housewife, *Real Housewives of Atlanta* (Season 2–Present)

Dolores Catania: Housewife, *Real Housewives of New Jersey* (Season 7–Present)

Bobby Ciasulli: Guest, *Real Housewives of New Jersey* (Season 6)

Lynne Curtin: Housewife, *Real Housewives of Orange County* (Seasons 4–5)

Raquel Curtin: Daughter, *Real Housewives of Orange County* (Seasons 4–5)

Ashley Darby: Housewife, *Real Housewives of Potomac* (Season 1–Present)

Eileen Davidson: Housewife, *Real Housewives of Beverly Hills* (Seasons 5–7)

Jo De La Rosa: Housewife, *Real Housewives of Orange County* (Seasons 1–2)

Luann de Lesseps: Housewife, *Real Housewives of New York City* (Seasons 1–5, 7–Present); Friend (Season 6)

Adriana de Moura: Housewife, *Real Housewives of Miami* (Seasons 1–3)

Kim DePaola: Guest, *Real Housewives of New Jersey* (Seasons 2–5, 7–9)

Cary Deuber: Housewife, *Real Housewives of Dallas* (Seasons 1–3); Friend (Season 4)

Mark Deuber: Househusband, *Real Housewives of Dallas* (Seasons 1–3)

Shamari DeVoe: Housewife, *Real Housewives of Atlanta* (Season 11)

Candiace Dillard Bassett: Housewife, *Real Housewives of Potomac* (Season 3–Present)

Robyn Dixon: Housewife, *Real Housewives of Potomac* (Season 1–Present)

Kelly Dodd: Housewife, *Real Housewives of Orange County* (Season 11–Present)

Aviva Drescher: Housewife, *Real Housewives of New York City* (Seasons 5–6)

Heather Dubrow: Housewife, *Real Housewives of Orange County* (Seasons 7–11)

Alexia Echevarria: Housewife, *Real Housewives of Miami* (Seasons 1, 3); Friend (Season 2)

Kathryn Edwards: Housewife, *Real Housewives of Beverly Hills* (Season 6)

Siggy Flicker: Housewife, *Real Housewives of New Jersey* (Seasons 7–8)

Quinn Fry: Housewife, *Real Housewives of Orange County* (Season 3)

Carlton Gebbia: Housewife, *Real Housewives of Beverly Hills* (Season 4)

Erika Girardi: Housewife, *Real Housewives of Beverly Hills* (Season 6–Present)

Teresa Giudice: Housewife, *Real Housewives of New Jersey* (Season 1–Present)

Brandi Glanville: Friend, *Real Housewives of Beverly Hills* (Season 2); Housewife (Seasons 3–5)

Jackie Goldschneider: Housewife, *Real Housewives of New Jersey* (Season 9–Present)

Melissa Gorga: Housewife, *Real Housewives of New Jersey* (Season 3–Present)

Camille Grammer: Housewife, *Real Housewives of Beverly Hills* (Seasons 1–2); Friend (Seasons 3, 8–9)

Kim Granatell: Guest, *Real Housewives of New Jersey* (Seasons 2–3)

Vicki Gunvalson: Housewife, *Real Housewives of Orange County* (Seasons 1–13); Friend (Season 14)

Yolanda Hadid: Housewife, *Real Housewives of Beverly Hills* (Seasons 3–6)

Marlo Hampton: Guest, *Real Housewives of Atlanta* (Seasons 4, 6, 8–9); Friend (Season 10–Present)

Tiffany Hendra: Housewife, *Real Housewives of Dallas* (Season 1)

Lisa Hochstein: Housewife, *Real Housewives of Miami* (Seasons 2–3)

Stephanie Hollman: Housewife, *Real Housewives of Dallas* (Season 1–Present)

Karen Huger: Housewife, *Real Housewives of Potomac* (Season 1–Present)

Charrisse Jackson-Jordan: Housewife, *Real Housewives of Potomac* (Seasons 1–2); Friend (Season 3)

Claudia Jordan: Housewife, *Real Housewives of Atlanta* (Season 7)

Margaret Josephs: Housewife, *Real Housewives of New Jersey* (Season 8–Present)

Tamra Judge: Housewife, *Real Housewives of Orange County* (Seasons 3–14)

Barbara Kavovit: Friend, *Real Housewives of New York City* (Season 11)

Dorit Kemsley: Housewife, *Real Housewives of Beverly Hills* (Season 7–Present)

Jeana Keough: Housewife, *Real Housewives of Orange County* (Seasons 1–5); Friend (Season 6)

Meghan King: Housewife, *Real Housewives of Orange County* (Seasons 10–12)

Gina Kirschenheiter: Housewife, *Real Housewives of Orange County* (Seasons 13–Present)

Tammy Knickerbocker: Housewife, *Real Housewives of Orange County* (Seasons 2–3)

Jacqueline Laurita: Housewife, *Real Housewives of New Jersey* (Seasons 1–5, 7)

LeeAnne Locken: Housewife, *Real Housewives of Dallas* (Seasons 1–4)

Adrienne Maloof: Housewife, *Real Housewives of Beverly Hills* (Seasons 1–3)

Caroline Manzo: Housewife, *Real Housewives of New Jersey* (Seasons 1–5)

Dina Manzo: Housewife, *Real Housewives of New Jersey* (Seasons 1–2, 6)

Amber Marchese: Housewife, *Real Housewives of New Jersey* (Season 6)

Jim Marchese: Househusband, *Real Housewives of New Jersey* (Season 6)

Eva Marcille: Friend, *Real Housewives of Atlanta* (Season 10); Housewife (Seasons 11–12)

Lydia McLaughlin: Housewife, *Real Housewives of Orange County* (Seasons 8, 12)

Leah McSweeney: Housewife, *Real Housewives of New York City* (Season 12–Present)

Dorinda Medley: Housewife, *Real Housewives of New York City* (Seasons 7–12)

Teddi Mellencamp Arroyave: Housewife, *Real Housewives of Beverly Hills* (Seasons 8–10)

Kenya Moore: Housewife, *Real Housewives of Atlanta* (Seasons 5–10, 12–Present)

Sonja Morgan: Housewife, *Real Housewives of New York City* (Season 3–Present)

Nicole Napolitano: Housewife, *Real Housewives of New Jersey* (Season 6)

Wendy Osefo: Housewife, *Real Housewives of Potomac* (Season 5–Present)

Marysol Patton: Housewife, *Real Housewives of Miami* (Seasons 1–2); Friend (Season 3)

Rosie Pierri: Guest, *Real Housewives of New Jersey* (Seasons 3–6); Friend (Season 7)

Larsa Pippen: Housewife, *Real Housewives of Miami* (Season 1)

Ana Quincoces: Housewife, *Real Housewives of Miami* (Season 2); Friend (Season 3)

Carole Radziwill: Housewife, *Real Housewives of New York City* (Seasons 5–10)

Marie Reyes: Friend, *Real Housewives of Dallas* (Season 1)

Cristy Rice: Housewife, *Real Housewives of Miami* (Season 1)

Kyle Richards: Housewife, *Real Housewives of Beverly Hills* (Season 1–Present)

Lisa Rinna: Housewife, *Real Housewives of Beverly Hills* (Season 5–Present)

Katie Rost: Housewife, *Real Housewives of Potomac* (Season 1); Friend (Season 4)

Lizzie Rovsek: Housewife, *Real Housewives of Orange County* (Season 9); Friend (Season 10)

Tanya Sam: Friend, *Real Housewives of Atlanta* (Seasons 11–13)

Monique Samuels: Housewife, *Real Housewives of Potomac* (Seasons 2–5)

Eden Sassoon: Friend, *Real Housewives of Beverly Hills* (Season 7)

Karent Sierra: Housewife, *Real Housewives of Miami* (Season 2)

D'Andra Simmons: Housewife, *Real Housewives of Dallas* (Season 2–Present)

Emily Simpson: Housewife, *Real Housewives of Orange County* (Season 13–Present)

Ramona Singer: Housewife, *Real Housewives of New York City* (Season 1–Present)

DeShawn Snow: Housewife, *Real Housewives of Atlanta* (Season 1)

Danielle Staub: Housewife, *Real Housewives of New Jersey* (Seasons 1–2); Friend (Seasons 8–10)

Sutton Stracke: Friend, *Real Housewives of Beverly Hills* (Season 10); Housewife (Season 11–Present)

Peggy Sulahian: Housewife, *Real Housewives of Orange County* (Season 12)

Kristen Taekman: Housewife, *Real Housewives of New York City* (Seasons 6–7)

Peggy Tanous: Housewife, *Real Housewives of Orange County* (Season 6)

Heather Thomson: Housewife, *Real Housewives of New York City* (Seasons 5–7); Friend (Season 13)

Elizabeth Lyn Vargas: Housewife, *Real Housewives of Orange County* (Season 15)

Lisa Vanderpump: Housewife, *Real Housewives of Beverly Hills* (Seasons 1–9)

Julianne "Jules" Wainstein: Housewife, *Real Housewives of New York City* (Season 8)

Kathy Wakile: Housewife, *Real Housewives of New Jersey* (Seasons 3–5); Friend (Seasons 6–7)

Kameron Westcott: Housewife, *Real Housewives of Dallas* (Season 2–Present)

Shereé Whitfield: Housewife, *Real Housewives of Atlanta* (Seasons 1–4, 9–10); Friend (Season 8)

Braunwyn Windham-Burke: Housewife, *Real Housewives of Orange County* (Season 14–Present)

Jill Zarin: Housewife, *Real Housewives of New York City* (Seasons 1–4)

Network Executives

Frances Berwick: Chairman, Entertainment Networks, NBCUniversal

Joshua Brown: Vice President, Current Production, NBCUniversal

Sezin Cavusoglu: Vice President, Current Production, Bravo

Ryan Flynn: Senior Vice President, Current Production, Bravo

Kathleen French: Senior Vice President, Current Production, Bravo; Executive Producer, *Real Housewives of Orange County* (Seasons 1–9), *Real Housewives of Beverly Hills* (Seasons 1–2), *Vanderpump Rules* (Seasons 1–2), and *Date My Ex: Jo & Slade* (among others)

Pamela Gimenez: Vice President, Current Production, Bravo
Jerry Leo: Former Executive Vice President of Program Strategy, Bravo
Shari Levine: Executive Vice President, Entertainment Content, NBCUniversal
Noah Samton: Senior Vice President, Current Production, Bravo
Rachel Smith: Executive Vice President, Development, NBCUniversal
Lauren Zalaznick: Former Executive Vice President, NBCUniversal

Production

Matt Anderson: Founding Partner of Purveyors of Pop; Executive Producer, *Real Housewives of Atlanta* (Seasons 2–3), *Real Housewives of New Jersey* (Seasons 3–4), *Real Housewives of New York City* (Seasons 3–4), *Real Housewives of Miami* (Seasons 2–3), and *Bethenny Ever After* (among others)

Alex Baskin: President of Evolution Media; Executive Producer, *Real Housewives of Orange County* (Season 9–Present), *Real Housewives of Beverly Hills* (Season 1–Present), *Vanderpump Rules* (Season 1–Present), *Date My Ex: Jo & Slade*, and *Tamra's OC Wedding* (among others)

Rich Bye: Founder and President, Goodbye Pictures; Executive Producer, *Real Housewives of Dallas* (Season 1–Present)

Andy Cohen: Executive Producer, *Real Housewives* franchise; Host, *Watch What Happens Live with Andy Cohen*

Chris Cullen: Executive Producer, *Real Housewives of Beverly Hills* (Season 1–Present) and *Real Housewives of Orange County* (Seasons 7–9)

Lucilla D'Agostino: Executive Vice President of Programming and Founding Partner, Sirens Media; Executive Producer, *Real Housewives of New Jersey* (Seasons 1–10)

Scott Dunlop: Original Producer, *Real Housewives of Orange County* (Season 1)

Lauren Eskelin: Executive Vice President of Programming, Truly Original; Executive Producer, *Real Housewives of Atlanta* (Season 1–Present), *Real Housewives of Potomac* (Season 1–Present), *Don't Be Tardy* (Season 1–Present), *I Dream of NeNe: The Wedding*, *Don't Be Tardy for the Wedding*, *Real Housewives of Atlanta: Kandi's Wedding*, *Real Housewives of Atlanta: Kandi's Ski Trip*, *Real Housewives of Atlanta: Porsha's Having a Baby*, and *Xscape: Still Kickin' It* (among others)

Bill Fritz: Executive Producer, *Real Housewives of Orange County* (Seasons 5–10), and *Real Housewives of Beverly Hills* (Seasons 1–2, 8, 10–Present)

Nate Green: Founding Partner, Purveyors of Pop; Executive Producer, *Real Housewives of Atlanta* (Seasons 2–3), *Real Housewives of New Jersey* (Seasons 3–4), *Real Housewives of New York City* (Seasons 3–4), *Real Housewives of Miami* (Seasons 2–3), and *Bethenny Ever After*

Abby Greensfelder: Cofounder, Half Yard Productions; Executive Producer, *Real Housewives of D.C.*

Lorraine Haughton-Lawson: Senior Vice President of Programming, Truly

Original; Executive Producer, *Real Housewives of Atlanta* (Season 4–Present), *Real Housewives of Potomac* (Season 1–Present), *Real Housewives of Atlanta: Kandi's Wedding, Real Housewives of Atlanta: Kandi's Ski Trip, Real Housewives of Atlanta: Porsha's Having a Baby,* and *Xscape: Still Kickin' It* (among others)

Thomas Kelly: Executive Producer, *Real Housewives of Orange County* (Seasons 14–15), *Real Housewives of Potomac* (Seasons 3–4), and *Real Housewives of Dallas* (Season 3); Co-Executive Producer, *Real Housewives of Beverly Hills* (Season 7) and *Real Housewives of Orange County* (Seasons 11–12)

Carlos King: Executive Producer and Founder, Kingdom Reign Entertainment; Production credits at Bravo include *Real Housewives of Atlanta* (Seasons 1–4, 6–9), *Real Housewives of New Jersey* (Seasons 1–2), *I Dream of NeNe: The Wedding,* and *Don't Be Tardy for the Wedding*

Bill Langworthy: Executive Producer, *Real Housewives of Orange County* (Season 10) and *Vanderpump Rules* (Season 1–Present)

Sheri Maroufkhani: Executive Producer, *Real Housewives of Miami* (Season 1)

Jennifer O'Connell: Former Executive Vice President, Shed Media; Executive Producer, *Real Housewives of New York City* (Seasons 1–5) and *Bethenny Ever After*

Jennifer Redinger: Casting Director, *Real Housewives of Beverly Hills* (Seasons 1–7), *Real Housewives of Dallas* (Season 4–Present), *Real Housewives of Orange County* (Seasons 5–12), and *Real Housewives of Miami* (Seasons 2–3)

Douglas Ross: Founder and President of Evolution Media; Executive Producer, *Real Housewives of Orange County* (Season 2–Present), *Real Housewives of Beverly Hills* (Season 1–Present), *Vanderpump Rules* (Season 1–Present), *Date My Ex: Jo & Slade,* and *Tamra's OC Wedding* (among others)

Dave Rupel: Executive Producer, *Real Housewives of Orange County* (Seasons 1, 13–14) and *Real Housewives of Beverly Hills* (Seasons 1–4)

Lisa Shannon: Senior Vice President of Programming & Development, Shed Media; Executive Producer, *Real Housewives of New York City* (Season 1–Present)

Dawn Stroupe: Casting Director, *Real Housewives of Orange County* (Season 13–Present) and *Real Housewives of Beverly Hills* (Season 8–Present)

Adrian Wells: Casting Director, *Real Housewives of Potomac* (Season 1–Present)

Not All Diamonds and Rosé

PART I

"Meet the Wives"

The Real Housewives of Orange County

PREMIERE DATE: MARCH 21, 2006

We were ready to kill the show before it ever made air.
—ANDY COHEN

Jeana Keough (Housewife): Vicki tries to pretend she was the first House-wife, but the bottom line is, it was me.

Vicki Gunvalson (Housewife): We started it together, but Jeana didn't last fourteen years. It was my show. When you start a job and you're the first employee and you work there for fourteen years, you have a sense of ownership. And I do believe if the show wasn't successful the first couple of years, there would be no other franchises. There would be no fifteen seasons. I set the map.

Scott Dunlop (Original Producer, *Real Housewives of Orange County, Season 1*): Of course Jeana would say I created the show for her, just like Vicki would say "It's my show." But Jeana actually was the first person I met when I moved to Coto de Caza, California, in 1986. I was unpacking the trunk of my car, and this woman in a white jumpsuit came up to me and asked, "What the fuck are you doing?"

Before Coto, I was living in Los Angeles. And Coto is a beautiful place—five thousand homes, fifteen thousand people, it's the largest gated community in America. But I was used to diversity, and it's very WASPy. All-white conservatives in this uber-wealthy area.

Kathleen French (Senior Vice President of Current Production, Bravo): It is the weirdest place. You go through this first gate—you have to give your name—and you're in this completely different land. Immediately, the world changes around you. It's a huge community, and there are gated communities within the gated community. More fabulous homes behind other gates of their own.

Scott Dunlop: The men would leave for work and the women were left to run wild on "the ranch," as they called it, playing golf and hanging out and shopping. These ladies who lunch, if you will. They were all such unusual humans. Entertaining, but also kind of annoying. There were the "Tennis Bitches," who were these violent femmes resolving their unsettled conflicts from high school in tennis matches they'd play while dripping in diamonds. There was the "Man of Leisure," who worked as little as possible to make as much money as possible. Oh, and the "Boomerang Kid," who was living back at home again and slacking on the couch all day, watching MTV, because that's way easier than finding a job.

All these archetypes started appearing for me, and I had an idea to do a short film that was kind of a send-up of life in affluent suburbia; something tongue-in-cheek and a little parodistic. Then, around 2003, reality TV was becoming big business. It made me think of the Loud family, who were on PBS's *An American Family*. And I said to myself, "There are plenty of characters here who are just as compelling. Maybe this could be a reality series? What would *that* look like?"

After marinating on his vision, Scott wrote up a one-page treatment and, beginning in 2004, started crafting a sizzle reel he could use to sell his concept to networks. Luckily for him, he had a strong anchor at the center of his presentation: his neighbor, Jeana.

Jeana Keough: Scott said, "You guys are like Ozzy Osbourne without the drugs."

Scott Dunlop: Jeana's family was very unusual. They were perfect for television, really. Jeana came from Hollywood—she was a *Playboy* Playmate of the Year, she had been one of the muses in ZZ Top's music videos, but she was now working as a real estate agent. Her husband, Matt Keough, was a retired baseball player. They were always gone, and their three children sort of roamed the streets of Coto de Caza wild. I remember seeing their son Shane one day, he must have been about seven years old, just standing at my door. I asked, "Shane, what are you doing?" He goes, "I'm hungry." I said, "Where's your mom?" and he didn't have an answer. That was the Keoughs. I knew we could get a lot out of them.

Jeana Keough: He was pretty excited about us. I thought, "Oh, how sweet. Anything we can do to help him out, we'll do." I've always been a networker and someone who helps people realize their dreams. It's coming from the Midwest, that's what we do.

With the Keough family in place, Scott began scouting for other people around Coto to participate in his reel. When it came to the "Tennis Bitches," he picked the leader of the pack: fitness fanatic, mother of two, and self-proclaimed trophy wife, Kimberly Bryant.

Scott Dunlop: Kimberly was one of the most eager to do the show. And she was fearless. The "Tennis Bitches" would always go out for cocktails and gossip, and while we were filming, Kimberly made this great backhanded comment about how her husband isn't in as good shape as the others' husbands because all he does is work. It captured my attention. She was also the one who was unafraid to say, "Eighty-five percent of the women in Coto de Caza have breast implants." We used that down the line in the intro for the show and people *hated* her here for saying that.

Jeana Keough: I actually thought 85 percent was a low number. It was probably more!

After flushing out the sizzle with more participants—including future actor Ryan Eggold, of NBC's New Amsterdam *fame, as the show's token "Boomerang Kid"—Scott began shopping it to networks under the title* Behind the Gates. *Bravo was the first to bite.*

Frances Berwick (Chairman, Entertainment Networks, NBCUniversal): I was in the very first pitch meeting. Scott Dunlop came in wearing white leather loafers—which in New York stood out—and talked about this gated community that he lives in and the antics that were going on. He really created a picture where these lonely, bored Housewives were staring out the window as these barely legal pool boys cleaned their pools. And we thought, "Well, that really sounds kind of up our alley." It was representative of the affluent, educated audience that Bravo attracts.

Shari Levine (Executive Vice President of Current Production, Bravo): You have to remember: Bravo had started out as an arts channel, so we were at a place where we were really defining ourselves and moving into uncharted reality programming.

Scott Dunlop: I was a first-time television producer, and this was a docusoap as we know it now, which wasn't as dominant at the time. But I knew that Bravo was kind of reengineering their brand.

Frances Berwick: The network was just coming on the other side of the huge hit that had been *Queer Eye for the Straight Guy*, which changed everything for us.

Lauren Zalaznick (Former Executive Vice President, NBCUniversal): Myself, Andy Cohen, and our head of marketing, Jason Klarman, all came to Bravo in 2004 from the Universal acquisition. By that point, Bravo had already launched *Queer Eye*, and it was a success. But what I didn't realize when I was put in charge of the network was that there was very little in the development pipeline that fit in with the *Queer Eye* ethos and, quite frankly, the *Queer Eye* audience. Nothing was working. With this vacuum in development, we sat as a team and really thought about our strategy, thought about our audience, and decided to make *Queer Eye*—our one hit—the blueprint.

Shari Levine: Lauren structured these development passion points to drive our programming decisions, and each of the *Queer Eye* guys represented those categories: Beauty, Fashion, Food, Design, and Pop Culture. We had just launched Fashion with *Project Runway*. We were in development on *Top Chef*, for Food, and knew we had something special there. *Blow Out* with Jonathan Antin hit Beauty, and *Flipping Out*, down the line, would be Design.

Lauren Zalaznick: *Real Housewives* was ostensibly going to be the Pop Culture launch show in our new mindset, with my tagline, which was "Watch What Happens."

Jerry Leo (Former Executive Vice President of Program Strategy, Bravo): I was looking for something that felt very noisy. And Scott's pitch, it felt like it could be *Knots Landing* for the new millennium. It had that CBS prime-time soap opera vibe; rich women living dramatic lives.

Scott Dunlop: When Bravo got it, they really showed a very honed interest. As a first-time television producer, and just from the business side, I said, "There's no way we want to walk away from that." They were engaged.

Rachel Smith (Executive Vice President, Development, Bravo): The sizzle certainly wasn't perfect. It had a scripted feeling. Like, the producing style was quite different from what we would go for now. I'd compare it to maybe *The Hills*; that very kind of stilted, staged feeling to it. But we could see that there was something fantastic there.

Lauren Zalaznick: The reel needed focus. There was something like two hundred characters in there. There was the tennis pro, the head of security, the head of the housing association, the real estate guy, this one, that one, and the other one.

Andy Cohen (Executive Producer): It was early 2005 when I first saw Scott's sizzle reel. I was in charge of production at Bravo at the time and Amy Introcaso-Davis, then head of development, handed me a VHS tape and a folder full of bios of women. She said to watch it, I'd love it, and it was coming my way. What that meant was: You and Shari (Levine) now have to go make this into a show. I watched and couldn't believe how sexy and *California* everybody seemed, how big their boobs were, and the way they spoke to their kids. I'm not sure Shari and I totally knew what it *was*, but I knew if it worked it could be like a soap opera. I remember being very excited that they lived down the street and went to the same tennis club, like they did in Pine Valley.

Shari Levine: When considering shows that we were picking for Bravo, having those larger-than-life personalities or distinct points of view was really essential. Things had to feel different. We'd come to say it has to have "The Bravo Wink," meaning it had a certain wink and a nod; a little bit of irony and fun. This had that.

Jeana Keough: We were breaking ground on a new form of TV.

Frances Berwick: None of us thought of it as a franchise at that time. We thought of it as really a social anthropological series—which in some respects, that is still what *Housewives* is—where we would follow these women, fly-on-the-wall, and see their lives.

Shari Levine: I don't know that any of us thought it would blow up to be what it is now.

Andy Cohen: No WAY could I have ever imagined how this show would change my life. It was at this point a very odd VHS tape!

After buying the series, Bravo gave Scott his marching orders, including the need to find more female characters.

Lauren Zalaznick: We cast the show for months and months and months and months.

Scott Dunlop: The network ultimately wanted more moms, more housewives, so we started leaning into the aspect that all of the narrative would come from women.

Lauren Zalaznick: There's really something to be said about the power of women living their lives on-screen. I wanted to celebrate that and celebrate women's programming—which at the time was not revered, it was disparaged. It still is. It's called this phrase that I really, really, really reject: "guilty pleasure." Men can spend ten hours every Sunday watching the NFL, and that's never called a guilty pleasure! That always bothered me.

Lifetime was also the No. 1 cable network for fifteen years, which shows you both how powerful women are in TV and also how desperate women are to see anything about themselves—even if it means being kidnapped, beat up, or killed off by cancer, which is all Lifetime seemed to do to women there. That's why I wanted Bravo, and *Housewives*, to tell women's stories in a completely different way. This wasn't Lifetime, it was a different ethos. Our women had the power. They were CEOs of their lives, come hell or high water.

Scott Dunlop: There was a lot of interest from women who wanted to be a part of it. One woman from the sizzle reel was marrying her plastic surgeon, but she never made it on because the plastic surgeon wanted a boatload of money. There was a divorced single mom who surfed every day—she was kind of a different beat than everyone else we had, but she passed. There was also this mother of twins and she was super religious. The network really liked her and I remember going to her home for a second time, third time, fourth time, until I finally said to her and her husband, "What's the real objection here?" And she said, "We're concerned because if there's a lot of focus on this show, our children could be kidnapped. A helicopter could come in and kidnap them." I couldn't get her past that.

> *To help expand his search, Scott put out two ads in the Coto de Caza community newspaper looking for subjects. A local kid named Michael Wolfsmith answered one of those ads, writing an essay about his family and his helicopter mom, insurance saleswoman Vicki Gunvalson.*

Vicki Gunvalson: Michael wrote in, expecting he and his friends to do the show. And in his letter, he talked about coming back home in between semesters of college to train with me to become a successful insurance agent. And Scott Dunlop contacted me saying, "We want to talk to you! Most women in this area don't work!"

Jeana Keough: Scott was shocked to find another woman who worked because there weren't many of us around.

Scott Dunlop: I was fascinated with Vicki when I first met her. She was frenetic. She was a workaholic. She was mercurial. She was not afraid. I just knew she was right for this. But she was hesitant, especially after I interviewed her and got her on tape. I remember, we were sitting in her living room with her then husband, Donn Gunvalson, it was the last time that I was going to try to get her to agree, and she blurts out, "Why would I be on television? I'm not pretty. I don't know anything about television and I don't understand what's going on." I said, "Vicki, maybe none of us know what we're doing, but I find you eminently interesting, and people will relate to that. Just be yourself." And so she agreed.

Vicki Gunvalson: Donn had said, "There's no way we're going to do a reality show. Everybody who does those ends up getting divorced." I said, "We're not gonna get divorced." That was the start of the crazy train, right?

Jeana Keough: I hadn't met Vicki until the show started, even though she practically lived next door.

Vicki Gunvalson: Jeana lives two houses down, but we live in a very spread-out community; there's about two acres between each of us, so we never crossed paths. Our kids knew each other, and she and I hit it off right away. It really was a nice friendship.

Jeana Keough: We really clicked. She was just fun. She's from Chicago, so we had a lot in common as Midwestern girls.

While interviewing Vicki at her home office, Scott saw someone else who caught his eye: Vicki's then employee, Lauri Waring.

Vicki Gunvalson: I met Lauri at this girl's house in Dove Canyon, where we were playing Bunco one night. I didn't like the other women, they were very pretentious and not women I wanted to hang around, but Lauri was going through a divorce and was complaining to me she didn't know how she was going to bring money in. So I said, "I train insurance agents from my house. I'll teach you."

Scott Dunlop: Lauri worked with Vicki, so we got a twofer there. She was going through a bitter divorce and was trying to move on with her life. And part of that next chapter included wanting to learn the insurance industry in an authentic way, which Vicki embraced because she loved women who work. It was a rebuilding time for Lauri, which we felt was a great story to tell.

Andy Cohen: I was particularly smitten with Lauri—she was that soap archetype of being from the wrong side of the tracks, striving for more. This is very un-PC to say but I also couldn't get over how big her boobs were. I just couldn't imagine she and Vicki selling insurance with these big boobs—I'd never considered that this could be a *thing*!

Jerry Leo: I was particularly fixated on Lauri. I'm a daytime soap opera fan, and I know Andy Cohen is as well, and she looked like someone you would see on *The Young and the Restless* or *The Bold and the Beautiful*. I just wanted to see her life.

Scott's cast was nearly complete, but he still needed a fifth woman to round out the group. Then he met twenty-four-year-old Jo De La Rosa.

Scott Dunlop: I was emceeing a fundraiser, and knowing we were in the final stages before going into production, I told my wife, "Keep your eye open for anyone who might be good for the show." Not long after that, Slade [Smiley] walked in. He lived up the street, but I didn't know him, and I immediately noticed the beautiful woman by his side.

Jo De La Rosa (Housewife): I was just a girl from Peru. I was never trying to pursue acting or TV or any of that. I wanted to go to law school!

Scott Dunlop: Jo was by far the most difficult to cast, but Slade really wanted it. Slade wanted in like dynamite. He smelled it and he wanted his fifteen minutes wherever he could get it.

Jo De La Rosa: Slade was definitely more interested. He was signed by an agent, because he had competed professionally as a cyclist for over ten years, and he had been an actor. We were dating for just under a year. And I was like, so not of that world. So I did it for him. I did it for love. I thought, "This will be an experience we can do together as a couple."

Scott Dunlop: By the way, Slade remembers this whole thing differently. He'll say, "I paid $2,500 to get on the show." That wasn't the case. There was a raffle and I had just mentioned onstage, while trying to get donations, that I was doing a television program and may be in the background of the show. I didn't ask for Slade's money, but he came up to me saying he wanted to be on the show. And I said, "I'll talk with your *girlfriend* about being on the show. . . ."

Jeana Keough: I remember it differently, too. I actually met Jo and Slade at that party and I was the one who pitched them to Scott. I thought they were so cool!

Scott Dunlop: Jo ended up being an extremely interesting cast member who provided a riveting dynamic because she opened up the whole definition of "Housewife," which ended up becoming a genius aspect in the brand.

With his cast nearly in order, production was finally able to begin on the series. There was just one more thing they had to address: the show's name.

Frances Berwick: We felt like *Behind the Gates* didn't really say what the show was, so we knew the name needed to change.

Rachel Smith: That title seemed like a more serious, tough documentary.

Jeana Keough: Our contracts all said *Behind the Gates*, which made me laugh hysterically because to get into Coto, you don't cross through a gate. It's like, a yellow Styrofoam noodle! I said, "We should call it *Behind the Noodle!*"

Scott Dunlop: Changing the title was a collaborative decision. There were a few names going around and I recall a discussion where the idea of *The Real Housewives* came up—because *Desperate Housewives* was such a hit on ABC.

Shari Levine: It wasn't just *Desperate Housewives*, because *The OC* was also a really big show at the time. Someone internally at Bravo suggested we combine those two thoughts.

Rachel Smith: It was Lauren Zalaznick who said we call it *The Real Housewives of the OC*. She came up with the title in an email.

Lauren Zalaznick: Network TV was still really important at the time, and *Desperate Housewives* and *The OC* were both very, very, very popular. Both shows were really sharp and campy; they appealed to at least two generations and sort of painted themselves as portraits of how people live their lives in extremes.

Frances Berwick: I liked it because it was sort of a nod and a wink to those two scripted series. It felt sexy and glamorous.

Lauren Zalaznick: What was lost on everybody was the irony of the title. Because yes, it was a play on *Desperate Housewives* and *The OC*. But more than being on the nose, it was thumbing its nose; it was rejecting that they were either real *or* housewives. Bravo was a channel about people's professional lives and our characters worked hard every day. They earned their own money, raised their kids, took care of their homes. On our network we were already elevating the status of being a style guru or a hairdresser or a chef or a fashion designer. And so here, too, the status of being a housewife.

Andy Cohen: I need to go on record that when Lauren added ". . . *of the OC*" to the title, which she said protected us in case we ever decided to do it in another city, Shari and I were vehemently opposed—worried the longer title was too clunky, and convinced we would never *ever ever* do this in another city. How wrong we were.

Filming began in 2005, but when Bravo saw the footage coming in, they began to question Scott's approach.

Scott Dunlop: I had always hoped that it would be more like *Curb Your Enthusiasm*; more of a hybrid show. Based on reality, but maybe some of that reality would be amplified in a weird way. But Bravo, they did not want that at all.

Frances Berwick: That was not at all what we were looking for, so every time he would give us something that felt like it was sort of pre-produced, we'd push back.

Andy Cohen: Shari and I were going nuts because the rough cuts sucked. The confessional interviews where the ladies spoke straight to camera weren't stylized—they weren't well lit, and the women didn't look their best. The women also weren't going deeply into their emotions or being honest about what was happening with their friends. And the stories didn't always make sense. What they were saying wasn't matching the way we saw them acting. The more we at Bravo asked the producers in California for answers to fill in the blanks, the less anyone knew.

Lauren Zalaznick: We would have weekly production meetings, editorial meetings, etc., and I kept seeing *Real Housewives* in the same place on the status report. This went on for months. I kept asking, "How's it going? When am I going to see a cut?" And one day Andy, Shari, and Frances came into my office and told me, "We don't have a show." I said, "What? It's been months!" And they said, "We don't have a show. It's not making any sense. The footage is just like, hundreds of hours of professional home videotape. There's no story, there's no arc. It's not compelling. It's not going to work."

Andy Cohen: Shari and I wanted it to go away. We were ready to kill the show.

Lauren Zalaznick: I stressed to them, "We need this. We don't have anything else." Because *Queer Eye* was dying. It had hit big and then fizzled quickly, never gaining numbers season after season. The future of Bravo was very much hanging on *Housewives*.

Frances Berwick: The question became, "Should we spend the money to fix the show or do we just write it off?"

Lauren Zalaznick: Frances is a very buttoned-up executive, very smart and levelheaded. She said, "We can call it a wash or we can go back into the field and shoot for a few more weeks with all our characters, because we don't know what's going to work and who's going to do what but we simply don't have enough story now." And I believe the amount to go back and shoot was something like $140,000. That's nothing for production, but it was such a big decision.

Frances Berwick: In the end, by shooting longer, we were able to get the footage we needed for that first season. To think, if Lauren said no, it nearly never would have happened.

Andy Cohen: Thank Lauren, and the Lord, that we didn't kill it! It would've been at that point a four-hundred-thousand-dollar loss to kill it. I would put in my own money today to make sure that never happened, and it would've been the best investment of my life.

> To help achieve their vision, Bravo took more control over production and hired Dave Rupel as showrunner. With writing credits on shows like General Hospital *and* Guiding Light, *as well as production credits including* The Real World *and* Temptation Island, *Dave's background in scripted soap operas and reality TV made him a perfect fit for* Real Housewives.

Dave Rupel (Executive Producer): I was brought in on the third day of shooting. And it's funny because Shari really, really pursued me for this job as if we had worked together before, which we never had. And that's because, back in 2005, it wasn't common for reality people to also have a scripted background. You had to have those storytelling skills.

Lauren Zalaznick: We didn't have a story editor. Someone had to help give it purpose and structure.

Dave Rupel: We would sit down with each woman and ask, "What's going on in your life? What's going on with your job? Your kids? Your husband? What's going on with your charities?" And then you start to build the schedule and follow the reality. It was a lot of the same process they still use now.

> But Dave didn't have relationships with the women like Scott did, and the original cast members resisted letting him in.

Dave Rupel: Vicki was notorious for not wanting to shoot. The show was not a known success at the time, so every time I saw Vicki, it would start off with a preamble—a five-minute complaint—about how every time we shoot with her we're costing her money. And every time I saw her, the amount of money she was losing just by being on the show went up.

Scott Dunlop: We had some bumps with Jeana, too.

Dave Rupel: It was hard for Jeana to adjust to the reality of just being herself. She had been known for her beauty, and here she was, struggling with her weight. And her relationship with her husband, Matt, wasn't in the best place. So it was tough for Jeana to put her life on display. She was like, "People are going to see my husband doesn't treat me that well and that my kids are a little bratty."

Scott Dunlop: Jeana wanted to control the show.

Jeana Keough: If you asked production, I thought I was the frickin' director! They always used to say, "Jeana's an actress, she's done this her whole life, of course she's going to try to come across better on TV. She knows." And there was some truth to that.

Dave Rupel: The hardest one for sure was Kimberly. While we were filming, Kimberly had a skin cancer scare and she totally shut production out. She would not allow herself to be on camera until she got the diagnosis, which turned out to be negative. But because of that, we lost all of that great drama, that human drama. I always tell anyone when I'm casting a reality show, "You may like me now but at a certain point, something is going to happen that makes you sad or angry or frustrated or upset and you're going to look at me and say, 'Dave, put the cameras down' and I'm telling you now, I'm not going to put the cameras down because it's those unexpected moments that the audience really craves and loves to watch."

I was disappointed that Kimberly wouldn't let us be in the process, but we needed to tell that story and that involved her talking about her fears and all of that. I knew Kimberly was resistant to me, so I turned to Brenda Coston—one of our nicest field producers—to do the interview, and told Brenda, "Kimberly has already told me she's not going to cry and that all she wants to say is, 'I am woman, hear me roar, and I am going to beat this.' Let her talk about that as long as she wants and get it out of her system and when she's done, you ask her the following questions: 'If it had gone the other way and you had cancer, which was potentially fatal, what would you miss about your husband? What would you miss about your thirteen-year-old daughter, Bianca? What would you miss about your seven-year-old son, Travis?" Brenda asked her those questions and Kimberly started crying for a solid hour. We got an amazing, emotional interview.

Vicki, Jeana, and Kimberly ultimately brought the stories Bravo was looking for. But doubts quickly surfaced from the network as to whether Lauri and Jo were the right fit.

Dave Rupel: Bravo was unsure if Lauri should be in the cast because she was divorced and single—oh, how times changed! But I lobbied hard for her.

Shari Levine: This was a show about people who lived in the gated community, and Lauri was someone who had lived that life, but lost it after she went through a divorce. It ended up being interesting to watch her come full circle because you got to see a privileged life from both sides.

Dave Rupel: There were some questions right away about Jo and Slade, too. The network was really attached to them as the "kept" younger woman and older rich man. But they tried a test scene and Shari worried they were too hammy.

Jo De La Rosa: Slade and I, we had seen the sizzle reel, and the way Scott shot that, it was a little bit more over the top and there was more of a comedic element to it. So we were really playing that up, but there were some moments I definitely wish did not happen on camera. Like, in the pilot, we were filming and I had too many glasses of wine and put on a hot pink boa and a zebra hat. And I climbed on top of Slade and took my top off, facing the wall so the camera only saw my back. That was definitely one moment I should not have done. I don't have a lot of regrets but taking your top off and straddling your fiancé? Probably not the thing you want to show all of America.

Dave Rupel: With any of these Housewives, there's always a first-season learning curve. Jo and Slade were really likable, and I thought we needed their story for the show—especially because Jo was Latina, which I knew was a well-needed bit of diversity among the group. Slade was also the most handsome husband among the group, and coming from soap operas, you always need a sexy leading man. So one of the first things I did was find a way to make them work.

Jo De La Rosa: There was one setup we did where I lost a bet doing this go-cart race with Slade and his prize was that I had to clean the house in a French maid outfit for the day. It was a million percent in good fun but also, I'm kind of horrified because cameras were there. And I swear, that costume will literally haunt me until the day I die.

Andy Cohen: I've never told anyone besides Shari this, but that first season I was not only very attracted to Slade, which won't be surprising to anyone, but also Jo was giving me some kind of feelings. She might be the only Housewife I've ever been physically attracted to. The two of them were giving me *feelings*! But I digress.

Jo De La Rosa: I was so, so nervous, the first time I met the rest of the women. It was actually the first scene I ever shot! I felt like I was coming into their world. I was so young. I barely knew what the heck I was doing. I really looked to them to kind of shape and mold me into this "housewife" that Slade wanted.

Jeana Keough: Jo was someone I felt very immediately protective over. We clicked, and I really liked Slade. Jo still calls me Mama Jeans, and the nickname stuck with all the women. I hate it. I'd tell Jo, "I'm not your mama, shut up! I'm older than your mama!" But the girls always mean it in a nice way, 'cause they know I know how to do everything.

Jo De La Rosa: I loved all the ladies. Vicki ran shit—ran her home, ran her business, ran the conversation. It was super impressive. And she was super outgoing with her "Woo-hoos" all the time. Lauri was cool because she was very social; she'd go to these parties and events in L.A. and I was really drawn to that world, so we bonded. And Kimberly would always give me advice behind the scenes on how to be a good homemaker, how to be a good girlfriend, things I could do for my man. And oh my God, she had such a hot body! Her body was incredible. You know, she had that Pilates sculpted physique. I said, "I would like to look like that one day, when I become an adult."

Jeana Keough: I was the glue that held everyone together. And we as a group started to get comfortable filming. It was practice makes perfect.

Dave Rupel: Late in that first season, Jo and Slade broke up. Again, it was Brenda in the field, and I remember her calling me being like, "Oh my God, they've produced this whole scene, it's so phony, it's so artificial." And I said, "Videotape is cheap. Keep rolling, keep rolling." And sure enough, Jo was drinking—she had a huge cocktail—and suddenly, their breakup became very real because Slade couldn't resist taking potshots at Jo and she started to get mad. It turned out to be a really emotional scene and that became the key with Slade and Jo for my field directors. "Just let them do their shtick and then keep going. It will get real."

Jo De La Rosa: That breakup was hard. I guess down deep, I wasn't really looking to be a mom at twenty-five. I didn't intentionally lead him astray, but I was really immature and very selfish, for sure. It sucked having to go through that in front of the camera. Fighting, splitting, packing, moving out—when you're ugly crying, you don't want cameras in your face. But I was always who I was, on or off the show. I just think it was difficult for me to process everything with the cameras there. You have a million emotions you can't control. I couldn't process it quickly enough.

Once filming on RHOC's *first season wrapped, Shari and Dave worked in post-production, putting in place many of the tentpoles of* Housewives *that fans see today.*

Andy Cohen: The material was better, but we still had a lot of problems in post. Some stuff seemed fake, and it was hard to tell some of the women apart.

Jerry Leo: I remember watching an earlier cut and saying to Frances, "All these blondes—Kimberly, Vicki, Lauri—I can't tell them apart! How do we find a way to make sure that viewers don't get confused?" That's how those establishing cards came about, the ones that show the women before each scene. It really became a staple across the entire franchise.

Andy Cohen: Shari Levine to this day is still giving detailed notes on the banners that come up before scenes. They identify each woman and give someone ownership over every scene. She came up with that whole system.

Dave Rupel: That's like taglines. They've grown over the years into this iconic thing, but I came up with the idea to use a signature line of dialogue to help define each woman in the opening credits. And that was inspired by Vicki getting Botox and saying, "I don't want to get old!"

Scott Dunlop: Those taglines have become so integral to the very fabric of the show, it's hard to imagine that they ever weren't there.

Lauren Zalaznick: Believe me, every corporate offsite that I ran, one of our best icebreakers was always, "What would your Housewife tagline be?" It just became a question you could ask and everybody instantly knew what that meant. And when you'd hear the answer, it was great because you knew exactly who that person is. It sums someone up pretty quickly.

Andy Cohen: For the opening credits, we had the idea to use the oranges. The opening of *Desperate Housewives* had the stars holding apples. This being Orange County, we gave them oranges.

Lauren Zalaznick: I was always meticulous about our packaging. Even during the process of designing the logo for the show, I wanted to make sure this was definable when we did other cities. The orange became an easy visual cue, so that was included in the final title treatment for the logo. And when we were shooting the opening credits, we made sure to have them holding oranges—not only to tie it all together, but to give another nod to *Desperate Housewives.*

Then we sent the art out and we're at the Television Critics Association right before we're ready to go on air and someone from NBC general counsel says to Jason [Klarman], "By the way, you can't use that image of the women holding the oranges. And you can't even call it *The Real Housewives*. Because ABC/Disney is going to say it's too close to *Desperate Housewives*."

Eventually, we had this huge meeting with the general counsel and I was adamant. I said, "Listen, the Walt Disney Company does not own fruit!" Obviously, a decision was made to move forward and there was absolutely no litigation or threat of litigation.

Actually, they were worried about "of the OC," too, because they thought it was too close to *The OC* on Fox. That's why we changed the name to *The Real Housewives of Orange County*.

Andy Cohen: When I saw the finished show open I thought the women were going to be pissed that we'd leaned into the most shocking aspects of their lives. I called Shari, who said they'd seen it and loved it! I knew if the wives loved it, we were off and running.

Bravo premiered The Real Housewives of Orange County *on March 21, 2006.*

Rachel Smith: None of us really expected that it was necessarily going to be a hit at the beginning.

Jeana Keough: Well, I did! I knew it would be big. Heck, I wanted ownership back then, but Scott wasn't going for it.

Jerry Leo: We wanted to protect the show, so we put *Blow Out*, which had a strong audience at the time, as our lead-in.

Scott Dunlop: The show started out and the first two or three episodes were "meh" in terms of numbers.

Lauren Zalaznick: You really have to understand how fragile that first season was. The way we made it strong was, we marathoned it to the max— the same playbook Jerry and I did at VH1 and the same playbook we did for *Runway* when it initially flopped. It picked up in the ratings as it went along. That's how we built the audience.

Scott Dunlop: By the end of the first season, the show had an audience. And it was basically a perfect storm. Right time. Right place. Right show. Right network.

Shari Levine: As I watched the end of the final episode, the iconic and very beautiful and bittersweet music (which now ends all the *OC* finales) started playing. I was flooded with the thought of how we didn't know anything when we started to make this series. There was no road map. It had never been done before. I looked at these beautiful women in the setting sun, and I thought of all the women, myself, and the viewers, and I was overcome with emotion. Something had happened here. I didn't really understand then how much had happened, but I knew it was important.

Andy Cohen: I wasn't expecting the show to win acclaim from the critics— and by the way, the reviews were mixed at best. I remember Tom Shales kind of getting that it was a sociological time capsule of a certain group of nouveau riche women, dressed a certain way (in what were called Sky tops), focusing on plastic surgery and their kids. When my friends started calling, I perked up. I'll never forget my friend Graciela Meltzer calling me after the first episode and going, "Who is this Vicki Gunvalson? Did you make her up? I'm obsessed. And Lauri? She's the Farrah. Doesn't Jeana look like Wynonna Judd? Her son is so hot!"

Jeana Keough: The first thing I realized, watching myself on TV when the show premiered, was that I needed to lose some freaking weight. I gained weight the first season, and throughout some of my time on the show. The other girls figured out before me that you cannot eat on camera. Those dinners that were planned for us? You just cannot eat. But I would be sitting there going, "Lauri, that looks so good, can I try that?" I would try a little of everybody's food, because we'd be at these fabulous restaurants and they'd order these really cool things. And I just blew up like a balloon. That's something I really struggled with, because I was always so thin! My top weight used to be 130 pounds, even after Colton. But it was menopause; it happens to all of us. It just happened to me first. And the viewers, they were all so mean to me.

Scott Dunlop: At the end of the first season, the ladies came over to my house and there was this feeling in the air of "Holy crap, we just did something that we never thought we could do." Every single one of them was in a really good mood. And it was there that the girls started to realize, "Wow, we're like a brand. This is bigger than us."

Jo De La Rosa: Never in our wildest dreams did the five of us, and definitely not little me, think that we were about to step into this world that would forever change our lives. The experience really connected us together forever. It doesn't matter how many years go by; nobody will be able to understand the life-changing experience that was being on that first season of *RHOC* except Jeana, Vicki, Kimberly, Lauri, and me.

Dave Rupel: As everything was wrapping up, Shari asked me, "What do you think? Should we do a season 2 with everyone?" And I said, "No, that would be a horrible idea. I would follow the *Real World* format and go to a different city because once you've shot with the cast, and they understand the system, it's not going to work." Of course, I was very wrong about that.

Lauren Zalaznick: That was an ongoing discussion. "Should we recast entirely? Should we go back to that tape of two hundred characters we had and pick some more people?" Because surely if you were real people doing real things, why would you ever be interested in living your lives out on camera for a second season?

Andy Cohen: This wasn't a question for me. If this was truly going to be a soap opera, we had to keep going with this group. I wanted to see what would happen next with these women. It sounds crass to say, but when I found out from production that Jeana was splitting up with her husband, the show felt like a hit to me because I had real feelings about it. *I cared.* That's what soaps do. I thought, "Wow, we could do this forever."

Conversations about a second season started at Bravo quickly. But a second installment of RHOC *would come with one big change behind the camera.*

Dave Rupel: Bravo offered me a chance to return and show-run *RHOC*'s second season. The day I got the call, I was lucky enough to get two other job offers on the same day. I was offered a job working in political advertising in Sacramento, though it was for a conservative-leaning firm, which I wasn't interested in. And I was offered a job to write for *Guiding Light*, this time as the associate head writer. I decided to go back to *Guiding Light* and worked there for the next three years until it got canceled.

Kathleen French: I was working at Evolution [Media] at the time, and we had a relationship with Bravo. We had done a special called *Gay Weddings* and a reality series called *Boy Meets Boy* way back in the day. And we also knew Dave Rupel, from his days working on a show called *Bug Juice*, a Disney Channel reality series we produced back in 1998 that focused around kids at summer camp. So when Dave decided not to return for *RHOC*'s second season, he recommended us to Shari Levine, and we got the phone call.

There was also a change in front of the camera: Kimberly Bryant decided not to return to the show for a second season.

Shari Levine: Kimberly ended up moving to Chicago at the end of the season, so we went in knowing she wasn't going to be around.

Scott Dunlop: She didn't even appear in the reunion.

Douglas Ross (Founder and President, Evolution Media): I don't think that Kimberly liked being famous. When she signed up for the show, nobody knew what it was going to be, and now that she saw it, it just wasn't her cup of tea. Over the years, she came back a few times for finale parties and we filmed when some of the girls went to Chicago. But she started pulling back. Subsequent times when we've tried to reach out to her to participate in things like the "100th episode special" or something like that, she just said she was not interested.

> *In Kimberly's place, Tammy Knickerbocker was cast. A friend of Jeana's, the down-to-earth divorcée and mother of three had a personal life rife with drama. Not only was she trying to rebuild her financial life after her ex-husband Lou Knickerbocker's business went under, she was also raising two opinionated teenage daughters while her ex-boyfriend, Duff Evans—the father of her four-year-old son—was trying to reconcile with her after their split.*

Tammy Knickerbocker (Housewife): Jeana and I had known each other for fifteen, sixteen years. Our girls had grown up together and we were buddies, we hung out all the time. Coto was a pretty lonely place back in the day; you held on to friends like that. Scott Dunlop used to work with my ex-husband, Lou, and Duff was working with Vick and Lauri, so I knew them, too. Coto is a big place but a small place.

Jeana Keough: She also had a connection to the show already. You know the gate in the opening credits? That was hers! We needed a gate for the show back in season 1 and I said, "Scott, let's use Tammy's gate." Because it was really big and grand.

Tammy Knickerbocker: You'd think I'd get some royalties for that, jeez! But they used mine because it was one of the biggest houses in Coto; a lot of the houses in the neighborhood didn't have that. Lou and I lived in that house when we were married, but I lost it after the divorce.

Kathleen French: Tammy had such an interesting story. You talk about rags to riches? She had gone from riches to rags; from living this unbelievable high life to losing it all after her divorce. And then on top of that, Tammy had this whole other life where she had been dating this man for ten years and they split because she wanted to get married and he didn't. But they were co-parenting, and he was this hunky guy that all the other women knew, too.

Andy Cohen: I loved Duff! He was iconic, a very OC archetype.

Tammy Knickerbocker: Everyone around me was going up in life, and I was going down. I was really rich, and then I wasn't.

As filming for season 2 began, it became clear Evolution had a different approach to storytelling than the cast had experienced before.

Douglas Ross: In those early days, we really wanted to elevate the way the stories were being told. Part of what we brought to it that hadn't really been there in that first season is Evolution's philosophy of dealing with the cast. We believe that you have to love your cast members and treat them with all the respect you can muster. If they feel that love, and if you can engender trust, then they'll open up and show you the more interesting real parts of their lives. They'll trust you. And part of our method for that is we told them, "Listen, we're not going to lie to you, but we're also not going to tell you everything, because we're making a TV show. We're going to have a real direct conversation, and a real direct relationship with you."

Alex Baskin (President, Evolution Media): The network noticed the ratings would spike when all the Housewives were together, too. It was inherently more interesting than everyone off on their own. So we made a conscious effort to get them together as much as we could, because the group dynamic is what propels these shows.

Kathleen French: But we tried to organically find ways to put them together. Was that someone's birthday party? Was that someone deciding to have a backyard pool party? Was that a shopping trip or a spa day? Were there things they would do naturally to bring them together and make it feel like it was true to how they lived their lives? That's really true to this day. We would never say to someone "You have to have a party" if they didn't want to have a party.

Douglas Ross: We started planting the seeds for that in season 2 and you can track, in those first couple of seasons of *RHOC* and increasingly over the years, how the show really shifted from it being only about personal stories to being about a group of friends.

The new approach brought a mixture of shocking, emotional, and dramatic moments that made up RHOC's second season. It started, however, with a big laugh, thanks to Vicki.

Andy Cohen: Whenever people ask me my favorite *Housewives* moment, I don't know why but I always go back to Vicki and that little family van.

Kathleen French: Here's what happened there, and this is classic Vicki—*classic* Vicki. When we were in pre-production, we said to Vicki, "We're going to start on this date." Well, when we went to start, Vicki was like, "Oh, I'm leaving for Greece for two weeks with the kids." We were like, "What?!"

Vicki Gunvalson: I wanted to take my kids to Europe because I had a really good year selling insurance. I deserved it!

Douglas Ross: Vicki has always been the kind of person who is used to getting what she wants and making things happen. She had survived her divorce, she created this business, the show was in its second season, she was starting to feel the power of stardom.

Kathleen French: Things like that happened with Vicki the entire time, but in this case, it was the beginning of season 2 and we had to shoot something with her before she left or she wouldn't have been in the first episode.

Vicki Gunvalson: Bravo said they wanted to film us leaving and I was like, "Well, this is going to be boring. We're just going to put suitcases in a car and leave." Little did I know it was going to be one of the most incredible scenes.

Kathleen French: The rest is history.

Vicki Gunvalson: I had ordered a full stretch limo, plus bagels and mimosas from this breakfast store nearby, because we had to go to LAX, which is like an hour and a half away from the house. So when this little blue van showed up, I thought Bravo was pranking me.

Douglas Ross: She just was 100 percent herself in that moment. She was angry and embarrassed and frustrated and, most of all, just flummoxed that whatever she said to the dispatcher resulted in that janky minivan and not a giant stretch limo. And of course, I often think about how our Housewives often think they've communicated something clearly in their heads but what comes out is hardly clear. So it's very possible that she did not do a good job of ordering the van in the first place but has no memory of that, of course.

Vicki Gunvalson: I ordered a limo, I did not order a family van! And I was pissed off! Donn was trying to calm me down, and the poor driver didn't speak a lick of English—he just kept waving at me and I kept saying, "No, you need to leave. I need a limo! I need my breakfast!"

Douglas Ross: I felt bad for that poor driver who didn't know what the fuck he got into and didn't know he was going to be filmed on a television show. In his eyes, he just drives up and then gets accosted by this crazy, screaming person!

Vicki Gunvalson: At the end of the day, we shipped six people and fifteen bags into this little family van.

Douglas Ross: That is to this day one of my favorite moments because it was so genuine, so real, and kind of relatable. Who hasn't had moments in life of extreme frustration? And God love Vicki, she seldom held anything back. Even in later years when she tried to hold things back, she wouldn't be able to control it and then it would all come out anyway.

As season 1 wrapped, not holding back was about to become a part of the very fabric of the Real Housewives *with the introduction of the reunion. . . .*

Lauren Zalaznick: The entire inception to do a reunion came out of Jerry Leo's brain.

Jerry Leo: Bravo, in the first few years, only had about two nights of original programming. Tuesdays and Wednesdays. So I was constantly looking to stretch the cycle out of the shows we did have for as long as I possibly could.

Lauren Zalaznick: *Housewives* was starting to pick up steam that first season, thanks to Jerry's brilliant programming strategy of constant re-airing, and I said to production one day, "Is there any way we can get an extra episode?"

Jerry Leo: We needed as many episodes of *Housewives* as we could get. They were the highest rated thing on at the time.

Lauren Zalaznick: Production said to me, "We can't do any more episodes. We've literally used every frame of every tape." So Jerry and his genius scheduling brain said, "Let's just get them back together and do a reunion."

Andy Cohen: Before *Housewives*, we had started doing reunions for *Project Runway* and *Top Chef*, and while they were a good way to extend the seasons, they also proved to bring good drama. There was a lot of tension in the first *Project Runway* reunion, where all the designers confronted Wendy Pepper over the way she played the game and called her "evil." The first *Top Chef* reunion was particularly chaotic. The chefs were chugging wine and got completely sloshed. A fist fight nearly broke out between two of our cheftestants, Ken Lee and Stephen Asprinio. I think Kevin also threatened our original host, Katie Lee Joel. And Tiffany Faison famously got so drunk, she ran off set to the side of the studio to throw up.

Jerry Leo: It worked in competition shows, we had proven that, but *The Real World* had been doing reunions, too, so I was inspired and thought it would work.

Scott Dunlop: Of course, our first reunion didn't really have that type of conflict because our show at the time didn't have that type of conflict.

Andy Cohen: We kind of gathered everyone to shoot at Vicki's backyard to see what everyone had been up to since the show premiered. It was quaint.

Jeana Keough: There was a monitor where we could see clips and we all sat together on high-top bar chairs in a semicircle, watching highlights of the episodes and laughing at ourselves.

Jo De La Rosa: I think we had champagne, too! It was totally chill and relaxed.

Jeana Keough: Everyone except Kimberly was there. I think she had already moved away at that point.

Scott Dunlop: It looks primitive if you look back at it now. But then again, I'm sure the whole first season does.

Jo De La Rosa: The first reunion versus the second reunion was so different. The second reunion, they stepped up their game. They brought us into a studio, gave us hair and makeup. There were lights, a fancy set, and the biggest difference, there was Andy.

Andy Cohen: By the time season 2 of *Orange County* started, I had been writing a blog on the Bravo website, offering behind-the-scenes scoops on *Project Runway*, *Top Chef*, etc. I was the only executive doing something like that, and it kind of upped my profile. Well, Lauren Zalaznick knew that one of my career goals was to be on television as myself. And in trying to figure out ways to help me and build BravoTV.com at the same time, she suggested I do a *Top Chef* aftershow online for season 2. "You'll have the eliminated chef on and we'll toss people to the website. It'll be like an extension of your blog." The first episode got something like 32,000 live-streams on BravoTV.com, which they thought was really great. American Express came in as a sponsor for the next season, meaning they were able to monetize it. And while this was going on, Lauren and Frances came to me and said, "We're going to do a reunion for season 2 of *Orange County*. Do you want to host this?"

Jerry Leo: We were already looking at Andy as on-air talent. We even talked about putting him on air for a few panel shows. We shot a few pilots for him and he was going to be our executive on the panel. One was called *Fashionality*, with Joan Rivers. Another, I think down the line, had Bethenny on it.

Andy Cohen: The network didn't really have a face back then. With the other reunions, Heidi Klum and Tim Gunn had hosted *Project Runway*'s while Tom Colicchio, Gail Simmons, and Katie Lee had hosted *Top Chef*'s. I guess the closest thing we had to the face of Bravo at the time was Kathy Griffin, who frankly would have been a hilarious and amazing host of these reunion shows. But with Kathy, she would have been expensive. I was cheap. I was getting, like, a thousand dollars a reunion. So I wasn't costing them anything. And there was the benefit of having me there because I had institutional knowledge of the show. I was going to be a team player.

Scott Dunlop: Having Andy as the face of the brand is genius. Andy has an energy and a work ethic like no one I've even known. It's mind-boggling. He's smart, engaging, charismatic. And because he was involved on the production side, he had the women's trust.

Jerry Leo: He had their trust and he had authority about him that the viewers immediately responded to.

Scott Dunlop: It was the best of all worlds, for the network and for the Housewives.

Andy Cohen: I was really excited to be hosting, but in those early days, I was very careful not to show it too much because I was head of production, too, and I knew the minute I slacked at doing my day job, I would be out. So I was like, "I can't act like this is all I want to do because this is not what they want me to do." I was working double time.

Jo De La Rosa: I first met Andy in the back of Vicki's backyard. He came to visit and check out the shoot we were doing that day, and he was super sweet, very nice, and funny. I immediately liked him. And then there he was, at that next reunion, hosting it!

Andy Cohen: For the record, I've sadly never been to Vicki's backyard. The first time I actually met Jo was at that first reunion!

Jeana Keough: How cool is that? He was sort of involved on the production end and then, boom, he was in this host chair. I didn't even know he could do that!

Andy Cohen: Jeana Keough came up to me at that season 2 reunion. We were in this actual studio rather than Vicki's backyard, and she said, "Andy, if you're here doing this, and if we're in this big studio, I think this means our show is a hit, right?" I was like, "Yeah. I think this means you guys are doing well. We wouldn't be doing this if the show wasn't."

Jo De La Rosa: All I remember about that reunion was that I had just changed my hair color to that caramel color, like Eva Longoria and Jessica Alba had back then. My publicist was like, "Everyone's doing it," and I thought, "I'm going to be trendy!" I look back now on it and think, "Why?"

Andy Cohen: If you look back, a lot of the questions I asked that reunion were a bit cheeky. I was kind of a nice Jewish boy, talking to women about their boob sizes and plastic surgery and their love lives. These were topics I probably couldn't get away talking about if I were straight, by the way. Certainly not in the same way.

Jo De La Rosa: It was easy to open up to Andy, because he's so warm and disarming. He had all of us talking about our plastic surgery secrets like he was our best friend.

Andy Cohen: I kind of had a sense that I was supposed to be the sane one in the room, especially in those early years, because the women just seemed so unusual to me and even to the viewers. I was really asking them the questions we all wanted to know. Like, what was the deal with those damn Sky tops they were all wearing?

Jo De La Rosa: Oh, those freaking Sky tops! Why did I wear those?

Jeana Keough: Sky tops were very popular back then in Orange County.

Lynne Curtin: The first time I went to meet casting producers, I was wearing a Sky top. I didn't even know they were a thing at that time!

Jeana Keough: I introduced the girls to how to get clothes from people, because people kept reaching out to me to give me stuff, and then the girls would go, "I want it, I want it, too." Those Sky tops, they always sent me a big box to wear each season. When we went on the *Today* show, Al Roker goes, "What is with you girls and these diamond-encrusted shirts?" We were getting them for free and we did really love them.

> *There was also an ongoing fight in season 2, as on-again, off-again couple Jo and Slade's bickering continued even after they reconciled. The pair wound up calling it quits by season's end.*

Jo De La Rosa: We were back together at the start of season 2, but our issues were still there. And obviously, I wasn't too happy that he had hooked up with Lauri when season 1 wrapped. I actually ran into them at a club in Los Angeles, on the dance floor!

Andy Cohen: What's more soap opera than Slade hooking up with another wife? It was delicious!

Kathleen French: Slade's a good-looking guy, he's a flirt. It didn't surprise me when I heard he and Lauri hooked up. He and Jo, they kind of messed with each other a little bit. There was always a little bit of game play between the two of them.

Jo De La Rosa: I was nervous it was going to be awkward between Lauri and me. And if I'm being honest, there were a couple of weeks of discomfort. But it didn't go on for a long time because Lauri did end up coming to me and we talked it out. I didn't want there to be any weirdness, we were working together. And I wasn't really upset with Lauri, as much as I was with Slade. Like, how could you go after somebody who is a cast member of mine? There's millions of people out in the world! But Slade and I, we really cared about each other. And I have a forgiving heart. And technically, he never cheated on me, we were on a break. So we gave it another shot.

Tammy Knickerbocker: I couldn't understand Jo and Slade's relationship, to tell you the truth. He was kind of like the wannabe Housewife. He was dating Jo, he hooked up with Lauri right before I joined, and then he was back with Jo when I started. It worked out for him—he lasted on the show longer than I did! But for a while, we were all joking about how we were going to give him his own orange.

Jo De La Rosa: We were just doomed from the start because he was fifteen years older than me. I mean, he threw my graduation party when I graduated college! Even if we had gotten married, it wouldn't have worked out in the long run.

Scott Dunlop: After season 2, Jo wound up leaving the show. There was a mutual parting of ways there. The women were leaning into the sail and exploring how the show could help make them money, but the network in those early days wasn't really interested in following these women as they sought out celebrity.

Jo De La Rosa: I was getting a lot of opportunities in L.A. and was always drawn to that city. So the minute we broke up, I left Orange County. It was that quintessential move-to-Hollywood-to-pursue-your-dreams sort of thing. My dad was a musician and I grew up singing and writing music, too, so there was a part of me that wanted to be someone like Kara DioGuardi. Never did I imagine I would actually end up getting a record deal.

Douglas Ross: I completely forgot about Jo's music career.

Alex Baskin: Every once in a while it'll come up on my iPod. "You Can't Control Me" was her single. It's really funny.

Douglas Ross: Alex and I went to the recording studio where she and Slade [who still helped to manage her music career] were, on the west side of L.A., and they were so proud of these tracks they had laid down and I remember looking at Alex and raising my eyebrow like, "Really?"

Andy Cohen: Kim Zolciak always gets credit for having the first *Housewives* song, but it was Jo!

Douglas Ross: We wound up doing a spinoff with Jo and Slade, which was the first *Housewives'* spinoff ever. That was Alex's brainchild.

Alex Baskin: Andy happened to be in Evolution's offices prepping for the *RHOC* season 2 reunion, and he told us that Bravo was looking for a dating series. On the spot, we pitched him a show that would involve Jo and Slade, where each would set the other up with their next great loves. It was an idea that was unproducible, so we tweaked it to be Slade setting Jo up instead.

Scott Dunlop: Only in reality television can two people who have split up come together to monetize a narrative. [Laughs] Sadly, the numbers simply didn't pull.

Jerry Leo: That was a real lesson for us that it's very hard to take the characters out of the real-life situations and put them in a format setup.

> *While Jo and Slade didn't work out in the long run, Lauri found her prince charming after season 1, when she met and started dating businessman George Peterson. They were engaged by the end of season 2, and had a fairytale wedding in season 3.*

Vicki Gunvalson: Lauri's whole motive was to marry money. That was it. She said, "I don't want to work. I want to find a rich man." She would go to the Playboy Mansion and all these parties in L.A., hoping to meet someone. I used to say, "You have three kids. Why don't you concentrate on work?"

Kathleen French: The first season Lauri was on the show, she was newly divorced. And in between season 1 and season 2, George saw her on the show and approached her. They really had a whirlwind romance. Right at the top of season 2, they went off to Saint-Tropez—he took her on this lavish vacation, and he bought her nice clothes and he wanted her to meet his friends.

Tammy Knickerbocker: Everybody in the beginning was like, "Wow, this is so stupid. It's never going to last. It's silly." And then when it started lasting, everybody was like, "Oh my God we're all so jealous!" It was hilarious. Vicki had an especially hard time with it. She thought Lauri was getting everything too easily, and Vicki was bitter because she worked really hard.

Jeana Keough: I was glad to see Lauri get her happily ever after.

Tammy Knickerbocker: Lauri got her little Cinderella story. They're so cute. And still together, so it's nice. It gives us all hope that good things can happen.

Bill Fritz (Executive Producer): At their wedding, they had these very expensive porta potties set up for the guests and above the urinals were these giant flat-screens playing the show. I couldn't tell if there was ego in it or irony. Was she promoting the show, or saying that now that she was married she'd be tossing the show in the toilet?

> Not everything was perfect for Lauri on the show, however. Her teenage son, Josh Waring, battled substance abuse issues and frequent run-ins with the law during filming. It was just one of the many stories involving the Housewives' kids that were told in the early seasons.

Frances Berwick: The show has always been about women protagonists, and, in that regard, their families are an extension of them and just as vital to the fabric of the show. The kids, especially back in the early days of *RHOC*, really drove story. These were teenagers and young adults, and their behavior was really affecting our Housewives.

Alex Baskin: *Orange County* had a great crop of teenage kids. We would give them their own scenes, independent of their moms.

Scott Dunlop: There was even talk of doing an *O.C. Kids* spinoff around them, before *Date My Ex: Jo and Slade*. The network was always having discussions about trying to get a younger target demo but in the end, they stayed the course with *Housewives*.

Dave Rupel: The kids helped you understand the parents better. In the first episode of the first season, we had Briana and Shane both graduating high school. And nothing super dramatic happened with either of their graduations, but we crosscut them because Vicki—being the helicopter mom that she was—flew her family in from the Midwest, had a huge, hundred-person party, and could not have made a bigger deal of it. Whereas Jeana forgot about Shane graduating and he was just floating in the pool. So showing them together, you really understood these women's different parenting styles.

Douglas Ross: One of my favorite moments ever in my entire career is when

Vicki surprises Michael at his college's fraternity house. And he does not like it at all and is mortified that his mother—who is completely oblivious to reading the room and just thinks he is loving it even though he's hating it—is there.

Kathleen French: That was Vicki's suggestion. She was like, "I want to surprise him, this will be great, he'll love seeing his mother." He didn't . . .

Douglas Ross: There was a turning point for Michael after that because he realized he wasn't enamored with being on television and was instead embarrassed by it. He started to move away from the show after that.

Jeana Keough: It felt like they didn't want to show any of the kids doing well. Shane was pursuing baseball back then, and they would always show him striking out instead of showing any of the home runs he got. He got really mad when Vicki and I went to one of his games in Illinois— this must have been back in season 4—and we went on the field to take a picture with him because it was fan appreciation day. He was angry and said, "Get off the field or I'm going to hit you with a bat." And they showed that. It was hard for him, especially when the show was airing. Shane had said to me many times, "Mom, I'm a professional baseball player. You cannot just walk on the field and take over the stadium like you own it. This isn't a Bravo production, this is my career. I don't want to be on a camera on the field, it's embarrassing."

Andy Cohen: The kids definitely took some lumps as a result of their behavior. People thought Shane wasn't nice to his mom, and I remember Shane calling his brother a faggot. We left it in the show because our feeling was that it had happened, and we don't editorialize or take a position on it. This was long before social media. I later discussed it with him at our first reunion and he apologized, but I'm sure the reaction was hard on him.

Frances Berwick: We respect what each family wants to do with their kids, as far as having them on the show. Sometimes there are physical barriers—like if a couple is separated and one parent doesn't want to give you permission for their kids to be filmed, obviously we respect that and don't put them on camera.

Jeana Keough: My kids pulled themselves off the show at a certain point. The boys were especially bitter. And I was like, "You know what? They're mad and they're right. And they deserve to be paid. You're taking their time away from their friends, the beach, whatever they want to be doing.

They should be paid." I kept pushing. Bravo agreed to start paying the kids, but by then, my kids didn't want to do it anymore.

Douglas Ross: Nobody knew what they were getting into in the first couple of seasons, and the kids really didn't sign up for it. It made their growing up a little bit more difficult. They were under the microscope. When you're a teenager or in your early twenties, you don't really like being under the microscope.

Kathleen French: Tammy's girls had it hard. They were going through their own personality struggles and, being teenagers on television, it was too much for Tammy. So we mutually agreed for her to exit in season 3. It was the best way to go.

Scott Dunlop: Lauri ended up leaving the show, too, partially because of what she was going through with Josh.

Kathleen French: That is a tragic story. Josh had been in and out of juvenile hall, and Lauri felt strongly he needed to get his act together. There was an incident in season 3 where Lauri wanted to have a therapist talk with her and Josh together. We set the meeting up, had cameras ready, and Josh didn't show up. She didn't know what to do and we said, "Well, why don't you talk through your feelings with the therapist?" And that's ultimately what she did.

Douglas Ross: A large part of that goes back to our philosophy of dealing with the cast and treating them with love and respect. The main message to Lauri was, "It's better to control the message yourself. These are the kinds of stories that get twisted out there in the world. So we will do our best to be as authentic, honest, and respectful to the story and what you as a mother are experiencing and how scary and painful this is. But you should put it in your words, not have other people on the show, in the press, in the world, tell your story." She heard that and wisely decided to let us work with her to tell the story in a respectful way.

Kathleen French: Josh was a sweet kid when you saw him, but between seasons 3 and 4, he got arrested. And at that point, it became such a painful thing for Lauri that she didn't want to talk about it on the show. But it would be impossible for us not to tell it on the show. We knew it was done. You can't make a show where you're going to cut around something that's on the national news. The other cast members are gonna talk about her.

Bill Fritz: For several seasons, they tried to bring Lauri back because audiences were always curious what happened to her. In season 8 she agreed to come on as a Friend. And that way, she didn't really have to talk about her Josh. (She instead accused Vicki of having a threesome.)

Alex Baskin: We replaced Lauri with a Housewife named Lynne Curtin in season 4. And she had a full household of rambunctious, rebellious teenagers—kind of that early formula.

Lynne Curtin (Housewife): Lauri and I have a mutual friend, and she gave my name to casting. I didn't know that I was actually supposed to be replacing Lauri.

> Lynne's tenure on Housewives *was just two seasons, but she had one memorable moment that reflected what was happening across the country.*

Kathleen French: There was a mortgage collapse going on in America and Lynne and her husband being evicted from their home was very much a representation of what happened in the housing market as a whole. We were there to capture, not cause.

Lynne Curtin: I think my landlord saw me on TV and thought I was living beyond my means. She probably saw that I got a face-lift and thought, "How did she have all that money to get plastic surgery and not pay me?" She probably got extremely upset. Viewers always thought I had all this money and was this extravagant person. I might have paid five hundred dollars to get my face done, they don't know. I wasn't a flashy person at all. I would shop at T.J. Maxx! I never overspent!

Raquel Curtin (Lynne's daughter): That eviction was one of the worst days of my life. My sister and I were just sitting on the couch, watching TV, when the doorbell rang. You could see through the frosted glass of the front door that there were a few people out there, so I opened the door. And this is how little I was expecting the producers to be there: I thought that it was Publishers Clearing House, those people who come to the house when you win the lottery! That's the scenario I expected. Instead, it was a man serving this eviction notice, and the producers and camera people behind him.

Lynne Curtin: That was really, really bad. I can't even talk about it because I'm still so upset. It still haunts me. That will always affect Raquel, the rest of her life.

Douglas Ross: It was a complete accident that we happened to be there when that person came. We were *all* surprised. But it was hard for Lynne to go forward on the show after that moment, so we parted ways at the end of season 5.

Before Lynne debuted on the show, another Housewife came and went. Filling the void left by Tammy's departure in season 3, producers cast Quinn Fry—a single mother of two and devout Christian who became known on the show for dating younger men, whether she liked it or not.

Kathleen French: Everyone was talking about cougars back then, that was all the rage. And Lauren Zalaznick came to us during casting and said, "I want a cougar." So we gave Lauren what she desired.

Quinn Fry: Production was hell-bent on painting me as the "cougar," which really annoyed me. Yes, I was divorced and dating this guy named Billy, who was ten years younger than me. I was fifty-two, he was forty. But I don't think of myself as a cougar and never have. And that dumb cougar thing followed me for years.

Jeana Keough: When Quinn came in, we all hated her. Vicki always hated the new girls, but that was the first time I didn't like someone. I didn't respect Quinn, I thought she was dating these younger guys just to make us look stupid. But later, I found out Quinn and Billy, they were really in love. They dated for years after the show, too, even though it looked like they broke up at the end of the season. And guess what I'm doing now? Dating guys ten, fifteen years younger than me.

Alex Baskin: I just think it's funny that in season 3, we added two new Housewives: Quinn Fry and Tamra Barney. I'd say we got one right.

A real estate agent and mother of four who confidently refers to herself as the "hottest Housewife in Orange County," Tamra Barney (now Tamra Judge) quickly became a fan favorite for her bold personality and unfiltered opinions.

Alex Baskin: The first few seasons of *RHOC* don't even feel like they're part of the same franchise. And that's all because of Tamra. She ushered in a new era for the show.

Tamra Judge (Housewife): I was a smartass from the beginning. When I first applied, I was sitting in [my then husband] Simon's office and my neighbor sent me the application while we were IM'ing on AOL. I was like, "Nobody wants to see me. I'm boring. I'm literally a stay-at-home mom. I don't have a whole lot going on." But I opened it up and I kind of filled it out like a fifteen-year-old boy. Every answer I gave, I just was obnoxious. And literally the next day, I got a phone call from one of the producers. When the casting director came to interview me, I was asked, "How do you feel about this person?"—like, going through the cast. They were small-town celebrities around here but I didn't know them personally. The only thing I could say was what I'd seen on the show. Jeana was always talking about her real estate businesses; I was working part-time in real estate. So I just decided to talk major shit on Jeana. I said, "Jeana? I can run circles around that bitch!" I was kind of brutal. And I don't think they were ready for that.

Scott Dunlop: Tamra was the first one to voice an opinion about another Housewife. Her words ultimately created conflict. Conflict matters; conflict moves the story forward. We didn't really know that until Tamra came on the show.

Alex Baskin: It wasn't until we were working on the hundredth episode special that we realized the impact Tamra really made. In hindsight we saw it was Tamra roping the other women into story and creating conflict back then. Having that negative commentary saw the show become, for better or for worse, very confrontational. It went from a sort of sleepy slice-of-life show with a bunch of suburban women getting together for trunk shows, into a much more aggressive, claws-out show. And the other franchises, which premiered after *RHOC*'s third season, kind of picked up from there. There was no going back.

Tamra Judge: The show was so different. It was just documenting women's lives and their kids and all that. It was boring. There was no drama. I definitely brought drama.

Vicki Gunvalson: She started going after Jeana, and I thought, "What in the world is going on? I thought this was supposed to be a nice family show?"

Tammy Knickerbocker: The show evolved into all drama all the time because of girls like Tamra. Which is great, by the way. We all like drama, a little bit. That's why people started watching and why they keep watching.

Tamra Judge: Part of me was pushing my way around to let them know I wasn't intimidated, even though I was, and the other part of me was just acting how I do in real life. I always call it like I see it, so why would I be any different on camera? If I had opinions about the other women and about what was going on, I was going to say them. But no one had voiced those on the show before.

Alex Baskin: In fact, now when we have scenes or when we cut to bites of other Housewives and no one is being judgy at all, it feels soft and that they're actually being fake. It has become so expected that they're going to have judgment toward each other that the show feels like it's missing a necessary ingredient when it's not there.

Tamra Judge: It wasn't like I was fighting with everyone right away. Vicki and I really hit it off. I felt like Vicki was real. I remember being on the photo shoot for my first season, I was wearing this short red dress and they put me right in the middle and I thought Vicki was going to lose her shit. Everybody was standing and I was basically lying on the table. She was pissed. She was always concerned about where she was standing in photo shoots, reunions, opening credits, stuff like that. And she'd be like, "Pull your dress down! Don't be trying to be so sexy!" But I liked that, you know? Because she was being herself.

I liked Lauri, too. I went to her wedding. And I liked Tammy Knickerbocker a lot. When I got hired, they knew *me* as Tammy, actually, because that's what everyone called me growing up. I recommended they call me Tamra, which is my birth name, to make it easier. When the show ended for me I told [my now husband] Eddie, "Okay. Now you can call me Tammy." He was like, "No, I'm not doing that!"

It was just Jeana who was a little annoying. Jeana tried to be a producer, she tried to tell people where to stand, what to do, what to say. And it got annoying. Nobody wants to deal with that.

Jeana Keough: In her heart, Tamra's a good person. But on a TV show, she knew she had to be a shit-stirrer. She had a smart mouth. She called me an old lady and said she was going to come for my real estate business. And I thought, "That's a pretty stupid comment to make on camera." I wasn't too worried. She'd never sold a house. Even when she sells her own house she hires a Realtor. I wasn't worried about her whatsoever.

Alex Baskin: *RHOC* is a show that started with very ordinary people who became reality stars. But Tamra, she was different. She was born a reality star. You meet her and you wonder if she actually exists when she *isn't* on a reality show—and I actually mean that as a complete compliment, because she just has all those qualities that you need to be interesting on TV. You don't meet someone like that every day. We instantly knew we wanted her on the show.

Douglas Ross: She has the "it" factor. She's ballsy! And most of all, she's competitive.

Tamra Judge: Evolution knew I was going to be that girl right from the get-go. Even during my casting, I got competitive. They had come back and interviewed me with my husband and the kids, and asked me to fill out all this paperwork, which I never did, thinking I would never get it. But then they called and said, "You've made the short list." And I met two of the producers at BeachFire—that restaurant we all went to back in the day—for another round of interviews, where they told me, "It's between you and another girl." And I said, "Wait, let me get this straight . . . you're going to interview her after me?" They go, "Right, she's up next." And I joke, "Well, not if I kill her first." I could see they were thinking, "This girl is too much."

A month went by after that, and I didn't hear anything. I was convinced I didn't get it. Then one day, I was sitting at this open house in Coto, and said, "Fuck it, I'm calling them." And I left a message for them, saying, "Hey, it's Tamra. Did I get the fucking job or not?" Minutes later, they called me back, laughing. "We just finished our meeting. You got the fucking job." And I was like, "Fuck you!" all excited and what not. And they go, "No, fuck YOU!"

Funny . . . I started my career like I ended it twelve years later: cursing out the producers.

Of course, every good competitor needs a challenger, and in season 4 Tamra found hers in budding entrepreneur and spunky blonde Gretchen Rossi.

Scott Dunlop: Gretchen, she was engaged to this guy named Jeff Beitzel, who was something like twenty-three years her senior.

Shari Levine: She had the most natural beauty of all of them. She didn't have plastic surgery. Her boobs seemed real while almost everyone else had implants. She looked like a breath of springtime.

Kathleen French: When I first met them, it was maybe eleven a.m. on a Tuesday morning and Gretchen came dressed up in a white fur with showgirl makeup, and Jeff looked like Kenny Rogers. I was just like, "I don't know what's going on here, but this is fantastic!"

Jeana Keough: There were rumors that Gretchen was just using Jeff and that she was a gold digger, because he was older and battling a rare form of leukemia at the time.

Shari Levine: We were concerned and talked a lot about bringing in someone who was clearly involved in a potentially sad and heartbreaking situation. There was a strong likelihood that Jeff might take a turn with his cancer, and it would all play out on camera. And was that something we and our viewers were ready for? Ultimately we decided to move ahead, but it took awhile for us to feel okay with that choice.

Kathleen French: It was all rather suspect because she was this cute little bouncy-blond cheerleader type. I mean, literally—she was doing back-flips at Jeff's house in Michigan. And in those early scenes they were always shopping together. He would buy extravagant things like expensive jewelry. He gifted her a motorcycle. She looked really committed to him, but you'd also wonder, "Okay, but if he had zero dollars, would this commitment still be what it is?" It did raise the question.

Alex Baskin: We knew Gretchen was another bombshell who would be a lightning rod on the show, because of her dynamic personality and her relationship with Jeff. But we didn't think Gretchen would necessarily be Tamra's foe. That just sort of naturally happened.

Douglas Ross: Tamra made that decision. Right away, by the way. She sized Gretchen up right away and thought she would fit the bill.

Tamra Judge: Gretchen and I were good for a while. The problem was, Vicki, Jeana, and I were out at an event at the St. Regis one night, and we saw Gretchen there with this younger guy, sitting on his lap and kissing him. We had just started filming and didn't really know her, but Jeana went up to her and said hello and asked where Gretchen's engagement ring was, because she wasn't wearing it. And she said, "Oh, it's in my purse, it's too big and it keeps falling off." And that was when we started questioning what the hell was going on. "Who is this girl? What is she doing? Isn't she engaged? Isn't her fiancé sick?"

Later on, Gretchen and I filmed together at BeachFire and, after the cameras went down, we had our first heart-to-heart. She told me, "Listen, I met Jeff, we dated off and on, it wasn't a great relationship. We were broken up and then got back together. Had I known that he was going to get leukemia and I'd have to be his caregiver, I would have left a long time ago." And I thought it was really brave of her to tell me that. So I never repeated it, never said a word about it while we were filming.

But as the season went on, it got a little disgusting to me to see her playing this role as if she's engaged and in love with this poor man who's dying, knowing full well that she didn't care about him. Her story line was just kind of bullshit. And then we found out there was more to the story with the guy we had seen her with at the St. Regis.

Alex Baskin: It was Tamra's thinking that Gretchen was a phony, that her story didn't completely add up. And then Tamra came across this piece of information that was really juicy, and she weaponized it.

Tamra Judge: We were at an all-cast shoot at the horse-racing track in Del

Mar. The night before we left, Simon and I were lying in bed when my phone rang. On the other end was a man who said, "This is Jay Photoglou. Gretchen's my girlfriend. I got your number off of her phone. She's playing it off like she's with Jeff. It's not true. We got into this huge fight and she just dropped me off on the side of the road. If she doesn't come get me, I'm going to Del Mar and I'm going to out her to everybody." I called Gretchen and she didn't answer, but Jay called back afterward, thanking me and saying Gretchen was on her way to pick him up. The next morning, she got in touch and basically wrote Jay off as an ex-boyfriend and stalker. But Jay kept calling us all season long, saying that Jeff was actually paying Gretchen to take care of him.

Alex Baskin: This goes back to the same point about Tamra ushering in a new era, because this was the first time a cast member was given a piece of information about her costar from someone off the show and used it against her. This happens all the time now, across every franchise, whether it's good for the show or not. In this case, Tamra had this intel and there was that part of her who was really loving the game.

Douglas Ross: And when it comes to playing the game, we've had several good Housewives over the years, but nobody does it better than Tamra. Other people may get close, but Tamra plays it better than anybody.

Tamra Judge: I was just so mad because so much stuff happened off camera, and on camera Gretchen didn't want to admit any of it. That's why we continued to fight as time went on. I felt like I was loyal to what she had told me about Jeff. I never repeated it, but knowing that I knew that, she treated me as if I was out to get her.

Kathleen French: In my opinion, Tamra's competitiveness with Gretchen went too far that season, especially with the "Naked Wasted" scene. I was shocked by it. To this day, I still cringe watching that.

Tamra Judge: Oh God . . . not this again. Okay, so, here's what really went down that night. I was having a party at my house, and up until then, every time I saw Gretchen out, she was a wasted sloppy drunk. You know, sitting on Jay's lap, making out with him. But when she got in front of the camera, she would always try to act like this little princess and be very proper. And Vicki and I had talked about how she never really showed her true self, so I made a comment to Vicki—"Let's get her naked wasted"—you know, to see if the real Gretchen comes out.

Kathleen French: At the time, our showrunner on the scene did not hear it on the headset. When they got back to Evolution, a story producer heard

Tamra say it on one of the audio channels and called our showrunner like, "You have to listen to this. What is she saying? Naked wasted?" And I was like, "Is that a thing? Do people say that?" I probably Googled it!

Tamra Judge: It was just an expression. And Gretchen actually got drunk, and she was fun! We were all having a blast together. There was no fighting. And then she went into the bathroom with my son Ryan, who's twenty-two at this point and closer to Gretchen's age than Jeff was. And according to Ryan, they were kissing in there and she was going, "No, I've got a fiancé, I shouldn't be doing this."

Andy Cohen: I was stunned by the kissing in the bathroom. That was one of the first times we caught someone doing something they shouldn't have.

Kathleen French: It felt like a setup. Like, "Was Tamra *trying* to show Gretchen in such a bad light?"

Tamra Judge: Absolutely, 100 percent, in no way was it a setup. Like I had this giant plan to get Gretchen drunk and then sic my son on her? That is sick.

Jeana Keough: Tamra said she wanted to get Gretchen naked wasted, but I was the one who told Ryan to help Gretchen go to the bathroom. She was so drunk, she would have fallen over. I assumed Ryan would stand at the door, not go in with her!

Kathleen French: Jeff died on September 13, 2008—about a week after we taped the season finale. And Gretchen called me the day he died. She was sobbing on the phone. Now, she didn't have to call me. We weren't taping. But she wanted me to know. She was genuinely, genuinely sad. So whatever their relationship was or wasn't, she was definitely involved with him.

Jeana Keough: What was going on in Gretchen's life at that time was tough. Jeff was dying, that Jay guy was putting the full-court press on her—he was pursuing her, which she didn't want, but she kind of needed somebody. She didn't want to be alone.

Tamra Judge: Gretchen denied it all at the reunion, claiming she and Jay were just friends. But I'll never forget, Jeana totally threw her under the bus. She was like, "Well, I don't know if they're dating, but I've been to Gretchen's house and his clothes were lying on the floor." Gretchen was like, "Shut up!" Jeana had a way of saying what she shouldn't. She thought she was trying to help, but instead she was being a bitch.

Scott Dunlop: Looking back, Tamra and Gretchen had the first Housewives feud ever—though obviously many more followed. It went on for years, too, on- and off-screen.

Tamra Judge: We just never recovered from that first-season fight, but the drama between us was good for the show. There was one year, I can't remember which, but they were sending out pickup letters for the next season and I got a call from Kathleen French, who said, "I don't think we're bringing back Gretchen." Gretchen and I weren't on good terms, but I told Kathleen, "You have to bring her back." Our fight *was* the show. I fought for Gretchen, who I didn't even like, because I knew we needed her.

> *If Gretchen's first season on RHOC was marked by conflict and loss, her second was much happier. Before the cameras went up, she began dating a familiar face to* Housewives *fans—Slade Smiley. Their friendship had blossomed into romance months after Jeff's death.*

Scott Dunlop: Slade always was the guy who was looking for the next Housewife. He went from Jo, to Lauri, and then to Gretchen. He would call himself the "Housewife Hunter." And there were a lot of people who thought, when he started dating Gretchen, that this was all for TV.

Kathleen French: When that relationship started, I was clueless. Jeff had died in September and two months later, in November, we were at the premiere party for season 4 and who shows up but Slade.

Vicki Gunvalson: Slade was not going away.

Andy Cohen: I found Slade coming back with Gretchen thrilling and hilarious, and brilliant for the show. Their pairing got under everyone's skin on the cast. It just made the ladies crazy!

Douglas Ross: Part of the reason they didn't like Gretchen and Slade is that it was annoying to them that Slade was glomming on to this other woman. But the other part is, I do really think that Gretchen and Slade are schemers, planners, and manipulators. They're both smart and when they teamed up, Vicki and Tamra in particular felt very threatened and distrustful of them. They didn't trust their intentions were genuine, and it led to conflict between them that still exists today.

Alex Baskin: We have always been fond of Slade because he's been nothing but nice to us and always wanted to make a good show. But for the audience, he was sort of this early reality TV douchebag.

Jeana Keough: Gretchen and Slade had some hard times on the show. I wish I would have been there to help them, so they had a friend on the show, but the fighting was all too much for me. That's why I pulled away and left the show. I just couldn't deal with the negativity and the superficial arguments we'd have during these long limo rides. "Your doctor made your lips bigger than her lips!" "No, your lips are bigger than mine!" It was all so stupid.

Kathleen French: We had been struggling with Jeana in production anyway, because unlike Vicki—who was an open book—Jeana was tough. She was always kind of putting on things to distract us from taping. One time, I was interviewing her in her home and she had all these things that kept popping up to divert us. First some guy came in the front door and delivered a five-foot wreath, then her husband showed up, then another guy dropped off the dog from the groomer. Her home was just a wild scene the whole time. And she would break the fourth wall all the time. Evolution, we want our team to create as little footprint as possible. They'd be rolling away, everyone was quiet, no one was talking to her, and she would just look right to the camera and go, "You get what you need here? Is it working for you?" It's like, "Jeana! Stop!"

> *With Jeana on the way out, viewers were introduced to Alexis Bellino, a married stay-at-home mother of three with two nannies and one overarching love for Jesus Christ.*

Alexis Bellino (Housewife): My husband at the time, Jim Bellino, knew Lauri and Jeana so when the show first premiered, we went to the opening party to watch the first episode. And Jim said to me, "You need to get on this. This is so you." A few years later, Jeana came up to us at Mastro's and said, "Hey, Alexis, I turned your name in." Jim was ecstatic. By that point, I had three kids. I couldn't even take a shower half the time! So I was shocked when I was cast. I didn't think I would be the right fit for it. I never thought anything would come of it.

Douglas Ross: Alexis was a great candidate for *Housewives*. When you meet her in person, it's hard not to like her. She's attractive, and fun to be around, and a bit of a nut, in a kooky way.

Alexis Bellino: Tamra was actually the first Housewife I met. As soon as they signed me on, she reached out and she was like, "Do you want to get together?" So she came over with Simon and I could tell it was all business with her. When I first met Gretchen, it was all fun. But with Tamra, it was all business. I could just see her wheels turning, I could see her trying to figure us out, which I thought was kind of odd.

Douglas Ross: Alexis also had this thing where she was so into her religion, but it didn't seem genuine.

Alexis Bellino: The one thing I did think about going in was that I wanted to bring as many people to the Lord as I could. I still feel that way, it's my heart. There's a lot of reality TV shows out there and nobody talks about Jesus or God. And I know I'm not the perfect Christian—I drink, and I have fake boobs and whatnot. But that's the beauty of Christianity: you don't have to be perfect because God takes you the way you are.

Tamra Judge: She played the God card, which really got under my skin because it was so self-righteous. I got so mad at her one reunion I called her "Jesus Jugs"—which is a nickname this artist David Gil-more, who used to draw caricatures of us, had given her. When I first saw that, I couldn't stop laughing and it just stuck in my head. I didn't plan on saying it out loud, but she was annoying me and it just came flying out.

Alexis Bellino: Tamra actually called me "Jesus Barbie" first, the previous year. So it went from "Jesus Barbie" to "Jesus Jugs."

Douglas Ross: The reason we were so into Alexis in the casting process is that she thought she was completely aware of who she is and what she had to offer and yet in our assessment, she was somebody who was completely unaware of who she was and how she was coming across. That has always made for a very good cast member: someone whose own perception of themselves is so radically different than the way everybody else sees them.

Tamra Judge: Alexis just wasn't authentic at all. She made it like she didn't care about the show, but she was very driven by money, very interested in fame. You could tell she was pretending to be someone she wasn't when the cameras went up.

Alexis Bellino: No reality star gives 100 percent of their life. Everybody hides a little bit. So yeah, there were things I hid because I didn't want to talk about them on the show. The biggest were the struggles going on in my marriage. But I wasn't lying, I was protecting my family. The show already had a reputation for ending marriages. I made a promise to my husband right in the beginning that we weren't going to be part of the statistic.

Alexis is right about that reputation. By the time she debuted on RHOC, the reality TV cameras had already captured the demise of a few relationships, while others were seriously on the rocks.

Jeana Keough: By the time I started the show, my relationship with Matt was pretty much over. He didn't like me very much anymore because my body had changed so much and he wasn't attracted to me anymore. During the season, he was scouting so he was always on the road. Off-season, he'd come see the kids for a couple of months and I just gave him a bedroom so he had a home base. But we weren't really together anymore.

Scott Dunlop: Jeana didn't talk about her problems with Matt on the show until season 2, and didn't really tell us they separated until season 3. And then Matt died on May 2, 2020, from a pulmonary embolism.

Jeana Keough: We stayed married even though we weren't together. Eventually, he wanted to get married again and I signed the divorce papers after sixteen years. And the divorce went through a month before he died.

Tamra Judge: Vicki was the next to get divorced on the show after Jeana. Or wait, was it me?

Scott Dunlop: It was Tamra.

Kathleen French: Tamra was this girl from Glendora, California, with working-class roots. Her mother was divorced, they didn't have a lot of money in the house, and then Tamra got pregnant with her high school boyfriend, ended up marrying him, divorcing, and really having to find her way in the world. And in comes Simon Barney, the son of a Greek diplomat, and a salesman at the leading car dealership in Coto, Fletcher Jones. He bought them a nice home. He took care of her. To an insecure woman, he represented sophistication and wealth. But he was also incredibly controlling. And he often was really, really tough on Tamra. I don't think Tamra felt like she had the voice or the strength to stand up to him.

Tamra Judge: Simon and I, our relationship wasn't great. We were always fighting, way before the show. And when casting called me, I thought, "There's no way in hell Simon's going to let me do this. No way he's signing up for that." So when he was like, "Okay, yeah, sounds fun," I was shocked. We fought more and more, and by the second season our relationship was getting worse. I was getting more independent, and Simon didn't like that.

By my third season, season 5, we went in knowing that we were going to get divorced. But we decided we were going to play for the cameras that everything was fine, and when the show ended, then we'd go our separate ways. It certainly didn't work out the way that we wanted it to.

Kathleen French: They ended up having this knock-down, drag-out verbal argument in the limo on the way to the finale party, and Tamra told him, "I want a divorce."

Tamra Judge: That wasn't supposed to happen. It really wasn't planned, but it just got to a point where I was like, "I can't even control this anymore. I'm out of here." I just blurted it out.

Kathleen French: Production in those days was not as sophisticated as it is now, so we only had a single-camera operator in the limo with them. No producer. So when the camera operator got out of the car and looked at me like, "Oh my God," I said to myself, "I guess something happened?" I couldn't ask about it because the cameraman was trailing them into the party. It wasn't until a good ten minutes later that he told me, and we moved the crew to follow Tamra, who was obviously upset. When I finally saw the scene back on tape, I was like, "Holy crap."

Shari Levine: I will never forget watching Tamra and Simon in the limo. The antagonism between them was intense. And when she said she wanted a divorce. I felt it. Viscerally. You felt that moment coming. And when they got out of the limo and Simon hugged her, you could physically feel her trying to melt away from him. Anyone who has ever been in a relationship that was pulverized into dust knows what that felt like. It was and is one of the truest moments of TV.

Tamra Judge: Our divorce went on for years. It got bad. And it didn't help when people like Jeana would talk to the press and stand up for Simon. That's why I threw a glass of wine in her face.

> *The scene to which Tamra is referring is one of the most infamous in* Housewives *history. Often parodied over the years, it's come to symbolize the type of over-the-top drama one would see on the series. And it all happened at the season 6 finale party, attended by RHOC alums and the full cast, including new Housewife Peggy Tanous—a married mother of two and former model who joined that year, filling the void left by Lynne.*

Tamra Judge: Simon and I were in a really bad place. He had thrown a dog leash at my face in front of our son. I took out a restraining order, and Jeana was going to the press alleging that I was falsely accusing Simon, ruining his life, making up his abuse, and that I was actually the one who had hit Simon in the past. It was total bullshit. She knew nothing about my marriage or what was happening behind closed doors.

Jeana Keough: Well, I know what the leash episode was. She's a klutz. He tossed her a leash, she didn't catch it, it hit her. That's not abuse. She just wanted the police report, she wanted the drama, and she wanted the attention. And she got it, but she cost him his job. It took him years to get it back. How is this man supposed to pay you support and alimony and you just made him lose his job? I was trying to be protective of her. It cost her money in the end. I'm sure if she looked back on it she'll say, "Jeana is right." I'm always right.

Tamra Judge: The press would call and everyone else would say no comment, but Jeana would say everything on her mind. I'd had enough. So I called my attorney and he suggested slapping her with a cease and desist. I asked, "Do I have to serve it to her?" and he said, "No, but it'll be more powerful if you do."

Jeana Keough: Tamra was doing it all for show. She had been planning it all day long. She knew how big it would be for her to do that to a popular cast member. She wanted the drama. She wanted to be the most talked-about incident.

Tamra Judge: I didn't care about that, I just wanted to get Jeana to shut up. I was legit mad. I'd had it with her.

Peggy Tanous (Housewife): I'm actually the one who instigated it. Everyone at the party was aware Tamra and Jeana weren't talking. It was the elephant in the room, and I was like, "This is so stupid, you guys need to just get over this." So I grabbed Tamra and said, "You need to go talk to Jeana," and pushed her Jeana's way.

Jeana Keough: I was clueless. You can see me, before it happened, asking everyone what Tamra was so mad about. Because she's such a bad actress, and I could see that she was scheming about something. I said, "What's she mad about?" And then I saw her coming up to me and I was like, "Oh frig, it's me."

Tamra Judge: When I approached her to give her the cease and desist, we started arguing.

Jeana Keough: Tamra called it a "cyst," like a pimple, and "deceased," like a dead person. Obviously she didn't know what she was talking about.

Tamra Judge: Jeana said to me, "You better watch it or I'm going to push your skinny ass in the pool." I remembered a producer telling me, "If she gives you a hard time, either push her in the pool or throw your drink on her." So when she said that, I assumed she had been tipped off and it triggered me. I thought, "Production obviously had the same conversation with her and she's about to throw me in the pool." Instinctually, I threw my drink in her face.

Jeana Keough: I don't think she wanted to throw it in my face, she just wanted to get my dress wet. But it went right in my eye.

Tamra Judge: After I did it, I took off running. I was like, "Holy shit, what did I just do?" I was scared shitless.

Jeana Keough: I was at the party for fifteen minutes, got drenched, and had to leave. Filming ended pretty much after that; everybody started going home. And then when we were walking out, Tamra came at us again, yelling and screaming. "You're a mean, nasty woman. Nobody wants you here. Leave." None of which is true. But that's okay. It made her feel good to say that. It was just to get more camera time.

Peggy Tanous: *The Real Housewives of New Jersey* had just premiered the year before we were shooting, and Teresa Giudice had flipped that table. That made headlines everywhere. So I feel like the girls were like, "We have to start doing some more dramatic stuff because that's what the viewers are liking."

Jeana Keough: Tamra did apologize the next day. I eventually forgave her.

Tamra Judge: I knew what I did was wrong. But she deserved it. She just wouldn't stop.

The funny thing is, Vicki was the one who was really upset that day because she had just announced that she and Donn were getting divorced and she didn't want to talk to anybody about it. Well, I don't have to tell you: after I threw that glass of wine, Vicki's divorce was the last thing people were thinking about.

> *Vicki and Donn's divorce came as a shock for* RHOC *fans. Though Vicki had lamented back in season 4 that her longtime husband was no longer filling up her love tank, the pair appeared to patch things up by season 5.*

Vicki Gunvalson: To this day I regret divorcing Donn. I regret it.

Douglas Ross: Donn was always a decent guy and a good stepdad. For the first couple of years, he was a good sport about the show. He would participate, and we saw fun moments and unflattering moments in his and Vicki's relationship, which made it real and relatable. But over the years, Donn experienced what a lot of husbands experience where they start to feel like, "I didn't sign up for this, it's the condition of the contract with my wife that I need to be a part of it, and I don't want to do it anymore."

He did not enjoy the limelight and did not like to see any of his dirty laundry portrayed on television.

Vicki Gunvalson: I started to see the show almost like a counseling session. I wanted viewers to see "Look, Donn's treating me bad," and it was not the right thing to do. I humiliated him. I pulled him down that path and couldn't stop it.

Jeana Keough: Well, fame pushed Vicki and Donn apart. She wanted bigger and better.

Douglas Ross: Vicki became a star, started acting like a star, and wanted to be treated like a star by everybody—including Donn. Donn was thinking, "Fuck that shit. You're my wife. If you don't love me, then I'm going to go live my life." He just got burned out on the shenanigans of being with Vicki as she was becoming a big celebrity.

Tamra Judge: It's hard to win when you're a househusband. The show wants to show any dysfunction in your family they can find, but the Housewives are always the ones explaining the dynamics of their relationships. And fans can be brutal toward the husbands. Unfairly so, I think.

Kathleen French: Every ounce of celebrity Vicki had, she loved. And every ounce of celebrity he got did not sit well with him. It was just a steady progression of them drifting in opposite directions.

Vicki Gunvalson: Fame, it's a drug. You know it's bad for you, but you can't get enough of it.

Kathleen French: They ended up doing that vow renewal for their fifteenth wedding anniversary, which was Vicki's Hail Mary attempt to save their relationship.

Douglas Ross: It was the first vow renewal in the history of *Housewives*, though it's now become a staple.

Andy Cohen: Over the years, vow renewals have earned a reputation with fans for being a relationship kiss of death.

Kathleen French: Ultimately, Vicki and Donn's relationship got to the point where it was just unsalvageable.

Vicki Gunvalson: It was just one fight after another with Donn and me, even after the renewal. We would never travel together. Never spend time together. Then I got insecure that he was cheating, and he got insecure. I talked about my love tank being empty and he told me, "I didn't even know I had a love tank!" It was just a slippery slope.

Shari Levine: There was a moment where we showed Vicki as she comes home alone, right after their split. And it's the first time that we're seeing her in an empty house. Donn's moved out and her kids are gone, so it's just Vicki. There's not a lot that happens, it's not an active scene. But it was actually a very telling moment that we played with very little music. You just see Vicki alone, making dinner for herself, walking around her kitchen, trying to figure things out, and not looking very happy. There was a real sadness and poignancy to it that was very quiet.

Meanwhile, other couples—like Lynne Curtin and Frank and Alexis Bellino and Jim—waited until after the show to get divorced.

Douglas Ross: Many of the women who sign up for this show are already in troubled marriages. What happens is, the show speeds up the natural process of a couple realizing or grappling with the fact that they need to get divorced. On one hand, we ask you to examine your life and your actions to the intensity and degree people often don't normally do in life. We're constantly interviewing you, pushing you to talk about things like "What were you really thinking? What was going on? Why did you do this?" That inspires self-discovery. On the other hand, for those couples who don't figure it out that way, well, then they see themselves on TV and how dysfunctional they are. The camera doesn't lie. So that usually inspires couples to address it in one way or the other.

Tamra Judge: The audience is always going to be able to pick up on a bad relationship. You can only pretend things are peachy keen for so long.

Kathleen French: Every split has been tough, from the standpoint of producers and the network. It's awful. Because we don't want to see anyone go through tough times. It's heartbreaking.

Douglas Ross: Except in the case of Alexis, because she kept her marital issues completely from the show.

Alexis Bellino: Jim and I, we didn't get divorced until 2018, but we were in eight years of therapy—the entire time we were on the show. I honestly never thought we wouldn't be together. I was going to fight for him as much as I could, but we just went the other way. You're either meant to be together or you aren't. I know that we gave it our all. We tried our hardest.

Douglas Ross: That absolutely hurt Alexis in the long run, and was part of her downfall. You can't claim to be authentic and then hide the most important part of your life, especially because none of these women are good actresses. The audience can smell a phony and they can smell obfuscation, and Alexis was not smart enough to navigate that very thorny path as the ladies voiced their suspicions.

One slight hiccup in Alexis and Jim's relationship viewers did see came in season 6, when it was revealed that Jim and Peggy had secretly dated years earlier. Feeling betrayed, Alexis ended her friendship with Peggy. And Peggy decided the show wasn't worth the drama.

Peggy Tanous: I had a lot of anxiety about going back for season 7. It didn't come out that Jim and I had dated until an episode of *Watch What Happens Live* right before the season 6 reunion, and once it was, I knew that was all my season 7 story line would be about.

As the first night of filming loomed, production asked if I would come film at a party Vicki was throwing. Well, of course, the Jim drama came up again, but I really freaked out and started crying. I was emotional and anxiety-ridden and I called my husband, who told me, "If you're not happy, then quit." So I did that. I left and told producers, "I'm done."

Kathleen French: Peggy had a little meltdown at Vicki's house and that was the last we saw of her. It was just too much for her. That was the thing that ended her relationship with Bravo.

Peggy Tanous: Bravo let me film an exit scene, because it didn't make sense for me to all of a sudden disappear. We had to explain why I was leaving.

Alexis Bellino: I was just so hurt and confused by what Peggy did, I could never look at her the same way again. She had that secret for so long, I couldn't move past it. I did not want her to return to the show.

Peggy Tanous: People online will say, "She was boring, she got fired, she wasn't going to come back anyway." That's bullshit. I wasn't fired, I walked away on my own. No one really knows because I distanced myself from the cast, so I'm sure they just made those assumptions, but I quit. And maybe I'm a dumbass for doing that, but the fighting just wasn't for me at that time.

Kathleen French: At the end of the day, people have to be ready, willing, and able to live their life openly in front of the camera. We don't want to twist arms, we don't want to put people in a situation that they don't feel good about. So we were comfortable with Peggy exiting if it was something she didn't want to do.

Lydia McLaughlin, a devout Christian and self-described friendship whisperer, also made the decision not to return to the show after completing her first season, in season 8.

Lydia McLaughlin (Housewife): The way the show is structured, if you have drama or a misunderstanding or you're mad at someone, it doesn't just live in that moment. You have to relive it again when the show airs, in front of the world, where everyone gets to comment. And so you get angry all over again. Then, by the time you calm down, you film the reunion where it comes up all over again. So this little thing that may not have meant that much becomes so big. And after one season of going through that, I was done. It became too much.

Kathleen French: Lydia had very strong religious beliefs. She knew who she was and she knew who she wasn't. Even when they went to Mexico and they brought in the strippers, she was like, "Yeah, I'm out of here." She was a girl who would get on the table and dance at Andele's, but something like this was too much. At the end of the day, the show did not sit well with her, and she decided to leave.

Lydia McLaughlin: In my mind, going into it, I thought it was fake. I thought, "Oh, it's a reality show where you get to promote your business, show off your family, and go on these great trips. And yeah, all these girls are being crazy, but that's just for the camera—everyone really likes each other when the cameras aren't rolling and you all have margaritas in the sunset." That's really what I thought. But then as the show progresses, you become involved in the drama, or even the target of it. And you realize that the drama is actually ten times worse off camera than it is on camera. It really never ends. I'm not used to having so many blowouts over and over again. It was so toxic and a very dark atmosphere to function in. I mean, a couple of the girls on *RHOC* are some of the worst people I've ever met. They're horrible human beings. I've never met people like this, they're vicious. It was eye-opening to me. It changed my view of humanity.

Andy Cohen: It's worth noting that Lydia is one of only a few Housewives who have left the show of their own volition.

> *Peggy and Lydia may have walked away from reality TV, but as the seasons went on, producers found plenty of women interested in giving it a shot. They were just outside the gates of Coto de Caza.*

Scott Dunlop: Casting within Coto didn't last long, because Tammy, Quinn, Tamra, Gretchen, Lynne—none of them were living within the gates when they joined the show.

Kathleen French: One doctor we were interviewing, his wife was a potential Housewife, he said, "We really consider Coto de Caza the backwash of Orange County." Which sounds ridiculous when you see how beautiful Coto is, but these were people with old money living in multimillion-dollar homes in these very exclusive neighborhoods of Laguna Beach, Newport Beach, and Corona del Mar. So we explored those areas.

Frances Berwick: The best Housewives are obviously people who are connected to multiple cast members. So we often ask the existing cast to open up their contact lists and say, "I know so-and-so, they might be good," and we'll reach out to them.

Dawn Stroupe (Casting Director): Every casting director does it differently, but I established a four-tier process for *RHOC* (which I also used for *RHOBH*) that has remained the same. And I let potential Housewives know the process right from the beginning, because I like to be open and transparent so that everyone knows what we're doing.

It starts with a phone call. We jump on the line so we can get to know somebody. It's almost like a pre-interview, but I don't call it that because it's more like you're meeting a girlfriend for the first time. We find out where they live, what they do, who their kids are—we just learn all about them. And we take copious notes as we do it.

Then, after that call, I would say 80 percent of the time we set up an interview. That interview may be in person, but most of the time it's via Skype or Zoom. And I tell the women, "You need to look like you're going to be ready to sit in the chair." Hair, makeup, outfit, the whole nine. Because Bravo, when they see these women, doesn't want to think, "I wonder what they'd look like in a confessional?" They want to see them.

That interview usually lasts about an hour, hour and a half. Sometimes we'll also interview anyone around them who might be pertinent—it really depends. I've interviewed someone's live-in mother before, I've interviewed someone's sister, I've interviewed someone's nanny! I like to include the husband, especially if he's very successful, because then I know that he's going to be sold into the process. And if he's super fun and the dynamics of their relationship is interesting, that's helpful because then we can see, "Oh, they're going to be amazing on the show together."

After that interview, we cut it down into a tape that's anywhere from six to eight minutes. And that's what goes to the network in our initial pitch. Once the network tells us who they're interested in, we do a meet and greet—that's the third part of the process. So they'll come up to the office and meet with producers at Evolution and the showrunner that season. Meet and greet is really the most important step of all because the women have to get producers excited about them potentially being on the show. Producers will then talk with the network and decide who is going on to the final round, which are the home shoots. Once you've gotten there, you're in good shape, but you still need to show them that you're ready to be transparent and be yourself on TV.

Frances Berwick: That honesty is so important. It's what's made the *Housewives* successful. If you scripted this, it would seem too hyperbolic and not believable, except this is who these people are. We show them warts and all, but by and large it's an accurate picture.

Dawn Stroupe: Kristy Swanson—the original Buffy the Vampire Slayer—interviewed for the show back in season 12. Doug and Alex had asked me to help do some additional casting for the show that year, and wanted to see if I could find any celebrities who might have ties to the area. In searching for folks, I found out that Kristy Swanson was from Orange County. She lived in L.A., but her mother and brother still live there, so I reached out to her agent. But before we even talked, she posted on her Twitter, "Hi fans! I've been contacted to do *Real Housewives of Orange County*. Should I?" I was in bed, it's like, eleven p.m. on the West Coast, and I got a call from someone at Evolution being like, "What the eff is going on? Call Kristy and get this down." I had to call her manager nonstop until he called me back. And I said, "If she's interested in doing the show, she has to take this down ASAP because the casting process is confidential." And she deleted it. That nearly ended her run right there, but we did interview her. When we came to do the interview, she was wearing a puffy vest and a sweater and jeans. She just didn't look like the glam they wanted for *Housewives*. And what we learned when talking to her is that her ex, Alan Thicke, had just died the day before and she was very upset. And ultimately, she didn't get cast.

Scott Dunlop: Mariel Hemingway wanted in, as well, in *Orange County*. That must have been like, 2012, 2013—season 7 or 8, maybe? I thought she'd be a great fit, I mean, she's an Academy Award nominee, after all. I passed her on and she went up to Evolution and the network and it didn't work out for one reason or another.

Jennifer Redinger (Casting Director): Kobe Bryant's wife, Vanessa Bryant? We pursued her every year and she was a no. She passed.

Douglas Ross: We also talked about making Vicki's daughter Briana a Housewife. That was something we threw around at Evolution, but the network never seriously considered it. It never got traction.

Jerry Leo: Actually, that was something Sheri and I discussed a lot. "Can we do a second generation Housewife?" But just as we were considering it,

Briana moved away. And we knew there was no way her husband would want to do it.

In season 7, Heather Dubrow—sitcom actress, stay-at-home mother of four, and wife of prominent Newport Beach plastic surgeon Terry Dubrow—joined the show, filling the spot vacated by Peggy.

Douglas Ross: Heather was someone we had looked at potentially casting back in season 5.

Heather Dubrow (Housewife): The way they often cast these shows is they call plastic surgeons' offices and see if they can recommend any of their wealthy female clients. They had checked in with Terry's office, and Terry came to me. Now, I had worked as a scripted actress—I had five series regular roles on TV shows—but took a step back after having four kids in seven years and was looking to return to television. I hadn't thought about doing a reality show but Terry had done *The Swan* and saw what it could do for your platform. So I interviewed with them; our house was under construction at the time but I had my designer stage a corner to look like a real room so we could shoot it. And they'd interview me, ignore me, come back to me, disappear again, call again. . . . It was like I was dating a guy who kept ghosting me and then reemerging.

Kathleen French: When Heather came in that first season to interview, we were at this restaurant in Newport and she was so great. I remember she wore this beautiful black dress, and she was so pretty. But you could see she was super conflicted about it. And it's a huge commitment; people really have to want the show. Afterward I said to Shari Levine, "She's going to have regrets if she signs on." It just wasn't her season.

Heather Dubrow: Terry was relieved. He goes, "That show, all they do is fight and throw things at one another, we're better off." And I, not knowing much about how the show worked, was like, "Why the hell did you ever tell me to do the show when you know I'm the most sensitive person? I wouldn't want to subject our family to that!" It felt like, bullet dodged.

Tamra Judge: People always say they audition for the show having never seen it before, and that's a crock of shit. Why would you apply for a job at a company you know nothing about? You've got to do your homework.

Heather Dubrow: A few years later, Terry and I started shopping a show around about opening a restaurant and Terry, who was really the brains behind the operation, wound up pitching it to Alex Baskin. Alex told

Terry, "I love the restaurant show, but do you think your wife would ever consider being on *RHOC*?" It was straight to offer from there.

Alex Baskin: Terry wanted to be on the show much more than Heather did. As a matter of a fact, we heard later that Terry may have forged Heather's signature on her contract.

Heather Dubrow: I was pissed at Terry. We didn't talk for two weeks. I was like, "I'm an actress, this is going to be bad for my career." But Terry, he's not stupid. He saw the opportunity and wore me down.

Kathleen French: Orange County has this laid-back, beachy-blond sort of sensibility about it, and Heather added an East Coast sophistication to the show that I really loved. She was well spoken and sophisticated. I really thought she classed up the joint.

Tamra Judge: She had the best homes, the best parties, the best trip ideas. Her husband was a character. We connected quickly. I liked her, and Vicki liked Heather, too. She always used to say she felt like Heather brought class and elegance back to the franchise.

Heather Dubrow: It's funny she says I brought class back because from my understanding, there wasn't a lot of that in the beginning [*laughs*]. The thing about *RHOC*, from what people have told me of the seasons before I joined, was that it was always perceived wealth, not necessarily actual wealth. It always felt a little more blue-collar—not in a bad way, almost more of a down-to-earth way, certainly lower than *RHOBH*. But you can see the shift, even in the fashions on the show. When I first joined, they were wearing all those Sky tops, and all of a sudden after I came around, the Chanel and Gucci started popping up.

Tamra Judge: Heather's rich. Have you seen her house? It's huge! I had a guided, in-person tour of it that took an hour and I don't think I even saw all the rooms!

Heather Dubrow: The girls gave me that nickname of "fancy pants." And I can understand; I came off looking a little elitist that first season.

Tamra Judge: There was totally an on-camera Heather and an off-camera Heather in the beginning, which isn't something that's uncommon with a lot of the girls. Heather's a little more down-to-earth off camera than she is on camera. She was very proper on the show, and wanted to be seen as being proper, so she would never even curse.

Heather Dubrow: Tamra used to laugh, she'd be like, "Off camera, she swears like a sailor!" And I do, but I wasn't showing that side of myself.

I really wanted to be me, and in the long run you can't not be you, it just took time to figure it out. The first party I threw, the painting party, the women were talking about blow jobs and oral sex, Terry was acting so inappropriate, and I was pissed off because I'm a control freak—I know that—and here I was, totally out of control. So, I looked like such a prude and so buttoned-up. I had a really hard time laughing at myself that entire season. That's why Gretchen and Alexis thought I was stuck up and had my nose in the air.

Alexis Bellino: Actually, I really liked Heather at first. I thought she was classy. But I really didn't like how she treated me on the show at all. That was my worst season, hands down. But that was really because of Tamra and Gretchen.

> *Once the greatest of enemies, Tamra and Gretchen decided to let bygones be bygones in season 7 and start fresh, leaving their problems in the past and working on their friendship. But not everyone was happy about how close they became.*

Douglas Ross: This show is about real friendships, and Tamra and Gretchen are a perfect example about how sometimes friendships shift—

Alex Baskin: —And how, whenever the women see a friendship of convenience on the show, they know they can expose it and undermine it.

Alexis Bellino: Gretchen and I were super tight. She really became my best friend, but it all changed with the next season when Gretchen decided to become friends with Tamra. They had talked so much smack on one another before that. Like, Gretchen *hated* Tamra and Tamra *hated* Gretchen. And then all of a sudden they're friends? That's where ego or fame comes into play, because Gretchen wanted stardom more than she wanted to be my friend. She wanted fame at any expense, which means true feelings and true friendships go to the wayside.

Tamra Judge: I really gave that friendship a shot. I was trying to move on from the fighting. We had been fighting about something year after year and it was getting old. I wanted to put that behind us. We weren't faking our friendship. Alexis was the one who faked everything.

Alexis Bellino: What did I fake? I would love to know what I faked.

Heather Dubrow: There was just a feeling with Alexis, especially that season, that she was putting on airs and flaunting her wealth all the time.

Alexis Bellino: I love that they called me phony because look at my lifestyle now. It has not changed at all, even after my divorce. I wasn't trying to keep up with the Joneses, I was just living my life. Gretchen was the one who was fake on camera. She faked her entire proposal.

Gretchen's proposal to Slade was an extravagant, over-the-top affair that wound up being one of the last things she did on the show as a Housewife.

Tamra Judge: So here's how that proposal even came about. We were at Mastro's one night, after filming ended on the season. Gretchen and I were on good terms back then, so I said to her, "I'm going to be honest. I'm worried you don't have enough this season to get you through another season." And the next thing I know, she decided to propose to Slade.

Bill Fritz: Gretchen's original pitch was, "I want to propose to Slade on the top of a snowcapped mountain, and we'd look across to another mountain and there will be fireworks." You know, real subtle.

Douglas Ross: Gretchen and Slade, by that point, were so in their heads about being TV stars that everything became a production for them. They knew that they were doing it to amp up the TV show. And viewers, they had gotten a little suspicious of them. If the audience had liked Gretchen better or didn't feel that phoniness, maybe her proposal would have been received better.

Tamra Judge: It wasn't even the helicopter. No one cared about the helicopter. It's that she just did it to stay on the show.

Bill Fritz: The proposal didn't save her. It's funny, Andy always gives notes on the shows. By the time a cut gets to him it's usually in pretty good shape, so he'll sometimes just point out a thing he's confused by or something he wants more of. But most of his notes are really fun. Something like, "This is so *Falcon Crest*, I love it!" And I'll never forget, when we cut together Gretchen's proposal, his note came back and said something like, "Great end to her run."

Andy Cohen: It didn't seem real. And that's always the kiss of death.

At the end of season 8, Gretchen and Alexis were both given pink slips.

Douglas Ross: It's never easy to figure out when it's the right time for one of the Housewives to exit the show. Gretchen had a really hard first season, and every season after that, it felt like she pulled back and protected herself.

Kathleen French: With Alexis, it just got to a point where she had moved herself away from the show so much that it didn't make sense to bring her back. She was on the outs with a lot of the cast members. You can't fake that. Many try, but really, you need to have a connection to the cast. And it's not a thing where they have to get along with everyone, but there has to be *something*. She was on an island.

Alexis Bellino: I felt like a failure because I was fired. It wasn't on my terms. I've never been fired from anything in my entire life, so I felt sad that I hadn't held up to the standard I expected from myself.

Heather Dubrow: Alexis got talked out of who she is. The thing that was fun about her was she was always a little dim, like in a Jessica Simpson, Chrissy Snow kind of way. It made her endearing. But she didn't want to be seen as that. She thought she was this upstanding citizen who was smart and does no wrong. If she had embraced her dimness and played it for laughs she probably would still be on, because she was hilarious.

> *Shannon Storms Beador, who joined the cast for season 9, proved to be an electric addition to RHOC. The holistic, feng shui–loving, married mother of three was an open book from the get-go, her unflinching honesty and kooky personality shaking things up among the OC gals.*

Chris Cullen (Executive Producer): I'll never forget meeting Shannon for the first time and instantly knowing, really within the first two minutes, that she was without a doubt a Housewife.

Shari Levine: A lot of women have been presented to us over the years. Shannon was memorable. Amazing, kooky energy, crystals built into the foundation of her home. We had never seen anyone like her, before or since!

Shannon Storms Beador: They asked, "Why should you be on the show?" and I said, "Because I'll go balls to the walls and be totally authentic. You guys don't show the wealthy part of Orange County like I'm in, and some of these people are fake. So if I do it, I'm going to be totally real."

Chris Cullen: Shannon was so open to everything. She spoke openly about her life and her new organic home that she built; she spoke freely about her husband and her children; she made us feel like we had a welcome mat into her life.

Kathleen French: I love Shannon Beador. I love her. She has this really fun, bubbly, eccentric personality. She's from California, but there's a relaxed confidence and generosity about her that's almost Midwestern. For example, when she threw a cast party that season, she made dinner herself. She didn't call a caterer, she got in the kitchen and made the roast. And guess what? It was delicious. And guess what else? The story you don't know is she made enough to feed the crew also. The producer had to say to her, "Shannon, this is so sweet, but you can't do this again." That's who she is.

Chris Cullen: Shannon had an epic first season.

Andy Cohen: It was like she was this lightning rod *RHOC* needed.

Kathleen French: It helped that she was filming for so long without any competition.

Shannon Storms Beador: They had taken three girls off the show that year but they could only find me to replace them at first. I started on October 13—I'll never forget the date—and filmed for six weeks with just Vicki, Tamra, and Heather before they brought anyone else in. I was able to develop a strong bond with them by that point, I wasn't the new girl anymore. So I was really lucky. No one had that opportunity before.

> *Though Shannon naturally fit in with the rest of the Orange County House-wives, she didn't exactly have a smooth season. In fact, she found a rival of her own in Heather.*

Shannon Storms Beador: From the moment I met her, Heather was very condescending. I mean, you see the first thing she did when she pulled up to my house was say, "Do we have taller ceilings than them?" She thought she was better than me.

Tamra Judge: That was kind of Heather's shtick. It was all in good fun.

Chris Cullen: Heather really liked being above everyone in season 7 and season 8. And then in season 9, Shannon came in. And Shannon lived in a gated community, Shannon had a big house, and all of a sudden, it was an even playing field. I don't think Heather liked that. Heather's insecurities got the best of her and she did not want to make Shannon welcome on that show and was going to make it as difficult as possible.

Heather Dubrow: That's a crock of shit. I wasn't jealous at all. I liked Shannon. I actually thought we were going to be friends. She was smart, she was educated, we lived near one another. But she kept saying, "When do I get to meet the other girls?" And her attitude toward me completely changed the moment I took her to the spooky party at Tamra's house, where I had the third eye on my forehead to cover a huge zit. She was so nice to me before but when we got to that party, she literally never spoke to me again. She made a beeline for Vicki and Tamra, and it was like I didn't matter.

Tamra Judge: Shannon and Heather were not getting along that season. Then, on a night before I was meeting Heather for lunch, Shannon called me and said, "David and I are splitting up. He just broke up with me in an email."

Shannon Storms Beador: [My husband] David and I had been fighting. What I'd later learn is that the day after we started filming, David left for a trip to Key West, Florida, and started an affair. I suspected something was wrong because I saw a change in David, but I didn't know about the affair. Still, we were arguing a lot. And one day, he sent me an email where he wrote, "I think we need to end our marriage." I got it and I called Tamra, very upset, and read her the email. But then she went and told Heather about it.

Tamra Judge: Only *after* Shannon said she was going to bring it up on camera.

Heather Dubrow: Tamra wasn't trying to hurt Shannon by telling me, she was trying to get Shannon and me to make up. She said on camera, "Shannon has a marriage that's falling apart. She's shared some things going on in her marriage that are really bad. Cut her some slack." And I felt sorry for Shannon, I did. But this is where life is stranger than fiction. When Tamra left, I went to the bar at Fig and Olive and met up with, like, nine girlfriends of mine. Shannon's name comes up—we don't have mutual *friends* but have mutual *people* in our lives—and I stupidly say, "Look, she hasn't been great with me, but she and her husband are going through a tough time." Something like that. It wasn't anything dire.

Shannon Storms Beador: Heather announced that David was divorcing me. It got back to me quickly.

Heather Dubrow: What happened was, this one fucking bitch at the table, who I didn't know that well, texted David Beador's girlfriend and said: "Heather Dubrow is telling everyone that the Beadors are having problems. Sounds like divorce." And the girlfriend calls David, and David then texts Shannon, who is in the middle of filming a scene with Tamra. It was like a game of telephone.

Shannon Storms Beador: David was flipping out.

Tamra Judge: Shannon hands me her phone, which has David saying, "Heather is telling people right now that I have a girlfriend." And Shannon looked at me, knowing that I was the only person she told, and goes, "Did you tell Heather?" And I just said to myself, "Oh fuck."

Shannon Storms Beador: Tamra insisted, "No, I didn't tell her anything!"

Not long afterward, Shannon went to Heather's home to get to the bottom of the rumor.

Shannon Storms Beador: That's when Heather kicked me out of her house. I've never been kicked out of a home before. She made it seem like I was disturbing her kids. I wasn't even talking loud! I was just saying, "Please, can you tell me how you found out about the email?"

Chris Cullen: Heather throwing Shannon out was a big, great moment.

Shannon was one of only two new Housewives that season. The other, Lizzie Rovsek, only made it one season as a full-time cast member.

Kathleen French: Lizzie was someone we liked right away. We liked her energy, we thought she was pretty, and, most importantly, she was actually a housewife. In *Orange County*, we always looked for Housewives who used their own vacuum, knew how to cook and things like that, because it's a different kind of a show than, say, *Beverly Hills* where you expect them to have a lot of staff in the house. So Lizzie, she checked a lot of those boxes.

Lizzie Rovsek (Housewife): To be honest, I didn't know what I had gotten myself into when I joined the show. I had people giving me all sorts of advice. Friends would say, "Be careful about what you say. Don't drink too much," stuff like that. And then producers were like, "Just be yourself. Don't be scared. Don't back down. You have to stand up for yourself." It was coming from so many different ways and I didn't know what to do. And in turn, I never let loose the real Lizzie. I don't think I acted like myself at all.

Shannon Storms Beador: That was the issue with Lizzie though, she was always afraid to get in the fray.

Lizzie only lasted one season, and the next year, she was replaced by Meghan King, a mom of one who had just moved to Orange County. But the biggest news as season 10 began wasn't the new cast member. After their season 9 struggles, season 10 opened with the bombshell revelation that David had in fact cheated on Shannon.

Shannon Storms Beador: One of the reasons why I wanted to go on this show in the first place is I thought it would bring us closer together and help reignite the intimacy that was lacking in our marriage. I was convinced David would see himself on TV and notice he wasn't spending enough time with me and he would change.

Douglas Ross: There were issues between the two they weren't addressing. I remember several times when we were editing scenes of Shannon and David that first season, I thought, "Oh my God. Stop the tape. Look at the expression in his eyes. Look at her body language."

The camera doesn't lie and picks up every dynamic between a husband and wife.

Shannon Storms Beador: That whole first season was "Shannon and David had marital problems but they worked on it and came out on top." Well, we finished filming mid-March. I found out, on April 1, that David was having an affair the entire time.

Bill Langworthy (Executive Producer): The thing about reality shows is, you show up every day knowing it could be really good or could be really bad, and you've got to roll with it either way. Well, when you're showing up to go to couples counseling because your marriage is in trouble as a result of an affair, you know it will be a bad, really long, tough day. So it takes a lot to show up and say, "All right, put the microphone on me, let's get in front of cameras and start talking about this."

Shannon Storms Beador: We wound up going to relationship boot camp, with the cameras, for season 10. It's crazy that never got out before the show aired. People saw that first episode and were like, "What?" How we kept that a secret, I don't know.

Bill Langworthy: At that point, this might have been the second or third time that I'd ever *met* Shannon. And this was a big story to tell, especially when you're putting together an entertainment TV program. People lying down on tombstones to commemorate the death of their old selves in the wake of an affair isn't something you usually see.

Season 10 was a major one. In fact, the biggest scandal in the history of the franchise unfolded that year, when the women began to suspect that Vicki's boyfriend, Brooks Ayers, who first appeared on the show in season 7, was faking his battle with stage 3 non-Hodgkin's lymphoma.

Bill Fritz: To understand how bad it was, you kind of have to go back to the start.

Tamra Judge: Vicki and Brooks first met when she was still married to Donn, but had started dating after her divorce. I was with Eddie by then and, off-season, the four of us would hang out a lot. That's when I started to see the red flags. He was an opportunist. He was really into the fame. But it was really hard to confront Vicki about any of this because she would get so defensive of him.

Bill Fritz: He liked to ingratiate himself to people and work his way in. When he first came on the show in season 7, he reached out to our show-runner and said, "Let me take you to a baseball game!" I wound up going along, which is how Brooks and I first met. And I was always a little dubious of him.

Shannon Storms Beador: I was happy for Vicki because I saw how her eyes lit up when she saw him. He was a little cheesy, kind of like a used-car salesman. But Vicki was happy and that's all I cared about. Then after season 9 finished airing, Vicki called me hysterically crying. Obviously, I was going through my own stuff with David, but she said, "Brooks has cancer."

Vicki Gunvalson: I was dating an incredible man, I thought. Brooks told me he had cancer. Of course I'm gonna believe it.

Tamra Judge: When I heard, I thought it was bullshit.

Meghan King (Housewife): I heard that Brooks had cancer before I met Vicki at that first party that season. [My husband] Jim's first wife was still alive, battling the cancer that wound up killing her, and I thought to myself, "We can bond over this." So I brought it up to her on camera. And I don't think they aired it, but her reaction to me having a friend with cancer was so curt and standoffish, almost like she was offended. Usually, in the cancer community, you embrace one another. It was a strange response. I thought I'd have an instant friend; instead I had an instant enemy. That was *my* red flag that something was fishy.

Vicki Gunvalson: I look defensive because I was! Absolutely. You know, I have an insurance business, I'm high on integrity and ethics.

Heather Dubrow: We all started questioning it in our own ways, on camera and behind the scenes.

Bill Langworthy: I do feel naïve saying this, because I'm a reality TV producer and I observe human behavior for a living, but it did not occur to me that he or that anyone could fake something like that. That someone would wake up one day and say, "I know what I'm going to do. I'm going to tell people that I'm suffering from this really terrible disease, when in fact, I'm not."

Shannon Storms Beador: Looking back there were signs, the first being the fact that I had been offering Brooks to see a highly respected oncologist at City of Hope since the beginning, and he just wouldn't. When Vicki first told me he had cancer, she said, "Brooks is going to City of Hope tomorrow. He doesn't have a doctor, he's going to see whoever will take him." So I called this oncologist, who happens to be the mother of one of my daughter's classmates, and she said, "I'm actually at the hospital today and have zero appointments because I just got back from Europe, so have him come see me." And when I passed the message on to Brooks, the story was, "I got two flat tires on the way, so I didn't make it to City of Hope today." Of course, I'd come to find out, the Mercedes he was driving didn't have any flat tires.

Vicki said the first round of chemo was going to be on December 5. I called her the next day to see how things went, and she said, "Shannon, it was horrible. He was so sick last night, we called Terry Dubrow, who sent over one of his colleagues to administer an IV, which really helped him."

Heather Dubrow: Terry never had been called. And even if they had called him, Terry was like, "You think I drive around with an IV bag in my trunk?"

Shannon Storms Beador: The next time Brooks had quote unquote "chemo," Vicki told me she wasn't going to be there because she had scheduled a trip with her friends. I was like, "Wait a minute. He's having chemo and you're going on a girls' trip?" It didn't make sense to me. But still, I believed he was sick.

Tamra Judge: I hadn't been around someone who was fighting cancer at that time, but even then, Brooks definitely wasn't a guy who looked like he was fighting cancer.

Shannon Storms Beador: And see, they had me go film with them and the second I laid eyes on Brooks, I thought, "Okay, he's really sick." Because he had lost a ton of weight. But I later learned he lost the weight because he went on a diet. Which makes sense since every time we went out with him when he supposedly had cancer, he was drinking 1942 tequila. Every single time. Always an excuse like, "This is my celebration." Whatever.

Tamra Judge: He was very convincing in the things that he would say when he talked about his apparent treatment, though. He gave you just enough information that you felt like, "That could be true."

Bill Fritz: That's what makes a good con man. Even though their excuse is probably not true, there's a shred of truth that it *could* happen that way. Brooks always did that.

Shannon Storms Beador: Then all of a sudden Brooks tells us, "I'm not doing chemo. I'm just going to do this juice program that starves the cancer cells." You know, I'm very educated about wellness. It wasn't like I was against alternative treatment options, but he still hadn't seen my oncologist friend—who by the way is world renowned in Western and Eastern medicine—so that bothered me.

Heather Dubrow: The moment I knew it was all a bunch of bullshit was when I looked up the name of his doctor. Brooks sat us all down one day to tell us he was stopping chemo, and brought up this doctor who claimed he had cured his own cancer by injecting himself with antioxidants. This doctor was putting Brooks on high doses of resveratrol, a chemical found in red wine. That was the big joke, because we were like, "Oh well good, I drink wine so I'll never get cancer!"

Anyway, Brooks kind of mentioned there, "You might know this doctor." Well, it turns out, I did know the doctor and had gone to him—not for cancer, but for cellulite. All my life I've had cellulite and have tried everything to get rid of it. And this doctor was doing this injectable treatment, which was really only done in Europe at the time. I went to him, I don't know, three times? The injectables made me nauseous and didn't work, so I stopped going. For some reason, Vicki and Brooks thought this would be embarrassing to me and told Tamra something like, "Heather should be careful questioning our doctor because she doesn't want anyone to know why she knows him." And then Tamra called me, warning me they were threatening to expose this. Which, I didn't care. So what, I have cellulite.

Meghan King: Before Brooks told us about that doctor, Heather and I went out with Tamra and her psychic friend, didn't we? The guy who said he didn't think Brooks had cancer.

Tamra Judge: He didn't say Brooks didn't have cancer, he said he didn't *see* cancer.

Bill Langworthy: Up until that point, no one had said on camera, "Brooks doesn't have cancer." Behind the scenes, I definitely heard the women say that, but this was the first time it was out there. And that was a clever way for them to bring that out into the world, using a psychic. I've never seen it done quite like that before.

Heather Dubrow: You never want to accuse someone of not being sick. It's like asking a woman if she's pregnant. You never do those things!

Bill Langworthy: And you never want to be the first person to bring an accusation like that up on camera, because you know you're always going to be associated with that claim. Once you say that, you're now accusing Brooks and maybe Vicki of lying. You can't unring that bell.

Shannon Storms Beador: When I heard about the psychic, I was angry. Maybe some people are psychic and know things, but that's frickin' ballsy. I was the one defending Vicki until the end. I was the last one standing saying, "Brooks isn't faking this. Brooks is sick!"

Heather Dubrow: Poor Shannon, man. That girl, she cared so much and she was so worried. I couldn't believe how gullible she was for the whole thing.

Shannon Storms Beador: In my defense, Vicki's story kept changing.

Heather Dubrow: Right, it went from, "Oh, I go to every chemotherapy appointment with him," to "Well, I just drive him there and sit out in the waiting room," to "Actually, I never go to appointments because he wants to go alone." Then it was, "I have this binder where all his medical records are organized, tabbed, and labeled." Guess what? The binder doesn't exist.

Kathleen French: Brooks's story was so convoluted and there were so many twists and turns—the story team built these boards tracking the cancer story in a way that it was almost like an FBI investigation. They had to produce the story like it was a *Dateline* piece.

Vicki Gunvalson: The way they edited it, they wanted to sensationalize this whole story.

Heather Dubrow: Eventually Brooks said, "I'm sick, I don't want to talk about my treatment." But by that point, it was too late. It just kept going and going.

Shannon Storms Beador: And he wouldn't show anyone his records, no matter how many times we asked.

Vicki Gunvalson: He would sit back and say to me, "I'm not getting paid anything. You're getting paid X amount of dollars. Why would I show anybody anything?" And I would say, "I get it. Don't show anything."

Shannon Storms Beador: At one point, Brooks said, "Okay, here's a chemotherapy bill." No one ever saw this, but it was hilarious. Because what he did was he went on Google and he searched "chemotherapy bill" and basically copied the first one that came up. It was an inflated chemotherapy bill, with every single number on his exactly as the one on Google.

Bill Langworthy: This was all heavy stuff. You can imagine what it was like to be getting weeks of footage with words like "oncology," "cancer," "lesions," and "chemotherapy."

Tamra Judge: I met with Vicki and Brooks and they gave me his supposed

Newport Imaging test results of a PET/CT scan he was claiming he had done.

Bill Langworthy: I remember the field producer called me afterward and I was like, "You know, it didn't necessarily sound like the doctor's reports I've read before."

Jerry Leo: Internally, we couldn't get our heads around what was going on. It was very murky. We knew that Brooks was definitely doing something devious, and Vicki seemed to be lying about something, but it was not clear to us what the lie was.

Ryan Flynn (Senior Vice President, Current Production, Bravo): One week we would think, "He definitely has it," and then the next we'd say, "He probably doesn't have it—God, I hope Vicki's not being used." We didn't know. Just like the viewers at home, we were watching it like, "What is the truth?" But Vicki was resolute to everyone—her friends, producers, her family—that Brooks was a good guy. As observers in production, the human instinct part of you wants to grab her by the shoulder, shake her, and say, "Snap out of it!" But that is not our role.

Vicki Gunvalson: Well, if anybody sits back behind their magazines or behind their TV or whatever and thinks for a moment: What did I gain? Nothing.

Tamra Judge: The one who actually took it to the next level was Meghan.

Meghan King: I've always had this sense of wanting to make things right. And I thought, "Oh, my gosh, this guy is doing this to promote juice. He's going to say he's cured because of the juice and that's so fucked-up. I'm not gonna let this happen. People are actually dying of cancer." So I started making calls.

Kathleen French: Somehow Vicki thought that everyone would bring her a casserole. How did she know that she had Meghan Sherlock Holmes on the trail?

Heather Dubrow: Meghan was like Nancy Drew, man. She was on fire.

Meghan King: First I called Brooks's doctor's office and said, "I have cancer, I was referred by a friend. I heard he administers this treatment using resveratrol." And they said, "This doctor does not deal with cancer at all." I also reached out to one of Brooks's exes, who had written on a blog that he had faked cancer in the past. And then I called Newport Imaging, the place where he said he got his PET/CT scan, and they said, "We don't do PET/CT scans."

Shannon Storms Beador: That's when I went, *"What?!"*

Bill Fritz: Meghan also went online and compared various City of Hope letterheads to discover that the document Brooks showed was actually on a letterhead that they stopped using five years ago, and was therefore likely forged because it would have been impossible that the letter was written now.

Meghan King: I totally blew up Vicki's life. Like, how crazy is that? I fucking figured out this dude doesn't have cancer . . . on TV. *What?!*

Kathleen French: People always say to me, "How do you think of these ideas for these story lines?" And it's like, "Are you kidding me? How can anyone think of something like this?"

Bill Fritz: Unfortunately for Brooks, it really was a perfect storm of events that took place. If Meghan King hadn't been on the show and hadn't been taking Jim's ex-wife to City of Hope to get cancer treatment, she wouldn't have known the kind of things that stood out as bullshit to her. If Jim wasn't in St. Louis most of that season, Meghan would have had more to do than just shoot the show and focus on this. But because of both of those things, she knew something was wrong, became obsessed with it, and had plenty of time to research.

Meghan King: Was it psycho that I was doing all this research? Probably a bit, but I had a lot of time on my hands. And it's just my personality.

Bill Fritz: Without Meghan, we would have had a season where Brooks was dealing with cancer and Vicki was just trying to help him.

Meghan King: And Vicki hated me for it. She would call me "little girl," really trying to create this narrative that I was this dumb, naïve person, which really pissed me off because I wasn't the one stupidly believing this dude has cancer.

Douglas Ross: Briana, who is a nurse, was in town, so we filmed a lunch with her and Tamra. And in that conversation, Briana said that Brooks previously told her he was a pancreatic cancer survivor but when she pressed him for details, he admitted he had pancreatitis—an inflammation in the pancreas that can be caused by alcohol abuse. That fueled the women even more.

Bill Langworthy: We tell cast members—and I do believe this—that the audience prefers someone who is honest to someone who is right. So do what you believe, say how you feel. It wasn't a tremendously sympathetic place to start from, to be going, "The guy suffering from a terrible disease is a faker and is lying." But they felt that they knew it and they went for it. And they were right.

Shannon Storms Beador: I wanted to give them one more chance. I said, "I get you don't want to produce medical records but you have to in order to justify that you're sick. Just pull a blood test out. Just show *one* document because this is getting out of hand." And Vicki said, "Fuck you," and stormed out of that lunch. Brooks then called me and said, "Fuck you," and hung up on me. It was bad. They really took it out on me, because they always thought I would back them. And here, I didn't.

Thomas Kelly (Executive Producer): I remember Shannon being so obsessed with finding out the truth. She even said to me, "Can you hire a private eye?" I said, "What? Are you kidding me? If you want to hire a private eye, that's going to be on you."

Shannon Storms Beador: I hadn't seen the PET/CT scans Brooks showed Tamra until I watched the show, but I freeze-framed the screen and took a picture of it and sure enough, it was a jumbled mess. So I went to Newport Imaging the day before the reunion. I asked, "Do you do PET/CT scans?" and Meghan was right, they don't. Then I showed them the picture. I said, "This is a report that's being used by someone to verify that he has cancer and he claims the report is coming from here." They go, "We have a proofreading department. A report would never go out like that, someone would be fired." And then they printed out my last CAT scan to bring to the reunion as an example of what all their reports look like.

Meghan King: Brooks actually sent me a cease and desist letter the day before the reunion. I ripped it up on camera. They didn't show that.

Bill Fritz: It had become such a big thing, everyone was invested. When it was airing, you could type in the word "Does" on Google, and "Does Brooks Ayers have cancer?" was the first thing that came up on a Google hit for months. It was like, "Holy shit!"

Andy Cohen: The question at a certain point became, is Vicki the victim here or the villain?

Heather Dubrow: Well, Vicki denied being a part of it. But how could she not be?

Meghan King: I didn't believe her then, and I still don't.

Vicki Gunvalson: That stupid Meghan, Tamra, and Shannon were like, "Vicki's in on a cancer scam."

Shannon Storms Beador: The plan probably was that at the reunion, he would announce, "I'm cancer-free!" and then finally everyone would embrace Brooks, this guy we've all been hating for so many years. Because Vicki just wanted people to like Brooks. That's all she wanted. So she thought, "This is a way that they're guaranteed to like him."

Vicki Gunvalson: Cancer is not a reason to care about somebody. Don't you understand? I got scammed! I paid over $350,000 to that guy, because he couldn't work, because he was sick or he needed child support. It makes me go absolutely psycho when I hear anybody think I was in on a scam.

Andy Cohen: I really don't believe that she knew. I don't believe she would have done that. The guy conned her.

Vicki Gunvalson: How did this get turned on me? It still pisses me off. You don't lie about something like that! I have integrity and ethics! I would never do something like that. Brooks told me he had cancer. Of course I'm gonna believe it!

Heather Dubrow: Honestly, she should have thrown herself on her sword, mea culpaed, and said, "He's a grifter, I know." But she just couldn't.

Jerry Leo: We filmed a one-on-one *Watch What Happens Live* special with Brooks to try to get to the bottom of it.

Andy Cohen: I've done a lot of ridiculous interviews, but this was one for the books.

Vicki Gunvalson: I didn't know Brooks lied to me. He was on Andy's show and said, "I fabricated the records." And Brooks said to me afterward, "I have the real records but your stupid show is never going to see them." I still don't know what the truth is.

Andy Cohen: As Brooks was leaving the *Watch What Happens Live* studio, he said to me, "This is it. This is the end. You'll never see me again." And I didn't take him seriously. I thought he and Vicki would be back together, but that *was* it.

Tamra Judge: No one has seen Brooks since.

Heather Dubrow: Well, he released that statement, where he fessed up to forging medical documents. And he still insisted he had cancer but said he acted alone in his deception and that Vicki had no knowledge of his scam. Which seemed like bullshit.

Tamra Judge: I really thought she was going to get fired, because the general public was pissed off. But the logical side of me was like, "She's a character who crosses the line and is causing controversy." Andy told me once,

"It's okay if they love to hate you, but when they hate to hate you, that's when you have a problem."

Andy Cohen: Here's this woman we've invested so many years in. Don't we want to figure out why she would stay with a man like this? Does she want love so much that she's willing to go along with this? I found it fascinating.

Vicki Gunvalson: Why wouldn't I come back? I had a lot to say. He broke up with me and I was handicapped. I mean, I was extremely sad, extremely confused. Of course they wanted to follow it.

Jerry Leo: One benefit to the situation was that it really drove the development of *Dirty John*. We had not had a lot of success yet with scripted but Frances had identified the podcast—I think her assistant flagged it up to her—and she said to us, "This story has shades of Vicki and Brooks." You know, Connie Britton's character was a version of Vicki and Eric Bana's character was as shady as Brooks. So that's how that happened, and it wound up being a great hit for Bravo.

> *Vicki wasn't entirely on the outs for long, though. In season 11, Kelly Dodd joined the cast. Not only did the outspoken mother of one quickly bond with Vicki, but she also found herself in heated battles with Shannon, Heather, and Tamra.*

Kelly Dodd (Housewife): I first interviewed for the show back when they were casting for season 8. I was divorcing my ex-husband Michael Dodd at the time and I was engaged to this guy named Jeff Caldwell. I thought I got the job then, but they ended up going with Lydia. I guess because my divorce was kind of messy? I don't know, they never gave me a reason, but I just remember watching that season and being like, "Oh my God they really picked this chick? Are you for real?"

Alex Baskin: For all the obvious reasons, Kelly's casting tape was not the type of casting tape you soon forget. So we looked at her again.

Tamra Judge: The show absolutely went downhill after Kelly. It just went to trash when she got on.

Thomas Kelly: I was in the field with Kelly her first season, holding her hand and guiding her through those early stages where she would lash out. I've always loved Kelly for her authenticity, humor, charisma, lack of self-awareness, and her big mouth. She was something we hadn't seen in a Housewife before. But when anyone new comes into this group, they're at a disadvantage because they're under a lot of scrutiny. And then on top of that, you add in Kelly's boldness, forthrightness, and crassness? Let's just say, a camaraderie quickly developed between the women who didn't like her. There was sort of an inner circle who wanted her off the show.

Kelly Dodd: Vicki came to me right at the beginning and was adamant about how she didn't lie about cancer. She was very convincing and loving and fun to hang out with. I immediately had a soft spot for her. Then she told me, "These girls are really mean and they really want me out." And, you know, I always like an underdog. So I formed an alliance with her.

Vicki Gunvalson: After the Brooks stuff, I started questioning how good of a friend Tamra was. It made me think, "Is she just somebody I work with?" Because, if she was a good friend, she would understand that I was the one who was hurting. She had nothing to be hurt about, nothing happened to her! So Kelly was there for me when Tamra and those other girls weren't.

Kelly Dodd: Shannon, Tamra, and Heather hated that we were friends. They said, "If you go on her side, it's going to be trouble for you." Well, I always like a challenge. I wasn't going to back down to these girls who wanted to run the show. Heather thought she was hot shit, and was always flexing how her husband was on *Botched* and they had this in with NBCUniversal. Tamra was always flexing about how close she was with the producers. Shannon is the leech, she's just a follower, but she was successful and smart. Even Meghan, who I didn't have a problem with, was on their side—she's a follower, too. So I had all these girls working together to get me off. They immediately felt threatened, wanted me off the show, and were going to do everything in their power to find out everything about me and make me look bad. I felt like they were bullies.

Shannon Storms Beador: We weren't bullying anyone or threatening to get anyone off the show. I still don't know the people who make the firing decisions!

Thomas Kelly: My job is to give everyone impartial treatment, to make everything fair and balanced. So I had to encourage the women who were against Kelly Dodd to give her a chance. It wasn't easy.

Tamra Judge: Everything kind of came to a head at that sushi party.

Kelly Dodd: Going into that dinner, I was like, "I don't need this show. Why the fuck am I doing this? I'm not getting paid enough to do this. These women are disgusting. I don't get along with them." I really wanted to quit. But I signed a contract and I knew I had to fulfill it. I wasn't going to let them walk all over me. You want to fight with me? Fine. Let's go.

Tamra Judge: Kelly came to that dinner and she was angry and foulmouthed and rude to people. She just started lashing out and saying things that were not appropriate at all.

Kelly Dodd: They had an agenda, and the agenda was to get me pissed off and riled up. They had already seen that if you got a little bit of alcohol in me, I was going to fly off the handle.

Shannon Storms Beador: I was sitting next to Heather, and Kelly just went off. She called me the C-word, and she called Tamra a dumb fuck.

Tamra Judge: It made no sense to me because we weren't even in an argument! I was fine with her and was calmly trying to talk to her and she's calling me a dumb fuck? That's how you talk to me? I'm not even fighting with you!

Shannon Storms Beador: Heather was holding, squeezing my hand underneath the table, like, breathe. So I just sat there. I don't know if I would have even normally gone after her. I never thought in my life that someone would call me the C-word. Ever. I don't hang out with people that use that word, for God's sakes.

Tamra Judge: We weren't used to that. It was embarrassing. We were at a restaurant and she's screaming, "You fucking cunt!" Like, "Oh my God. Shut up." There was a feeling, in that moment, of "This isn't what our show is." Because it's not.

> *No one felt that more than Heather. Though Kelly's anger at that dinner was directed toward Shannon and Tamra, Heather wound up so enraged by Kelly's behavior and the turn the show had allegedly taken that she lashed out behind the scenes—and consequently dug her own grave on the series.*

Heather Dubrow: That sushi dinner was a breaking point for me. Screaming "cunt" in the middle of a restaurant was so abrasive and vulgar. I remember thinking to myself, "What kind of a person am I on this show with? I'm teaching my young kids, 'You're known by the company you keep,' and I'm hanging out with this girl?"

Kelly Dodd: Oh please. Behind the scenes, nobody has a worse mouth than Heather Dubrow.

Heather Dubrow: It wasn't about the cursing. I am not a wilting lily. I'd heard the word before. I can say the word. It was bigger. Here we are in a family restaurant with paper-thin walls, filming a television show, and this Kelly is yelling "cunt" like a psychopath. It was just beyond unnecessary and disgusting and made me question why I was even on the show to begin with.

Shannon Storms Beador: Heather got really, really upset. That was a restaurant she knew, and she was embarrassed. So she left and immediately started screaming at producers.

Thomas Kelly: She was on a tirade, her finger in front of my face the whole time. And I was on crutches at the time, at the monitors while Heather lashed out at me in front of twelve of my crew members.

Heather Dubrow: I took off my microphone, walked to video village, and I said, "Aren't we better than this? Is this really the show you want to make?" I certainly wasn't this composed, actually. I was more going crazy like, "Are you fucking kidding me? This is disgusting! How could you bring a person like this on? We have families, we have children that are going to watch the show!"

Thomas Kelly: I find it really fascinating how Heather's reaction was not to deal with it on camera with Kelly, but to try to deal with the producers in order to rectify the problem. That's fine, you can express your grievances, but ultimately you're gonna have to handle that all on camera. We can't do the show for you.

Heather Dubrow: After the sushi dinner, I was really done. I understood Kelly was bringing drama to the show, I just didn't want to *be* on that show. It was time for me to go. But it's very, very difficult to get a show—and to get a show that's successful, at that. So I couldn't walk away. Instead, I just basically gave them every reason to not want me on the show.

Alex Baskin: Production didn't think they were getting what they needed from Heather. And as we pushed harder, that caused Heather to offer up even more resistance.

Heather Dubrow: I really just started shutting down, pulling back, and closing myself off—which isn't exactly what you want when you're making a reality show. I didn't want the cameras in my house. I didn't want to show up for certain events. I stopped telling my personal story. Like, I sang the National Anthem at Angel Stadium, which was a bucket list thing, but I wouldn't let them film it.

Andy Cohen: We also filmed her building her dream house for two seasons and she refused to show it on camera when it was done. That was beyond annoying.

Alex Baskin: The network was over it and, at a certain point, circled Heather as a problem.

Heather Dubrow: After the season finished airing, I was sitting around and waiting for them to call with my offer. And when they did, it was for a reduced role. I went back and sat down with them and said, "For me, I either have to be all in or all out." And that's how I left. I pissed them off and really gave them no other place to go. If I were in their position, I would have done the same thing.

Alex Baskin: I don't think Heather's being honest. She's taking ownership in pushing the show away, but I don't think that's what she intended, even subconsciously. Because she wanted to continue with the show.

Kelly Dodd: Heather's never ever come out and said exactly what went down. She likes to pretend she left on her own recognizance; no, they didn't want her back!

Tamra Judge: Losing Heather was hard for the show. It lost a level of class that it never got back. There was no turning back.

> *Before Heather's exit, however, there was another season 11 showdown to be had between Kelly and the rest of the cast. This one came during the trip to Ireland, where Kelly once again felt she was being set up by her castmates.*

Kelly Dodd: I was so alone on that trip because Vicki was trying to get back in Shannon, Tamra, and Heather's good graces, so she was scared shitless of going against them, and Meghan—well, she was pregnant and not feeling well, but she also was so scared of those women and didn't want to involve herself.

Meghan King: Kelly's a victim. To say that I'm scared? That's just her insecurity showing.

Kelly Dodd: It was just bad right from the get-go. We were out having a beer at a pub and Tamra came out and lied, saying I had been looking into Heather's finances. That wasn't the truth. What happened was, my friend was Heather's Realtor and she told me Terry inherited his money after his dad died and his brother died—which makes sense because you don't make that kind of money being a plastic surgeon, you just don't. So Terry's a trust-fund baby, who cares? There's nothing wrong with that. But I told Tamra all this, and she turned around and painted me like I was being deviant, which I wasn't.

Heather Dubrow: Kelly kept coming after me that whole trip for no reason.

She did that thing in the bar where she said, "You're Jewish, so you should be funny and understand my jokes." Like, "*What?*"

Kelly Dodd: Then we go shopping and while we're there, I tell Shannon something like, "Even Tamra's own daughter hates her because she's a liar." Because Tamra set me off! And of course, when we're in the store, Shannon tells Tamra and Tamra flips out.

Shannon Storms Beador: I should have waited. I'm stupid. But I thought I had to tell my friend what Kelly said because it really wasn't nice.

Tamra Judge: When I heard what Kelly said about me, I saw red. I was furious.

Shannon Storms Beador: Tamra just took off and said, "Fuck that bitch," and ran through that store. I was running after her. You can kind of hear it because we were still miked.

Kelly Dodd: Suddenly Tamra came up and hit me—like, pushed me hard in the chest. I was like, "What the hell?"

Heather Dubrow: We wound up getting kicked out of the store. It was crazy.

Things really came to a head on the last night of the trip.

Heather Dubrow: [Tamra, Shannon, and I] went down to the hotel bar with the crew, to kind of celebrate the last night.

Shannon Storms Beador: Tamra, to hurt Kelly, called Vicki and said, "Come meet us but don't bring Kelly." So Vicki came to the bar and it was Tamra, Vicki, Heather, and I with a bunch of crew people.

Tamra Judge: While we were at the bar, Vicki told me all this shit Kelly was saying about me—calling me a mean girl and stuff. And so I texted her and told her off.

Vicki Gunvalson: Kelly wasn't invited down to the bar; they didn't want Kelly down there. And when she found out that I went down with every-body, she got upset with me.

Shannon Storms Beador: As we were going back to our rooms, Kelly came out, and a whole argument exploded, and Heather took out her phone and started filming it.

Kelly Dodd: Now it's time to head to the airport, and I told producers, "I'm not going on that fucking bus. I will pay for my own taxi to go there by myself." But producers were like, "It will be okay. There's no camera in there, no mics. We'll have Thomas sit next to you. Everyone is tired and drunk. They're not going to bother you. Just sit there and be quiet."

Vicki Gunvalson: It was, like, three a.m. when we got picked up to go. It was weird. I felt like I was in *The Twilight Zone*.

Shannon Storms Beador: I was the last one in the van, and I sat right behind Kelly because that's where the empty seat was.

Kelly Dodd: Shannon was adamant that she was going to get under my skin and come after me. She started antagonizing me, and I finally had it, where I couldn't take it anymore, so I told her to shave her chin because a floodlight was shining right on her chin and there was a bunch of hair on her face. She looked like Sasquatch!

Shannon Storms Beador: Well, first Kelly said, "You can dish it out but you can't take it." Then she called me an alcoholic. And *then*, she said, "Shave that hair off your chin," and I went, "What?! You only *wish* you'll look like me when you're my age."

Kelly Dodd: She said, "You should hope you look like me when you're my age without any physical altercations." She meant "alterations," but she said "altercations." That was funny.

Meghan King: At first, as things were unfolding, I was like, "Oooh, this is good drama!" I was excited because I could be an observer; it wasn't about me. And then it got so, so nasty.

Kelly Dodd: Production saw what was happening so they whipped out their iPhones and started filming it.

Thomas Kelly: We shot it all in the back of the van. Everyone looked like monsters, but that was less because of the lighting and more because there was some monster behavior.

Heather Dubrow: My impression of Ireland is that filming it was completely different than how it played out on TV. Sometimes that happens; you think the story is going one way but it's going another. In the moment, I thought Kelly was being crazy. She did and said some really crazy things. And when I watched it, I was surprised. She definitely got a very good, sympathy cut to that trip.

Thomas Kelly: Kelly held her own. She fought back, but she didn't lose it. She didn't swing and hit anyone, like some of the women wanted her to do. That's the beauty of Kelly: she's always been able to use restraint in moments that matter the most.

Shannon Storms Beador: Then, Kelly turns and says to me, "Your husband beats the shit out of you. Vicki told me." That's when everyone went crazy.

Meghan King: Kelly's like a child. Whenever she feels attacked she goes on the defense and just says whatever is on her mind. It's like dealing with a toddler.

Kelly Dodd: I would never have brought that up but I was backed into a corner. I was provoked! They were attacking me, and the only recourse I had was this information about Shannon. And it was brilliant on my end because I deflected the narrative. Everyone just turned on Vicki.

Shannon Storms Beador: I was beside myself because what she was saying was completely untrue. I screamed at Vicki, "What the hell are you doing to my family right now?" David had just done a vow renewal for me and we were supposedly trying to repair our marriage.

Tamra Judge: Then I went up to Kelly and asked her if Vicki had told her anything about me. Now, the thing is, earlier in the season I had found out that Vicki and Kelly had a meeting with Gretchen, Slade, and a few other ex-cast members at Starbucks to try to come up with stuff to make me look bad. Vicki was mad about the Brooks thing and wanted to get revenge, so they were all brainstorming ways to take me down. They had no facts, but they wanted something, and one of the things that they settled on was that they were going to spread a rumor that Eddie was gay. They were going to film a guy in a CUT Fitness hat jacking off and send the video to another guy so it looked like it was Eddie. A real fucked-up thing to do.

Vicki Gunvalson: I absolutely wanted to get revenge on Tamra for hurting me, yes. Hurt people hurt people, so you can't go around hurting people and expect to sit there and never expect to be hurt back.

Kelly Dodd: When I got that job, Gretchen and Slade contacted me—I'd known them for a while, they're friends—and they told me all this stuff about the dynamics of the group, including warning me that Tamra was evil. I don't like to listen to people at all; I want to be a judge for myself. Just because Gretchen had a bad experience with Tamra doesn't mean I was going to. But then Vicki would tell me things like, "Tamra is an awful person." They hated her.

Vicki Gunvalson: I really didn't want to hurt anybody. I was always potentially the victim of people hurting *me*.

Tamra Judge: I got tipped off about it by Uncle Richie, Jeana's friend. Remember him? He was like, "I don't want to get in the middle of this, but this is what they're doing and it's so nasty." And then Kelly later verified all this but made it look like it was all Vicki's idea and she didn't want to be a part of it. So I knew it was going on but I never gave it any attention because I knew it was all stupid. I never gave it any attention—well, until that bus ride.

When I went up to Kelly and asked her if Vicki had told her anything about me, you don't hear what I actually said next, which was, "Let me guess, Eddie's gay?" And Kelly said, "No, she actually said you were having an affair." That's why I flipped out, got in her face, and screamed, "Fuck you."

Shannon Storms Beador: When we got off that bus, I was in fucking shock. My mind was racing, "This is going to be on the show. This is going to destroy my marriage. This is going to hurt David's business, his reputation, our family." Because when you put ideas out there like that, there's always a chance people might believe them.

Vicki Gunvalson: I just sat there crying, thinking, "How did this just happen?" We had just had a great time down at the bar, and now we were in this weird place again.

Shari Levine: I was shocked by the bus ride. I had never seen people on this series be so mean and so determined to destroy each other. It had gone to a place we'd never been before. I still cringe when I think about it.

Thomas Kelly: The best reality TV is caught off the cuff, and that bus ride in Ireland, that was a great moment. There's a point where the viewers need to see the women being caught off guard because it reminds them they're seeing something real. That bus ride was one of those moments where viewers said, "Holy shit, we are really in these women's worlds."

The next season Tamra and Shannon had to figure out how they were going to continue being on a show with Vicki.

Vicki Gunvalson: I talked about how addictive fame is before, but your fame can be good or bad, depending upon what season you're in. Some days I hated it and wanted to get out. Other times I was like, "I have to stay on long enough to make my character what it truly is." Because it's edited reality, it's not 100 percent you. So you think to yourself, "I need to fix this."

Shannon Storms Beador: I couldn't believe they were going to keep Vicki employed after what she did. She's already faked cancer and lied; now she's making allegations against my husband for a criminal act. And you're still going to keep her? I don't know how they decide what cast members come back or not. I've been told there's market research, but I can't imagine that Vicki came out with glowing reviews after that. What does it take? Does she have to murder someone?

Douglas Ross: Vicki has always been questionable. So I would have never thought of getting rid of her for being kooky enough to think that she could get away with what she was doing. It made for a great story. It was a producer's wet dream!

To help bring some positive energy to the group, producers brought back sunny season 8 Housewife Lydia—a casting choice that surprised many people.

Tamra Judge: Lydia had only been on for one season, so I was shocked to see her return. We'd just lost Heather, a huge part of the show, and nothing against Lydia—she was a sweet girl—but I don't always think sweet works as a Housewife.

Alex Baskin: There was such a strong division in the group and we were coming off such a heated time, there was a feeling among us of, "Well, we can't bring in two completely new people." And we wondered whether Lydia could help bring people back together. She was sort of, like, neutral territory. It felt like the right solution.

Shannon Storms Beador: None of us needed Lydia to put us back together. She was the peacemaker that never was.

Kelly Dodd: She was very nice and very kind, but she didn't have any backbone. She's just not cut out for this.

Lydia wasn't able to help orchestrate a truce, but Shannon and Tamra did finally mend fences with Vicki, the three coming together at the season 12 reunion in the three-way hug seen 'round the world.

Shannon Storms Beador: I wasn't super excited about that group hug.

Tamra Judge: Here's what happened. I was going back and forth that season, because it took me a long time to consider forgiving Vicki. But I got there, and definitely before Shannon did.

Shannon Storms Beador: I was happy to forgive Vicki, I just didn't want to be her friend. I told that to Vicki directly. But Tamra was very phony. She'd say on camera she was willing to make up with Vicki, but behind the scenes, she'd call me and talk shit about Vicki all the time.

Tamra Judge: I was really, really wavering on what to do. Because at the reunion, all the stuff that happened during the season resurfaces. You bring stuff back up and you say to yourself, "Wait, why am I forgiving you?"

Kathleen French: Reunions are always emotional days for the ladies. And this one was where Shannon announced her separation.

Shannon Storms Beador: That was incredibly difficult, but I don't know that David and I ever got back to normal after his affair and after doing relationship boot camp. By the end of season 11, I was literally eating and drinking myself into oblivion, and by the time season 12 began, I was forty pounds overweight and David wanted nothing to do with me. He was pulling away. The decision to separate finally came at the end of August 2017. We went on a family trip to Hawaii, but David left early and when I came back with the kids, he said, "We're done."

At the reunion, I was finally ready to talk about it. And that's when I finally saw true remorse from Vicki. She had tears in her eyes and said, "If I caused any of this, I'm so sorry." Then she got into a tearful conversation with Tamra, and I was like, "Oh Jesus, are they really going to make up now?" Sure enough, Vicki got up, came over, and hugged Tamra.

Tamra Judge: I wanted to move forward.

Shannon Storms Beador: It just felt fake, phony, phony, phony, phony. And then Vicki apologized to me and reached for me. And I'll tell you—for one split second, I hesitated, going, "Oh fuck me, now I've got to get up again?" But she showed what I considered to be true remorse.

Andy Cohen: It felt real to me. I saw the moment Vicki broke through.

Vicki Gunvalson: I still don't know how we were able to get through it. I don't know how.

Kelly Dodd: It was just completely weird because all season, Tamra and Vicki hated each other. Now all of a sudden, they're best friends? It was like *The Twilight Zone*.

Meghan King: I'm sorry, but that was fucked-up. I was sitting there with Shannon and Tamra at the reunion, and their anger toward Vicki was not going that way.

Lydia McLaughlin: For me, I knew once they made up that I was going to be on the chopping block. Because I didn't fit in with this group of girls anymore. So I actually called the producers the next day and I said, "I will not film again with them. They hate me. They're all going to pretend to be best friends, and I can't be around people who aren't authentic." They were like, "You're just upset. It's fine. Everyone's upset after the reunion." But I said, "No. I'm out." And that was that.

Alex Baskin: Lydia didn't choose to leave the second time around. We actually moved on. Frankly, her return just didn't completely work. She did her job well, so it wasn't like she didn't bring it. We felt like we should start over.

Kathleen French: It was strange that she returned in the first place, given why she left.

Alex Baskin: The idea was almost to pretend that season 12 was a dream sequence and just move on altogether.

Meghan King: I ended up quitting after the reunion, too. I went to dinner with Andy in St. Louis and I told him I didn't want to come back, because I was pregnant with twins and just knew I couldn't devote the amount of time that the show demanded. He was very supportive. He told me, "You're always welcome back anytime." And then I went home and cried because the decision was so hard.

Alex Baskin: Meghan retreated! Her life was pulling her toward St. Louis and it almost felt like to us that she didn't want to be doing the show anymore. It just felt like time. It was pretty obvious to all of us at that point that she wouldn't be returning.

Meghan King: Oh, I would have surely been fired had I not quit, don't get me wrong. Because remember how I said after my first season I begged to keep my job? I did that for my second, too. So I could see what was coming, I figured I'd be fired. Being fired sucks! Nobody wants to ever be fired from a job. So I took that power and control back.

> *Another Housewife also left after season 12: newcomer Peggy Sulahian. The married mother of three and a proud immigrant who was born in Kuwait to Armenian parents, joined RHOC that year as a friend of Lydia's. But like Peggy Tanous before her, this Peggy was a one-season wonder.*

Andy Cohen: Nick Rizzo—my incredible head of research at *WWHL*—figured out that Peggy was very famously our hundredth Housewife in the franchise. I wish she'd been more iconic.

Peggy Sulahian (Housewife): I didn't learn about that until Andy said it one day, and it was like, "Wow." It's an honor to be the hundredth Housewife in the franchise. Even though I was only on one season, that's something they can't take away from me.

Shannon Storms Beador: She still hashtags everything "100th Housewife." She's going to have that on her tombstone.

Peggy Sulahian: They had been asking me for several years to audition but I always had that attitude of "You guys need me, I don't need you." My husband is the founder of the custom auto company Giovanna Wheels, which has been in business for nearly twenty-five years and is very well known in the industry. We'd been on TV in the past, doing interviews here and there. I've also known celebrities like P. Diddy, Khloé Kardashian, and French Montana. But I was never someone who was drawn to fame; I've never been starstruck. And I've always wanted to keep my family behind the scenes; I'm very, very careful with them and kept them a secret just in case of kidnapping. So I thought, really, the show wasn't for me.

My husband was the one who pushed me to do it. I was going through a difficult time in my life, a very sad time, because my dad's health was deteriorating and they had found cancer cells in my breast. My husband thought doing this would help lift my spirits and take my mind off things. And he was right, but the time line was crazy. I made the decision to have a double mastectomy because my mom had cancer and I had seen the experience she went through before she succumbed to her death. I had my surgery in January and then, five weeks later, I started filming.

Alex Baskin: Peggy had an active, fun family, and we thought that casting her would bring a lively household into the show.

Peggy Sulahian: Most of the women were not at all supportive of me. They were horrible and not compassionate; very selfish people and very inconsiderate.

Lydia McLaughlin: It was horrible to see the way Peggy was treated, especially when we went away to Iceland. The viewers didn't see the worst of it!

Peggy Sulahian: Iceland was where Kelly called me ISIS. It wasn't on the show, but I have proof. I have a recording of it. What happened was, there was a big bee in my room and I called downstairs to the concierge and said, "Please come up and get this bee out." As I was waiting for them, I stayed out of my room and a few doors down, I could hear Meghan's daughter crying, so I walked down there. Meghan's room was connected to Shannon's room and they were both in Shannon's room, drinking with Kelly and Tamra. It was like, "Are you kidding? You are drinking when your baby is crying?" And when I got there, I could hear them laughing at me and saying very, very, very horrible things about me.

Kelly Dodd: We were having fun. Tamra and I went out in the hallway—I think we had to get something from Meghan's room?—and Peggy opened up her door and said, "Why are you guys laughing at me?"

Peggy Sulahian: I was recording it because they were drunk and I knew they wouldn't remember.

Kelly Dodd: We said, "We're not laughing at you." Because we weren't, though we started laughing in her face then. And then Peggy said, "Do you know who my family is? Do you know who I am?" And I go, "Who, ISIS?"

Peggy Sulahian: I couldn't believe it. How could you call someone ISIS? Just because I'm an immigrant and talk with an accent? Did she not see what was going on in the world?

Kelly Dodd: I wasn't calling her ISIS because of her ethnicity. I wasn't being racist or anything. I know she's Armenian and Christian. But at the time, ISIS was the big terrorist group in the news and she was over here threatening us, so it was like, "Who are you? A terror group? Am I supposed to be scared? I'm not scared of you!" That's how I meant it. If I said it today, I would say, "What are you, Antifa?"

Shannon Storms Beador: Kelly kept saying, "ISIS! She's ISIS!" I pulled out my phone and filmed it, but they never aired it.

Tamra Judge: The next day, Peggy stayed in her room the whole time.

Kelly Dodd: After that fight, Peggy left Iceland early.

Lydia McLaughlin: Peggy brought up the ISIS comments at the reunion. She actually said a bunch of stuff that didn't air, which sucks because it looked like she's overreacting about nothing.

Douglas Ross: In the earlier days, outrageous comments like that would have been kept in because they're polarizing and would create a story. But by then, political correctness had bypassed everything.

Alex Baskin: It was also to protect Peggy, in a sense, because being called something like that on television would be damaging to her and her family.

Shannon Storms Beador: The bombing at Ariana Grande's Manchester concert happened this same year and that was an ISIS attack. It would be too much; it was too close to a tragedy.

Heather Dubrow: Yeah but Kelly talks about Black people, she talks about ISIS, she talks about Jews—I don't understand why she's Teflon?

Peggy Sulahian: After we finished filming, I went into surgery because I had to delay my second surgery due to filming. And then I had to wait another two months for recovery. By that point the show was airing and with everything happening in my life, I just felt like the bullying and the drama wasn't worth it. My health was more important than the show.

Meghan, Lydia, and Peggy's exits left openings in the cast. In their place producers found two new Housewives. First up was Gina Kirschenheiter, a Long Island transplant now living in the OC with her husband and their three children.

Dawn Stroupe: Gina walked in with her Chanel earrings on and a full-sequin dress—I mean, she really looked like a Housewife. But then she opened her mouth and she had this thick Long Island accent, which was so unexpected. And she was telling these hilarious stories; I was howling with laughter. She was so fun and so fresh; really different from anybody else I had met. And after our interview, I said to my staff, "She's going to be on the show." I hardly ever say that, but I just knew because she popped off the screen.

The other Housewife was Emily Simpson, a married mother of three, attorney, and part-time party planner.

Dawn Stroupe: It was clear Emily was a good fit for the show. She had all the inner workings of a Housewife. She wasn't a "perfect mom," her sister carried her children, her husband hadn't passed the bar but had tried twice. That imperfection was attractive. She wasn't stick thin. She didn't look like anyone else. That, to me, that is gold.

Shannon Storms Beador: I won't lie, I questioned why Emily and Gina were brought on. And I had enough going on in my life with my divorce, the last thing I wanted to do was get to know two new girls.

Gina Kirschenheiter (Housewife): Shannon was never friendly or nice to us. She, Tamra, and Vicki would ice us out at group dinners. One night I flipped on them because it was clear they were talking shit and whispering to each other about us. It was driving me fucking nuts! So Emily and I, we had to just stick together.

Emily Simpson (Housewife): Shannon actually ignored me for the first *two* seasons. She didn't speak to me at all. We had no relationship. I never filmed with her unless it was a group thing. It was like I didn't exist. That's how Shannon operates. She just pretends like you're not there and that you're not good enough to breathe the air that she breathes. I don't know what her endgame is. Maybe it's just part of the whole strategy to ice out the new people so they don't last very long.

Kelly Dodd: Gina and Emily were lucky. When I started, I didn't have anybody. I always thought it was so nice that they had each other.

As Emily and Gina began to learn the Housewives *ropes, another friendship was starting to crack.*

Shannon Storms Beador: This was the season everyone painted me as the asshole friend who makes everything about me. Which was untrue.

Tamra Judge: Was it?

Shannon Storms Beador: I was in the midst of a very difficult few months. I had just filed for divorce two months prior to starting filming. I was still so fucking fat, I hadn't lost the weight yet, and my confidence was shot. I actually wasn't there for the first two days of filming because I went to the Golden Door Spa. I wanted to just get away. And then I started to date someone in my neighborhood, but he wasn't being kind to me. So overall, I just wasn't in a good place emotionally. I was really down.

Tamra Judge: This was the season Eddie had been diagnosed with atrial fibrillation. He was undergoing a series of procedures to address the problem, and Shannon never seemed to care about how he was doing, how I was feeling, anything. She would get drunk and call, at all hours of the night, venting about her problems.

Shannon Storms Beador: Did I call Tamra when I was upset sometimes? Yes. I was going through a nasty divorce! I had some hard nights. But you're my best friend. Don't start bitching about taking a few phone calls. Let's go back and scroll through your footage when you are going through your divorce with Simon, crying all the time.

Tamra Judge: It got to be exhausting, always having to deal with her shit. She was being so needy and so negative, and I had bigger things going on in my life that she was never even asking about. My feelings were hurt! So I vented my feelings to other people because I had a hard time expressing myself.

Shannon Storms Beador: I was totally blindsided. What happened was, Vicki and I had a joint golfing birthday party on a Friday. And while we were at lunch, Tamra got super drunk and started attacking me for comments I had made about Emily's husband. It completely came out of the blue, and I was upset. I wound up walking off.

We didn't talk again until we filmed a scene together at Roger's Gardens that Monday or Tuesday. And looking back, knowing Tamra, she sat there that weekend going, "How am I going to spin this?" So when we sat down, she started crying and telling me I haven't been a good friend to her. I couldn't believe it. I wanted to go, "Are you fucking kidding me? I haven't been a good friend to you?" But I thought instead, "You know, Shannon, you better bend over and take it up the ass. Just take the bullet for the friendship, because it's not worth getting in a tit for tat with her." So I just dropped it, without realizing she was going to take that conversation and turn it into her story line for the season.

Douglas Ross: One of the things Tamra did that drove Shannon crazy was that she would be forthcoming about her relationship with Shannon in the interview bites. And Shannon was so devastated when she watched the show and saw that Tamra didn't have her back.

Shannon Storms Beador: It was shocking to me. I say all the time that filming is the most fun part of this show, but watching it back is horrible because you see all the things people say about you behind your back. To see that Tamra was filming with Gina and Emily, saying things about me, it hurt.

Gina Kirschenheiter: Hello, you're filming a show with other people! There's going to be times you and the person you're fighting with aren't together.

Shannon Storms Beador: All of it culminated in Jamaica, where Gina went after me at dinner saying that I hadn't been a good friend to Tamra. And Tamra was silent at that table, which was completely devastating to me. I couldn't believe that this was the worst year of my life and they were all making me out to be the asshole. It was like a feeding frenzy of rats.

Tamra Judge: When we got back to the hotel, Shannon had a complete meltdown.

Gina Kirschenheiter: The day after she freaked out, Shannon spent the entire day refusing to film. And all the women were bashing Shannon while she was gone, talking about how she's a raging alcoholic, how she wasn't taking care of her children, how she would sleep all day and then call them at all hours of the night. And then, boom, the next day Shannon and Tamra hashed things out in a private conversation in a hotel room in twenty minutes and we were all supposed to just pretend everything was fine. It's like, "What happened to all the other shit we just witnessed? You made us feel like this woman was mentally unstable. You were saying you were afraid to leave her alone because you didn't know what she was going to do to herself. Is it really all now hunky-dory?"

Shannon Storms Beador: Clearly it wasn't. That was probably my most frustrating season because I didn't say everything I wanted to say. I wanted to protect my friendship with Tamra, and I thought that being a best friend was more important than being right in the argument. But looking back, I should have, because Tamra took every opportunity she could to cut me down and make me look unstable.

Tamra Judge: I cared about Shannon. I was hurt. But that didn't mean I was ready to throw the friendship away. We worked through things.

Shannon and Tamra were able to patch up their friendship, but Kelly and Vicki weren't so lucky when they had a surprising fallout in season 13.

Kelly Dodd: The second I saw that three-way hug at the season 12 reunion, I was nervous because I knew that Vicki, Shannon, and Tamra were now going to band together and take me down.

Tamra Judge: Here we go again, with the conspiracy theories.

Shannon Storms Beador: Jesus, get off your fucking high horse, Kelly.

Kelly Dodd: But sure enough I was right, because Vicki turned on me the second she could. I thought we were friends. We went to Cabo together, I would go to BBQs at her house. It felt like a legit friendship. But then one day, I got a call from the *Daily Mail* to tell me that Michael—who I had divorced by that point—was dating one of Vicki's friends and they all went out to dinner recently on a double date. I felt like she stabbed me in the back.

Tamra Judge: The two of them went at each other, back and forth, all season long. Then Kelly started attacking Vicki on social media, calling [Vicki's new boyfriend] Steve a douchebag and Vicki a pig. Then at the reunion, Vicki accused Kelly of doing coke—which, if you watch back, you'll see my jaw drop when she says that.

Shannon Storms Beador: That's how Vicki operates. I know because she did it to me in season 11. She'll hear a rumor and repeat it just to cause you pain.

Kelly Dodd: There just was no basis for Vicki's accusation. It was a complete and utter lie. I don't want to be on a show where you can just say whatever you want and there's no recourse and no validity to it. Though, I guess there were consequences in this case because they demoted Vicki that next year.

That's right. After fourteen years of holding an orange, Vicki was moved to a "Friend of" role—though it didn't have anything to do with her allegations against Kelly.

Andy Cohen: Over the years, there were times when we knew viewers were not connecting with Vicki, but we felt like it would be too dramatic to take her off the show. We would have conversations within Bravo or elsewhere, like, "Should this be the year we pull Vicki out?" And I never could see it. Until that last year . . .

Alex Baskin: The network was concerned, at that point, that Vicki didn't have enough personal story left.

Douglas Ross: Vicki had been pulling back over the last two seasons. And there were two important factors at play here. On one hand, her relationship with her daughter Briana had gone through so many ups and downs (especially through the Brooks years), and Briana was really over participating in the show. She was involved with her family, living in North Carolina, and wasn't around to film. You may not realize it but Briana's participation, through the years, was really key to making Vicki interesting and rounding her out. So when she wasn't around, that didn't help Vicki.

On the other hand, Vicki was now in this relationship with a retired homicide detective named Steve Lodge. Though Steve was supportive of the show in the beginning because he knew how important it was to Vicki, both emotionally and financially, he wanted to be part of it as little as he possibly could. And because he was conservative and was running for office at the time, she started clamping down on her own behavior. The Vicki who showed her boobs, who whooped it up, who said whatever came to her mind—all of that stuff, she not only wouldn't do that anymore but she was now vocally critical of others like Tamra for being loose and free.

Alex Baskin: She changed. She wasn't as unfiltered as she had once been. We couldn't eke out much more personal story. But Vicki is great in group scenes, and particularly on trips—on a vacation, you know shit's going to go down and she's probably going to end up in an ambulance—so it felt like she could be the perfect Friend.

Douglas Ross: Alex and I told her what the network wanted, that her role was going to be reduced, and she didn't want to do it. We were at a restaurant, Vicki had arranged for a private dining room, and we sat with her and Steve and had to lay out all the reasons why we thought it was important for her to do it.

Vicki Gunvalson: I didn't understand it, and I still don't. Not enough story, are you kidding me? It's so stupid. I mean, what is Kelly's story? What is Gina's story? What is Emily's story? I mean, come on, it's ridiculous. I thought this was a reality show? If it's a reality show, you never know what your reality is going to be each year. There's no preplanned "story," so how would they know?

Alex Baskin: I can't even count the number of conversations we had with Vicki about why the decision was made. Yet she kept saying she was never given an explanation for it. The truth was, she was given an explanation for it many times but she never, ever accepted it.

Meanwhile the network did everything to make sure Vicki didn't have to suffer the indignity of being called a "Friend," even not referring to her as that in the press releases. They wrote, "The Tres Amigas will be back with Vicki in a supporting role"—so not "Friend" but, instead, "Friend" in Spanish.

Tamra Judge: That didn't make a difference. Vicki was pissed.

Andy Cohen: Vicki hated every minute of being a Friend. She asked me on the phone if being a Friend meant she wouldn't be holding an orange in the opening credits. The answer was no, she wouldn't be, and she was embarrassed. That was a rough call. I think I walked my dog five miles while we talked.

Kelly Dodd: When I learned Vicki was getting demoted—Oh my God, it was like being suffocated and all of a sudden getting oxygen again.

Vicki Gunvalson: I never felt like I was a "Friend." I filmed every day, just like everybody else. I got paid almost the full amount I got before. I gave it my all, was on every episode, was part of every story line, had my engagement party. It didn't feel handicapped at all.

Alex Baskin: She was miserable the entire time. Vicki really thought it was complete bullshit. She would say, "I created this franchise! You can't demote me!"

> *Braunwyn Windham-Burke filled the spot in the cast left open by Vicki. A married mother of seven children, the spitfire California native had a unique tie to the series.*

Jeana Keough: I've known Braunwyn since she was a kid.

Braunwyn Windham-Burke (Housewife): The Keoughs were good family friends of ours growing up, so I had watched the show for years. And when a casting director slid into my DMs on Instagram all these years later asking me, "Have you ever heard of *The Real Housewives of Orange County* and would you be interested?" I freaked out because this was something I really wanted. I'm not one of those people who will be like, "Oh, I didn't really want to do it." No, I have thought about this since I was a kid. Some people dream about being an Olympic athlete. I dreamed about being a Housewife.

Dawn Stroupe: We're always looking for people with big lives, because then there's a plethora of stuff we could shoot. So Braunwyn having seven kids, that felt like there were a lot of possibilities there. I remember going to her house and meeting her and Sean. They had an eight-month-old and an eighteen-year-old at the time. And in that interview, Braunwyn was great—probably not as vulnerable as she is now, but still very open. It was a home run.

Braunwyn Windham-Burke: When I got the final phone call in January, I screamed so loud, my kid ran in the room thinking something was wrong. I was jumping up and down. I mean, having babies was nice, but this was better.

Dawn Stroupe: Braunwyn was a member of the Balboa Bay Club and so was Kelly Dodd, so there was a connection there.

Braunwyn Windham-Burke: I didn't meet Kelly until a few days before we started filming. I went to lunch with her and Thomas at the Balboa Bay Club, and I was starstruck. I couldn't wrap my brain around the fact that Kelly Dodd was sitting there. I don't think I spoke for five minutes. There is a weird thing when you're a fan coming onto this show that not a lot of people talk about. I had very preconceived notions of everyone and it took me a little bit to shake the fact that I was interacting with them in real life. Even my first all-cast event, I was dropping food on the floor, I was so petrified to be around everyone. They never showed me walking into Tamra's house because when she answered the door, I had this stupid, giggly reaction to meeting her for the first time. I couldn't even fake it. They were like, "Welp, we won't be using that!"

There certainly was a lot of off-camera drama in season 14, as the Tres Amigas each found themselves in their own bitter battles with Kelly.

Kelly Dodd: Those girls wanted me off, and they banded together to kick me off.

Emily Simpson: I agree. The Tres Amigas thing was nothing more than a conspiracy to get Kelly fired from the show. It doesn't take a genius to see it.

Tamra Judge: How many more times do I have to say that's not true?

Gina Kirschenheiter: It didn't even feel like they were really friends. They were coworkers who had this common ground. They knew that together they were stronger than apart.

Kelly Dodd: The thing was, filming with Vicki as a Friend was worse because she was on attack mode toward me! She was so thirsty to come back and get me off, because in her mind, she thought I was the reason she got demoted, so she wanted to take me down.

Emily Simpson: Vicki in season 14 was entirely different than the one I met in season 13. My first year, she wasn't as close with Shannon and Tamra and she was really nice to me. She filmed with me a lot, and I found her to be amusing. She acted like a tenured professor who sits in the back of the room and just does crossword puzzles; she didn't try very hard. But in season 14, they formed that Tres Amigas thing and she was an entirely new person. All of a sudden she was mean and was lashing out at everybody. She got caught up in Tamra and Shannon's ways, even though she isn't as conniving, manipulative, or strategic as they are. And she was fighting for her job back. She had been demoted and she came in, wreaking havoc everywhere, ready to fight.

Gina Kirschenheiter: And see, I liked her better in season 14 because she shows up. My first year she was so low-energy. You'd be talking to her and she'd be typing on her laptop, or would just leave a scene. She was comfortable. Whereas, after she was demoted, she came to play. She kind of made everything into an issue and stirred up shit, probably because she thought that would save her job.

Dave Rupel: The Tres Amigas alliance sort of did them all in. Tamra, Vicki, and Shannon were all totally likable when they were interacting with other people, but as a threesome, it hurt them.

Alex Baskin: On one hand, secrets and gossip are really fun. That's essential to the formula. But the challenge for us always is when the cast gets fixated on their standing in the cast. When it looks like they're trying to control each other or exterminate someone else. The relationships between them aren't real at that point. It becomes just a battle of information against each other or reputational damage. It crosses a line.

Andy Cohen: It just became clear after that season that something had to change.

> *Something sure would change. Season 14 wound up being Vicki's last on* The Real Housewives of Orange County. *In January 2020, the "OG of the OC" announced her departure from the series, after not being asked to return for another year.*

Andy Cohen: We called it after season 14 with Vicki. She'd been a "Friend" that last season, which she was completely demoralized by. By the end of the season, the network felt it was time to move on. The final straw was the reunion, which was a really bad day for her, starting with her flipping out that she wasn't going to be onstage the whole time, and that we originally didn't have her seated next to me. We did move her next to me.

Alex Baskin: Vicki's frustrations had been building up all season. All of this culminated in the moment at the reunion where we had a champagne toast. If you remember, it was full-time ladies only, and getting Vicki off the stage infuriated her and led to her epic meltdown backstage.

Douglas Ross: Alex, Andy, and I have discussed this several times since then. The plan was that Andy was going to say, "Thank you, goodbye," and have her leave before we reset to do the toast. And we debated, should we have Andy warn her? Instead we thought, "She's going to have a meltdown. Let's just do it in the moment." And after it happened, we agreed that Andy should have bent over to her and said, "When we're done with this I'm going to thank you and have you exit," so she could have mentally prepared a little bit. But she was so flummoxed, didn't understand it, and didn't *leave*. We didn't really show that, but it was bad.

Andy Cohen: It was a meltdown that came as close to *The Comeback* as anything I've seen in fifteen years. It was a reality star who hated the cameras but seemingly couldn't survive without them. Pure Valerie Cherish.

Vicki Gunvalson: I was extremely loyal and passionate about my job. I definitely had pride in it. I employed a lot of people. Think of the cameramen, the people behind the desks at Bravo. Think about Andy Cohen who really was not where he's at now when I first met him. There's a lot of people who, because our show was successful, I helped employ.

Alex Baskin: She still, even at the end of the season, hadn't come to terms with the fact that she was no longer full-time on the show.

Vicki Gunvalson: Getting fired, that was really tough. You know, when the show was airing, I was seeing how they twisted and turned the realities and wanted to quit all the time. But when it's decided for you . . . I remember getting the call from Doug telling me, "The network has decided to go in a different direction," and I had a complete meltdown afterward. I couldn't breathe, I was crying so hard.

Lauren Zalaznick: When I think back to Vicki, she was always *the* Housewife. You know, a lot of these women were born at the wrong time. Society caught up to them. And Vicki, she's this incredibly complex person who was striving for something bigger.

Kathleen French: You saw her really reinvent herself from the Midwestern girl with bad hair and unattractive teeth to this Orange County gal. She had left her first husband, the father of her children, because of his substance abuse issues and now was in this gated community with Donn, drifting away in that marriage. She always showed all those sides of herself. She showed the good, the bad, and the ugly. To the end of my career, I'll always have a soft spot in my heart for Vicki because she was always an open book, and I always appreciated that.

Andy Cohen: I will say, the level of comedy that Vicki brought to that show, I don't know that will ever be replaced. She is like a Ramona in my mind, comedy-wise. They can't get out of their own way. They are just so uniquely themselves that it's funny.

Braunwyn Windham-Burke: Since she left the show, I saw Vicki do an interview where she said she equates the show to doing a drug. And when I read that, I was like, "I get it." Filming is addictive. It's an adrenaline rush. I do see how when someone says, "I'm taking that away from you" after fourteen, fifteen years, it's scary.

Shari Levine: It's like having a husband you really don't like anymore divorce you. You hate him, but you remember loving him, and you can't believe that it's over and that he's the one who called lights out.

Vicki Gunvalson: Leaving the show, it's like a death. You feel like, "What did I do wrong? How can I fix this?" And when you're being told you can't fix it, that's the hard part. When you're being told, "This is a decision made in the upper level," I'm like, well, "Who do I need to call? Because they obviously have this wrong." And that's when you find out that the decision has been made over a table about my fate. Like, I didn't have a say. That's the hard part. You don't have any say.

And then from there, every day, it's people in your DMs saying, "Are you coming back? You should come back!" You absolutely can't escape it. It's difficult. So you move on, but you never really can. You still have a little bit of a burn on your side because you're trying to figure out, "What's my new normal?"

Shari Levine: It is hard to not be a part of a show that has been such a big part of your life for many years.

> Vicki wasn't alone in her exit. A day after announcing her departure, news broke that Tamra would be leaving Real Housewives of Orange County after twelve years.

Andy Cohen: For years, I called Tamra the perfect Housewife, and she really was. She had so much personal story—she really opened up her life—

plus she was beautiful, funny, confrontational, dynamic. I mean, she had it all.

Alex Baskin: She really changed the game for *Housewives*. She was sort of the model Housewife all others would be compared against.

Tamra Judge: In the beginning, I was the girl who put it all out there. I don't hold anything back. I don't know if I'm brave or just ignorant, honestly, because I would talk about anything I was going through, problems I was having, or how I felt about other people. I didn't feel the need to hide things.

Thomas Kelly: Tamra's downfall was that the viewers got so used to this brilliant reality star that they caught on to what she was doing. They could see it coming and they just got tired of it. It was fresh and new for a long time but we now needed someone else to bring it in a different way.

Alex Baskin: Calling Tamra to tell her she wouldn't be returning as a Housewife was one of the hardest phone calls we've ever had to make.

Tamra Judge: I was at Ocotillo Wells on a camping trip at the time. A couple of days prior, I had gotten a call from the Evolution office to schedule me for the kickoff meet, where we talk about what we have on the books for the next season. So I'm in the desert and I have no phone service. But because my daughter was with her dad, I would periodically go up the road where there was like, one bar, and check in on her. And on one of those trips, I see I had a text from Alex.

Alex Baskin: We couldn't get her; it was going straight to voice mail and we *had* to talk to her. So I texted her, "Please give me a call." And of course, she knew where it was headed and wrote back, "Are you firing me?"

Tamra Judge: They said something like, "It's better that we talk on the phone and not through text." And the second I saw that, my heart kind of sank.

Alex Baskin: We offered her three episodes to wrap up her story because it would be weird for her to just disappear.

Tamra Judge: I was totally taken aback. I had no idea. So I just said, "You can fuck off." I started crying. It was miserable for me. Twelve years of my life, over just like that. I sat on the side of the road, sobbing.

Gina Kirschenheiter: Afterward, Tamra did unfollow us all on social media.

Tamra Judge: That wasn't anything personal, I just needed some space.

Heather Dubrow: When I left the show, I unfollowed everyone, too. You don't follow your sorority account when you graduate college, you kind of move on. And of course, there's a certain level of FOMO. "Is it going to be better without me? Are people going to like the fact that I'm gone?" I'm human. I totally thought about stuff like that. It's not easy.

Kelly Dodd: Tamra's firing, I mean, we were all just ecstatic when we heard about that.

Emily Simpson: I honestly was, like, pinching myself. I thought maybe it was a joke, or just a false rumor going around the Internet. But when Tamra gave the statement herself—like it was actually on her own Instagram—I was like, "Damn, that is karma at its finest. That is what you get for spending an entire season trying to get somebody else fired."

Lydia McLaughlin: It was Lizzie's birthday. I think there were, like, eight past Housewives, all with champagne, toasting to the news. That speaks volumes of what people thought about working with her.

Emily Simpson: Gretchen and Lizzie sent a text like, "Ding dong, the witch is dead!" They were having their own private party. I'm sure every ex-Housewife was happy about that.

Heather Dubrow: Don't you think it's weird, if you listen to these former Housewives, how much they hate these other Housewives? I love Tamra. Tamra plays this show like no one else—and I did use those words properly. She has a directive for the year, she knows what she's going to do, and she's very, very good at it. It's one of the things I actually admire about her, and it's one of the reasons why we've always remained friends. She was a young single mother and that mentality still stays with her. This is her bread and butter. She's doing what she needs to do for her family.

Lizzie Rovsek: She does know how to make a good show, I'll give her that.

Alexis Bellino: Yeah, she's good TV, that's the thing.

Gina Kirschenheiter: At the end of the day, you need an ensemble of people who are willing to do different things to make this show. You need someone like Tamra who will stir the pot and help move the story along. You need someone like Kelly who is going to sling shit for no reason even if it doesn't make sense. You need a voice of reason like Emily, a loyal friend like me, and someone who makes you laugh like Shannon. Like, all these personality types balance one another out. No one is better or worse than the other.

Bill Fritz: Tamra knew how to recognize the opportunities in a scene and take advantage of them to further push her personal story. Take that time she spoke at that women's conference, I think it was season 8. That was a scene where, going in, we didn't think it would make the show. We call those scenes "cast management," because we'll cover them but we know we may not actually use them as they tend to not be about anything other than self-promotion, and the audience just doesn't care about that. So we shot that thinking, "No one's probably going to see this, because who wants to watch an inspirational speech from Tamra?"

Well, the footage came back, and I'm watching it, and that's when Tamra admitted onstage in front of everybody that twice she tried to commit suicide. It was like, "Holy shit, this is really powerful." It wound up being a beautiful scene and taught viewers at home what makes Tamra so hard and such a street fighter. And again, that was just her recognizing the moment and saying, "I'm going to be vulnerable here." That's radically different than making up drama just to be the center of attention. Because Bravo smells that, instantly, and usually cuts that out. Tamra never did that.

A fresh start came in RHOC's *15th season. Adding to the action was new Housewife Elizabeth Lyn Vargas, an ambitious and outspoken Missouri native.*

Elizabeth Lyn Vargas (Housewife): I run an online music company, and I was working with this rapper named Too Short—who is quite a strong, opinionated rapper based in California—and one day his manager, David Weintraub, called me and asked me if I'd audition for a show in Burbank. He said, "Dress in your finest, do your hair and makeup, and bring your Bentley." I said, "Wait a minute . . . what is this? Is this a porn?" And he said, "No, it's *The Real Housewives of Orange County*."

Dawn Stroupe: We were almost finished with the casting process when Elizabeth came to us. A mutual friend who has known Doug, Alex, and myself for twenty years recommended her. He said, "You need to interview this girl."

Elizabeth Lyn Vargas: I couldn't help going online and doing my research before going in. I already knew Kelly Dodd—she's a friend of my neighbor and I had met her hanging out on the beach one day—so David told me to be sure to mention that. And then I went and watched the first episode of every season because I had to know what was going on and who the rest of these girls were, and everyone that I researched looked like a strong-ass bitch. I was so impressed with their strength. To be able to get on a show like this and really be raw and dirty?

Dawn Stroupe: We really liked that Elizabeth didn't hold back. She told everything about her life.

Shannon Storms Beador: When I first met her, before the show started, she was drunk and told me, "Hi, I'm the richest bitch in Newport Beach." I just kept walking. I was like, "Oh God help me." Richest bitch in Newport Beach? Who says that?

Gina Kirschenheiter: There were a lot of inconsistencies in Elizabeth's story, especially pertaining to her finances. And a lot of the women got pissed because we've shared so much and we've exposed so much of our lives, and she wasn't. So it definitely left her disconnected from the group. Oddly enough, it bonded the rest of us because having someone like that who literally no one connected with made us look at each other like, "Oh well, at least we have each other and know what we're doing."

Shannon Storms Beador: I'm not sure about that. Look, was I happy with the cast? No. I didn't think there was real chemistry.

Braunwyn Windham-Burke: We definitely weren't a bonded cast.

Shannon Storms Beador: All I know is, I have learned one lesson after what happened between Tamra and me. In the future, if I am still cast on the show, I'm never going to become best friends with a cast member because their job is always going to be more important. It's not worth it to become best friends with someone that you work with on a reality show like this.

Elizabeth Lyn Vargas: Everyone told me, before I did the show, "Oh, it's fake." Well, I'm here to tell you: "No, it's not!" It's actually real drama. And I'm someone who runs from conflict usually. I'm a mediator! I'm one of eight children, I've always mediated the crises and discrepancies of personalities in the family. I assumed I could handle it with this group but I wasn't used to people coming at me with dumb, stupid things.

Gina Kirschenheiter: I see Elizabeth as very confused. She was plucked out of Missouri at a young age and given a lot of money. She freely admits that she got it by basically being a high-class hooker. Now she's divorced and a billionaire and having to stand on her own two feet, but she's still that confused, small-town girl, trying to figure it out.

Elizabeth Lyn Vargas: My problems are so, so much different than "Why are you wearing those shoes? I bought the same shoes last week. It's annoying you bought the same shoes." That's not really an issue.

> Elizabeth wasn't the only one in the hot seat in season 15. Braunwyn became a divisive figure among the cast, after she admitted she was an alcoholic and was finally ready to get sober.

Braunwyn Windham-Burke: I got sober twelve days before we started filming. Literally twelve days before cameras went up, I hit rock bottom. Once I kind of faced the truth and knew what I had to do, I didn't have time to second-guess doing it on television. I was like, "Fuck, I signed the contract." But I actually said to producers, "Please don't make my getting sober my story line this season." I begged them. Because I had so much else going on in my life I wanted to focus on. Looking back though, how could it not be?

Kelly Dodd: Braunwyn is full of shit. Her whole sobriety thing is contrived and fake to get her a spin-off.

Shannon Storms Beador: According to Kelly and other people that we know, Braunwyn said before the season that her agent told her she could get her own show if she stopped drinking. That's hearsay, I wasn't there, I didn't hear it, so I don't know. But I didn't have an agenda when we came on the show, I was just myself. So it feels calculated.

Gina Kirschenheiter: And that's my issue with Braunwyn. It's less about her drinking and more about, she's just obsessed with fame.

Kelly Dodd: Everything is about her image. She hires professional photographers to follow her around.

Braunwyn Windham-Burke: I don't need to defend my sobriety to Kelly Dodd or anyone else. Anyone who's been around me knows, I'm really going through this. Some people have to lose everything before they realize what their issues are. I was the opposite, I had to gain everything. There was a hole inside of me, and I thought the show would fill it, but it took me getting *Housewives* to realize there was nothing external that was going to fix me. It wasn't another baby, or a bigger house, or a fancy vacation, or the right pair of shoes. I needed to look inward. And I'm still exploring what that is for me.

It actually ended up being a really powerful season for me because I got back to the roots of who I am. And if I can make "alcoholic" not a dirty word, that will be great.

Amid all of this, the RHOC *cast faced the COVID-19 pandemic, which forced production to halt halfway through and put the women in charge of filming their own stories.*

Emily Simpson: This was the first time in three years I was actually excited to film. I felt like a weight had been lifted without Vicki and Tamra—like a dark force had been taken away—and there was an opportunity for real friendships without someone trying to destroy them. And then COVID hit.

Elizabeth Lyn Vargas: We filmed for about five weeks before we had to shut down. And my heart really broke for the crew who couldn't work during that time, because I've been in the media for years and I know how much these positions mean to them. I've got the easy job; all I'm doing is showing up and being myself. They're the ones really working. They did ask us to film ourselves at home, and they set us up with servers so we could upload and transfer the files at five p.m. every night. I mean, they really knew exactly how to navigate the storm.

Braunwyn Windham-Burke: I sent in 449 videos, I think. It's pretty incredible how much we captured.

Elizabeth Lyn Vargas: It wasn't a bad experience. The only thing that put a damper on things for me was that I didn't feel like a Housewife at all. It was very odd. It was only when the trailer came out that I felt, "Oh, I guess this is real."

Gina Kirschenheiter: We were all worried coronavirus would cut the season short. Even just from a moral standpoint. Like, how are you going to sit around and fight about who said what about the size of my house or whether Elizabeth is as rich as she says she is when we're in the middle of a fucking pandemic? People are dying, half the world is unemployed, I'm trying to get my kids through home school—like, isn't it all so stupid?

Braunwyn Windham-Burke: Not to mention during this all, the Black Lives Matters protests began. And we don't typically want to get into uncomfortable conversations, like politics or race, because those aren't polite conversations and we want to appeal to everyone. But I was on a text chain with the other Housewives and I said I was going to a protest in Newport Beach with my kids if anyone wanted to join me, and Kelly basically called me a terrorist and said I'm a horrible mom for bringing my kids. So I called Thomas and said, "I'm out. I'm done. I'm not doing this. It's bullshit. I'm not fighting over hairpulling." And he promised me we could have real conversations this season and talk about the hard stuff.

Thomas Kelly: Politics would have seeped into the show no matter what because Braunwyn is a bleeding liberal, which is amazing because she speaks to a lot of our core values and we need that in Orange County, which has been so dusty and conservative for so long. But she's naturally going to clash with Kelly. You can't help that. That conflict is at the core of your characters.

Gina Kirschenheiter: I appreciated that they let us talk more about what's really going on. Maybe that's not the worst thing? It's scary and uncomfortable and it may not be the best territory to enter into, but we are a great group and can have adult discussions when necessary.

Braunwyn Windham-Burke: It's not like I'm the expert on this. I hadn't confronted these topics at all, either, so I was learning with everyone else. I was just trying to read and take in as much as I could. I'm not woke, I'm just waking up. There is a difference.

Gina Kirschenheiter: Braunwyn and I had a great conversation about it. I wish there could have been more diversity within our cast to give that perspective.

Heather Dubrow: There's always been a lack of diversity in Orange County, so I can see why there's a lack of diversity on *Real Housewives of Orange County*.

Braunwyn Windham-Burke: Orange County has a race problem. Thomas actually said to me, "Bring your Black friends around more," and I said, "Thomas, I don't *have* any Black friends in California. They're all in Miami." That's not because I am racist, it's because there are no Black people in my neighborhood. None. I know one woman who has a Black husband and I know one mixed-race woman. That's it.

Fifteen years after The Real Housewives of Orange County's *premiere, the show is still going strong.*

Scott Dunlop: I'm still in awe. That Bravo was able to take this idea, replicate it, build it into a franchise that's become so embedded in pop culture and entertainment? I mean, what an accomplishment! That's hard to do! It's Herculean! And it's been a joy to watch it grow; to see my concept become what it is now, create all these jobs, launch all these stars, and reengineer an entire network along the way. I can't take credit for it, they did what they did. I just feel so lucky to be a part of it, and so proud of them.

Shannon Storms Beador: I have to say, I've had many dreams in my life but being in front of a camera has never been one of them. To start filming a television show in HD when you're about to turn fifty? It's just mind-boggling to me that I would start something like this so late in life. But despite all the hardships along the way and difficult times, I'm incredibly grateful to have been a part of this.

Heather Dubrow: You'd be hard-pressed to find a Housewife who, no matter what happened, isn't a little proud to be a part of it deep down. We participated in this slice of television history and can all look back at the show as a time capsule for our lives. I mean, I can trace my children's growth. My youngest daughter, Coco, took her first steps on camera—though they never aired it or gave me that damn footage! I would have pulled out my phone and recorded it but didn't because we had a whole crew standing there!

Tamra Judge: I definitely think that I spiced things up when I came on. It was a very simple show documenting your life and going to lunch and playing tennis, and that's it. I mean, it wasn't so much about fancy things. Nobody was wearing Gucci. And, you know, it was more low-budget. And then it kind of evolved into this drama. I definitely brought drama.

Vicki Gunvalson: As Frances, Shari, and I say, "Be thankful you had that time on TV for so long." Well, I am, but I'm not. I'm also bitter you fired me. Because I know I'm good TV.

PART II

"Bite of the Apple"

The Real Housewives of New York City

PREMIERE DATE: MARCH 4, 2008

My mind was totally blown by the idea of making this a Housewives show. The thought gave me goose bumps, actually. Because the women we had were so New York—aggressive, controlling, and totally opposite of Orange County.

—ANDY COHEN

Shari Levine: While *The Real Housewives of Orange County* was in production for its second season, we got a pitch for another female-led ensemble series, called *Manhattan Moms.*

Frances Berwick: There were really great characters in there, including Jill Zarin.

Jill Zarin (Housewife): I was really trying to sell myself as fabulous; I took producers to Zarin Fabrics, I went out for dinner with, like, six girlfriends. I had a Bentley and on the way to dinner I went through all the invitations I'd gotten for parties, dropping celebrity names and talking about the conflicts on the social calendar. I wanted to be famous, and I had no problem telling people that.

Andy Cohen: Jill was such a yenta, which is a term I use with great affection. From the second I saw her, she had this energy about her that was instantly familiar and instantly New York. You know, she's this fast-talking Upper East Side type.

Jill Zarin: Alex McCord and her husband, Simon van Kempen, were originally going to do another show about kindergarten kids and their families, but that show didn't happen, so they were offered this instead.

Andy Cohen: You couldn't write characters like Alex and Simon. Alex's thing was all about speaking different languages to her sons, Johan and Francois. Simon was this Australian guy with this eccentric style. Do you remember those glossy red leather pants he wore?

Jill Zarin: I'll never forget those pants as long as I live.

Jennifer O'Connell (Former Executive Vice President, Shed Media, and Executive Producer): What was great about Alex and Simon was they were their own people. Yes, they were slightly off-center. Yes, they didn't quite fit in. Yes, they were seen as social climbers. But they were young and had good intentions. That "Let me in, how do I get in?" struggle was something interesting to follow and fun to study.

> *The next Housewife to join the cast was Ramona Singer, whom producers noticed while doing a test shoot for a different potential cast member.*

Ramona Singer (Housewife): It was this event teaching women how to make sexy dinners for their husbands. And of course, I'm always popping up, asking questions, being animated. I found out later that producers were like, "Who's that girl?"

Jill Zarin: Ramona and I were friends back then, or so I thought. I mean, I was good enough to play tennis with her in the Hamptons, but she would never say, "Stay for lunch," which hurt my feelings. But anyhow, they got her name, they got her number, and they found her.

Ramona Singer: They really pursued me. They called me up and said, "We want you, we really want you."

Andy Cohen: If you've ever watched Ramona, you know she's one of those people who is just funny without trying to be funny. She makes people laugh.

Jennifer O'Connell: She doesn't have a filter, which was just one of the many things she had going for her. She had a big social life, a beautiful house in the Hamptons, was a self-made woman . . . I don't think we realized how much she loved Pinot, but that worked out, too!

Ramona Singer: My then husband, Mario Singer, and I had come up with the concept for True Faith Jewelry, which would be a whole new direct-to-consumer business. That's ultimately why I ended up doing it. I wanted to showcase the business.

> *With Jill, Alex, and Ramona in place, casting was past the halfway mark. But finding the last two women for the show would present challenges.*

Andy Cohen: Jill brought us several women in her circle, all of whom would have been perfect. But for one reason or another, women kept dropping out. One couldn't get her boss to agree to her appearing on the show. Another woman couldn't convince her husband to go for it.

Ramona Singer: One of those people who dropped out was Sonja Morgan.

Sonja Morgan (Housewife): They were looking for women with certain kinds of jet-set lifestyles, and they read about me while flipping the pages of different social magazines. I had studied at the Fashion Institute of Technology, I had dated Prince Albert and George Clooney. I was married to J.P. Morgan's grandson John Adams Morgan, and my philanthropy work often had me—I hate the word "socialite"—but I was on the boards of charities and would raise money for things like children's education, LGBTQ+ rights, animals, artists, and other causes while entertaining many of these very wealthy Park Avenue women at the Morgan Library. They liked what they saw.

Jennifer O'Connell: We were really trying hard to get her for season 1, but she was in the middle of a messy divorce with her ex.

Sonja Morgan: My daughter was only six years old. I was going to court all the time. So I turned it down. I didn't want to be in the limelight or in the press while I went through that.

> *Fortunately for the* Manhattan Moms–*to be, two more personalities soon entered the show's orbit.*

Jill Zarin: While all this casting was going on, I went to the premiere for Michael Moore's new movie *Sicko*. And who did I meet at the after-party? Luann de Lesseps.

Luann de Lesseps (Housewife): I'm at this event and I see this older man buying my twin nieces, who must have been twenty-three, shots of tequila. I said, "Who is this guy? If you're going to buy them a shot, you're going to buy me a shot!" And lo and behold, it was Bobby Zarin.

Jill Zarin: Bobby was always scouting for me, even when we weren't casting. He was Mr. Social when he drank.

Luann de Lesseps: Over to the bar walks Bobby's wife, and I was kind of blown away by her character, with her bright red hair and her bold attitude and her Long Island accent.

Jill Zarin: We just hit it off really great. Afterward, we were invited to another party at someone's house and Luann and I went and hung out the whole night together.

Luann de Lesseps: That night, we became fast and furious friends. But I was going to Europe the next day, so I said I would reach out when I got back.

Jill Zarin: She gave me her pink business card, which I still have today, by the way.

Andy Cohen: Casting wasn't going well at that point. We still had these two open roles to fill and had missed our filming start date. At a certain point we told the producers and the women that we would have to pull the plug. And, just then, the reality TV gods smiled upon us.

Jill Zarin: One of the producers came to stay at my house in Bridgehampton to help with casting, and I took her to the VIP tent of this big polo event that was going on that weekend.

Andy Cohen: Brideghampton polo is a madhouse. It's famous people and people who want to be famous, weighted more toward the latter. But the gods smiled on us that day.

Jill Zarin: Bethenny has said that the show discovered her. That's not true. I knew Bethenny socially, we were casual acquaintances, and I went over to her to say hi. We were just chitchatting and Bobby turned and said to me, "Why don't you ask Bethenny to be on the show?" So I said to Bethenny, "Oh, listen, I've got this producer I'm with, I would love you to meet her. She's casting for this show I'm doing called *Manhattan Moms*." She said, "But I'm not a mom." I said, "Yeah, but you're a mom wannabe." That was the introduction.

Andy Cohen: The story I heard is that Bobby brought over the producer and when Bethenny met her, she just shut down. She had nothing to say. And it was her boyfriend at the time, Jason (not Hoppy), who went into action, opening up about their life together, his kids. He was selling it and selling her.

Jill Zarin: Bethenny didn't really want to do it at first. She had aspirations of doing other things, like acting. She was working as a natural foods chef and was writing a diet cookbook. And she had been on *The Apprentice: Martha Stewart* and lost, so she was worried about failing again on television. But she realized this was the best opportunity she had in front of her.

Jennifer O'Connell: When I saw that Bethenny was on this list, all I thought was "Genius," because I had just seen her on *The Apprentice: Martha Stewart* and she should have won!

The problem was, Bravo was not really excited about her because she did not have a lot of the attributes we were looking for—she was not married with children, accomplished in her career, or living in these luxury, amenity apartments. She wanted that, that was her dream, but she hadn't gotten there. And then the network found out she had been on reality TV already. . . .

Andy Cohen: I thought it was weird that we would put her on this show after she had been on *The Apprentice: Martha Stewart*. Like breaking the fourth wall right when we started.

Jennifer O'Connell: This was earlier in the life cycle of unscripted programming, and the idea that someone had been on another reality TV show was kind of this taboo thing.

Andy Cohen: I'm so glad I was overruled on that, because that would have been one of the great mistakes of my career.

Jill Zarin: Bethenny was set, but we still needed someone else. Then one day I saw the pink business card in my closet and came running down the staircase like the house was on fire. Remember, there was a producer staying at my house. "Oh my God! This is the girl, I completely forgot about her! She's a countess! She wanted to be famous—she was on Italian television and had her own lifestyle show in the United States! She's beautiful! And her kids are in private school! She's perfect!" And that was a message from God. It was really meant to be.

Luann de Lesseps: That's how I got on *Housewives*. It really kind of came to me.

Jill Zarin: When Luann got back from Europe, the producer went to her house, and it was all out of my hands.

Jennifer O'Connell: The royalty thing was huge for all of us. She lived the lifestyle. She had an apartment in the city, a beautiful home in the Hamptons, kids in private school, the whole thing.

Andy Cohen: I remember seeing Luann's audition tape, and I just thought it was hilarious and amazing that she was a countess. She took it so seriously. She talked about etiquette and her husband's family gifting the Statue of Liberty to America. There was a lack of self-awareness there that I thought was funny.

A complete cast now in place, filming on the inaugural season of Manhattan Moms *kicked off. And unlike the Orange County Housewives in their first season, the New York ladies knew exactly what they were doing.*

Jill Zarin: Filming in the beginning was very exciting for us. You know, it was an adventure. We all knew how to turn it on and have fun with it.

Luann de Lesseps: The show was very different at the time—it was about the children and life in the Hamptons—but the friendships were real, which is what made *New York* tick. We all knew and would see each other socially, on and off camera, and especially in the Hamptons. There was history. And Jill was kind of the glue.

Jill Zarin: I felt connected to everyone early on except for Alex and Simon.

They were kind of on an island that first season, and not just because they lived in Brooklyn.

Luann de Lesseps: I actually liked them at first. Alex was bright, and Simon was very social. Of course they were social climbers, but I didn't really know that at first. I had never been to their apartment in Brooklyn, and I certainly had never been to their house in the Hamptons. I never really saw their lifestyle or how they lived. They were just a couple from Down Under.

Jennifer O'Connell: Alex came into it naïve. She and Simon were not self-aware at all. And that is tricky when you're putting yourself out there, because what you see and what the world sees may be two different things.

Luann de Lesseps: I told my husband, Alex, the count, "You have to meet these people." We had dinner and he said, "I never want to see them again, ever."

Andy Cohen: They were sort of putting on airs for the camera—going to the opera, looking for themselves in the *New York Times* Style section, vacationing in St. Barts off-season. It wound up biting them in the ass because once the other women got hold of them, they tore them apart. They were just like red meat.

Jennifer O'Connell: Jill and Ramona certainly looked down on them.

Ramona Singer: I didn't like their codependent relationship at first. It really irked me.

Jill Zarin: People hated Simon and Alex, and they both blamed me for that because I would point out some of their flaws. But the funny thing is, they didn't go after Bethenny, who was probably the meanest about them. But when she said it, it came out funny and snarky. So she got away with it.

Jennifer O'Connell: In the beginning, Alex was always playing catch-up with the group.

Ramona Singer: Over the years, I warmed up to them. There's one thing I've learned from being on the show, especially fifteen years later. If you're happy, you're happy. Who am I to judge? I shouldn't be critical. I shouldn't be so vocal. But that's why I'm good TV, I'm unfiltered!

Jennifer O'Connell: Adjusting to being on TV was difficult for some of the women. We had some tough conversations with Luann in particular. She got some blowback for what people saw as hypocrisy in how she treated people versus how she, as "the countess," expected to be treated.

Luann de Lesseps: It's not easy to see yourself on TV at first. And in the beginning, I was not sharing certain things on the show, as a way of protecting myself and my children. Like, I didn't want to talk about my divorce because I didn't want it to be fodder for the press. But now, I'm much more myself and I have much more fun with the "countess" thing. The fans get it.

With filming of the first season underway, and RHOC *gaining momentum, the decision was made before the show aired to adopt the title of* The Real Housewives of New York City.

Shari Levine: Lauren Zalaznick had given these marching orders to start finding more Housewives cities. Someone brilliantly said, "Maybe *Manhattan Moms* could be *The Real Housewives of New York City*?"

Andy Cohen: My mind was totally blown by the idea of making this a *Housewives* show. The thought gave me goose bumps, actually. Because the women we had were so New York—aggressive, controlling, and totally opposite of *Orange County*. They had nothing in common with the OC women. But the show's packaging and structure would be similar, which meant we could have endless possibilities. Suddenly I understood Lauren's brilliance in adding a location to the original title.

Jennifer O'Connell: My understanding was that producers said to the cast when they were hired, "This is not *The Real Housewives of Orange County*. That show is trashy, it won't be like that at all." So I had to reassure them that what they were shooting wasn't changing, and tell them, "Good news: *Orange County* is doing well so you'll now be seen as part of a successful franchise!" There was definitely a little bit of handholding.

Season 1 of The Real Housewives of New York City *premiered on Bravo on March 4, 2008. Unlike* Orange County, *New York clicked instantly.*

Jerry Leo: Everybody was talking about it from the get-go. It had huge gay appeal and grew a quick cult following.

Jennifer O'Connell: It really snowballed after it premiered.

Andy Cohen: It was so funny to me in a totally different way than *OC*. The women were real but like no one I'd ever met in the city. My mom and I started talking about the show like we did *All My Children*.

Jill Zarin: I'll never forget, one day I was in the car with my daughter Alison on Thirty-fourth Street between Third and Second Avenues. Right in front of me is the back of a bus—and I'm on it, right in the middle! I almost had a stroke. I followed that bus to the last stop and jumped out into the freezing January air, and Ally took pictures of me. That was the first time I'd ever seen myself on a bus, and I'd never been so excited in my life.

With season 1 a bona fide hit, a second season was quickly ordered, but Bravo wanted another Housewife added to the cast.

Lisa Shannon (Senior Vice President of Programming & Development, Shed Media, and Executive Producer): Bravo, coming out of the first season, really wanted a socialite. That was the big directive. We needed somebody of real clout—of real importance and money. And we were meeting with some pretty incredibly wealthy and connected people who ultimately just didn't want to do it. And then Kelly came along. . . .

Andy Cohen: Kelly was a legit Page 6 name, with the lifestyle to back it up.

Kelly Killoren Bensimon (Housewife): I had been invited by an executive producer at NBC to discuss potential projects, and afterward he pulled me aside and was like, "I can't believe you have such a big personality. We have this show called *Real Housewives of New York City*. Would you be interested in going on it?"

Jennifer O'Connell: We saw her tape and thought, "She's a supermodel. She's got kids. She's got this great lifestyle. She's gorgeous. She seems fun. She seems positive. Let's throw her into the mix."

Kelly Killoren Bensimon: I'm not your typical model. Yes, I've had this incredible career in front of the camera, but I'm also so much more. At the time, I had just finished as the editor of *Elle Accessories*, one of two magazines I would help start, and was writing *The Bikini Book*. I had also gotten divorced from my husband, Gilles Bensimon, six months beforehand. And I thought to myself, "It's time for me to spread my wings."

Lisa Shannon: Kelly had this very cool, downtown vibe, unlike anyone else on the show at the time. It was such a New York story. This gorgeous supermodel and hands-on mom, living in this great apartment in Chelsea and this house in the Hamptons with these supercute kids. She was very well connected to the social scene. And she was divorced from this famous photographer. Our intention with her was to showcase a new part of the city through her story.

Kelly Killoren Bensimon: My agents at IMG—I have legitimate agents—they were like, "Do not go on this show." But I viewed things through a different lens. I wanted to celebrate women. I wanted people to know that you could bring home the bacon and fry it up in a pan while still being fun and sexy and flirty and charming. There was no Stepford wife anymore. It was 2009, a new era. So in the beginning, I was having a good time, meeting everybody and going to parties. I was really happy to be a part of it. And then it turned.

Turn it did. Within the first weeks of filming, Kelly found herself in a vicious battle with Bethenny. Their feud would last all season long.

Jennifer O'Connell: With Kelly, we saw for the first time something that would happen over the years—the OGs would try to ice out new Housewives by not agreeing to film with them. Maybe they didn't like them, maybe they were threatened or didn't think they belonged. They would just refuse to shoot scenes with them—and usually it backfired. In this case, Bethenny and Jill were icing out Kelly when she first started.

Andy Cohen: The "I'm not shooting with them" trope, not relegated to one city in particular, has been quite annoying—and unsuccessful—over the years.

Lisa Shannon: Kelly interviewed very differently than she came off on the show. She seemed very approachable, very funny—intentionally and unintentionally—and like she would be such a natural, easy fit. But Kelly came on the show, and her buttons got pushed very quickly by Bethenny. They really just did not get along from the jump.

Kelly Killoren Bensimon: Bethenny and I had met before the show because she came to an event at my house. Bethenny was dating a photographer I knew, and she was his date. I didn't even really notice her, she didn't make an impression on me, bad or good—and I don't mean that in a nasty way, I mean that in a genuinely honest way.

Jill Zarin: Bethenny hated Kelly even before the show because she felt that Kelly snubbed her at that party. Then she got even more upset when they met again on the show and Kelly had no idea who she was. She didn't recall Bethenny being at her own house. And listen, I don't remember a lot of people who come to my house, especially when it's a party! But Bethenny was very offended and treated Kelly very badly because of it.

Kelly Killoren Bensimon: When I started the show, I thought things were fine between us. The only time I found out there was a chip on her shoulder was when we were meeting to talk about this charity function. We were all together, and I heard Bethenny calling me "Madonna" under her breath. She could have come up to me and been like, "I met you once before and I feel like you don't really remember me." I'm a sweet girl, I would have listened and apologized.

Andy Cohen: "Evidently she's Madonna" was a moment.

Lisa Shannon: It's hard, while casting, to know how somebody is going to do in the face of an opponent.

Kelly Killoren Bensimon: Bethenny was just looking for attention. She was so insecure. Remember, she was the old guard and I was the new, pretty, fun girl. She didn't have kids, I was a mom with young kids. She was struggling in her career, I was accomplished. There were just so many things about me that—I don't like to use the word "threatened" because I don't like it when women talk about each other in those kinds of terms— but she felt a certain way about me that I somehow became her nemesis, immediately. Anything unconventional about me, she didn't understand and it was automatically wrong. It was a game. She could make herself relevant by tearing me down. And she did, over and over again.

The two came together for an epic chat that would soon become one of the most quoted battles in Housewives *history.*

Kelly Killoren Bensimon: Production wanted us to sit down together and talk. The second I arrived, she gave me attitude and I just wasn't into it. It was so tacky. So I said to myself, "If she's going to act like a child, I'm going to treat her like a child." I was in full-on parenting mode. That's when I said, "This is you, this is me." Everyone thinks that had something to do with social class, but really what I said was, "This is you, this is me, I'm an adult and you're a child." Like, "Maybe this is not the conversation you want to have with me right now, because you're not going to win."

Jill Zarin: Kelly was pummeled for that line, though. Because Bethenny was the underdog at the time. She had no money, she was poor—well, that's not true, she wasn't poor, but that's what she wanted everybody to think.

Jennifer O'Connell: Bethenny realized immediately, like, "Oh, I just cemented her in the show."

Andy Cohen: It was the first time a Housewife called me after they'd filmed something. She said, "You can't believe what just happened…on camera."

Jill Zarin: By the way, at the time, Kelly was right. Kelly Bensimon was a supermodel and Bethenny Frankel couldn't sell a cupcake in a grocery store. Honestly, she was a nobody.

Kelly Killoren Bensimon: I mean, people come up to me all the time and do it. NeNe Leakes, when I first met her she was like, "Girl! I'm up here, you're down there! You're amazing. I love you!"

In season 3, Sonja Tremont Morgan, the Housewife who got away in season 1, joined the cast as "the straw that stirs the drink."

Luann de Lesseps: With Sonja, so many of us knew her, so it felt like she was always a part of the show.

Sonja Morgan: It took a while for my negotiation; I didn't start until the middle of the season because, to be honest, I wasn't going on the show to become well known. I didn't need to social climb. I wasn't looking to meet a man. Some of these girls, they do it for fame or for the spotlight. That wasn't me. I prefer to be at home. The only reason I did it was so that my daughter and I, as a family unit, could afford to stay in the town house.

Jennifer O'Connell: People forget Sonja was not part of season 1 because she's just such a huge part of the DNA of that show.

Andy Cohen: Her perky, Upper East Side–Streisand vibe did not immediately convey the hilarity that would ensue with Sonja over her run on the show.

Sonja Morgan: I hit the ground running because I knew everybody around town. Ramona and I went to FIT together, we were in the stock market together, bought our first homes together, and, back when it was okay, we got our first fur coats together. Luann, I knew her ex-husband because I was always jet-setting as a young woman. I'd be off to Gstaad, Phuket City, Saint-Tropez, Paris, Rome, and Alex de Lesseps was always around. Kelly Bensimon, same story, I knew Gilles Bensimon. And Jill Zarin— did I know Jill before she was married to Bobby? Was there a Jill before Bobby?

Jill Zarin: I didn't meet Sonja until the show.

Despite this fresh face, season 3 was dominated by the dissolving friendship between two OGs. To this day, the dramatic demise of Jill and Bethenny's relationship remains a devastating split in the eyes of Housewives fans.

Jennifer O'Connell: Jill and Bethenny had a very special relationship. They were like Lucy and Ethel, Laverne and Shirley.

Andy Cohen: Viewers loved their friendship. It's one of the reasons *New York* was such a big hit.

Jill Zarin: When the show first started, I liked that Bethenny needed me because I am very motherly and I liked giving. She was broke, single, and just starting out in her career. I wanted to help, and I did. But that got hard for Bethenny because she's not a taker, it's not her nature. So Bethenny grew to resent my wanting to help her, especially as she got more successful. I wanted to celebrate in her wins and stay involved in her life. Instead, she pushed me away.

Andy Cohen: Weeks before we began shooting on season 3, I remember running into Jill at Bridgehampton Polo and she said to me, "I'm so fucking mad at Bethenny. She's been horrible to me and I'm going to confront her this season. It's not going to be pretty!" And I was like, "You have to make up with her before the season starts. We can't have you guys not being friends!" I knew viewers loved seeing these two together and I was nervous about how a ruptured relationship would play on the show. Today, if someone said, going into the show, "I'm so mad at this person," I would be like, "Well, okay, we'll see what happens." At that point, I was trying to impede the reality of what was happening. And it wound up being the driving story line all season.

Jill Zarin: I was mad at her because when Bobby was diagnosed with cancer and he was told he had limited time left, she sent me a small thing of flowers. She never called me. She never came over. And looking back, I should have forgiven that quickly. I should have afforded Bethenny that grace.

Ramona Singer: Jill always thought she was better than Bethenny. That whole season, she was after Bethenny. So many times I tried to get them to make peace. It was just heart-wrenching.

Andy Cohen: I was scared this would all ruin the show. I was scared viewers wouldn't want to watch anymore. But what happened was, that story line really blew up that series and that season. I mean, no one will ever forget Bethenny in that red dress crying outside on the street and Jill saying, "Get a hobby, we're done." Viewers were enthralled. They related to watching these two friends fall out, and the ripple effects it had on this group.

Jerry Leo: It was must-see TV.

Andy Cohen: That fight, ironically, wound up doing so much for Bethenny. It turned Bethenny into the real underdog, and viewers really rooted for her. And on the other side, that was the year they saw Jill really becoming something they didn't like as much.

Jill Zarin: The fans really ganged up on me, and a lot of the criticism was unfair. Like that scene when Bethenny and I spoke over the phone and I told her, "We're done." First of all, I put the call on speakerphone. When it aired everyone was like, "How could you put her on speakerphone and not tell her Luann was in the room?" Well, you dumb idiots, we're making a TV show. In any other situation, I would have had the phone to my ear but how else would the camera get the call? And second of all, I had no idea producers were on the other side of the call, filming Bethenny while she was crying on the street. No one told me that. So I just looked like a monster!

Andy Cohen: Jill was becoming really difficult to deal with behind the scenes, too. If you look at Jill at that reunion, her hair is huge. She has all these pieces in her hair. And I said, "Look at you. You were this nice girl from Long Island. Now what have you become?" I just remember I was like, "Wow, there's something profound about that." I had kind of seen the transformation starting. It was the first sign Jill was no longer the person who we had all fallen in love with.

Luann de Lesseps: At a certain point, Jill realized that she might have gone too far and taken this TV feud to the point of no return. Bethenny had become this fan favorite.

Jill Zarin: When the horses come out of the race, one wins and the rest of them are in the back. That's what happened with *Housewives*. Right away, Bethenny shot out, and we were all left behind.

Lisa Shannon: Bethenny got to a place where she didn't need Jill anymore. And Jill didn't like that.

Jill Zarin: I'm a really loyal person and in truth, I wanted loyalty back. But I did not get that back from everybody.

Luann de Lesseps: And she was also jealous. Jill let that get the best of her.

Andy Cohen: There is no guidebook for how to behave when you become famous. Some people handle it well and some don't. I think it took a while for Jill to get her equilibrium.

Jill Zarin: Yes, I'm a jealous person. I'll admit that. But when you're on an ensemble cast and some girls get picked to do certain things that other girls want to do, it creates hostility among the cast. *Entertainment Weekly* once did something with us. I think it was the Entertainers of the Year. For the spread, they had a photo shoot—NeNe Leakes, Padma Lakshmi, and Tim Gunn were in it. Maybe Tom Colicchio? And they could've picked any of us, but they asked me. Which was so nice, it made me feel like a superstar. But one of the things they said to me is, "You can't tell anybody else." Now I understand, they didn't want to have to hear from the other women, but the girls become jealous and you become the one who's in trouble for hiding that from your costars. And then you start to get suspicious. Like, "Well, what are *they* keeping from *me*?"

Andy Cohen: Ironically, that shoot was not Jill's finest moment. She was a beast at the shoot, and she got in trouble.

Ramona Singer: Jill's her own worst enemy.

Jill Zarin: I knew secrets were being kept, and that drove me insane because I hate secrets. I became paranoid, sometimes rightfully so, and other times, wrongfully so. But it was hard for me. I didn't know how to handle my jealousy.

Ramona Singer: She would get mad if Bethenny did anything without her. Bethenny would tell me all the time that she'd get a spot on *Kathie Lee and Regis* or whatever, and then Jill would be pissed off and call the production company and say, "Why is Bethenny on? I should be on!"

Jill Zarin: That's not true. I liked sharing the spotlight, that wasn't my problem. I just didn't like that she didn't want me anymore.

Ramona Singer: That fight was very hard to live through.

Jill Zarin: Bethenny was very cruel to me. And I understand why people think Bethenny's sharp laser tongue is funny, but it wasn't funny when it was about you. She was vicious.

Jennifer O'Connell: Jill was especially stubborn. There were many points when Bethenny would have made up with her, but Jill held out too long. And then when Jill was ready Bethenny was like, "You have basically rejected me over and over and over again."

Jill Zarin: I wanted to make up with her desperately, and I didn't understand why Bethenny wouldn't forgive me. My mother loved Bethenny like a daughter and called Bethenny for a month straight. Bethenny didn't call her back.

Andy Cohen: By that point, Bethenny had really had it with her.

Jill Zarin: I was spiraling because there are so many things that happened that season. She got pregnant, I didn't know; her father was sick and died, I didn't know. And as I said, I don't like surprises.

> *Speaking of surprises, season 3 was also marked by one of the series' most shocking vacations—a trip to the U.S. Virgin Islands that quickly became known to fans as the infamous "Scary Island."*

Kelly Killoren Bensimon: I'm the one that dubbed it Scary Island. Those are my words. I thought we were going to Fantasy Island!

Sonja Morgan: Here's the thing: When we go on those trips, it's almost like spending time in quarantine with your family. It looks fancy, and you're in a beautiful home, great food, and a lot of alcohol. We have to look at ourselves day after day after day. So we learn a lot about ourselves.

Jennifer O'Connell: When people are socializing and partying, your authentic self comes out because there's no escape unless you go to sleep. It just escalates everything—especially if there are underlying issues between people. You see a deeper side of everyone, and it's a really good source of drama because they can't escape each other.

Kelly Killoren Bensimon: Let me give you the behind-the-scenes of that trip. I was filming six days a week, from the very beginning to the very end. I filmed all the time, and I thought I was doing great. It was one of my best years. But my agent was like, "They are really mad at you and they don't know if they're going to bring you back." I don't know why all this pressure was on me, but there was a lot of animosity and they told me that they were going to cancel me if I didn't go on the trip. That's why I said at the reunion that I was forced.

Jennifer O'Connell: No one's forced to go on trips.

Matt Anderson: Scary Island is, without question, the hardest cast trip I've ever done for any Bravo show. People forget, this was one of the only Housewives trips where two main characters did not go. Jill and Luann were fighting Bethenny, Ramona, and Alex, and they thought that by not going they would tank the trip and stop it from even happening. But we were like, "No, we're going." And the remaining five women just carried it.

Kelly Killoren Bensimon: I found out when I got there that producers had originally planned another trip to someplace nicer than St. John (not that St. John isn't nice), but they had changed it last-minute because they spent all this money filming Bethenny on back-and-forth trips to L.A. to visit her dying father—who, by the way, producers told me wouldn't even see her—and they no longer could afford the first trip. And then I learned that Bethenny had this spin-off show they were filming for her because she'd just gotten pregnant, and Ramona was freaking out because she wanted to be a part of that show so badly. Actually, every single person on that trip wanted to be on Bethenny's good side to get on her show. So I quickly realized that no matter what I did, I was the underdog. She was the one with power. It didn't matter if I was the most amazing, nicest, sweetest, most charming person. I was going to lose.

Jennifer O'Connell: Kelly and Bethenny were not in a good place. Kelly was struggling. And it just spiraled. I mean, it went off the rails.

Kelly Killoren Bensimon: So that's all the backstory. But here's what you need to know: I didn't have any anxiety going into Scary Island. Anxiety was not a word I would use to describe me on that trip. The night before, my hairdresser Bradley Irion—who works with major celebrities like Brooke Shields, Elizabeth Hurley, the best of the best—put extensions in my hair, and I felt gorgeous. My hair was amazing. I had the best bathing suits, we had incredible weather, the cutest little rooms, great food. I was really loving life.

Sonja Morgan: We started that trip staying on this beautiful yacht, and that first night was really where Kelly started losing it.

Kelly Killoren Bensimon: It actually started in the morning with the whole "cook and chef" thing between me and Bethenny. I was just making fun of it because she was constantly telling me how proficient she was in the cooking world. In my eyes, a chef is someone who owns a restaurant and a cook is someone who makes amazing soup.

Sonja Morgan: Oh God, not the "cook and chef" thing again. Can't we just move on from that?

Kelly Killoren Bensimon: Bethenny really felt, because I called her a cook, that I was defaming her brand. That season, Bethenny was literally wearing all of her paraphernalia, constantly branding every single scene that she was in with me. It was very strange. She even gave us these Skinnygirl Cocktails goodie bags when we got to the villa. Bethenny had her minions, and she was armed and ready to go. Plus, she was pregnant and her dad had just died, so everyone was sympathetic toward her. She had all of the keys to the kingdom.

Sonja Morgan: That night, on the yacht, I went down to Kelly's room and said something like, "It smells like cat pee." Because it did. And then I guess the bloggers said some drug has an ammonia-like smell so they thought that's what Kelly was doing. But I have no idea about that. I don't know that Kelly does drugs. She doesn't seem to do drugs. She doesn't even drink, which pisses me off. I caught her doing shots of water when everybody else was doing tequila. That irked the shit out of me! We're all in this together!

Anyway, something was wrong with Kelly. She was off that whole trip. She thought Bethenny was trying to kill her! She called Jill when we got to the villa and said she was having nightmares that Bethenny was stabbing her.

Matt Anderson: It was a super, super hard shoot. There was a limit to how many people could be on that yacht, so we didn't have what would normally be our extensive coverage. So it was very raw. Like, "Turtle Time" was happening with one camera. The other fight with Bethenny, Kelly, and Sonja on the yacht? That was one camera. That's just not how a lot of the shows are covered now. There's typically multiple cameras, and a lot to cut to. It turned into a documentary where we were all on walkie-talkies in different locations. Someone would be like, "Ramona's walking into a random yacht right now." "Okay, just follow it!" "There's a crazy fight going on in the hull of the yacht right now between Kelly and Bethenny." "Great, get that." It was complicated!

Kelly Killoren Bensimon: By the time I called Jill, I was really done. I was like, "Get over here. The woman is psycho, and she's doing whatever she can to try to make me feel terrible about myself and make me feel super insecure. She's trying to make everyone say that I'm crazy."

Sonja Morgan: Kelly's behavior that night was very odd. And the fact that we were on TV? To act like that? She looked insane. She was telling everyone she threw up the night before she came on the trip because she was worried Bethenny was going to come after her.

Kelly Killoren Bensimon: How could I have thrown up the night before when I was feeling gorgeous with my new hair? I was loving life.

Sonja Morgan: When we sat down at the table, she was screaming nonsensical things like, "Al Sharpton!" I was trying hard to chat with her but nothing was making sense. She kept talking about the press and her friend, that Paltrow girl.

Kelly Killoren Bensimon: Well, at the time Bethenny was floating all these negative stories to the press about me, my family—really, whatever she could get her hands on. She was doing all this stuff and just going crazy, trying to get as much press as possible. Her technique was to get more people to look at her. She was always like the little girl in the back going, "Look at me!" And she went on these Twitter rants, too, attacking celebrities so people would see who she was. Like, she said things about Gwyneth Paltrow. Of all people, you don't want to attack Gwyneth Paltrow. She's not an attackable person. It was the weirdest thing!

Sonja Morgan: I don't think they'll allow you to put this in the book, but she was going off on the side like a crazy person. She kept repeating the producer's name over and over again. At one point, they had to put the cameras down and tell her to go to her room and stop. It was crazy.

Kelly Killoren Bensimon: I stopped the filming. I was literally screaming the producer's name like a thousand times. I knew if I just screamed her name over and over and over again, they would stop production—they would stop filming.

Matt Anderson: They had that "Go to sleep dinner," and Kelly was really agitated. She kept breaking the fourth wall and kept calling my name and the other producer's name. She'd go, "Matty, Matty, Matty, Matt, Matt, Matt." That's when Sonja was like, "I think something's going on with Kelly."

Sonja Morgan: We've never had a situation like that again on the show where somebody was actually not in a healthy situation. That was real.

Luann de Lesseps: I'm sure today they would have stopped filming. They didn't do that then.

Sonja Morgan: I felt very bad for Kelly. Eventually, I put an end to it. I said, "You guys need to stop engaging with her because she is cuckoo. This person has a real problem." I said, "She has a chemical imbalance. We need to protect her. She's a crazy person."

Kelly Killoren Bensimon: That was not chic, what Sonja said about me. You don't say things like that. But I mean, having said that, consider the source. . . .

Sonja Morgan: I slept in Ramona's room that night. Because one thing about Ramona is, you know, nothing is going down with Ramona. Luann, she'll run into the closet and leave you hanging there. But Ramona's a fighter. And I was very nervous for my life.

Matt Anderson: After that, two of my other producers went and walked Kelly up to her room, which was in the crow's nest. They were talking to her and calming her down.

Jennifer O'Connell: At a certain point, I know that I got a call. I was in New York but in touch with the team in the field, and they were saying, "What should we do? Kelly doesn't seem happy and it just feels like this might not be a good place for her to be right now." I was like, "Well, if people are becoming unhinged and if it's not safe for them, they should leave. Don't keep people there if it's not feeling comfortable or mentally healthy. Get her out of there."

Kelly Killoren Bensimon: I didn't leave Scary Island because of Bethenny or the girls. It had nothing to do with what happened at that last dinner, because production knew I was leaving before that. I had childcare issues back at home.

Matt Anderson: We booked her a flight. The next morning before she left she wrote a thank-you note to every producer and every person on the cast, on her own personalized stationery—it was very sweet. It was a very nice gesture.

Little did the women realize, just as one storm was clearing out, another was on the horizon. . . .

Jennifer O'Connell: When we had been planning the trip, Jill had said she wasn't available. She was uncomfortable and didn't want to go for whatever reason. She and Bethenny were at odds, so that was fine by us. We were like, "You're missing out, but whatever. Fine. Don't go." But Jill was smart, and she realized if she didn't go on a trip, she'd be missing a couple of big episodes. So eventually she said she was going to come with Bobby because she didn't want to be left out.

Kelly Killoren Bensimon: Jill was always supposed to come to Scary Island. I knew that, production knew that, we all knew that. That call I made to her two days before was just production's way of giving her the reason to come check on me.

Jill Zarin: It was my fucking idea. I only have myself to blame. Ramona had invited me, but Ally was doing her applications for college and I wasn't comfortable leaving unless I knew it was all done. When Ally finished early, and we were flying to St. Barts Tuesday for Thanksgiving anyway, I said, "Why don't I fly to St. John just for one day and one night on my way to St. Barts?" I was going there to support Kelly, who was by herself, basically, and also to make up with Bethenny. The producers loved it. But then, the night before I was scheduled to go, I got a call from the girls and they told me Kelly was having a nervous breakdown. I should have told them right then that I was coming the next day, but I kept the secret because I wanted to surprise them. When the plane landed and I walked on the tarmac into the airport, I saw Kelly on the other side of the window waving at me. I have a picture of this, by the way.

Nate Green: I doubt there's a picture. If there was, we all know Jill would use it.

Jill Zarin: I walked up to the window and we were like, nose to nose with glass between us. And I said, "What are you doing here?" And she said, "I gotta go back. My babysitter has to go home." I'm like, "What?" I didn't know what to do.

What Jill did was head to the house, greeting the women with her signature, "Hiii."

Jill Zarin: By the time we pulled up to the house I was hungry, I was cranky, and all I wanted to do was take a shower. Did I ever think that I would get kicked out of the house? No!

Sonja Morgan: I'm intuitive enough to know if Bethenny is hurting, she's going to go into her cave and lick her wounds. You can't get in Bethenny's face and convince her not to be upset with you. Jill crying like that? That wasn't going to help!

Jill Zarin: People thought I was stirring up drama or was calculating—not at all, I had no clue.

Jennifer O'Connell: We knew she was coming, but I don't think we had told the cast. It was dramatic.

Nate Green: Nothing like this had ever happened before. And we were toward the end of the trip. No one expected she would show up like that.

Andy Cohen: The fact that Jill was going down there (on her own dime, I might add) was like a drama bomb waiting to happen. Thrilling!

Jill Zarin: It was like walking into a war zone. Who was there? Ramona, who hated me. Bethenny, who hated me. Alex, who hated me. And Sonja, who was new—we didn't like each other or not like each other, we didn't know each other.

Sonja Morgan: I was new to the show and I was like, "Who does that?" If I'm not invited, I'm not invited. I found that so bizarre. I couldn't believe Jill had the balls to do that. I was just mortified.

Jill Zarin: The girls were fucking pissed. All they wanted to do was go to the beach after they had worked all four days in a row. Fighting with Kelly was the end, and they just wanted a break because they were leaving the next day. And then I walked in the door.

Kelly Killoren Bensimon: I wasn't shocked when they kicked her out—they were feeling gorgeous. They were like, "We won. We're the new A-Team."

Jill Zarin: I was, like, hysterically crying when I got in the car and left. I was so upset. I was so hurt. I was hungry. I was tired. I hadn't had a glass of water. It was five p.m. at that point.

Kelly Killoren Bensimon: After it was over, producers told me, "Scary Island is going to be big episodes for us." And that's when I knew it was going to be bad for me. I actually broke up with my boyfriend at the time because he was very successful and on TV, and I said, "I have to break up with you because I cannot put another person through this." It was really bad. But there's nothing you can do about it. You can't fight it.

Scary Island may have been bad for Kelly, but it only made things worse between Bethenny and Jill. By season's end, their friendship was beyond the point of repair, and its demise made it easier for Bethenny to move on to her own show.

Andy Cohen: Jill was becoming really difficult to deal with behind the scenes. It was exhausting (and she'll agree with you, too). She was a different person at that reunion—her hair was huge, full of pieces. Bethenny said, "Look at you. You were this nice girl from Long Island. Now what have you become?" Jill's greatest moments were when she was just being her true self. When she tried to produce herself, things didn't always play out the way she intended. I think she thought the viewers would be on her side in the Bethenny saga, and none of it went the way she expected. Meanwhile, Bethenny felt like she'd outgrown the show, didn't want to be on with Jill anymore, was pregnant and madly in love—if ever there was a moment for a spinoff, it was then. It felt like a win-win for both of them to remain on Bravo. And that's how *Bethenny Getting Married* and *Bethenny Ever After Started*.

Ramona Singer: She never told us about the spin-off, you know. We had to hear about it in the press. She couldn't even give us that respect. Here she had filmed with us for three years, got her spin-off show because of us.

Luann de Lesseps: It wasn't the proper way to handle that, I'll just say.

Ramona Singer: Then in her silly book she wrote, "No one ever said congratulations for getting my own show." Because bitch, you never told us! That was a slap in the face.

Jennifer O'Connell: There was obviously jealousy among the women when Bethenny left. Like, "Why is Bethenny so special that she gets her own show?"

Ramona Singer: I was fine with it; our ratings when she left were much higher than when she was there—which I'm sure she didn't like.

With a Bethenny-sized hole in the cast, RHONY had to deal with the fallout in the group dynamic and find a new Housewife. Enter Cindy Barshop. . . .

Cindy Barshop (Housewife): I owned a national line of spas at the time called Completely Bare, and they were very successful and getting a lot of recognition in the press. I made an appearance on Kimora Lee Simmons's reality show that kind of blew up the business in a really unexpected way.

Everybody and their grandmother came out saying they saw me on that show, which was weird to me because I was kind of clueless to this whole reality TV thing. So I asked my publicist, "What's the biggest show that's available?" because I wanted to promote my company. They said, "*The Real Housewives of New York City*." And I go, "Great, get me on that."

Jill Zarin: I loved Cindy, and I still love her. She's a little kooky and very bright.

Cindy Barshop: The casting was closed already, I remember, but they called me and then came to interview me at my West Village apartment. Next thing I knew, I was a Housewife.

> *While producers may have welcomed the tough-talking single mother of twins, the cast did not—her downtown energy never quite meshed with the Upper East Side crowd.*

Luann de Lesseps: Cindy came in and was kind of like a deer in headlights. She didn't know what was happening. She was afraid to speak out too much. For a lot of people, it can be overwhelming to be around all these strong, established characters.

Cindy Barshop: For most of these women, this show is their whole identity. They need to protect that. It was almost as if they decided early on that the only way to ensure they'd keep their jobs was if I failed. They would ignore me when we filmed, completely cut me out of conversations.

Andy Cohen: It was crystal clear from the start which Housewives were not on Team Cindy.

Cindy Barshop: Jill was actually very nice to me. She always kept me in the loop. And Luann, I remember, gave me a good filming tip. I wore this beautiful skirt in one sit-down dinner party, but I paired it with a T-shirt top and she said, "Darling, you have to think about how they'll be shooting you. It looks like you're wearing a T-shirt to a black tie affair." So that was helpful. But from a lot of the other girls, I didn't get that kind of kindness.

Sonja Morgan: Cindy just didn't fit in. She thought she could just come in and be No. 1, but I told her, there's a pecking order!

Kelly Killoren Bensimon: I really liked Cindy. She was a fun, sweet girl, and a great businesswoman. But she was kind of . . . out of the scene. She's not a drama queen.

Andy Cohen: That whole season was off. Cindy wasn't the greatest fit, and it felt like the women weren't really progressing.

Cindy Barshop: It was all new to me, but producers eventually told the other girls, "If you don't step it up, you're going to be fired." I don't think they had heard that before. I later learned they were calling each other up saying, "Don't film with Cindy. If they're going to fire someone, it'll be her." And it came back to bite them in the ass, because they fired a lot of people at the end of the year, not just me.

> *Cindy's right. A mass shake-up before season 5 saw Bravo parting ways with not just her, but also Kelly, Alex, and, to the surprise of fans, Jill. It was the biggest casting changeup in the history of* Housewives, *at the time and still to this day.*

Luann de Lesseps: When the fans are so animated about disliking people, you sometimes have to weed the garden.

Andy Cohen: That was the first season that the women's (and husbands') social media behavior became part of the story on the show, which was kind of annoying. At the same time, there was a wave of really nasty social media from the fans surrounding certain Housewives (*New Jersey*'s fans also became equally pointed around that time). Getting rid of Alex, Kelly, and Jill also was like jumping off a bridge.

Lisa Shannon: It was a hard pivot, but it also was a necessary shake-up.

Ramona Singer: I was shocked. I said to Andy Cohen, "You have a lot of balls to fire half the cast."

Sonja Morgan: None of us were surprised about Cindy. Or Kelly—Kelly was someone who was definitely going.

Luann de Lesseps: Kelly had blamed a lot of things on production.

Kelly Killoren Bensimon: I wasn't bitter. I had an amazing time in season 4. There was so much less drama and conflict without Bethenny. I was proud. I was grateful. The only thing I feel bad about is that I never got to show my fans how I am as a mother, how I am as a friend, how I am as a girlfriend. All I showed was how I could be the seed who fueled the fire—of course, that was my job.

Sonja Morgan: Who else went that year? Oh, Alex!

Andy Cohen: The viewers felt that she was inauthentic.

Sonja Morgan: Obviously everyone has their fans, but Alex didn't have enough to stick around.

Jill Zarin: I wish they didn't fire them. They were great TV—a couple you'd love to hate-watch.

Andy Cohen: Alex and Simon went for blood after we didn't pick them up. They became incredible thorns in our side. Simon left his job and started a website called BravoRatings.com, where he analyzed our ratings. He would live-tweet *Watch What Happens Live* and troll my guests. It was a brilliant—albeit seemingly time-consuming and not at all profitable—way to try to get under our skin. Then Alex started a vlog where she would critique episodes of *New York Housewives* and talk about areas where she thought that production had gotten involved. It was unprecedented. I've never seen anything like it since.

Sonja Morgan: The shocking one for all of us was Jill. But because Ramona and I were such gold, they didn't need Jill anymore.

Lisa Shannon: She loved being a star. And when she didn't have it anymore, it was a huge slap in the face. There was a sense of, "You're cutting me out from something I helped build," and I get that. It's a shitty feeling.

Jill Zarin: I tried to be a team player. I tried to do everything they wanted. You know, I was kind of a self-appointed ringleader, but I thought in a good way. Obviously, it wasn't always seen that way.

Andy Cohen: When the show starts to define the women and they become so into their own image, they become their own worst enemy. There comes a tipping point where it becomes not worth it to us. And so there you go. That's the sad story of Jill. There was too much bad behavior behind the scenes, and it got too much to handle.

Sonja Morgan: The rumors are that Jill's a pain in the ass. Surely you've heard that? That she calls all the time, trying to get back on the show. People do spoofs about it all the time. Like "There she is! Hiding in the bushes, still trying to get back on the show!"

Jill Zarin: Even now I don't understand why Bravo never asked me to come back full-time. All the girls are still friends with me. Luann wants me back, Sonja wants me back, Dorinda wanted me back. The only person who didn't was Ramona, and that's only because she's afraid of me. But that's what would make the show good. Everybody would watch!

Ramona Singer: Jill's still desperate to get on the show. I mean, the show was her life. She's not fulfilled in her life. Bethenny, I believe, is fulfilled in her life. Luann is fulfilled in her life, I'm fulfilled in my life. Jill . . . there's something missing.

Jill Zarin: It just doesn't make any sense to me. Maybe it's my ego and maybe everyone gets this, but I get thousands of messages every day, "Please come back, we miss you"—all of it. Why won't they have me back? I wish I could know the truth. Not the party line, but the *truth*.

Andy Cohen: There were so many moments during the years where we almost brought Jill back for a party or tennis game or special something, and something would happen that would kill it.

Lisa Shannon: The truth is, the show has evolved past when Jill was on it. I just don't think she fits in anymore. A full-time spot wouldn't make sense.

Andy Cohen: She'll always be one of our great Housewives. Without a doubt, *New York* wouldn't have been the success it is if it wasn't for Jill. And over the years she has mellowed, and our relationship is good after years of it not being amazing. I would like to work with her again.

> With Jill, Alex, Kelly, and Cindy all out of the picture, there was room for some fresh Housewives. In their spots, three women were cast: award-winning journalist, Polish princess by marriage, and best-selling author Carole Radziwill; mother of two, celebrity stylist, and shapewear brand owner Heather Thomson; and mother of four and amputee Aviva Drescher, whose ex-husband Harry Dubin had previous romantic entanglements with not one, not two, but three (!) Housewives: Sonja, Luann, and Ramona.

Andy Cohen: This was the moment where we could prove that this franchise, in this city or others, could lose important cast members and figure out a way to repopulate to take it in other directions. If this worked, it could prove to help other cities do the same and extend the lifespan of the series. We'd already survived without Bethenny, now this was the true test.

Jennifer O'Connell: One no-brainer casting choice was Carole Radziwill, a woman who embodied a sort of downtown yet down-to-earth chic. She was a widow who held ties not only to the Manhattan elite but also American and European royalty by way of her late husband, Anthony Radziwill, a cousin of the Kennedy clan.

Andy Cohen: I'm the one who asked Carole to be a part of the show. I was at dinner at Kelly Ripa and Mark Consuelos's house and it came up somehow that Carole was a princess. I had known Carole for years, but I didn't know that. We weren't close friends, but she was in my orbit—we traveled together in groups on fancy trips and saw each other at parties—and I always really liked her. So I asked her if she wanted to do it, because we were about to do a major recasting in New York and it hit me that she would be a big get for the show. The timing felt right for her, too. She was at a crossroads in her life looking for something to do.

Jennifer O'Connell: What was appealing about her was that she was really smart. She was a journalist. She had written books. She had married into the Kennedy family. And so we felt like she brought a new level to the table.

Carole Radziwill (Housewife): At that point, I didn't know about *Housewives*. I just knew Andy had a talk show that was really funny and had these funny, quirky, crazy women on it. So I said, "Okay, I'll do it. I don't care." It's part of being a journalist. You have a natural curiosity about things.

Ramona Singer: I liked Carole fine, but she was a wallflower. She faded into the background—unlike Heather, who was so annoying and in-your-face that season.

Andy Cohen: Heather brought a spark plug energy to the mix. I was hoping there were shades of Bethenny there.

Heather Thomson (Housewife): It was literally out of the blue for me. The marketing director at my company, Yummie Tummie, got a cold call from a casting agent and interrupted me in the middle of a meeting being like, "You might want to take this." When I got on the phone, I was a bit distracted and thought they wanted to do something with my brand for *The Apprentice*.

Jennifer O'Connell: We liked Heather because she was another self-made woman. We appreciated that she had a real business, that she was super successful, that she was strong, that she didn't seem like she'd be bossed around very easily. She knew her shit and was confident.

Heather Thomson: They told me it was for *The Real Housewives of New York City*. And I said, "Oh my God, hell to the no!" That was my exact answer. I said, "I'm nothing like any of those women. I would never fit in." These women didn't have all that much going on, and they had to create story lines for themselves. They're fake socialites, you know what I mean? Ramona's no fuckin' socialite. Jill Zarin was as close as you got to one because her husband was so fucking loaded. But real socialites in Manhattan would never go on this show. There's nothing for them to gain.

Jennifer O'Connell: She didn't need us, which was another component— she would have been just fine with or without the show. If people desperately wanted to be on the show or were fans, it usually didn't work. She seemed like she'd be along for the ride and have some fun with it.

Heather Thomson: It was totally out of my comfort zone, but I knew it would help my business. And aside from that, as a parent, I had been through this emotional experience where my son had this rare disease, biliary atresia, and received a liver transplant at six months old. So that became another motivating factor for me: to talk about organ donation and what it's like being on the other side of having a sick child at home.

Andy Cohen: And then there was Aviva, who had no shortage of connections to the series. We had put her on tape a few years before but I don't think she was a contender. Bethenny called me one day and said, "Are you insane not to hire a beautiful woman with one leg whose ex-husband has slept with half your Housewives!" She was right!

Aviva Drescher (Housewife): I auditioned twice. The first time I was nine months pregnant and made it to the top three before I realized I would be nursing and didn't really have time to do the show. And then the next year they came back and, I guess, Bethenny was like, "You've got to hire that woman with the fake leg!" I figured I could help other people who had physical differences.

Heather Thomson: I loved Aviva and was so excited she was cast. Here was this beautiful, smart woman with this dynamic personality who had suffered an unspeakable tragedy but was a survivor. I thought she was going to be so inspirational and could stand for so much. I said, "This is a chick I like."

Jennifer O'Connell: Aviva also brought immediate drama with her connection to Harry Dubin.

Aviva Drescher: Everybody wanted me to be jealous and annoyed that he'd had this relationship with my cast members. But by the time I was on *Housewives*, I was happily married to my husband, Reid.

Sonja Morgan: I was supportive of Aviva because of her being a mom. I wanted her to do well to support her child—she needed the money!

Lisa Shannon: Aviva was the most neurotic person I've ever met. I understand what place that comes from. You get your leg caught in a machine at the age of six and have your foot amputated? I'd be terrified of most things, too.

Aviva Drescher: In the beginning, I definitely was planning on just being myself. I did not plan at all on getting into the muckety-muck of this show. I planned on being elevated and refined.

Things didn't go exactly as Aviva planned, though. And the reception she, Carole, and Heather got from the veteran Housewives could have had something to do with it.

Jennifer O'Connell: As much as Ramona, Luann, and Sonja were probably relieved they hadn't been fired, in a way it only empowered them more.

Andy Cohen: It was the new girls versus the old girls. It was not the immediate vibe we hoped it would be. One does hope, but why did we expect otherwise?

Heather Thomson: I felt the former Housewives didn't want us to succeed. They were intimidated.

Sonja Morgan: When those three came on at the same time, I was at Luann's house and they all went to bed at nine o'clock. I go, "WHAT THE FUCK? Who are these girls?!"

Lisa Shannon: Ramona, Sonja, and Luann wanted to really establish "the way we do the show," so to speak, and impart this bad behavior on the three newbies, who were eager and hardworking, and it was frustrating for us as producers. We were trying to make sure that the new ladies didn't get poisoned by them.

Andy Cohen: One of the reasons we were excited about the new blood was how tough the New York women were with some of the producers, I'll just say that.

Ramona Singer: I was having a bad season that year because they brought three new people on, who I felt were all vanilla. They really didn't have big personalities. Aviva only had a big personality when she got angry, and I don't consider that having a big personality, that's just called having anger problems. They didn't have any depth.

Heather Thomson: Oh please, Ramona has the depth of a dried-up creek.

Carole Radziwill: In the press, Ramona would say how difficult it was because we were new and we didn't understand how to do it. We understood how to do it, we just weren't playing by their unspoken rules.

Lisa Shannon: Heather and Carole, in particular, were very savvy. They thought Ramona was ridiculous and rude, and they didn't want to be associated with that bad behavior.

Heather Thomson: Ramona was so mean to me in the first season. One time, Sonja and I were posing for a picture and Ramona said to Sonja, "Don't pose with her! Don't promote her!" I was like, "Oh my God, these little fucking queen bees."

Lisa Shannon: Heather and Carole hit it off right away. It's always helpful to have an ally.

Heather Thomson: Carole and I have been friends from the minute we met on the show. Like, genuine friends. And during our first scene Aviva was so honest. We were at this French restaurant called Orsay on the Upper East Side and really bonded, the three of us. We all kind of agreed that we would have one another's backs and wouldn't do the mean-girl stuff. Of course, that didn't last long!

Carole Radziwill: I thought a lot of what the other Housewives did was crazy but I had a good sense of humor about it. I used to say, the difference between me and the other Housewives is I'm on a comedy and they think they're on a drama.

Aviva Drescher: As time went on, I began to realize, this is really a show about creating entertainment through drama. So I began to make drama.

Jennifer O'Connell: We didn't realize how much drama Aviva was going to bring to the table when we first hired her. But she was not easy. Everything about her was just extra.

Heather Thomson: I didn't know it when I first met her, but Aviva had applied to be on the show several times, so she wanted to be a Housewife. When she finally got her spot, she was going to play the game hard. I was totally naïve, but she was very strategic. She had her whole story arc planned out: beginning, middle, and end.

Aviva Drescher: The truth is, I didn't really care about these women. I'd just met them and I didn't really care about who invited who to a party, who was fighting with who about what. I certainly had no stake. But I knew I had to get into it to keep the job, which I felt was important. So I leaned into that.

Ramona Singer: Aviva was terrible. She would just get very upset and say horrible, horrible things. Remember when she came to St. Barts and called me and Sonja "white trash"? I had no idea what that meant.

Sonja Morgan: We had to Google it!

Carole Radziwill: After the "white trash" comment, I really could not look Aviva in the eye again. I called her and I said, "Listen, Aviva, you need to do damage control. That is not okay what you said." She just laughed and said, "Are you kidding me? This is the best episode ever! I watched it ten times."

Aviva Drescher: I was caught off guard by being seen as unlikable because I didn't think it would be that harsh. I went from being super light to being such a snob, so quickly. But I don't blame editing because it was me.

Carole Radziwill: Aviva loved it all. She, more than any of them, got caught up in this idea that she had to play an alternate person for show. With all that she had going for her, she could have been perfect if she just played all that—but she wanted to play the evil character.

Aviva wasn't the only source of conflict in season 5. Heather and Sonja butted heads when Sonja enlisted Heather's help to launch a new product: a luxury toaster oven.

Sonja Morgan: Everybody loved the toaster. I was cooking all the time in it on the show and the idea of releasing my own? I thought it was a no-brainer.

Heather Thomson: I really wanted to help Sonja. Here was this woman who was struggling. She kept talking about this luxury toaster oven. I believed she could make money off the idea, because you don't have to have any type of expertise to have a toaster oven. Her story was great: "I'm home in this big house alone, I don't need to cook out of this big oven for myself, I'd rather just cook out of my toaster oven—it's easy, it's simple, and I can make great things, so I created one of my own with more room in it and three tiers." I'm a storyteller, that's something I can sell.

Sonja Morgan: I went to see my FIT adviser, and he goes, "Honey, you can't start with the toaster. Sonja, you're not going to be a Martha Stewart. You are an international fashion lifestyle brand. You went to FIT for marketing. You have to start with fashion and then build your brand into homeware later. You're a much more sensual brand." So I pulled the toaster deal.

Heather Thomson: What pissed me off the most about Sonja is that I'm a real business person. I mentor fashion designers all the time, early in their careers, and they're working their asses off just to get a fucking nut. And here's this girl standing on gold leaf. She's got a platter and a waiter there just ready to say, "Here, girl, here's Sonja Morgan's brand." She had everything going for her and she just wasted it away. Do you know how many people out there would have fucking hung by their toenails for an opportunity like that?

Sonja Morgan: I still get requests for the toaster! People still want it. They're desperate for it!

The season 5 casting refresh brought some new dynamics to the group, but producers still weren't done tweaking. In a shocking season 6 surprise, the countess herself was downgraded to a "Friend of" role—the first such move in Housewives *history.*

Lisa Shannon: Luann, Ramona, and Sonja had developed a lot of very bad behavior in season 5. And Luann was probably the worst offender. She wasn't really available, she had a very noncommittal attitude toward everything. She'd cancel filming whenever she wanted. I would get calls at two a.m., "I'm not going to film this manicure tomorrow," and you'd have to spend hours trying to convince her to go get a goddamn manicure at the salon for forty-five minutes. It was horrible.

Carole Radziwill: I'm guessing the demotion was a way to pay her less money and scare her into actually participating in a more real way.

Andy Cohen: The *RHONY* negotiations, in my opinion, have always been hard, and in that instance, the tip of the iceberg was that Luann had a representative who missed our deadline, and we said, "Fine, we're now demoting you."

Heather Thomson: That was the biggest slap in the face for her. The countess was so degraded by that.

Luann de Lesseps: It wasn't like I was a supporting player. I was in every scene of the show that season. And then they didn't have me in the opening.

Heather Thomson: She lost her mind when that happened.

Jennifer O'Connell: Diva behavior brings the ultimate payback because they only bite themselves in the ass. If you don't show up, that means you're not really in the show. And at the end of the day, these women want to see themselves in the show as much as possible, even the ones who don't want to take the time to shoot as much as we want them to.

Heather Thomson: She came back with a vengeance and was out to make sure that something like that would never happen again.

Andy Cohen: Luann is someone who has kind of saved herself despite herself.

Luann de Lesseps: That's called resilience, baby!

To grow the group more, producers added a young, married mother of two named Kristen Taekman.

Kristen Taekman (Housewife): Brandi Glanville is one of my best friends. She was a bridesmaid at my wedding, we've known each other for a million years. One year, Brandi came to town and brought me to the Bravo upfronts. So there I am, holding Brandi's drink while she took pictures with fans, and Andy Cohen walked into the room. Brandi said hello to him and then looked at me and was like, "This is Kristen, your next New York Housewife." It was completely random! We'd never even talked about it; she just said it. Andy and I both were like, "What?" The next day, I got a call from whoever does the casting.

Andy Cohen: Brandi has a good sense of who would be a good Housewife. How could we not check her out?

Lisa Shannon: Kristen was one of those people we liked right away when we saw her tape. She was very self-deprecating about how beautiful she is. She and Heather, they had a really great rapport. Kristen's marriage was captivating to watch; she was very open about their issues. And the kids were really young—Kingsley was like, barely two, and Cassius was what, four? There was a lot to like.

Heather Thomson: I was excited to have Kristen join, because it felt like, "Yes, here's someone with a similar, young, cool energy like Carole and I have." But she had no idea what she was in for.

Kristen Taekman: I didn't really do a ton of preparation before filming, so I went in pretty blind. And it wasn't at all what I expected.

Ramona Singer: She was one of those girls who had no personality. I didn't quite get it.

Kristen Taekman: Ramona is so interesting to me. She has a soft, loving outside layer, but she has been doing this show too long and it's hardened her. So she wasn't very sweet to me. But fair enough, she's an OG—like, how many of me has she seen throughout the years? I'm sure she looks at a girl like me and under her breath is like, "I give this bitch two seasons."

Lisa Shannon: Kristen just rubbed Ramona the wrong way. And of course they got into an infamous clash when, during a trip to Heather's house in the Berkshires, Ramona threw a glass at Kristen and cut her lip.

Ramona Singer: First of all, it was a plastic cup, okay? It was plastic shaped like a wineglass. And what happened was, it was in my hand and it was a reflex. She splashed me and got me wet, so I just tossed it at her—not knowing that it would hit her in the face and hurt her!

Kristen Taekman: I tasted blood. And to be honest with you, I was literally treading water at the time, so my first reaction wasn't to retaliate. It was like, "Holy shit! a) I don't want to drown, and b) Something is bleeding. I'm going to get out of this gross lake, take care of myself, and then maybe I'll deal with her later." Of course, once I knew I was okay, I was like, "Whoa, this girl is crazy."

Ramona Singer: It was never my intention to hurt her.

Kristen Taekman: You have to remember, she threw a glass at me *because I splashed her*. It was ridiculous.

Ramona Singer: We were on this trip and we didn't have glam there with us, so I had gotten my hair done before we left, hoping it would last the whole trip. And then she purposely splashed my hair, and it just got me so infuriated!

Kristen Taekman: Everybody always asks me about that moment. And my personality is, I can take care of myself. I would never, ever, ever throw something back. It's not something I would teach my children to do, and I wouldn't have done it myself—that's not how I was raised.

> *Ramona and Kristen's feud was far from the biggest drama in season 6. Most of the tension stemmed from Aviva, who found herself on thin ice with production after alienating her fellow Housewives in season 5. In order to save herself, Aviva showed she would be willing to do almost anything to hold an apple.*

Carole Radziwill: Aviva nearly didn't come back full-time in season 6.

Aviva Drescher: They were concerned that at the end of season 5, especially during the reunion, I was self-censoring. Because I was sort of backing up from my bad behavior and trying to be more likable. So for season 6, they wanted to see what I would produce.

Andy Cohen: That was the problem, even with everything Aviva had going for her, she was coming off as inauthentic and producing herself.

Carole Radziwill: No matter how much drama she made, for some reason, the audience did not like her. And the more time we spent with Aviva, the more obvious it became why.

Aviva Drescher: Carole was my best friend our first season. But Carole's like a chess player, and when I became a little unpopular and called the girls "white trash," she started to distance herself from me.

Carole Radziwill: Between seasons, I had seen how crazy she was and started backing off. The first thing I filmed for the new season was the lunch when the whole "BookGate" thing came out.

Aviva Drescher: Here's how that started. I was telling Carole about my book. . . .

Carole Radziwill: The season before, she asked me legitimately about writing a book. And I remember telling her, "Listen, you're smart and capable. I'm sure you can write it yourself. But it's probably going to take you a year or two, and you're on a reality show, you're not necessarily going to want to become a writer and live a writer's life. You're doing this for the show—which is totally legit—so you should get a writer to help you if you want it to come out during the season." And she totally agreed and asked me if I knew any ghostwriters. I didn't, but I gave her the name of someone who knew someone. So the next time I saw her, she said something about the book and I said, "That's great! Did you end up hiring the writer?"

Aviva Drescher: She sort of came at me like, she was the writer and I was some pathetic Housewife just doing a book. It was very condescending and one-upping.

Carole Radziwill: So she looked at me and said, "I did it myself, it was really easy, it was like writing a long email."

Aviva Drescher: If she was such a secure writer, she would be warm and welcoming! Her attitude was just really rude.

Carole Radziwill: Then she brought up *What Remains* and said, "It was your first book. Did you have a ghostwriter?" At that point I realized, "Oh my God, she's trying to flip the story and make the drama about me." I wanted to say, "That wasn't for a TV show! I didn't write it in a month to be published during the season!" But at the time, I didn't want to break the fourth wall.

Ramona Singer: I heard that rumor was true! That someone did really write her book and that she didn't write it.

Aviva Drescher: I never really intended on BookGate becoming a thing.

Carole Radziwill: This was the first week of filming and I just thought, "Oh my God."

Heather Thomson: For Aviva, it was all about throwing Carole under the bus to give herself a story line and make sure we were talking about Aviva's book over and over and over again.

Carole Radziwill: I confronted her and said, "What are you saying about me? What do you know about my career?" To have Aviva demean something that took two to three years of my life and was incredibly personal to me, I was shocked. I was being slandered.

Heather Thomson: It was a terrible, terrible thing to do to someone. Because that rumor is so damaging to Carole's career, and for what reason? So that Aviva could sell more copies of her book? Like, that rumor followed Carole. And people believed it. I remember being on Bethenny Frankel's talk show and she was like, "I really think Carole did have a ghostwriter!" She didn't even know Carole! I was like, "She did not!"

Carole Radziwill: I will say, I don't think Aviva expected me to be as angry as I was. It was my life story, it was about my husband and my friends. It was something I really cared about, and I didn't want it to get dirtied up.

Aviva Drescher: I didn't intend on hurting Carole so deeply, I really didn't. If I had known, I wouldn't have brought it up. All she had to say was, "No, I didn't have a ghostwriter."

Carole Radziwill: I tried to correct her but it's funny how when you're defending yourself, the audience is like, "You're so defensive!" I'm like, "Yeah! I'm defending myself. That's what it looks like. That's the definition!"

Heather Thomson: That was the beginning of the end with Carole and Andy, too.

Carole Radziwill: It was a big lesson. Though I will say, the end of that first scene was one of the best exits of any *Housewives* scenes ever. We had this blowout fight, I left the room, walked downstairs, walked into the kitchen, saw Reid, and said, "Your wife is a terrible person," shut the door on his shocked face, walked over to Harry, who I just met an hour earlier, and I said, "Harry, it's so nice to meet you, I totally understand the reason for the divorce." And then I walked out. To this day, I think that was brilliant.

Lisa Shannon: The kiss of death for a Housewife is to turn nasty and not have growth from it. Aviva was vile toward Carole, just vicious and vile, and that's not fun to watch.

> *In a cast with no shortage of drama queens, Aviva's antics were wearing especially thin by the time season 6 was rounding the bend. She may have extended her contract in the short term by bringing drama, but by the finale, it was clear she was on her last leg.*

Lisa Shannon: The problem with Aviva was, she was very rehearsed.

Aviva Drescher: Maybe that's why I wasn't a good fit for the show, because it's all just nonsense to me. It was all very petty. Most of the things I did on the show I would never do, so I was doing a lot of acting.

Andy Cohen: Aviva is awesome but she's not a great actress.

Carole Radziwill: There was one scene I thought was touching amid the theatrics, when she returned to her hometown to revisit the place where she'd had the fateful accident that resulted in the partial amputation of her leg.

Aviva Drescher: The most real moment for me never aired, even though it was filmed. I went back to the barn where I lost my leg as a kid and reunited with the girl who was there with me when it happened, Becky Morgan. Now, they showed that and it was very emotional—that really was the first time I had seen her and the first time I had been back. What they didn't show was that Becky's mom gave me a bowl she had saved since 1977. And that bowl belonged to my mother. The night before my accident, my family had eaten dinner at Becky's house and my mom, who was an incredible cook, brought over a cordon bleu and potatoes gratin in that bowl. I slept over that night and the next day I lost my leg and in the chaos, she never gave it back. So now, thirty-five years later, here was the bowl that Becky's mom had saved. And it was very moving. My mom had passed away years earlier. It was meaningful to me to have that piece of her.

Carole Radziwill: But you know what's weird? When that episode aired showing her seeing this machine that dismembered her, I remember she got slammed. The audience didn't care. They were like, "I hope the other one gets cut off!" I mean, they *really* hated her.

Sonja Morgan: Eh, you know, fan is short for fanatic. They love you, and they hate you.

> *It only took one fell swoop for Aviva to seal her* Housewives *legacy and secure her own exit papers.*

Andy Cohen: You're going to talk about the leg toss, right?

Aviva Drescher: Okay, here's how that came about. I hadn't gone on the group trip to Montana because of my health issues. I was newly diagnosed with asthma. None of them believed me and when they all came back, it was everybody ganging up on Aviva. I got really annoyed. So I got copies of my X-rays and my medical records, and if they came into the finale and apologized and seemed interested in how I was doing, we'd be fine. But if they came in guns blazing, I was going to make a splash.

Carole Radziwill: This was the first time we were all seeing her, and we all knew she was going to make some excuse or cause some drama.

Aviva Drescher: I felt a moral obligation to entertain people. That's what I was hired to do. And I was annoyed because they were all being so unsupportive. So I basically looked at all those women, who were telling me that they didn't believe my health issues were real, and confronted them about it.

Carole Radziwill: She was clearly angling for us to try to say she was a fake. But if you watch it, none of us said that she was a fake! The closest thing was Heather saying something about the fact that she was not authentic.

Aviva Drescher: Under the table, I took my leg off. And putting it on and off takes only a second, so it didn't take me long to get ready.

Heather Thomson: She kept trying to bring it back to Carole's book being written by someone else, and I kept walking away because it was such bullshit. And then she threw the X-rays at me, saying that she had never lied to any of us at the table and that we had all hurt her.

Carole Radziwill: Aviva raised her voice, and she said, "I'm just tired of this group always questioning me and I am tired of being called a fake." And then she was like, "The only thing fake about me is this!" That's when she put the leg on the table.

Heather Thomson: My immediate reaction was to walk away. I got really far from her. Like, "This is fucking ridiculous."

Luann de Lesseps: I couldn't stop laughing. Who does that?

Kristen Taekman: What does Ramona always say? Déclassé. It was just such a big shock.

Carole Radziwill: It was a little awkward because her leg was just sitting on the table. Right in front of her. And that wasn't enough of a theatric because she could easily just put it back on and walk out. That's why she threw it.

Heather Thomson: She threw it at me, you know? It was right at me. And then she said, "Heather, you'd sooner see me crawl out of here!"

Kristen Taekman: When someone is throwing a limb at you, like, your first thought is, "This is a horror movie." I couldn't believe she did that. It was just so crass and disgusting.

Aviva Drescher: My goal wasn't to gross anybody out or anything. I made sure there was a tablecloth so I wouldn't flash my residual limb at anybody, which could make you queasy, understandably.

Heather Thomson: At a certain point, the leg was just in the middle of the floor by itself.

Carole Radziwill: I went over, picked it up, and gave it back to her, saying, "You need to get help," and walked away. And then she put it on.

Aviva Drescher: I knew one of the girls would grab it for me and bring it back. I wasn't worried about that. I wasn't going to hop over to get it or anything. Throwing it was as far as I was going to go.

Andy Cohen: I thought it was incredible television. I thought it was hilarious. I loved it. The music, the reactions, the shock of it being at *Le Cirque*!

Aviva Drescher: People say, "She was just trying to get airtime!" I wasn't vying for airtime, it's not like you get more money if you get more airtime. I was trying to create good entertainment! And I did.

Despite the iconic television moment, Aviva would not get another chance on RHONY.

Andy Cohen: The irony was that we had already shot the season and knew the leg toss was coming and would be an incredible ending to the season, but that Aviva otherwise really didn't work on the show. I think she bet it would go in another direction. Her husband called me as the season was airing, asking for more money for Aviva given how exciting he thought the leg toss would be. That was a first.

Heather Thomson: She got fired, which was just such a fucking slap in the face for her because she really thought taking off her prosthetic leg and throwing it across the room at Le Cirque would have been the thing that saved her.

Carole Radziwill: But the audience wasn't on her side. The audience is really smart. They can see through people who are being fake and not good at it. And Aviva more than anyone was playing a character. She was so over-the-top and camp and hyperbolic that none of it rang true.

Andy Cohen: On one hand, throwing her leg was absolutely hysterical and brilliant. On the other hand, it was kind of a nail in her coffin because you were like, "Okay, well, where do we go with this? What more can you do?"

Lisa Shannon: It always comes down to, "Are we going to see something new?"

Aviva Drescher: When Lisa Shannon called me as I was driving out to the Hamptons and said, "We're not going to have you back this year," I was really relieved. I didn't have any ego attached to it whatsoever. It's not like this was a job based on any kind of skill that I spent my whole life building up to. That's why I had no problem coming out saying that I was fired. So what? It wasn't an insult to me. "Awww, I'm not going to be a reality star?" Oh well!

Aviva's spot was filled quickly. Luann was given back her apple, and Dorinda Medley also joined the gang.

Dorinda Medley (Housewife): I heard about the show way back when it was *Manhattan Moms*. I didn't want to do it then, as I had just married

Richard and was really focused on our life together. But when Richard passed, Ramona started talking about it again and said, "Why don't you try it for a year? It will be a no-brainer. Andy would love to have you." I remember the first day I was filming at Ramona's house and I was like, "Wow. I like the camera and the camera likes me." It became almost like my therapy. It was a great way of reconnecting to something that was all mine. It had nothing to do with me being Mrs. Something, or being someone's mother. For the first time, I didn't care what people thought. I'm a grown-up, my daughter Hannah's a grown-up, I'm not a wife to anybody. It kind of gave me a freedom to explore that part of my life.

Andy Cohen: Dorinda was perfect casting with a capital P. A natural connection with the group that went back years, opinions, likeable, and relatable.

Heather Thomson: But listen—and I'm friends with Dorinda, so I say this from a place of love: she was a fucking nightmare when she first joined the show. She would tweet like she was a fan. "Wow, Heather was a real bitch in that scene." I was like, "You're on my fucking team! I've got enough fucking trolls on social media giving me shit, I don't need you!"

Dorinda Medley: Hey, I definitely don't have a filter. I've always been someone who speaks her mind. With me, unlike a lot of the girls they had on the show before me, you had someone who was a full-fledged person. I've lived a life. People who stay on the *Housewives* have to have layers. You've got to be like an oyster that keeps throwing them pearls. And that's what I gave them.

Dorinda shined in her first season, a big feat considering there was another major addition to the cast. Three seasons after leaving the show, Bethenny returned as a full-time Housewife.

Andy Cohen: Bethenny was arguably our most successful Housewife. After the show she had gone on to sell her cocktail company and made a ton of money. She had a syndicated talk show. She was a mother. She seemed so far over the *Housewives*. And when Bethenny leaves something, she has a way of really putting it in the past, like she's totally done with it. It felt impossible, but I felt like there was an organic opening, that this was the moment.

Lisa Shannon: She had gotten separated. Her talk show was ending. It felt like there could be a new chapter to explore.

Andy Cohen: I sat in her kitchen in the Hamptons and she started to see the sense in it. As she entertained the idea she was getting amused; her wheels were turning. We agreed to keep it a secret from the other women. I was so excited and proud we were able to make that happen. It felt huge for the show.

Ramona Singer: Well, she needed to come back on the show because she couldn't get a show any other way. Her talk show had failed, her marriage had failed . . . she didn't have anything else.

Andy Cohen: She'd sold Skinnygirl Cocktails for a ton of money, so she didn't need to come back per se, but she was smart enough to know the exposure it provided; it was an even bigger show than when she'd left.

Heather Thomson: I had been clued in to the fact she was coming back to the show, or at least considering it, when I did her talk show. Her producer, before I went on, asked me, "What do you think about Bethenny coming back to *RHONY*?" And I said, "That's great!" She's such a nightmare, the show needs someone like Bethenny, because that's what makes it tick. And the producer said, "Would you be willing to ask her on the couch if she would consider coming back?"

Carole Radziwill: I didn't know anything about Bethenny except that she really crushed it in business. By design and luck she had managed to do something pretty extraordinary on that show, so I was like, "That's pretty admirable."

Dorinda Medley: In retrospect now, they were really putting a lot of pressure on Bethenny's return. They had a whole advertising campaign, "The B Is Back." I didn't really understand that then, but I understand it now. It was a big deal.

Sonja Morgan: I couldn't have been happier. My cup runneth over for Bethenny. You can never go wrong with Bethenny on the show. I needed her to tell me the real deal—I don't want someone on the show that's going to blow smoke up my ass.

Dorinda Medley: If the other girls had negative feelings about her return, they never said anything to me.

Heather Thomson: No one will tell you, but they hated Bethenny. And I know that they all hated Bethenny because they talked negatively about her all the time. Ramona, Luann, and Sonja especially were not happy about her coming back. Mainly Ramona and Luann. They thought they had gotten rid of her for good.

Andy Cohen: I remember everyone thinking it was ultimately great for the show. Were they bullshitting me?

Ramona Singer: I always call Bethenny a cat. You don't know if she's going to purr up next to you or scratch your eyes out.

Carole Radziwill: Ramona, in particular, wasn't happy to see her at all.

Ramona Singer: She's nice to you as long as she needs you for something. As soon as she doesn't need you, you're not in her life. That's why most of the people she hangs out with are people who work for her. So when she came back, we didn't have a relationship. We weren't really friends.

Dorinda Medley: It definitely felt like we were out in the wild and people were sort of sniffing around each other.

Heather Thomson: Dorinda was a huge fan of Bethenny—that's another thing that skeeved me out. She wanted to be Bethenny's friend because she was enamored by Bethenny as a Housewife. I was like, "Uh, whatever."

Ramona Singer: Every season Bethenny would take someone under her hat, love them, and then dump them.

Dorinda Medley: People try to sway you to form alliances, and if you're strong enough, you know how to manage it. When someone would say to me, "I can't believe you're friends with her," I was like, "Well, I don't care if you believe it."

Carole Radziwill: I remember defending Bethenny to the group before I even met her—and Heather did, too—because Luann claimed to have invented Skinnygirl margarita. She claimed she was an integral part of creating it, and her proof was that Bethenny wrote a Skinnygirl book and she gave it to Luann with the inscription: "To Luann. I couldn't have done it without you," or something like that. And you know how narcissists are black and white. She was like, "You see? This is evidence! She could not have done that without me!"

Kristen Taekman: The OGs knew well enough that it was really good for ratings—but at the same time, they were kind of freaking out because a lot of the airtime got split up.

Heather Thomson: Bethenny knew that the girls didn't want her back on the show. But then she showed up at the first filming and they were, like, fucking crawling up her asshole. "Oh Bethenny! Oh Bethenny!" I was like, "What the fuck's going on around here?" I couldn't believe it. They knew how powerful she was, and they wanted to get on her good side.

Carole Radziwill: I wasn't close with Bethenny at all at first because we barely filmed together. But I had none of the underlying issues that the other women had with her.

Ramona Singer: You could tell she felt awkward coming back, especially around me. She knew I knew all the times she had bad-mouthed the show. "This is a show that projects women in a bad way. I'll never do that show again." And yet here she is again, as if it's a different show. Bullshit.

But Ramona had bigger concerns that season than Bethenny. After twenty-two years of marriage, she and her husband, Mario, were going their separate ways.

Dorinda Medley: That was really tough on her, because you know what? She really loved that man. They had something special.

Ramona Singer: I caught Mario cheating. Never in my world did I ever expect him to cheat on me. I was just an emotional wreck.

Sonja Morgan: Singer shed a lot of tears that year. She was crying to everybody!

Ramona Singer: Since then, he's apologized deeply. He said, "I felt emasculated but it wasn't you, I emasculated myself and I'm sincerely sorry and I miss my family. I'm so sorry about how I handled everything." And we've moved on. We have a daughter; when you have children, you have to look at the bigger picture. You can't use your children as pawns. It's just not healthy for your children or for yourself.

One budding relationship surprised everyone that season: the one between Carole and twenty-three-years-younger chef Adam Kenworthy. Sparks immediately flew—but it was Luann who was fired up, since her niece had previously dated Adam. The relationship led to seasons of acrimony and allegations between the countess and the princess.

Heather Thomson: We were all there when Carole and Adam met. The whole world saw it on television, right in Luann's kitchen.

Carole Radziwill: Believe me, I knew the history and asked Adam if he was dating Luann's niece, because if he was I didn't want anything to do with him. He assured me they had broken up a year earlier, though during the course of that year they had hooked up, like exes do. But I made sure he and Nicole were on the same page and it wouldn't cause any drama.

I know they wanted to couch it in this way that I was a cougar and he was a boy toy and this was a fling, but we definitely had a connection. Plus, he was thirty years old—he was a man. I was married by the time I was his age.

Sonja Morgan: I was certainly not judging her for going younger.

Carole Radziwill: When I told Luann I was seeing Adam, it had been two

The OG Casts

Orange County: Kimberly Bryant, Lauri Peterson, Jeana Keough, Vicki Gunvalson, and Jo De La Rosa

New York: Ramona Singer, Jill Zarin, Luann de Lesseps, Bethenny Frankel, and Alex McCord

Atlanta: Lisa Wu, Shereé Whitfield, NeNe Leakes, DeShawn Snow, and Kim Zolciak-Biermann

New Jersey: Jacqueline Laurita, Teresa Giudice, Danielle Staub, Dina Manzo, and Caroline Manzo

D.C.: Catherine Ommanney, Stacie Scott Turner, Mary Schmidt Amons, Lynda Erkiletian, and Michaele Salahi

The OG Casts

Beverly Hills: Taylor Armstrong, Camille Grammer, Lisa Vanderpump, Kyle Richards, Kim Richards, and Adrienne Maloof

Miami: Marysol Patton, Lea Black, Alexia Echevarria, Larsa Pippen, Cristy Rice, Elsa "Mama" Patton, and Adriana de Moura

Potomac: Charrisse Jackson-Jordan, Robyn Dixon, Karen Huger, Gizelle Bryant, Katie Rost, and Ashley Darby

Dallas: Cary Deuber, Brandi Redmond, Stephanie Hollman, LeeAnne Locken, and Tiffany Hendra

The "Tres Amigas"

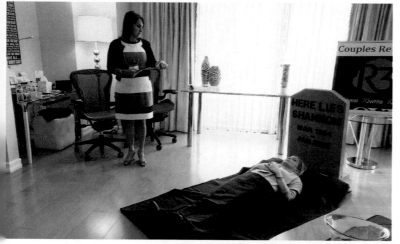

Shannon faces her fear of death as she grapples with her divorce.

Tamra Judge being baptized in the holy waters of a hotel.

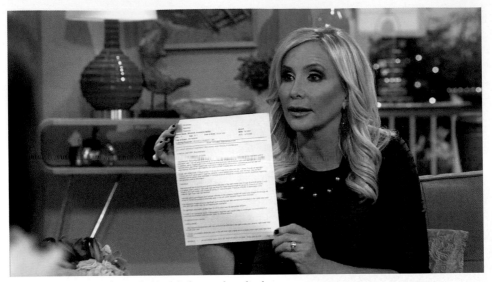

Shannon with Brooks Ayers's doctored medical records, further proving he was faking cancer.

"She. Broke. The. Bow. Off. My. Cake. And. Ate. It."
—**Heather Dubrow**

"You couldn't write characters like Alex and Simon. . . . Do you remember those glossy red leather pants he wore?" —**Andy Cohen**

"I'm the one that dubbed it Scary Island. Those are my words. I thought we were going to Fantasy Island!" —**Kelly Killoren Bensimon**

Turtle Time

"I knew one of the girls would grab it for me and bring it back, I wasn't worried about that. I wasn't going to hop over to get it or anything."
—**Aviva Drescher**

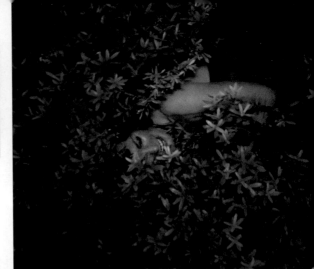

Luann in the bushes

Jovani

Bethenny and Jill reunite at Bobby's funeral.

Tiki torches and skinny dips

Shereé, Kenya, Cynthia, and NeNe in true ATL glam

BTS moment with original Housewife Shereé

"Linnethia 'NeNe' Leakes was an instant standout. She was popping with personality. And she kind of anchored this group of friends." —**Andy Cohen**

"Who gon' check me, boo?"

Kim and Kandi writing
"Tardy for the Party"

Just peachy: Cynthia, NeNe, Marlo, Kenya, and Malorie

weeks—it wasn't like I had kept it secret. Mind you, I didn't have to tell her or anyone. But she seized the moment and said something like, "I knew you were friendly but I didn't know you were fucking." I should have probably defended myself more. I probably should have thrown my drink in her face, but I was like, "Okay, Luann. Calm down." I should have taken the moment, but she did, and then she ran with it.

Dorinda Medley: You have to adapt. The show is about adapting, taking your fights and deciding if you're going to go all the way with it. In this case, Luann leaned in.

Carole Radziwill: Depending on how drunk Luann was, Adam was either family or he was the help. In fact, Adam was still cooking for her once or twice a week, and he was babysitting her son Noel. So she couldn't quite decide which would be a better narrative—was it more to her advantage to paint me as a peasant dating the help of the countess, or for her to play up the family angle? And ultimately she went with the family angle. She realized she could turn it into a story line that made her look like the Mother of the Year who's protecting her family against some cougar predator.

Dorinda Medley: Sometimes on *Housewives* you feel like you're playing Emperor's New Clothes because there is an art form to it. If you say something enough, it becomes the truth. It's not *60 Minutes*. And that sometimes can be frustrating because the audience doesn't see what you see.

Carole Radziwill: The thing was, I knew it wasn't true. I knew she wasn't wounded by this at all—nor was her niece, by the way, who had a boyfriend! But it just got nasty. It got to the point where she was saying out loud, "Carole is a pedophile." It was like, "Are you kidding me?" She said that in reference to me dating Adam, a thirty-year-old *man*. To conflate that with pedophilia? Abuse like that is a real thing—people's lives and families get destroyed. So to use that as an insult in some dumb story line was really offensive to me.

Dorinda Medley: It's like football—the players get on the football field, they beat each other up and then they shake each other's hands at the end. It's just the way it is.

Carole Radziwill: Probably the most personally offensive thing was that she turned it on me for not having kids. "Oh, if you had a child." She smartly used this whole fake drama as a way to put herself on a pedestal and say, "It's family, you don't understand family." As if she was raising the Brady Bunch.

I never claimed to know more about kids or family than she did, but let's just say, she was not Mother of the Year.

There was another clash in season 7 that occurred in an unexpected place: the vestibule of Sonja Morgan's iconic town house.

Sonja Morgan: We were all going on a party bus to the Borgata in Atlantic City. I was upstairs, and my sister called to tell me that someone we knew had died. She was supposed to come take care of my daughter, but because of this death, she couldn't. I didn't have a housekeeper, and I had my daughter there who doesn't film. I couldn't leave on a trip and leave my daughter alone with an au pair in a town house with animals. Anything could go wrong—the cat could get hit by a car, or the elevator could crash, or someone could fall in the pond. My daughter could be kidnapped. So Heather, being fake, decided to come in and film and say, "We're outside and we're freezing." She was playing it up for the cameras.

Heather Thomson: That was real as real can be. That's actually when I turned on Sonja, because I had literally carried that woman home. I had scraped her off carpets. I had taken her out of a vestibule where she was letting guys put lit cigarettes in her vagina. I had done so much for that woman. And here we are, waiting to go to Atlantic City. We all arrived at her house, but the limo wasn't there yet. And it was raining out. Well, she would not let us in.

Sonja Morgan: They all had their coffee and breakfast paid for by production and had separate Town Cars to sit in. The schedule said "Not to be filmed in Sonja's town house." So they were supposed to be in their cars waiting to get into the party bus, and I was on the phone upstairs with my sister, and I was upset and crying about this death. And I've got the bitches downstairs complaining they can't come in and I don't have a seat in my front entrance?

Heather Thomson: I went into her house and called up the stairs, "Sonja, the car's not here yet, we're going to come inside and just sit on the couches." So I'm walking up to the second floor and one of the interns comes barreling out being like, "Lady Morgan asks if you can please wait in the vestibule." So I go downstairs and call her on the phone, but she doesn't answer. "Sonja, we're downstairs in the vestibule and it's fucking freezing in here. The walls are leaking from the rain. Can't we just come inside and wait?" And the fact that she would not let us in her house? I was so fucking incensed.

Sonja Morgan: They needed to stay in their car and eat their muffins and coffee. This wasn't a free-for-all. If the situation were reversed, I wouldn't go running through Heather's house. Wait in the fucking car! Rudeness! And they spilled coffee on my gold-inlay family table. You know, the Morgan antiques are in the Metropolitan Museum. They're up in Hartford, New Haven. Everything that was Morgan that I don't have is in a fucking museum. They were all sitting on a sixteenth-century chest in my front entrance that's worth at least half a million dollars. No one sits on that. The red chair that I had in my front entrance has hundred-year-old antique velvet—it's not velvet that you just come in and sit on. I mean, I wasn't ready for this.

> *As season 7 wound down, production realized that the biggest cast in* House-wives *history needed a little paring down, and both Kristen and Heather said goodbye. Meanwhile, season 8 brought the addition of Julianne "Jules" Wainstein, a Hong Kong–born beauty, entrepreneur, and married stay-at-home mother of two.*

Jules Wainstein (Housewife): Dorinda and I were friends—we met at a wedding and just clicked. I guess, after her first season, she submitted my name to casting and I wound up getting a call that summer.

Dorinda Medley: Jules was such a sweet girl. She was so beautiful, so kind, and had this bustling family. And you know, she was half Jewish and half Japanese!

Jules Wainstein: Oh God, I didn't realize how much I said that until I watched the show!

Dorinda Medley: She always made jokes about it and herself, which I loved. She was very funny.

Jules Wainstein: I did the show because I had nothing to hide—and that included talking about my eating disorder. I'm eighteen years in recovery now and while eating disorders are so secretive, I've always lived by the mantra "Secrets keep you sick."

Dorinda Medley: She really did an amazing and courageous thing, talking about her struggle.

Jules Wainstein: It was a very difficult thing for the rest of the cast to understand. You're never cured of an eating disorder, just like you're never cured of alcoholism or addiction. But unlike those, you can't cut yourself off entirely from the source of your pain. Alcoholics can give up drinking, but I still have to eat. So I would be eating in ways that made me comfortable, and they didn't understand that. They picked on me and made it so that I was always justifying and always explaining myself.

Carole Radziwill: I'm sorry, but she was just nuts.

Jules Wainstein: These women were not supportive. I felt like, "I gave you information as a gift about myself because I felt like I wanted to share something personal with you, and you guys are just using that information to pick on me." Bethenny was especially brutal.

Sonja Morgan: Jules got a bad shake because she went after Bethenny too soon, right away.

Jules Wainstein: I thought, "Here's a woman who wrote a book about weight loss, has a brand called Skinnygirl, is a natural foods chef." And on top of that, Bethenny's mother had an eating disorder, that's one of the reasons why I told her my story. But rather than being compassionate, she decided to just pick on me and make me feel worse.

Carole Radziwill: Bethenny does pretend to be an expert in everything. In this case, though, there was an instability about Jules that had us all concerned.

> One of Jules's most infamous scenes came, unsurprisingly, during a girls' dinner when she loaded up her make-your-own calzone with silverware—yes, you read that right—much to the other ladies' bafflement and concern.

Jules Wainstein: That calzone scene had nothing to do with my eating disorder. When I was on the way to that scene, I was on the phone with my best friend. And this place was somewhere kids have birthday parties to build your own pizza. So my friend said, "Why are fifty-year-old women filming there? Whatever you make, you should just put everything in it. It'll be so funny!" So that's what I thought I was doing.

Carole Radziwill: It was disturbing to watch, and being there was difficult.

Jules Wainstein: I was mortified. I called the producers and begged them to change it. I was like, "I look crazy! I look like a crackhead, and I don't do drugs!" I wanted to die.

Lisa Shannon: We don't love to have one-and-done Housewives, but Jules was not in the right place in her life.

Dorinda Medley: I've always felt that Jules was gone too soon. She was a great Housewife.

Jules Wainstein: Everyone always says the world gets to know you better if you do a second season. I didn't really have that chance. But I didn't have what some of those girls had. They were experienced reality stars; they knew how to put it on for the cameras. Like, Sonja Morgan plays up the Lucille Ball ditz act on TV, but off camera, she's a really educated, smart, pulled-together woman. Maybe if I would have had the smarts to do that, they would have kept me on.

One of the season's biggest dramas swirled around Luann and her lightning-fast courtship, engagement, and marriage to Tom D'Agostino, who'd also been involved with Sonja and Ramona.

Dorinda Medley: Luann's spiral really started when she moved into Sonja's town house. That was not a smart choice for her, I think.

Sonja Morgan: I asked Luann to move in with me because she didn't have a place in New York. She was always in the Hamptons. So I invited her to live with me, and the viewers loved it. And at that point, she was seeing five or six guys, at least, playing bingo, as I say.

Andy Cohen: It's worth noting the change that happened in Luann in Turks and Caicos. When the once buttoned-up countess appeared in a bikini, robe, and sunglasses begging Heather to chill out, we said hello to what seemed like a new woman. The ride she took us on in years to come drove an incredible amount of story on the show, sometimes at the expense of hardship in her personal life.

Carole Radziwill: Luann was desperate. She wanted to make something happen. She had one boyfriend one week, and then she had another boyfriend. She had a couple of these guys.

Sonja Morgan: Tom and I are real friends. We have a history. That said, there are certain men in their fifties who will always be your friends with benefits. They're great guys, very generous, you call and they're there, but they're philanderers.

Carole Radziwill: Two weeks into filming, suddenly Luann comes in and she's gone on a date with this guy Tom, who was Sonja's fuckbuddy.

Sonja Morgan: She says she was introduced to him through Dorinda, but she met him at a fashion event I hosted. Maybe Dorinda did introduce them at the party, but it was my party. Either way, it was October when they met, and at the same time, Tom was talking to me about coming to his family home for Thanksgiving. Mind you, we were just friends that fuck. But he was saying to me, "I'm ready to get married." I'm looking at his apartment and thinking, "It's kinda small, I don't know if he has enough closet space for me." Next thing I know, Luann's telling everybody she's getting married—to TOM!

Ramona Singer: I think they were dating three months? It was very fast.

Sonja Morgan: People were like, "You were living with Sonja and you got with her guy?" Ramona was going apeshit over that because she had been on a date with him, too, and I guess he had talked about marriage with her as well.

Ramona Singer: We went on a few dates, but Luann downplayed that as if it never happened. Hello, I was there!

Luann de Lesseps: If it happened "Before Lu," I didn't care.

Sonja Morgan: The most painful thing for me was that Tom had betrayed me. I thought he wanted to be married to me. So I was hurt that he would marry Luann out of the blue. But I didn't blame Luann for going hook, line and sinker. In fact, when Luann told me she was getting married, I said to her, "Hos before bros. I will always be there for you no matter what. No one knows better than me that men come and go."

Dorinda Medley: But Luann really became obsessed with that wedding. She was hell-bent on it.

Sonja Morgan: Luann might have thought, "A wedding is going to be great on the show!" It might have started like that, but I really think she got on that merry-go-round and never got off.

Lisa Shannon: Things came to a head when the ladies went to Miami for the couple's engagement celebrations and that photo came up of Tom cheating on Luann.

Carole Radziwill: Bethenny got a picture of Tom kissing a girl at the Regency Hotel. It was a total setup. Bethenny knew this woman and found out that she was in contact with Tom. And Bethenny was like, "The next time you go to see him, text me." And that's what happened. Bethenny knew that they were going to this hotel, and she sent her friend or probably her assistant to take a picture. I mean, Bethenny doesn't have a lot of friends—and she certainly didn't just happen to have a friend at the Regency at ten o'clock on a Tuesday night when Tom just happened to be there kissing some chick he used to bang.

Ramona Singer: Bethenny totally planned that Tom thing. She knew what was going on and sent someone to photograph that. For me, there are certain lines you don't cross. And something like that? I don't think I could ever do that.

Andy Cohen: I still don't know where Bethenny got the picture.

Luann de Lesseps: I always felt like Bethenny was trying to take me down. She just had a hard-on for me from day one.

Ramona Singer: And here's how calculating and smart Bethenny is: When she told Luann about Tom having a kissing moment with someone else, she was like, "Hold on, I need a drink. Give me that bottle"—which happened to be a Skinnygirl drink. She wanted to make sure it was in the film.

Carole Radziwill: As for Luann, when Tom got caught cheating, she doubled down. He went on this apology tour and she forgave him, professing their love to the press and whatnot. We all had to kind of move on and pretend like they were the happiest couple on earth, when behind the scenes, no one in her circle felt that way. I mean, just ask Barbara.

> *Barbara is Barbara Kavovit, a close confidante of Luann's and the owner of one of the largest construction firms in New York City. During season 9, while appearing as a guest at a charity event, she famously confessed off camera to Carole that she questioned the countess's marrying motives. Little did she realize her words were caught on a hot mic.*

Barbara Kavovit (Friend): About a month before the wedding, Dorinda asked me to donate to a charity auction that would be on the show. I did not plan on filming, and I never signed a release or had a mic on. Carole and I were walking around, and the cameras were following us—just looking at the auction items, not saying anything important. I didn't think I was being filmed more than just showing my tools. At the end of the night, Carole came up to me and started talking about Luann. At that point, there was no camera crew around—and in my mind there was no mic.

Carole Radziwill: Since there were no cameras around, it didn't occur to me that I still had a mic on. It wasn't premeditated.

Barbara Kavovit: Of course she knew she was miked. Now that I've been on the show, I know that as soon as you're done filming, those audio people are on your ass taking the mics back.

Carole Radziwill: She started confiding in me, and she just kept talking.

Barbara Kavovit: At that point, there had been twelve incidents in the month before when Luann came crying to me like, "I can't." It was very bad what was going on with her and Tom, but nobody knew except me and maybe one other person. She was frazzled because of the fights she and Tom would have. I would be like, "Luann, you need to get out of this relationship."

Carole Radziwill: She said the only reason she's going through with this is because she sold the exclusive to *People* magazine, and she's going to go through with it, deal with it, then get divorced. That was Luann's plan.

Barbara Kavovit: At this point, Luann cared more about the press than her own emotional well-being. She was so wrapped up in "Am I in *People* magazine? Am I in *Us* magazine? Did they take a picture of me and Tom?" All she cared about was the spotlight. I do believe in my heart of hearts that there was love there. But those are two people who should have gone out for six months, gotten their rocks off, and then realized that there is no way that two egotistical narcissists like that could ever cohabitate.

Dorinda Medley: Look, I wasn't a proponent of the marriage. But if you want to marry someone and you love them, I'm not going to be there to try to destroy it.

Sonja Morgan: No one was going to stop her going down that runway.

Barbara Kavovit: Luann's wedding was in Palm Beach on New Year's Eve, and she called me in the middle of December and said, "I heard there was a hot mic, and that you said some really fucked-up things about me getting married." My heart sank because I didn't want to do anything to hurt Luann, that was my last intention. I thought Carole was legitimately a concerned friend, and I was legitimately a concerned friend.

Dorinda Medley: Barbara showed up to the wedding and Luann wouldn't even acknowledge her.

Carole Radziwill: They didn't film the wedding for the show, because Luann had sold it to the press. None of us were really invited anyway except for Dorinda.

Dorinda Medley: Three weeks after we shot the reunion, they got divorced.

> *Meanwhile, a different kind of princess came on the scene in season 9—one with a mug shot. With Luann out of Sonja's town house, Lady Morgan welcomed a new roommate in Tinsley Mortimer, who was coming off a public scandal after she'd trespassed on her ex's Florida home.*

Sonja Morgan: I brought Tinsley on the show. When she was arrested and her mug shot came out, I called her and told her, "I'm devastated for you because I know how it feels to have a last name like Mortimer or Morgan and be in the news." The same thing happened to me with my Chapter 11. I was devastated that everyone knew my business. I told her, "You need to get out of Palm Beach. It's a fishbowl." So she came to stay with me, and after a while, she said, "Can you get me on the show?" She had tried to be on the show before and I didn't think they were looking for a single girl, but they were looking for an ally for me.

Carole Radziwill: The thing about Tinsley is, she was easy to talk to because she didn't talk much. She would just nod a lot. There were no layers.

Sonja Morgan: Right away Bethenny was gunning for her. Tinsley wanted to look like this Southern, wealthy trust fund girl, and Bethenny saw right through it—she went after her about being fake. At first Tinsley wanted to hide the fact that she needed to live with me, so she was looking at these nine-thousand-dollar-a-month apartments. She was complaining about the cost. She also wanted to hide the fact that she came to New York to find a guy.

Carole Radziwill: Tinsley was desperate to land a rich guy, so I fixed her up with my boyfriend Adam's friend Scott. I knew he was very successful. I knew the kind of women he had dated, they were always kind of like, boozy and emotionally crazy, and he liked that. So I thought, "Oh my God, I know someone for you. She's really cute. She's boozy, you'll love her. And she'll really like you."

Sonja Morgan: Tinsley friend-jumped to Carole because it was a better look for her. And she wanted to look like the trust funder rich girl who didn't need to eat day-old sandwiches out of my fridge.

Carole Radziwill: Obviously the money is something—Tinsley's motivated by money. Then, because of the boyfriend connection, we ended up doing a lot of scenes together.

Sonja Morgan: She dropped me for Carole, and suddenly I was Mommy Meanest. I was very hurt because I had helped her a lot. You don't bite the hand that feeds you. She acted like, "I have to get out of Sonja's, and I couldn't." That was not true. She could have called a Suburban at any moment, moved out, and rented an apartment for ten thousand dollars a month like everybody else.

But the season's biggest blowup came in a series of confrontations between Bethenny and Ramona that spanned from Vermont to Tequila, Mexico.

Ramona Singer: Bethenny was always angry at me because I was the only one who would ever speak up to her. If you disagreed with her, she would cut you out of her life, cut you out of the show, and not want to film with you. And would just be revengeful.

Kristen Taekman: Bethenny, in her core, has got the most loving, caring heart. But she's also got this hard shell on the outside that she's developed from her childhood. She feels like she's got to protect herself. Ramona's the opposite. They were never going to meld.

Ramona Singer: She would also start wars with you over nothing. Like when I said her house was on the highway and she got all angry. It was on the fucking highway! I've lived in the Hamptons much longer than she has. South of the highway is more desirable than on the highway. That's just a fact! Or there was the time she didn't want me to come to Mexico, as if it was her trip. It was a bumpy season for us. We had a heart-to-heart in the pool in Mexico that helped her understand me more, but with Bethenny, it was always temporary. You never really felt like your friendship was unbreakable.

> As the antipathy between Bethenny and Ramona grew, an OG returned briefly for a somber occasion. In season 10, Jill Zarin returned to say goodbye to her beloved late Bobby Zarin. Ramona, Luann, Sonja, Dorinda, and Bethenny all attended the funeral.

Lisa Shannon: When Bobby passed, Jill's rep called and said, "Jill is open to you guys filming a part of this. She recognizes Bobby was a big part of the show."

Jill Zarin: I never spoke to the network. Bobby and I were in the hospital. He was dying. I was not on the phone with anybody about filming anything those last days. I was planning the funeral. But then the network showed up with the cameras up.

Andy Cohen: I'm not sure it's fair to say we just "showed up." In any case, Bobby was such an important part of the foundation of *RHONY* that I was so glad we were able to say goodbye to him on the show.

Lisa Shannon: I was very grateful to them for allowing us to do that because Bobby and Jill played a huge part in the show, and it did close a chapter. Bobby was beloved, he was a gentleman, such a sweet man, so it was nice to be able to pay that kind of tribute.

Carole Radziwill: Ramona, Luann, Sonja, and Dorinda were legitimately friends with Bobby, so they were all going to go, but Dorinda and Ramona didn't want to go with cameras.

Lisa Shannon: They felt very strongly that it was gross to attend with cameras and that Bethenny was using it as an opportunity.

Ramona Singer: It was a funeral!

Carole Radziwill: Bethenny set up her own filming. She was in Aspen, but the minute she heard about the death, she flew right back to New York.

Jill Zarin: They were all mad at Bethenny. They said, "How could you go to the funeral?"

Carole Radziwill: It was all for the show. Nobody was better at that than Bethenny.

Jill Zarin: The footage of me and Bethenny hugging and making up made the promos for the show. But for Bethenny, it was all about the story line because afterward when I tried to keep a relationship with her, she wouldn't. She blocked my number. She wouldn't talk to me.

Andy Cohen: My sense was she wanted to say goodbye to Bobby, and yes, she is smart enough to know that it was a moment. She did spend time alone with Jill at her apartment without cameras, so clearly it wasn't completely for the show.

> *While Bethenny and Jill at least appeared to reconcile, the longtime frustrations between Bethenny and Ramona finally boiled over. Ramona criticized Bethenny for committing a mortal Housewives sin: being a woman who doesn't support other women.*

Ramona Singer: Bethenny had a lot of success in business, but we all helped her get there. When she was doing her book, we promoted her book. We went on her talk show. We'd drink the Skinnygirl. We'd promote whatever she was promoting. Do you think she ever promoted my Ramona Pinot Grigio? Do you think she ever promoted my skincare, or anyone else's product lines? No. But we always did it for her.

Jennifer O'Connell: Starting way back in the early seasons, with Bethenny Bakes, Bethenny was determined to get her brand off the ground. And she succeeded. So when the other women saw that, they were like, "Oh, well, if she can do that, I can, too." They didn't fully grasp that Bethenny lives her brand. Bethenny was a hustler.

Lisa Shannon: Other franchises, too, they all tried to follow in Bethenny's footsteps.

Alexis Bellino: By the time I'd been on *Orange County* for a season, Bethenny had taken off. As a Housewife, you think to yourself, "A reality show only lasts so long. Might as well capitalize on the moment." That's why I did Alexis Couture. But the thing is, when you start a business, you have to go full steam ahead. And I found that hard to do. My foremost job was to be a wife and a mother, so as soon as it started eating into some of that family time on top of production, it was too stressful. My kids needed me 150 percent, not just 20 percent. I had the passion, but I had to weigh my pros and cons. It was either my family or my business, so I let my dress line go.

Carole Radziwill: Sonja, more than anyone, tried to follow in Bethenny's footsteps, but she was just not good at it. A toaster oven, a fashion brand . . . there was no thought process to it.

Ramona Singer: Still, there's room for everybody. There's enough success to be had. But Bethenny didn't see it that way. She was so unsupportive, that's why I told her, "You don't support other women." And she freaked out when I said that. I hung up the phone and I heard she was crying on the other side, because I had really put her in her place.

Kristen Taekman: Bethenny really came for my Pop of Color nail polish brand. It kinda sucked, because she had all of these super successful brands and like, Who am I that you even care? She was comparing my brand to Colourpop, a popular makeup brand. I never talked about all the other "Skinny" brands. I definitely felt like it was kind of messed up on her part to bring up other brands and basically confuse my potential customers, maybe even driving them to other brands. That wasn't nice.

Carole Radziwill: The thing is, Bethenny claimed to have a business but really, as far as we could tell, she was just setting up licensing deals each season for a different product. Sparkler drinks, candy, wine, margarita mix, jeans. She didn't have an office. Her office was her two employees and her driver and a museum of Skinnygirl products. It looked great on TV. I'm handing that to her—she got it, she played it. But she wasn't taking meetings and she didn't have any direct reports. She didn't have inventory to deal with. Still, she knew how to integrate and promote her products subtly, in a way that looked and felt organic. She was really good at that, and we were expected to play along.

Andy Cohen: We got a lot of complaints from viewers about Bethenny shilling on the show. We actually cut a lot of Skinnygirl stuff out. We were mostly covering the fact that this is what Bethenny was doing in her life, versus showing the brand attributes. So while you may be giving the brand exposure, it wasn't a formal integration. But the lines became blurred a lot with Bethenny because she surrounded herself with product and she was really smart about it.

Over time, the business of Bethenny made the other Housewives resentful.

Carole Radziwill: Bethenny wanted to only work part-time. We'd have to cram our scenes around her schedule or Bryn's school schedule or her many vacations. She was always very busy being busy and being Mother of the Year and Businesswoman of the Year. And we would all sort of go along with this idea that she was so crazy-busy with work and crazy-busy with being a mother, but it wasn't always true. Like, Heather has two kids, was running a huge business—one much bigger than Bethenny's. She was much busier than Bethenny, but she wasn't trying to get out of work every time she had to take her kid to the doctor. You're a working mother, that's what it is.

Ramona Singer: While we were filming she would say, "I'm not going to this scene, I'm not going to that scene." She would cancel coming to the events. She wasn't a team player and it really affected our show.

Sonja Morgan: My costars would say, "Why does Bethenny get to come late? Why does she have the weekend off?" Well, Ramona, why do you get to scream at the cameramen and be rude? Everybody has their thing, so I don't compare myself. If you do that, you'll never be happy.

Lisa Shannon: Bethenny was difficult to schedule, more difficult than anybody has ever been, but she had a different circumstance than the rest of the ladies. She only had her daughter half the time, whereas the other women's kids are grown, and as parents we respected that. She also had a huge career she was juggling, so scheduling with her was not easy, but we made it work.

Andy Cohen: It was not easy, and the women felt she was treated differently. They had a point. But the ratio of the footage we shot and used of Bethenny was also higher than the others.

Dorinda Medley: I looked at it as a job. If they say I have to go to Timbuktu, I just go because it's part of my job. I didn't know that there was leeway to not show up or to leave early, to push the times of production, all that. I'm not that Housewife. I get my schedule and I do it. So I was surprised even from day one how Bethenny operated.

> *The biggest rift of all in season 10 was between Bethenny and her longtime friend Carole. They butted heads over (among other things) Carole's boyfriend Adam's supposed unwillingness to volunteer for charity, Carole's friendship with Tinsley, and a text conversation gone awry.*

Carole Radziwill: The Adam story is this: Bethenny hired a friend of mine to manage her "charity," B Strong. (I say charity in quotes because it's really a PR effort.) Bethenny had that friend reach out to Adam on her behalf to ask him to go to Houston with her on this boondoggle for a soup kitchen. She asked him to bring all his photography equipment and film her the whole time. At this point in his career, Adam was hustling—he was like Bethenny when she was hawking muffins in the supermarket. He doesn't have Skinnygirl money. So he says, "Is there a budget for it?" And she flips out. She says, "I need you to do this. How dare you question it?" She never told me, ever, that this happened, but then Bethenny told Dorinda that Adam didn't care about charity and that he'd asked for money. And then we go to the Berkshires, and Dorinda finally tells me that Bethenny said Adam was a terrible person for not going along with her to Houston. It totally blindsided me.

Sonja Morgan: Bethenny and Carole had been a team for many years. Bethenny was such a good friend to Carole. But Bethenny, when she is not jiving with you, it's done.

Carole Radziwill: Not long after that exchange with Adam, we start filming season 10. Bethenny didn't film for the first week.

Sonja Morgan: Tinsley was there for Carole to film when she didn't have Bethenny. And Tinsley was there at the finish line when Carole ran the New York City Marathon—Bethenny wasn't.

> *Carole and Tinsley had also spent some time together—including a few days on vacation in Spain—because their boyfriends were friends.*

Carole Radziwill: Tinsley's a nice girl. I liked her, but we weren't BFFs. But Bethenny wanted the story line to be that I had dumped her, spent too much time with Tinsley, and she felt left out. None of it was true. So I certainly didn't expect to see Bethenny saying, "I understand why she really likes Tinsley—she's never had a career, no kids, no husband." I'm like, "What? Are you really saying that I don't have a husband when my husband passed away? And are you talking about my career? We're in the same business, honey. It's called reality TV."

Ramona Singer: I do think Bethenny cared for Carole more than she's ever cared for anyone else. And she just got upset when Carole started having a life where she didn't need Bethenny one hundred percent because Bethenny needed Carole one hundred percent.

Andy Cohen: And I still don't understand what happened. I think they were both outgrowing each other.

> *The final straw between the onetime besties seemed to come over the holidays, when Carole was in California.*

Carole Radziwill: I was visiting a friend whose husband had recently died. Bethenny was texting me over the holidays like a lunatic, wanting to hash everything out. She was so rude, she kept going on and on, totally not respecting my boundaries. So I said, "Gee, Bethenny, this is a lot for a text. Let's talk as soon as I get home." In a moment, she just saw me as the enemy. So, when we're filming, she flips it—she said, "I was reaching out and I was so upset at the holidays, I was so vulnerable, and I get this text message back from Carole: 'Gee, Bethenny. That's a lot.'" But on *Housewives*, the person who talks the most, their story is going to get out. In my mind, it wasn't true. I was making boundaries, and I wasn't as available to her as I had been before. I'd always had to be that loyal friend who said, "Bethenny, you're great! Good for you!" And the minute I didn't want to do that, it looked like I was being a terrible friend. Even though, if you look at the evidence and the facts, she was a terrible, terrible friend to me—maybe never was genuinely a friend.

Ramona Singer: Carole felt that Bethenny used her.

Lisa Shannon: Things got so dark with Carole and Bethenny, but Carole wasn't able to own her side of any of it.

Andy Cohen: As that final year went on, Carole just got angrier and angrier—angry with the crew, angry with the producers, angry with me, even angry with my staff at *Watch What Happens Live*. She was unpleasant—not the light, free woman she'd been when she joined the show.

> *In the midst of all of this, toward the end of season 10 came a vacation to Cartagena, Colombia, that would live in* Housewives *infamy. And this time, it wasn't about a fight between women, but a fight between the women and the open waters (and, later, the women and their digestive systems).*

Sonja Morgan: We got to the boatyard. It looked . . . it looked iffy. It wasn't chic.

Carole Radziwill: But we were being good soldiers. And it was actually fun, the island. But we left late. We left at like three, three thirty. And we got into really rough water.

Dorinda Medley: They didn't even take the back route, they went straight into the ocean. And they left at a time when they knew there was a storm coming.

Sonja Morgan: It was very choppy coming back. Tinsley was playing it down, and I was like, "Shut the fuck up, child!"

Carole Radziwill: I've been in rough water before and get seasick often, but the key is to go to the deck and just stare out the horizon and then you don't feel sick. Here, it was so bad, you couldn't even see the horizon because the waves were crashing. And I've been in some seriously scary places in my career at ABC—I went to wars and stuff—but this was not a good situation for us at all. I'm not trying to be hyperbolic about it, but holy fuck.

Dorinda Medley: It's happened on a plane with me before where you're like, "This is it. This is really happening." You almost have this overwhelming sense of peace. I kept thinking, "I just want Hannah to be okay. Please, please, please, please."

Carole Radziwill: Eventually the anchor dislodged. We were probably two miles from the coast and in very, very rough water. And now the anchor was attached to the bottom of the ocean, so we were no longer able to float. It probably went on for—well, it felt like an hour but it was probably two minutes. The cameras went down before that happened because the seas were so rough that we couldn't film anymore. The crew had no idea what was happening. They were alarmed. You could smell smoke because the engine was revving but it couldn't move the boat forward. We were getting hit on both sides with waves.

Sonja Morgan: Ramona and I were clinging to each other and crying like it was our last minutes. I peed all over Ramona, I was so scared.

Dorinda Medley: Honest to God, I really thought we were going to die that day. I literally went home and had my will done after that.

Carole Radziwill: The next morning, everyone was sick. We had parasites.

Sonja Morgan: We all got sick.

Dorinda Medley: People were literally shitting their pants. We had to move out of the place because every toilet was clogged. We were physically ill. They didn't want to send us to the hospital. They were afraid it was too dirty. I couldn't stand up. I had no electrolytes left in my body.

Carole Radziwill: And then basically production just said, "It's a wrap." They checked us out and they filmed us packing up. We go to breakfast. Bethenny's sorta not talking to me again even though I come in and say good morning. She doesn't even look at me and say good morning. But that went over everyone's head. Then Bethenny announces that she got rooms for us at this suite down the street, and we're all going to stay there for the night and leave in the morning, and get spa treatments, as if she planned it.

Andy Cohen: We did everything we could. We realized that the boat was subpar and they had a really bad experience. We needed to do something for them. We sent all of them away to a spa. I know that we tried to make it right with them. But that was truly a bad scene.

In the end, the decision was made by Bravo that Carole would not return for another season.

Andy Cohen: Up until that point, Carole had managed to maintain a distance between the show and her life. She really kept things in perspective about it just being a show. But in my opinion, toward the end, she got sucked into it in all the ways she had been trying to avoid. The show had gone from being a fun sociological experiment to being her life.

Heather Thomson: I wanted her to get off the show so bad. I just felt like she was getting sucked into being a Housewife. It wasn't healthy for her anymore. The show wasn't bringing out the best in her.

Andy Cohen: People think that moment at the reunion where Carole said to me, "Are you afraid of her, too?" is the moment that sealed her fate. It wasn't. It had no effect.

Carole Radziwill: I think worse things have happened to him in the reunions. He actually was good-natured about me saying he's full of shit and scared of Bethenny. They all walked on eggshells around her.

Andy Cohen: We went into the reunion knowing that we were not going to pick up Carole for another season.

Carole Radziwill: When Lisa Shannon called and said, "We need to talk," I thought, "This is when they say, 'We're not going any further.'" I ended up crying because I was so upset. Now I think back and it's almost comical, but then I was so emotionally distraught over what had happened the whole season—it just didn't end up the way I felt it should have.

Andy Cohen: As we do with all Housewives, we allowed Carole to craft her own statement about leaving, but we put a little pressure on her to do it within a certain time frame because we were worried the other women were going to find out and leak it to the press.

Carole Radziwill: My statement went out, and then I took a trip to Aspen. And while I was there, I posted something on my Instagram Story like, "Did you ever do something for money that you thought was against your values but you did it anyway?" It was a poll, and after the results came in and, like, 80 percent of people said "yes," I posted the results and said, "That's how I've been feeling this year." Something like that.

It was just soul-searching, I wasn't trying to criticize the show. I wasn't trying to say I was better than the show or above it. The show is a show. It's funny and entertaining. I was on it! But there were times where I felt like, "What am I doing? Should I be doing this?"

Andy Cohen: Carole's post basically implied she was leaving a really toxic situation and, you know, "Wouldn't you, too?" It really rubbed me the wrong way because I really felt like I had changed her life over, what, six years?

Carole Radziwill: Andy went ballistic that I had somehow, like, affronted him. It got to the point where I said, "Andy, if you email me again, don't ever speak to me again."

Andy Cohen: She emailed and said, "Don't ever speak to me again." And I haven't. She is not the person I used to know.

> *Bethenny and Carole's relationship wasn't the only thing falling apart in season 10. After the collapse of her short-lived marriage to Tom—and an arrest in Florida—Luann was struggling to keep herself together even with the help of many friends.*

Dorinda Medley: Tom was the beginning of the end. Luann really wanted the marriage to be something it couldn't have ever been.

Sonja Morgan: I stayed at Luann's house during that time, and she was off the rails. She was manic and had a bunch of people around her who were hangers-on. They didn't care if she was in a danger zone. But I didn't want to be part of it. I have a daughter.

Barbara Kavovit: That was a tough summer. Luann was not of sound mind and body, she was a shell. There was nothing inside. She would drive boats, she would drive cars, she would drive mopeds—just completely annihilated drunk. She was out of control. She thought she was invincible.

Luann de Lesseps: It's hard to revisit this time. It was very, very painful, and I'd prefer not to go back into every detail of it because I'm all about moving forward in life. But I made mistakes and I'm proud of the person I am today.

Sonja Morgan: Bethenny had the balls—you know, the strength—to get her help. And Bethenny got her all the help she needed. And listen, Bethenny didn't have to do that. She really helped Luann with PR management. Her boyfriend at the time, Dennis Shields, got Luann a lawyer. Barbara stepped in and helped with the finances.

Barbara Kavovit: Bethenny suggested I should be Luann's power of attorney. Everybody who knows me, including Luann, would always say, "Barbara's my smartest friend," because I am the fucking smartest. It's just who I am. And I spent an inordinate amount of time working on saving Luann's financial life.

Sonja Morgan: We all intervened.

Andy Cohen: If she hadn't gone to rehab or had refused treatment or seemed unwell when she came out, then we just wouldn't have put her on television that season. It was a tough time for Luann, but everyone really rallied around her. Bethenny did a lot on her behalf with no cameras anywhere.

Luann de Lesseps: I have to say, as much as Bethenny has loved to tear me down, that was a time where she really came to my rescue. And the network was very supportive. They were behind me 100 percent.

> *After standing by her friend's side through her darkest days—and with space in the cast in the wake of Carole's exit—Barbara Kavovit was given an official role in season 11, initially as a Housewife and eventually as a Friend. And though she had preexisting connections to many on the cast, she still received a chilly reception from all sides that would prevent her tenure on Housewives from being longer.*

Barbara Kavovit: They sold me by saying, basically, "We're going to show this badass woman who runs a construction company in New York City." And I was like, "Wow, this is going to be great for women. They're going to see how a woman from the Bronx who comes from nothing starts a business and turns it into a multimillion-dollar company."

Ramona Singer: To be honest with you, I didn't really understand why Barbara was brought on. She didn't make any sense to me. She was just kind of . . . frumpy.

Barbara Kavovit: My contract was as a full-time Housewife. I did all the photo shoots and attended all the filmings as a full-time Housewife. My construction company, my mom, and my son were all filmed—so many things that you never saw were filmed. But I never felt welcomed. I was such an outsider. For someone like me who's tough and strong, being iced out like that makes you feel unattractive and unimportant. It really tests your self-esteem when you're up against six people who aren't embracing you in any way or being kind.

Dorinda Medley: If Barbara hadn't been so tied to Luann, she would've had two or three seasons, if not more, and the show would have been a great platform for her business.

Barbara Kavovit: When I found out I was going to be a "Friend of," I was upset. The problem was that I was protecting my friendship with Luann. I should've thrown her under the bus ten fucking times over. And I wish I did now. Then I would have been on the show for another season probably.

Carole Radziwill: Except then she had her *second* hot mic moment.

Barbara Kavovit: Here's what happened there. My sister visited from London. She's not a *Housewives* fan, and I told her I was taking her to see Luann perform, so she was just like, "What kind of show is this? Is it like an Adele kind of a performance?" And I was like, "No, she can't really sing, but it's a fun show."

Dorinda Medley: To be taken down by not one but two hot mic moments? That's something.

Andy Cohen: It was actually Luann-esque, but happening to her bestie. Meanwhile, it was about whether she can sing which made it kind of ridiculous.

Barbara Kavovit: I begged them not to air it. Begged them. But Luann found out prior to it airing, and she was so fucking mad at me. She threw away our relationship over that comment.

Dorinda Medley: Barbara saved Luann's life—literally—with Bethenny. And basically in return, Luann was like, "I'm done with you."

Barbara wasn't the only one struggling with Luann that year. The New York Housewives' frustrations with the countess came to a head during filming. Bethenny, especially, exploded on her longtime costar—who, post-divorce, post-arrest, and post-rehab, had now embarked upon a new endeavor as a cabaret star.

Luann de Lesseps: I come from an entertainment background—I was a model and a showgirl in Italian television. And on the show, I wanted to sing. I wasn't quite sure what I wanted to sing about, but I had just written a book, and "Money Can't Buy You Class" was born from excerpts of that book. And from there, I released "Chic C'est La Vie." It just grew and grew.

Sonja Morgan: Luann is a great master of ceremonies. She has unstoppable energy because she loves the attention.

Lisa Shannon: The cabaret act was interesting because it became a whole new source of tension in the group. And it spanned multiple seasons.

Carole Radziwill: Dorinda was really upset in season 10 with Luann, because she'd been a good friend, had stood by Luann throughout the whole Tom thing, and had gotten her all the dresses from Jovani for her cabaret show. And Luann kind of ignored her.

Luann de Lesseps: She came to my show and she heckled me from the crowd, screaming "Jovani."

Carole Radziwill: Which, of course, Luann then turned into her whole personality. Everything about "Jovani." She capitalized on that moment from Dorinda.

Dorinda Medley: The underlying thing with me and Luann was that after helping her through her rehab, I provided her entire wardrobe for her cabaret. I mean half of our show was what she was wearing! And she wouldn't acknowledge or thank me. I did a nice thing and I was turned into a mockery, and the viewers never let go of it. Plus they just bought into this countess cabaret character.

Carole Radziwill: Luann is a terrible, terrible friend. What she did to Dorinda was terrible.

Luann de Lesseps: It was played for laughs on the show, but people don't understand that cabaret saved my life. Being able to sink my teeth into a creative outlet like that, and then getting the love from fans onstage every night was extremely helpful in helping repair the damage that had been done. It motivated me. I felt like, "I'll show you."

Sonja Morgan: The cabaret thing, she got too big for her britches. She wanted me to be a part of it but she wouldn't pay me! I don't care if I'm a shoe salesman; if I'm going to come and get up there and do something, I got to get paid! When Luann has me on the stage, it gives more power to the show. And then she gives me two hundred dollars? She just wants to be the No. 1 at everything, and that's why I call her my diva. But when she said on the show, "You're not a Broadway actor"—no, I'm Sonja Fucking Morgan, bitch.

Dorinda Medley: Bethenny got so mad at Luann that year, because Bethenny had put all this energy into helping her get sober and then Bethenny's boyfriend, Dennis Shields, had died of an overdose. You think Luann was there for Bethenny? She didn't check in with her about it at all.

Lisa Shannon: Here's where Luann saves herself, though, because she came into the season 11 reunion really apologetic. After a season where everyone was criticizing her for being so full of herself, she really owned her behavior.

That goes a long way, which is why we had Luann back for season 12, which was a fantastic season for her.

In an off-camera bombshell, Bethenny broke the news that she would not be returning to the show just days before season 12 filming started, leaving everyone on shaky ground.

Andy Cohen: I knew months before the season that we were not going to be able to make a deal with Bethenny. I wrote her a goodbye and thank-you email at the beginning of the summer!

Lisa Shannon: The sticking point was contractual. It wasn't a title. She wanted to be paid more.

Andy Cohen: There was a very specific thing Bethenny wanted in her contract that Bravo refused to give on and I knew they weren't going to give her. And that's why she left. I knew that what she was asking for wasn't going to get by Bravo. The irony was that all the women thought Bethenny was treated differently by Bravo but here they were drawing a line in the sand at treating her differently.

Lisa Shannon: She pulled the plug a day before filming.

Andy Cohen: It was the dead of August and I was on vacation when I got a text from Bethenny saying to call her. She could not believe that Bravo wouldn't cave on this one issue and told me she was not going to come back—this was after she had been telling production, "I'm coming back. I'm coming back. It's going to be fine." And she announced it immediately. I mean, it was in *Variety* moments later, and that was that.

Dorinda Medley: We found out the night before that Bethenny wasn't going to be there.

Ramona Singer: She fucked us over. We had a whole season planned, and she was gone.

Andy Cohen: Again, I wasn't surprised. I was disappointed, but I wasn't surprised. And I'm glad Bravo didn't cave on the contract. It would've set a bad precedent.

Sonja Morgan: You know I love my Bethenny, so I would have thought you would have seen a lot of anarchy like, "I'm not watching without Bethenny!" But we didn't see any of it. I was shocked.

Dorinda Medley: Everybody took Bethenny leaving differently. For me, I missed her. She's great reality TV, and it's like, you can't lose Tom Brady and not acknowledge that you miss him.

Bethenny may have been out of the picture, but there was a new Housewife in season 12. Leah McSweeney—a self-made fashion mogul, single mother, and straight-shooting New York native—joined the cast.

Lisa Shannon: Before the season, Bethenny had given us like forty people's names. All the Housewives did that. She didn't even know Leah's last name. She was calling her "Leah Mob" based off her social media handle.

Leah McSweeney (Housewife): In the winter of 2019, I got a text from my facialist of eighteen years who, it turns out, also has Bethenny as a client. I guess Bethenny had asked the facialist, "Do you think Leah would be interested in being on the show? Can you ask her if I can give the producers her name?" I said yes.

Sonja Morgan: We've had so many people come on this show, and when I've been asked about Leah, I say, "She's a real New Yorker." Tinsley's not a New Yorker. She never paid New York taxes, she lived with her mother in a condo in West Palm. She married a guy from Virginia and stayed in New York, but she doesn't even know where the shoeshine is, doesn't know where the dry cleaner is. Then we have other upstate girls like me, Heather, Ramona. Luann is a Connecticut-er. So that's number one. Number two, what I like about Leah is she's like me, she's very real, she's not judgmental. But ironically, she comes off as judgmental 'cause she's such a fucking fighter.

Dorinda Medley: Suddenly, we had this new girl who was fifteen or twenty years younger than us that none of us knew. So Leah coming on definitely sparked the fear in a lot of girls about their position on the show.

Leah McSweeney: Ramona was very nice at first.

Sonja Morgan: When Ramona feels you're getting more popular, it's good to the point that it's good for her, then she starts to ice you out because you start becoming competition. She wants you to do well—but not as well as her.

Season 12 was defined early on by boozy chaos and thrown tiki torches, and the party lifestyle was especially concerning given Leah's early admission that she had been to rehab and had been sober for years prior to filming.

Leah McSweeney: I started drinking again six months before we started filming. I knew I should probably stop for the show, but I wasn't ready.

Sonja Morgan: I was off the rails that whole season, from tiki torching all the way through the Halloween party show to Newport.

Leah McSweeney: It's very hard for me to manage my drinking—that's why I don't drink anymore. I'm an alcoholic.

Andy Cohen: There was a discomfort at Bravo with the amount of alcohol this season and with the lack of awareness of it on behalf of some of the women. And that has been a recurring thing with the New York Housewives. There's already a negative association with the New York Housewives and alcohol that we've always been sensitive to. And this season it seemed to be worse than ever.

Leah McSweeney: I stopped drinking again on March 31, a few days before the show aired. I didn't need to wait to see myself because it wasn't about how I looked, it was about how I felt while I was drinking. But if you are on this show and you don't use it in a positive way to look at your behavior and change things that you don't necessarily like, then you're not doing it right.

During a girls' weekend in Rhode Island, things got heated when Ramona objected to Leah inviting her sister to tag along.

Sonja Morgan: God, that sister was a nightmare off camera. She went apeshit on me. She had me and Ramona hiding under a table to get away from her. She just kept coming at me and coming at me, and Ramona started crying because Leah was like, fucked-up, daytime, nighttime, everything. It was so bad. And that's why, when we went out to a restaurant one night, we didn't want to sit at the table—because the way they were acting was embarrassing. Instead they made us out to be these lecherous old women trying to pick up guys. Ramona was very concerned about how those nights in Newport would look. Afterward, she was calling and saying, "I can't do a show like this, this is too trashy."

In the middle of the season, Tinsley departed the show, and New York City entirely. Her not-exactly-forthcoming behavior regarding her on-again-off-again relationship with Scott resulted in hostility with Dorinda, and a bitter-sweet send-off as she moved to Chicago.

Sonja Morgan: Dorinda did come in hot, and people didn't realize why. But she was aggravated because Tinsley's a faker who was mooching off whoever she could and living with whoever she could for free for years.

Luann de Lesseps: You have to be transparent on this show. That word was used so much this season in terms of Tinsley not being transparent and Dorinda calling her out.

Dorinda Medley: No one wanted to talk about the reality that all of us knew Tinsey was still dating Scott but was saying she wasn't.

Lisa Shannon: Tinsley and Scott broke up and got back together so many times that I think she just didn't want to keep saying, "Oh, we're back together, now we're broken up." It was humiliating. I don't think she wanted to shine a light on that and then be embarrassed again.

Dorinda Medley: I'll be the first to tell you that it's very hard to have a relationship on the show.

Sonja Morgan: Tinsley's always been a jumper. A friend jumper. A job jumper. She has never committed.

Leah McSweeney: It was very hard for her, obviously, because any time she tried to talk, she wasn't being heard.

Dorinda Medley: You run into a little bit of a problem as a Housewife when you create smoke and mirrors because eventually that will come out. So you should try to be as transparent as you can be. Of course, some Housewives keep their cards close to their chests more than others.

Luann de Lesseps: Dorinda's anger about Tinsley not talking about Scott was kind of unfair because we didn't really know what happened in her breakup with John. I don't think she was very transparent about that. She didn't want to talk about it. And that was her right. But then don't expect Tinsley to talk about Scott.

Dorinda Medley: One week she and Scott were broken up, and then the next week she was moving out and ready to get married. It was like, "Wait, what? Where was I for this discussion?"

Sonja Morgan: Dorinda was very angry about Tinsley climbing and using her. She felt like, "Wait a minute, I was there for you. I supported you."

Leah McSweeney: Tinsley was treated badly and unfairly by the women.

Sonja Morgan: Dorinda came off looking like a total bitch who's jealous of Tinsley. For Dorinda, it was like, "Why are they demonizing me for telling the truth that Tinsley's a faker?!" I can tell you Dorinda is not jealous of Tinsley.

Lisa Shannon: For Tinsley, getting back together with Scott wasn't really real until she decided to move to Chicago, which is when she made it public. Tinsley was very professional and respectful about that decision. She called and said, "I can do the rest of the season, but I want to move to Chicago. I can still come back and film." And we said, "If you're in Chicago, be in Chicago." We want to follow the truth of what's happening in all of our ladies' lives.

Andy Cohen: We agreed to let her out of her contract, and I remember watching an early cut of Tinsley's final episode, and it was just like she drove off and it was over. I go, "You guys, this is falling flat for me. It's her last appearance as a Housewife. She's moving to Chicago. She's getting her man. He's proposed. We should do a freeze-frame and say goodbye to her properly." It wasn't about giving her some storybook ending, it was just the truth. I know Dorinda hated that ending.

Lisa Shannon: She came back for the reunion. And she did all of her interviews throughout. She really was very professional about it. At no point was Bravo ever pissed off that she was leaving. We made it work.

Leah McSweeney: At the end of the day, she totally won. She's, like, living her best life ever. She followed her heart, regardless of what happened, and I don't think she would have done anything differently.

Tinsley Mortimer and Scott Dunlop have since called off their engagement. As season 12 was still airing and producers were looking toward season 13, millions took to the streets in global protests for Black Lives Matter, bringing renewed attention to a lack of inclusivity in the cast that producers had been trying to remedy for years. For season 13, Bravo cast attorney and broadcaster Eboni K. Williams, making her the first Black Housewife on RHONY.

Leah McSweeney: It's awesome. Not only do I think it's great that Eboni is representing Black women and is the first Black Housewife of *Real Housewives of New York City*, which is pretty historic for the show, but she also has a lot of substance. She has so many great qualities.

Andy Cohen: It's embarrassing that it took this long for diversity on this show, but it's not for lack of trying. I don't think anyone could argue this show has ever been about, you know, six woke women. Sometimes there is a tone deafness about it that is funny. But you want a breadth of opinions just like you want a breadth of ages, and you want to be reflective of what's going on in the world, and reflective of New York itself. So it's about that balance.

Carole Radziwill: I honestly would come back on the show for those episodes when Ramona and Luann are meeting the first Black Housewife. Ramona is obviously gonna step in it and say "All Lives Matter" or something insensitive. And it's going to be game on.

But just as a newcomer signed on, another RHONY *Housewife bade farewell.*

Andy Cohen: We went into the reunion thinking Dorinda was potentially on the chopping block. She seemed very angry, and the relationship with alcohol was tipping the balance of the show. And she really doubled down on everything at that reunion. So we left there thinking, "We can make a change."

Dorinda Medley: Here's what happens: You film for four months, then you're off and you forget about it for a couple of months. Then the promos start, and the season starts, and you're in it again. Halfway through the season you're like, "I'm over this, I'll never do it again." Well, then you go to the reunion and you resolve a bunch of stuff and you're back in it. Then you get another month off before your contract shows up. And when that happens it's like, "Well . . . it's really only four months of my life. What else am I going to do? They're paying me well. I'm just going to do it one more time." I cannot tell you the amount of women, not only on my franchise but on others, who say "I'm never doing it again" and then there they are the next year.

Lisa Shannon: I think that Dorinda put pressure on herself. She told Leah, "I'm going to be the new Bethenny." And that's never good. When they get in their own head and forget that it's an ensemble, it's a problem.

Andy Cohen: Dorinda's lack of awareness about herself contributed to a negative reaction from viewers and within Bravo.

Dorinda Medley: My mother always said to me when I was little, "If you are in a good mood, the world smiles. But if you're in a bad mood, you're like a terrible storm. So just do me a favor. Learn this lesson early. If you're not in a good mood, stay home."

Lisa Shannon: We told Dorinda, "You've got to stop being so mean to Tinsley. It's not worth it. It does not look good. It's like beating a puppy." But when they get in those headspaces, they won't listen. And it's like, "I have no skin in this game if you want to keep going down this road. I'm just telling you that, from a thirty-thousand-foot view, this is not looking good." She just did not take our advice. She was very relentless.

Andy Cohen: She was pretty unrepentant about Tinsley. The level of anger seemed unusual.

Lisa Shannon: With Dorinda, frankly, she just needs some time off. I don't think it is necessarily the end of Dorinda on the show. I hope it's not. But she does need to take a year.

Andy Cohen: I do hope she comes back to the show.

Dorinda Medley: Andy said it perfectly one day. He said, "It's like the Mafia. Once you're in it, you're in it forever."

PART III

"Just Peachy"

The Real Housewives of Atlanta

PREMIERE DATE: OCTOBER 7, 2008

There's no fame like Housewives *fame.*
—CYNTHIA BAILEY

Lauren Zalaznick: *Atlanta* was the one that took us all by surprise.

Andy Cohen: We'd been sitting on a casting tape for a show called *Hotlanta* for a while.

Lauren Eskelin (Executive Vice President, Programming, Truly Original): It was *Ladies of Hotlanta*. A woman named Princess Banton-Lofters started the whole thing. She put together the cast and brought her idea to Truly Original, who then fleshed out casting before we went to Bravo.

Shari Levine: It was a really vibrant tape. You had these outspoken women filled with attitude. Some were wives and ex-wives of prominent professional athletes, which felt *very* Atlanta, while others were being kept by these affluent men. And at the center of them all was NeNe Leakes.

Andy Cohen: Linnethia "NeNe" Leakes was an instant standout. She was popping with personality. And she kind of anchored this group of friends.

Shereé Whitfield (Housewife): Princess was looking for women who lived a certain life behind the gates, which is why she thought of me. NeNe, she wasn't living the lifestyle. I mean, her apartment wasn't even behind the gate! But, you know, she kind of takes over.

Andy Cohen: Shereé had been married to Bob Whitfield, who was a defensive tackle for the Atlanta Falcons, Jacksonville Jaguars, and New York Giants. They were just getting divorced when we started, but her lifestyle was highly aspirational.

DeShawn Snow (Housewife): NeNe and I had both worked in real estate.

We were real cool, and she thought I might be a good fit so she reached out to me and asked if I'd want to be involved.

Shereé Whitfield: None of us knew DeShawn, but NeNe was searching around for people and found her. She was sweet, but very quiet. She didn't really say a lot the whole damn show!

DeShawn Snow: My ex-husband, Eric, and I loved *The Real Housewives of Orange County*. So when the offer came to do a reality show, even before it was called *Housewives*, we were excited. Our kids were young, Eric had been playing basketball, I had a foundation helping teenage girls. We were already in the limelight, because of Eric. But this was the first hurrah for me as DeShawn Snow.

Shereé Whitfield: The other person NeNe pulled in was Kim Zolciak.

Andy Cohen: Kim was someone who really confused me. I didn't understand her role within the group, not just because she was white, but because she looked like this country singer with a big blond wig. She didn't look like she was living the upscale lifestyle like the rest of the women were.

Shereé Whitfield: Well, here's how Kim got on. Princess, me, and NeNe were at this restaurant—this was way before the casting reel was ever solidified. And Princess was saying, "We need to find some other people." Now, Kim happened to be at that same restaurant, but at the time, she and NeNe were not speaking. They hadn't talked in years. So Princess is like, "Do you know anybody?" And NeNe goes, "Well, if you want a white bitch who got it goin' on, then that's your girl right there."

Shari Levine: For me, NeNe and Kim really stood out. Nobody had seen those two before on television. Their friendship was really remarkable.

Shereé Whitfield: Friendship? Did I not just tell you they weren't friends! They fell out because NeNe, being the shady person she was, went behind Kim's back and tried to befriend her ex. Kim had been dating a rich guy, the original Big Poppa, and when they broke up Kim had to move out of the house he was paying for, so NeNe—who worked in real estate—tried to befriend him to get the listing. It was a whole mess. They only reconciled right before we got the show. It was all for TV.

Andy Cohen: Whatever their friendship was or wasn't—they had crazy chemistry. And just like with Bethenny, I was wrong about Kim. She wound up being a really integral part of that cast.

Shari Levine: There was Lisa Wu, too. At the time, she was married to Ed Hartwell, who was a big football player.

Shereé Whitfield: Lisa Wu wasn't in the reel, though. She came later. We were supposed to start taping but there were two other girls who ended up not working out, so they kept on delaying our start date. So I started reaching out to people. "Hey, do you know anybody who is living a good lifestyle?" One of the names I was given was Lisa Wu.

Shari Levine: It became pretty clear that we were green-lighting this thing. It had a completely different sensibility than the other two franchises.

Lauren Zalaznick: It opened Bravo up to an entirely different audience—female, African American viewers who were completely underserved at that time by our channel. We had diverse casting on *Project Runway* and *Top Chef*, but this was a group of mostly African American women who were organically friends with each other. It was new.

DeShawn Snow: We were the first African American *Housewives* show. Some people felt pressure to represent Atlanta in a certain way, as it's a city with a lot of prominent African Americans, many of whom are athletes and entertainers. But I never felt like we were there to represent all Atlanta African Americans. We were just who we were. We were going to be true to who we were.

Lauren Zalaznick: As more and more of these franchises premiered, we learned a lesson: There'd be viewers devoted to *Orange County* who would never in a million years watch *New York City*, or people watching *Atlanta* who never saw *Orange County*. People gravitated to different attributes of each of these shows, even though we saw them as being generally alike and fitting the same format.

> *Production company Truly Original was at the helm of* The Real Housewives of Atlanta, *which would become the third installment of the franchise. One of their newest hires behind the camera was an associate producer named Carlos King, who would go on to be one of the franchise's most influential behind-the-scenes figures.*

Carlos King (Executive Producer): I got a call from a friend who'd been hired as a production manager, and she wanted to know if I'd be interested in joining as an associate producer. I had only heard of *The Real Housewives of Orange County*. The *New York* installment wasn't out just yet, it was coming out a few months later. But I said, "Listen, I'm obsessed with *The Hills*. It's my *Young and the Restless*; my *Bold and the Beautiful*. I want to get into reality." So I jumped at the chance.

DeShawn Snow: All the producers were cool, but I remember Carlos the most. He and NeNe were really close.

Carlos King: My first day they said to me, "Every producer at the associate level is going to be assigned to a Housewife. You're going to have NeNe Leakes." I didn't know who she was at the time, but I went to her house and the moment I met her, it was love at first sight. I'm a whimsical gay guy, and she laughed at my mannerisms. And then she would mimic them on camera. My friends would call me being like, "Why does she talk like you? Why does she act like you?" but I was her producer. She fed off me. We were two peas in a pod.

Shereé Whitfield: She wanted to portray herself as this person she wasn't. She's always presented herself as having this big, huge personality, but it's so put on.

Carlos King: Now just because I was NeNe's producer in season 1 didn't mean I didn't love me some Shereé Whitfield. I was this young gay boy, fascinated with Shereé. She was so delicious, so grand, so over-the-top—but also subtle, you know? She is a badass chick.

Shereé Whitfield: Carlos has always been good to me. But with NeNe, I told him at the end of that first season, "You have created a monster." And that was what, twelve years ago? Can you imagine how much worse she got from there?

There was bad blood between Shereé and NeNe from the start, which producers learned on the first day of filming, when NeNe's name was left off the security list for Shereé's birthday party.

Carlos King: None of us saw that coming. NeNe was making it out like she and Shereé were friends.

Shereé Whitfield: When we filmed the reel, we were fine. But NeNe and I were never really close friends. She was fun, but she was also really wild and sometimes it was a little embarrassing. By the time we actually started filming, NeNe and I had fallen out. We were not talking.

DeShawn Snow: There was a lot of tension between them.

Shereé Whitfield: What happened was, I would always invite NeNe to a lot of parties, because she was not a socialite—she was not on the scene, no one knew her—and I wanted to include her. Well, about a month before we started filming, I was invited to a private birthday party with a plus one and invited my girlfriend. But NeNe wanted me to get her in, plus her husband, Gregg, and two more friends. That's four people! I couldn't do it. There were three checkpoints to check for your ID before you even got upstairs! There was no chance. Well, this bitch got so mad at me that we never talked again. I done got this ho into five hundred parties in the past, but she could not get over this one, so she stopped talking to me.

DeShawn Snow: NeNe is who she is, on and off camera. That's what I like about her. She isn't fake. If she loves you, you know it. And if she doesn't, *you know it.*

Sheré Whitfield: A month later, we have a dinner at this nice restaurant with all the producers. She was sitting at one end of the table, and I sat at the other. And I don't even remember what we were saying, but she got loud. She stood up and stood over me. I was sitting calmly, 'cause I know this bitch ain't about to touch me. And it took everything out of me not to throw water in her face. I'd never seen anything like that in my life. Not in a restaurant. Now, take you around the corner in the alley or something? That's different. But we are literally in a restaurant! People are looking! That was the start of it.

Carlos King: I was so green back then, I didn't know what the fuck was going on. When we started filming weeks later, I thought we'd just be following NeNe and Kim heading out to Sheré's party. I had no idea what was in store.

DeShawn Snow: Everything we were doing was very authentic. Those fights between Sheré and NeNe, nothing was ever made up or set up or anything like that.

Carlos King: It started when we were at NeNe's house, watching her glam squad beat her face as she got ready for Sheré's party. And even there you had NeNe saying she wanted her "lashes poppin', her lips bustin.'"

Andy Cohen: NeNe always had the best one-liners. She made me howl from the jump.

Carlos King: Then we go pick up Kim, and she had a dress that needed last-minute alterations, so she makes us pull into a Shell gas station where she meets up with the designer and proceeds to get butt-ass naked to change into this dress. I was like, "You cannot script this shit!" I was salivating. Again, my homework was *The Hills.* All I was thinking was, "Heidi and L.C. aren't doing this shit!"

DeShawn Snow: Kim was funny. She was good TV!

Carlos King: By the time we got to Sheré's house, I thought it couldn't get better. And boom—NeNe walked up, and her name wasn't on the security list.

DeShawn Snow: We all went there knowing that NeNe was going to be on that list, so when she wasn't on it, that was surprising.

Carlos King: Now, did Sheree do that on purpose? That will always be an urban legend. Who knows?

Sheree Whitfield: I don't know how it happened. I gave them the list and she was supposed to be on it. I guess she didn't make the cut.

Carlos King: I truly am telling you, not one producer knew that was going to happen. And NeNe broke the fourth wall immediately. We didn't show it, but she said, "I'm on this show. These cameras are following me." But security was adamant. They said, "Ma'am, you cannot enter this party. You are not on this list."

Sheree Whitfield: I gave them good TV. How about that?

Carlos King: What I learned from that is, you have to let the reality play out. Because we just stepped back and followed NeNe's reaction. NeNe was like, "Fuck that." And even when Sheree's assistant tried to apologize and let her in, NeNe wouldn't budge.

Sheree Whitfield: NeNe and I were not getting along. It didn't make sense for her to come to my house. I wouldn't want anyone in my house who isn't my friend. And a girlfriend of mine, she was working the list and . . . I don't know, NeNe somehow wasn't on it.

Carlos King: Ultimately, it made for an iconic scene.

Sheree Whitfield: It turned out how it should have turned out. You see the fool she was outside? She didn't need to be inside. Because she was going to bring nothing but negative, bad energy into my home and that's where I gotta lay my head.

> *Sheree's birthday party was just one of the memorable parties she threw in season 1. She ended the season by throwing a party to debut her clothing collection, She by Sheree. Well, sort of . . .*

Carlos King: She by Sheree! Is there anything more iconic?

Sheree Whitfield: I had a high-fashion boutique that I closed right before I started doing *Housewives*. I had been running it for five years, in hopes that I would one day be able to carry my own line, but it wasn't in the best area and even though it did well and I had lots of celebrity clients, it was a hassle to keep it open. With the business closed, I started to think of what was next, especially knowing that I was on this show and was about to get major exposure. So I said, "Let me start my own line." But it didn't work out because there just wasn't enough time. We had what, seven episodes? There's a lot that goes into starting a line. I just couldn't do it that fast.

Carlos King: That's where Dwight [Eubanks] called it a "fashion show with no fashions."

Sheré Whitfield: I could have had fashions there, but the clothing just wasn't up to par for me. It was pretty upsetting.

Carlos King: Sheré kept pursuing it, bless her heart. And that's what I love about her; she's determined.

Andy Cohen: Like Sonja's toaster oven, I'm still hoping to one day see Sheré dressed in She by Sheré. I have possibly spent more time talking about She by Sheré than Sheré herself! This is a brand with major name recognition, by the way!

Sheré Whitfield: Andy asks me that all the time. And fans to this day still come up to me and say, "I want She by Sheré."

Meanwhile, as Sheré and Kim grew closer, NeNe and Kim fell out.

Sheré Whitfield: NeNe always had a problem with that friendship, because she introduced us but we had more in common with each other than we did with NeNe. Like, Kim's a fun person to be around. It's a jealousy thing. NeNe felt like she brought Kim on. But mind you, before the show, they had not spoken in years!

Carlos King: That feud felt like it happened overnight. We knew there was beef between NeNe and Sheré, but when tension started to brew between NeNe and Kim, it was like, "Where is *this* coming from?" And I can say, none of us in production were happy about it. We loved them together. We didn't want them as adversaries, we wanted them as friends.

Sheré Whitfield: You forget how *real* it all was back then. Our fights weren't around "You didn't show up to my party." Our fights were real fights. These girls, a lot of them really don't get along.

Carlos King: It all came to a head at the reunion, which NeNe really made happen.

Andy Cohen: NeNe might think that she invented the reunion show, the way that she tells it now, but I had already hosted reunions in *Orange County* and *New York*. But at that time, reunions were not a given for every show. And an *Atlanta* reunion was not yet picked up. There were questions of "Would we fly to Atlanta to do this?" These discussions were still going on when I got a call one day from NeNe, telling me she wanted to do a reunion.

DeShawn Snow: Kim had been saying things in her confessionals that NeNe really wanted to address. So NeNe pushed for that reunion. She had a bone to pick!

Shereé Whitfield: NeNe always has a problem with everybody.

Andy Cohen: She was so funny on the phone. She was like, "I'm watching this Kim and the shit she's saying about me. I want to confront her! You have to do it, it'll be a great show!" And that call certainly motivated me.

Carlos King: That was the reunion where NeNe said to Kim, "Close your legs to married men." Because Kim was dating Big Poppa at the time—which, by the way, we all wanted to know who Big Poppa was, behind the scenes. We were all very curious.

DeShawn Snow: We all knew who Big Poppa really was. Kim just gave him that name to protect his identity because he was legally married and going through a divorce.

Carlos King: I got a chance to meet him, and it was shocking because you hear the name "Big Poppa," you think you'll be meeting someone like Notorious B.I.G., right? Well, he's the total opposite. He's the tiniest man. He did not look like the person we thought he would be.

Shereé Whitfield: We actually filmed at my house with Big Poppa, but it got cut. It was an episode where I was sick and Kim came over with Big Poppa and bought me some medicine. He's actually a really cool guy, very fun.

Andy Cohen: I met him at one of the reunions. Season 2, maybe? I couldn't believe he was there in the flesh. After all that buildup, it was a little bit of a letdown. He was a little fella!

Carlos King: The reunion that year belonged to Kim and NeNe. They just went after each other. The other girls were like, "I guess I'm just here to be an audience member."

Shereé Whitfield: Kim, she's not going to let you walk all over her. She sticks up for herself. She keeps it real. And she tells it like it is.

Andy Cohen: NeNe low-key was starting to lunge at Kim. I was really nervous. I didn't know what was going to happen. I didn't feel in control on any level and I didn't know what kind of TV this was going to make.

DeShawn Snow: Lisa Wu was, like, sitting on NeNe to keep her from jumping up.

Andy Cohen: The reunion aired the night before Thanksgiving and got something like three million viewers. It was insane. It was definitely one of the highest-rated reunions we've ever done. Jeff Zucker, then CEO of NBCUniversal, emailed me the next morning like, "Wow, nice numbers. Congratulations." I was like, "Whoa!"

Lauren Eskelin: The show did well in the ratings, but the reunion really sealed the deal that *Atlanta* was a hit.

Andy Cohen: That's also when I started pushing for multipart reunions, because it seemed ridiculous not to air more of this great material we were getting. I still think about footage we never aired from that reunion.

> *To no one's surprise, season 1 of* The Real Housewives of Atlanta *played to big ratings. In fact, the series would go on to be the highest-rated of all the cities in the* Housewives *franchise. And while all five of the Atlanta House-wives were thrust into the spotlight, NeNe found her way into the zeitgeist like no other.*

Carlos King: NeNe became a huge star after season 1. I saw it coming. Two weeks before we wrapped, I said to her, "You're going to be a huge star." She didn't believe me. She was like, "Shut up, bitch. No, I'm not. Girl, bye." Sure enough, I saw her during the Thanksgiving holiday while the show was airing, and she said, "Remember when you told me I was going to be a huge star? Bitch, you were right."

DeShawn Snow: We all knew NeNe was going to be a breakout star.

Carlos King: She just made everyone laugh. She was fun and hilarious. She had *it*.

Sheree Whitfield: NeNe, she wanted to act. She wanted to be on TV. This was her passion. She was taking acting classes back then. So for her to even get this opportunity to do this show, she jumped at it. She worked her way in there. She did what she had to do to stay relevant.

Carlos King: NeNe knows the moment the camera is on. She doesn't want to be interrupted. She doesn't want you to tell her what to do. NeNe is savvy.

Sheree Whitfield: It's just not genuine. She puts it all on. NeNe would do anything to be famous.

Carlos King: Fame can change people. But I'm happy to say, NeNe was the same the first day I met her as she is now. She's always remained 100 percent real.

DeShawn Snow: I'm not sure if other girls were jealous of NeNe, I can't speak to that. But the way I saw it, they should have been worried about themselves and doing what they needed to do to take advantage of this platform. 'Cause we were all given the same opportunities, it's what you do with it that matters.

> *DeShawn knows that all too well. As producers planned for season 2, the network decided she wouldn't be returning as a Housewife.*

DeShawn Snow: The biggest misconception about me was that I left! I would have come back for a second season, but my option wasn't picked up.

Sheree Whitfield: I was not surprised about that.

DeShawn Snow: Me either! I get it, too. I had a pretty drama-free experience on *Housewives*, and that's because I didn't really have any contact with them. The only person I'd talk to was NeNe.

Carlos King: She was just one of those Housewives who didn't pop. And that's okay, the show's not meant for everyone.

DeShawn Snow: It's funny, I still watch the show—I'm a big fan—and there are times I'll be like, "This is boring, I don't want to watch her." So I get why nobody wanted to watch me. I was boring!

> *In DeShawn's place came a big star: Kandi Burruss. The Grammy-winning songwriter and singer was known for penning songs like the TLC hit "No Scrubs" and Destiny's Child's "Bills, Bills, Bills"—not to mention her time as member of the female vocal group Xscape. But* Housewives *would introduce Kandi, the single mother.*

Sezin Cavusoglu (Vice President, Current Production, Bravo): Kandi is almost the linchpin of the group. She's friends with everyone. She's such a true Atlanta personality, born and raised there. She represents the city and the culture.

Kandi Burruss (Housewife): *Real Housewives of Atlanta* caught a lot of flak after the first season, especially from the African American community. They were like, "Oh, it's painting Black women in a bad light." So when I would mention that I was thinking about joining the show, a lot of people were like, "Oh, don't do that! That's not a good look! You should never be a part of something like that!" And I was like, "Well, I don't understand—if you feel that the women on the show don't really represent well for Black people, and you feel that I am a good representation of a Black person, why wouldn't you want me to be a part of the show?"

Sheree Whitfield: Kandi was cool. We had met before, but didn't talk because she used to date one of my ex-husband's teammates. I used to listen to her music, though. I thought she was a good addition.

Kandi Burruss: I didn't think the show was going to change my life at all, because I'd already had some celebrity. But it became kind of overwhelming when A.J., my ex-fiancé, died after we wrapped filming on my first season.

Sheree Whitfield: That was so shocking.

Kandi Burruss: Our relationship was featured that year, and having something so emotional happen, the fans really connected with me. Just walking down the street, people would come up to me and cry. It made me see the power of this reality TV platform.

Kandi wound up being a great addition for Kim. The two forged a friendship (albeit a short-lived one), with Kandi even helping produce Kim's debut single, "Tardy for the Party."

Kandi Burruss: When I met Kim, I thought she was really cool. Obviously she had this whole drama with NeNe and they were making fun of her, but I was like, "Well, dang! She's just a person who has a dream and they're hating on it." I mean, I never entertained it like she was a great singer, but there are a lot of people out there who are not necessarily the best singers but have hot records because they have the right person who believes in them. Something in me just wanted to help her, and that's what I did.

Carlos King: In the first season, Kim sings "Tardy for the Party" in this hilarious scene with NeNe, but it's an entirely different song.

Kandi Burruss: It was pretty easy for me to take "Tardy for the Party" and make it what it needed to be. It turned out superhot apparently!

Sheree Whitfield: None of us thought it would be as good as it ended up being. I had no idea Kim even sang! Kandi did her magic on it.

Kandi Burruss: I knew how to get what I needed from Kim in the studio. When you deal with somebody who is not necessarily the best vocalist, it can be challenging to record them. But, you just have to be patient and you have to have a great engineer that's great at editing. It's as simple as that, really.

Andy Cohen: What Kandi did with that song was pretty remarkable. I mean, it's such a hit.

Kandi Burruss: Looking back, I don't really look at it as a thing I was necessarily proud of. No dis to Kim, it's just that I take my writing career very seriously, and it's almost like a mockery for me as a writer-producer when I work with somebody who's not really an artist. So, for me, it's not a bad thing, but it's not necessarily a highlight.

Andy Cohen: There wound up being some kind of controversy between Kandi and Kim about the royalties.

Kandi Burruss: That was a big drama. See, when we were making the song, Kim and I agreed to split everything equally between us and the producer who helped me put together the track. We did a friendly handshake. Well, when the song came out, Kim was saying she shouldn't have to split it with us equally. Instead, she wanted to only give us a writer's royalty. It was like, "Now you want to change the agreement? Fine, let's play it that way."

Sheree Whitfield: It basically ended things between Kandi and Kim.

Kandi Burruss: The friendship fell out over business. If we had just done everything properly and done the paperwork like we needed to, we probably would have never run into those issues.

> *Of course, you can't talk about season 2 of* The Real Housewives of Atlanta *without mentioning its most infamous moment: when Sheree and her divorce party planner, Anthony Shorter, got into an epic, expletive-filled argument.*

Carlos King: "Who gon' check me, boo?"

Sheree Whitfield: He was crazy. What kind of so-called professional person acts like that?

Carlos King: Sheree is the best to work with it, because it doesn't take a lot to get her gears going.

Sheree Whitfield: I didn't even know this guy. We met, and he was over-promising stuff, like saying he would fly a helicopter in. People get on TV and they want to make sure they make the cut, so they'll say anything. But this is my real party. I like over-the-top stuff but I felt like, "Don't promise me stuff I can't have."

Carlos King: This was right in the beginning of season 2, which is why that scene is in the season premiere.

Sheree Whitfield: I met him at his pretend office and the second I got there, I knew this was going to be some mess. There was tension in the air. So, of course, when I sat down with him, it didn't take darn near nothing for him to explode on me.

Carlos King: It was just incredible. I wasn't in the field that day; I had an office day, and my phone was blowing up. "Sheree and the party planner are going at it!"

Sheree Whitfield: He was so ignorant. They cut it out but he stood up, raised his hand, and was like, "Bitch I will smack the shit out of you!" That's when I stood up and said, "I wish the fuck you would." Sometimes people just take you out of your character and there's nothing you can do. I wasn't going to sit there and let him talk crazy to me. I tried to be calm when he said, "You better watch yourself before you get checked." That's why you see me ask, "Who gon' check me, boo?"

Carlos King: It's an iconic moment in reality TV history. And one of the most-quoted lines of all time.

Kandi Burruss: I watched it over and over again because I thought it was so funny.

Carlos King: A week later, Shereé pulled Kim's wig. And I remember being like, "Who is *this* Shereé? She went from not having NeNe on the list to checking bitches and pulling wigs. What is going on? I don't know, but I like it."

Shereé Whitfield: That wasn't a pull, it was a shift. I was just wanting to get her attention. Kim was walking away from me and you grab a girl's wig, that definitely gets her attention.

Carlos King: Everyone made up after that and then boom—NeNe and Kim were fighting again, over "Tardy for the Party."

Shereé Whitfield: NeNe hated to see Kim succeed.

Carlos King: I will say, NeNe understood her worth by season 2. She was way more confident in herself and she spoke her mind more. She wasn't a diva in the bad sense of the word, like hard to deal with. But I saw this growth in her. I was like, "Oh, she's aware. She knows she is NeNe Leakes, honey. And she ain't going to put up with this shit."

Shereé Whitfield: TV changed her tremendously. She wanted to be the only one of us to stand in the spotlight. There was one big ego among the group, and her name was NeNe.

Kandi Burruss: The cool thing about Kim, Shereé, and NeNe is that they had a lot of history before coming into this, so their arguments were more authentic. Like, "You really want to come at me on this other stuff? Because I knew you *when!*"

Carlos King: The arguments between Kim and NeNe were always next-level. All season 2, they went back and forth, fighting and making up. And then there was an incident that happened off camera where NeNe allegedly tried to choke Kim in a Target parking lot. . . .

Shereé Whitfield: They were at Atlantic Station. Kim and NeNe were waiting to film a scene shopping at a boutique. But NeNe was upset because Kim had supposedly been talking about her behind her back at the A-List Awards. While they were waiting to film, Kim was sitting in one of our producers' car and NeNe went to talk to her. They started arguing, and NeNe went for Kim's neck and was choking her. She lunged at her twice. Kim ended up calling the police but dropped the charges. The cameras were inside the store, so they missed the whole thing.

Carlos King: We had to address it because it was obvious they were not going to get past their problems. I mean, they couldn't even do an interview together. They went on Ryan Seacrest's radio show to promote the season and just blew up at each other.

Sheré Whitfield: As soon as you're not getting along with NeNe, she has no need for you. She throws you out.

Carlos King: I'll never forget, right when we premiered that year, NeNe was on *Watch What Happens Live*—which had just started—and Kim called in. I was in New Jersey, watching, and I spit out my protein shake because I could not believe the shit NeNe was coming up with on the fly. She just dragged her. Andy, he was sweating. He tried to cover his face with a cue card but you could see he was laughing. Unfortunately, it was at Kim's expense. But it was epic.

Andy Cohen: NeNe was on fire and I never recovered.

> By season 3, the network decided to part ways with Lisa Wu, leaving her peach up for grabs. Rather than hire one Housewife, Bravo expanded their cast and added two. Even so, when the cameras went up, supermodel Cynthia Bailey had no idea if she'd made the cut. . . .

Cynthia Bailey (Housewife): I went into this whole thing blind. They told me during my initial casting meetings that they were interested in bringing on a Housewife and a Friend that season, and that whoever had the more interesting story would be the Housewife, while the other person would be the Friend. So I shot my entire first year not knowing if I was going to make it as a Housewife, if I was going to be the Friend, or if I would make the cut at all. I got married my first season—walked down the aisle, completely clueless if anyone was ever going to see it.

Sezin Cavusoglu: Cynthia was really transparent about the issues surrounding that wedding and the way her family felt about her relationship to Peter. There was a lot of ugly, uncomfortable shit happening and she put it all out there.

Cynthia Bailey: We were told to show our reality, and our reality, at that time, was very tumultuous. As soon as I got on the show, we started having financial issues. We were getting married and, to be completely transparent, we could not afford to pay our wedding planner. We had to pay him in installments. I kept trying to beg him to like, "Can you cut out some drinks from the bar? Maybe we don't have to have a salad before dinner?" It was really sad. Bravo had given us, like, ten to fifteen thousand dollars, but that was just to pay for what they were interested in, like making sure the lighting was good. Finally my wedding planner just said, "I'm giving you the wedding you deserve. Pay me when you can pay me." And, you know, I have a lot of things I'm proud of in my life, but driving that check over to his place was probably one of my proudest moments.

> As Cynthia focused on her special day, Bravo's other potential Housewife that year—attorney to the stars Phaedra Parks—was getting ready to welcome her first child with her then husband, Apollo Nida.

Cynthia Bailey: They told me they were filming with a young lady named Phaedra Parks, who I'd never met. In the end, it turned out that Phaedra and I were like night and day—two completely different personalities—so they ended up going with us both as Housewives.

Carlos King: Phaedra resonated with people because she was super funny in a way we hadn't seen before on *Atlanta*. Prior to Phaedra, Housewives were loud and boisterous and aggressive. She was none of those things. But she was still able to make her mark by giving the audience a different side of a Southern belle in Atlanta. It was just perfect casting.

Andy Cohen: I'd first met Phaedra when she was Bobby Brown's attorney and I was overseeing *Being Bobby Brown* for the network. She was pretty reserved in our dealings, but really popped on-screen.

Cynthia Bailey: My only thing with Phaedra was that, for some reason, we never got close. I don't know if she saw me as competition since they were probably telling her, "It's you or Cynthia." But there was a wall up. We were cool but we weren't *friends* friends.

Sheree Whitfield: Well, no one was close with Cynthia at first because she kind of jumped in NeNe's underwear. She was so stuck up NeNe's ass.

Cynthia Bailey: That's true. You're at the mercy of who you end up coming on with and when I joined, I was NeNe's friend. That meant that there were certain people I couldn't really be friends with. I couldn't be friends with Kim because I was Team NeNe, whether I chose to be or not. Me being NeNe's friend meant I was Kim's enemy. And that's just the way the show works. In real life you can play the middle; in reality TV, you have to pick a team. It seems silly and high school–ish, but fans are like, "You're supposed to be NeNe's girl and you're over there hanging with Kim?"

Sheree Whitfield: When you're friends with NeNe, you can't be friends with anyone else. NeNe won't allow it. That's how it works.

Cynthia Bailey: It's unfortunate because at the end of the day, coming on with NeNe, I got stuck in NeNe Land. It held me back from ever really getting close to anybody else.

> *One major moment of Cynthia in NeNe Land came when Cynthia presented NeNe with the infamous friend contract.*

Cynthia Bailey: That friend contract was the best and worst thing I ever did.
Carlos King: I'd vote best!
Andy Cohen: It seemed so weird!
Cynthia Bailey: Here's what happened: One day NeNe kind of snapped at Peter on the phone. When that happened, I asked myself, "Wait, are we friends or not? Is she going to be dogging him to the other women in scenes?" Because I was starting to learn how the reality TV game was played. So I joked, "I might have to put her under a contract just to assure that she's being my friend behind closed doors, too." So that's how it started. It was fully meant to be funny. Even as I was walking into filming, I was like, "This is hilarious. This will show my personality more. She's going to laugh because it's totally ridiculous." Like, who would *actually* ask someone to sign a friendship contract? That sure backfired, huh? It turned out, everyone thought I was crazy.
Carlos King: There's nothing harder than being a first-season Housewife. It's a learning curve.
Cynthia Bailey: Oh, I learned. None of those girls liked me after my first season, but I watched and I figured out the game. Like, it never occurred to me to be mean-spirited in the interviews. I was going in there like, "Everything's unicorns and rainbows." I learned we're supposed to defend ourselves against people who we've seen saying shit about us on the show. I learned you can't trust these girls to have your back.

> *Season 4 found the Housewives making major moves in their personal lives. NeNe was dating after a divorce from Gregg while Shereé battled her ex for child support. Kim had left Big Poppa behind and was deeply in love with NFL linebacker Kroy Biermann (the couple would welcome their first child and walk down the aisle by season's end, their wedding airing in a special appropriately dubbed* Don't Be Tardy for the Wedding*).*

Shereé Whitfield: I was there when Kim met Kroy, back in season 3. She came to support me while I was dancing in a local charity event that

Kroy was also participating in, and she was like, "Shereé, who is that?" They definitely hit it off, and have done amazingly well ever since. It's crazy how things have really progressed for them. They have a genuine connection.

And there was a new face on the scene, in Marlo Hampton, a pal of NeNe's. She'd first appear that season as a guest, recurring in a similar role in seasons 6, 8, and 9. In season 10, she was made an official Friend, a role she's held consecutively for four years. But the "Housewife" title seems to have eluded her.

Marlo Hampton (Friend): I auditioned for a full-time Housewife—they came to my house and filmed a scene between me and my mother. But my family was too *Love & Hip-Hop* for Bravo's brand. My mother was eating out of the refrigerator, yelling and cursing and drinking a Colt 45. My truth was not what they wanted. It was not their truth.

Lauren Eskelin: I met Marlo when I was casting for season 4. She was being kept by a very wealthy man, and was very open, fun, fascinating— definitely *Housewives* material. She was very comfortable with herself. We came to film her home visit, went into her closet to pick out an outfit, and she fully stripped down naked in front of me within five minutes of meeting. I was like, "Oh, my God!" It was the most epic casting I'd ever seen. I loved her immediately.

Marlo Hampton: I was dating Charles Grant, the big NFL star, at the time. And part of me thinks I would have been full-time if I would have stayed with Charles. But I wasn't happy, and I wasn't going to fake it like a lot of these other girls do.

Sezin Cavusoglu: We saw that with Porsha, we saw that with Cynthia. But that's because their lives evolved along with the show. Marlo hasn't had that evolution. To cast someone who doesn't bring that same kind of diversity in terms of our access to people around them, it's just not interesting.

Andy Cohen: That's all true, but her mug shots didn't help her case with the network, either. NeNe really tried and continued to push for her year after year, though.

Marlo Hampton: It hurts. They're more for the new girls they try out who only work for one season instead of being loyal and dedicated to someone who's been around for eight years.

Sezin Cavusoglu: The other thing that didn't help her is that there was a time when, every time she would come on, all she would do is start fights with people. She fought with Shereé, she fought with Kim; she was best friends with NeNe, then she had a falling-out with NeNe; she was friends with Kenya, then fell out with Kenya; she fought with Porsha, fought with Eva. And as fun as that can be for the drama, all of her messiness in the years past contributed to our decision not to make her a Housewife.

Marlo Hampton: I feel like, sometimes, I'm holding back because I'm so afraid of, "Oh my God, the network isn't going to like this." I censor certain aspects of my life because I'm afraid to really give it all to them with no sugar on top.

Sezin Cavusoglu: Marlo is a perfect Friend on the show. She's a great sounding board for the women, and she's fabulous and shady and over-the-top—all of that. She's still a very important part of our show. And she's mellowed out over the years and really forged friendships on her own with so many of the women. I'm such a fan of who she has become.

Andy Cohen: I wish these women would remember the power they have as a Friend. They can say anything, do anything, light it up, have fun, and you don't have to show off your family life. It's a good gig!

> As for the dynamics among the group in season 4, the more things change, the more they stay the same. NeNe and Shereé were once again at odds, coming together in the season 4 premiere for an explosive face-off.

Carlos King: It took us forever to get NeNe and Shereé to sit down in season 4. I spent weeks begging them to talk through this dumb argument they were having. But they did not want to see each other. They did not want to talk. And they each wanted to be summoned by the other. That's the thing with *Housewives* that most people don't know: no Housewife ever wants to be the one to call the one-on-one. "Well, she needs to call *me*"—like, that's important to them. So we finally got them to agree by telling the other person that the other one invited them. Whatever it takes to get them in the room!

Shereé Whitfield: Carlos knew I could make good TV. He knew I wasn't afraid of NeNe.

Carlos King: What was interesting about that face-off is, it was the first time we could actually acknowledge and address—at least a little bit—that these women were celebrities. Because if you remember, their beef was over these speaking gigs they were doing with Tyrone [Gilliams], a promoter who was booking NeNe, Kim, and Shereé at the time.

Shereé Whitfield: People wanted to book me, Kim, and NeNe together, but NeNe felt like, "I'm above Shereé and Kim." She would say, "Why don't you just book *me*?" She wanted to be by herself. Now, to be clear—me, Kim, NeNe, and Lisa Wu all started using the same attorney in the second season. We all received the same amount of money. So boo, you're not above anybody.

Carlos King: NeNe was fresh off of *The Celebrity Apprentice*, and she felt she was the richest bitch in the room—which, she said it! "I'm a very rich bitch!" It rolled off her tongue like syrup. I didn't see it coming, but this is the genius of NeNe: she was able to deliver that line, stand up, and point her finger in Shereé's face the whole time with such ease.

Shereé Whitfield: She acted like everyone was jealous of her. I didn't even watch her on *Celebrity Apprentice*! I just heard she quit. So how are you cashing Trump's checks if you didn't even finish?

Carlos King: It was just super funny. And mind you, this was happening at this tiny winery in Atlantic Station in Atlanta. That's the equivalent of Times Square. NeNe left, and there were tons of people outside, and Shereé was chasing her down saying her car was repossessed. In Atlanta, to see NeNe Leakes and Shereé Whitfield scream at each other on the sidewalk during rush hour was everything.

Shereé Whitfield: I should have said "Fix those doggie dentures" because they had just started airing commercials with a dog with these big old teeth that looked just like hers! She's had those done a couple of times because they're not as big as they were at the time. They were horrible!

Carlos King: They kept going, too, at that season 4 reunion. That's the "Fix your body, fix your face" exchange. I can watch that all day.

Shereé Whitfield: She needed to fix that body!

Carlos King: A lot of people ask, "Do they come up with these lines on their own?" They do! They're not coached. They're not prepped. It's all theirs.

Shereé Whitfield: In the moment, I don't really feel like I'm that good, to be honest. I'll leave filming and be like, "Damn, I should've said that!"

Cynthia Bailey: Oh no, Shereé's one of those people where she seems cool in person and then you see her go off in interviews, and you're like, "Oh shit, I better watch out for her!"

Carlos King: There will never be a rivalry as good as Shereé and NeNe's for me. I had a lot of love for them both. Even though I was assigned to NeNe, I wasn't always on Team NeNe. When you're a professional, you don't get involved in their disagreements or hold biases against talent.

Sadly, season 4 would close the chapter on Sheree's first RHOA run.

Sheree Whitfield: We could not come up with a mutual agreement for season 5. It wasn't working.

Andy Cohen: A lot of women feel, at the end, like they need a break.

Carlos King: But notice, they brought on two new people to replace one Sheree. That's how important she is.

> *Those two women—former Miss USA winner Kenya Moore and Porsha Williams, then wife of NFL quarterback Kordell Stewart—would wind up carrying* RHOA *through its next generation, while also forging one of the deepest, most-sustained rivalries in* Housewives *history.*

Kenya Moore (Housewife): I would come to Atlanta all the time to see my aunt and spend time with Miss Lawrence—we are very, very close. But I had hit a brick wall where I was just not happy with the course of my career, my personal life, and so on. So one day, I said, "I'm going to move to Atlanta. This is the perfect time." And not long after I arrived, I got a call from a producer saying, "We hear you're in town. Do you want to go on tape for *Real Housewives*?"

Carlos King: No one knows how to make her mark better than Kenya Moore. She stuck like glue.

Cynthia Bailey: Kenya came, she showed out, and she's been showing out ever since. She's reality TV gold.

> *Kenya and Porsha's casting brought the number of full-time Atlanta Housewives up to seven, the largest its cast had ever been. However, one Housewife wouldn't last the whole season. . . .*

Andy Cohen: Kim Zolciak quit in season 5. She just got up and walked out, pushing a cameraman away in the process. She and Kroy called me from the car. And he ripped me a new asshole about how unfairly Kim was being treated. I don't remember being yelled at by anyone as much as he did that day.

Carlos King: I was not surprised when I heard Kim was leaving. During season 4, it was a struggle to get Kim to participate in any group scenes. She did not want to leave her house. Kim would be like, "Why can't these bitches come and see me?" It's like, "Kim, you have to interact with your cast!" But she was over it.

Lauren Eskelin: She made it very clear to the women that she did not think she needed to give to the show what they were giving to the show, and that really pissed them off. The cast was very united in their feelings about Kim. It was the first time in a long time they were on the same page about something.

Cynthia Bailey: Kim can be disrespectful as hell, that's for sure. And we all felt that because she was white, she wasn't held to the same standard as we were. Kim got a pass on stuff. She would show up late to a scene, eating McDonald's. They'd tell her she couldn't eat it while filming and she'd say, "Fuck you," and just eat it while filming anyway. And then would get up and leave whenever she wanted. Like, if I did that, I wouldn't be on the show.

Lauren Eskelin: The breaking moment came at a brunch where the entire cast was talking about going on the trip. They had been planning these dates and moving around their schedules to accommodate Kim. But now Kim revealed she wasn't going to come because she was pregnant and didn't feel like she could leave her family.

Cynthia Bailey: For me—I don't care who you are, I don't care what color you are, I don't care how many kids you got—when it's time to come to work, bring your ass to work. Because Cynthia Bailey shows up for work. I film when I'm asked to film. I don't torture production. I don't make it difficult. I love and appreciate my job, and I'm getting paid very well to do it. So be a professional.

Lauren Eskelin: None of them were buying Kim's excuse. They were really tired of her trying to get out of everything, while they were on the hook to do everything. And when Kim was being held accountable by the women and by the producing team, she wasn't having it. She didn't like it. So she got up and left. And just like that, that was the end.

Carlos King: Kim felt like the show wasn't a reflection of her life anymore. You know, that Big Poppa chapter had closed. She met Kroy and was in that nesting phase.

Sheree Whitfield: I'm not surprised that happened. To be honest with you, I don't watch the show when I'm not on the show, but who did she have left?

Carlos King: That's right. Without Sheree, who did she really have on that show anymore? She and Kandi weren't close. She didn't talk to NeNe, didn't talk to Phaedra, didn't talk to Cynthia. And it was like, "Who are these new girls, Kenya and Porsha? Why should I talk to them?" You could see her taking inventory of her circle and realizing, "Maybe it's time to move on."

Lauren Eskelin: It wound up being very necessary for the other women. It really bonded them. They were happy to move on without having to deal with somebody who wasn't a team player.

Cynthia Bailey: Look, I never really got a chance to connect with Kim, but I could see she was good for the show. I had never met anyone like her before. A white lady in a wig, chain-smoking cigarettes and cussing up a storm? That was different. But when these ladies get to the point where they think they're bigger than the show and the network, it's disrespectful. Now, if you want to be a diva and do all this stuff after we're done filming, by all means. But do not waste my time.

> *In the wake of Kim's absence, the drama focused on Kenya and Porsha, who weren't exactly fast friends.*

Kenya Moore: I didn't know her at all. I'm not going to say that she was a nobody, but she wasn't a known person. She was the wife of a known person. They billed her to be this really prominent Atlanta socialite, and when I met her in person I was like, oh my God, she's like a total airhead cheerleader. I just really did not mesh with her. Then when she invited me to come and be a guest at an event, I took the time to come, get dressed and glam, and she got my title wrong. And people confuse Miss America and Miss USA all the time. That wasn't the insult. The insult was how she reacted when someone corrected her. She was like, "Oh, whatever." And I was like, no, it's not whatever. The Queen of So-and-So does not want to be mixed up with the Queen of Whatever. . . . They're two totally different things and you need to respect the difference. So I went outside, and she came out and was just so aggressive and nasty. I had never insulted her, and she was like, "You're on the curb where you need to be." I will never forget those words. I didn't understand where all that aggression was coming from. And that's when I decided, with everything about her that I knew so far, it was a hard pass for me.

Carlos King: "*Gone with the Wind* fabulous" was such a moment.

Kenya Moore: I felt like I opened a door for her. I had been on TV for twenty years. I made my way and I fought to be where I am. I earned it. And for her to diminish my role in history as the second Black Miss USA, I was upset. So I immediately thought of how Vanessa Williams paved the way for me as an actor, or how Hattie McDaniel was the first Black woman to ever win an Academy Award. That's why I said I was *Gone with the Wind* fabulous. It was like, you can't take away my accomplishments from me. I will always be relevant. And not long after it aired, people around me started saying it. I got my life when Beyoncé quoted it after performing at the Super Bowl with Destiny's Child.

Andy Cohen: She followed in the footsteps of our other Housewives and did a song next, naturally. The more songs the better, as far as I'm concerned. It's theater of the absurd.

Kenya Moore: I lost my damn mind in season 5! I don't know what happened, but I was just having fun.

Cynthia Bailey: "Now twirl! Twirl! Twirl! Twirl!"

> *Meanwhile, Kenya also found herself on the outs with Phaedra, their initial friendship falling apart over competitive working tapes, rumored boyfriends-for-hire, and claims that Kenya was making moves on Phaedra's then husband.*

Kenya Moore: I had at one point considered her to be my friend, I really did. I had no idea that she was as diabolical and evil as she is. But eventually I told people on air, "She's evil, she's trying to destroy me." And I was right. But because I came on and I rubbed people the wrong way, nobody cared whether or not it was true. It was a newbie going against a fan favorite. So fans are going to stick with the girl they know. She said I was crazy, that I propositioned her husband. But that was all because she knew that it's the perception that hurts people. It's not truth. It's the perception. And listen, I don't really start anything. Coming into the show, I just wanted to be myself. I didn't want to do anything to intentionally hurt someone *first*. But once I taste blood in the water, it's like, "Now I'm really coming after you."

Carlos King: Those clashes were epic. Legendary. It's a game of sportsmanship. They are great adversaries.

> *Throughout seasons 5 and 6, Kenya continued to butt heads with her costars, emerging as one of the franchise's biggest villains. And while there may have been tensions on camera, behind the scenes, the Housewives knew it was good for the show.*

Carlos King: As much as they bitched and moaned about one another, the women understood and appreciated being Number 1. When you are Number 1 you want to stay Number 1.

Kenya Moore: I had never been the subject of any controversy or negativity until I came on this show. I was a quiet girl in Hollywood. I would come to the set on time, had a great work ethic, was friendly and very professional. There was never any scandal. So I really thought I would continue to have that persona on this show. I said, "I'll come in and be America's Chocolate Sweetheart. People like me, so I'll just be my unapologetic self." Well, that is not the way I came across.

Carlos King: If you don't like Kenya Moore, then you don't like reality television. You have to know she's a necessary evil for a show. Same with Brandi Glanville, same with Lisa Rinna, same with even Bethenny Frankel sometimes. There are certain people who are polarizing that you either love to hate or you hate to love, but you understand their reason for being there.

Sezin Cavusoglu: The thing is, Kenya is an incredible Housewife. She's so good when she's on. She understands how this works. She gives it her all. She doesn't shy away from conflict.

Cynthia Bailey: Kenya lights up a scene like no other. She's someone who knows how to make a moment on TV, even if it's coming for you.

Kenya Moore: You need a protagonist and an antagonist for any story to work, right? I get that part. What I don't like—and I don't know if I've ever leaned into it—is the one-sided portrayal, or people being so ready to vilify you when you're actually not trying to be that way. I have a love-hate relationship with the villain concept. But the girls respect me for it. They don't think they could do the show without me.

RHOA *was firing on all cylinders in season 6. Among its biggest dramas was a twist no one saw coming—the end of NeNe and Cynthia's friend contract.*

Cynthia Bailey: Peter, my ex, was the most vocal Househusband they ever had. And you forget, but up until that point on *Atlanta*, the husbands weren't saying anything. Peter came around and changed the game. He defended his wife and he voiced his opinions, which I thought was admirable. But the other women didn't like that. It became, "He needs to stay out of women's business. What kind of man argues with a woman?" And that's why NeNe called him a bitch. But I will say, I learned a lot from that. Now with my husband Mike, I try to protect him. I want him to have a voice, but I don't want him to be reduced to just being Cynthia Bailey's man on *Real Housewives of Atlanta*, because he's so much more than that. I don't want him to have to feel the brunt of the things Peter had to go through. I told him, "You can have my back behind the scenes, but let me fight my own battles in front of the girls." It's not easy. But most girls would agree, if we didn't have to show our husbands and families on the show, we wouldn't. It's not really fair for them. It's not really their show, so they're not as invested. And the audience always sides with us. It's not really fair.

But season 6's biggest moment came early into the reunion, when Porsha and Kenya got into a shocking physical altercation.

Carlos King: Those reunion shows are twelve-hour-long days, or sixteen hours when you incorporate glam, production—all that shit. Now, we were shooting for maybe thirty minutes when Kenya started pulling out her props. And as soon as she did, we were all like, "Don't you just love Kenya? She's amazing! Iconic! She's the first Housewife to bring a prop to a reunion!" Andy was laughing, even the other Housewives, they were laughing. Because that's who Kenya Moore is. That's her shtick.

Cynthia Bailey: Kenya was definitely making her mark with those props.

Kenya Moore: I brought the scepter for NeNe because she always talked about herself as if she was the Queen of *Atlanta*, so I wanted to taunt her with the subliminal message of "I'm the new Queen." Same thing with the bullhorn, that was also for NeNe, because she loves to get very loud and yell, drowning people out.

Carlos King: But Porsha? Porsha wasn't into it.... There was something different about Porsha's headspace that day. Even before that scepter was pointed at her, or the bullhorn, you could tell something was off. She was not playing.

Cynthia Bailey: You don't know what people are going through. You don't know how people are going to react to stuff. Porsha was just coming off this divorce from Kordell. She was finding her own self on the show, her own identity. That could not have been easy. And Kenya's antics, for some reason that day, were hitting her the wrong way.

Kenya Moore: I wasn't even thinking of Porsha at that point because I didn't have beef with Porsha. She wasn't really an issue for me. But as the reunion went on, Porsha and Phaedra were both gunning for me. Every little thing I would say, they would start in on me. And Porsha, because she was on my couch, was throwing these jabs at me, left and right.

Carlos King: All of a sudden, Porsha snapped the scepter out of Kenya's hand. Now, I'm a Black boy from Detroit, Michigan, right? I grew up around Black women. I knew their behavior. So the second that happened, I inched my chair a little closer to the stage. My Spidey senses were like, "This could go bad." I was alert.

Andy Cohen: This was the same season as NeNe's pillow talk slumber party, which also got violent. And a lot of the women, NeNe specifically, really felt like Kenya had provoked that argument by standing up. I was totally clueless as to where this thing was headed. But I might've been the only one in the room who was surprised.

Kenya Moore: People will say, "Oh, Kenya provoked Porsha." But go back and watch the scene. *She's* the first one to start with me, saying crazy, nasty things. Porsha called me a slut. Porsha said no man would have me. People don't want to see that—because I was the villain, right? That's the role they were painting me to be. When you're the villain, it doesn't matter who's fucking with you. It doesn't matter what they're saying. You're always going to be the one to blame.

Carlos King: By the time Porsha stood up out of her seat and got in Kenya's face, what people don't know is that I was already running. I ran the moment Porsha stood up. Because I know, when Black girls stand up, they fight. And I said to myself, "Oh shit, a fight's about to happen." No one knew that; I didn't tell anyone that. But that's why, two seconds after Porsha latches her hand on to Kenya's hair, I was pulling her back. If I had gotten there two seconds earlier, it wouldn't have happened.

Cynthia Bailey: It just happened so quickly. I don't even remember Porsha snatching Kenya or seeing Kenya being dragged across the floor. I don't remember my titty coming out. All I remember is Porsha stood up, Kenya stood up, and next thing I knew, Porsha was lying on the floor screaming. That's how fast it happened.

Carlos King: If you look back at it, you can see that we all fell backward together—me holding Porsha, and Porsha pulling Kenya's hair. Kenya got up gracefully and walked away. She's a bad bitch. But I stayed on top of Porsha as the other girls circled around her to get her to calm down.

Kenya Moore: I was just in shock. I truly never saw it coming. I know I have my differences with Porsha, but most of the time people know that it's not okay to get up in each other's faces. We may yell, we may call each other out of our names, but the cardinal rule is that you never put your hands on someone.

Carlos King: Porsha said she blacked out, and she did. I remember looking into Porsha's eyes, she wasn't coherent. She really was gone. And as everyone was calling her name, she came to life. I saw it in her eyes. She realized what she did, and she was super remorseful. She started crying, kicking herself, screaming, "What did I just do? I'm so embarrassed. I ruined myself. I ruined my career."

Kenya Moore: What you did not see was that Porsha was screaming, "I quit! I quit! I quit! I don't want to do this!" while she was kicking and stomping her feet like a toddler, her fists all balled up. "I quit! I quit! I quit!"

Andy Cohen: Well, maybe, but Kenya was also saying, "You're fired! You're fired!"

Carlos King: NeNe had her hand on Porsha's mouth, saying "Shut up," because she didn't want Porsha to say anything she'd regret.

Kenya Moore: I remember just being stunned, standing there looking at her. I was like, "I can't believe this . . ."—I'll reserve the name I thought to call her in the moment.

Carlos King: Porsha was upset. I wound up picking her up and carrying her offstage to the lobby area, where I confronted her. And I really saw in that moment that she was damaged. She had a really difficult season 6. She was going through a divorce, her entire world was changing. The timing of the reunion, it was just too much. That's why she was so quiet; she wasn't mentally in the right headspace to deal with anything that day.

Cynthia Bailey: She was asked to leave the reunion after that.

Carlos King: Andy came into her dressing room and said, "You're not in the right headspace for this. It's in your best interest to just go home." And she agreed and apologized. I applaud Andy for at least saying, "Look, this is not something we're celebrating. This is something we realize is too much for you to handle today."

Sezin Cavusoglu: That altercation was not something that we condoned or approved of. There's a reason why we don't show flashbacks to it the way we used to in the beginning. It really is not an image we want to perpetuate. And it's also not who Porsha is anymore.

Kenya Moore: I never thought that I would be involved in a physical altercation on a national TV show. That's the worst thing, not only as a former Miss USA but as a Black woman. It's the worst imagery you ever want to see yourself in. The only step that would be worse would be if a wig would be pulled off, because then you're no worse than the buffoonery you see on *The Jerry Springer Show*.

Carlos King: It was a very sad moment overall, probably the darkest day in *Real Housewives of Atlanta* history.

The following season, Porsha was moved to a Friend-of role.

Carlos King: A lot of people think Porsha was demoted for that fight. That's not true. Porsha came back in season 7 as a full-time Housewife. There was no demotion.

Lauren Eskelin: We started shooting with Porsha, and she just wasn't giving much by way of personal story. In group scenes, she was great and would pop, but alone, there wasn't much there.

Carlos King: In order to have that status, you have to give everything. Porsha just wasn't invested in being on the show and giving us that story. It was like, "Wow, maybe she's not capable of handling being full-time right now." So the network made the decision—pretty late in the season, too—to make her a Friend.

Andy Cohen: If you ask Porsha, it was absolutely because of the fight.

Lauren Eskelin: And that should be a warning for all Housewives and future Housewives. The biggest crime you can commit is to not be honest with your personal story. You really need to be open and honest, and if you don't, then you shouldn't be holding a peach or an apple or an orange or whatever it is.

> While they lost Porsha as a full-time Housewife in season 7, Claudia Jordan was added to the cast. The actress, model, and former beauty queen had appeared on unscripted TV before (including The Apprentice, Deal or No Deal, and The Price Is Right) but was new to Atlanta.

Claudia Jordan (Housewife): I was doing a show in L.A. and got a call from producers that my contract wasn't being renewed. Down on my luck, I went out for drinks with some friends in West Hollywood and they were like, "You should meet Carlos King." So they called him (he was in town) and he met us at our next stop. And the minute he saw me, he said, "I have been wanting to work with you the longest time. I'm gonna change your life." Within a couple of weeks, I was interviewing for *Housewives*.

Carlos King: I never had a say in casting, but I would give opinions. And when I met Claudia Jordan I was like, "Oh, she's going to be a good Housewife." Because Claudia is effortlessly funny. Claudia can hang with the big dogs. Claudia stands her ground. Claudia's organically connected to the women. And you never know what's going to come out of her mouth.

Claudia Jordan: People think I was brought on to take NeNe out. That was never, ever, ever the case. Before I got on the show, Carlos told me, "People think when they get on the show that they need to come for NeNe.

That's a mistake. Just do you." Kenya said the same thing. "My fights are not your fights." So I came into it ready to make my own opinions.

Carlos King: We tested Claudia, and I thought she was a *great* Housewife. But they thought she would be a good Friend. That's how we were originally considering her.

Claudia Jordan: I wound up moving to Atlanta because I got a gig working on Rickey Smiley's radio show. So I was connected to Kenya *and* Porsha, who was doing Rickey's television show.

Carlos King: We were actually looking at Demetria McKinney, who was dating mega TV producer Roger Bobb at the time, to be our new Housewife.

Claudia Jordan: Demetria had the boyfriend with the money and the connections in the Atlanta film scene. She was more primed to get the peach.

Carlos King: What happened was, Roger was okay doing the show until he realized that we needed to shoot with him all the time. He wasn't ready for that. There were tons of conversations where we'd say, "Roger, we need you!" and he wouldn't show up to film. He was trying to control his own narrative. And unfortunately, it cost Demetria her peach because in order for this show to work, you have to have stars who are willing to show their entire lives. You can't introduce your boyfriend or husband to the narrative and then he never shows up.

Claudia Jordan: It was not until we went away to Puerto Rico, and I got NeNe together for being extremely rude to Demetria and myself, that I was made a Housewife.

Carlos King: NeNe and Claudia had that epic argument in Puerto Rico. Think back to that: Claudia didn't blink an eye. Didn't sweat. She gathered NeNe right the hell up.

Claudia Jordan: Never in my wildest dreams did I think, "This one scene is going to make me a Housewife." But by that point, I had filmed enough to know that these girls turn it up when the cameras come on. And have a lethal mouth. I will say what everyone's thinking. So I dug in.

Carlos King: And NeNe respected it! NeNe was like, "Oh, she's good." She saw Claudia as a formidable opponent. And NeNe is the one who said to me and another producer, "Y'all got the wrong bitch. Claudia, that's the one, not Demetria." And that was *after* their fight.

Claudia Jordan: I heard NeNe said I was good for the show. And I give her credit for that. She knew that it's not fun to watch everyone kiss her ass, or not put up a fight.

Carlos King: It goes to show you how much these girls respect it when you can come in and make your mark. There's a feeling of "If you can hang with us, you deserve to be around us."

Claudia Jordan: The problem was, by that point, we only had a month left of filming, so there was a frantic rush to cram things in that would flesh out my story line—which wasn't enough time, really. I didn't get a fair shot. People would say, "She didn't have a story line outside her fight with NeNe," and they're right! I didn't have time to!

Andy Cohen: I always thought we didn't give Claudia a fair shake. She'd just moved to Atlanta, we couldn't decide if she was going to be a Friend or what, and her introduction was clumsy.

Sezin Cavusoglu: *Atlanta* is a unique ensemble. It really is. I have to say, it's probably one of the hardest shows to cast for. The women are so glamorous, so funny, really well connected. They now have decades-long friendships. It's hard to bring somebody into that. It's intimidating. And even though the Atlanta Housewives are the nicest group of women I work with, being an outsider coming in, it's hard to keep up with that kind of dynamic. As a group, they're fire.

> Claudia didn't return after season 7. But surprisingly, neither did NeNe. The Atlanta OG announced she would be leaving the show that made her a star, amid a sea of new acting opportunities including TV roles on Glee and The New Normal.

Sezin Cavusoglu: It was nerve-racking when NeNe wanted to walk away from the show because she felt like the engine that kept it running. I mean, NeNe made the show. I won't mince words about it. It's an ensemble show, but without NeNe Leakes, we weren't sure what the show would look like.

Kenya Moore: When she left and got on that series, she seemed so happy. In her mind it was, "I have surpassed all of you. I'm moving on. I'm a Hollywood actress now. That's all I've ever wanted."

Carlos King: But also, NeNe had a rough season 7. There was a disconnect with her and the rest of the cast. She and Cynthia weren't friends that year, and she had been fighting with Kenya and Claudia. At the same time, she was making moves in Hollywood, doing Broadway. She had her sights set on moving on.

> There were big shoes to fill in NeNe's absence. But season 8's casting of actress Kim Fields wound up being a bit of a misstep.

Sezin Cavusoglu: The casting people at Truly Original pitched Kim Fields's name, and we were like, "Hmm, that's interesting. Would she do it?" You know, for a lot of these franchises, famous actresses' names get thrown around all the time. Most of them usually back away and change their minds at the last minute. And Kim Fields was someone who was surprisingly interested. The idea really tickled us.

Carlos King: I'm not going to lie to you, I fanned out when I met Kim Fields. Obviously, Kim Fields is a legend. She's Tootie from *The Facts of Life*, Regine from *Living Single*. I said to her, "You're an icon and I love you." I was really excited about working with her.

Andy Cohen: I was *thrilled* with the prospect. It seemed genius.

Sezin Cavusoglu: If I'm being honest, though, we knew from the beginning that Kim Fields wasn't going to be around for too long. Obviously she was a big name. And she had a connection to the group, through Phaedra; they were both young mothers and cared about social causes, so there was good synergy there. But really, you can never become a successful Housewife if you're not committed to doing this show fully. And we could see, very early on, that Kim didn't realize how involved it was going to be.

Carlos King: The problem was, Kim Fields had no idea what she was getting herself into. She had never watched an episode of *Real Housewives of Atlanta*. And unlike other women who came on the show before without any experience in this genre, Kim did not even understand the institution of reality television. She was a child star. The only thing she knew was scripted and structure. And she never adjusted.

Sheree Whitfield: Kim Fields was great as Tootie and Regine, but this was the wrong platform for her. She was a household name. People like that, they get on TV and they're like, "I gotta protect my brand!" They can't really be themselves.

Carlos King: I was in constant dialogue with Kim Fields, all season long, trying to get her to understand the structure of reality TV. Remember Jamaica, when Kenya pulled Kim Fields's chair back? So Kim Fields got up after that and bolted. So of course, we follow her and I say, "In your real life, who would you want to talk to about this?"—because we wanted to film her processing her feelings to someone in her life—her husband, another Housewife—about what had just happened. And she said, "Andy Cohen." I said, "Kim, you can't call Andy Cohen on camera." "Why not?" "Because in this world, Andy Cohen doesn't exist." She goes,

"I'm confused, Carlos. You want to follow my reality? I'm telling you, I'm going to call Andy Cohen right now and tell him what Kenya Moore did." I said, "Kim, this may sound crazy to you, but on this show, Andy Cohen is the host of the reunion show and that's it. So you cannot call fucking Andy Cohen on camera." It just, it didn't click for her.

Sezin Cavusoglu: I will say, Kim isn't the first person to think Andy is going to step in and fix things for them. That's not an uncommon perspective. It takes a while for them to learn that lesson.

Andy Cohen: We spoke throughout the season and I kept thinking I was getting through to her, but the results were mixed. I liked her a lot. She wanted to do a great job.

Cynthia Bailey: I filmed with Kim a lot. Every time I had the chance. She's a great person. I respect her personality. But on this show, it just didn't feel like the right fit.

Kim wasn't the only addition to the cast in season 8. With one OG out, another OG came back—Sheree Whitfield.

Carlos King: I left the show after season 7 to start my own company. But they were filming season 8 and a month and a half into filming, nothing was happening. The showrunner left the show, and the production company called me and asked to take me out to dinner. And I'll never forget, they said, "We need you. *Your* show is suffering. This is *your* baby. Will you come back?" Within twenty-four hours, I had spoken to the network and agreed to come back. But there was one thing I wanted: to bring Sheree back with me.

Sheree Whitfield: Shut your face, Carlos said he'd come back if he could bring me back? Oh my gosh . . . we really worked great together.

Sezin Cavusoglu: Bringing Sheree back as a Friend was a no-brainer. Not only did Sheree have a history with these women, but she still had maintained relationships with many of them. She was very much in their orbit.

Carlos King: Plus, I knew the fans missed her. Sheree had been off the show for three years. They wanted her back.

Sheree Whitfield: You know, I'd had interest in coming back before but the timing was never right. But this time, I was no longer going through my divorce, or fighting for child support. I didn't have the stress of building my house. And I was ready to just have good times with the girls.

Carlos King: Listen, I knew Sheree was this lightning rod. And she proved that in the first scene she filmed for us, when she showed up at Cynthia's party in all black—like the villain she is—and had this iconic face-off with Kenya over the building of Moore Manor vs. Chateau Shereé.

Shereé Whitfield: I hadn't even met Kenya before we started filming, and she came for me right away. I walked into that party, feeling so happy to be back. Everyone was like, "Shereé! Shereé! Shereé!" which made me feel good. But then this bitch wants to act like a fool. I was like, "Damn, bitch, I don't even know you. Who are you? What are you doing?"

Carlos King: This is the beauty of Kenya, by the way. Kenya saw Shereé walk in and said to herself, "Okay, we've been filming this show for six weeks and ain't nothing happened. Now Carlos is back, Shereé is here. I know what I need to do."

Shereé Whitfield: Well, that was unbeknownst to me! I knew I had come back to save the show but I didn't know I was going to be the target as soon as I walked in the door! Especially by someone I didn't know!

Kenya Moore: I just lit her up about her house. I was building mine not too far away, and everyone was talking about it.

Shereé Whitfield: I built that house from scratch. That took me four, five, six years to build. Anyone who knows new construction knows a bank is not going to approve a loan over that many years. So I went through it, really. But it ended up fine, baseboards and all.

Kenya Moore: It was fun shade, until she took it too far.

Shereé Whitfield: People always want a moment. And of course, they want it with me because they know I will come back. I'm not going to sit back and let you talk to me any kind of way.

Afterward, I got a call from someone who was like, "Kenya wanted me to tell you that she hopes you didn't take any of that personally." And I said, "Oh hell no. It's personal. It may not have been if you had given me a heads-up, but you ain't given me no heads-up. So it's personal."

Carlos King: Kenya's the best villain *Atlanta* has ever had for this very reason. And I always say, you gotta protect the villains and respect the villains. Because they're necessary.

Shereé Whitfield: Yeah, Kenya knows how to make good TV. Even if she's not getting along with you, she knows it's good for the show. She's not gonna take it so personal where "I'm not gonna work with this person ever." She knows at the end of the day, it's a bigger picture than just her. She sure did piss me off and I sure did piss her off, but we're good.

Meanwhile, Porsha got her peach back in season 8 but found herself in the middle of another physical fight—this time with Cynthia.

Sezin Cavusoglu: That was another unfortunate incident that left us all shocked.

Cynthia Bailey: We were on a boat, drinking and having fun. I hadn't eaten. Nobody had. At some point, after a lot of drinks, Porsha said something like "whatever, bitch." Now, while we can call each other bitch all day long, at the time—in that moment, in that context—it rubbed me the wrong way. She was hovering over me, antagonizing me as if to say, "I know you ain't going to do nothing." Which pissed me off more because people definitely mistake my kindness for weakness. And I don't want to fight a bunch of grown-ass bitches, but will I defend myself when I'm cornered, without question.

Shereé Whitfield: That fight was so crazy. I remember looking over and seeing them tussling, and I'm like, "Oh my gosh!" None of us knew that it would elevate to that level.

Cynthia Bailey: I may have overreacted with some things that I was saying during our first back-and-forth. But the moment I decided to excuse myself and go to the other side of the boat, now she should've stayed where she was and let me the hell alone. But that's not what happened. She came to where I was, sat herself down on the chair where I was lying down, and continued to come at me. And knowing that Porsha had gotten physical in the past, my instinct was, "If she tries to hit me, I'm going to defend myself." So once she stood up and raised over me—remember, I was in a vulnerable position, lying down—my instinct was just to kick her off me.

Carlos King: I saw it getting there again and pulled Porsha back, just holding her down until she calmed down.

Cynthia Bailey: I'm grateful for Carlos King to this day because if Porsha had gotten loose from him, I would have been toast, probably. I'm not a fighter, that's not what I do. Porsha would have thrown me off that boat.

Lauren Eskelin: Porsha was not disciplined for her fight with Kenya but she was for her fight with Cynthia, because it was like, "Okay, this can't be happening again." So we required Porsha to go to anger management on camera. It was the network's way of saying, "We take this seriously."

Sezin Cavusoglu: We wanted to send a very clear message to all of our cast members that this wasn't okay. We loved Porsha and wanted to keep her on the show, but this wasn't a way she could continue behaving.

Cynthia Bailey: I was nervous I would get in trouble for defending myself, but I got a call from the network and they told me, "We watched the tape, Cynthia. You had every right to defend yourself." Still, it was not my proudest moment. I felt bad immediately because I have compassion for people. I'm not a monster, and I'm not crazy. But I'm not on this show to be beat up, either.

Sezin Cavusoglu: It was all a part of Porsha's growth, because today, Porsha would never do anything like that. There were other issues she was dealing with back then, and she's learned to tackle them. Porsha's journey on *Housewives* is one of the most impressive journeys we've seen any of these women go through.

> *Porsha's journey was about to hit a major bump, though. In season 9, she revealed she'd heard a rumor that Kandi and her husband had plotted to drug and rape her. The shocking claim, which Kandi and Todd both denied, was later traced back to Kandi's former BFF, Phaedra.*

Kandi Burruss: That was a hard falling-out. That was horrible.

Carlos King: It all started on that camping trip. Shereé told Marlo, "There are people around us accusing Kandi of being a lesbian." And immediately, Marlo wanted to get down to the truth of it all. And when she posed the question at the dinner table, that infamous exchange of "Who said that? Who said that? Who said that?" occurred. And we were watching from behind the scenes thinking we were just watching something funny unfold. We thought it was pure comedy. Kandi rolled with the punches; everyone laughed. We had no idea that moment would turn into what it did. Next thing we knew we had Kandi saying that Porsha wanted to . . . let's just say, service her.

Kandi Burruss: When they came at me at the campground and Marlo said, "I heard you're an in-the-closet lesbian" and all that bullshit, I was just sitting there like, "I've already told you guys that I've dipped my toes in the lady pond, so where is this coming from?" Then, when I found out that Porsha was the one who said it, it completely threw me off. Completely. Because in my mind I was like, "Wait a minute, sis, you in the same boat as me—like, what the hell are you talking about? Who are you to make it seem like I'm doing something crazy?" I was completely shocked.

Carlos King: Then, when Kandi and Porsha saw each other for a one-on-one after that camping trip, it only got worse. Accusations were flying around, one after the other. And in the midst of it all is when Porsha said,

"Well, I heard you wanted to drug me and take me to your sex dungeon," which was like, "What?! What the fuck is happening right now?!"

Kandi Burruss: When I had that lunch with Porsha, I was just like, I really gotta put her on blast. Basically at the top, I was like, "If you want to talk about somebody being in the lady pond, we gonna let the people know you in the lady pond, too!" I was being open about the moment she and I had in the club, with the whole kiss situation off camera. That was a year and a half prior to us having that argument, and it was something that neither she nor I told anyone—it was our own personal secret. So when I said, "When you kissed me in the club and said you wanted to eat me till I came," and then she was like, "Oh you mean when you tried to drug me?" It completely threw me for a loop. I was like, "Wait, what?!" I honestly almost laughed at her because I thought she was joking. And when she kept going with it I was like, "Okay, wait, this bitch is serious!" I was so furious. I could not believe she said that. I called production, like, "Obviously y'all cannot let this bitch go on national TV talking about how I tried to drug her"—like, that's insane! And they were like, "Nobody's going to believe that. Why are you worried?" But I was like, "She can't just put that bullshit out into the world."

Carlos King: I'll be very honest. At the time, none of the producers thought anything of what Porsha said. We know Kandi. We knew she would never do anything like that. We never thought this was something to follow. We saw it as, "Okay, Porsha, that was shady but let's move on." But Kandi would not let it go. She kept bringing it up, she kept talking about it.

We didn't get why this was becoming something bigger when we were all looking at it as nothing more than shade. It wasn't until Kandi said that she refused to be around Porsha because she thought Porsha was trying to ruin her brand that we got it. She was upset. She wanted to clear her name—and rightfully so, it's her reputation on the line. But it was unexpected for us.

Kandi Burruss: I was boiling mad at that point because I realized a person can say anything about you and just put it out there. I mean, how can someone say something like that with a straight face? I was like, "This bitch is trying to make me look like a lying, crazy person."

Carlos King: Porsha kept saying, "That's what I heard." But we had no idea who she heard it from. We were all perplexed. We kept asking, "Well, who did you hear it from?" But she wouldn't say. None of us knew. I left the show not even knowing. Believe me, if Porsha told us she heard it from Phaedra, we would have used it. That's not something you save for the reunion.

Cynthia Bailey: We filmed a whole season not knowing. And then at the reunion, Porsha said that Phaedra was the one who told her—which was just a total shock to all of us.

Andy Cohen: I was speechless.

Sezin Cavusoglu: That really was a watershed moment for this show. And it really was as raw as you saw. Our reactions in the control room as it was happening were exactly the same as the women's on the stage that day.

Carlos King: I'd guess the reason Porsha brought that up at the reunion was because she saw how the story line played out on the show, she saw what people were saying about *her* on social media, and she felt the need to tell her truth and save herself.

Cynthia Bailey: Once it was revealed that Phaedra was behind everything, Kandi was done. Kandi wanted no part of her. They had a genuine friendship for many years, but Kandi was devastated Phaedra would involve herself in a plot to take her down like that.

Kandi Burruss: Phaedra and I had gotten super close and had a lot of fun— Todd, Phaedra, Apollo, and I would all hang out as friends. But over the last two seasons, we started having a falling-out. She got mad when I told Andy she should take the kids to see Apollo in prison, and there was the whole thing of her saying she was upset about Apollo having his motorcycle at our house, as if we were letting him hide stuff from her. It was just a bunch of little things. But on this show, not only do you have the drama when it happens, but then it comes on TV and happens again, which makes it worse because the fans are chiming in, and then you have it again at the reunion and that makes it even worse. You never really have an opportunity to talk it through and dead the issue. So the things that were happening in seasons 7 and 8 were messed up in our friendship, but what happened in season 9 . . . to me that was the ultimate low.

Shereé Whitfield: I sat on the stage like everybody else with my mouth open, literally crying, because I couldn't believe it and was so upset.

Kandi Burruss: You know that feeling when you find something out about someone and it triggers your mind to go in reverse and think about every moment that person was sitting right there with you, and you didn't know they were the ones pulling the strings the entire time? That's how I felt about Phaedra. So that's why I was like, "Yeah, I can never come around her again or be involved with her or do business with her."

Cynthia Bailey: And then Phaedra blamed everything on Carlos King, saying that *he* had been the one who told her that.

Kandi Burruss: She blamed Carlos, but it was a fucking lie!

Carlos King: I never said anything to Phaedra about it, ever.

Kandi Burruss: I guess Porsha had a conversation with Phaedra right before the reunion to be like, "Are you sure Kandi said that to you?" And Phaedra said yes, so then when she blamed Carlos at the reunion, Porsha was like, "No, but you told me Kandi said that to you out of her own mouth."

Andy Cohen: None of us believed that was true. Phaedra had told Porsha she heard it from Kandi directly but was now pinning it on Carlos. It felt fishy.

Kandi Burruss: To be clear, I don't just blame Phaedra. I had issues with Porsha for a long time because I was like, "You knew what Phaedra said wasn't true." Like you know goddamn well that we had a moment where it could have gone there and nobody made you. So stop trying to say that you believe anything this woman told you. But the fact that Phaedra said this to Porsha off camera, and then came back and tried to be like, "Oh well, the producer told me to say it"? Hell no!

Cynthia Bailey: All I know is, Phaedra is one of the smartest women on the show. I don't know if God Himself could convince Phaedra to do something that she didn't want to do, let alone Carlos King.

Carlos King: By that point, I had left the show. The season was wrapped and both Bravo and Andy knew I was moving on from the show. So when the allegations were made that I told Phaedra that rumor, and people started saying I had been fired from Bravo because of it, I was furious.

Sezin Cavusoglu: Carlos was not fired. We loved working with Carlos. What Carlos brought to the show was just as important to *The Real Housewives of Atlanta*'s success as anything. But Carlos was going in his own direction. His production company was taking off and he wanted to work on his own projects. It was a natural parting of ways.

Carlos King: I'm usually a cool, easygoing guy, but I was shaking. I screamed, I cried. I thought my career was over. It was really bad. I remember Andy Cohen called my cell phone the day after filming the reunion and told me, "I just want you to know we do not believe this. We support you."

Cynthia Bailey: I just remember walking away from that reunion thinking, "Wow, this has gone to a scary level of lowness now. If people can just make up stuff that's hurtful to your character and your brand, and you have to watch it play out all season long, live on the TV and social media, before you can ever be vindicated, that's a problem. Because we're never going to get everyone to see the truth. So I got to be real careful now." A lot of people don't realize, those rumors stuck around for a long time. Not every viewer makes it to the reunion. I'll still hear people be like, "Oh, isn't Kandi the one who was trying to drug and rape Porsha?" Like, "You didn't see that that ended up being exposed to be not true?!" But it's still out there, on the Internet. It stays out there.

As a result, Phaedra was not asked to return to the cast for the show's tenth season.

Kandi Burruss: Nobody assured me Phaedra wouldn't be coming back. I just said, "I'm not going to be here if she's here, so if y'all want her to be here, that's fine. I'm just not going to be here." That was their own call, because obviously it wasn't just me she lied on—she lied on production. Either way, I knew I would never ever deal with her again.

Sezin Cavusoglu: I don't think it was a huge surprise for Phaedra. She saw it coming. She was caught red-handed at the reunion. Even when you watch that episode back today, you can see that she just gave up. She could have said some things to make it better, but she didn't. It was like she knew she could not come back from it. The whole situation was just beyond anything we had dealt with as a network before. It was important for us, at that moment, to show Kandi that we did not take what Phaedra did lightly.

Cynthia Bailey: I had no idea Phaedra would be fired. I knew it wasn't a good look, but she was a big player on the show. She had a great relationship with Andy. She had a great relationship with the network. She would come to work and she knew how to play her cards right. So I didn't know if this was big enough for them to do that.

Andy Cohen: I *loved* Phaedra on the show. She made me laugh as consistently as NeNe, which is saying something! And at the reunion I felt like she was letting her peach slip away before my eyes. I kept throwing her life preservers to try to save herself, to explain *why* she might've been so angry at Kandi to make something like that up, or to profusely apologize, but she couldn't save herself.

Cynthia Bailey: Andy pretty much all but said, "Girl, just apologize! Can you please just open your mouth and just say something, can you show some kind of remorse?" And she didn't. It was just the weirdest thing.

Sheree Whitfield: He kept asking her for an explanation, but she didn't have any.

Cynthia Bailey: Phaedra's a lawyer, so maybe she saw an apology to mean an admission of guilt? Maybe that's why she was stuck? Because I couldn't understand for the life of me why she just wouldn't apologize. Whereas Porsha got it right away. That is the one thing that saved her in the situation because a lot of people felt she was just as guilty. To this day Kandi wants no part of Phaedra.

Kandi Burruss: I'm glad she was able to go about her life and do what she got to do, I'm going about my life, but we just never need to communicate or do anything together ever again. Period.

Sezin Cavusoglu: Meanwhile, people always ask for Phaedra to come back—which I get. Fans miss her, and we miss her, too.

Kandi Burruss: I'll tell you what: if she comes back, you will not see me on this here show ever again.

Andy Cohen: A boy can dream. . . .

After an explosive season packed with headline-making allegations, producers turned to some familiar faces for its milestone tenth anniversary season, inviting NeNe and Kim back into the fold.

Sezin Cavusoglu: Going into season 10, the draw really was for us: "Let's bring the OGs back."

Sheree Whitfield: I don't know why they would bring the OGs back, when I was already there. But they brought Kim back as a Friend, which was nice. And then what's her name?

Sezin Cavusoglu: NeNe.

Sheree Whitfield: Yeah, NeNe.

Sezin Cavusoglu: With NeNe, when she left after season 7, we told her the door was always open. We said, "Do your thing, and whenever you want to come back, we're here."

Sheree Whitfield: I don't know why she came back, because we all loved filming without NeNe. It was amazing without her. Perfect, really. It was so easy! Because NeNe has a lot of negative energy, and it was nice to not have to deal with that.

Kenya Moore: When her show got canceled and she was actively looking for other work—which wasn't happening—that's when she decided to come back.

Sheree Whitfield: She came crawling back!

Kenya Moore: That's when she turned on me, by the way. Before it was like, "I don't mind passing the crown to you, I'm not going to be here. Go have at it, be down here with these reality stars. I'm over here in Hollywood." And when that didn't happen and she saw that her position was compromised, she changed.

Sheree Whitfield: We were cordial on camera, when NeNe returned. I don't kiss people's asses on camera but we learned over the years to just leave each other alone.

Andy Cohen: It felt like we were getting the old gang back together. As a fan of the show, just the idea of all of them in the same *room* together felt unprecedented.

Cynthia Bailey: When Kim came back, in my opinion, it was almost like you were starting over with a clean slate.

Sezin Cavusoglu: We missed that friendship between Kim and NeNe. And it looked like there was a door open where we could find a way back there. Obviously it didn't happen like that. . . .

Sheree Whitfield: The problem once again was Kim hanging out with Sheree. NeNe couldn't take it.

Cynthia Bailey: And Kim wasn't interested in us at all. When you come back, you have to recognize that you've been out of the house for a while. You can't come back and disrespect the house just because your room has been taken.

Sezin Cavusoglu: Every friendship you've seen fall apart on *Housewives* has to do with the show. Every single one. Somebody gets more famous than the other, or somebody is more popular and the other one catches up to her. We see these all the time. Jacqueline and Teresa. Bethenny and Jill. LeeAnne and D'Andra. That's what happened to NeNe and Kim.

Sheree Whitfield: NeNe's the one who started first. We showed up to her house party and she was going, "I can't believe Sheree brought Kim to my house when she wasn't invited!" But NeNe knew I was coming to her house with Kim. We were taping! But fans don't realize that. So they're like, "Yeah, that was shady of her to bring her to her house." This is why it's hard to be on the show. Fans start thinking a certain way and you can't say, "NeNe knew, the producers told her!" You have to take the beating and hope they hurry up and forget about it.

Lauren Eskelin: NeNe did *not* know Kim was coming to her house. That was very risky because NeNe could have reacted very badly, but she didn't. She was very gracious and welcoming. Kroy even came in with Brielle and joined Gregg and Brent.

Cynthia Bailey: For whatever reason, nobody really was feeling Kim except

Shereé. And then that didn't work out for Shereé because we were looking at her like she was crazy for not acknowledging the fact that Kim was being out of line with everybody.

Carlos King: Shereé, by that point, had been made a Housewife. She was a "Friend of" in season 8. Then in season 9, I rallied for her. I told the network, "I really want Shereé back full-time. I want her to be a Housewife. She delivered, she's got some great personal story line, and she's capable of handling it full-time." And I was right, because she came in that season and she was just fantastic. But by season 10, she became the bone collector.

Cynthia Bailey: The problem was, Shereé forgot to collect the biggest bone of all that year. Now how you gon' be the bone collector and do that?

> The "bone" in question was a video Kim's daughter shot during a visit to NeNe's new house, which showed a bug crawling in the reality star's bathroom. Kim showed the video to Shereé during a night out, claiming that NeNe had "roaches," but Shereé kept quiet about it. Later, Kim sent NeNe the clip while questioning the cleanliness of NeNe's home—sparking the biggest battle of the season, as well as claims that Kim was racist.

Sezin Cavusoglu: The women were split. NeNe felt like the roach comments were racially motivated. There were other people in the cast who knew Kim and did not necessarily think so.

Cynthia Bailey: I personally have never had any interaction with Kim where I felt as though she was being racist to me. Now I've definitely heard that she's done and said things to other people over the years, but she's always been very nice to me.

Sezin Cavusoglu: We always look to our Housewives to lead the way in these sorts of discussions. If a group of Black women say they felt something someone said was racist or racially motivated, I don't think it's up to us to argue otherwise. We have to honor that and hear that and accept that. Our position always is if there are these grievances, they need to be aired out and hashed out in a way that's hopefully constructive and can help change some of the behaviors moving forward. That's why we wanted to get into it at the reunion.

Shereé Whitfield: You guys didn't even get to see the half of it. They were being so horrible to Kim and bad to me because I was trying to protect Kim. It was almost like NeNe had gotten everyone together beforehand. Like, Porsha was coming for me, but Porsha and I never had a problem. NeNe gets in people's ears!

Sezin Cavusoglu: Kandi did a really good job of explaining things to Kim at the reunion in a way that could maybe help Kim understand. She was able to do it in a way that didn't come from anger or hate because she wasn't in that fight with NeNe and Kim. It was almost like an outside POV to lay this bare at Kim's feet.

To no one's surprise, the reunion wound up being Kim's last appearance on Housewives.

Sezin Cavusoglu: After that season, Kim felt like her own show is where she wants to be. The safety her husband Kroy provides, her kids provide, her house provides, she needs that. *Don't Be Tardy* has a very different flavor than *Housewives*. It's basically a half-hour family comedy. *Housewives*, you're getting Kim Zolciak; *Don't Be Tardy*, you're getting Kim Biermann. And Kim's return to *Housewives* in season 10 reminded her which Kim she wants to be.

Cynthia Bailey: I still don't know what Kim's strategy was, but she just came in very negative. Like, guns blazing, for no reason. She was clearly coming for Kenya—which, no surprise, a lot of people come for Kenya—but she was saying shady stuff about all of us.

Andy Cohen: I just remember Kroy yelling at me in the bathroom after the reunion, telling me I didn't protect Kim enough, or focus on enough positive things that had happened to her that season on the show. I sheepishly said, "Well, there was really nothing positive to focus on." It was the only time during this whole run where I ever felt like I was going to get punched. I thought, "This is it, dude, there are so many Housewives and husbands who are tired of your shady shit and you're about to get your reckoning." What I'm relieved I didn't know at the time was that Kroy had a gun with him that day (Georgia is an open-carry state) and production made him leave it in the car.

Sezin Cavusoglu: I have to say, in a perverse way, it gave us closure on the friendship and closure on Kim that we didn't get when she left in season 5. It felt like a very definitive end to Kim and NeNe's friendship.

Unfortunately, Kim wasn't the only one to leave RHOA that season. Sheree's time as a Housewife was over, again.

Sheree Whitfield: They asked me to come back in season 11, but as a Friend. "You can come back as a Friend again and when the season gets going, you may end up being a Housewife. You can always be upgraded." And

I said to myself, "Do I need to prove myself again? Because I've already proven myself. If you don't want me to be a Housewife now after everything I brought to the table, then we don't need to do this."

And right behind Sheree came another shocking RHOA exit. After six seasons as a Housewife, Kenya Moore was MIA.

Sezin Cavusoglu: The problem with Kenya was, she went off and got married two weeks before we started filming season 10. It was just such a blatant "screw you" to all of us. This is a woman we watched on the show from day one looking for love, wanting to get settled, wanting a husband, wanting a baby. And after following that journey, all those years, she went and did it without us. We were happy for her but at the same time, it didn't sit right with anyone at the network for us to then not have any access to Marc Daly. We realized at the end of season 10 that it wasn't going to work out with Kenya for season 11. She needed time away to be a wife and to have her baby and do life without the show for a little bit. And when she returned in season 12, she gave us a lot about her marriage. Obviously, none of it went the way any of us hoped it would go, which was heartbreaking to see, but I'm really grateful that she put it on camera.

Kenya may not have been around in season 11, but there were a few new girls to help stir things up. First, Eva Marcille—a mom and multifaceted entertainer known to reality TV fans as the cycle 3 winner of America's Next Top Model. *She had been in the mix on RHOA since halfway through season 10, as a Friend.*

Eva Marcille (Housewife): My agent called and said *Housewives* was interested. At the time, I'd been living in L.A. but my now husband was running for mayor of Atlanta and I had been in Atlanta for, like, eight months. I had a lot of connections to the group through the entertainment industry and knew NeNe personally.

Sezin Cavusoglu: Eva was someone who had organic connections to our cast, but she hadn't even moved to Atlanta full-time yet when we started filming with her. And one of the things we look for when we're casting Housewives is for someone to have real footing in that city, so we decided to bring her on as a Friend to see where she would end up. You know, her now husband—who was her fiancé at the time—was running for mayor, so there was a chance she could be the First Lady of Atlanta, which would have been amazing, although very complicated for us to shoot. But there was also a chance, if he lost, that she would move back to L.A. at the end of the season. So we weren't comfortable enough to commit, even though we loved her and wanted her around.

Eva Marcille: I was not there five minutes and they were pulling me into some mess with Cynthia and her boyfriend. It was so dumb. I knew some of them might like to fight, but I assumed the women were just going to let me be on the side and smoke my little vape and chill. But oh no, that was not the case.

Sezin Cavusoglu: She wound up moving to Atlanta full-time, getting married, having kids. And once we saw roots were being put down, it was a no-brainer to bring her on as a full-time Housewife in season 11.

Eva Marcille: I struggled a bit to navigate because I didn't fit into any box that existed before. Like, on these shows, there is a company person, a villain, a girl next door . . . I was none of those things, and didn't want any of those roles. That's why I was so taken aback all the time. It felt so foreign.

Sezin Cavusoglu: Eva was a great Housewife. Not only did she fit in with the cast, but she also stood out. She beats her own drum. She didn't try to portray herself as something she's not. In group situations, she really found her voice. She didn't hold back from giving her opinions, and formed good bonds with these women, especially Cynthia.

Eva Marcille: You gotta remember the first time I did reality television, it was a competition-based show, *America's Next Top Model*. That was extremely new, and we lived together for three months in the same house. But everything was centered around a structured competition on a given day. We were trying to make it to the next level of this "game," and the drama between us was just the filler. So going into *Housewives*, obviously I knew it wasn't a competition, but I thought they were just gonna follow whatever it is we did in life. Like, I didn't realize the beast that it was to do this kind of reality show. I had no clue.

> *Eva wound up being promoted from a Friend to a full-time Housewife in season 11 but departed the series at the end of season 12.*

Sezin Cavusoglu: With Eva, it was a mutual parting of ways.

Eva Marcille: I'm not green. I understand that there needs to be some level of spice and drama. I just don't think I'm willing to give this genre the kind of drama they want. I can't generate it. With the climate of the world right now—the way Black women are on the front lines of social change and racial change and equity for so many people across the board—I had no guarantee that this show was going to dedicate a season to trying to eradicate that at all costs.

Sezin Cavusoglu: There were a lot of things in Eva's life that were off-limits. She wasn't opening up very much in her personal life. She found a house and moved while everybody else was on a cast trip. We weren't getting a lot of Michael or her home life. And it felt like, "Okay, maybe Eva's life is moving in a different direction."

Eva Marcille: I'm glad I stepped away from reality TV when I did because unless you have a proper handle on this, it can literally ruin the best of the people, the best friendships, and the best relationships.

> *Another new Housewife—Shamari DeVoe, a married mother of two, best known as the lead singer in the R&B group Blaque—joined Eva as a full-time Housewife in season 11, though she only lasted one season.*

Shamari DeVoe (Housewife): They reached out to me for season 10, but at the time I declined because I was pregnant with my twin boys and I didn't want any extra stress. But when they came back the following year, I figured I'd give it a shot. Kandi and I were label mates at Columbia Records at one point, and she did the remix for Blaque's first single, "808." And Porsha, we were on the drill team at Southwest Dekalb High School together.

Sezin Cavusoglu: Shamari had the best energy. And we loved that she had natural ties to some of the cast members. Plus, her husband, Ronnie DeVoe, of New Edition and Bell Biv DeVoe fame, was big in the music community.

Shamari DeVoe: Ronnie didn't really want me to do the show in the first place because of the drama and the cattiness that comes with reality TV. He knew that it was just going to be a lot of conflict. But we figured this would be a great opportunity to have a platform for our marriage ministry. We wanted to be transparent about the challenges we faced in our relationship and how we overcame them, to help save other couples with similar stresses.

Sezin Cavusoglu: We loved having her around, and she and Ronnie were really honest about their marriage—you know, how they had started an open relationship because Shamari was bi-curious. But unfortunately, the women on the cast just didn't take to her. She couldn't connect with the larger group.

Shamari DeVoe: When you're on a show like this, you really feel the pressure to be confrontational and stir up drama, because that's what people want to see. But I was more interested in having fun.

Sezin Cavusoglu: We kept watching, hoping she would build those bonds, and she never did. And that comes from the women, not us. She just didn't gel. And Shamari also knew it wasn't working. I don't think there were any hard feelings or anything.

> *And then there was Tanya Sam, a tech-savvy businesswoman and philanthropist, whose Canadian roots helped her stand out from the crowd. She was considered a potential Housewife, but . . .*

Tanya Sam (Friend): A casting agent had been pinging me on my social media—Instagram, LinkedIn, etc.—trying to get my attention, but I had been ignoring it because a) I thought it was fake and b) I just wasn't interested. And then I was at a dinner party sitting beside Mariah Carey's then manager, Stella Bulochnikov, and she said, "What? Are you kidding me? Of course you should do this! You're stupid."

Sezin Cavusoglu: We liked that Tanya was so different from the women we normally meet. She has such great energy—a ball of positivity. And she's very analytical.

Tanya Sam: I had watched as a casual fan on and off over the years, but I would lose at a *Housewives* trivia game for sure. So I said, "Okay, let me go study this *Housewives* show!" And I was like, "Ahh, there's a formula here. They always have boobs out. They usually wear some sort of godawful necklace. . . ."

Sezin Cavusoglu: With Tanya, we wanted to make her a full-time Housewife but we could not agree on a contract.

Tanya Sam: We were negotiating a peach—and the offer was there—but we figured out pretty early on that there would be no way to get past some structural thing in the full-time contract around businesses and exposure of businesses on camera. So I was like, "You know what? I don't have time to go back and forth arguing with you and you wasting my lawyer's time and money. I don't want the Housewife contract. But I can test these waters as a Friend?"

Sezin Cavusoglu: I really like Tanya in the Friend role. She's able to build genuinely close relationships with the women, and it's great to have her around. She also has a very full life that we wouldn't have access to if she was full-time, so I don't think we'd get the well-rounded picture we want.

Tanya Sam: As much as I love being on the show, I'm a business person before I'm on *The Real Housewives of Atlanta*. That's something I'm much more protective of. It was a very easy decision for me!

> *Despite some new blood in the mix and the lack of her longtime foe Kenya, season 11 wound up being a tough one for NeNe as she struggled to take care of her husband, Gregg, amid his battle with stage 3 colon cancer. She hit her breaking point during a "Bye Wig" party, when she ripped a cameraman's shirt as he followed Porsha and Kandi into her closet, even though she had explicitly asked them all to stay outside.*

Marlo Hampton: That was a nightmare. There was a lot going on in her head. It was Gregg, it was the alcohol.

Sezin Cavusoglu: The closet situation was stressful. Obviously, she ripped the cameraman's shirt. And one of our producers went to the hospital, I believe, to get checked out. It was scary.

Marlo Hampton: NeNe's closet is fucking amazing. Even when it's junky, it's amazing. It's a whole damn studio apartment! I wouldn't care, but she just felt something was out and she didn't want someone—or the TV—to see it that way. You have to respect that. But it got a little out of hand.

Sezin Cavusoglu: NeNe really feels like *The Real Housewives of Atlanta* is her show and nobody else's. Behind the scenes, she'll tell you that she made the show. And she brings a lot of that energy to her dealings with Bravo, with Truly, with showrunners, and with costars.

Marlo Hampton: You saw her grab the cameraman's shirt but there was a lot more that night. There was yelling and fussing. It was a whole lot.

Sezin Cavusoglu: That season, NeNe was genuinely having a hard time with Gregg's illness. There was a lot going on in her personal life that I have a lot of sympathy for. But you could see she also had a lot of frustrations and disappointments with the show. She felt like she wasn't being treated the way she wanted to be. And the closet incident was almost the capper of that. And again, it was that thing of showing no remorse about it that was upsetting. Because our crew works so hard. They're there for these women all the time. So that really should not happen. And there should have been an apology, but we didn't really see that from NeNe.

If you remember, at the reunion, she completely shut down. She wouldn't acknowledge any of her castmates' feelings or her behavior. It was upsetting.

Andy Cohen: That was one of several reunions where NeNe completely shut down. I asked her a hundred questions and got no energy back.

Shereé Whitfield: NeNe can dish it out but she can't take it.

Sezin Cavusoglu: NeNe also really believed that all these girls were coming for her crown. I promise you, those girls were not ganging up on her. They were not in an alliance. They did not have a plot to take her down. But she wanted everyone to respect her as the queen bee and for them to show up and treat her as such.

Andy Cohen: The queen bee stuff gets exhausting in any city.

> *Just when NeNe thought it couldn't get worse, Kenya made a surprise appearance at the season 11 finale. She was there to surprise her pal Cynthia, but NeNe believed Cynthia knew Kenya was coming and set her up.*

Cynthia Bailey: I don't like to break the fourth wall. I don't like to throw production under the bus, because I know they are there to be messy and to get a good TV show. But you cannot make someone look like a liar. And that was very hard for me at the reunion. One of the main reasons NeNe and I fell out was because she felt like I knew Kenya was coming and didn't give her a heads-up. Now, and I've always said this, I invited Kenya, without question. But she said she wasn't coming. Why did she say she wasn't coming? Because she wasn't getting paid to come. She wasn't part of the cast, she didn't want to come and film, she was not in a good place with the network. Fast-forward to, she shows up with Kandi, who got her to come and surprise me. Then you see me whispering in Mike's ear but you don't hear me saying anything.

> *NeNe's last few years on the show were tough. She spent season 12 on an apology tour, rebuilding her friendships with many of the women, so fans were surprised when the virtual Zoom reunion ended with her walking off in a fury.*

Lauren Eskelin: She did not like how she had been treated at that reunion—like when she came to the reunion wearing black, and all of the women were in white. She blames us for letting her be the only one not wearing white, which was not at all the way it went down. They were all going to wear white when we were going to do the in-person reunion, but that reunion got canceled because of COVID-19. So when we decided to Zoom-union, we just told the women to find a gown of their own and they all came wearing white. Whether they had their own group text about that or not, and whether NeNe saw the group text or not, I don't know. But it wasn't our call.

Kandi Burruss: The possibility of wearing white was brought up, but nobody really confirmed it. Obviously me and Kenya, we talk all the time, so I knew she was wearing white. I knew Cynthia was talking about wearing white, as was Eva. And I decided to wear white. But I don't think it was a discussion between everybody; it just so happened that other people were having their own discussions and they all showed up in white, too. I guess nobody gave NeNe the memo, so when she came on the computer, she was wearing black and it just made her look like she was bucking the system.

Kenya Moore: And she was upset that Kandi got all those spin-offs and she didn't.

Kandi Burruss: I just didn't like the negativity and hate because when it comes to anything anyone does, I always try to support. I always try to post, even when we don't get along. I'm not upset when Porsha gets opportunities, I think that's dope for her. NeNe was the first one out of us to get opportunities, none of us got upset. But it was just, like, this unnecessary negativity coming toward me, and I just feel like it wasn't cool. I was just sick and tired of it, you know?

Sezin Cavusoglu: NeNe had a wedding spin-off, and we tried to do a spin-off show with NeNe and Kim called *NeNe and Kim: The Road to Riches*. It was going to be almost like *The Simple Life*. This was back in 2015; NeNe wasn't coming back for season 8, and we thought this could be a really fun way to bring these two stars back together. The problem was, they weren't in a great place behind the scenes and NeNe decided she didn't want to do it.

Cynthia Bailey: See, I don't know why NeNe didn't have her own show on Bravo. She has all of this personality and she has all these things going on. I've always just been waiting for that announcement.

NeNe announced she would not be returning to the show for season 13, along with a flurry of accusations against the network.

Lauren Eskelin: She had an offer to come back as a Housewife in season 13. The back-and-forth and negotiations just took forever, and ultimately she was not feeling that coming back was the right thing for her. We had many tearful conversations about it, and about the way she felt she had been treated at the season 12 reunion, which upset her.

Sheeé Whitfield: It's like she forgets that she tried to get everyone on the show fired. If you did not get along with her, she'd go out there and say you should not be here. So now that *you're* not here and they don't want *you*, you say that *you* were done wrong? It's like, "Girl, you were one Black girl trying to sabotage every other Black girl on here! Are you crazy?"

Claudia Jordan: Don't hijack the real movement of social justice that's happening in our country right now because of your personality short-comings. Just because you don't get a spin-off doesn't mean it's racism, it means they don't want to see that much of you. Certainly the network, if they thought they could make a lot of money off your spin-off, they probably would have done it. Why would they not? Networks are about money!

Kandi Burruss: For years, NeNe has preached to everybody about how she was the highest-paid woman for the network, regardless of whether that was true or not. Some people said I was the highest paid; I'm certainly not comparing our coins. What I do know is that *RHOA* is the most popular franchise on the network and those of us who've been on it for a long time, we're all paid more than most of the other Housewives. And we're all Black. So you can't say, "Oh yeah, we make the most money" and then when you get mad say, "You're racist!" You know what I'm saying?

Sheeé Whitfield: It's strange, because now NeNe's talking about how she was treated unfairly, whereas a lot of us who were on the show with her feel like it was not equal because they would always cater to *her*. NeNe always had the upper hand. They bent over backward for her. She would talk to the producers and the network like shit, but they allowed NeNe to get away with a lot of stuff.

Lauren Eskelin: Regarding NeNe having the upper hand with producers, I will say that is always the impression cast members have when another cast member is more vocal. Just because a cast member is demanding with producers does *not* mean producers prioritize that cast member over the others, but the others often assume that to be true. It's inevitable with an ensemble. But the truth is, producers balance the demands of all cast members.

Andy Cohen: I'm really sad about how my relationship with NeNe played out. There's been no one in the run of Housewives who I've celebrated more or has made me laugh as much as NeNe. No one! Through some of the negativity, there was so much humor, heart, and, I thought, a real friendship and mutual respect. I loved her and celebrated her publicly, much—I'm sure—to the chagrin of her costars. The year 2020 was a horrible year for so many reasons, but the dissolution of my relationship with NeNe was absolutely heartbreaking to me.

Kenya Moore: I believe NeNe's problem is insecurity. This is a woman who used to be a stripper, single mom, struggling, doing all kinds of things to find an older gentleman to basically get her out of the strip club, legitimize her, buy her nice things or give her a certain lifestyle, and then put her on a platform on which she became famous overnight. Because *Real Housewives* made her. It didn't make Kandi; it did not make Cynthia; it did not make me; it didn't make Eva. Quite honestly, it didn't make Phaedra because she was an attorney, and she was known in that world. Then you take your Porshas and your NeNes; the show literally made them, and so they come in differently. They cling to it more than somebody who can say, "Well, I'll get another job. This is a launching pad, not the pinnacle of my career."

Lauren Eskelin: I adore NeNe. It's not fun to see somebody leave feeling so unhappy about their experience on the show. Especially somebody who is a founder of the show and a trailblazer of reality TV. She put her everything into this show and has become an icon. That's very hard to choose to walk away from.

Andy Cohen: When NeNe was "on," there was no one better. She was the show's greatest cheerleader and star, and sometimes its biggest public detractor. I think her relationship with the show ultimately became toxic and she wasn't loving it like she once had. She was great for a *long* time, though!

Cynthia Bailey: Leaving the show doesn't take away from her success. Like, when you ask me about NeNe Leakes, the only thing I'm ever going to consistently say is she's great TV. She was hands down the breakout star of *Real Housewives of Atlanta*. I'm always going to give her her props. She never has to give me mine—she can call me boring until the day I die, and I could care less. You think of *Real Housewives of Atlanta*, you think of NeNe Leakes.

Eva Marcille: NeNe and I are not the best of friends but listen, I don't kick nobody when they're down. NeNe definitely was instrumental in building the machine that is what we are talking about right now. She has everything to do with the greatness that is the show.

Lauren Eskelin: But sometimes, the story is just done and it's time to move on. It's hard not to be sad and nostalgic about that, but that's the reality of it. The only way these shows continue is if they evolve, and the only way they evolve is if there's movement in the cast. Kenya, Porsha, Cynthia, Kandi—eventually, they'll all move on, as they should.

As Atlanta's *success continues on, its legacy is not lost on its creators and stars.*

Sezin Cavusoglu: I feel like *Real Housewives of Atlanta* is one of the more important shows on Bravo.

Andy Cohen: No show has made me laugh more or given us more fodder for fun on *WWHL*.

DeShawn Snow: To be part of something so groundbreaking? I'm beyond proud. But I'm even more proud of how the show has evolved into this phenomenon. It's so entertaining. The women, the reads—they always make me laugh. They're hilarious. And the audience has embraced them so, so much.

Cynthia Bailey: There's no fame like *Housewives* fame. I remember driving my daughter to school and passing through the drive-through to get McDonald's breakfasts. The lady who was ringing us up flipped out. "It's you! You're the model! I saw you on TV last night!" It was instant celebrity. I was well known in the fashion industry, but never this level of famous.

Kandi Burruss: I was apprehensive because *Real Housewives of Atlanta* caught a lot of flak after the first season, especially from the African American community, because they were like, "Oh, it's painting Black women in a bad light and that we weren't represented well as far as television is concerned." So when I would mention that I was thinking about joining the show a lot of people were like, "Oh, don't do that! That's not a good look! You should never be a part of something like that!" And I was like, "Well, I don't understand. If you feel that the women that are on the show don't really represent well for Black people, and you feel that I am a good representation of a Black person, why wouldn't you want me to be a part of the show?" So I just went ahead and did it . . . and it's turned out all right to me!

Sheree Whitfield: It's amazing to be part of this legacy. When they first pitched the show I was like, "Okay, a show about mostly wealthy African American women. I don't know about this." But there are so many people who would say, "I never thought Black people lived like that!" I don't know if they thought we were all in the projects, but it helped people see Black people in a new way.

Sezin Cavusoglu: Through the years, it's given a platform to so many really strong, powerful, beautiful Black women. I love how our cast has changed over the years; how they're not afraid to show us the good, the bad, and the ugly.

Sheree Whitfield: We were able to share our stories. And so many people related to a lot of things we've gone through. I have people all the time tell me, "I've gone through a divorce. I've had to fight for child support. I'm dating someone in jail." They've been in the same predicaments.

Sezin Cavusoglu: Representation matters. This is why it upsets me how much the press leans on a few negative moments or a few negative interactions. Because our show is so much more than that.

Sheree Whitfield: I will admit though . . . I never thought it would ever go past *Atlanta*. I never thought in a million years that *Housewives* would be this big. I was thinking, "They'll do *OC*, *New York*, and *Atlanta*. That'll be it." What did I know!

PART IV

"Flipping the Table"

The Real Housewives of New Jersey

PREMIERE DATE: MAY 12, 2009

Family offered a new spin on the Housewives.
—ANDY COHEN

Dina Manzo (Housewife): It all kind of stemmed from Chateau Salon. I went there, Jacqueline went there, Danielle went there. Victor, the owner, said to me, "I've been approached to find some girls." At the time, they were saying it was a show called *Jersey Girls* and it was about women who could do it all.

Jacqueline Laurita (Housewife): My five-year-old son was entering into full-day school that year and I was a little bored, so I was ready to go back to work.

Lucilla D'Agostino (Executive Vice President of Programming and Founding Partner, Sirens Media): We were calling it something like *The Ladies of New Jersey*—the kind of boring working title you give a show when you don't want to acknowledge that maybe it'll be a *Real Housewives* show.

> *Jacqueline and Dina were a win for casting. Not only were they close friends, but they were also sisters-in-law, with Jacqueline married to Dina's brother, Chris Laurita.*

Lucilla D'Agostino: We loved the sister-in-law angle—sort of the outsider in the close-knit family. She had to always be aware of that unspoken line and navigate those complicated relationships.

Jacqueline Laurita: I liked the thought of making money while just living my life, so, after a long negotiation, I signed on.

Lucilla D'Agostino: As for Dina, she was very glamorous. She was that pretty girl in high school with a nice car and good hair. It seemed like everything would go right for a girl like Dina. Yet she also had this mysterious husband who was never around.

Dina Manzo: We were going through issues. When we were casting, I caught my husband cheating. So I was sitting there in my preinterview saying, "My husband and I are going to remain friends, but we're getting separated." Then when I forgave him and we were back together, I told Andy Cohen, "You need to burn that casting reel. I said things in the heat of the moment of a scorned woman."

Carlos King: I had just come from *Atlanta*, and when I met Dina, I saw NeNe-like star quality. There's nothing like a pretty woman who is snarky, because it shows you she has personality and spunk. If Dina would have stayed on that show, I promise you Dina Manzo would have been a legend. Dina Manzo would have been among the greats.

> *From there, Jacqueline and Dina began recruiting—though they didn't go far. Jacqueline quickly recommended her other sister-in-law, Caroline Manzo, a fiercely loyal and perhaps overprotective mother of three who always put family first.*

Lucilla D'Agostino: Caroline and Dina are sisters. Caroline's older, but they're like, two of eleven children. And they happened to marry brothers, which was obviously a unique story to tell.

Andy Cohen: It was so confusing to me that Caroline and Dina were sisters. They looked nothing alike. And they were married to brothers. I couldn't wrap my head around it.

Lucilla D'Agostino: The thing that made it exciting was that this was now shaping up to be a group of women, most of whom happened to be from an Italian cultural background, who not only lived within a seven-mile radius of one another but who were also mostly related.

Andy Cohen: *The Sopranos* was big at the time, and here we had a cast made up of real Jersey Italian women. They spoke the language of New Jersey. Family offered a new spin on the *Housewives*.

Shari Levine: What did Caroline say? "Blood is thicker than water"? That made the series compelling in a totally different way because you can't get away from family. Those bonds are very deep and can be quite tortured. Everybody relates to that.

Lucilla D'Agostino: Plus, unlike all of the other cities that had called themselves *Real Housewives*, these were actual stay-at-home moms—they were *real* Real Housewives. They made their families dinner every night and cleaned their own homes. They had the kinds of problems that come with being sisters and sisters-in-law and mothers—it wasn't a glimpse behind the gates of glamorous McMansion communities like you got on some of the other franchises.

Caroline Manzo (Housewife): When they were doing the audition tapes, they were at Jacqueline's house and she said to them, "You really should go see my sister." When she called and told me, I said, "Jacqueline, what am I going to do with that?" At that point, I didn't know anything about *Housewives*, but I didn't think it was a good fit. By the time I hung up the phone, they were at my door because Jacqueline literally lives down the block. So I just pointed to my chest and said, "These are real. And I love my husband. I don't belong on reality TV." But they wanted to film anyway, and I'm the kind of person who's, like, "You're here, you unpacked all your stuff, I won't be rude, just do it."

Lucilla D'Agostino: What I loved about Caroline was that she was like that sane sage we all know in families like this. The person you go to on the side like the consigliere to ask, "What should I do?"

Andy Cohen: Caroline reminded us of Edie Falco as Carmela Soprano. And her family was funny. I mean, in the original casting, her son Chris Manzo talked about wanting to open a car wash strip club. You know, they just popped.

Caroline Manzo: My husband said to me, "Do me one favor: Do not try to be anything but yourself. I love you the way you are. Just be you." And I was like, "Well, I can't sell anything but me. So if you're looking for the person with heels and makeup and glamour, you got the wrong girl."

Lucilla D'Agostino: Caroline was not trying to say she was glamorous. She was not trying to say she was rich. She was a hardworking woman with a really strong opinion. You hadn't seen that type of Housewife yet. Instead of bragging about her cars and her houses, she was bragging about her kids.

Among the girls gathered were two friends from Paterson, New Jersey: a sweet stay-at-home mom of four named Teresa Giudice, and Dolores Catania, a divorced mother of two and tough-as-nails former cop.

Dina Manzo: I recommended Teresa and Dolores.

Teresa Giudice (Housewife): Dina told the producers about me. They were looking for beautiful women with beautiful houses who had it all going on.

Lucille D'Agostino: There were a thousand things we loved about Teresa. She was obsessed with her kids, dressing them in bows and taking pictures of them. And her husband, Joe, was the guy you see in the movies about New Jersey—this hardworking, blue-collar guy in construction, trying to give his family everything he thought they deserved. These people worked very hard. People make fun of New Jersey, but Teresa was building this castle of a house, and she was proud of it!

Jacqueline Laurita: I talked Teresa into joining. She was reluctant at first, but I knew she was a character, so I was persistent and got her to sign.

Dina Manzo: We were all friends. Teresa and Dolores, they'd known each other since they were kids.

Dolores Catania (Housewife): Teresa was doing it, and Dina and I were very close back then.

Jacqueline Laurita: Dolores Catania was almost one of our cast members, but she backed out because her boyfriend at the time didn't like the idea of her doing it.

Dolores Catania: I backed out because after I had my first interview, they started asking me all these questions about my friends. Back then, friends were friends—I would never say anything bad about my friends. But the next day I got a call from Jacqueline and Teresa, both saying, "What did you say about my husband?" That's when I was like, "You know what? I'm out. I don't want to do this. I don't like the way it feels."

With Dolores out, a space on the cast opened up, one that would be filled by one of the most talked-about figures in Housewives *history.*

Dina Manzo: There was room for one more, so I said to Victor, "What about that girl that goes to the salon, Danielle?" Because they were always telling us stories of this woman who came to the salon. And Victor was like, "You don't want her."

Jacqueline Laurita: I suggested Danielle because the scouters liked the idea of recruiting a single divorced mother to the group. Dina had heard she was a wack-a-doo, which I figured would most likely make good TV.

Danielle Staub (Housewife): I went for my hair color at Chateau Salon, and in came the characters who would in the future be known as the cast of *The Real Housewives of New Jersey*. I was at the tail end of a six-and-a-half-year divorce, but at the time, I was still pretty loaded up with my gems and was driving a different car almost every day because nothing had been liquidated or divided from the divorce. So apparently they were watching me and I didn't even know.

Dina Manzo: Jacqueline and I were supposed to take her out to lunch to kind of see if she was good crazy or bad crazy, but instead Jacqueline went to the salon and saw Danielle sitting there and was like, "You want to be on TV?"

Jacqueline Laurita: Of course Danielle was interested.

Danielle Staub: Had I not just gotten divorced, I would have never ever signed on for anything like this. But Jacqueline was quick to become my friend, and she was very insistent on me doing this. I was looking for something new. These women led me to believe we'd be a group of friends and this would be a good time for all. So I said to my kids, I said, "What do you think?" They were like, "Well, you need new friends." Famous last words.

Carlos King: I was mesmerized by Danielle. She had a lot of baggage that she was open about, and it was interesting to dig deep and peel back the layers with her.

Lucilla D'Agostino: In my opinion, Danielle was one of the most fascinating characters. She was truly the outsider. She was going through a horrible divorce, and raising these two daughters by herself. So you have a single mom and then you have this close-knit family that's going to rally around one another come hell or high water. Put that all together at a dinner table and you have a real interesting cross section.

With the cast in place, Bravo ordered the show to series as the fourth install-ment in the Real Housewives *franchise.*

Jacqueline Laurita: When we were finally told it was a *Real Housewives* franchise, I watched the first season of *Orange County* and decided I would be fine doing a show like that. I really didn't think anyone would watch it. But I was very open with my life anyway, so I was fine with it.

Dina Manzo: I was a fan of *Orange County*, but we were signing our con-tracts just as *Atlanta* started airing, and I knew the direction of that show was different than *OC*. So when they told us, "Guess what, we're going to be part of this franchise," my stomach just dropped.

Carlos King: When you are an Italian family, you don't just electively spread your business to a bunch of strangers. So season 1, it was very protective. It was very much like, "I'm only going to give you what I want you to know."

Lucilla D'Agostino: There are little moments of that first season that are burned into my brain, like Danielle walking around her pool in high heels and a bikini. That was pure, classic Danielle. That, in my opinion, is one of the best Housewife entrances in season 1 of any *Housewives* show.

Carlos King: And when Teresa went on that all-cash shopping spree—that was her own money. We didn't think she would bring that much money. We were like, "Oh, stacks on stacks. Okay, get it, girl." We were floored. At that time, of course none of us in production is thinking like, "There's some shady shit going on behind the scenes." We just thought she was a rich bitch.

Lucilla D'Agostino: I was always trying to make a show that was about what was really happening. I wasn't trying to come up with fake country club scenes. I wasn't trying to throw fictitious white parties to entice women to get drunk and be the worst versions of themselves. I'm just trying to tell their story. And that's why I do love them all, because I know the humanity in every single one of them.

Carlos King: It's a learning experience when you first start these shows. Keep in mind I had only done one season of *Atlanta* at this point. But like the Atlanta Housewives, the Jersey girls quickly adapted. That had it.

Lucilla D'Agostino: The ladies were each iconic and unique in their own right. If we needed funny, we would always go to Jacqueline. If we needed someone to just tell the truth, no bullshit, and say what the viewer would say, that was Caroline. If you needed someone to deliver a line that was meme-worthy, cutting, super bitch, and delicious, it was Dina with her "She wants to skin me and wear me like last season's Versace." She was the girl you'd want to have brunch with because she's pretty and smart, but she's got a mouth. Teresa's in her own world. What comes out of Teresa's mouth! One time we told her we had to wrap up filming because a nor'easter was coming, and then she went on set and said, "You guys, we have to wrap up filming because a Norwegian is coming." And we put that in the show. It's not ditzy, but it's kind of like she's on her own fucking planet. And Danielle—a lot of people have burnt and hurt Danielle. As she got older, she found her voice, so when all of the other women were worried about looking too aggressive or too mouthy or too tough, Danielle would go in and say the thing you don't say.

But some of the things Danielle said gave Caroline and Dina pause. And soon, a rivalry grew between family and friend that left Jacqueline conflicted.

Carlos King: It was painfully obvious the Caroline and Dina didn't like Danielle. Painfully obvious. Dina doesn't have a poker face. So whenever they were in the same room, Dina's piercing, beautiful blue eyes would just go across the room and give Danielle the death stare. Everyone knew. Teresa tried to be cordial because Teresa was the sweet one. Jacqueline was Danielle's friend, so Jacqueline was in the middle between her sister-in-law and her girl. But we all knew that the Manzos did not like Danielle. Danielle was not paranoid.

Danielle Staub: In hindsight, I realize Dina was very worried that I was going to expose their family secrets.

Dina Manzo: I was so innocent. Like, my first husband was my first kiss, my first everything; I never even cursed until I was thirty. Danielle wanted some of that. Sometimes you hate people because they're a mirror of what you're not. That's why I was her target, because I was such a Goody Two-shoes.

Danielle Staub: Dina had a problem with me because she wasn't happy with herself. For some reason, I rubbed her the wrong way. But Jacqueline was a sweetheart. She was a pretty good friend to me. Not that I asked her to be, but she seemed very interested in my life. And I felt bad for Jacqueline. I felt like she wasn't being treated like a part of her own family. According to her side of the story, Caroline had a big opposition to Jacqueline and her mothering skills. She was being treated pretty unkind.

Not helping Danielle's footing in the group was Cop Without a Badge, *a 1996 book about the life of Danielle's felon-turned-informant ex-husband, Kevin Maher, that found its way into the hands of the Jersey Housewives. The tell-all inspired a sea of questions about Danielle's past, including her alleged run-ins with the law and her nineteen engagements.*

Dina Manzo: Here's what happened: We were at a party at the Brownstone, and I walked in the office and my niece Candace was at the computer and she's like, "You'll never guess what I found." A friend of hers tipped her off and said, "You might want to look into this Danielle character." Caroline and Jacqueline and I all crowded around the computer and we were shocked. So Caroline and her friends went to the library and got the book.

Carlos King: We kept asking them, "What is it about Danielle you girls don't like? We don't get it." Because it's hard to produce this show when everyone's just saying, "She's wacky." It needs to be deeper than that. So we were pushing them and that's when they said, "Read the book." We were five weeks into shooting the show before I heard a peep about this book.

And I was shocked because I was assigned to Danielle at that time and Danielle told me nothing about a fucking book!

Lucilla D'Agostino: It's not like we started off the first episode going, "This whole season is going to unfold about a book." We didn't know. And we were capturing it in real time. That's one of the things I miss so much about some of the reality shows I see nowadays—you can tell women come in with an agenda for the season. That first season of *New Jersey* was as organic as a reality television show can be.

Carlos King: The book was saying she had been through these terrible things. We were like, "We did not sign up for that shit. What the fuck is happening here?" We were all shocked.

Danielle Staub: I was hearing this buzz and I was like, "This doesn't make any sense. Why are they talking about that?" I didn't understand. I couldn't make the correlation of why this was relevant now. It was about me prior to turning twenty years old. We all have a past, but they tried to make it look like thirty years ago was my present.

Caroline Manzo: In my mind, if we figured out this was all ancient history, she wouldn't pose a threat. She might be a little crazy, but we could deal with crazy. I just didn't want to deal with dangerous. There was no malice toward her. It wasn't that we had our guns blazing to get her off the show or ruin her. But we were talking the Colombian drug cartel here; we were not talking jaywalking. It was us being responsible adults doing our due diligence to figure out who this person was and say, "What's going on? Is the cartel going to come after her once she's out and about on television?" According to the story, she turned in some very big people in that world, and now she was living the high life and showing off her wealth and her mansion on TV. I would have to believe that there's some sour grapes along the way. So my question was, "How sour are they?" It was a matter of protecting ourselves against something that could possibly turn very bad.

Danielle Staub: It was written by an ex. Think about that for a minute. Who wants an ex's letter read out loud? And not just a current letter, a letter from many, many years ago. This guy basically wrote a journal. But they weren't looking for proof of anything. Nobody was giving me the benefit of the doubt, and I didn't feel like this was going to go good for me any way I approached it. Defending it was a mistake. Not defending it was a mistake. I was starting to become a complete outsider.

Carlos King: I could see why Danielle would think this was all unfair. In her eyes, these women were behind her back, digging up dirt on her and bringing up the deepest, darkest secrets that she didn't want out. Now, what their intention was is up for public fodder. But as producers, we had to follow the reality. The reality was that these girls felt this book was their proof that this woman on the show with them wasn't stable.

Caroline Manzo: As we investigated, we saw her personality start to emerge. We were all like, "Guys, listen, this has got to be looked at."

Lucilla D'Agostino: It was the first time that any *Housewives* show had this kind of plot—it was like a show on Investigation Discovery. It was an investigation.

Danielle Staub: The things that they were starting to gather up about my life were things that I'd already put to rest. It's like a suitcase. You pack that suitcase and it's packed up nice and neat. You know where it is. You know where it's stored. When you're ready to pack it, you want to pack it slowly and carefully because each part of that is a trigger. Each part of that is your memory. For whatever reason, you packed it up. It's yours to pack up and keep packed until you're ready to unpack it. The ladies decided to unpack a bag that, quite frankly, they didn't know where any of the belongings went. So they just applied it where they needed it to hide behind and make people laugh at me. It was to bully and humiliate me. The moment I started to see all my things scattered about, I started to feel shame, guilt, uneasiness. All these things I had put away.

Lucilla D'Agostino: Would it have been better for Danielle if no one ever found that book? One hundred percent. But there was no way once everyone found out about the book that they weren't going to talk about it.

Dina Manzo: Caroline always had the book in her purse. We'd be at a party that had nothing to do with the show and she'd start telling people about it.

Danielle Staub: You can bet your bottom dollar that the judge who granted me full custody didn't think my past was a big issue. So why was it that these four complete strangers felt entitled to give that perception?

Caroline Manzo: Because of the show, we were inserting ourselves in this woman's life. Then we read something like this—and then when we Googled it, it was crazier than what we read in the book. How do you not address that?

Danielle Staub: They did that to me because I was beautiful. I was strong. I was getting out there on my own, raising two daughters after being treated like a queen by my husband. I was strong enough to walk away from something that wasn't working with two kids in tow.

Teresa Giudice: Back then I was very naïve, so as I heard all this about Danielle, I was like, "Oh my God!" But I always judge people for who they are at the present time when I meet them; I don't really judge them based on their past. 'Cause she was cool to hang out, I had fun with her, I liked her at first, you know? I did.

Carlos King: We all felt bad for Danielle in season 1. Everybody in the world knows what it feels like to be isolated. Danielle just wanted to be with the cool kids, and when the cool kids don't want to be around you, your feelings are hurt. The audience would have received it and understood it if she was able to articulate it that way: "I just want to belong and I feel like I'm not belonging in this situation." But because she went to the dark side, it was really hard for the audience to have any sympathy.

> *The rising tensions surrounding the book culminated in an epic moment that would reverberate throughout the* Housewives *universe for years to come. It all started with the cast and their families gathering for a dinner party at a local restaurant.*

Lucilla D'Agostino: There was trepidation from everyone going in.

Danielle Staub: The night before the finale, I told my producers, Carlos and Erica, that I was thinking I'd bring the book and put it on the table very quietly. Then I'd wait to see if anyone really wanted to talk about it, since they all seemed to want to talk about it behind my back. Carlos jumped off his seat so high, he nearly hit my vaulted ceiling. He was like, "Oh my God, this is going to be the best ever. You're really going to do that?!" I said, "Yeah, I'm gonna do it. Just one thing: Give me a hard copy, please."

Lucilla D'Agostino: There was no way Danielle wasn't going to go down swinging.

Danielle Staub: I knew they wouldn't have liked it if their kids found out about their pasts when they were that young. They protected one another from that happening.

Dina Manzo: Before the final dinner, we knew something was up. I said to Caroline, "If this book comes up, you better have my back, because you know I wasn't the one spreading it around."

Carlos King: Danielle had handed me her purse when she arrived to set with the book in it. And when the time was right, I crawled under the table and put the book next to Danielle.

Danielle Staub: I brought a bag and I still have the book in that bag to this day. I reached down and I put it on the table.

Caroline Manzo: Bam! There was the book. Half of me was like, "You are crazy. What are you doing?" The other half of me just wanted to laugh. And I was like, "Okay, let's go. What do you got? Bring it on."

Dina Manzo: When I said, "Caroline?" I didn't want her to say, "It was me." I just wanted her to say, "I know for a fact it was not Dina." I didn't need her to own up to it.

Carlos King: They had shut down the restaurant for us and the cast was sitting in the main dining area, while we were all huddled in another room two doors down watching the monitors. When Caroline Manzo, this boss-ass bitch who we all loved, said, "Look at me. I'm the one who did it. I showed the book," we were screaming. Screaming! It was like the fucking *Sopranos*. I'm like, "Am I on HBO? This shit is great."

Caroline Manzo: It really was me that spearheaded this—not because I wanted to be rotten, not because I wanted to be nasty, but because I owed it to myself and everyone around me to investigate it. So it was me that did it all, and I'd do it again.

Danielle Staub: All I ever wanted to do was say, "Yeah, I have a past. I made it through." I had so many things I wanted to say that were clever, but I was too busy telling Caroline to get her finger out of my face.

Carlos King: All of this, of course, led to Teresa's table flip. And we had never seen this side of her. Teresa was just the sweetie pie. I did not know she could become that person if provoked or pushed. It was a switch.

Teresa Giudice: I'm Italian. I have a fiery Italian temper. But my true personality doesn't really come off on the show. I'm the sweetest person. Everybody thinks I'm this bitch, this hard-ass, so tough and so mean—meanwhile, I'm so not! I'm like the opposite. I'm so cool, so easygoing, I'm really down-to-earth. I don't act like a diva or anything like that. I just stand up for myself if somebody comes at me. The same way anybody else would, you know?

Caroline Manzo: I will say that Teresa's emotions got the best of her. I don't think any of it was planned at all. She's very hotheaded, and that's just the way she reacted.

Danielle Staub: For hours, Teresa was banging on that table. There were a few times I kind of flicked her off, like those gnats that fly around your head. Well, she kept getting louder and more annoying. There was no swatting her away. There was this moment when she said, "Will anybody look at me? This is my party." I whipped my head around and I looked at her and went, "This is a party? Oh, no, no, no, no, no. I throw parties. This is some fake bullshit here."

Teresa Giudice: Danielle was attacking Dina. And Dina's not a fighter—I mean, not that I am, either, but Dina really doesn't like confrontation, you know? But when I'm your friend, I'm really your friend. I'm very loyal. So I just got mad at that moment and that's when I went after Danielle. I was doing it to defend Dina.

Carlos King: Next thing we knew, Teresa flipped the table. And all the other producers ran for cover, but I ran into the dining area because my instinct was like, "Okay, let me make sure no one got hurt."

Teresa Giudice: I flipped a table, big deal. It had nothing even to do with me and her. I had my own issues with Danielle because I didn't like how she acted at my Shore house. Remember how she had hooked up with Joe's friend Steve there? That young guy? Back then I thought she was being very inappropriate, doing that in front of my young daughters. Now, you can fuck anyone you want, I wouldn't give a shit. But that's what I was screaming at her.

Danielle Staub: When Teresa called me [a prostitution whore], at first I just wanted to say, "Well, that's redundant. Either I'm giving it away or I'm selling it. Tell me, which is it? Brain surgeon. I mean, NASA is not calling you anytime soon." But nothing could have prepared me for her calling me those names after that. Nothing could prepare me for it being done in front of my children.

Andy Cohen: "Prostitution whore" makes zero sense, by the way.

Teresa Giudice: I don't know if anyone could actually hear what I was saying. Did you hear it? Joe was pulling me away but I was like, "She was fucking a guy in my Shore house! You fucking whore!" That all got lost in the noise.

Lucilla D'Agostino: It was chaos.

Caroline Manzo: It was the craziest thing I've ever seen. My sons were holding Teresa and Danielle apart. Then Joe Giudice got into it and was grabbing Teresa. But initially, both my sons jumped up and Albie had Danielle, trying to push her away.

Lucilla D'Agostino: You had the kids running over trying to figure out how to push people back. And then poor Danielle's daughter was making sure that they were safe and went to the other room.

Danielle Staub: When I stood up, I went, "Oh, that was classy." Maybe she was used to talking that way in front of her own, but she shamefully did that in front of my children without my permission. My past was something I had hoped to share with my daughters when it was age-applicable, not on the heels of a six-and-a-half-year divorce litigation, and certainly not at the ages of thirteen and eight. It just wasn't fair. I'll never be able to erase that from my kids. I'll never be able to give them back the childhood that they deserved. What they took from my children, I'll never forgive them.

Carlos King: Listen, it just goes to show you how epic that show is because Teresa's cussing out Danielle, screaming, "You fucking bitch" as she's being escorted by Juicy Joe. And Joe's like, "Shut up, shut up," gives Teresa a kiss, and it immediately calmed her down. The fact that his lips were able to do that was hilarious to me. She immediately turned back into the Teresa we filmed for two months.

Dina Manzo: To me, she had always been silly, fun Teresa. I never saw her get angry. We'd been friends since we're twenty. So I was mostly in shock, and I was just mortified that this was going to be on TV.

Caroline Manzo: If you look at the footage, you see I am laughing. It's because I have a nervous laugh. I'd never seen a table flip. Of course, when you're home in an Italian family, there's always screaming and yelling. But never out in public like that. So I was laughing because I couldn't believe what was happening.

Lucilla D'Agostino: I feel like this is the most ridiculous statement, but as a fan of the Godfather movies and anything Coppola ever did, there was something to that moment that was like a tragedy playing out in real time.

Danielle Staub: I just wonder how many people realize how difficult that must have been for me. Never once did anyone defend me and say this is a really messed-up thing to do to a mother of two daughters who's really just trying to make her way. They had a gang mentality. They wanted to act like they were the Sopranos.

Carlos King: After that table flip, you would have thought that everyone would have run out of the restaurant. They did not. The men were like, "Who gives a fuck? Let's get some wine." And look, I don't care if you like Danielle or not, everyone in that room felt bad for her. Everyone. So the guys said, "Danielle, come have a drink with us." Teresa was like, "What the fuck? Don't talk to her, Joe!" Joe goes, "Teresa, shut up. Enough." And that was that. The women all kind of gave up. And they all had drinks at the bar.

Caroline Manzo: Literally the second that died down, either my brother Chris or Joe Giudice said, "Do you want to go get a drink?" There was a bar right next to the room in the restaurant, and we all sat and had drinks. I remember sitting there and Joe Giudice said to me, "What do you want to drink?" And I was looking at him like, "Am I in *The Twilight Zone*? You just trashed a room over here. You just were at each other's throats. And now we're sitting here having a drink?" That was crazy. I was just stunned.

Dina Manzo: That was the most mortifying part for me. Everyone was at the bar having a drink together, and I was just like, "Does anyone realize what just happened?" I was like, "This is going to be aired on television." I said to my daughter: "Don't ever be like us. I don't want you to be like this."

Teresa Giudice: At home that night, I was like, "Oh my God, what did I do?" I never did something like that before and I got really angry with myself.

Carlos King: Teresa called me afterward. And if you know Teresa, you know that Teresa loves a compliment. So Teresa's like, "What did you think?" I said, "Teresa, that is going to go down as the most epic moment in reality TV history. Period." She said, "You liked it?" She wanted reassurance.

Teresa Giudice: It ended up being the best thing ever because everybody loved it.

Carlos King: Teresa is a big star now, but she was born that night, honey. None of us saw that in her.

Andy Cohen: When I heard someone flipped a table, I just didn't understand what it meant. I couldn't get a visual of it. And then when I saw it, I just completely—I just thought it was one of the most perfect episodes of television. It was epic.

Lucilla D'Agostino: Watching that footage back for the first time, I knew it was gold. We had so many camera angles and so many POVs, it felt like a game of Clue. Every single woman's perspective told a different story. From Danielle's perspective, she was absolutely horrified that this was happening in front of her children. From Teresa's perspective, she was just so disgusted that this was going down, that someone told her to pay attention, that was egregious. From Caroline's perspective, the whole thing was absolutely beneath her. Each one of them had their own point of view.

Caroline Manzo: It was a great episode and Teresa's table flip is an iconic moment that will forever be ingrained in everyone's mind. For reality TV, it was a tipping point.

Lucilla D'Agostino: I don't think any of us knew how iconic it would be, but we knew it was going to be a dramatic moment. That was the first time that Bravo ever did a director's cut of an episode.

Andy Cohen: By the way, that clip of the table flip was in the opening montage at the Emmys that year. I was sitting in the audience as the nominee for *Top Chef*, and my mouth was on the floor.

> *As expected, once the first season aired, audiences couldn't get enough of the table flip. But for Danielle, it was anything but entertaining, and in season 2, she focused on a new set of friends.*

Danielle Staub: Bravo called me up and said, "We're going to give you a gift in exchange for all of the bad stuff that's happened." I'm like, "Yeah, I hope it's a huge paycheck." There was nothing else that would help. They were like, "You'll see, this is going to be a really big deal. We're going do this show called *Watch What Happens Live*." And I'm like, "So I'm going to do something else for you? That's it? That's what I get?" They brought me into a studio in SoHo. It was 180 degrees, I kid you not, inside the building—there was no AC in the studio. Andy and I shot the debut episode of *Watch What Happens Live*. I was the first and only guest on his big premiere. I was like, "I don't understand how you can't see that this is not funny. It's ruining my career." This was destroying my reputation, and nobody seemed to care.

Andy Cohen: She's complaining about it now, but my recollection is that Danielle was tickled pink about being the first guest on *WWHL*, and about the notoriety that *RHONJ* was giving her.

Carlos King: Danielle was really upset by that table flip, and she blamed us for it. We were close in season 1, but in season 2 she wouldn't talk to me. She thought we were all out to get her.

Danielle Staub: I came back for season 2 because I was offered a book deal. I figured that, with a second season, all eyes would be on me. This would be mine, and I would run with it.

Andy Cohen: Season 2 was really Danielle versus the other women.

Carlos King: She was on an island the entire season.

Lucilla D'Agostino: There was a really long time where it was difficult to get everybody together. Nobody wanted to be the first person to have the sit-down.

Andy Cohen: They were all talking about each other, but they never interacted.

Lucilla D'Agostino: We spent a lot of time exploring what kind of life Danielle had being on the outside of the clique, especially when you're going up against, essentially, an entire family.

Carlos King: Out of nowhere, Danielle brought people and said, "Well, these are my friends now. This is my crew."

Andy Cohen: *Jersey* had the best side characters of any show—and thank God because by season 2, nobody would be in a room with Danielle.

Carlos King: We knew the thirst was real when Danielle was hiring friends to round out her story. Smart girl.

Danielle Staub: None of these people were really my friends. They don't know my life. My real friends, all those scenes, were taken off the show.

Carlos King: She brought on two forces—Kim G. and Kim D., the femmes fatales.

Lucilla D'Agostino: Kim D. owned Posche, which was the store where they all shopped. That was a safe space for Danielle.

Kim DePaola (Guest): When it was time to film the opening credits for the second season, Danielle was afraid of all of them. And I'm a really tough street girl. People respect me. They're not going to start with me, so she asked me if I'd come with her. I helped her with clothes and helped style her.

Kim Granatell (Guest): I saw Danielle as a quality woman, a good mother who was misunderstood. When someone says to me, "Don't hang around with her. Stay away. She's not good," I'm not going to listen to that person. I'm going to judge by what I see. And I'm going to tell you something—whatever Danielle was, she was interesting. She did some crazy, wild, foreign things. But those other girls couldn't hold a candle to her personality—outgoing and, like, drama. Come on!

Caroline Manzo: When they started bringing in all the side pieces, that's when it started to turn. Those people had an agenda coming in because they wanted to hold the apple or the diamond or the peach—of course, in Jersey, we didn't hold anything. So there became some underlying animosity, like, "You're trying to steal my spot."

Carlos King: Before Marlo Hampton, before Faye Resnick, there was Kim G. And the *G* stands for "Gangster." Because she did not give two fucks. Kim G. caused the nonsense. She definitely knew she was there to cause a stir and have more camera time. She was a fucking firecracker.

Andy Cohen: There would be no "Square Tits" without Kim G.!

Kim Granatell: I made a lot of the season happen.

Andy Cohen: We couldn't believe we got away with that season being so good with so little interaction. It seemed very dramatic, though. There was always the suggestion that something very untoward was going to happen.

There was one untoward thing that even today fans may not know happened. Before production began on season 2, Dina quit the show.

Dina Manzo: I quit. I was working really, really hard. When I say I was struggling, it was because I was so successful, my business was really booming. Even before this show started, I had the foundation, I was kind of a single mom because my husband was never around, so it was just a lot. And then filming on top of that, I felt like I was just missing Lexi's moments. Like, all of a sudden she had bubbies and I was like, "When did this happen?"

Lucilla D'Agostino: Dina wasn't having any fun anymore with it, and you could tell. She wanted to move on with her life. We tried our hardest to give her a thousand reasons why she should stay, but ultimately it wasn't worth it anymore.

Dina Manzo: They had talked about me maybe coming on part-time, but this was before anybody was part-time. They said, "We would want more of your husband," and I was like, "No. I don't even want to be on anymore, and I'm not going to make him do something he doesn't want to do."

Caroline Manzo: She did what she had to do for herself, and that was her decision to make.

Lucilla D'Agostino: Obviously that was a big disappointment for us because we always loved the sisters and the sister-in-law dynamic. We loved Lexi. And we loved the glamour that Dina brought to the show. She was our lone blonde.

Dina Manzo: I was still under contract, though, so I spoke to Andy. He was like, "I need you to wrap up some scenes for season 2," which I willingly did. I filmed, like, three scenes and they milked it for seven episodes.

Andy Cohen: That's how we got that great confrontation between Dina and Danielle.

Carlos King: I remember being in Dina's bedroom selecting her outfit, and she said, "What should I wear? You know this scene is going to be replayed ad nauseam." I was like, "You have to look bomb." So we were in her closet for, like, thirty minutes selecting her wardrobe and it was game on. Dina is a professional. She knew.

Danielle Staub: Dina called me and I was out and about. I was told by production, "You're getting a phone call. Pick it up and say yes."

Carlos King: Danielle was driving in her Range Rover. Dina was driving in her Range Rover. It was very *Sopranos*—two gangsters about to meet up at the pizza parlor. Dina was very focused. She walks in and we were all in the video village, like, "Let's go!" The scene in real life may have been eight minutes. Dina came in and she had a mission. She knew what she was going to say. She saw the wheels turning in Danielle's head and knew she was going to go for a low blow. So Dina was like, "I said what I had to say," and Danielle was like, "Oh, you're running away. That's all you do. You run." And Dina was like, "Fuck this shit." She turned her back, flipped that blond hair, and was like, "Let's get one thing clear, bitch. I'm not running from you. I am choosing my peace." And then Danielle was like, "Run, Dina. Run." It just turned into something more funny than dramatic. But that was it for Dina. She was like, "I did it. I'm done. I'm out."

Lucilla D'Agostino: As sad as it was to see Dina go, it was the best decision for her.

Even without Dina, there was no shortage of conflict for Danielle. By the middle of the season, she and Jacqueline were on the outs. And during a fashion show for Posche—where Jacqueline's daughter Ashlee would walk the runway—Danielle came head-to-head with Teresa for the first time since their epic season 1 showdown.

Kim DePaola: That night was bad. We were at a very elegant country club, and they banned all New Jersey Housewives from coming back to the club after that night!

Danielle Staub: It was a setup. I didn't want to go. Even my kids didn't want me to go.

Kim DePaola: Teresa and I were having a great time. We were drinking our Posche-tinis. We're having a ball. Then, Ashlee, who is only eighteen, walks the runway and Danielle calls her a cokewhore? Who says that about a young girl?

Danielle Staub: Ashlee had been saying stuff on social media that was horrifying. Her mother had been doing it, and her grandmother had been doing it—they were all doing it. They were attacking my children and me. I never fought on social media. Not once. The worst thing I did was reply and tell the truth.

Kim DePaola: There's no gray area with Danielle. Danielle doesn't understand that you don't attack a young girl. Even though Ashlee was a little bratty, she was still a teenager.

Kim DePaola: That's when the night really ended. When Teresa sat outside by the bathroom.

Carlos King: Little did we know that hello would turn into a whole chase, hair pull, cops being called, a broken heel, 911, police sirens. Madness.

Danielle Staub: I had locked the doors and got myself regrouped with my girlfriends. When we were all good, we went back out and there was Teresa.

Kim DePaola: Danielle came out, and a rip-roarin' fight started.

Danielle Staub: Teresa was like, "Aren't you going to say hi, honey?" I was like, "Don't call me honey." She said, "Is bitch better?"—which, everyone thinks that was a really big deal for Teresa to say "Is bitch better?" How innovative. Really, really clever.

Teresa Giudice: "Is bitch better?"—that was funny, though.

Danielle Staub: I am a button pusher when I'm pushed. So Teresa said a few more things to me, and I said, "Honey, take a seat, your house is in foreclosure." I didn't know they'd start physically coming at me after that! I should be able to say what I want to say and not get physically accosted for it.

Kim Granatell: It was so chaotic.

Danielle Staub: Teresa took a fork to my back! I had a fork stabbed and dragged down my back! So I started running. One of the security guys was holding on to my arm. I remember saying, "Let go of me—you're holding me back." This was like *Jerry Springer* on steroids. Like, these women were dangerous.

Kim DePaola: These women were running through the country club like lunatics. The frickin' tables were flying up in the air. All the glasses were broken, the dishes. I wound up getting a bill from the country club that made me go, "What the?!"

Danielle Staub: I got chased through the country club and ended up hiding behind shrubs. I was triggered all over the place and in fear. I wanted to go home. I was very disoriented because it came as a shock to me that I was allowed to be treated this way.

Kim Granatell: That's when the hair-pulling happened, when Ashlee grabbed Danielle and her extensions came out. Oh my God, it was bad. . . .

Jacqueline Laurita: Ashlee was told by someone there (a producer, maybe?) that Danielle had hit me, so Ashlee was reacting to hearing Danielle hit her mother. Some people may have done worse in that situation.

Danielle Staub: They just showed a little yank. That's not what happened. They clipped out my head going all the way back.

Andy Cohen: We don't like it when it gets physical. We tend to cut away from it. We'll show that something happens, but we kind of do flashes on the screen. It was not in keeping with what we want the *Housewives* to be.

Danielle Staub: I had come back that season thinking they would make right, that Teresa would make right, that they would clean up the mess they made—but they just made a bigger mess. So no good deed goes unpunished.

Kim DePaola: That night was madness. Thirteen cop cars showed up. Teresa was giving the cops a hard time. I calmed them all down. Everyone that was at my fashion show was like, "That was the most disgusting thing I've ever seen."

Danielle Staub: I don't know how people think that was funny. I don't even care to know why someone would think that that was a great scene for TV. A whole chunk of my hair came out.

Kim DePaola: I have extensions, and I gotta tell you something. That's pretty darn hard.

Jacqueline Laurita: I was told by Kim G. that Danielle actually pulled her own hair out in the car to make it seem worse. All Ashlee did was yank on it.

Carlos King: Let's get one thing straight. Although it was madness, mayhem, stampede, all of those things, I did not see a chunk of hair being pulled out of Danielle Staub. Did Ashlee pull the hair? One hundred percent. Did she pull it from the root of Danielle's scalp? Absolutely not.

Danielle Staub: I had to go to the hospital! I didn't even go home from production—I went straight to the hospital. Stitches in my head. Nervous wreck.

Kim DePaola: Jacqueline was so mad at Ashlee for getting involved. I was like, "Oh, stop it. She got emotional. She pulled her hair. Big deal." Come on. . . .

Jacqueline Laurita: I still feel that it was still not okay for Ashlee to pull Danielle's hair, but I see where her anger was coming from. However, I do believe Danielle absolutely overexaggerated how bad it actually was.

Carlos King: In Danielle's confessional, she pulled out this chunk of hair. It was like, "Danielle, if this much hair was pulled from your scalp, I would see a bald spot." It was so ridiculous. I was banned from Danielle's house at that point, but watching it back, I was like, "Okay, girl. You got that hair from a Party City wig."

Jacqueline Laurita: Danielle even went on to further exaggerate about it years later.

Andy Cohen: She brought the wig head to demonstrate at the reunion, and what you didn't see was Caroline Manzo trying to keep a straight face on the other end of the couch.

Lucilla D'Agostino: Well, Danielle decided to take Ashlee to court!

Danielle Staub: I pressed charges because I thought that was the best way to wake that kid up. I was asked if I would minimize the charges against her so she could do community service. Being as she was only eighteen years old and didn't really have a bright future at the time, I wanted to give her the best chance. So rather than have her tried as an adult, I let her be tried as a juvenile.

Carlos King: Jacqueline was upset because Ashlee gave Danielle reason to press charges. She was like, "I keep telling you, you can't give this woman an excuse to do things because she's not a rational person. She's going to do it."

Lucilla D'Agostino: *RHONJ* wasn't and still isn't just about following five or six women. You have to remember their children are involved. A lot of times their parents are involved. So it was a village of a show. And when you have real mothers who are super protective of their children, it's always very sensitive. There were always heartaches going on behind the scenes because every single one of these women, whether you like them or not, loves her children and would do anything for them.

Jacqueline Laurita: Fast-forward to season 10 and Danielle, as a grown adult, pulled Margaret's hair on camera after Teresa asked her to! What a hypocrite!

> *Danielle's legal battle with Ashlee was a cloud over the second half of the season. Hoping to end the madness, Caroline met with Danielle and tried to convince her to drop the charges. What happened instead was an evening that ended with Caroline calling Danielle a "clown" and "garbage."*

Lucilla D'Agostino: That conversation had to happen, and if it could have happened civilly, it would have been amazing for people to see. We didn't want to force a conversation in a way that felt produced, and that's why the sit-down between Caroline and Danielle was so awkward. Because it really was awkward between them.

Caroline Manzo: I remember walking into the restaurant and there were these two bouncers at the doorway of the restaurant. They had to be six foot five, six foot six. They were bears. And I'm all of five feet tall, I'm not a big person. But it wasn't just for show in her mind. She thought she needed protection from me. I walked in there with all good intentions, I don't like conflict, and I started to explain to her where the issues were. I tried to have her understand our way of thinking. But she just started being Danielle and I got frustrated. I haven't called anyone a clown since, hadn't called anyone a clown prior, it just came out.

Carlos King: And Danielle's clapback was, "But you're the one sitting across from me with orange hair."

Danielle Staub: My producer at the time had taken a big gulp of water because it was a quiet moment, and he blew it all over the screens laughing. He said that was the most hilarious thing he's ever heard.

Caroline Manzo: I remember when I was done with filming, I was shaking.

Kim DePaola: Caroline hit her pretty hard. Caroline really was very demeaning to Danielle in a terrible way. I don't think Danielle's the nicest person, but to call her garbage, that's pretty low.

Danielle Staub: I was like, "Is this really happening? Does she think she's on *The Sopranos* right now?"

Caroline Manzo: The biggest conflicts I've ever had in my life were on that show. And when it's not your personality, or it is an arm of your personality you never knew you had, it takes a toll on you. I remember being sick about it for the rest of the night. You have these moments, and you feel bad about it because you are in the moment and you react the way you react. But all my feelings were honest and true.

Carlos King: Eventually the charges were dropped.

Danielle Staub: She had to do community service and she got a fine.

> *By the time the season 2 reunion rolled around, relations between Danielle and the rest of the women were not any better. Except this time, an unsuspecting bystander got caught in the crosshairs.*

Danielle Staub: As soon as I sat down, they started in, and Andy was like, "Oh my God, we're not even rolling yet, everyone shut up." I was like, "Damn, these are some angry bitches here. Maybe you should put them in a cage and I'll be back." I put my mic down and left, with thirty or forty security around me. There were armed guards there for me that day. As part of my conditions for coming to the reunion, there was a safe room built for me.

Andy Cohen: Thirty or forty security? Um . . . I will say it was electric. It was so electric in the room because they really hadn't seen Danielle all season. Then the show had been airing, and they were seeing what everyone was saying about each other. They were ready for blood, and finally they were in the same room.

Danielle Staub: All I cared about was getting as far away from that set as possible. They were literally like caged animals; when I would walk into a set or into a scene, they would turn vicious.

Andy Cohen: When Danielle said that one line—"You didn't even go visit your niece or nephew in the hospital"—that's when Teresa lost her shit. And that's when she said, "Don't talk about my family."

Danielle Staub: Teresa stood up viciously. She was so close to my face that she was spraying. I said, "Bitch, either fuck me or get off of me." And she goes, "You're disgusting." I go, "And you need a Tic Tac." I walked away quietly, and she physically threw Andy Cohen!

Andy Cohen: Teresa pushed me and, it was so weird—after the taping, I got all the way back to New York from the Borgata, where we'd filmed in Atlantic City, and I was having drinks with Mark Consuelos and Kelly Ripa on their roof at, like, ten or eleven at night, and I said, "I think I got pushed. I think Teresa pushed me." I was in shock. I didn't see the footage until I saw the first cut of the supertease, and I thought it was hysterical. I watched it twenty times. I couldn't believe it. That summer when it aired, I was in the Hamptons, and when I went back to the city, everybody on the street knew who I was. It was so crazy, people were saying my name. It was like that push actually kind of it made me famous. It was incredible. Teresa inadvertently wound up making me famous!

After two chaotic seasons, Danielle's time as a Housewife was done.

Danielle Staub: Sitting on the couch at the reunion, I told them I didn't want a renewal. I didn't want to be signed back on. I couldn't take it anymore, and my kids begged me never to return until Jillian graduated from high school, and that's what I did. I did that for my children. Did Teresa do any of that for her kids? Even after going to prison? Her mom dying? Her marriage being destroyed? Then her father dying? Has she done that? I want everyone to know that. I want that printed. I want people to scratch their heads and think to themselves who they are putting on a pedestal and why.

Andy Cohen: We felt like we had kind of gotten away with Danielle being on the show that second season even though she barely saw any of the other women. So in our mind, there was no place to go with Danielle.

Lucilla D'Agostino: It became harder and harder to figure out what to do because there was no real relationship, and there was no way to make a show like this when we were not coming from a place of truth. And the truth was that the friendship had broken. Danielle couldn't live on an island forever.

Andy Cohen: One thing I regret is that we really fucked up Danielle's departure. Bravo promoted before the reunion that it was the last appearance by one of the Housewives. It was clear that Danielle wouldn't be on the show because it was four against one, but we hadn't explicitly told Danielle we weren't picking her up. I just remember apologizing to Danielle after that reunion, and then publicly on *WWHL*. It was really poorly handled.

> With Danielle gone, producers decided to increase the family ties in the cast. Rather than go back to the Lauritas, this time they added some branches from Teresa's family tree: Melissa Gorga, Teresa's aforementioned sister-in-law, and Kathy Wakile, Teresa's first cousin.

Andy Cohen: The misunderstanding among the Tree Huggers is that we cast Melissa and Kathy to take Teresa down and rip her to shreds. That was not it.

Melissa Gorga (Housewife): We were not trying to take Teresa down.

Shari Levine: *New Jersey* was always the hardest show to make changes in the casting. This was a family show. Family dynamics. Unique in that respect. And we were determined to protect that and keep it going. Which meant we looked to Teresa's family.

Lucilla D'Agostino: Melissa and Kathy coming on the show wasn't a long-plotted endeavor. It all came together pretty quickly, actually.

Andy Cohen: They were her family, that was all. And this was a show about family.

Lucilla D'Agostino: As difficult as it was for Teresa, it was an incredibly honest telling of what was going on in her family at the time.

Shari Levine: *New Jersey* has always had these moments with Teresa and Joe that are pure documentary. The crew would slip into their home early in the morning . . . and literally be in the bedroom with them when they woke up. And you could tell it was a real wake up. Tre had no makeup. Her hair was bedhead. Joe also looked like he'd just woke up. So we looked toward Teresa's family to expand when we needed to.

Melissa Gorga: Teresa and I were really not on great terms when I joined the show. We weren't not speaking, but we were definitely not besties. And that's not because of *The Real Housewives of New Jersey*; we were like that way before the show. Our whole family suffered from our bad relationship.

Kathy Wakile (Housewife): You have to understand that Teresa and Joe Gorga were best buddies. Their whole life it was the two of them, and then Melissa came into the picture. At first, Teresa really wanted to be close to Melissa because she never had a sister. But she also wanted Melissa to know the pecking order. And when Joe, who had always turned to Teresa for advice, didn't need her anymore because he had Melissa, Teresa got jealous.

Andy Cohen: I remember Melissa's audition tape. She was kind of a younger version of Teresa, married to Teresa's brother—who was cute and hysterical—and she was comparing herself to Teresa on the tape, kind of gently ribbing Teresa. It wasn't overtly anti-Tre, and they also sold themselves as great characters in their own right. On a show about family, they fit!

Lucilla D'Agostino: We actually did not explore Melissa for a really long time. It just didn't seem like there was much there initially. She wasn't on our radar.

Melissa Gorga: At the time, the show was very family driven, so as the years went on, the producers went to Teresa's page and started searching for her family. That's how they found me—a producer from Sirens hit me up via DM on Facebook or something. Actually, they found Kathy first and *then* they went to me.

Kathy Wakile: I got a message on Facebook from a casting producer for a lot of different shows on Bravo and TLC. She kept mentioning food things, and I was very into cooking and still am, so I thought they wanted me for a food show. I honestly thought it was a joke at first. They came to my house and filmed. We'd only seen Italian families on *New Jersey*. My husband is Lebanese. I'm one of the girls that married outside my culture. It was a chance for us to share our differences but make people realize how alike we are.

Lucilla D'Agostino: With Kathy, she was kind of the outsider in that family, but was also someone who wasn't afraid to speak her mind and spill the family beans. That was an interesting family dynamic.

Rosie Pierri (Friend; Kathy's sister): Kathy was hesitant at first. I told her, "Go do it! Do it!"

Kathy Wakile: I used to say I would never do this show because I saw how the women were being portrayed the first two seasons. My privacy would be so exposed.

Lucilla D'Agostino: When we started looking at Teresa's family, we then realized she had this super-young, supercool sister-in-law and were like, "Why don't we explore the sister-in-law relationship with Teresa and Melissa?" Because we loved the sister-in-law dynamic between Jacqueline and Dina, and we loved the sister dynamic between Caroline and Dina. It was a logical next step.

Teresa Giudice: They never cared about Melissa and Joe before. I remember asking Carlos King once, "Do you want my brother on the show?" He was like, "No, the show has nothing to do with your brother." Carlos King told me that Melissa would DM him constantly on Instagram, trying to get on!

Danielle Staub: Melissa was filming for two seasons prior in the background and she wasn't getting seen. She was so mad about that, and Joey was mad. They are opportunists at their best.

Teresa Giudice: It was like this whole jealousy thing because Melissa kept telling my brother, "Your sister doesn't put us on the show!" How could I put them on the show? It wasn't my show to put them on, you know what I mean? But she was putting that in my brother's head that it was my fault.

Melissa Gorga: That's not true.

Teresa Giudice: It never really came out on the show, but my sister-in-law Melissa was emailing Danielle back then, too, telling her bad things about me to try and hurt me. That's why I went crazy at the season 2 reunion and got so upset. Because I did go see my nephew, I did! But Melissa told Danielle I didn't.

Melissa Gorga: I wasn't using Danielle to get on the show. I had written a post on Facebook about the sprinkle cookies, saying, "What would you do if you brought sprinkle cookies to someone's house and they threw them in the garbage because they thought they were cheap? Is that rude?" And I didn't say Teresa's name, but Danielle in-boxed me on Facebook and was like, "Hi, I feel so bad about your story. You should come have lunch with me on camera"—you know, thinking that I would go on camera and rip my sister-in-law a new one.

Danielle Staub: Melissa blew up my phone constantly during the filming of season 2. Every single day, she would call me. Andy Cohen, Lucilla—they knew because I would send them every message and tell them everything Melissa was telling me; how she and Joey wanted me to come to their house and film with them, how she wanted to expose Teresa and get her locked up from fraud, how she and Joey were going to help me look good.

They were like, "Nobody in production will listen to us, we've desperately tried. We want to get a hold of TMZ, but they won't take our calls either because they don't know who we are. We deserve to be famous!" It just went on and on and on.

Melissa Gorga: I did know my sister-in-law was giving Danielle a hard time, so Danielle and I vented to each other about how difficult Teresa was. But that's as far as that went. Literally, that was it. I was not a Housewife; I was eight months pregnant or something; I wasn't going to go on TV and dog Teresa out.

Danielle Staub: Eventually I started to realize I was going to be used as a pawn between Melissa and Teresa, and this was not the look I was looking for. So I told Melissa, "I don't get involved in family drama. . . . I want nothing to do with that. Absolutely nothing. To me, that sounds like a bunch of sick, twisted stuff you're willing to do to your sister-in-law. I can't play a part in this."

Melissa Gorga: The only reason Danielle brought up that not seeing her nephew was because she knew it was a sore spot for Teresa. And you can see Teresa lost it because she didn't want to speak about Joe and me on the show.

Teresa Giudice: That was fucked up, what Melissa did. Excuse my French, but it really was. And nobody ever . . . like, do people really know that? 'Cause she got away with it.

Lucilla D'Agostino: My personal opinion is that Melissa was young, beautiful, and interested in being a part of this thing that she saw her sister-in-law doing, but I don't think it was like plotting.

Danielle Staub: Melissa seemed really excited she got under Teresa's skin by supporting me, even though Teresa wasn't putting it together. And by that point, I was leaving. I said, "It's all yours. I'm going to put you in my spot." And that's what I did. I put her on that show.

Teresa Giudice: When my family came on to the show, I didn't even know they were coming on. I was talking to Kathy, Melissa, and my brother the whole time I was filming, telling them everything that was going on on the show. Meanwhile, they were interviewing behind my back! And when I found out, that was so hurtful.

Melissa Gorga: Did the producers go behind Teresa's back and message us? Yes. But everybody knows that's what they do. They've contacted every family member and friend that I know. That's what casting agents do!

Lucilla D'Agostino: Teresa has always said she was blindsided by it. And

I always knew that at some point I was going to have to answer for it, because I knew it wasn't going to make Teresa happy.

Andy Cohen: I remember Teresa calling screaming—and she never called me. She was really pissed about the casting. I didn't think they were best friends, but I never expected Teresa to be pissed like she was.

Teresa Giudice: Family is everything to me and so is loyalty. It's like *The Godfather*. I'm so loyal. I'm loyal to a fault. If you don't have loyalty, you have nothing. My brother and Melissa aren't like that. In fact, I even asked Melissa once, "Did you ever watch the movie *The Godfather*?" She said, "No." I said, "You should watch it. You should watch that."

Melissa Gorga: The way it was portrayed as though "we came on behind her back" was just so frustrating. Because it's not like I was interviewing for months before this happened. It was like a day or two after casting DMed me. Teresa called me before I even interviewed with them! She found out through the grapevine—I'm sure one of the producers told her, "We're going to interview your sister-in-law."

Teresa Giudice: Casting agents contact my friends sometimes and ask to interview them. As soon as they get the call, they call me right away to tell me. Melissa and Kathy should have done the same thing.

Melissa Gorga: Kathy didn't even tell me at first! When I let her know producers were in-boxing me, asking to do an interview, she was like, "I already did an interview." I was shocked!

Rosie Pierri: The producers told Kathy not to say anything. And by the time she was going to tell Teresa, Teresa had already found out. It was a mess.

Kathy Wakile: I didn't tell her because I didn't have the chance! I was told I was one of the top people under consideration, but then I heard nothing for months, so I didn't think anything of it. And I wasn't going to have that conversation with Teresa over the phone. Unless you actually physically sit her down or throw a brick at her, she doesn't listen. So my plan was to have Joe and Teresa over to talk to them when and if I found out anything. But then I got a phone call from Teresa. She said, "I can't believe you're going to do the show, you are going to be the next Housewife." And I said, "What?"

Melissa Gorga: Teresa called me, too, after she found out I was being considered and said, "I heard you're interviewing for *Housewives*." I said, "Yeah, they asked me. I figured it's a great opportunity, so I might as well do the interview." And she was like, "Why are you going to do that?" before giving me a very sarcastic, "Good luck."

Rosie Pierri: Look, I understand how Teresa must've felt. But she had to open her mind up, which she can't fucking do because she's stubborn as a rock.

Teresa Giudice: If they were on the show first, I would never do what they did to me. I like to be different and do my own thing. I like to be unique. I would never ride anybody's coattails.

Kathy Wakile: I knew there would be a reaction, but I didn't expect it to be so inflamed. It was out of control. I couldn't get a word in edgewise. She said, "Bravo just called me, and I find it incredibly disgusting that you would do this without even telling me." And I said, "Do what? They interviewed me. We had a phone conversation. That's all it was. I have no contract. They didn't pick me."

Rosie Pierri: Teresa didn't want Kathy and Melissa on the show because she didn't want any competition. She was the star, she didn't want anyone else having any light. That sucks. That's a bad human being to me.

Teresa Giudice: Why would I stop them from coming on the show? They were my family! I would have looked like the bad one if I tried to keep them off the show! If they would have asked me, "I want to be on the show," I would have told the producers about them!

Kathy Wakile: She goes, "You're never gonna make it, this show is about drama." I go, "You are all about drama, aren't you?" I said, "You know what? I can't believe you. This is what you call me for? Fuck you." And I hung up the phone. That's the only way you could talk to her.

Rosie Pierri: They used to be with each other all the time. All three couples— Joe Gorga and Melissa, Teresa and Joe Giudice, Kathy and Rich—were together every weekend.

Teresa Giudice: Kathy especially was at our house . . . when I tell you religiously, I mean, it was all the time. They were moochers. My ex and I, we used to be big entertainers. We'd go all out, buying the best liquor and going all out to the nines. But people take advantage of you and that's what they were doing. So when I started *Housewives*, we started distancing ourselves from them.

Kathy Wakile: When I got a contract, I called her and said, "Hey, Teresa, listen, I know that you were really upset when you found out that I was interviewed. And I want you to be the first to know that I'm holding my contract in my hands, okay? Bye!" I hung up on her again. I know it was childish of me to do that, but I didn't want to hear what she had to say.

Melissa Gorga: She refused to sign her contract unless Bravo would not sign ours. She held out as long as she could, but Bravo held out, too, calling her bluff. I told her I had signed already and that they were filming the baby's christening for the first episode of the season. She knew the cameras would be there.

Kim DePaola: I was on the phone with Teresa talking her off the ledge the night before the christening. She was like, "I don't know what to do. I don't know if I should sign." I go, "Listen here, Teresa. You got a good thing, honey. You're making good money. Sign the contract and show up. Yes, they went behind your back. Are you going to lose your job because of it? It's your show."

Melissa Gorga: She held out until, I want to say, ten hours before the first day of filming.

Andy Cohen: When we cast Melissa, she said she and Teresa didn't always get along. It was clear that there were some issues, but it was not, "I'm going to rip her to shreds. We don't speak. Our christening is going to become a bloodbath."

Lucilla D'Agostino: Obviously, none of us anticipated that on the very first day of filming with Melissa, craziness would happen. That was far beyond anything any of us could have ever imagined.

Kim DePaola: Teresa walked into the christening and all hell broke loose. Her own brother called her garbage.

Teresa Giudice: That's terrible. Who calls their sibling garbage? I would never have called him that on national TV. Like, I really wouldn't have, you know? That was like, so hurtful for my parents.

Lucilla D'Agostino: I would let the showrunners do their jobs in the field, but I was always the phone-a-friend—like when everything goes bad, I would be the person they'd call. So they said, "Lucilla, we need to let you know, a brawl broke out in the middle of the christening. Joe Gorga ended up outside on his knees screaming in Italian to his father."

Kim DePaola: There was fist-fighting and name-calling. It was pretty ugly.

Danielle Staub: I didn't think Melissa and Joe would go on quite as violently as they did. To have a baby's christening party, a religious event, that turned into a horrifying fistfight? And to think at the end of my last season, Melissa would tell me, "Oh, we do not condone anybody being physical." I'm sorry, did they forget their first scene on the *Housewives*? Going for their own family?

Kathy Wakile: After it was all over, I ripped my mic off and said to producers, "Are you fucking kidding me? You kept poking the bear and this is what you got. I didn't sign up for this." And we left. We actually had another party around the block, so we went to that.

Melissa Gorga: That night, I remember coming home and just climbing under my bed. I wanted off the show.

Kathy Wakile: Me too. I told them, "Fuck this shit, I'm not doing this. I'm not putting my kids' lives in danger. I'm not being associated with this shit."

Shari Levine: We have never stopped a Housewife who wanted to leave the show from doing so.

Lucilla D'Agostino: There's a time in every Housewife's existence where they either beg or demand that something not make television. The christening was an example of everyone being so in the moment and so upset, and then waking up the next morning and being like, "Oh my God, the cameras saw me act that way."

Melissa Gorga: Joe would have to pull me out of bed to go pick up our kids from school because everyone would be looking at me—they knew our drama, and I was not happy.

Lucilla D'Agostino: To his credit, Joe Gorga was always the one to say, "That's the truth, that's what happened."

Melissa Gorga: We don't even talk about that christening. When they replay it on Bravo, we turn it off. It's really hard for both of us to watch. We're not happy about it. We're not proud of it. It brings back really sad memories for us.

And that was just the first episode of the season! From there, things between Teresa and her now castmates only got worse.

Teresa Giudice: I want people to know the truth about Melissa. I want to be vindicated. I had never done anything against her, it was the other way around. I'm not a vindictive person at all, especially to my family. But I got thrown under the bus!

Melissa Gorga: Teresa turned this whole thing into a "smear Melissa" campaign. "Let's pretend she's the younger wife of my brother and just wants him for money. Let's say she came on the show because she wants fame." When that wasn't the case.

Teresa Giudice: My brother, I don't even think he wanted to be on the show so much. It was definitely Melissa more. 'Cause wives, you know, they do control their husbands. They have the power of the pussy, they do. They tell their husband to jump—my brother's like that, and he says, "How high?"

Lucilla D'Agostino: Melissa really wanted to be able to coexist with Teresa on the show in a way where they could both enjoy it. She didn't want to feel like she did something wrong by coming on the show.

Melissa Gorga: This version of the story was jammed down everyone's throats by Teresa. It was like, "Melissa just wants my brother for money. She came on the show behind my back. All she wants is fame." Teresa already had a crowd of people who knew who she was, and I was introduced as this evil sister-in-law who just loved her brother for money.

Teresa Giudice: Why would you want to go on national TV and hurt your family? Look at Caroline and Dina. Even though they don't speak now, they always stuck together on the show. They should have done the same thing.

Kim DePaola: Melissa would walk in like, "I'm the new, young hot Housewife." Who introduces themselves like that? She's very much like Teresa in that manner. They're kind of mirror images of each other. Melissa is maybe kinder inside, not as hard-core as Teresa, but there's definitely some similarities between the two.

Melissa Gorga: It wasn't just a one-sided thing. We were both going at each other. I don't think I went down and dirty—it's not my style—but I would defend myself. I would call her out and say, "Okay, you're here, you're portraying one life but you live another." So, yes, I definitely had my part in it as well. But I was trying to explain to her, "You're making this such a negative. Let's show everybody our great family."

Teresa Giudice: Could you imagine like your family comes on the show? If this was me, I would have done it all different. I would have showed the world how amazing it would be to get along with your family. People would have been like, "Wow, that family is amazing. That's how they get along?" To me, that's impressive. Not like fighting with your family. To me, that's disgusting. That's like, you know, unclassy.

Given their history with Teresa, Caroline and Jacqueline approached their new castmates with caution.

Melissa Gorga: Caroline and Jacqueline were basically told not to like me, not to film with me.

Kathy Wakile: They knew how the show worked and they couldn't really go against Teresa on camera if there wasn't any evidence supporting that, because then they would look bad. So they kept a little bit of a distance.

Caroline Manzo: I heard stories about Kathy from Teresa, so I had this predetermined expectation of who she was going to be. Your natural instinct is, "I'm going to not like you." But eventually you realize there's nothing wrong with these people.

Kathy Wakile: It wasn't until I had a goddess party at my house that Caroline started to open up. She saw that I was legit. I did cook and I did entertain and I was doing all the work. Jacqueline saw that, too, and so they had respect for me in that way.

Melissa Gorga: Caroline was very supportive of Kathy, which would bother Teresa.

Caroline Manzo: I told Kathy later, "Kathy, I was terrible to you in the beginning because I believed the stories." That's the machine that Teresa became—nothing was off-limits, nothing was out of bounds. It didn't matter who got bulldozed.

Kathy Wakile: I have always been really good to Teresa. Always been an ear for her, like an older sister. For her to say things about me that were not true was shocking to me. Why would you try to poison people against me, when I don't want to hurt anybody?

Teresa Giudice: What Kathy did to me after the christening, saying I left Audriana unattended? First of all, it was all family. Nobody would take my child, are you serious?!

Kathy Wakile: All season long I prayed the cameras caught me with the kids because I knew I did that. And it wasn't just Audriana, I grabbed all the kids and got them out of the room. I had Gia by the hand. They just focused on Audriana because she was in a stroller and I wheeled her out.

Teresa Giudice: For Kathy to even go there as my first cousin? It came down to her just doing that for TV, for the fame and money. That's all she cared about.

Kathy Wakile: Listen, had I been in that same scenario, and my husband and my father were going to blows, I probably wouldn't be worried about my kids, either. I'd be more worried about breaking up the fight. But Teresa didn't want to hear it. She was backed into a corner because I was advising her, "Teresa, you've got to talk to your brother, you've got to straighten this out," and her response was, "Stay out of my issues because when the going got tough, you ran out of there." But I said, "Yeah, I ran out because my kids were there and so were yours. I was concerned about everybody's kids. Audriana was left unattended." It made her look like her priorities weren't straight, so she turned on me. I'm just glad the cameras caught me and proved me right.

Rosie Pierri: They portrayed my sister as a troublemaker, and that's so far from who she is. She never tries to start trouble. She's always the one to try to put things back together. That's why she did the show.

Kathy Wakile: I wanted us to be a normal family. I thought I could be the person in the triangle with Teresa, Melissa, and Joe who could bring them together and get them to resolve their conflict. But Teresa wouldn't let that happen.

Lucilla D'Agostino: It took a while for the other ladies to see that, but they did. And they rallied around Melissa at a certain point, too, and said to Teresa, "She's here, she's staying, we like her, let's just get past it."

Melissa Gorga: I never asked them for their support or any of that. They truly, authentically were watching what was going on. They could see that Joe and I were a real couple who loved each other.

Kathy Wakile: Teresa would be like, "You and Melissa are such buddy buddies going against me." You were either with her or against her. There was no way you can be friends with everybody. Somebody had to be a villain.

Teresa Giudice: That's what ultimately ended my friendship with Caroline. She got on the bandwagon. I did nothing to her. What she did with my family, she was disgusting. We were friends and then she paired up with my family and went against me. I was on an island all by myself and I still survived.

> *That may have been why Teresa felt the need to end her friendship with Caroline, but Caroline's relationship with Teresa would hit a more serious rough patch off camera, during a trip to the Dominican Republic. It was an incident the RHONJ stars have never discussed publicly before, until now.*

Melissa Gorga: We were a younger crew back then—I mean, I was just thirty-one when I started—so when we wrapped filming on our first trip, we were really ready to party it up. That night, we went to the nightclub at the Hard Rock in Punta Cana. It was me and Joe, Teresa and Joe Giudice, Jaqueline and Chris Laurita, Caroline and Albert Manzo, and then their kids, Albie, Chris, and Lauren. Oh, and Greggy Bennett.

Caroline Manzo: If my memory serves me correctly, we were only there twenty minutes. There was a little area with couches they had us in, and I was standing at the railing, looking at the crowd because I'm a people-watcher. All of a sudden, I felt something wet hit me on the back of the head.

Melissa Gorga: Everyone was drinking and as Teresa opened up a bottle of champagne, she decided to shake it up and spray it on us—you know, just to have fun. But she accidentally sprayed it on some other people at the club.

Caroline Manzo: Teresa was just flailing the bottle around, spraying everyone on the dance floor area. But after it stopped, I saw a woman rubbing her eyes as if they were burning.

Melissa Gorga: Her group, they thought, "Oh, these reality stars come in here, thinking they were tough shit." Meanwhile, it was a complete accident. But this woman came up and started yelling at Teresa.

Caroline Manzo: They were being very aggressive toward Teresa. And my sons, Chris and Albie, stepped in and started to defuse the situation. They said, "Guys, we're not looking for trouble. She's just being silly, she drank a bit. Our apologies, let's buy you a drink." And they walked off together to the bar, but the guy who was with this woman turns around and goes, "It's a good thing you apologized, because I wouldn't want to have to fuck you up"—at which point, you know when a basketball player palms a basketball with his hand? Well, he took his palm and smashed it into Albie's face, pushing Albie backward.

Greg Bennett (Friend of the Manzos): When I saw that, I got nervous for Albie because there were two or three people there and they shoved him backward. So I kind of jumped. And I don't really do that stuff, I've never been in a physical altercation in my life, but I was worried for him so I jumped in between to try to push him out of the way.

Caroline Manzo: Then, one of our producers—who was a person of color—goes to step in to stop it from escalating. But the guy says, "Shut up you fucking N-word." And my boys are like, "Yo, no one needs that disrespect. We're not looking for a problem, we don't want a problem." But the guy is just, over and over again, calling them the N-word. He said to my sons, "You hang out with N-words? You're an N-word lover?" And then another guy with him started calling Greg and my sons gay slurs, too. "You're F-words?" Just going in, like, bad.

Greg Bennett: One of the guys pushed me and fell and then I fell on top of him, because it was very slippery from all the liquid on the floor.

Melissa Gorga: From there, the two Joes got involved. And of course once they were involved, all hell broke loose.

Caroline Manzo: I turned around and Joe Giudice—I don't know how, but he and Joe Gorga were in *another* fight with the other people of the party. And Joe Giudice is like a friggin' ninja warrior. I haven't been privy to a lot of physical violence in my life, aside from what happened that year at the Brownstone, but Joe was literally just throwing people around left and right.

Greg Bennett: These guys were there for some wedding party, so I don't know now how many of them were there in the club, but they just kept coming out of the shadows. Albie and Chris are arguing with the guy dropping the N-word, I've got the guys calling me homophobic slurs, then the Joes are dealing with another dude. It was like, these different scenes all around.

Caroline Manzo: I'm standing there and I'm in a state of shock and all of a sudden, my husband picks me up from behind like I was a bale of hay and tosses me on a couch to get out of the way. When I get up, I hear him scream like a madman and I turn around and see a man winding up to punch my twenty-one-year-old daughter right in the face. And I don't know how but my husband, by the grace of God, pulled her away just in the nick of time where the guy's fist only grazed her face.

Melissa Gorga: A big fistfight broke out. Just punches flying everywhere.

Caroline Manzo: You have to remember, the lights never came on and the music never stopped, so all this is happening when it's dark and loud. It was bedlam. A full-out brawl.

Greg Bennett: It was just chaos. I started sobbing after it was over. [*Laughs*] As the lights came on, I was crying and didn't know where to go or what was going on.

Caroline Manzo: I don't know how it ended. The police were never called, that I recall. But when we got back to our rooms that night, Lauren had a nasty cut on her leg 'cause she had fallen on some broken glass. And Joe Giudice sat in the bathroom with her, pulling shards of glass out with a tweezer before cleaning her cut and bandaging it. He took such good care of her. That's what people don't know about Joe, he's got a good heart.

Greg Bennett: The next morning, the police came to question all of us, including the people who started the fight.

Caroline Manzo: It was my belief that they knew who we were and they were looking for a problem from the beginning. Because before the fight even started, my daughter was going to get a drink and they called her "reality trash" or something. And then, when we were talking to the police, the guys described my boys and Greg Bennett, but they had never seen Joe Gorga because he wasn't on TV at that point—he had been filming but it hadn't aired—so they didn't bring him up.

They did say, "Some guy named Joe," talking about Joe Giudice (which also tells me they knew who we were because there was no way they heard the name Joe in such a loud place). They kept saying, "The guy with the beard." And we kept saying. "We don't know who that is," because Joe was not implicated by that point and we were trying to protect him. But then Teresa goes, "Oh, my husband's name is Joe!" So that's how he got detained too.

Greg Bennett: They took away our passports—me, Albie, Chris, and Joe. And we were told we couldn't leave the country until this was figured out.

Caroline Manzo: At this point, Bravo then says to us, "You need to go home." And I say to Bravo, "Good luck with that. I'm not leaving. I don't give a fuck what you tell me, I am not leaving."

Melissa Gorga: Joe and I got out of the country safely. We were allowed to go, and we left to get home to the kids.

Lucilla D'Agostino: It was devastating, knowing that my cast was in a foreign country and detained. I can tell you that for five days, I didn't leave my office. I had trash bags covering my windows so no one could see in because I was sleeping there. We were spending twenty-four hours a day trying to get in touch with lawyers and officials down in the Dominican Republic to figure out what was happening and how we could help.

Caroline Manzo: They weren't exactly arrested or incarcerated, because there weren't any official changes, but they had to sit in the lobby of the jail every day. I would not leave my sons, so we sat there with them. And exactly across from us were the guys who started the fight. This went on for at least three days. We'd arrive at eight a.m. and be allowed to go home around dinner time. They fed us water and a cheese sandwich. At one point, I went to the bathroom, and to get there, you had to walk through the women's holding area. I'm talking a dirt floor, women sitting on a bench, bars on the window. It was so filthy. I said, "I'll be goddamned if I'm walking out here without my boys."

Lucilla D'Agostino: It was horrifying. I just remember at the time calling a friend of mine and saying, "What happens in a Dominican jail?"

Greg Bennett: I was pretty terrified. It was not the most above-board operation we were dealing with. There were requests being made to give money to get out of it, and we were just waiting it out.

Lucilla D'Agostino: A lot of the accusations were being thrown their way in

Spanish, and nobody spoke Spanish. So they didn't even know what they were being accused of because they couldn't understand!

Dolores Catania: I was supposed to be on that trip. I had filmed a few times that season, and even went on the Catskills trip. They asked me to come to the Dominican Republic, and I have mad connections there. Like, I know the president and general. So I had the whole trip planned. We were going to stay at this mansion on a coconut farm. They were going to take us there on a helicopter. And at the last minute, they cut me out of the trip, replaced me with Greg, and had to stay at the Hard Rock hotel. Maybe if I went, they wouldn't have wound up in jail!

Caroline Manzo: One of the things that sticks in my mind was when Bravo called the NBC attorneys in. They came rolling in, wearing these gorgeous beautiful black suits, one more beautiful than the other. Me, Teresa, and Lauren were going, "Holy fuck. Look how beautiful the guys are!"

Lucilla D'Agostino: In the end, there weren't any formal charges. It all became a whole bunch of people pointing fingers. Authorities couldn't figure out who was at fault. It was like a great big mystery.

Greg Bennett: The lawyers got us released and we transferred to a new hotel to await our passports. And we just waited there every day until the passports came in.

Caroline Manzo: Every day we packed our luggage to be ready to go at a moment's notice. Wherever we went, the luggage was right with us. When we finally got them, the producers looked at us and said, "Let's get the fuck out of here," and we ran. We had cars waiting by that drove us right to the airport. Producers had us literally running as if we were missing a flight to get on the plane. "Excuse me? Excuse me! Coming through! Out of the way, please! Sorry, sorry, sorry!" They ran us to the front of the line at TSA and got us on that plane and got us home.

Greg Bennett: It was like *Argo*. I kept waiting for Ben Affleck to pop out. It was a wild thing that happened to us. To this day I can say I was in jail with Teresa Giudice and her husband. Just one of many people who can say that, I suppose!

Dolores Catania: None of them will go there anymore.

Caroline Manzo: Oh, the Manzo family will never set foot on Dominican Republic soil again. We used to go often over the years, but it was such a wild thing that there truly is in us a little bit of fear going, "Well, what if we go back and they see this passport?" We're not going back.

Greg Bennett: You know, I think that was the real catalyst for the Teresa and Caroline fallout. It all started to go downhill after that. Everybody had kind of had enough of Teresa throwing a champagne bottle around and starting a brawl in a bar. Caroline thought, "This is not as cute as funny as it was in the beginning."

Because of the ever-changing dynamics between the castmates and family members, producers decided—in a Housewives *first—to film seasons 3 and 4 with no break in between.*

Melissa Gorga: There is nothing like our seasons 3 and 4. They were crazy! They were twenty-two or twenty-three episodes each, filmed without a break.

Lucilla D'Agostino: It got increasingly difficult to tell the truth of what was happening because every time we went down between seasons, the dynamics would shift. It was like, you go to the reunion, you leave the reunion, everyone picks their corner and chooses their side. Then four weeks later, after the dust settled, I'd see that so-and-so and so-and-so went to lunch. And it's like, "How the hell did that happen?" That would blow my mind. Then I would have to backtrack and explain it on the show. So I thought, "What if I could capture the rationale in the moment?" At a certain point it's cheaper to keep filming than it is to step down. Because then I had some way of at least explaining to the viewer that this is not lies.

Melissa Gorga: There was just so much real shit going on, they were scared to give it the nine-month break they normally do. We had a two-week break and started up again.

Kathy Wakile: Our producers told us, "Check your email. Pickups for next season already came," and we were like, "What do you mean? We didn't even film a reunion."

Lucilla D'Agostino: Even though I'm the person who pushed for it, filming two seasons back-to-back was exhausting for everybody.

Andy Cohen: Oh, that was a disaster. We will never make that same mistake again. There was a moment when we considered doing it again with *Potomac* around the time of the pandemic and we said, "Remember *Jersey*?"

Melissa Gorga: Watching it and filming at the same time was rough. I was crying every day. The producers would tell me, "Don't worry. You'll see, the truth comes out at the end of the season." I was like, "I can't wait." It was honestly the longest season we ever had—twenty-three long weeks.

Caroline Manzo: I remember it taking its toll on everyone because it was very dark. It was completely consuming in every aspect of your life.

> *One consequence of shooting two seasons back-to-back was that when it came time for the season 3 reunion, filming for season 4 was underway. And though it still hadn't aired, season 4 filming had caused enough chaos that, at the last minute, Jacqueline refused to attend the season 3 reunion.*

Andy Cohen: The night before the reunion, there was a huge fight revolving around Strippergate, and Jacqueline refused to leave her house. I was so pissed at her. Furious!

Lucilla D'Agostino: She and I were on the phone for four or five hours the night before. I was trying to convince Jacqueline to come. Rebecca Toth, another executive producer, who was pregnant at the time, even got in a car and drove all the way to Franklin Lakes and stood outside Jacqueline's house talking to her through the door.

Andy Cohen: I was like, "Well, we're not going out there until Jacqueline shows up."

Caroline Manzo: We were all like, "We're here, we're doing it. We don't care."

Lucilla D'Agostino: We kept pushing an hour, thinking maybe she would change her mind.

Andy Cohen: I remember Caroline Manzo came to my dressing room in the most Caroline way. She was like, "I want to be clear with you. Jacqueline is not showing up. So you're going to either send us home or not. But once Jacqueline makes up her mind about something like this, she's not showing up." She got through to me.

Lucilla D'Agostino: Credit to Andy, it was the first thing we addressed at the top of the reunion.

Andy Cohen: It was so confusing to the viewers that we were in the middle of production on season 4 during the season 3 reunion and something happened the night before that was so bad that all of their allegiances had shifted. Everyone was so mad at Teresa, but they couldn't explain why because it was a spoiler for next season. It was a disaster.

> *Season 4 had plenty of dark moments, but one heartwarming exchange took place between Kathy's kids and Rosie, Kathy's out-and-proud sister (and a fan favorite from her first moments on-screen).*

Rosie Pierri: The first season Kathy was on the show, everybody would see me and be like, "Who's that?" I didn't even know the cameras were on, to be honest with you. Then they wanted to mic me up the second time around, and I was a little nervous. I didn't know how the audience was going to take me, because I am who I am. I don't hide much. I did enough of that when I was younger—all my life I hid, hid, hid. Now I'm just who I am and that's it.

Andy Cohen: Thank God for Rosie.

Lucilla D'Agostino: I always loved the honesty that Rosie brought to the show. It takes a lot for someone to put themselves out there that way, especially on television. And she was charming. Rosie could be the toughest chick in the room and the sweetest and biggest heart in the room.

Kathy Wakile: I've known my sister was gay since we were kids. But she never came out, and it wasn't my business to ever ask her. That's not my truth. That's not my business. If she wants to share it, great, but I don't want to overstep. And so when she finally did, it was like, "Ah, what a relief. What took you so long?" But when they wanted to film her, I remember saying to her, "Rosie, listen, if you want to be a part of this, I want you to be because you're my life, we're besties forever. But you have to be ready to be out publicly. And then I need you to have a conversation with my kids." They were both in high school and neither had a clue.

Rosie Pierri: Kathy told production, "Look. She's not going to film before she talks to my kids about being gay." They automatically said, "Holy shit. We've got to get this on camera." So then I had to speak to our mom and explain to her that it would educate so many people out there. I told her, "People are going to be thrown out on the street and have nowhere to go because their family doesn't accept them. If I could help three or four or ten, or even one, family out there, then it's all worth it for me." She said, "Okay, go ahead." And we did it. It was very emotional for me. I have other nieces and nephews, and I love them all. But my sister's kids—I gave them their first baths. I love them like they are my own. I go back to that day and get emotional because they were just kids. Victoria was tearing up because she saw me tear up. And then Joseph—he's so, so funny—he goes, "So, Aunt Ro, do you have gaydar?" He just broke the ice. It was so natural.

Kathy Wakile: We raised them just to see love. It didn't matter. When they were kids, they asked me, "Mommy, what does 'gay' mean?" And I said, "Well, 'gay' means 'happy.'" They really never dug any deeper. I wanted them to know that their first interaction with the word "gay" is "happy," you know? And I wasn't lying.

Other moments, like one caught on tape between Joe Giudice and an unknown woman were . . . less touching.

Sezin Cavusoglu: We film for so many hours, you don't always catch every little thing that happens. That phone call with Joe at the vineyard? Nobody even knew it was there until I isolated everyone's audio tracks and listened.

Lucilla D'Agostino: Listening to that audio was just like, "Holy shit!" It seemed clear to us that he was having a conversation of a romantic quality. And also, in that conversation, he called Teresa a cunt.

Sezin Cavusoglu: There were a million other conversations going on at the same time and the most interesting one ended up being this side conversation Joe was having on the phone when he stepped away from the table.

Lucilla D'Agostino: Putting the episode together was one of the only times that I have ever allowed a Housewife to see something more than a day or two before it aired. We knew that conversation and that particular verbal insult to her was just explosive. So I created a preview link that would expire in thirty minutes so she could see it and emotionally deal with it in advance. We sent the link, and Teresa called me right after watching. My understanding is they watched in the house together, and Joe was so upset after watching it, he left the house.

Teresa Giudice: When that came out, I was like, "You guys must have did something because Joe's never said that word to me." And Andy Cohen called me and told me, "Teresa, he did say that." I was shocked!

Andy Cohen: File that under "awkward conversations with Teresa."

Kathy Wakile: I was getting calls from all the magazines and gossip sites after that, and I would say, "No comment." They would ask me if Joe ever cheated, and I'd say, "I never saw anything like that." And it was the truth. I never saw anything like that.

Teresa Giudice: Joe was drunk, and for two weeks he didn't know what to do. He felt so bad for doing that, you know. He was drinking. He was drunk and I don't know what because I never heard him say that word before.

Lucilla D'Agostino: Teresa was devastated and honestly in shock. And she remained in shock about that for a while, but there was no way to say it didn't happen—you could see him saying it, you could hear him saying it, it wasn't taken out of context. It wasn't like he was telling a dirty joke to a buddy, it was all there. I'm glad we handled it the way we did, because it gave Teresa time to make the decision she ultimately did, which was to forgive him. Of course Joe remained very, very mad.

Teresa Giudice: By the way, those cheating rumors never bothered me because I never caught him with a girl. And trust me, I'm the type like if I would have caught him, I would have been like, "Bye!" Like I would never give anybody a second chance. You have to be faithful. There's no way he's going to stick his penis in another girl, come and stick it back in mine, that would never happen. I'm serious.

> *Hostility between Melissa and Teresa simmered throughout seasons 3 and 4, eventually poisoning Teresa's relationship with many of her fellow cast members. It all came to a boil during a conflict that came to be known as Strippergate.*

Kim DePaola: Teresa is the one who told Caroline and Jacqueline that Melissa was a stripper, that they did not want her in the family.

Teresa Giudice: I had nothing to do with any of that.

Kathy Wakile: We went for drinks at the Hudson Terrace. We were just being silly and there was a pole there and Melissa was dancing by the pole or whatever. Jacqueline goes, "Was Melissa a stripper?" And I was like, "What the hell are you talking about? I know she was a barmaid, but I don't think she was a stripper." She goes, "Well, Teresa told me she was." I was like, "Come on, get the hell out of here." And that was the end of it. We laughed it off.

Kim DePaola: People would come to me with all the stories. Remember, I owned a local store. It was very easy for them to just walk into my boutique and tell me. I already knew she was a stripper. When Teresa and Caroline and Jacqueline were very, very close and Melissa was nowhere to be found, Teresa told them the truth that she was stripper. And that Joe would go around to bookers and whatever. Teresa was upset because he'd had a nice fiancée and had broken up with the fiancée for Melissa. She moved right in and they got married right away. The family didn't like her. It was an ongoing thing from day one. I knew. Jacqueline knew. We all knew. Then when Melissa came on the show, all hell broke loose. Word spread like wildfire that she was an ex-stripper.

Kathy Wakile: I felt bad because I didn't think it was relevant. She was or she wasn't, who cares? That's her business. I didn't really see how it mattered, but they made it to be like being a stripper was so bad—so dirty, and, like, Oh my God! Even if she was, who cares? She's not a stripper now. She's happily married. She's got kids. Why would you bring that up?

The final straw was when Kim D. invited Angelo Vrohidis, who claimed Melissa danced for him at the strip club he managed, to her Posche fashion show.

Kim DePaola: I was talking to Teresa every day, seventeen times a day, but I never said, "Angelo's going to come and call her out on being a stripper." I didn't trust any of them to not open up their big mouths and I wanted it to go down the way I wanted it to go down. It was my plan. It was my fashion show. I told the producers what I was going to do, because it wasn't my place to go ruining their show. But it was my place to bring what I needed to bring. But Teresa found out at the salon and she never told Melissa. She had every chance in the world to text Melissa and say, "I was just at a salon and this guy Angelo says he was your boss." Teresa didn't care that Melissa was being set up. She couldn't stand her.

Teresa Giudice: Kim D. has admitted that I had nothing to do with that. She was just trying to do that to get a paycheck, you know?

At the fashion show, Angelo showed up as planned. As always happens with the Jersey ladies, things got dramatic.

Kim DePaola: I was told to come outside. And there was Joe Gorga, screaming. I wondered, "How the hell did Joe Gorga and Richie Wakile get all the way up to Montvale—an hour and fifteen minutes away—to my fashion show that fast?" What happened was, when Melissa saw her ex-boss Angelo, she texted Joe under the table and Joe flew over there. There's no question in my mind. The minute she saw him, she knew something was going down because she knew she'd worked for him. Here's the thing: I didn't care about Melissa. I was friends with Teresa. I was part of a reality show. But Teresa knew a lot more than I admitted on the reunion. I didn't lie. I just omitted. I think Teresa denied it so heavily because the whole cast turned against her. They all hated her guts. She lost her position. It wasn't because she set up Melissa. They could care less. It was just the real Teresa was coming out, and they didn't like her.

Teresa Giudice: Thank God my brother did not believe that. I was set up. They made it look like I would do something, and I would never do something like that. I actually think Jacqueline was behind all of that. Did you see how she was smiling at the end? Her and Kim D. planned that whole thing and tried to put it on me.

Tensions in the Giudice-Gorga-Wakile crowd continued to build, and in season 5 they culminated in a brawl between the Joes on a family retreat.

Kathy Wakile: I don't even know whose idea that retreat was, but we really got in there and did the work. And I went to bat for Teresa when Joe called her scum. I said, "Joe, that was not right. You don't talk to your sister like that. What are you doing?" I continuously told him he needed to let it go. But I also told her she didn't need to bring her husband into it. She didn't need to let her husband know that her brother just called her scum. What did she think was going to happen?

Teresa Giudice: I just walked away and then my ex freaked out because he's like, "I have a sister. I would have never said that to my sister." And Joe's family, they're very loyal. In fact, they asked Joe's brother to come on the show, and I don't get along with Joe's brother's wife, but they both didn't come on the show because they didn't want to go against us. It takes a certain kind of person to do that to a family member.

Rosie Pierri: Kathy, Rich, and I were trying to stop the conflict. We wanted the best for the brother and sister. We didn't want them to fight—and we didn't want to fight with them, either. That's not who we are as people.

Caroline Manzo: Their family was there for one day, and I got a phone call: "You got to come up here. Joe and Joe just got into a massive fistfight. Nobody's talking. Everybody hates each other. Everybody's in their room." I was like, "What could I possibly do to fix this mess?" But producers wanted to bring in a neutral party to talk to each of them." A car came and got me at like four o'clock in the morning. I had to drive four hours to Lake George. They all come down for breakfast and who's sitting at the breakfast table? Me. They all looked at each other like, What is she doing here? But they needed a moderator. So I was the only player left.

But perhaps the biggest fallout of season 5 was a mass exodus from the interconnected cast. Jacqueline, Caroline, and Kathy all left their full-time roles.

Jacqueline Laurita: I actually wanted to quit after the fourth season. I only came back to bring awareness to autism and tell our family's story. But filming just became burdensome and felt too forced. The energy on the show was changing.

Lucilla D'Agostino: Jacqueline needed to take care of Jacqueline and her son. She was very vulnerable and honest about Nicholas's struggles and eventual triumphs. But it became evident to Jacqueline and to Chris that the show wasn't a positive experience for her anymore. It wasn't a healthy place.

Like Jacqueline, Caroline had been anxious to leave for a couple of seasons— though her departure came with a bigger payoff.

Caroline Manzo: I was done season 3. I was done and I remember having conversations with Lucilla and she was like, "You're not going anywhere." So at season 4, I said to Andy, "I have to go," and he was like, "No." I felt like I had too much respect for what we'd built—because it was a phenomenon—to drag it down. I said, "I don't want to ruin your show and I'm going to because I'm done. I have nothing left to give you." And they said, "Okay, give us one more season and we'll give you *Manzo'd with Children*."

Kathy Wakile: I'm sure Teresa was jealous because she and Melissa both want spin-offs. I know Melissa desperately wants a spin-off.

Teresa Giudice: Oh, I didn't care. They always ask me for my own spin-off. I don't want it. My kids don't want it. I would never want my own show.

Andy Cohen: Everybody wants their own show. Everybody.

Caroline Manzo: I would have left either way, with or without the new show. I'm not that person that's going to hang on just because I want to be on TV. It's fun, it's great, it's all those things—but at the same time, you're in a whirlpool of nasty. Why would I want to subject myself to that? I walked away from a lot of money. But your sanity comes before money.

As for Kathy, she made appearances for the next two seasons as a Friend— Rosie even joining her in the role in season 7. But eventually, they, too, departed.

Lucilla D'Agostino: We tried with Kathy for as long as we could to stay honest to what her relationship was with Teresa, but it was repeating itself over. Kathy would try, Teresa would say no, Kathy would try, Teresa would say no. Rosie would try, Teresa would say no. And it doesn't work when someone's on an island.

Kathy Wakile: I was happy to come back part-time because my daughter had a recurrence of her brain cancer, and I was checked out pretty much any-way. But I kept trying with Teresa and asking production, "Can I have a sit-down with her to clear the air and let her know we're here for her?" And then one day, I had just gotten to my house in Florida, I got a text from production saying, "Teresa's agreed to a sit-down tomorrow. We've convinced her. You and Rosie have to be here." So I booked a flight back to Jersey, only to be told by Teresa that I was a cancer she needed to cut out of her life. (This was right after my daughter had brain cancer surgery, mind you.)

Rosie Pierri: I stayed pretty quiet in that scene because my sister had asked me, "Let me do the talking. I don't want this to be an explosive scene." So I kept my fucking mouth shut. But let me fucking tell ya, it took everything for me to not say what I wanted to say and not jump over the table and fucking punch her face. I don't like liars, and I get infuriated when I feel I'm being manipulated. I just get like a caged animal. I'm a reactor. A switch goes off and I'm ready to fucking kill. It took everything for me not to beat the fucking piss out of her for calling us fucking cancer.

Kathy Wakile: Teresa was very contradictory in that whole conversation, saying, "I love you guys. You'll always be my family. But I need to cut the cancer out at that." I don't know what her deal was. So I just said, "I'm so done."

Teresa Giudice: I stopped talking to Kathy when I realized I was giving her a paycheck every week. I didn't get that at first because I was so upset that my family was doing this to me. And when I put it together, I was like, "I'm so stupid! By entertaining her, I'm making her relevant." So I was like, "I'm done," and I cut her and Rosie out of my life. That's why they got fired. They didn't have anything without me.

Kathy Wakile: Afterward, Teresa was, like, sobbing in the car. Because she knew she was wrong, but she couldn't change it. That was it. How much more could she do to us? It was the end.

Teresa Giudice: If she never came on the show, I'd probably still have a relationship with Kathy. But it is what it is, you know? You live and learn!

Kathy Wakile: Teresa never forgave me. Never. She doesn't know that word. She didn't forgive Melissa or Joe, either.

Rosie Pierri: Meanwhile, Joe Gorga was there the whole time and did nothing. Which, I knew Joe and Melissa would turn on my sister because that's who they are. They're not loyal. Especially Joe Gorga, that little two-timing fucking two-faced fuck.

Melissa Gorga: Kathy was very hurt that she was no longer on the show.

She thought I could make Teresa reconcile with her, or that I could have fought harder to keep her on the show. I can't make Teresa do anything and I can't make Bravo do anything. Nor can Teresa make Bravo do anything! Teresa said that she was not filming with them, and Bravo made the decision not to stay with Kathy. She just had hard feelings about it.

Kathy Wakile: Melissa says I was upset with her, that I was part-time or whatever. That wasn't the case at all. I didn't care about the show. I was upset that the phone calls stopped. I was like, "What the fuck is going on here? We were friends. I accepted you with open arms into this family. It's our real-life family. I was there for you. And then you turn your back on me?"

Rosie Pierri: My sister stuck up for Joe Gorga and his bitch wife and got beat up. When my sister needed them to stay by her side a little bit, they fucking dogged her. And they turned their back on her. So they're pieces of shit for doing that.

Melissa Gorga: We have no relationship anymore.

Kathy Wakile: Melissa's life is wrapped up in this show. My life is still the life and relationships that we had before the show. And I value those. For them, it all became about story line. And I was just like, "This is just plastic bullshit." And I backed away.

Teresa Giudice: I'm still waiting for my thank-you card from Kathy. If it wasn't for me, she would have never built her house in Franklin Lakes. You're welcome, Kath!

Kathy Wakile: I'm not kissing anybody's ring anymore. Teresa thinks that she won. But what did she really get?

> Season 6 of RHONJ saw a major cast shake-up. To start, producers decided to expand beyond Franklin Lakes and cast a wider net. The results were . . . not well received.

Melissa Gorga: I was a little nervous for our show. With no Caroline, no Jacqueline, I was like, "I don't know that our franchise can handle the switch-up."

Andy Cohen: I lost a lot of sleep over what was to become of this massive hit show. It's next to impossible to replace family.

Shari Levine: I loved watching New Jersey because the family connection is not replaceable. You choose your friends not your family. And the dynamics we saw play out over the different seasons were relatable to everyone, because we all have family that we both love and pull against. The show was truly at a crossroads.

Lucilla D'Agostino: So much of the show took place in that bubble of northern New Jersey. At a certain point we said, "Let's open this up."

Amber Marchese (Housewife): When I was a kid, I wanted to be famous. I even practiced my autograph, though I had no talent whatsoever. I met Jim when I was in my twenties and started a family pretty young, and then I was diagnosed with cancer when my second child was six months old. So after that, I said to Jim, "I want to do acting. I know what it's like to face uncertainty in life, and I just want to do what I want to do."

Jim Marchese (Househusband): I belittled the whole idea of her being an actress. Of course, she proved me wrong.

Amber Marchese: I started taking acting lessons and was doing anything that came across my desk, so long as it wasn't porn. I was on a lot of casting calls for networks, and I applied for something that was very open-ended, looking for "affluent" women to do a reality show. I had no idea it was *Housewives*.

Lucilla D'Agostino: I'm not shocked to learn Amber saw it as an acting gig. In hindsight, that was part of the problem.

Amber Marchese: I also knew Melissa Gorga—though when I knew her in school, she was Melissa Marco.

Melissa Gorga: I hadn't talked to her in fifteen years. I was very surprised because I heard through the grapevine, "They found one of your old friends." When I found out it was her, I was like, "Oh my God, I forgot about her. I used to go to clubs with that chick."

Amber Marchese: Melissa immediately looked to me as her competition. I know this because she called me and basically said, "Don't fuck with me. I own this show." I felt like Spock—"I come in peace." We weren't there to take away money. We were all working together and should all have been able to sit at the table and give drama. But after she called me, I was like, "I'm the outsider." So I thought it would be cool if I had a bit of a posse going in. My intention was to have the twins as backup.

The twins were Nicole Napolitano and Teresa Aprea, sisters who brought a new family into the cast.

Nicole Napolitano (Housewife): I truly feel Amber would have never got chosen without us. Not to be pompous, but that's how I truly feel about it.

Amber Marchese: Production said to me, "Do you have any friends? Because you're in Central Jersey. All the girls are North Jersey. It'd be cool if we could have a couple people in your camp." So we started recruiting people. Then one day, our friend Bobby Ciasulli said he met these twins at Dunkin' Donuts. No shit. Literally, Dunkin' Donuts.

Nicole Napolitano: I'd lived in Colts Neck at that time for like, oh my gosh, it had to be over fifteen years. And I would always go into town and I would have my coffee and I would see Bobby at Dunkin' Donuts. Our kids went to school together. But we would never talk, we were never introduced. Then one day, Bobby asked me out on a date. And then, it was weird, he was just like, "Oh, you know what? Would you be interested in doing some kind of, like, reality TV?"

Teresa Aprea (Housewife): Nicole really got me involved. I knew nothing about it.

Bobby Ciasulli (Guest): The twins, they had a certain look, a certain attitude about them. I thought they'd be great.

Teresa Aprea: Bobby lived in the same development with Amber and Jim. They were good friends, so he introduced us to Amber and Jim.

Jim Marchese: Bobby told us, "I literally met these Bobbsey Twins. They're dumb as the day is long, but they've got big boobs and they're really loud." I was like, "All right! We'll try them!" So we met them for a glass of wine and they were all insane. They were perfect!

Nicole Napolitano: Because Amber always, always wanted to be a Housewife and they needed us to get her on. Bobby, Amber, Jim, they always watched *Housewives*. She lived and died by it.

Teresa Aprea: No, but I think she didn't know it was—

Nicole Napolitano: —She had a promoter, Teresa!

Teresa Aprea: You're right, you're right.

Nicole Napolitano: Teresa didn't want to be a part of it, but you know how twins are. I was like, "You are my dynamic duo. You have to do this."

Teresa Aprea: I was like, "No, no, no way." My sister told me, "We're going to be filmed for three days. It'll be nothing."

Nicole Napolitano: Before I knew it, it was all decided and we were cast. We had no idea it was *Housewives* when we agreed. It wasn't until I got a letter like a few weeks later, in the mail, we got something that said, "Welcome to Bravo's *Real Housewives of New Jersey*. You're going to be a Housewife this and that."

Andy Cohen: The twins were really cute. They brought Teresa's husband, Rino, with them. There was the whispered allegation that Rino had had an affair with his mother-in-law. It was all very *Jersey Housewives*. The trappings were there.

Bobby Ciasulli: At that point, me and Nicole had actually started dating. It wasn't a made-for-TV relationship. We'd been together about seven months when the phone calls started coming through again from Bravo about wanting to take a deeper look at our group.

Nicole Napolitano: Let me tell you something: That relationship was real. We cared for each other and we happened to get along very, very well. We even dated for almost a year after the show ended.

Season 6 also saw the return of the snarky favorite from the early seasons, Dina Manzo.

Lucilla D'Agostino: Getting Dina back took begging, lots of begging.

Dina Manzo: They had asked me back every season. Andy even came over one day with rosé and tried to get me back.

Andy Cohen: She didn't want to be on with her sister, so Caroline leaving opened up the door for her to come back. Getting Dina back was crucial to me.

Dina Manzo: I wouldn't do it while my family was on. I just couldn't do that to my parents.

Andy Cohen: She really just wanted to support Teresa.

Dina Manzo: They said, "We need you because we're going to give Teresa a break, and we want it to be fun, the way season 1 used to be, where you guys hung out and had a good time." And I said, "Okay, I will have her back. Nobody is going to talk about her on my watch."

Teresa Giudice: That was sweet, that she did that for me. I'm grateful. I love Dina. We've always been friends, we've never gone against each other, and that's the way they should be.

Lucilla D'Agostino: It was really exciting to see her again for a hot second. It was like the Beatles were back together in a weird sort of way.

Andy Cohen: It was very big that we got her back.

Despite all the new additions, the biggest story line of season 6 centered around the longest-running Jersey girl. Teresa and Joe Giudice were facing serious legal troubles. As their struggles were captured on film, some questioned the show's role in promoting their behavior.

Teresa Giudice: I feel like everybody on the show had something to do with Joe and I getting in trouble. I feel like they called the government. I really do believe that in my heart. I mean, that's really upsetting.

Andy Cohen: It was an interesting dialogue. On the one hand, you had an argument being made that these were criminals we were glorifying. On the other hand, I certainly felt like these were people who'd been sharing their lives with us for years, and now we were seeing arguably the most dramatic thing that could happen to them. How could we not show that?

Amber Marchese: She committed a crime. Taxpayers are still cleaning up for her crime. There are banks that were hurt by them. Everyone goes, "Oh, big banks." No. There were some small banks that were hurt by that crime. There were companies that were hurt by her crime.

Andy Cohen: People could say, "Well, you're paying them to do the show, so you are actually rewarding their behavior." But to me, this was a story we were all invested in and we had been following for so many years. How were we going to bail out of it now?

Dina Manzo: I know how Teresa is, I understand her at her core. She's not malicious in any way. Does she always say the right thing? No. A lot of times she says the wrong thing or she'll believe someone she shouldn't believe. But I was fiercely protective of her on and off camera that season, because I love her kids like they're my own, and I could see past the show and see what was happening to everybody in real life.

Lucilla D'Agostino: Teresa did not want to talk about her personal business. She did not appreciate people shooting scenes where they discussed it, because everything was speculation at the time. Mostly it was all playing out behind closed doors in Teresa's house. We didn't know the extent of how bad it was, and at the time, Teresa was just learning herself how bad it was. I don't believe for one second that she knew the full extent of how this was going to shake out. The gravity of the situation, and what ended up happening, was a constant shock for her. There was always a feeling that something could be worked out, that it wouldn't involve jail time. And then it became abundantly clear that at the very least Joe was going to go away. Obviously, every one of the ladies on the show had their opinions, but it was Richie Wakile who was always the most vocal. He was the one that was like, "Joe's going to go to jail." He was one of the first people that I ever heard emphatically believe that.

Kathy Wakile: Richie has no filter. He's like Joan Rivers—he says whatever everybody else is thinking. It was like, "Shut up, Rich. You can't say things like that," but it was not mean-spirited.

Rosie Pierri: What did she expect? She knows the game better than any of us. So why would she be upset over us talking about it? And we were just saying that we felt bad. But she got upset because we were getting airtime.

Teresa Giudice: Her husband was such an asshole.

Lucilla D'Agostino: Honestly, as angry as any of the women ever were with Teresa, every single one of them felt horrible. It all goes back to being mothers, knowing that there are kids involved and that these kids are the ones who are going to suffer. Not that they agreed with the choice to not read the documents your husband makes you sign, or to not look at the credit card statements. For Caroline, it was always like, "Wake up!"

Andy Cohen: How's this for weird timing, we were pretaping an episode of *Watch What Happens Live* and had Caroline and the Manzo kids come in to promote *Manzo'd with Children* the day Teresa and Joe were being sentenced. We realized we couldn't tape the show until the verdict came in because I would want to ask Caroline her opinion about it. And I remember it was just so surreal sitting with the Manzos in my greenroom waiting for this verdict to come in. It was very sad that day. We were all very sad. Nobody wanted them to go to jail.

Teresa Giudice: For Caroline to say that she knew what was going to happen to me. It was fucked up. She predicted what was going to happen. Like why, bitch? Why you predicting that? You're on to something. You're doing something, right?

Rosie Pierri: When she went away to prison, my heart broke for her. It did. I felt bad for her kids. How could I not? But Joe and Teresa brought it on themselves. I'm not saying their punishment was the right thing. I would have liked to see them not go to jail and pay back all the money they stole.

Teresa Giudice: I was mad at the show because obviously all eyes were on us. But it was Joe's fault. We're on national TV. It's like, you should just do the right thing, you know?

Andy Cohen: I'm a very nostalgic person. I do feel a special connection with the women who have been on the longest because we've been working together and I feel like I got famous because of them and with them. I feel a connection to many of them that is very real and goes beyond a working relationship. So I was sitting there and I just thought, "Wow, here's this woman who's going to jail for something that her husband did. And she seems pretty in the dark about it." I really didn't know if she would ever be back on the show. I really didn't know if I'd ever see her again. Or if the show would go on. There was just so much unclear. So as we were sitting there, I was starting to get really emotional. And that was when, in the season 6 reunion, I held her hand.

Lucilla D'Agostino: That day on set when she grabbed Andy's hand at the reunion, all of us were crying in the control room. Every single one of us. And we all cried when they walked off set because it felt like a death.

Teresa Giudice: I really thought I was not going to come back and I figured I was going away and that would be it. I thought my career was over.

Andy Cohen: I did a couple of interviews with them when they were first charged and before they went to jail. They were just terrible interviews. Joe was totally unrepentant, unsympathetic. And I can't say Teresa was very clear, she was so sedated.

Teresa Giudice: You know, for years I felt like Andy hated me because he always asked me the hardest questions. I was very sensitive. I didn't realize he was just doing his job, you know?

Andy Cohen: I didn't know what was going to happen to her, I didn't know if she would ever come back to the show, and we didn't know if we were going to wait for her. I drove out to see her in Jersey a week before she went to jail. I wanted us to be clean before she left, in case I never saw her again. There was so much that was uncertain, and she seemed willfully in the dark about what this prison experience was going to be. She was asking me what I thought she should do with her hair in prison. I mean, it was all very, very Teresa.

Teresa Giudice: I absolutely adore Andy, I love him so much. We kept in touch the whole time I was away. He was such a sweetheart, he was there for me and it meant a lot.

Andy Cohen: To access emails to a prisoner, you have to go to a website and enter all kinds of information. Every email I got from Tre had the subject line, "It's Teresa." It was totally unironic, like her!

While the series' longest-running cast member was dealing with her legal troubles, the cast's newest members wasted no time starting their own drama.

Melissa Gorga: The twins and Amber thought to be on *The Real Housewives of New Jersey*, you need to bring it, you need to scream, you need to go fucking crazy. And that's what they did.

Lucilla D'Agostino: Amber had Danielle vibes. She's fit and smart. She has a smart mouth. She's educated and has the husband who had the job that wasn't the blue-collar job. It was very different for us. She also had that Danielle vibe in the sense that you just didn't know what was going to happen. Amber could frickin' hold her own.

Melissa Gorga: I honestly think Amber and her husband were both fighting for the spotlight twenty-four hours a day. She was performing. She literally would say to her husband behind the scenes, "Oh, we did good. Did you see what we did there?" I would look at her like, "That's not how we do this."

> *Though Amber and the twins joined the cast as friends, a season-long falling-out began on a trip to Atlantic City and quickly escalated when Amber caught wind of a rumor that Teresa Aprea's husband had slept with her mother.*

Amber Marchese: I get this call from production like, "Hey, Teresa Giudice really wants you to go out to Long Island for her book signing." So they sent me a car to go out, and who is also there? Victoria Gotti! We ended up going to her house, which was sketchy. I was really fucking nervous. But then she was like, "You know, I know the twins." I'm like, "Oh, there we go." So she starts telling this big story about Teresa Aprea and Rino and the mom. My jaw went down to the floor because that's not what I thought I was going to hear. On any level. I come to find out later that Teresa Giudice is using me as a pawn—the backstory I heard was that Teresa had done a lot of digging, found this out before the twins were even brought on, and then used me to bring it out into the world. Fucked up.

> *On a trip to Florida that Dina hosted, the rumor was made public—but it didn't come out of a Housewife's mouth. . . .*

Amber Marchese: Jim said, "I'll just do it for you." And that's what he did. It was going to come out regardless.

Bobby Ciasulli: One night after we all came back from dinner, Jimmy started taunting me and Nicole in a very passive-aggressive way. He was talking about how he knew Amber was the girl for him the moment they met, and how he proposed right away—basically saying to Nicole, "I don't know why Bobby hasn't gotten engaged to you yet." She and her sister were drunk, so they were buying into this bullshit, taking the bait.

Teresa Aprea: Everybody was drinking a lot that night.

Bobby Ciasulli: I was not going to fight with her on TV, so I left the room and went upstairs. That's when Jimmy tried to get Nicole pissed off at me, twisting some story about how I had a girl living in my place in Florida—which, by the way, Nicole already knew because she'd seen the damn rent checks. He was like diarrhea of the mouth, stirring the pot. Finally, Teresa came up and told me, so then I had to go down there because if I didn't defend myself, it would look like I was guilty. And in all this mess, that's when Jimmy broke out this big secret that wasn't even true, how Teresa and Nicole's mother slept with Rino.

Teresa Aprea: You can call me whatever you want—sticks and stones. Call me a whore, call me a this, call me a that, I don't care. I know who I am. You want to talk about my husband? He's fine, he's a man, let him go handle himself. But don't ever talk about two people in my life: Don't ever talk about my mother who gave birth to me, and don't ever talk about my son who I gave birth to. Because then we're talking war.

Bobby Ciasulli: When I tell you all hell broke loose, it was completely out of control. I'm surprised the roof didn't blow off the house. They lost their minds when this happened. I thought, this kid has really gone over the deep end. I understand he wanted to be the villain breakout star, but there's got to be a fucking line somewhere that you just don't cross.

Jim Marchese: I mean, I knew if I told a guy to go have sex with his mother on national TV, it would not be well received.

Bobby Ciasulli: Eventually we all wound up back at the house, and me and Nicole's bedroom bathroom connected to Amber and Jimmy's room. And what did we hear for two hours? They were laughing hysterically about what just happened, both of them. They were high-fiving each other, saying, "You really brought it."

Dina Manzo: I told production I was throwing him out.

Teresa Aprea: They wanted to stay in the house. They wanted to go on that yacht so bad, they were practically begging.

Nicole Napolitano: They were humiliated when they got asked to leave the house. Humiliated. He got his balls cut off.

Jim Marchese: I had my tickets a month and a half early for the Florida trip. I knew I was only going to be there for two days. I had my return tickets. Everyone else got to stay for the week. We were going to get thrown out. That was the gag.

Dina Manzo: Maybe they gave him a heads-up that this was going to happen, but it was definitely me saying, "He's disgusting, I will not film with him anymore. I want him out of here."

Lucilla D'Agostino: Amber and Jim held on to this belief that Rino had sex with the twins' mom. And in an effort to make exceptional television, what better time to drop the bomb than on the group during the trip? So they probably knew they were going to say that and get kicked out.

Dina Manzo: I really pushed back against the story line in season 6. I even asked, "What can I do to change it? What can I help with to make this not about somebody's mother?" But that doesn't fly in reality TV—they want the most salacious thing. And it backfired because season 6 was the worst season ever.

Andy Cohen: Yeah, it was terrible. I mean, it was bad. It was just bad.

Melissa Gorga: We lost a lot of fans and we bottomed out for a minute.

Andy Cohen: Amber's husband was just too awful for TV, what can I say? Not since that Simon van Kempen has there been a husband that went after me so hard—he was after me on Twitter for years, and he kept saying that he was writing a tell-all book about me. People who get spat out of the system, it's difficult sometimes. They have a very strong love-hate relationship with the show. On the one hand, they want to do anything they can to sink it. And on the other hand, they want to do anything they can to get back on it.

Jim Marchese: I take it as a compliment. I joke around that I should've gotten an Emmy or an Oscar or something. Imagine not knowing any of these people and having to pretend.

Bobby Ciasulli: He has to have gone down as the worst, most hated man in *Housewives* history.

Andy Cohen: Let's just say I don't get tweets from people saying, "Bring Amber and Jim back." They're the only two people who have asked for their return.

Lucilla D'Agostino: There was a feeling among everyone that that particular experiment didn't work. We had stretched our arm entirely too far from the center of the world we had created.

> *Needless to say, Amber and the twins did not return for season 7. Neither did Dina, who said her final goodbye to the Garden State.*

Dina Manzo: I moved to California right after the reunion. I talked to Bravo about maybe being on *RHOBH* at the time, because I lived in Malibu. All around we felt like it wasn't the right fit because this is when they were on private jets everywhere. I was by no means poor, but that wasn't me.

> *After the failed experiment of season 6, producers weren't sure what was next. Four cast members were leaving. One was going to jail. The show's future was in jeopardy.*

Melissa Gorga: We went on a pause because after season 6, we were like, "We're lost here. This is not our show, this is not what we are."

Andy Cohen: Taking a hiatus was unprecedented. It certainly pained us, but it was the only thing we could do. If we had been more successful at introducing the twins or if Amber had been better liked by the viewers, then we would have kept shooting with them and brought in someone new or someone from the past. We would have shot while Teresa was in jail. But really it was slim pickings for us.

Kathleen French: That was a little bit of what we call a transitional year.

Lucilla D'Agostino: We had long conversations with Teresa and Joe and their attorney about the possibility of tracking Joe being the single parent while Teresa was away.

Teresa Giudice: They held the show for me and I was so surprised, so grateful, and so thankful. I was just saying, "Wow." It really meant a lot to me, you know? It did.

Kathleen French: While she was in prison, the network did a couple of specials where we showed Joe at home taking care of the kids, taking the kids to the Jersey Shore and different things.

Lucilla D'Agostino: And that was just part one—part two was Joe taking his turn going away.

Kathleen French: The months leading up to Joe going to prison, he was a very unhappy man and you could feel it in the show. Production knew it. They treaded very lightly around him. I'm sure he was reliving a thousand things he did right and a thousand things he did wrong, and you could see it on his face the whole time.

Lucilla D'Agostino: It was really difficult and it was very brave of both Teresa and Joe to agree to let us film during that time.

> *Though the relationship between Teresa and her sister-in-law had been strained for years, Teresa's time in prison seemed to change her attitude toward Melissa.*

Melissa Gorga: We were on bad terms pretty much until Teresa went to prison. She basically went in without us speaking to each other. But prison changed things a lot. By the time it was time for her to come out, she was ready. She wrote me a letter saying, "I can't wait to see you when I get out."

Teresa Giudice: Nothing really changed about me when I was in prison. I was more like, "God, is this what you have to do to me?" I never went away to college, so I guess this is my way to go away to college [*laughs*].

Lucilla D'Agostino: We were so sick and tired of the same conversation over and over again. They got tired of it, too.

Kathleen French: I do think they probably talked and said, "You know what? This is bad for the family, it's bad for our girls." Teresa's husband was about ready to go to prison, and she really needed her brother. They needed to put it to rest. I just wish they would have done that on camera.

Melissa Gorga: Maybe her going to prison brought to light, like, "You never know what could happen in this world." She realized I was not going anywhere.

Lucilla D'Agostino: The truth of the matter is, Teresa's family is very tight-knit and at a certain point it became easier for everybody in the family to just drop it. The parents were getting older—this was before Teresa and Joe's parents died.

Teresa Giudice: I only made up with Joe because of my parents. I did it for them, that's why. My parents, it broke their heart, you know? They had two children, they didn't want us to fight. So I let it go with him. And Melissa was an extension of that. Obviously if I wanna make peace with my brother, I gotta with her, too.

Melissa Gorga: We wanted for Teresa and Joe's parents to see us happy, so we fixed our relationship—and that's why I don't think Teresa and I will ever go back there. None of us would ever do that to my in-laws.

Kathleen French: I also think they realized it was just a bad look.

Danielle Staub: I know positively beyond a shadow of a doubt they're not on good terms. The only reason Melissa is around is because Teresa needs that whole element of someone to film with so she can stay on top. It's all fake. They hate each other. They just do all this stuff to make themselves look good for TV.

Kim DePaola: Teresa hates Melissa, and Melissa hates Teresa. That is just the bottom line. Anything else anybody tells you is a bald-faced lie. They cannot stand each other. That is it.

Teresa Giudice: I still hold a little bit of animosity toward Melissa. I'll never trust her again. Believe me, I keep the peace because I love my niece and my nephews, but I'll never forget. I forgave, but I'll never forget. How can you forget when somebody's done that to you? My own friends called me right away and my own family didn't? It's crazy. It still bothers me inside.

Melissa Gorga: As much as anyone wants to say the show ruined us, I totally say it brought us together. It forced us to go on vacations and girls' trips together and to have us bond outside of Joe and Joe, which was what we really needed. It forced us to rely on each other when newbies came in, because at the end of the day, our kids love each other and we're still family. Who are you going to back up if not family?

Teresa Giudice: They never said sorry about it. Melissa never admitted to me like, "Yeah, I did this. I came on the show behind your back to hurt you." That would go a long way. But yeah . . . I'll never fight with them again like that.

> *After nearly two years off the air,* RHONJ *season 7 began with Teresa's return home to her family after eleven months in prison.*

Kathleen French: It was like an *Ocean's Eleven* jailbreak. They were letting her out in the middle of the night, probably like three or four o'clock in the morning, because they wanted to try to avoid the press. I was in L.A., and I had my phone next to my bed and they started texting me as things started to unfold. "We're inside the jail," "She'll be coming out any time," "She's here," "We're now driving away," "We're being followed by the press." It was the craziest thing.

Lucilla D'Agostino: We had to hide Teresa under a blanket while we were on the highway with cars all around us.

Kathleen French: The press in front of Teresa's house was insane.

Lucilla D'Agostino: We wanted to authentically capture that first moment when she walked in.

Andy Cohen: I cried and cried watching her reunion with the girls. And it made me glad we kept following her story.

Lucilla D'Agostino: She was very, very nervous. Very quiet. If you look back, she looks so different. She did all that yoga, she had a different body and she was a different person. It was like she had been a boiling pot before and someone put her on simmer. She was just soft and mild and completely focused on seeing her daughters. Nothing else mattered in the entire world.

Melissa Gorga: Teresa changed for the better. After being judged by everyone, she realized that some of the things she used to worry about or that used to matter to her, like the material things, don't mean anything anymore.

Lucilla D'Agostino: Teresa graduated mentally from a place where what happened on the show ruled her life. By that point Teresa's life was so much more dramatic than the television show, and at a certain point she sort of put it in perspective. I give her credit for that.

Kathleen French: She and the network took a few knocks from people saying, "This is a person who is a convicted felon." Personally, I respected that she was found guilty, she did her time, she came back and was moving on with her life. She had shown herself to be a good mother, a good person.

The seventh season also added some new names to the cast, including Dolores Catania, who had appeared on-screen from time to time in previous seasons.

Lucilla D'Agostino: If you go back and watch early episodes, Dolores is in a number of the scenes—she's at Christmas parties, she's at Teresa's housewarming.

Dolores Catania (Housewife): Jacqueline pushed for me over the years. And I remember Caroline kept saying, "You're missing out by not having Dolores on." But I saw people going to jail, sisters and friends who weren't talking, so I never had FOMO. But that season, it just worked.

Kathleen French: She reached a point in her life where she and the ex were in a good place, the kids seemed like they were interesting and at an age where they would be a great added element. It just seemed like the perfect fit.

Dolores Catania: I also knew Teresa very well.

Andy Cohen: She "speaks Teresa." She could kind of translate. It was a perfect fit.

Dolores Catania: She was so timid that first day when I picked her up because it was her second day home from jail. She would jump when I pulled too close to a car. She was a shell of what she was before she went in. Not for long, though.

A second addition was Siggy Flicker.

Siggy Flicker (Housewife): I was introduced to *Housewives* through Jacqueline Laurita, who rejoined the cast that year. She basically said to me, "Listen, we have a situation where Teresa's coming out of jail and we need a fun, bubbly show. It's gotten too dark."

Lucilla D'Agostino: With Siggy, we were excited to bring on someone with an entirely different life experience and cultural background. Her passion for being Israeli and being Jewish, I've never seen anything that has equaled our cast's passion for being an Italian American. She brought a whole new flavor and awareness to our cast.

Kathleen French: Siggy was such a Jersey girl. She's funny, really funny. She was an accomplished person and an educator with such personality who was raising two kids. She just brought great energy to the group.

Lucilla D'Agostino: And Siggy does not suffer from a lack of opinions, so it was exciting to see her almost in Caroline's role, offering up advice, being the sophisticated adult in the room.

As Siggy said, the third new cast member was actually a returning one. After a season away, Jacqueline was back. But her return was short-lived.

Jacqueline Laurita: Toward the end of season 6 filming, producers called me and begged me to help save their show because filming wasn't going well. By that time, I missed my paycheck so I agreed to film again. You sort of get this temporary amnesia in between filming seasons and you forget how stressful it is.

Lucilla D'Agostino: The breakup of Jacqueline and Teresa's friendship was painful, so on the production side, we were all hopeful there could be a reconciliation.

Teresa Giudice: I hold grudges when you screw me. When I'm your friend, I'm loyal to the core. So with Jacqueline, I never trusted her again. I was trying, and I did try, but I just never trusted her.

Siggy Flicker: When you had Jacqueline and Teresa filming, it was just so real. There was tension there. And Jacqueline was an OG. She put a lot of heart and soul into that series.

Melissa Gorga: Honestly, Jacqueline could not take the stress.

Andy Cohen: She had become very, very polarizing to the viewers. She was really overly active on Twitter in a way that was detrimental to her own mental health, to the mental health of the other Housewives, to the mental health of the show. Her relationship with the show and the viewers' relationship with her just became too toxic.

Teresa Giudice: Jacqueline was my best friend. Was my best friend. That hurt me so bad what Jacqueline did, siding with my family and turning on me like that. It's like when a boyfriend cheats on you. How do you ever forgive them? You can't.

Melissa Gorga: Jacqueline's life was 24/7 *Real Housewives of New Jersey*. She never turned it off. So I knew that it was really affecting her. I almost wanted them to take her off for her own good.

The Housewives spent season 7 finding their footing after a long hiatus, and when season 8 rolled around, there was a familiar face returning to the show.

Noah Samton (Senior Vice President, Current Production, Bravo): The stories were getting a little tired and dark, and the audience wasn't thrilled. We were trying to inject some new life and take a little bit of a new approach. And when we were meeting before the season started shooting, it came up that Danielle and Teresa had reconnected.

Teresa Giudice: When I was away, I thought about Danielle and I felt bad that her job was taken away from her. She's a single mom, and I was getting ready to be a single mom. I wanted her to know that I did not take her job away from her, that was Caroline and Jacqueline who took her job away from her because they refused to film with her. I always wanted to work with her again. She was great TV. That's why I wanted to go have yoga with her.

Danielle Staub: Teresa reached out to me when she was finishing up her stay at the country club prison or whatever you want to call it. She said going away had changed her. She knew I'd always loved yoga—I didn't just find it in prison—and she wanted to write and sell a pretend book so she had to make people believe yoga was her thing. She was like, "Listen, I'm really sorry. I'd never take a paycheck from you again. I know now what it feels like to be a single mom." I go, "You really don't. You have your mother and your father raising your children." I mean, it's different. But I gave her a chance because I felt like she was being genuine. Like she genuinely needed a friend. The rest of them had turned on her.

Noah Samton: Of course, when we heard the two of them did yoga together, our jaws dropped. Like, "How's that even possible?"

Jacqueline Laurita: I heard Teresa thought I was coming back to the show and was using Danielle to come at me because she knew I didn't like Danielle and didn't want to film with her.

Danielle Staub: Yup. Teresa thought Jacqueline would be coming back and she wanted me to go after Jacqueline for her so she could look sweet as pie, like she'd learned everything she needed to learn in prison and was just as clean as could be.

Teresa Giudice: Listen, Danielle's her own person. I'd never tell somebody to go against someone else. Because then we're on a TV show, and they could go against you, you know?

Jacqueline Laurita: Danielle used Teresa, too. The week before they made up, Danielle was trashing Teresa on social media! It was a connection to get back on the show. Teresa was her ticket in.

Danielle Staub: They'd asked me back since season 4, but I said, "There's no way if I don't have an ally." Then enter, stage left, Teresa, fresh out of prison.

Andy Cohen: She had asked to come back pretty much every year. There were many emails, but I kept telling her there was no natural way in to bringing her back. As the years went by, and then Teresa started interacting with her, Teresa thought it would be interesting for the show, and I did too.

Noah Samton: Danielle is a lightning rod. We had a big internal discussion of, "Is this somebody we want to bring back?" Danielle certainly made for very interesting television, but she was controversial and had a dark history that was not necessarily exactly what we wanted our shows to be.

Danielle Staub: They offered me a Friend role, and I couldn't understand why I would want to return for a limited role and limited pay. But they convinced me that I would eventually be asked back full-time. I wasn't thrilled about it, because my gut told me that the limited role would leave me wide open for those who needed to make a name for themselves. Those people needed somebody to shit all over so they could look like a big deal.

Noah Samton: It was almost forced on us. Danielle and Teresa were suddenly friends, which happened completely organically. Before we knew it, she was there for the entire season and actually doing well.

Lucilla D'Agostino: Obviously it ended disastrously, but for the brief period of time that it was real, it was very real for Danielle. It was very real for Teresa.

Another new face in season 8 was Margaret Josephs.

Margaret Josephs (Housewife): They wanted me to do it in season 6, but I was signed for my own reality show to a different production company. Two years later, they needed somebody new. I was like, "All right. It's time." This was the dysfunctional family I was meant to be with. I was like, "I put the 'fun' in dysfunction."

Noah Samton: We looked at Margaret and it was like, "Wow, this is somebody who feels completely different." There was just something about her that was so interesting and compelling.

Lucilla D'Agostino: Margaret has a style of sarcasm that I'd never seen on this particular *Housewives*.

Andy Cohen: Margaret is amazing. She's a Jersey woman who tells it like it is, and she really makes me laugh. She was like the Dorinda of that show, but without as much history with the cast. She's really grown to be a fan favorite.

Noah Samton: If you watch her casting tape, there's just one-liners all across. People focus so much on the drama, but the humor is so important to us. And she was a home run in that regard.

Lucilla D'Agostino: And how can you not love a grown woman in pigtails?

Noah Samton: We always look for someone who has layers about them and fodder for storytelling. She had this cast of characters around her and the story of her ex-husband, who she's super close with.

Margaret Josephs: I was not going to pretend I didn't have an affair because people were going to ask me how I met Joe. I had to be up front about it. If I said I didn't have an affair, then people would find out and go, "Oh, you cheated." I had to be honest about my life. It was nothing I was ashamed of.

Danielle Staub: She needed to fit in with a group that didn't quite like people who cheated—Dolores got cheated on, Teresa got cheated on, I got cheated on. Everyone said, "If a woman cheats, I'm never going to allow them into the group." This woman was bragging about cheating on her husband for four and a half years while still living under his roof.

Margaret Josephs: They had a fucking hemorrhage. My daughter was very upset that I shared any of it, very devastated. But it was my story. I was telling them how I felt about mistakes I made. It was about my heartbreak.

One of the biggest feuds of the season was between newcomer Margaret and Siggy.

Margaret Josephs: I knew Siggy, but I was not friends with her—believe me, I could not stomach her at all before I got on the show.

Siggy Flicker: She's not my type of girl and I'm not hers. I would never hang out with somebody like that. We have an organic dislike.

Margaret Josephs: She made my life fucking miserable from day one. She was a total fucking douche. She was unhinged.

Siggy Flicker: From scene number one, when Margaret Josephs said she put pot on her pussy, I was already grossed out. Then she talked about her mom swallowing and talked about cheating on her husband? I was done. I said, "This is not my type of girl."

Dolores Catania: Siggy felt the producers were closer with Margaret—which they were. Margaret knew what to do to stay on the show. She went for Siggy—she called her "Soggy."

Margaret Josephs: They loved it. As soon as I said it, everybody started cracking up.

Dolores Catania: Siggy looked at her like, "What'd you just do to me?" Like she had shot her. That was the beginning of the end. Siggy never got over that moment.

Margaret Josephs: I was encouraged to apologize to her. I was like, "Grow the fuck up." But everyone was like, "She's hurt." I'm not used to people like that. She was crying. She took it to heart. She still cannot dial it back. *Housewives* is not for the faint of heart, the overly sensitive, and first-class pussies. You have to be able to move on.

Dolores Catania: Siggy went out of her fucking mind.

Margaret Josephs: From then on, shooting with her was horrible.

Noah Samton: Siggy is a very emotional, sensitive person.

Siggy Flicker: All I have to say is, thank the Lord for Dolores Catania. She stood by me. Even Teresa called me and said, "Siggy, I see what's going on. I love you. Hang in there." It was so hard. Teresa Giudice and Dolores Catania saved me from not walking off the show.

Noah Samton: It was complete torture. When I saw Margaret or Siggy calling or emailing me, I would cringe because there were two people at complete odds. The number of phone calls I had from both of them, the issues they had with each other, who did what and how upset they were—it was absolutely awful. There was no middle ground. It went on for months.

Trouble between the two women built up all season, culminating in a major blowup and accusations of antisemitism.

Siggy Flicker: It started because I said, "I'm going to so-and-so's charity event." Margaret right away says, "I don't like them." I said, "But you don't know them. You've never met them. They happen to be an angel and a doll, so shut up." And then she says, "Hitler wouldn't have killed me. Does that make him a great person?" Now if somebody would've brought up the KKK to a woman of color on *Housewives of Atlanta*, that would be meant to hurt them. This was an antisemitic remark and it was meant to hurt me. I know plenty of self-hating Jews. She said that to hurt me. When you're not getting along with somebody and you claim you want to make up with them, you apologize. You're not going to bring up Hitler's name, knowing I'm the daughter of a Holocaust survivor and scholar, and the only Jew in the room. Why was Hitler even on her brain?

Margaret Josephs: Her big thing is that she judges people only by the way they treat her. I said, "Well, that's the stupidest thing I've ever heard." I tried to explain it to her twenty-seven different ways. And I said, "Siggy, that's like saying Hitler would have been good to me. But that doesn't make him a good person." That's not antisemitic, but you know, she has a fucking pea brain. Then she said I was antisemitic knowing well and good that I was married to someone Jewish previously, that my son had a bar mitzvah, that I raised Jewish children.

Dolores Catania: Siggy wanted it to become something and it didn't. And that drove her crazy because, once again, she wasn't vindicated for something. It bothered her.

Margaret Josephs: Teresa felt sorry for Siggy. Dolores felt loyal to Siggy. It did divide the cast. Siggy was so crazy. After she called me an antisemite, it really put a rift in the whole thing.

Lucilla D'Agostino: It was not good for anyone. It wasn't good for the show. It wasn't good for Siggy, and it certainly wasn't good for Margaret. All of the hurt and all of the accusations were truly inflammatory. For Margaret to be called an antisemite is very powerful, very painful. And it wasn't done for a television show—that's really how it got between them.

Margaret Josephs: I knew they were going to put it on there. I don't think I ever asked them not to air it. I just said, "I'm so devastated. I'm so upset." They were like, "Obviously, we know you're not antisemitic." Basically, I was like, "I can't work with someone like this. She has to fix this." But she was trying to push me off the show. Little did she know, it backfired. Everybody who was Jewish came to my defense.

Noah Samton: It didn't have to blow up like that. We didn't want them to hate each other, but there was no stopping it.

Siggy Flicker: They really had hopes for her, but she fell short. You don't have any girl out there saying, "When I grow up, I want to be Margaret Josephs." Come on. She's a joke. She's a clown. That Margaret Josephs was always very, very jealous of me.

In the end, season 8 would be Siggy's last.

Noah Samton: She was just done. She was not having fun, and she didn't feel supported by the people she thought were her friends. And they were having a hard time understanding what she was so bothered by. There was no way to come back from it all.

Lucilla D'Agostino: If we're going to say Jacqueline would get obsessive behind the scenes, I feel like Siggy would have been second in line to claim that title. Behind the scenes the show really upset her.

Andy Cohen: Her relationship with the show and the producers turned really toxic. How many times can you relitigate that cake?

Melissa Gorga: You have to have a thick skin. Siggy and Jacqueline were great Housewives and they made great stories, but they personally could not handle it.

Andy Cohen: The viewers kind of turned on Siggy. There is love to hate and there's hate to hate. And unfortunately, as that season went on, people were just very annoyed.

Siggy Flicker: I really went in there with all the best intentions and I have to say, it was like *Mean Girls*. Every day they took that knife and they stuck it in deeper and deeper. I used to call the Bravo executives all the time and report the producers, and they knew it. I would call them out, which would infuriate them. It became draining for me and after about episode 6, I no longer wanted to be there. It took the life out of me. Now, Bravo was nothing but amazing to me. Andy Cohen was nothing but a gentleman to me. At the end, I had to just write the resignation letter, give it to my attorney, and say, for the sake of my health, I can't do it. It was too much for me.

Margaret Josephs: I didn't really know Andy, but I knew he sided with me.

Andy Cohen: Siggy was very upset at Margaret for mentioning Hitler's name in an analogy. (Sidenote: Analogies never work on *Jersey*!) I mean, listen, I'm Jewish. I talked to my rabbi about it. I talked to my parents about it. No one I know who's Jewish had a problem with using Hitler as an analogy. But she did and now it became a huge thing.

Margaret Josephs: She claims they let her walk away, but they were going to not ask her back. It was very clear. She couldn't take me being happy. She felt that I was favored or I was treated better. Meanwhile, I wasn't. She just did crazy, crazy things. But when she left, I felt like I hit the lottery. Like I hit the fucking lottery.

Siggy Flicker: I just know that in the two seasons I was on *Housewives of New Jersey*, I made my mark. The thing that I'm most proud of is leaving the show when I did. That was the best. My whole life, I was always about "Know your worth." And when you're not being treated correctly, you walk away.

As Siggy departed, two new castmates joined the gang. Meet Jackie Goldschneider and Jennifer Aydin.

Jackie Goldschneider (Housewife): They reached out to me on Facebook, and at first I said, "I'm sorry. I'm really not interested." That night I went home, took a screenshot of the text, wrote "LOL" on the bottom, and sent it to my three best college friends. All of a sudden they started texting me going, "Are you nuts? Call her back right now! Tell her you want to do this!" Then I sent it to my mother and she was like, "You don't say no until you know what it is."

Lucilla D'Agostino: Jackie came from a whole other life experience.

Jackie Goldschneider: Evan and I live around the corner from Siggy Flicker. We would drive by her house, see the vans outside, and say to each other, "I don't know what kind of person would do a reality show." Like, who would want all these cameras in their face all the time, the whole world knowing their business?

Andy Cohen: We loved that she had been a lawyer. She was professional, but she still seemed Jersey—very ballsy and unafraid of anybody.

Jackie Goldschneider: I texted Siggy the same night I texted my friends. I said, "Bravo casting reached out to me. Should I go for it?" She wrote back and she said, "It's the worst thing I've ever done in my life. I did it only to sell books. And I sold books. And then I got the hell out of there. It was horrendous, and you put your life in the hands of editors. That's all I have to say about it. Good luck." Still, at that point, I thought the chances I'd get it would be one in a thousand, so I called the casting producer back and we just went from there.

Shari Levine: Jennifer was perfect for *New Jersey*. She came from an old-world, traditional family dynamic. She still had family in "the old country." It was a different culture but felt very in line with the old-world Italian culture that was at the heart of *New Jersey*. She and Teresa and Dolores understood each other in a very core way.

Jennifer Aydin (Housewife): I had originally applied in season 6, but I was instructed that Bravo was on the prowl for a group connected through a family member or neighbor or something. So I pitched my cousin who lived in Franklin Lakes.

Noah Samton: By season 9, we were looking for a reinvigoration for *Jersey*. We wanted something that would breathe new life into it. Jennifer and Jackie both felt different from anything we had seen before. And Jennifer knew Melissa and Dolores, so they had real relationships.

Lucilla D'Agostino: I'm always excited by the prospect of showing people who are exactly what people think Italian American New Jersey women are like. But Jennifer also brought that Turkish background, this different idea of what families do and how husbands and wives behave. It was fun to explore her role in her family.

Andy Cohen: Jennifer seemed like a Jersey Housewife from the get-go. A plastic surgeon's wife, big McMansion, and she loved to flaunt it.

Jennifer Aydin: Of course, the vanity got the best of me and I decided to interview so I could say no to them after what had happened before.

Noah Samton: I went out to her house and it's this amazing sort of excess.

Jennifer Aydin: My house is a castle like the Taj Mahal. I pinch myself every day.

Andy Cohen: When Margaret talked about how close the mansion is to the Paramus Mall—I mean, it's so funny.

Noah Samton: It was visually overwhelming. Her house is giant with this huge pool and a basketball court and a movie theater. She's got five kids and two maids and an intercom system. But she would be on the intercom calling for help, and it was like being on the New York City subway in the seventies—you couldn't understand a word. She had a lot of elements that you look for in a Housewife—excessive glamour, the loud family.

Jennifer Aydin: I have the house. I got the husband. I got the kids. I got the crazy extended family. I'm willing to show it all: the good, the bad, the ugly. Of course, I would be perfect. So they called me up to tell me I got the gig and that Melissa would introduce me on the show. Boom.

Noah Samton: The thing that cemented Jennifer for me was when she said, "Let me show you my Siggy impression." And she did a dead-on impression of Siggy. It was perfect.

Dolores Catania: I liked her when I met her. She reminded me of Fran Drescher.

Lucilla D'Agostino: I also love anybody who has an unabashed love for plastic surgery and is unafraid to talk about it and to call people out on it.

Jackie Goldschneider: The first time I walked into Jennifer's house, I was like, "Oh my God. This house is enormous." And she kept showing off all the shit she had. I'm thinking to myself, "Bitch, I could buy this house without a mortgage with what I've got in the bank right now. I could buy this and not even notice a dent in my bank account." But I was hiding that. I hid my wealth for a season and a half. I've heard people say it's the first time in the history of *Housewives* somebody wanted to appear poorer than they actually are. But I have a lot of family money. It's not a lot of money that's liquid, sitting in my bank account. I invest everything, and I've got tons of real estate. But if I want to go buy something, I can. So when she was bragging about a big empty house in Paramus and I had to listen to all of this and have to be impressed by it, I didn't like her from day one. I fucking hate people who brag. I fucking hate it because I know I have more than you. So shut your fucking mouth because I'm not impressed by any of it.

Dolores Catania: Jen's always trying to prove something.

Jackie Goldschneider: She said a few times to me that first season, "We always have to stick together. We have to be each other's allies."

Lucilla D'Agostino: She likes to call people out on their bullshit.

Jackie Goldschneider: It's no secret that I don't like Jen. I'm glad she's there, though, because she throws herself under the bus for the sake of the show.

Melissa Gorga: Jennifer is another one of those who would just do whatever she had to do to make herself seen.

The season 9 reunion brought a big revelation. One of the staple relationships of the show could be coming to an end: the marriage of Joe and Teresa Giudice.

Andy Cohen: I was surprised when Teresa said at that reunion that if Joe got deported they were splitting up. That was the first we had heard of it.

Rosie Pierri: Come on! She wasn't going to say, "I'm moving to Italy." No way. I don't know what their marriage was like. I don't even want to speculate because I didn't live with them. It's not my business. But I always thought if he had to stay in Italy, she wouldn't go there. She wouldn't be able to live there. It's not a life that she could deal with.

Teresa Giudice: There were people that wanted to take us down, which they did. I have to say they did take us down, which is sad. But, you know, we both rose back up. I wish he wouldn't have got deported 'cause it's sad for my children. But I guess this is the way life was supposed to go. I don't know how else to look at it. I can't keep crying over it.

Dolores Catania: Those two, they have a special bond. They'll forever be connected because of those girls.

Teresa Giudice: Joe was a great husband and is a great father. The way he acted on the show was so different than the way he acted with me in person. The thing was, he didn't like to film and I would make him do it, and then he would be an ass on the show. Believe me, he was horrified by his behavior on the show, looking back. He was. I should have just not made him film. You see how some husbands get into it? He didn't like the cameras. He wasn't trying to become famous. He's just a normal person.

Season 10 saw an all-returning cast for the first time in years—but that didn't mean it was short on drama. One unexpected showdown stemmed from a pair of twelve-year-olds' birthday party.

Jackie Goldschneider: Producers asked me, "Are you going to throw your kids a party?" When I think of *Housewives* parties, I think of Taylor Armstrong throwing that party for Kennedy in the first season of *RHOBH*. I told them, "I do not do over-the-top birthday parties for my children. So I'm going to show you the real party I would have."

Jennifer Aydin: Number one thing at a birthday party is entertainment. All right, we've got twenty kids here. Now, what are we going to do? We're going to sit here and twiddle our thumbs? Run around in circles? "No, pick a team, kids! Basketball, blue or white." I had a six-year-old wearing fucking heels—you think she wants to play on the white team of the basketball game? I don't think so, honey. Where's your gender-friendly activity table?

Jackie Goldschneider: When you're twelve years old, it's a fucking drop-off party. I'm not going to have food for adults at a drop-off party.

Jennifer Aydin: When you're inviting adults, it's common courtesy to have a little bit of something other than just pizza and cake. There wasn't even a fucking balloon in sight.

Jackie Goldschneider: Jennifer said it was sweltering heat and that everyone had to stand in a driveway. It was a beautiful April day, but it certainly wasn't sweltering heat. It was sixty-five degrees. I was in a fucking turtleneck.

Jennifer Aydin: And then the Amazon box came.

Jackie Goldschneider: The thing with the Amazon box is like me at my core. Me throwing that Amazon box on the floor, I didn't think, "This is such a great filming moment." I just put it down because I didn't want the kids to leave without their party favor. People went to town on it. People fucking loved it. Every mom in America fucking loved it.

Jennifer Aydin: The fact that it was called the goody bag was actually an oxymoron because there was no bag inside, honey.

Jackie Goldschneider: The people who are fancy schmancies thought, "How could you do that? You ruined the party." People still talk about it!

Jennifer Aydin: At the end of the day, I just felt she was being stingy.

Jackie Goldschneider: I am the least cheap person in the world. But I don't spend money on nonsense. I don't see any point in it.

In what can only be described as a full-circle moment, the most dramatic showdown of the season involved Danielle and a hair pull. But this time, Danielle wasn't on the receiving end.

Margaret Josephs: When I first joined the show, I wanted to give Danielle a fair shot. I figured years had gone by, maybe she was better, she probably had therapy. I thought she was misunderstood. If you look at her first season, she was very sweet, very nurturing. I liked her, we spent a lot of time together, and I really wanted her to be a Housewife. I truly wanted good things for her.

Danielle Staub: I allowed her to get in and know my damages while she was sharing all of hers.

Margaret Josephs: Everything I did, she wanted to do and do it better. She moved to Englewood, New Jersey, to be by me. She shopped in the same boutiques, used the same hairdresser. She was very *Single White Female*. I know it sounds crazy, but I was getting pissed off at her. She would say that I talked crap about her and about my friends. One day she said to me, crying, "I don't know who to trust!" I said, "Don't trust anybody. You talk too much." I said that because she tells everything to everybody all the time.

Melissa Gorga: Margaret was not happy with a lot of the things Danielle was saying and doing. She wasn't happy with the friend that she was, and she didn't want to be a part of it anymore.

Jackie Goldschneider: Once Danielle started fighting with Margaret, it all went downhill. She thought I took Margaret from her. I didn't have to take Margaret from anyone. Margaret has more friends than I've ever had in my life. Margaret is her own person.

The bad blood escalated during a shopping trip gone terribly wrong. After an exchange of harsh words on both sides, Margaret dumped a bottle of water out on Danielle. In retaliation, Danielle threw the contents of Margaret's purse on a candle. Just after things had seemingly died down, Danielle came back for more, yanking Margaret's ponytail.

Margaret Josephs: We were arguing for probably an hour and a half to two hours. She was acting crazy. She pushed me twice.

Noah Samton: Margaret poured the water on Danielle.

Margaret Josephs: I did think she was going to hit me. That's a Housewife move. Instead she set my purse on fire. She did. She ruined the stuff. She burnt my Valentino bag. My makeup. My money. My lipstick. All that stuff was smushed into that candle. Everything. She poured wax into my bag.

Jennifer Aydin: Let's put ourselves in that situation. Would we let someone pour water over us in an aggressive and hostile manner, especially on camera when they're going to make us look like a punk in front of the whole world? Hell fucking no! That is a sign of attack. An attack deserves retaliation.

Noah Samton: Danielle sort of thought about it for a few minutes. She didn't react immediately. But she was not going to let Margaret get away with that.

Jennifer Aydin: Danielle could have played that scene any way she wanted. Maybe she could have gotten the pity card and Margaret would have looked like the villain. Instead, the way she retaliated was so aggressive that nobody cared what Margaret did anymore. You pulled her hair, you risked physically harming her—that's not what we signed up for.

Margaret Josephs: Dolores, Melissa, Jackie, and I were talking about how crazy Danielle is because she set my purse on fire. We were cleaning it up. I had no idea she was coming back over to me, because I was bent over. We were all so taken aback. I didn't even know what was happening.

Noah Samton: There are many people in the world who will say if you pour a glass of water on somebody's head, get ready to get punched in the face. And then there are people who will say pouring a glass of water on somebody's head is not something you should do, but it certainly doesn't justify physical assault. And I'm sure if you ask fifty people, you're going to get a lot of different opinions on which is right. But believe me, Margaret thinks very strongly that there's a vast gulf between pouring water on somebody's head and pulling somebody's hair. And Danielle thinks one action leads to a reaction. So that was what we were in the middle of.

Jennifer Aydin: Danielle claims to be a pro on this show. If you're so much of a pro, don't do it on fucking camera. You want to win this game? Hold your own. Keep it together. Walk out like a lady.

Noah Samton: Dealing with the immediate aftermath, Margaret was incredibly upset, understandably, at what had happened. She wanted to be done shooting the show. She didn't want Danielle to ever be on the show again because of this.

Jennifer Aydin: I told Teresa it was fucked up that Danielle pulled Margaret's hair. I didn't know Teresa was in on it. None of us knew. We all found out at the finale. That was very, very real.

Noah Samton: We didn't find out about that until days after the incident, when one of the audio guys came to the producers of the show and said, "Hey, Teresa said something to Danielle before she pulled Margaret's hair." That sort of shifted the entire story for us because suddenly we now had this whole other layer that Teresa was actually the instigator.

Teresa Giudice: It wasn't my idea. Steven Dann, the owner of the shop we were in, he's the one who said it first and then she came up to me and asked me. I wasn't in the right state of mind because I was drinking, so I said, "Yeah." What I didn't know then was that it was on camera. Like, Danielle was trying to be discreetful [*sic*], but they caught her and I was miked when she came and asked me in my ear.

Noah Samton: Margaret thought Teresa was her good friend, not knowing that her good friend betrayed her this way. As producers, that was important information for Margaret to have. It was challenging for us because we didn't like that Margaret was sort of living a lie and was unaware of Teresa's role in what happened to her. But at the same time, we didn't want to engineer what happened. So it remained a secret until Danielle brought it up on her own to Melissa, and Melissa brought it back to Margaret.

Jennifer Aydin: Danielle ratted Teresa out! You don't bite the hand that feeds you! You don't burn the bridge that crosses you over to the other side. What is she, an idiot? Teresa was her only anchor to this group.

Noah Samton: There were layers to what was going on. Danielle was being dumped on by everybody. There was talk of her getting kicked off the show because she was being violent. And Danielle was telling us on the side that Teresa encouraged her. She was trying to defend herself.

Margaret Josephs: When I found out I was in shock. Why would Teresa do this? I was like, "What is going on here? How did they plot it? What happened?"

Noah Samton: Teresa thought she had gotten away with it. Then, suddenly, the conversation came up. I'm sure she felt like, oh, now I'm in trouble for something I thought I'd gotten away with. And, you know, she wasn't happy about it.

Teresa Giudice: When Melissa told me what Danielle had said, I got upset with production and cursed them out because I realized at that moment they had that footage.

Melissa Gorga: Deep down, Teresa was probably making Danielle do it for the show, and now production was calling her out. She was pissed.

Jennifer Aydin: Well, Teresa saw that Margaret did pick on Danielle. Yes, Danielle was an easy target, but when Margaret goes in, she goes in hard. There are times when Danielle doesn't go in and Danielle looks like the punk. So Teresa was a little fed up.

Noah Samton: I don't think Teresa really meant to encourage violence.

Jennifer Aydin: If someone poured water on Teresa like that, can you imagine what Teresa would have done? She would have been like a jungle animal! Like, straight for the throat.

Teresa Giudice: Yeah, I mean . . . if somebody treated me like we were great friends and you did what you did to me that day? It was bad. But at the end of the day, Danielle's her own person. You don't have to listen to me, you know what I mean? Like, do your own thing.

Margaret Josephs: In Teresa's head, she probably thought Danielle was going to come and give me a little yank on my ponytail. You know? Teresa doesn't think things through.

Teresa Giudice: I got blamed for it but I really was apologetic. I apologized to Margaret.

Margaret Josephs: Teresa truly cares about me. She knows I've been good to her. She was mortified when she thought about it. I just think that can't be an excuse anymore. She has to take accountability moving forward.

Teresa Giudice: I'm not like Jackie Goldschneider, who, like, starts crying, you know?

Jackie Goldschneider: Margaret was absolutely adamant that if Danielle was ever in one scene with her again that she would never come back to the show. So I knew that if Danielle wasn't coming around Margaret, she probably wasn't coming around me anymore. Once you put your hands on somebody, you throw yourself off the show. I hate her, but I wouldn't mind filming with her because I could fucking tear her apart.

Margaret Josephs: Listen, I didn't blow it up. I could've made a big stink. But I was like, I'm not even gonna. I was so disgusted. She attacked me. She was trying to say I poured the water, I pushed her. I was like, "Cut me a fucking break."

Noah Samton: What ultimately happened was that Danielle wanted things to unfold in a way that worked for her. And Margaret wanted Danielle to be done forever at that moment. And neither one of them was getting exactly what they wanted. To Margaret's credit, she ultimately rolled with some punches because she understood that having Danielle on the show in some capacity is something the viewers wanted to see. They wanted to see resolution after that hair pull.

In the end, season 10 was Danielle's swan song.

Noah Samton: There was nobody on the show who was friends with her by the end of the season. There was nowhere for her to go on the show. You cannot be on *Housewives* and not be friends with anybody else in the cast, it just doesn't work. So it's not as simple as Margaret got her fired or Danielle quit. There's a lot of gray area in there.

Andy Cohen: At Danielle's request, she came on *WWHL* and announced that she was quitting the show to focus on her YouTube cooking show, and that she would never, ever come back. That was the last I saw of her. A year or so later she put out a podcast completely trashing me as a human being and a father.

Teresa Giudice: She made a mistake because instead of going after Melissa, who kind of wrote her off back in season 3, Danielle went against me when I'm the one who brought her back on the show, I'm the one that got her a paycheck again. And then she's the one who threw me under the bus! I was like, "Really, why would you do that? Now you don't have a job anymore." I couldn't believe that. Talk about loyalty.

Margaret Josephs: Danielle's entire life was *Housewives of New Jersey*. Obsessed. Her only goal in life was to get back on and prove herself. And she proved herself to be exactly what she was: a psychopath.

Dolores Catania: The thing about *New Jersey* wives: everybody had their part in how their story ended. No one can make you do anything. They can't make you look like you're doing something that you didn't do. The producers aren't photoshopping you on the floor under the table drunk. You're doing it. You've done this. You have to own it.

Teresa Giudice: Everyone thinks I'm not smart. Believe me, I'm smarter than everyone thinks. I may play that role, but trust me, I'm not going to go down that way. I know how to make good TV. If you come at me, I'm coming guns blazing.

PART V

"Capitol Wives"

The Real Housewives of D.C.

PREMIERE DATE: AUGUST 5, 2010
FINALE DATE: OCTOBER 21, 2010

---

*When the FBI subpoenas your raw tapes,
you're not bringing the show back.*
—ANDY COHEN

The D.C. franchise of Real Housewives *lasted only one season—but it certainly made headlines. That's mostly thanks to cast members Michaele and Tareq Salahi, the now infamous "White House Party Crashers" who may or may not have had an invitation to the White House State Dinner they attended.*

Lauren Zalaznick: D.C. was a great example of flying in the face of every critic who said it's produced reality, it's manipulated, it's controlled, it's this and that. Well, first of all, the show was interesting because it was very hard to cast in D.C. The people are interesting, but it's such a tight little society. It was a pretty good season. And it was going fine. And then honestly, we got grifted. And we were stunned. Stunned. As was our crew, when the grifters actually grifted their way into a very exclusive event.

Andy Cohen: I was really proud of *RHODC*. It was a racially diverse, eclectic group who discussed politics, and where access to power meant everything. That access—or attempt at access—is what ultimately sunk the show.

Amy Argetsinger (Writer, the *Washington Post*'s Reliable Source column): Let me set the stage for you. It was the first state dinner for the Obama White House. It was a big deal.

Roxanne Roberts (Writer, the *Washington Post*'s Reliable Source column): The first state dinner of any administration is an important social and political moment. That the Obamas—arguably the most popular presidential couple in decades—were finally having their first state dinner almost a year after the election meant that anybody who was anybody within the Democratic political establishment wanted to attend.

Andy Cohen: The Salahis were real characters. Michaele was kind of a bubbly space cadet who was longing to be a society lady. She was zany, untrustworthy, likable, and fragile all at once. Tareq reminded me of an incredibly litigious used-car salesman whose suits needed a good dry cleaning. Still, when they told our producers they were invited to the White House for the state dinner honoring India, no one had reason to question them. One of the first scenes we'd shot with them was a polo match featuring the ambassador from India and a friend of theirs from the State Department.

Abby Greensfelder (Cofounder, Half Yard Productions): My company was developing the franchise, and to us what's most interesting about D.C. is that it's really not about money or fame but about proximity to power. So we thought the state dinner would be a true access moment for the *D.C. Housewives* viewer. It's like the prom on steroids for Washington. We tried to get filming access—we needed permits and approvals—but we never heard back from the White House, which wasn't surprising. I never expected they would allow us to film—those things are very cornered off. So we decided to just follow them to the point where we couldn't anymore.

Andy Cohen: We shot plenty that day: Michaele trying to figure out how to pin herself into her elegant red sari, Michaele looking for the invitation that may or may not have existed, then the two of them climbing into the limo and heading toward 1600 Pennsylvania Avenue.

Amy Argetsinger: My guess is that they walked out of the limo knowing they were being filmed as they walked up to the White House gate. I don't think they expected to get in, necessarily. For all I know, they figured they would tell Bravo the next day that they had been at the dinner even though they hadn't.

Roxanne Roberts: It was a chilly, rainy night in November, and the White House had invited some three hundred guests. So the White House staff and the staff at the various security checkpoints were under a lot of pressure to get a large number of people in the door as quickly as possible. And these are all people who are important to the White House in one way or the other—people who are unaccustomed to standing in lines, much less outside in the cold.

Abby Greensfelder: Somebody checked the list and allowed them in. We thought it was all good.

Roxanne Roberts: The fact that they got in must have been stunning to them.

Lauren Zalaznick: The Salahis were shady as hell. I'm thinking back, like going over the episode or at least that footage in my mind, thinking we remember they're in the back of the limo, and the producers are saying, "But do you have the invite? Could we see them? Could we see it? We can't go in. We've called. We the producers have called to get a permit to shoot even on the ground and this and that. They don't have a record of you."

> *They just might have gotten away with it, had it not been for Reliable Source columnist Roxanne Roberts, who had been covering the casting and filming of* RHODC *for the* Washington Post.

Roxanne Roberts: I had covered state dinners at that point for twenty years. I was really familiar with the routine. And when Michaele and Tareq walked in, I took notice. And honestly, if I hadn't been there, it's entirely possible no one would have ever noticed. The Venn diagram of people who had a close awareness of the *Real Housewives of D.C.*, which was still filming and hadn't yet aired, and were also intimately familiar with how state dinners happened was very, very small.

Amy Argetsinger: That night, Roxanne called me and said, "You'll never guess who managed to get into the dinner: Tareq and Michaele Salahi."

Roxanne Roberts: They were announced by the military attaché, and my first thought was, "Could that be? Is it really them?" She was wearing a red sari. He was in a tuxedo. I immediately checked the guest list to see if I had overlooked their names. I hadn't.

Amy Argetsinger: When Roxanne told me, my immediate reaction was, "They must've crashed," because I knew instantly that no one would have put them on that list. Roxanne's reaction was, "I don't think it's possible to crash the state dinner."

Roxanne Roberts: The idea that anybody could crash the White House—theoretically one of the most secure places in the entire world—was just stunning to me.

Amy Argetsinger: Later that night, I saw all the pictures that the Salahis were posting from inside the reception and I freaked out.

Abby Greensfelder: The moment we discovered something was askew was the next day. The *Washington Post* publishes a list of the people who attended the state dinner in the paper, and I looked at the list and I was like, "That's weird, the Salahis are not on here." But I didn't think much more about it. And then I got a call that was like, "There's an issue."

Amy Argetsinger: We posted some photos online early that Wednesday morning saying, "Look who showed up at the state dinner." It took us several more hours to be able to write with some measure of confirmation and legal confidence that these people appeared to have crashed.

Roxanne Roberts: The White House had to verify that they were not invited guests.

Amy Argetsinger: The White House Press Office's reaction was, "I don't know what you think you saw, but those people were not invited. No one let them in. They were not seated." They were almost denying that these people could possibly have been there. To us, that was confirmation that they had gotten in without an invitation.

Roxanne Roberts: No one would have noticed they shouldn't have been there until it was time to sit down, because every table at a state dinner is obsessively considered, and each table has someone who serves as the host and knows where everyone is to be seated. So if you're not supposed to be at a state dinner, you can't just sit down at any table. Even so, they basically had a ninety-minute ride before the coach was going to turn back into a pumpkin.

Amy Argetsinger: Once we published, it was a front-page story.

Andy Cohen: I was on a friend's boat in Indonesia, of all places, and that morning I got up and on the cover of the *New York Post* was a photo of the Salahis with the headline, PARTY DUPERS. I was looking at them saying, "I think I know them . . ." Well, then I checked my email, which was filled with frantic emails from Bravo: "Urgent! Urgent!" That's when it clicked. I was like, "Oh my God, this is a Housewife."

Abby Greensfelder: I called Michaele and asked what happened. She and Tareq were pretty much like, "No big deal." They had that "all press is good press" attitude.

Amy Argetsinger: It was one story after another for more than a month because there were so many pieces here: Who is this couple? How did they get in? What was going on at the White House that people who were not invited were able to get in and shake hands with the president? That was the shocking photo—when they went into the receiving line. There were some serious national security questions to be answered.

Andy Cohen: The press went after Bravo as hard as they did the couple.

Lauren Zalaznick: We really had to fend for ourselves, PR wise. NBC News was really against us, I remember distinctly. There were a lot of people up on high horses saying it's the end of civilization again because of this little show.

> Soon a federal investigation was launched to try to determine how this alleged security breach had occurred.

Andy Cohen: This wasn't just some tabloid media firestorm. It was literally a federal case.

Abby Greensfelder: There was a federal investigation, a Committee on Homeland Security hearing, and then a grand jury investigation— which some of our staff testified for. Imagine, here we were asking some twenty-year-old producer who just happened to be helping with a sheet of paper that day: "Do you mind going in and testifying in front of the grand jury?"

Mary Schmidt Amons (Housewife): My understanding is that the authorities right away implicated Bravo and producers.

Abby Greensfelder: At first our take was, "It's a *Real Housewives* franchise. It's not a documentary, it's not news, it's an entertainment program." But when the Secret Service got involved, all of a sudden, the truth became vitally important.

Andy Cohen: A massive debate was ignited over the ethics of reality TV, which I found incredibly frustrating and very upsetting.

Abby Greensfelder: Being in Washington and having a business here, I had people working for me who were savvy about managing government. Before we even started filming, we made sure we were very buttoned-up on the types of procedures we needed to follow. And luckily, as part of our production process, we had very diligent notes and call sheets, so everything was very documented.

Andy Cohen: Everything was basically turned over to the investigators.

Abby Greensfelder: There was a big focus on making sure that we could both assist any investigations the government would do and make sure that we had the evidence that this was not a TV stunt.

Andy Cohen: Because it wasn't.

Abby Greensfelder: During our investigation, we combed through footage as evidence. We had footage of the Salahis speaking with the person stationed outside the gate; we didn't really have hearable audio on what that full conversation was, but you hear the security person say they're not on the list but let them go to the next checkpoint. And remember, we couldn't film them after that point because we didn't have a permit. So any further conversations happened out of earshot from us. We still don't know exactly what was said between the Salahis and the final Secret Service person who let them in, but it was clear it wasn't on us.

Amy Argetsinger: No charges ever came out of it on the production end.

Mary Schmidt Amons: The Secret Service wound up taking the blame for it all.

Amy Argetsinger: Desirée Rogers, the White House social secretary, ended up stepping down from her position. There was some perception that she just wasn't running a tight enough ship.

Mary Schmidt Amons: Of course, Tareq and Michaele got off scot-free.

Abby Greensfelder: Tareq and Michaele remained defiant about their innocence the whole time. To this day, I don't think anybody knows the exact truth of what happened. Even those who investigated it.

Mary Schmidt Amons: I mean, it was an international incident that was captured and unfolded on reality TV cameras. It's mind-blowing, looking back on it, that the whole thing happened.

> The Real Housewives of D.C. *premiered on August 5, 2010. Its eleven-episode season would be its last, making history as the only franchise to get canceled after just one season.*

Andy Cohen: When the FBI subpoenas your raw tapes, you're not bringing the show back.

Abby Greensfelder: Now that we've officially had a reality show president, Andy Cohen has joked about rebooting the *Housewives of D.C.* with Kellyanne Conway. Television will always have a role to play in Washington because that world we showed, it's still there whether we're filming it or not.

PART VI

"Shine of a Diamond"

The Real Housewives of Beverly Hills

PREMIERE DATE: OCTOBER 4, 2010

*These bitches are jealous. They really can't be happy for each other.
A lot of these women are like, "It's my show, I'm the star."*

—BRANDI GLANVILLE

Andy Cohen: I was against it in the beginning. I was like, "Look, we already have four franchises. How much is too much?"

Alex Baskin: We pitched the network for a few years on the idea of doing *Real Housewives of Beverly Hills*. And the network was concerned that *RHOBH* may be unnecessary and duplicative of *RHOC*. They sort of said, "What's the difference?"

Kathleen French: You could be doing a show in Orange County and a show on Mars. That's how different Beverly Hills is.

Dave Rupel (Executive Producer): For me, *Real Housewives of Beverly Hills* was more akin to *Dynasty*. I remember telling the crew, "We're doing soap operas. We're doing cliffhangers and flashbacks and long pauses." We're watching rich people here. And we should be envious of their lifestyle, but we should also know their lives aren't perfect.

Alex Baskin: That's why one of the candidates for season 1 of *Real Housewives of Beverly Hills* was none other than Lisa Rinna.

Lisa Rinna (Housewife): I went in and made a tape and they came to the house and filmed a little sizzle reel. Usually when you get to that point, you're on the short list.

Alex Baskin: We thought Rinna was an interesting choice because she was very much a Hollywood type—sort of the actress/entertainer who was still hanging on and has a famous husband. But at the time, Bravo didn't want actresses on the show because they thought it would take away from the reality.

Andy Cohen: Lisa Rinna had been on so many reality shows, it just seemed like a parody. For me, it needed to be about real women. I didn't think we should have an actress, and I didn't think any of them should be famous.

> *A few early entrants into the franchise would set the tone for RHOBH: stunningly aspirational for viewers, extremely competitive for insiders. Kyle Richards—known as aunt to Paris Hilton and sister to Kathy, and a beloved former child star—was the first to catch the attention of production.*

Jennifer Redinger: I remember my producer was like, "I watched an *E! True Hollywood Story* on Paris Hilton last night and it showed Kyle Richards's home. We need to get in touch with her." Kyle has all the glamour and the lifestyle of Beverly Hills, but she's so down-to-earth and relatable as a woman.

Alex Baskin: She's somehow sort of completely of L.A., but not totally defined by it.

Douglas Ross: And she grew up in Hollywood.

Kyle Richards (Housewife): I knew Bethenny but I hadn't really paid attention to the series, to be honest. I didn't really get what it was.

Andy Cohen: I remember there was a pitch from the Richards sisters going around, centering a show on Kyle, Kim, and Kathy. That brought in Kyle and Kim, and now of course, we have Kathy, too, so that germ of an idea really blossomed into the show.

Kyle Richards: No. What happened was, they kind of said they may not do Beverly Hills because of the OC thing. And I'll never forget, I was sitting in the parking lot of Porsha's preschool. It was her Mommy and Me. E! had offered us a show with my sisters and me. E! had. All three of us. At that time, E! wasn't the sister network, so my manager called me. I guess when Bravo heard about the E! show they were like, "Wait a minute, hold on, we're going to lose these girls if they do this." So my manager said, "They will greenlight *Real Housewives of Beverly Hills* if you say yes right now," and I was like, "Right now? I need time to think about this!" The whole time I was like, "Is this really going to happen? Am I really going to do this?" And they said, "Well if you say yes, it's a go." And I was like, "Okay, let me just called Kim." And I said, "Listen, we could do the E! thing or we could do this. This is already an existing successful franchise." And I don't know, I kind of . . . in my mind, I didn't always want to be "Paris Hilton's aunt" or "Kim Richards's sister." Growing up, I had my own acting career—Kim and I both did—and then when Paris became so famous, it was like, "Oh, that's Paris Hilton's aunt." And I was like, "Okay, if I do this E! show with Kathy, it's going to be a lot of that." So I wanted to do my own thing. And then I brought Kim into it with me, and that's how it started.

Alex Baskin: We met her at the Polo Lounge and we just fell in love with her. I knew she was the linchpin.

Next up, a pink-clad queen of hospitality and bone-dry zingers who'd established her reputation in London . . .

Alex Baskin: Lisa Vanderpump—

Douglas Ross: You mean Lisa Todd. That's who she was then.

Kyle Richards: Lisa and I knew each other because she was my husband's client. I didn't know her well, but we went to business dinners and stuff like that.

Lisa Vanderpump (Housewife): Sylvester Stallone's wife, Jennifer, basically said, "You should watch this show called *Real Housewives of New York* because they're doing one in Beverly Hills." And I remember sitting on the bed watching it and I thought, "Oh, it seems kind of contentious. All these verbal altercations? That's something I just couldn't be part of, that's not my thing at all."

It was Robert Kovacik, who is a news journalist from NBC, who got me there. He said, "Come on, I'm going to drive you over to the audition, let's go." It was over in the valley and I remember he waited outside. And I didn't take it that seriously. I remember they said, "Tell us about your sex life." Now, I'm English. I didn't understand why on earth these people were asking about my sex life. So I joked, "My sex life with my husband or with everybody else?" And they laughed. I guess they liked me.

Alex Baskin: Lisa was so Beverly Hills—this extravagant, over-the-top, beautiful woman. At the time, she had the restaurants Villa Blanca and SUR, and we liked that she had businesses that sort of anchored her.

Lisa Vanderpump: I was sort of the quintessential Beverly Hills Housewife. After all, I had one of the most prominent restaurants in Beverly Hills at the time, Villa Blanca, drove a white-on-white convertible Bentley, and lived in one of the premier gated communities, Beverly Park. I had always been a little eccentric—what with my love of dogs and Giggy, my lap dog, always by my side.

Andy Cohen: Lisa Vanderpump really tipped it over for me personally as a gay man when I saw her in casting. I really responded to the fact that she was like a character out of the book *Hollywood Wives*—she was like a Collins sister.

Jennifer Redinger: When we did her callback at her house, she was telling us interesting, fun stories. Cedric [Martinez] was there, and we were like, "This is so Beverly Hills. You have a houseboy who's great-looking, walks around looking all studly, and you've also got your husband."

Jennifer Redinger: I remember looking at her closet and her jewelry. I'm like, "Oh, my gosh, this is every girl's dream." Lisa really embodied glamour and aspirational living.

Lisa Vanderpump: When they came to my house and filmed some test scenes, I started to become interested. But that's also when they put the project on hold for a while. And it's funny: often you learn what you want when someone's going to take it away from you. And I wanted it.

When I finally got the call, it was quite a few months later. Ken and I were in London and at two o'clock in the morning my phone rang. Ken and I were fooling around in bed, as you do, and I saw the number and told Ken, "Get off! It's an 818 number, it could be them!" That's how much I wanted to be part of the show.

Once Lisa and Kyle were in place, young mom Taylor Armstrong's name was thrown into the mix.

Alex Baskin: Taylor represented more of a striver, the outsider in Beverly Hills who was looking to fit in, someone who had moved to California from Oklahoma and was sort of trafficking in those circles. She didn't have the money, wasn't as established.

After RHONJ had shown how complicated and explosive family dynamics could be on-screen, RHOBH followed suit by extending an offer to Kim Richards, Kyle's older sister and a fellow former child star.

Andy Cohen: The truth is that there would not have been a show without Kyle and Kim. I know I said I didn't want actresses, but Kyle and Kim Richards were a different type because their stardom had faded. Kim, especially, kept talking about how iconic she was.

Dave Rupel: I'm old enough to remember Kim Richards on *Nanny and the*

Professor and the Disney movies. It's funny, when we were filming, she would occasionally smoke off camera. I was trying to get it on camera and literally she looked at me like, "Dave, you can't do that. I'm a Disney girl." And that really is the way she views herself, even all these years later.

Jennifer Redinger: During the interviews, Kyle and Kim talked about each other, and you could tell there were things they needed to say to each other. They were telling me stories about Thanksgiving dinner and who sat where at the table. You could see there is so much love, but I was a little bit of a therapist listening to each frustration.

> *Producers had long had their eye on Adrienne Maloof, a member of the famed casino dynasty who brought mover-and-shaker energy to the group. Her proximity to Lisa Vanderpump also established a frenemy vibe that any good Housewives series needs.*

Dave Rupel: Adrienne Maloof, her family owned the Palms Casino in Vegas and also the Sacramento Kings basketball team.

Adrienne Maloof (Housewife): My husband Paul had heard about the show through his publicist, so he was thinking, "Wow, this could really help my business." But we had children, so I was initially hesitant.

Alex Baskin: We had some meetings with Adrienne and Paul, and it was very clear to us right away that Paul wanted to do the show much more than Adrienne did. Paul had been on television, featured on *Dr. 90210*, and really thought that the show would be good for his practice. And was a little bit of a ham anyway.

Jennifer Redinger: She and Paul were hilarious. I asked one question and the rest of the time they were just back and forth, bickering. It was funny, it wasn't mean. I was like, "Oh my God, they have such a crazy fun connection." And I can see that they're going to be really interesting on the show. Sometimes you have to pull a little bit more out of the husband, but that never happened with Adrienne and Paul. It was almost like he wanted to be just as fabulous.

Adrienne Maloof: For me, it was, "Okay, I'm going to go from known family to well known all over the world," and that's kind of a scary thought.

Alex Baskin: I'll never forget a meeting we had with Paul and Adrienne, where Adrienne was on the fence about the show. She turned to me and said, "If you were me, would you do it?" So I said, "No. And I'd be making a mistake."

Adrienne Maloof: Lisa Vanderpump had also pushed for me to be on the show.

Alex Baskin: Beverly Park, where Lisa and Adrienne lived, is the wealthiest of the wealthy. Huge stars live there. It's one of those places where on Halloween kids get in buses to go from house to house because the properties are so big they can't just walk the neighborhood. So the idea that we would have not one but two cast members who live in Beverly Park really set the show apart.

Andy Cohen: Vanderpump and Adrienne Maloof lived across the street from each other in these, like, fiberglass castles.

Dave Rupel: One of the network's favorite gimmicks was to have them walk to each other's houses because they'd have to go out their huge yard, gates would open, they'd cross the street, other gates would open, and they'd have to go up another huge yard to get to their doorstep.

Chris Cullen: Right from the beginning, it felt like they were the two alpha dogs in this game.

> *Even as production for season 1 was imminent, producers still felt the puzzle wasn't quite complete.*

Alex Baskin: Doug and I were thinking, "We are one cast member short, we need someone else, we're just not exactly sure who it is." One day I was on the phone with Kyle and I said, "You sort of know everyone. Can you just rack your brain, go through your Rolodex? Is there someone we're missing?" And she's looking at her phone. And she got to Camille Grammer. And then she started describing having seen Camille at a party, dancing wildly.

Kyle Richards: I saw her at a Christmas party. She was, like, dancing on a pole.

Camille Grammer (Housewife): I received a phone call from Kyle Richards a few days after I ran into her and Lisa Vanderpump around town. She started talking to me about this project that she had going with the network, and it was a *Real Housewives*. My initial reaction was no. I said, "Kelsey will never allow me to do this. He's never going to okay this." And she just went, "Oh, well, you know, this is the time that we really need to start thinking about ourselves and not just our husbands, and Lisa and I know you'd be great. Would you think about coming in for an audition?"

Kyle Richards: She said, "I don't know, I don't think Kelsey would want me to do something like that." And we all know what happened there.

Dave Rupel: I remember the first interview, we were talking about her life, homes, whatever. And she says, "Oh, you know, we have a house in Malibu and we have seven or eight other houses." And she had no awareness of if she had seven or eight, or that that would sound like an enormous amount to the average person.

Alex Baskin: At the time she was incredibly unfiltered, didn't give a shit. She had spent the past four years as the wife of Kelsey Grammer, the biggest star and highest-paid actor on television.

Camille Grammer: To be honest with you, we didn't watch the show. My mom watched it and had a lot more information than I did. She said, "They will eat you alive. You're pretty naïve at times, and they're going to tear you down and pick at your bones until there's nothing left." And I was like, "This doesn't sound good." So I thought there was no way Kelsey would be for it. He had been really private after he went through his recovery. So when he said to me, "This is a good opportunity for you," I was very surprised.

Douglas Ross: I will never forget the time that Alex, Kathy French, and I went out to Camille's house in Malibu. I was thinking to myself, "I can't believe it. I'm going to Kelsey Grammer's house." We sat down, and it was very friendly, but Camille kept saying she didn't know if it was right for her. And Kelsey kept pushing her, saying, "Oh honey, I think it would be fun." And it was just so weird that a big star was pushing his reluctant wife to do this show.

Camille Grammer: They said they were going to make it different than the other *Housewives* shows—more of a *Lifestyles of the Rich and Famous*. And when they said that I thought, "Well, you know what? That's more appealing than girls fighting."

Kathleen French: I got in the car afterward and I was like, "Why in the world is Kelsey agreeing to do this?" He was an A-level celebrity choosing to participate and something didn't sit right with that. And I said, "He's parking her. He wants out." He was on his way to do *La Cage aux Folles* on Broadway, and she was going to stay in California with the kids. I was like, "I got a funny feeling about this." And sure enough.

Alex Baskin: We found out later that Kelsey was pushing her to do the show because he had another life that he was tending to in New York. He later told Oprah that *The Real Housewives of Beverly Hills* was his "parting gift" to Camille.

With season 1 locked and loaded, and the Housewives *brand a certified success, the production values were through the roof.*

Dave Rupel: The franchise and the network had gotten so big over the years so the expectations were a lot higher. Suddenly you're in Kelsey Grammer's home and you're looking at all of his Emmys and you're like, "This is not like Jeana Keough's house."

Lisa Vanderpump: I was so unsure of what we were getting into. The first day of filming, we were going to Vegas and they were filming us getting ready in our bathroom. Ken was packing his bag. I said, "What are you doing packing four things of neatly folded underwear? You normally only wear one a week!"—you know, joking. And he looked at me like, "Are you nuts? That's going to be on television, why would you say something like that?" I just laughed but he was like, "Oh shit, what have I gotten myself into?"

Camille Grammer: I was terrified going into filming! I had gotten that warning from my mom, and sure enough, that year I was the target.

Alex Baskin: The tension started even before filming.

Kathleen French: Whenever we start a season, we do a general dinner with the cast to go through the ins and outs of how the show is going to work and also have a glass of wine and get to know each other. The field producers, the showrunner, and Doug and Alex were there.

Alex Baskin: Camille had called in advance to say she needed to leave early to go to a Bon Jovi concert. And as much as her leaving early would go against our plan to have everyone together the entire time for bonding, we thought, Why not let her tell everyone the situation herself? We knew it would probably ruffle some feathers, but we had no idea that in addition to leaving early, she would also show up to the meeting really, really late. So we'd all been seated for at least an hour. And Camille sort of busted in and interrupted wherever we were in the conversation. She said basically, "I'm sure you guys have spent a lot of time talking. Is there anything you want to know about me?" So everybody was sort of already at high irritation at the beginning.

Andy Cohen: I knew from the first few episodes that Camille was in for a really rough time. As a TV producer, I absolutely loved it, obviously, and found it wildly entertaining. She was outspoken in a really polarizing way.

Dave Rupel: Tensions heated up when we were coming back from a quick trip to Vegas. I made a decision we weren't going to shoot the trip home, as sort of a reward to the cast and crew. And so Camille and Kyle and Kim were waiting for their cars, and they were the only people there, there were no other witnesses. Some holiday was coming up, and Kyle asked Camille, "What do you have planned?" And Camille said, "I'm going to Hawaii, and the crew is coming with me."

Camille Grammer: I remember Kyle being disappointed at production for filming me in Hawaii without Kelsey there.

Kyle Richards: What I said to her, off camera, was, "What are you going to do for spring break?" And she said, "They're filming me in Hawaii." And I said, "Oh, they're filming you? Is Kelsey going, too?" She said no, and I said, "Oh really?"—because I didn't know how it worked! It was our first trip, we had just started! But she said, "Oh, you don't think I'm interesting enough without Kelsey? They wouldn't want to film me?" And I was like, "What are you talking about?"

Dave Rupel: The point of contention became whether or not Kyle said, "The crew's coming with you without Kelsey?" In Kyle's mind, she was saying, "I'm surprised you're going without Kelsey." In Camille's mind, she heard, "Why would the cameras shoot you if Kelsey's not there?"

Camille Grammer: I felt that she was pressing a little too much. And it made me feel uncomfortable.

Dave Rupel: It played into Camille's insecurity of always being overlooked because she had a very famous husband.

Kyle Richards: I literally just didn't know that we could go on spring break, if we got a spring break, if they filmed with us. It was all new to me! But then when I said, "Don't be insecure," that sent her over the edge.

Camille Grammer: I was excited about my trip to Hawaii, still thinking the show was supposed to be like *Lifestyles of the Rich and Famous*. I wasn't thinking about whether my husband would be there. I felt like her line of questioning was backing me into a corner. So that's when I said, "Obviously you're not happy with this. And I don't like your attitude about it." And then the fight started.

Dave Rupel: I know Andy Cohen hates the fact that that was off camera, but to me, it's genius. It would have been much less interesting if we had seen exactly what was said. That mystery drove a whole season of tension.

Andy Cohen: I was also annoyed that it was a fight that broke the fourth wall. It was about cameras. What I didn't realize then was that fourth-wall breaking fights would become pretty common on *RHOBH*.

Camille Grammer: She apologized at one point—but she didn't really. It was more like, "You don't have to be so insecure." What kind of apology is that?

Tensions continued to build during another girls' trip, this time to New York City. It all started at dinner on the first night.

Dave Rupel: Camille had gone to the bathroom with Taylor. They went in very calmly. . . .

Camille Grammer: Taylor was telling me what the girls were saying about me at the airport before they flew to New York. It wasn't nice.

Dave Rupel: About five minutes later, the door flew open and Camille was just red-hot angry.

Camille Grammer: I was very, very upset that I had become the target, the butt of the joke. I think some of the girls knew more about how these shows work—I know Kyle was very close to Bethenny Frankel. But I was so green, and I was learning under fire. So I said, "You're not doing this to me. You're not going to make me look like the bad guy." When Kyle started yelling at me, I was just shocked.

Dave Rupel: The next morning, we had an early morning shoot between Lisa Vanderpump and Kyle. They were laughing about how ridiculous the previous night had gotten, and Lisa said, "I feel like I've been shagged through a hedge backward." Even though it had been chaos hours before, they were having so much fun. And that's what I loved about the show. They could fight and recover. I've always said that women are sort of like steel magnolias—they can be the best of friends or the worst friends, and then they bounce back.

Camille Grammer: Even today, I still think I'm in the right, and I'm sure Kyle still thinks she's in the right. That will never get resolved.

Camille's relationship with Kyle and the women went up in yet more smoke later in the season when she offered to host a night fueled by strong cocktails and shocking predictions.

Alex Baskin: Camille had been pitching doing a dinner party and having Allison DuBois give readings. Allison was a good friend of Camille and Kelsey, and she was the basis for *Medium*, the show produced by Kelsey's company, Grammnet Productions. She was saying to us, "She's great— and if you get a couple of drinks in her, she's even better."

Camille Grammer: She was hesitant, but I said, "We can talk about *Medium* and promote it. Kelsey thinks it's good publicity."

Dave Rupel: We went into that dinner not thinking Allison would give us much. If anything, we were expecting Kyle to start something because she insisted on bringing Faye Resnick. She came with a wingman.

Kyle Richards: Going there, I knew Camille was going to be coming after me. She just had that cat-with-the-canary look on her face all the time. She felt I brought Faye as my "wingman," but that's not why she was there. Camille was just nervous that I had someone in from the outside who would see what she was doing.

Camille Grammer: Faye wasn't very nice to me when she showed up at my house that night. She was just snarky and acting like a high school catty girl, even though she was an adult. That immediately put me on the defensive. But it was really at the very end of the night that the fireworks happened.

Dave Rupel: We were almost done shooting. There had been very little contention. They literally were, like, five minutes away from having had a nice dinner party. I think we already started wrapping one crew, and then that's when it all kicked off.

Camille Grammer: All the girls had been drinking these very large cocktails, and Allison wasn't eating any dinner. She got feisty because they were asking her to give them readings, and she just wanted to support me. She finally said, "I'm not here to be anybody's show pony."

> By the end of the night, Allison's plan to be "off the clock" went down the tubes, cementing the "dinner party from hell" in Housewives history.

Chris Cullen: Allison had a mouth. And Faye has a mouth. So they both went in and did some of the heavy lifting for our cast members.

Camille Grammer: The other girls weren't innocent that night, either. They came after us pretty hard. But Allison did say those things.

Kathleen French: From the viewers' standpoint, people felt Camille had a hand in Allison going after Kyle. And it certainly looked like that to me, too.

Andy Cohen: I remember watching that for the first time, and I was in a state of euphoria.

Kyle Richards: I found it entertaining myself, even in the moment. I had never seen an e-cigarette before, because they were new at the time. I was like, "What on God's green earth is that?" But she just looked so evil.

Camille Grammer: Allison said to me, "These are not your friends, you know, they'll kill their own. This is about the business and making money. They're not even each other's friends. They're just backstabbing, don't trust them." But she was devastated by how the night turned out. She thought I threw her under the bus.

Andy Cohen: The thing that pushed it all the way over the top—besides the e-cigarette—was the women getting drenched by the sprinkler on their way out. I mean, that was such a beautiful little cherry on top of the entire affair that I couldn't believe it.

Camille Grammer: I did not plan the sprinkler system going off on the girls as they left!

Adrienne Maloof: That made the whole episode so iconic. Nothing was planned. It was very real. And yes, it blew up within seconds.

Camille Grammer: After dinner, they were all in the car on the way home, and they were showing naked pictures of me from *Playboy* and laughing like it was some joke.

Kathleen French: The funny thing was, the women are all forty-plus and they're in the back of the car and Kyle's trying to show them the pictures but no one can see them. They're like, "Where are my glasses? Can you see them? I can't see the pictures!" I thought it was the funniest thing in the world. Here was Kyle's "Look how trashy Camille is" moment—and no one can see the pictures.

Camille Grammer: That was one of the few scenes I didn't want producers to show. It hit below the belt.

Dave Rupel: So much about that night went to hell and we have a great episode because of it.

> At odds with the women, Camille slowly began to realize she had no refuge in her home life, either. Over the six months of casting and filming, her marriage completely dissolved.

Camille Grammer: When I talked to Kelsey in December about being on the show, he said something that sent up a red flag. He said, "Well, when is the show filming?" I told him it would be February through June or July, and he goes, "Oh, that's perfect timing for me." I thought he was just nervous about Broadway.

Alex Baskin: Pretty early on, I remember some of the women speculating like, "Oh, he must be doing Broadway because he wants to live in New York away from his wife." And others were like, "No, that's ridiculous."

Camille Grammer: I flew out to New York in February to look at apartments and schools. I had no idea that he'd already met somebody and was planning to end our relationship. We filmed the whole process of meeting with the interior decorator, discussing how to make this apartment feel like a home and bringing our furniture into it. And I said this stupid thing about this thirty-five-hundred-square-foot apartment being too small for me. I look back and laugh at how ridiculous I sounded. But at the time, my kids were being raised in this house that had a tennis court, a pool, a pond, a riding stable, barn—it had everything. So for them to go from living on five acres in Malibu to an apartment in Manhattan would be an adjustment. Suffice it to say, we never moved into that apartment.

Chris Cullen: The first time we realized something was really wrong was when we went to New York and we shot in his dressing room before the show. He was really icy to her. She was like "I love you," and he just said, "I know."

Camille Grammer: When we filmed in New York, Kelsey would give me a cold embrace and kind of fake play with the kids. It was forced and very uncomfortable. I just thought he was not happy that the cameras were there, like, "Keep them on Camille, not me. I want to stay private."

Alex Baskin: We started to sense the distance. And she became aware of it and was insecure about it. She thought she derived her status from him, so to acknowledge that he may have had one foot out the door would diminish her power. I don't think she wanted to admit it to herself.

Camille Grammer: It was what they say, the wife is the last to know. Most of the theater world knew that Kelsey had a girlfriend because she would go to the shows and she was in his dressing room. I would get these phone calls from the front desk at the building in New York City: "Your vegan burger's here." And I'd go, "My vegan burger? I'm in Malibu." The third time they called me telling me my vegan burger delivery was there, I said, "Can I talk to your manager? Because I don't know who is ordering these vegan burgers, I'm here in Malibu." And they said, "Ah, don't get me in trouble, I'm new here." And they hung up the phone. So, you know, she was shacked up in the apartment that was supposed to be rented for my family and ordering food and the restaurant was calling me about the delivery.

Alex Baskin: The other women were sensing it. There was definitely a lot of speculation.

Camille Grammer: I wasn't handling it well. I cried a lot. I lost a lot of weight. I think I went from 116 to like ninety-eight or ninety-six pounds.

Chris Cullen: She developed this kind of protective attitude. She definitely put up a big brick wall around herself because she was worried about what this all meant and how this all was going to play out on TV.

Camille Grammer: Kelsey and I were arguing over the phone a lot, and I was starting to get nervous. Finally one night I called him at twelve thirty or one a.m. my time. He sounded drunk, and there was a woman in his bed. He didn't want to talk, but I pressed it and he was so cruel and basically said, "I don't want to be married anymore. It has nothing to do with another woman." But I could hear somebody in the background. I said, "What about the kids?" I was crying. And he's like, "Oh, the kids, they'll be fine. Kids are resilient. They'll get over it."

Dave Rupel: After we finished shooting for the season, the news broke that Kelsey was leaving her.

Alex Baskin: One of the questions at the time was, "Well, you already know they're going to get divorced. Do you even care to see it play out?"

Dave Rupel: The audience wound up appreciating that they could sort of play detective and see a clue. When we went to New York to see Kelsey in his play, and he gave her that very stiff hug, now the audience could watch and go, "Oh look, there's a sign."

Andy Cohen: When you watch it going down, it was all there.

Alex Baskin: Now you see that all the time in our *Housewives* series, where there are leaks about what's happening on the show well before the current season, and it makes the audience want to watch even more in some cases.

> While Camille's estrangement had been captured on camera, Taylor spent that first season desperately trying to keep troubles in her own marriage out of sight.

Kathleen French: Taylor came in for her first interview and put on the most spectacular show I'd ever seen. She was funny and hilarious and amazing and had great stories about what she did in her business. My gosh, she was a superstar. And the minute we started rolling, it was like trying to hold on to water—there was nothing there.

Taylor Armstrong (Housewife): There were days on the show when the stress and the anxiety were so high, I was shaking from fighting with friends and all the stuff that was coming out of people's mouths. But even in the middle of all the arguing with the girls, it was more scary for me to go home to Russell.

Alex Baskin: As we got deeper into filming, we would get calls where Taylor would describe arguments with her husband that were not outright physical abuse but sounded really concerning. And we would say, "Listen, if you're fearful for you and your daughter's safety, please let us know and I'll put you up at a hotel and we'll take care of you. What can we do?" And she would say to us, "No, I'm fine, no big deal, it was a misunderstanding."

Taylor Armstrong: Russell believed he would absolutely be loved by America. He thought he was going to win everyone over because he was extremely charismatic when he chose to be. But instead people were like, "Do you two have problems?" They could tell by our spacing and the way he would look at me and grab hold of my hand. It was very forced. I remember doing *The Wendy Williams Show* while season 1 was airing. And in the middle of the segment, Wendy said, "He abuses you, doesn't he?" And I literally almost fell out of my chair because clearly that's something your abuser cannot find out—that other people know. I mean, that's like a death sentence. So I was like, "What! No." In that weird frantic, breathy way. And she just looked at me. I don't know if she has a history or has worked with people who've been abused, but she didn't go any further with it. She just looked at me with a blank stare. Basically like, "I know."

Douglas Ross: She was denying it always.

Taylor Armstrong: The cameras, I believe, did provide some protection. The problem was that as I saw season 1 unfolding, I would think, "Oh my God, who is that girl?" Because I was constantly trying to transform to keep him happy. With abusers, there is no winning. "Your dress is too long. You look like a nun. Now your dress is too short. You look like a whore." You're constantly trying to mold who you are to keep the lid on the pot. But watching the season back I was like, "Oh my gosh, guys, I look like a Stepford wife." It was hard to watch. But, you have to remember, Kyle and Lisa could have drama with us all day or all night and then go home to a support system. For me, I had drama all day with the girls and then I go home and I have frightening drama at home. So I was living in a constant state of anxiety.

> Every cast member in Beverly Hills had something to hide, but season 1 saw carefully buried truths unearthed about the Richards sisters, resulting in a dramatic finale feud in uncomfortably tight quarters.

Chris Cullen: There had been tension between Kim and Kyle all season and everything came to a head at our final party. Things started going wrong that night when Kim and Kyle had a fight by the ladies' room. Kim got mad, took off her mic, and said, "I'm leaving." Another producer and I chased her down and said, "You can't leave, this isn't settled. You still have things to say. If you walk away, you're handing the narrative over."

Dave Rupel: She continued her meltdown off camera, running through the lobby saying, "Fuck you, fuck me, fuck you."

Chris Cullen: Here's the truth: We didn't know Kim was struggling with alcohol at this point. We had no idea. So when we got to the lobby, I said to Kim, "Let's have a drink before you leave." We sat and had a drink in the bar, and I said, "If you don't want to go back to the group, who *can* you go back to talk to?" She said, "Adrienne's the only one who's ever been fair to me, she's the only one I trust."

Dave Rupel: We'd hit our wrap point, because the city of Beverly Hills had a law that we had to be wrapped up on the rooftop at a certain time. The hotel wouldn't let us shoot in the hotel room. We weren't even allowed to shoot on the sidewalk. So the only place physically where we could shoot was the limo.

Chris Cullen: We drove around the block like ten times while they talked, and then as we came up to the hotel that last time, Kyle opened up the door and said, "What's going on? What are you doing, what are you saying?" In came Kyle and boom! All of a sudden, like Camille's dinner party, we were in it.

Dave Rupel: I actually tried to talk Kyle out of getting into the limo because Kim was really upset and Kyle was just red hot. She said, "I'm getting in the car. You can shoot it or not." So, of course, I had to put a cameraperson in there.

Kyle Richards: I was so mad about the things she was saying that calling her an alcoholic just came out of my mouth.

Chris Cullen: Kyle was feeling like, "Oh my God, we're on television. My sister, who's been sober, has fallen off the wagon. I know she's drunk, the producers don't know she's drunk, and I know how this is going to play out." There was tension building up in Kyle all season and it all came vomiting out in an explosive, very provocative way.

Kyle Richards: When people drink, they're not the nicest people in the world, let's just put it that way. And it doesn't bring out the best in others around them, either.

Adrienne Maloof: At that moment, I was thinking, "This is really real.

They're furious with each other." The passion they each had in what they believed, it was so shocking. But there was a long history there.

Dave Rupel: In Kim's viewpoint, going back a long way, her sisters wouldn't have the lives they did if Kim had not been a successful child actress. Kim took them to all of these Hollywood parties, which is how Kathy met her husband. Kim's husband was a rich oil guy, so she had been at the top of the heap, but when she divorced him and her drinking became a problem, she lost everything. So in that limo, when she said, "You stole my goddamn house," in her mind, she was going back years. She felt like they owed her.

Chris Cullen: It's insane to be that close to family drama and know you are part of the team documenting it and putting it on television.

Andy Cohen: The sisters were begging Evolution and Bravo to take the scene out of the show. That didn't happen.

Shari Levine: All of the Housewives series are based on shooting people in their lives and documenting their real interactions. The series really does capture life as it happens. And everyone has moments that they want to keep off the air. The great equalizer for all the franchises is that it's all out there. If it's shot, we will edit it in.

Once the show premiered, RHOBH *was must-see TV—not least of which because Camille instantly became a Housewife viewers loved to loathe.*

Andy Cohen: I remember the night of the *Beverly Hills* premiere. I had all of the Beverly Hills Housewives on *Watch What Happens Live* and I said to Camille, "This is going to be really rough this season and you should stay off Twitter. You will have vindication at the end when people see what Kelsey did to you, but it's going to be really rough." And it was.

Kathleen French: There are times when viewers really don't like something that cast members have done, and they can be really vicious. My husband, Bill Fritz, was working on the structure of the reunion, including the questions from viewers. And every single one was another expletive: "Camille, you're a blank. Camille, I think you're a blank. Camille, you're . . ." I mean, I was blown away. I thought she made missteps, I thought she mishandled things, but I never saw her that way. It was just like, "Oh my God."

Andy Cohen: It's really hard to put stuff back in the bottle once it's out there. But I wouldn't say Camille got a bad edit, I would say we used the most interesting material. And she handed it over very freely. She did live a super-fabulous life in these amazing homes, so in her mind she was just harmlessly flaunting it. But it obviously came off differently.

Shari Levine: She was hands down the most jaw-dropping Housewife to watch that season. She was fearless in saying whatever she felt. Especially in the first half of that season. And that included some pretty caustic comments, but she delivered them with style and verve.

Alex Baskin: There was such a wide gap between who she thought she was and who the audience was telling her she was. And it was exacerbated by the fact that her husband was leaving her. She felt very alone and vulnerable. To have been Mrs. Grammer for all those years, she had ass-kissers all around her. And then to have the audience just flood her with that hate, it gutted her.

Kathleen French: What was that magazine cover? "Most Hated Housewife in America"? She was devastated.

Douglas Ross: She didn't see how she was coming off when she watched the episodes. And then when the audience response would come in, she'd have a complete reversal and call up Alex and unload on him for hours—screaming, crazy angry. If she could have embraced the idea of being the villain on the show, she could have gone on to be one of the biggest reality stars of all time—a sort of love-to-be-hated type. But she couldn't handle the negative feedback from the audience.

Camille Grammer: My mom's cancer was coming back right around that time, too. So even without knowing Kelsey was leaving, I had a lot on my plate. I was very lost during filming.

Andy Cohen: I talked to Camille a lot before that reunion. Reunions are meant to be about retribution, but also rehabilitation. It's a place where you confront the worst and hopefully come out for the better. And Camille did that. She clearly had thought about what she wanted to say, and she did a really good job. She took my shit and she owned it.

Camille Grammer: Lisa Vanderpump and I were talking a lot during that time. And she told me, "Camille, you'll have a better season, it's not going to be like that again. Things change the second season."

Despite the fact that season 1 had been a smashing success, the women of Beverly Hills acutely felt the sting of their secrets coming out, making season 2 a bit of a challenge from production's point of view. Luckily for producers, they had a firecracker with a short fuse coming along.

Brandi Glanville (Housewife): I was going through a very public divorce from Eddie Cibrian, who'd left me for LeAnn Rimes, and I have a big fucking mouth, so all the tabloids were calling me and instead of saying, "No comment," I was like, "He's a scumbag. She's a whore." I think it caught the producers' eyes.

Chris Cullen: Brandi did not tiptoe her way in. And I'm glad she didn't. But we had limited access to her life because her ex-husband certainly didn't want to be on the show and wouldn't allow the kids to be on the show.

Brandi Glanville: My ex-husband was holding out on me in every way, probably to torture me. I was a thirty-six-year-old single mom. All I'd ever done was model. I had to do whatever came my way. If I had been rich like Camille and had forty million dollars, you would never see me again. I didn't ever want to be famous.

Chris Cullen: Because she wasn't married, she was very different than the other ladies that we had on the show, and it changed the playing field a little bit.

Brandi Glanville: I did all of these interviews to be a full-time Housewife. I went through all of this craziness, and then months went by and I didn't hear anything. And then I got a call from one of the producers and she was like, "Hey, you want to come to a party tonight? On camera?"

Chris Cullen: The ladies weren't welcoming to her. They didn't like someone coming on to the show in season 2, so they weren't going to make it easy for her.

Dave Rupel: That game night went so disastrously bad from the start. Kim and Kyle went low first.

Chris Cullen: Kim showed up with a Starbucks cup or Dunkin' Donuts cup with booze in it. She had already been partying.

Brandi Glanville: When the game started, they were just super cocky to me. They were mean girls. I had never even met Kim, so I didn't understand why she hated me so much. I just felt like I was being attacked.

Chris Cullen: I knew Brandi would be at her best if she was really focused and called the ladies out and was honest about everything. There's nobody like her and you can't hide from Brandi—she'll come for you with a big flashlight. She let them have it that night.

Brandi Glanville: I really don't like to fight with people. I just happen to have a temper. And if somebody hits me, I stab them. I'm very reactionary. It's something I can't control.

As the evening unfolded, things got increasingly heated between Kim, Kyle,
and Brandi. Kim hid Brandi's crutches, and Brandi accused Kim of doing
crystal meth in the bathroom.

Brandi Glanville: The night before, I had learned about crystal meth in a
drug awareness class I took as part of a DUI I'd gotten, so it was just on
the top of my head. Kim had come in acting loopy and immediately went
into the bathroom multiple times, but everyone was pretending like she
was fine. So I was like, "Are we all just not going to state the obvious here?
This is kind of insane."

Kyle Richards: That was horrible because our minds went straight to, "Our
kids are going to see this." And it wasn't true! But as we know, in reality
TV, you say something and put it out there, it just sticks.

Chris Cullen: Kim wasn't doing anything in the bathroom. I had to go into
the bathroom many times with her because her mic was falling off, so we
had to readjust her. But she was a little messy.

Andy Cohen: I thought it was mean that they took Brandi's crutches. That
was a little ugly for me.

Kyle Richards: Because Kim and I are sisters, we're always lumped together,
no matter what. So that night, Kim hid Brandi's crutches. For years people
have said, "You and your sister hid her crutches!" That's not what happened. Kim hid the crutches because she had a bone to pick with
Brandi.

Brandi Glanville: I had broken my leg right before filming because I was
drinking and walking. When my crutches were hidden, it's like there
were bullies standing right next to me. I looked at them and was like, "I
can't leave. I need my crutches." I was crying and I had to wait for one of
the girls to get my crutches, and that was when I realized, "Oh, they don't
give a fuck about me, they're making a show."

Taylor Armstrong: There are a couple of scenes that people refer to when I
would say, "Enough!" and one of them was that game night. I really thought
that Kim and Brandi could potentially get physical with one another.

Brandi Glanville: I grew up fighting, so I do have that in me where, if things
escalate, I can get physical.

Taylor Armstrong: I got in between the three of them and kind of pushed
them apart. It really touched a nerve for me because there was physical
abuse going on at my house and it was like, I am dealing with this enough
at home, I can't watch this happen here, too.

Andy Cohen: I know that night resonated with viewers, but it was too dark for me.

Brandi Glanville: It was fucking hell.

Chris Cullen: It cemented Brandi and created a dynamic where the other women knew that even if they didn't like her, she was formidable and was worthy of her place on the show. She wasn't going to let them get away with anything.

Brandi Glanville: After the party they were like, "We'd like to have you be a 'Friend of.'" I was broke. I had no money. So I basically worked for a small fee my first season. Like, literally no money. And of course I did the most and I got the least.

The allegations at the game night were part of ongoing concerns surrounding Kim's sobriety. Throughout season 2, worries escalated until she had to skip the reunion in favor of a one-on-one interview with Andy Cohen as she tried once again to pursue a life of recovery.

Kathleen French: Kim had mostly kept her shit together through season 1. Season 2 was the beginning of the spiral down.

Chris Cullen: That season was emblematic of a conversation we've had with Kim for years—she wants to keep coming back to the show and she wants to show her sobriety. So, okay, we will document that. But then if she falls off the wagon again, do we pack up our cameras?

Andy Cohen: When it was clear that it was a real problem, we wanted to be responsible and we didn't want to put her in a situation where anything could be exacerbated. We considered her family and wanted to work with her to get her better. Bravo paid for her rehab.

Problems only worsened as the pressure Taylor felt to hide her domestic trauma became too much to bear.

Chris Cullen: Taylor and Russell, that was an enormous crisis of conscience.

Kathleen French: It had been hinted at between seasons, even toward the end of season 1, that there was something off in the marriage.

Chris Cullen: The ladies started hearing rumors that Russell was abusive to Taylor. Lisa had heard something. Kyle had heard something. Adrienne had heard something. We would go into a scene in Taylor's house and all be like, "Let's just watch for anything. Let's watch for Russell being annoyed with her. Let's look for the eye rolls. Let's look for if they're frustrated with each other. Let's try to find these moments that support the rumors that we're hearing and see if we can capture that on camera." Within those first seasons, you could see they didn't have a loving relationship. It was pretty apparent things weren't great there.

Adrienne Maloof: I knew from my own marriage that it's hard—and it's on your mind the whole time—when you have issues you can't really discuss on camera.

Taylor Armstrong: Looking back, subconsciously I thought the show was going to give me an opportunity to have some income of my own and maybe give me a little bit of power in the relationship. And I hoped the cameras might keep him under control. That if I had cameras at the house and there were cameras filming me the next day, he wasn't going to leave marks on me. I believed that the cameras would make him better. Because that's all I really wanted. I just wanted him to be good all the time—to be a good husband and to be the person that I knew he had the potential to be. But unfortunately, he couldn't control himself.

Kathleen French: Everything was just off. He was a man who could never really look you in the eye. There was always something, you know, the hair on the back of your neck would sort of go up—at least for me. Maybe as a woman it was different. He literally looked through me. As if I didn't exist.

Dave Rupel: In season 1, when we traveled to Las Vegas, Russell had forgotten his driver's license, so I wound up spending about an hour with him one-on-one at the Burbank Airport. He was very soft-spoken, I'd never seen him lose his temper.

Camille Grammer: He was very quiet. You didn't understand why they were still together.

Adrienne Maloof: She would occasionally tell me about some of the abuse that was going on. I would always tell her, "Listen, you probably need to get some professional help." But did we know the extremes she was living through? Oh no, I had no idea. None of us did. Kyle was very close to her at the time, and I don't believe Kyle even knew the depths of how dark that was.

Chris Cullen: In the early seasons, we would wrap that day's filming at ten o'clock and go home. The ladies would stay back and continue drinking. We would never leave them alone now—now we're there with iPhones and little mini cruiser cams. But back then, they would stay after filming to hang out, and that's when Taylor would get wasted to the point she would start confiding in Kyle and Lisa, telling them, "Russell beats me." She was telling them off camera, and then we'd come up with cameras again and she would act like everything was fine and normal.

Taylor Armstrong: It's tough for production, from their perspective. Because they're making a show about someone's reality. But no, I definitely would not have gone to production to say, "By the way, I'm being abused."

Adrienne Maloof: Eventually Lisa, Kyle, and I talked to the production company.

Chris Cullen: The ladies came to us and told us, but we couldn't break their trust and go to Taylor and say, "Hey, we've heard this, your castmates are talking about you behind your back. What do you have to say about this?" We needed to be the people on the sidelines and couldn't have our hands in the story, so we needed to wait for Taylor to come forward.

Unbeknownst to the other women and production, Camille had the clearest idea of what Taylor was enduring behind closed doors.

Taylor Armstrong: I had gone to meet Camille when she and Kelsey were divorcing. I wanted to talk with her about custody because I was trying to figure my own way out. Not long prior, Russell and I had been at the Super Bowl and things got really dangerous. He knocked my jaw out of the socket. I remember literally lying over the toilet with my jaw out of the socket, and there was saliva running out of my mouth. He wouldn't call me an ambulance, and I couldn't talk. So I was just lying there, trying to figure out how to lower my jaw so I could get it in place. After we got back from the Super Bowl, I went to Camille and shared with her what had just happened and asked her about what to do about custody.

Camille Grammer: It was heartbreaking. She was trapped. There's no question. I went over to her house, she showed me photos, we talked for hours about what had happened and how it transpired. It was really very upsetting, she was terrified of him.

Taylor Armstrong: I was trying to help Camille understand that my situation had become severe enough that I was fearful. I wanted her to understand why I needed to get away safely and with custody over my daughter. I felt like she was someone I could confide in privately.

As tensions came to a boil, Lisa invited the ladies to a tea party where Taylor had planned on confronting Lisa about not being a real friend to her. . . .

Camille Grammer: It all came to a head that day.

Taylor Armstrong: My understanding was that Camille would have my back if I brought up some other stuff about Lisa at the tea party—but when I brought up that stuff, that's when Camille blurted out about the abuse.

Camille Grammer: When she said, "Yes, I want you to tell the truth," I said, "Do you really want me to tell the truth?" And she nodded yes. I thought she meant about the abuse. I didn't realize she was talking about Lisa.

Taylor Armstrong: When Camille said, "We don't say he hits you, but now we said it," I was completely in shock.

Camille Grammer: I was really disappointed in myself for not reading her signals the right way.

Dave Rupel: By this point, Taylor had told all of them in various ways, but never during filming.

Taylor Armstrong: I don't even think I said anything in response because I was literally so awestruck that it possibly could be coming out. But Camille had been prompted to bring it up and was panicking a little.

Camille Grammer: I felt a lot of pressure on different sides. Certain people wanted me to talk about it. I know Adrienne wanted to bring it up. She thought it was important. Lisa thought it was important to have an open discussion. Production, too. Everybody was so fearful that she was getting hurt and nobody was addressing it and she wasn't getting any real help.

Taylor Armstrong: The cat was out of the bag and it was definitely going to make the air.

Adrienne Maloof: There was a pain on Taylor's face in that moment that was so real and so raw. Maybe it was too raw? It was even tough for the audience.

Taylor Armstrong: I knew my personal life was about to be completely uprooted. And it was going to go one of probably three ways. One, he was going to be forced to do anger management and the odds of him getting better from that were slim to none because he had done two years of court-ordered anger management before I ever met him. Two, we were going to get divorced, which would have been a long-fought battle. Or three, he was going to kill me.

He had threatened to kill me multiple times. After things would get violent, when he would finally calm down the next day, many times he said, "I'm afraid I'm going to kill you some day." Like, almost in a remorseful way.

Camille Grammer: After I said it I felt like shit. It was just one of those moments, and I regretted it every moment after. I felt so bad that I would put her in harm's way at all. And, you know, she got really upset at me, reasonably so, because she was afraid.

Taylor Armstrong: I don't know that I would have found a way out otherwise. I definitely have friends and I have a very supportive family, but I didn't want my parents to go through that with me. And frankly, I was afraid of what he might do if I left.

> *Desperate legal maneuvers were quickly threatened on multiple sides, complicating not just the group dynamics but also production for the remainder of the season.*

Chris Cullen: Taylor and Russell served Camille with legal papers, some sort of cease and desist.

Alex Baskin: Camille turned around right away and threatened to sue us if we aired that show. She was worried that if we put it out there Russell would sue her.

Dave Rupel: All this time, we're still filming, and at the end of season 2, Kyle had her annual white party.

Chris Cullen: Because of the legal papers, the cast said we couldn't have Taylor and Russell come to Hawaii with us after the white party.

Dave Rupel: But we wanted Taylor and Russell to go to the party to find out they'd been disinvited from the trip.

Chris Cullen: And so they arrived in front of Kyle's house at the white party, and the group came out and said they weren't invited to Hawaii.

Dave Rupel: Obviously, Taylor was very upset. And I pulled her aside, outside of Russell's earshot, and I said, "Are you safe if you go home with Russell?" And she said, "Yes, I'll be safe."

Chris Cullen: Taylor and Russell got in the car and left and apparently that's the night he punched her in the face.

Taylor Armstrong: When he made that last blow to my face and I ended up in Cedars-Sinai Hospital, it was inevitable it was coming out. The nurses were coming into my room saying, "Oh, we love you on the show." And there was no question that I had been hit. Also, I have friends in law enforcement in Beverly Hills, and they were saying, "You know, the D.A. is going to have to press charges whether you do or not, because you're a public figure in Beverly Hills. It would be irresponsible of them to let this one go." And I was having to miss filming due to corrective surgery. So there were a lot of questions brewing. That's when it felt like everything was really tightening around me. I knew this was becoming more and more public and I didn't know what his reaction was going to be.

Chris Cullen: As far as witnessing any physical abuse, that was the first time anything was clear to us in production. The next day, Taylor called Lisa and Kyle on the beach and said, "I'm leaving Russell." So we really needed to step in at that point because she started the separation procedures. They never got back together after that.

Taylor Armstrong: I had my reconstructive surgery in July and we filmed the finale not long after that because I still had a black eye when we filmed. I remember being in a limo with my psychiatrist, Dr. Charles Sophy, because he went with me to SUR to talk with the girls. Doug and Alex got in a limo with Dr. Sophy and me, and they really were adamant about the fact that I needed to say the words "I've been abused." It was for legal reasons because they needed to hear it from me directly before they could air it, because it's a criminal allegation.

Any hope to repair Taylor and Russell's broken marriage was shattered just before the season 2 premiere.

Taylor Armstrong: Russell and I were still trying to sort everything out. He had moved out and I was staying in our home. We were going through financial and custody discussions, and we had a meeting scheduled in the middle of the day at his office. He was so adamant about trying to make me happy at that point because he didn't want me to press charges and he was trying to find a way to get himself out of this mess. I showed up at his office, and the office was dark. He was a major workaholic, so he was never out of his office, and I thought, "This is weird." I started calling him and I waited around, but he never came back. Then I started calling his colleagues, but no one knew where he was. And he wasn't answering his phone, which was completely bizarre. As the day went on, I started getting a really weird sinking feeling, like, "This is just not right." I had a bad, bad feeling. Finally I called one of my girlfriends whose husband was a world championship kickboxer, and I asked if he would go with me to the house to look for Russell, just in case things got violent. So he went with me, my assistant, and Kennedy to the house. We buzzed the gate multiple times. No answer. He had someone living in a guesthouse upstairs, who said he hadn't seen him since Friday. But he came down and let us in. The tenant banged on the door, no answer.

"It all kind of stemmed from Chateau Salon. I went there, Jacqueline went there, Danielle went there. Victor, the owner, said to me, 'I've been approached to find some girls.'" —**Dina Manzo**

"I flipped a table, big deal. It had nothing even to do with me and her. I had my own issues with Danielle because I didn't like how she acted at my Shore house." —**Teresa Giudice**

Joe Giudice and Joe Gorga erupt into a brawl at a family retreat.

"It was like an *Ocean's Eleven* jailbreak. They were letting her out in the middle of the night, probably like three or four o'clock in the morning . . ."
—**Kathleen French, SVP/Current Production, Bravo**

Viewers never knew that after Teresa poured champagne on someone in a club, Melissa and Joe Gorga fled home from the Dominican Republic — and the rest of the cast was detained for a week.

The holy trinity of *RHONJ*: Melissa, her husband, Joe, and Teresa

"All the girls had been drinking these very large cocktails, and Allison wasn't eating any dinner."
—**Camille Grammer**

Kim and Kyle's season 1 limo fight

The Richards sisters

"Yolanda came in beautiful, married to David Foster, a gorgeous house, those gorgeous kids. . . . She kind of checked a lot of the boxes that Lisa Vanderpump had been filling over the past two years." —**Chris Cullen, Executive Producer, *Real Housewives of Beverly Hills* (Season 1–Present)**

Giggy with a wine glass

"To this day we still don't know what Harry supposedly did. I'd love to know. He'd love to know." —**Lisa Rinna, on throwing her glass down when Kim Richards came for her husband**

Erika Girardi as Erika Jayne

Always bring receipts

Email and call sheet from Bravo production proving Dorit had the same call time as Teddi

Goodbye, Kyle!

"That entire story line was a lot of misunderstanding . . ."
—**Dorit Kemsley**

Bravo, Bravo, Bravo

Lea Black, the unofficial "Mayor of Miami"

"Elsa lit up the room. There was something so charismatic about her. . . . When he [Andy] saw her in the first cut, he was immediately like, 'More Elsa—we need her in every episode.'" —**Sheri Maroufkhani, Executive Producer,** *Real Housewives of Miami* **(Season 1)**

"The White House Press Office's reaction was, 'I don't know what you think you saw, but those people were not invited. No one let them in. They were not seated.'" —**Amy Argetsinger, writer,** *The Washington Post*'s **Reliable Source column**

"I was never going to stab anyone with that butter knife."
—**Candiace Dillard Bassett**

Monique with her bird, T'Challa

"All I was thinking was, 'I cannot let my wig come off on this camera. I cannot live in infamy on the Internet as a Black woman whose wig has been ripped off and I'm fighting in my cornrows.'" —**Candiace Dillard Bassett**

"I always felt that if Bravo ever came to Potomac beating the grass for Housewives, my name would come to the top."
—**Karen Huger**

"I'm the only person on the cast who was actually born and raised in Dallas. I'm sixth generation. I'm old school Dallas." —**D'Andra Simmons, pictured here with her mother, Dee Simmons**

"I was more upset about the camera. Which is why finally I yelled, 'Stop filming me' and pushed the camera. I had already asked them not to film me. In my world, if I tell you to stop filming me, that is your warning. You get one." —**LeeAnne Locken**

It still fits!

But we could see his car was there. So we went over to the window of the bathroom and my friend pulled the windows open. When we went inside we were able to see into the bedroom. He had hanged himself. I ran into the street in front of the house and was screaming and crying— and the 911 tapes, unfortunately, are public. I was on the ground in a ball on the street. And all of a sudden I realized that Kennedy was in the car with my assistant. And I started screaming, "We've got to get Kennedy out of here." So my assistant called my nanny, and they got Kennedy away. And then police, ambulance, fire trucks, helicopters, everything started coming. That's how all that went down.

News of the suicide spread quickly. . . .

Chris Cullen: It was early in the morning, and all of a sudden I saw the headline on one of the Internet rags: REAL HOUSEWIVES OF BEVERLY HILLS HUSBAND COMMITS SUICIDE.

Alex Baskin: TMZ had it right away and reached out to our cast, so I remember getting those calls from the cast incredibly early in the morning.

Andy Cohen: I just remember feeling light-headed. It was bad.

Brandi Glanville: When I got the news about Russell, I literally didn't get out of bed for a week. It hit me so hard because I just feel like, to take your own life, like, I could never imagine what your head space has to be. It broke my heart.

Taylor Armstrong: After it all happened, I somehow got home. I spent the next few days in shock. My friends and mother were there. People were sending flowers. It was just a blur for quite some time.

Adrienne Maloof: It was horrible.

Everyone involved with the show faced a dilemma as the clock ticked down to the season 2 premiere. . . .

Douglas Ross: Nobody exactly knew the right thing to do and how to handle the show.

Andy Cohen: We were on a mission to not only find out what happened, but to check in with Taylor. We were weeks away from the premiere and there was a conversation about whether we were going to air the show at all.

Douglas Ross: In the end, we decided that we had to deal with it head-on, so we reedited the first episode and brought the cast together to talk about how shocked and sad they were and how badly they felt for Taylor.

Taylor Armstrong: They did not ask me to talk about it. I wouldn't have been ready.

Dave Rupel: We actually had Adrienne and Paul host both husbands and wives—everyone except Taylor—at the house just to sort of talk about, were there signs? Did they see this potentially happening? Did they feel guilt? And it turned into a really heartfelt, emotional scene and the right way to open the season.

Douglas Ross: We felt like we needed to follow the same advice we always gave the Housewives: Talk about it, deal with it, confront it, and be real with your emotions and the audience will embrace you.

Alex Baskin: We screened the first episode for Taylor after giving her space, and it was one of the few times that we were looking for cast approval because we wanted to know that she was okay with what aired. She saw it and she said, "This is really well done and the show should go on. I stand behind my story, I stand by my truth, and I stand by the way that you guys have portrayed it." So with that we had her blessing.

Andy Cohen: The season turned out to be a story of domestic abuse and a woman hiding it and trying to protect her husband. We did not want to air it if Taylor was against it.

> *Next came the anxious wait to see how viewers would respond to the House-wives' darkest chapter to date. . . .*

Alex Baskin: Our show became the referendum on reality TV.

Andy Cohen: There was really relentless, upsetting, asinine coverage surrounding his death that looked at what had happened in the most base, broad way without any nuance whatsoever or any exploration into who this guy was or where he was in his life or what was happening in his business. It was literally just, "Reality TV killed this guy." It was unfair.

Adrienne Maloof: The truth is, it wasn't reality television that brought him to that very dark, dark place. He had many years of issues that he had to deal with. Reality television showcased it, but it was not the reason.

Andy Cohen: I have to say the women were really great. They all worked together, and everyone wanted to protect Taylor and be mindful of her and respectful of her and somehow turn this into something that could wind up helping someone.

Adrienne Maloof: Season 2 is very difficult to watch. Very difficult. That was just a situation that turned really bad.

Taylor Armstrong: At this point in my life, when I tell this story, it feels like the story of another person, you know?

Douglas Ross: Taylor was a tough one, but she never blamed or accused us of a bad edit. We were very fair and measured. We wanted to do right by her—but also tell the real story.

Shari Levine: We hoped that by telling her story we were shining a light on a truly terrible problem. Domestic abuse affects so many people. The fact that this was happening to Taylor, who had money, friends, and family, meant it could happen to all kinds of people.

Taylor Armstrong: I do a lot of public speaking these days, and I tell people, "You would be so surprised—you have so much more strength inside you than you would ever believe."

In season 3, Yolanda Hadid, then Foster, joined the cast. To the frayed group she brought a grounded spirit—not to mention the world's most magnificent walk-in refrigerator and a trio of soon-to-be-globally-famous teen children.

Dave Rupel: Yolanda used to be married to Mohamed Hadid, who is Lisa Vanderpump's good friend, and the network was so in love with Lisa Vanderpump that the idea of another European with an accent was appealing. She was also married to David Foster, so it was just a very rich background.

Yolanda Hadid (Housewife): David was cautious about it on the one hand. But on the other hand, he wanted me to work and have my own income.

Chris Cullen: Yolanda came in beautiful, married to David Foster, a gorgeous house, those gorgeous kids. She had amazing taste and was fashionable and sophisticated and a world traveler and she kind of checked a lot of the boxes that Lisa Vanderpump had been filling over the past two years. And I don't think Lisa liked it at all—Lisa didn't want any focus being taken away from her.

Yolanda Hadid: Lisa was the most dangerous one on the show for sure. To your face, she was really nice. And then behind the scenes, she was cooking up all kinds of situations to make good TV. I'm very Dutch, very black and white. I'm not good at playing the game and kissing ass and that was read by some of the women as being high and mighty.

After an alienating but action-packed first season, newly promoted full-time Housewife Brandi was playing a thankless but key role in the group as she formed a surprise alliance with Lisa.

Andy Cohen: Lisa Vanderpump was legitimizing Brandi by taking her under her wing and finding humor in her.

Brandi Glanville: Lisa Vanderpump is beautiful and funny. I kind of fell in love with her. She was very intoxicating. When she walks into a room, it's like, "Oh, she's arrived." It was fun to watch the queen.

Andy Cohen: It was an interesting new wrinkle in the group.

Brandi Glanville: When I got promoted to full-time Housewife, Lisa started to make me believe that she was the reason I was on the show. She would make sure I knew she was responsible for my success, so I did feel indebted to her. And I believed her because it seemed like she ran the show. Everything she wanted to happen seemed to happen. I thought she really did have the producers' ear.

With Brandi allied with Lisa, Adrienne found herself squarely in their crosshairs.

Brandi Glanville: Producers had made it seem since season 1 like there were two queen bees: Adrienne and Lisa. The public loved Adrienne and thought she was the voice of reason, but Lisa wanted to be number one. It was a power struggle.

Alex Baskin: Pretty early on, Lisa's humor rubbed Adrienne the wrong way. So Lisa would get in little jabs at Adrienne, who didn't like it, and then Lisa would react to that.

Adrienne Maloof: Lisa has a hard time saying when she's wrong—that's just her personality. But that can eat away at you, because if you can't admit wrongdoing and move on, then every time you see it replayed, you get angry again.

Chris Cullen: Lisa specifically had an ax to grind with Adrienne after she'd accused Lisa of giving stories to the tabloids at the season 2 reunion. Lisa was going to go after her, and she used Brandi.

When Brandi eventually brought up a forbidden topic, she set off a chain of events that would have major consequences. . . .

Brandi Glanville: I had learned about Adrienne using a surrogate through someone who worked for Lisa, not from Lisa herself. I mentioned it to my boyfriend at the time, and he told me it was kind of an open secret that Adrienne would walk around in a prosthetic belly. Of course, in hindsight, if you're wearing a prosthetic belly, you clearly don't want anyone to know you're not having your own kids. Adrienne was trying to keep things on the DL because surrogacy wasn't really an open thing at the time, even though there was nothing wrong with it.

Dave Rupel: The women had sort of an unspoken understanding—everyone knew, but no one talked about it.

Brandi Glanville: When I told Lisa, she said, "Are you going to say anything?" She kept on harping on it. Clearly she wanted me to say something, because I don't have anything against Adrienne. But I was so thankful that Lisa was my best friend. I wanted to make her happy.

Dave Rupel: It came out at an all-Housewife event at SUR, Lisa's restaurant.

Brandi Glanville: We were sitting at the table and everyone already knew and was laughing behind her back. I was just the first one to say it out loud. And everyone gasped, like, "I can't believe you said that!"

Kyle Richards: That was just so, so low to me. To do something like that to a woman on television. Nobody knew that. Her children didn't even know! To say something like that? Who knows what would come next?

Camille Grammer: I had also gone through surrogacy and chosen to be very open about it, but that was my choice. I thought it was wrong of Brandi to just blurt that out.

Brandi Glanville: Every time Lisa wanted me to say something, she was like, "You know, Brandi, I would never tell you what to say." But then she'd make a few points about whoever she wanted me to take down, and it would just get the ball rolling in my head so if anything came up, I had ammunition and it would just come out.

Chris Cullen: In hindsight, Brandi was the first example of Lisa recruiting other people to do her dirty work for her.

Kyle Richards: Brandi became friends with Lisa Vanderpump and I knew the second that happened that if Lisa ever wanted to get to me, she'd use Brandi to do it. That's how Lisa operated; she would silently send Brandi to do stuff for her against everyone.

Brandi Glanville: She always liked to have someone nearby she could manipulate. It was a very unhealthy relationship that I had with Vanderpump.

Adrienne Maloof: I'm not giving Brandi a pass, but Lisa encouraged her to come forward with that. Maybe Brandi looks like a bad person, but behind the scenes, it was also Lisa.

Brandi Glanville: I have to take responsibility. It did come out of my mouth. Is that a crime? No. Did I say it? I did. So, I'm an asshole.

Adrienne Maloof: I wish it was done on my time, not on her time. That's what was so difficult. My initial response was, "Screw this, I'm out of here. This is too much. Now it's affecting my children and invading my privacy."

Andy Cohen: We kept saying to Adrienne, "You don't understand. This is going to be reported in a magazine. It's going to get out. Wouldn't it be better if it just played out on the show and you could turn it into some sort of a teachable moment?" But she refused.

Dave Rupel: Adrienne stopped shooting with us for a while. She just couldn't go along with it. And ultimately, because it's a HIPAA issue, we're not allowed to talk about a medical situation without the person's permission. So we had no choice but to take it out.

Chris Cullen: She threatened to sue because we were airing private medical information. That was the technicality. So we bleeped out the word "surrogacy" or "surrogate" anytime it was said. And we warned her, "Look, it's out there. And once people hear these bleeps and can't quite figure out what you or Brandi are talking about, they're going to be digging. And they're going to figure it out."

Adrienne Maloof: There was just no turning back at that point.

Dave Rupel: Then she tried to sue Brandi.

Brandi Glanville: That was just my first cease and desist letter. Nowadays I joke that I'm going to make a coffee table book out of all of them.

> As the season 3 reunion approached, Adrienne—still reeling from the surrogacy revelations and the collapse of her marriage—had a choice to make.

Chris Cullen: We tried everything we could to get Adrienne there, to convince her that the best thing to do would be to not run from the story but confront it head-on.

Adrienne Maloof: Everything kind of came crashing down at once. They were coaching me to come forward, but I was also going through a divorce, thinking, "Now I've got to deal with a custody battle." I really didn't feel like I had anybody in my corner.

Chris Cullen: My husband and I, we adopted our two children. So I kept telling Adrienne, "Look, I'm in a situation like you. Families are created many, many different ways, and you did this for a reason. Get out there and be proud of it." And we also tried the other side: "Throw it back on what a horrible person Brandi is for bringing this up. Ask her why in the world she would do that. Make her answer for this."

Adrienne Maloof: I just needed relief, and I needed to step back and focus on my children.

Chris Cullen: As much as our show was pitched as *Lifestyles of the Rich and Famous*, the audience also wants to find something that they can relate to. And Adrienne could have really become a fan favorite by dealing with this topic in an honest way. And she could have put Brandi in her fucking place. But she just couldn't find the strength to do it.

Alex Baskin: The truth is, had she shown up to the reunion, we would have kept going with her.

Andy Cohen: I was bitchy on air about her not showing up at that reunion and I regret it now.

Adrienne Maloof: I'm so much stronger now and I should have just pushed through it. But I was struggling at the time.

> *Adrienne was just one of many women, both OG and new, exiting* RHOBH *in season 3.*
>
> *Still struggling to get her bearings after the wreckage of season 2, it was time for Taylor to step out of the spotlight. And Camille was still dealing with the fallout of a broken marriage that made it difficult for her to commit completely to the show.*

Chris Cullen: Camille exited because of the legal situation. Her divorce was in full swing. She was in court all the time. All of that was untouchable on the show. We weren't allowed to talk about it because we were under all these rules of Kelsey Grammer and this lawsuit over their divorce and custody arrangement. So she was stressed beyond belief, and we recognized that we weren't going to get any content about what was really happening in her life.

Camille Grammer: I'm proud to have been a part of pop culture history. And it was good to wake up and have a job to go to—it gave me a focus other than the divorce and crying over my ex-husband. Was it a painful experience at times? Yes. Was it a learning experience? Yes. Do I regret it? No. Are there aspects of things I've said and done I regret? Yes. But on a whole, no. I'm glad I was part of it.

> *In the middle of season 3, Lisa Vanderpump added another feather to her cap when her spin-off,* Vanderpump Rules, *premiered. Vanderpump's role as executive producer escalated long-simmering tensions for the other women, who were growing increasingly wary of her influence over* Housewives.

Dave Rupel: I'm sure the women weren't happy that Lisa had two shows on Bravo. You'd have to think she had more power, and I know that rubbed the women the wrong way.

Lisa Vanderpump: I always felt that *Vanderpump Rules* was very provocative. The fact that I had a spin-off when everybody else tried for a spin-off incited a lot of demons.

Chris Cullen: I don't think the other women were pissed off about *Vanderpump Rules* specifically. It was more Lisa's way of presenting it—it was like, "I'm holding the center diamond, and now I have a spin-off because I've got this special relationship with Andy and Bravo."

Douglas Ross: She never hesitated to tell the other cast members how close she was with Andy, how much sway she had as the executive producer of her own show. I don't think she helped herself.

Andy Cohen: Every so often I had to call one Housewife or another to promise them that they were as important to me as Lisa, that all were equal. And they were!

Chris Cullen: She would constantly cut down the ladies' confidence in order to build herself up. She tried to make other ladies feel insecure, and that's what they resented.

Yolanda Hadid: Obviously there was a lot of jealousy of Lisa Vanderpump's success.

Kyle Richards: No. Not even a little bit. Lisa used to say that all the time: "They're jealous. They're jealous." I've never, ever—and none of the other cast members, I promise—have ever been jealous of anything the other one is doing. It's funny that Lisa is the only woman who ever said that on the show. That's how she thinks, that's not how we think.

Brandi Glanville: These bitches are jealous. They really can't be happy for each other. A lot of these women are like, "It's my show, I'm the star."

> *After the clearing of the decks in season 3, season 4 brought two new faces: practicing Wiccan mother of three Carlton Gebbia and Joyce Giraud de Ohoven, a native Puerto Rican Miss Universe runner-up, actress, and mother of two. The results were . . . mixed.*

Dave Rupel: Joyce was a beauty pageant contestant and was very sparkly and dynamic and from Puerto Rico and feisty. But the moment the camera started running, she gave us pageant queen.

Carlton, on the other hand, didn't hold back. But there were concerns from all sides about her Wiccan faith and how the show would present it.

Dave Rupel: Kyle got wind that we were hiring a witch, and she said, "I'm not going to work with somebody who will put a spell on me." Kim had the same fear.

Carlton Gebbia (Housewife): The one thing I said from the start was, "I'm extremely wary about my faith being exploited because I'm not traditional. And it's something that's very sacred to me. And I will have a big problem if you go a way I'm not okay with."

Dave Rupel: I said, "You know, there's gonna come a point where you're going to hate my guts. That happens with every Housewife. That just happens." And I said, "I need to know you're not putting a bad spell on me." So I understood Kyle and Kim's fear. But she told me a very convincing story that when you invite dark magic into your life, you don't have control over it. And she said, once I had my children, there was no way I would ever invite dark magic into my life because it could affect my kids. And that seemed very reasonable to me.

The renewed group dynamic was fraught from the start.

Carlton Gebbia: It was just high school shit. Apparently Kyle and Lisa wanted to paint me as the villain because I was a fucking witch. I started to get pissed off because I felt like I was being exploited and my faith was being exploited. Kyle would say shit to me and she took it too far when she accused me of being antisemitic. I had gotten a tattoo that Kyle thought was the Star of David. I was like, "No, it's a fucking pentagram and you should know this—you're Jewish." I went from zero to sixty in a split second because it was just so predictable. Meanwhile, the bitch was walking up to my house saying it was like Harry Potter's house. She was a soulless troll that would sell her soul to make money or to be in the spotlight. I fucking was horrified.

And with new perspectives came fresh accusations, the biggest of which were against Lisa Vanderpump, whose behind-the-scenes maneuvering had become increasingly apparent to the other Housewives over the course of the show's early seasons.

Brandi Glanville: *Housewives* was Lisa's baby. She would set up what she wanted to happen down the road.

Chris Cullen: She thought the best way to do that was to have these big, impactful, explosive secrets revealed or big gossipy moments where other people looked bad so she could then console them or advise them. But she didn't want her hands dirty. She didn't want to be the one who's bringing up gossip and rumors.

Brandi Glanville: Even when we weren't shooting, all we would talk about was the show. It was really exhausting, to be honest.

Alex Baskin: The cast started to question her.

Chris Cullen: Beverly Hills is a small town, and Lisa had a reputation for manipulating and dropping her friends. I wish she had embraced that sneaky part of her personality a little bit more. But she wanted to appear different on camera than who she really was.

Yolanda Hadid: I always said, "My God, these women, they walk over dead bodies to get camera time and to be famous." That was the hardest thing for me to learn.

Chris Cullen: I'm guessing Kyle was getting a bad taste in her mouth, too, because remember she said during the season 2 reunion that "being friends with Lisa is like playing chess with Bobby Fischer."

Kyle Richards: Lisa and I . . . people like to focus on the drama of *House-wives*, but we had so much fun. We have the same sense of humor and we laughed our asses off. We could be naughty at times and it was fun for me to have someone to do that with. We laughed harder than anybody. So it was like, "I love you, I have fun with you, but I don't trust you at all."

Carlton Gebbia: There was so much drama between Lisa and Kyle. They were both sort of desperate to be the queen bee.

> *Tensions came to a head when tabloid accusations about infidelity in Kyle's marriage showed up on a girls' weekend to Palm Springs. A major dispute broke out over who brought them.*

Chris Cullen: The ladies were getting very suspicious that Lisa was supplying information to Radar Online and TMZ.

Brandi Glanville: I still don't know for certain how the rumors about Mauricio having affairs—which were never even proven—got out. I feel like it was probably Lisa behind that story. Why else would she want me to bring it up? It was all too convenient.

Chris Cullen: The tabloids in the suitcase—it happened off camera, but it happened.

Brandi Glanville: Yolanda came over to my house prior to leaving, and we were looking at these tabloids. Then Lisa got there and she said, "You have to bring these." And she put them in my fucking bag.

Chris Cullen: Brandi took them out of the suitcase and Lisa put them back in.

Brandi Glanville: I said, "No, I'm not bringing these. Listen, I'm not here to ruin a marriage over a fucking rumor." It's one thing if it's true and I have exact proof of it and a reason to bring it up. And listen, when you're on reality TV, you have to share things when you know they're 100 percent true—that's what you do. But if it's a rumor, I'm sorry.

Kyle Richards: Everybody knew Lisa put the tabloids in the suitcase. She will deny it until the day she dies. She was trying to create drama, but she didn't want her hands dirty.

Dave Rupel: We did not have that on camera so that's another case of there's no smoking gun to trace it back to.

Chris Cullen: Once they were in Palm Springs, Brandi kept bringing up the tabloids because Lisa Vanderpump was making her do that. Lisa wasn't going to do it herself.

Yolanda Hadid: Everybody was afraid of Lisa Vanderpump because she was the head honcho. She was the big boss, she was the one that created a lot of that show and the content of it. That's just business. That's just a fact.

Brandi Glanville: We were a little afraid to be honest because, if you go against her, you're not going to have a job.

Dave Rupel: Brandi never shared that fear with me, although it doesn't surprise me. And, you know, Lisa talked about the show a lot. But if Lisa had called Andy one day and said, "Get Brandi off the show," I don't think she had that kind of sway. No one has that sway.

Andy Cohen: Every so often, someone will mention to me that someone should be shown the door, or say that they won't come back if someone they dislike is on the show. I can't think of a situation where another Housewife has made that demand and it's worked.

Brandi Glanville: I was sitting in my backyard one day and got a call from Andy, who was like, "Listen, no one has special privileges. We are showing everyone's story. And don't think you're here because of Lisa. You just have to be true to yourself and not be afraid of her." He made me feel very comfortable, so I decided I was going to be the one to call out her bullshit.

Andy Cohen: It just got to this point where Lisa was boxed into a corner. None of the other women liked her. She was an island.

Brandi Glanville: I didn't want to cross her. I was in love with her. I loved her more than pretty much anyone. She took care of me for quite a few seasons, and she was like my mom. And you don't cross Lisa without getting fucked. Even one word that's negative. But when I met Yolanda, and then Kim and I became friends, I was like, "You girls let me be me." From Lisa, I would get lectures like, "Brandi, you shouldn't say that." But they never said, "Say this, do this, do that." We're actually friends. So it was very refreshing. I could be my authentic self without having to be someone's sidekick. And Lisa just wanted to ruin my fucking life. Of course, there is a part of me that still loves her in a weird way. But she's the biggest asshole on the planet.

> *Carlton and Joyce both left after one season, but season 6 saw two iconic soap opera stars join the cast—and the drama ramped up accordingly. First up was someone the producers had been eyeing since the very beginning: Lisa Rinna.*

Lisa Rinna: When producers approached me again, I was colder than cold. I could barely get an agent. So I just started looking at everything. We were talking about possibly creating my own reality show. I thought to myself, "What is the best real estate on television right now if you're going to do a reality show? *Housewives*. Look at Bethenny." I saw what had happened with her and her business. So I thought, I'm going to meet with Evolution, but I'm going to drop some hints about being on *Housewives* without saying I should be a Housewife. And I guess on the flip side, they were doing the same exact thing—meeting me about doing a reality show, but really wanting me to be a Housewife.

Andy Cohen: Six years later, the idea I was so against now seemed brilliant. Rinna had existing relationships with many of the women for years. She just fit.

> *Rinna was joined by longtime friend Eileen Davidson, who was hitting a career high as she started filming for RHOBH.*

Jennifer Redinger: Eileen was on a soap opera and lived in Beverly Hills and won actual awards—like, who doesn't want that?

Eileen Davidson (Housewife): My husband Vinny used to make fun of me for watching reality TV. He didn't really get it. It was an "ignorance is bliss" type of situation for him.

Lisa Rinna: It was a really happy surprise when Eileen was cast the same season because I've always loved her. The last time I had seen her we were doing *Days of Our Lives* at the same time.

Eileen Davidson: Before I even signed a contract, they decided to cover me getting ready for the Daytime Emmys. I'd been nominated and Chris Cullen and I had been speaking and it was kismet because they were able to shoot me coming out after I won—but I wasn't even under contract when they shot that.

> But once Eileen did officially join, she had to meet Brandi at a dinner with Yolanda and Lisa Rinna, in which Brandi took her soap opera fandom a bit too far. . . .

Eileen Davidson: I'll tell you what happened. I knew Brandi was a *Days of Our Lives* fan. So, she's like, oh, come on, do some of those little soap opera moves and she wouldn't let it go. And then she threw the wine in my face and I actually laughed. But the reason why I got emotional is because after she threw the glass of wine in my face she started saying, "You bitch, you cheated on your husband, how could you do that?"

Brandi Glanville: I don't throw wine. I mean, I do throw wine but not like often, but she actually laughed after I did it. We were all laughing.

Eileen Davidson: What made me cry was realizing that I was in this really fucked-up world, a really crazy, fucked-up world, and Yolanda ended up driving me home, and I remember saying, "Yolanda what the hell are you doing on this show?"

> Eileen soon found herself in the middle of one of the season's big dramas when a poker night at her house highlighted Kim's worrying behavior.

Eileen Davidson: Lots of things had been said off camera about Kim's behavior over the years. Lots and lots and lots of things.

Lisa Rinna: It was clear as a bell that night that she was on something. It was really frustrating to watch and be like, "Why isn't anybody helping her?"

Eileen Davidson: She had her sister there, she had Brandi there, so I wasn't thinking, "I've got to get this person help." I just didn't get why she was on camera clearly inebriated. It didn't make any sense to me.

Lisa Rinna: It's really tough when you're dealing with somebody who is not themselves and maybe is on something that is affecting their mood. So I was more in shock than anything else.

Eileen Davidson: We found out later that she had taken some kind of a pill or whatever, and then it became, maybe this is something we should bring up? I didn't feel great about it, but she brought her personal problem into my home.

> *The questions surrounding Kim's behavior came to a head when the ladies flew to the Netherlands. Tensions hit a fever pitch at a dinner that ended with Kim making vague accusations about Lisa Rinna's husband, Harry Hamlin, and Lisa lunging at Kim and breaking a glass.*

Yolanda Hadid: Obviously, the explosion that first night out to dinner was not fun.

Lisa Rinna: To this day we still don't know what Harry supposedly did. I'd love to know. He'd love to know.

Chris Cullen: I really think Kim just tried to throw something out there just to be provocative. I've had many conversations with her about this, and she has never told me what she meant.

Brandi Glanville: Kim didn't know anything, she was just posturing. But the fact that Lisa got so upset kind of makes you think there was something to it.

Eileen Davidson: All that weird shit with Lisa Rinna and Kim was kind of emotionally messed up—Rinna's eyes looked like she had PTSD. When you threaten somebody with a glass, I mean, that's crazy shit!

Chris Cullen: That was a fucking real moment. That was as real as it gets. There was nothing manufactured there. That accusation, that anger, all of that was, you know, insanity.

Eileen Davidson: Bravo had no idea what they were getting when they got Lisa Rinna. I saw her in action that first season, and I was like, "Holy crap, you were born for this."

Lisa Rinna: The show brings out things in you that aren't necessarily triggered in real life. So there are times when I see myself in the third person, and I'm just like, "Who is that?"

Andy Cohen: This may be contrary to what everyone thinks I would say, but I do not like it when a glass is broken or thrown. It is an overused trope. You're taking a very real moment, where someone's really mad—like when someone is insinuating something about your husband—and turning it into a TV show.

Lisa Rinna: I remember being in the moment and almost putting my hands on Kim. And I remember I had like a divine intervention. I'm not even kidding, something from above said, "Do not touch her or you will go to prison." That's why, if you watch the scene closely, I back up because I've got this energy. And that's when I grabbed the glass and broke it because I was going to literally put my hands on her.

Kyle Richards: When the glass flew, I ran out. I suffer from anxiety, and when there's anything uncomfortable that stresses me out, I flee. We were in a public place! So I don't know where I was going, but I had to get out of there because my anxiety couldn't take it.

On the final night of the trip, a playful moment between off-again friends Brandi and Vanderpump turned accusatory. . . .

Brandi Glanville: We were on a canal cruise, joking around, and I was like, "Either kiss me or I'm going to smack you." If you're going to kiss someone, you don't hate them. I just want wanted to make up and make it funny. And then I went in for the kiss—and we were on a fucking boat, you can't escape—but she wouldn't do it.

Lisa Rinna: Brandi has that thing where she likes to make something happen. It really wasn't that big of a slap.

Brandi Glanville: I literally gave her a love slap. She was definitely shocked, but it was completely playful.

Eileen Davidson: She barely touched her. I mean, Brandi was an asshole, but that was Lisa Vanderpump trying to capitalize on the fact that Brandi was an asshole. If Brandi had done that a few years earlier, they both would have laughed about it.

Chris Cullen: Brandi did it to get a rise out of Lisa, and she was doing it to keep her job, and she was doing it for the shock value. I'm sure all of those things are true. But, you know, she hit Lisa and Lisa reacted to it.

Brandi Glanville: The next day I woke up, I had all these texts from Yolanda and everyone like, "Did you slap Lisa?" I'm like, "Not really, we were playing around." And then Lisa took it to a whole other level.

Eileen Davidson: Vanderpump had a lot of power, but I don't think it was just her because a lot of people had problems with Brandi. She just crossed lines.

The brighter the flame, the faster it burns. . . . Sensing her time on the show was nearing its end and happy to leave a trail of destruction in her wake, Brandi decided to take action into her own hands.

Brandi Glanville: I was an asshole. I was pissed at everyone. I went after Andy on Twitter, and then I wrote a fuck-off email to every single producer, including Andy, telling them all to go fucking fuck themselves. Not the best move if you want a job!

Yolanda Hadid: She's highly emotional. Highly.

Brandi Glanville: I thought I was being treated unfairly, I don't actually remember exactly why. I was depressed, I was mad at production. Lisa was after me. It was too much to take on. I was fed up.

Jennifer Redinger: Brandi, as much as she can definitely get crazy on the show and is very outspoken, I will say she's one of the most thankful, humble people. And a lot of people may not see that side of her. There's a softer side.

Brandi Glanville: Luckily, from that point on everyone hired me. They're like, "You're great TV. Do you want to do this show?" I'm like, "Yes yes yes yes yes yes yes." So I was very blessed. *Housewives* saved my life in a lot of ways.

> *Too much diva energy? Never! Season 6 saw the entrance of Erika Girardi, a high-powered lawyer's wife by day, who stormed the gay clubs at night as dance music sex kitten Erika Jayne.*
>
> *She found her way into the show during a night in with Yolanda and David Foster.*

Yolanda Hadid: She was sitting on the couch and I had this vision come to me like, "Oh my God, she should be a Housewife."

Erika Girardi (Housewife): Yolanda just interrupted me and goes, "Have you thought of being a Housewife?" And I said no. And she's like, "I think you'd be perfect. I'm going to text my boss right now."

Yolanda Hadid: I remember going to the bathroom and texting Alex Baskin like, "I have your next Housewife on my couch. Nobody knows her, but she'd be perfect."

Erika Girardi: I thought nothing of it. Alex called me and said, "You know, this could be a five-minute phone call or it could be something else. Who knows?" The next week I went in and put myself on tape. They asked me a bunch of questions and I just answered them as honestly and as thoughtfully as possible with no agenda. And then I got the job. I mean, it was as simple and as complicated as that.

Yolanda Hadid: I was hoping she would stay herself and be cautious. I wanted her to make it work.

Erika Girardi: When I got the job, David Foster gave me a piece of advice. He said, "Erika, I don't want you to believe in the good, and I don't want you to believe in the bad. I want you to be neutral because none of it means anything. On this show, one day you're great and the next day you're a piece of shit. So you cannot buy into it. This is a different type of celebrity, and you need to understand that." He was very savvy that way.

Lisa Rinna: Erika was so different from anybody that had ever come on the show. She is larger than life, performing and traveling with her glam squad. I saw her fabulousness right away. And so did Eileen.

Eileen Davidson: Right out of the gate I liked the fact that she was doing something different with her life and taking chances as a performer. I felt like she was an underdog, which—I'm dumb, because she really never was.

Erika Girardi: Rinna and Eileen were both very kind to me. Oftentimes you just strike an understanding with some more than others.

Eileen Davidson: I remember once in the Hamptons, Bethenny was saying something mean about Erika Jayne and I stood up for her. And Erika goes, "Thank you so much, but I'm not going to make it in this crowd if I can't fight my own battles," and I went, "Whoa. Gotcha." She knew what she was doing.

Erika Girardi: I was open. I wanted to stick up for my friend Yolanda, which I did. And I wanted to watch—I watch everything. I look very deeply at people. And I listen to what they say. I think that people tell you a lot. And sitting back and watching is never a bad thing.

Lisa Rinna: I learned from her that first season. Erika is very smart. And she's in on the joke. She gets it. She's been selling Erika Jayne for a long time.

> *Also entering the fray was new Housewife Kathryn Edwards, but the biggest through line of the season was the doubt swirling around Yolanda's Lyme disease diagnosis. As the women tried to make sense of the elusive condition taking their friend out of the group dynamic, a word was uttered that couldn't be taken back: Munchausen.*

Kathryn Edwards (Housewife): Yolanda wasn't coming out at all. She was just lying up in her bed in that dingy robe she wore all season.

Yolanda Hadid: I didn't even know what was wrong with me, but it was so bad at the beginning. I couldn't read or watch TV. I was struggling with severe brain and neurological issues. All I remember from that time is that it was such a struggle for me to get diagnosed and once I was diagnosed, I was doing IVs two times a day.

Eileen Davidson: It was causing a lot of weirdness on the show that she wasn't filming a lot.

352 NOT ALL DIAMONDS AND ROSÉ

Kathryn Edwards: Everyone knew that she was depressed. There was more going on—it wasn't just about her having Lyme disease.

Yolanda Hadid: I was suffering from severe depression from not being able to use my brain. I mean, I didn't go to college, but I've always been very successful because I had a pretty brilliant mind, and when that mind wasn't working anymore, I lost such a big part of myself.

Eileen Davidson: Before the season starts, they'll come and talk to you about what you have going on that year. They'll ask, "Have you heard any of these rumors? How do you feel about those tweets?

Chris Cullen: Kyle and Lisa Vanderpump were saying, "Hey, rumor has it that Yolanda's not really sick, that she has Munchausen—do you know what Munchausen is?" We all would look up Munchausen.

Kyle Richards: When Yolanda was sick, Rinna knew somebody who said she thought Yolanda had Munchausen's. Rinna told me that, and I told Vanderpump. But I was only repeating what Rinna told me her friend said, I didn't even know this woman. Still, Vanderpump wanted it brought up on the show.

Yolanda Hadid: I'm sure Lisa Vanderpump was part of it, that it was something they cooked up together.

Chris Cullen: Lisa Vanderpump was pushing Lisa Rinna to bring the Munchausen up because she'd heard the rumor from one of her friends.

Lisa Rinna: I had been getting calls from Vanderpump for a long time. Kyle was involved, too. Lisa and Kyle could see that I was perplexed by what was going on, and I started to question it with them. They kept being like, "Doesn't that bother you?" I was being produced without knowing I was being produced.

Eileen Davidson: Vanderpump was the sniper. She would have Lisa Rinna do these things and take the hit, and she would stand on the sidelines watching all the havoc that she'd helped create. But Rinna and I both decided before that season that we were not going to go near Yolanda with this Munchausen thing. It was gross. It was picking on somebody who was not doing well.

Lisa Rinna: I said something like, "I'm not doing it. I'm not going to be the one to do it. I don't think it's fair. She's sick."

Chris Cullen: The day that Lisa Rinna came into Vanderpump's house and read that definition off her phone, none of us knew that was happening.

Eileen Davidson: I came from work to Lisa Vanderpump's house. Kyle was there. Lisa Rinna was there. Rinna was upset because she had just mentioned Munchausen. She and I went outside and I said, "What the hell? You said you didn't want to go there." She was like, "I know, I got manipulated."

Chris Cullen: Lisa Vanderpump could be very persuasive, and she might have said something like, "This is your second season on the show. You want to establish yourself. You want to have impactful moments, you've heard this information, you might want to bring this to us so we can have a conversation about it." I could imagine Lisa Vanderpump producing Lisa Rinna in a way that felt like it was in Lisa Rinna's best interest to create a big conversation for them to all have about Yolanda.

Eileen Davidson: I said, "Just tell everybody that you made a mistake by bringing this up and you don't mean it, if that's what you want to do—because you are doing something right now by opening this door on Yolanda." So Rinna started backpedaling and I heard Lisa Vanderpump—I was standing next to her—say, "There goes our story line." I would hear things like that and they would just make my skin crawl.

Lisa Rinna: In that moment, I knew the story line was going to be about Yolanda no matter whether I stepped in or not. And I didn't want to displease Lisa Vanderpump. Remember, she was the queen. She was the grande dame. And in a sense, you felt like you wanted to please the grande dame.

Brandi Glanville: When people were saying that Yolanda wasn't sick, it was so bothersome to me because I would go to her house; she literally was gray in color.

Yolanda Hadid: I'd never even heard the word "Munchausen." It was devastating. But, you know, it was really a time for me to go deep within myself and go, "Okay, I have some balls. I can't take this personally. This is somebody that is highly uneducated about chronic disease and just wants to be famous."

Lisa Rinna: I fell into it so quickly and so easily because I truly did question it. I really was confused by it because I knew Yolanda before this, and I hadn't seen her in this position.

Andy Cohen: Lisa Rinna is always so hell-bent on finding out the truth.

Lisa Rinna: I didn't understand it and nobody took me aside and tried to explain it to me, so I was very easily manipulated into carrying that torch. And I took it, hook, line, and sinker. I mean, I'm the one who did it.

Brandi Glanville: To say that she was faking something? That's when I was like, "I'll fucking murder all of you because you guys don't hang out with her outside of the show. I do. And I know she's not faking."

Eileen Davidson: Something that never aired was that Lisa Rinna, just in passing, said something about how Yolanda was getting paid even though she wasn't working. I said basically, "Whether she has Lyme disease or is faking it, there's something wrong with her, isn't there? So either way, she's not well." Of course, I was going to take her at her word—not in a million years did I think she was making shit up. But either way, you don't turn on people who aren't well.

Andy Cohen: In Rinna's mind, she was making a show and we had to be truthful.

Lisa Rinna: It's super frustrating when someone will say to us, "I wish you would have pulled her aside and just done it in private." And you go, "Well, yeah, but then we wouldn't have a fucking show!"

Yolanda Hadid: It really worked against her. She lost a lot of respect with a lot of people because of her ignorance.

Eileen Davidson: It does leave a bad taste in your mouth. But it's different rules in that world.

Lisa Rinna: Believe me, I've had my years where I am hated. That's been hard.

Yolanda Hadid: Part of me wanted to get off the show, but maybe this was the higher purpose of my journey. To show that, regardless of your status in life, nobody's spared from this kind of disease.

> *After never quite clicking with the women, Kathryn joined the one-and-done club. And after a season of relentless questioning, as well as the behind-the-scenes collapse of her marriage, Yolanda no longer had the energy to fight anymore. Season 6 was her last.*

Yolanda Hadid: I got sick and I was only there because of my work ethic. But I could not get well, and I just had to acknowledge that and take the step of moving away from it.

Chris Cullen: Yolanda was asked to do a diminished role, and she said no to that and never looked back.

Yolanda Hadid: We talked about a lot of different scenarios for me to maybe stay on. And then I was in Tahiti and I went for a swim and I was just like, "God, just give me a sign. I need clarity." I was swimming for an hour and I came back and I got out of the water and I said to my best friend, "I'm going to quit the show." And she's like, "What, are you crazy? You have a book coming out. You've never done any business. You went through all these years of struggling. You've got to stay." And I'm like, "No, I'm done. The journey is done." It felt so true and so clear to me that it wasn't even worth a conversation.

Andy Cohen: Yolanda was passionate about bringing attention to Lyme disease on the show, and she was very clear when she left that she'd done all she wanted with the show. She had a fantastic run, and not only brought a lot of elegance and class to the show, but if you think about it, the Hadid girls were launched on *RHOBH*. We were there for their early modeling shoots and had an insider's view of the beginning of their now stratospheric careers.

Chris Cullen: I don't think she has any regrets about that whatsoever.

Yolanda Hadid: It took me quitting the show, getting divorced, moving away from Beverly Hills, and finding my life on a farm on the East Coast to really start my healing journey. But I love that I did that. There's a whole other life out here that I didn't know.

> With a glamorous model-sized hole in the group, producers recruited a new blond bombshell in Dorit Kemsley, a fashion plate whose styles would inspire as many conversations as her accent. Between Dorit's connection to Queen Vanderpump, her conflict-prone husband, PK, their globally famous live-in client Boy George, and her two adorable children, Dorit provided no shortage of conversation.

Dorit Kemsley (Housewife): Lisa Vanderpump was friends with PK, so we became friends by extension.

Jennifer Redinger: I just remember thinking, "This is so crazy—Boy George is living in your house!" Plus, she was naturally friends with Lisa and Kyle. I'm like, "This is great."

Dorit Kemsley: But I had just had our baby girl, Phoenix. So I said, "Oh my God. Absolutely not. Never in a million years."

Jennifer Redinger: She had just given birth and was feeling self-conscious, like, "I feel so overweight," and I'm like, "Don't worry about it. That's part of being a woman."

Dorit Kemsley: Long story short, after several interviews, they came back and said, "You're the newest Housewife." And, you know, as much as we've struggled at times, it's definitely part of my destiny.

> During her first season, Dorit found herself in an unexpected feud after Erika revealed at a party that she was going commando. "Pantygate," as it came to be called, revolved around Dorit's insistence that Erika intentionally flashed her husband.

Jennifer Redinger: I will say, a lot of these Housewives love to not wear underwear. They don't want their panty lines to show. I've been Sharon Stoned more than anybody.

Erika Girardi: After your first year you kind of see where things are going and how small things—like underwear or lack of underwear—will be seized upon. It becomes this giant snowball and gets a life of its own.

Alex Baskin: Early in Dorit's run, PK got involved in the women's affairs and caught some flak for it.

Dorit Kemsley: PK's British. He's got a certain character about him. When he first started, he put his foot in his mouth a couple of times when he was feeling very protective of me.

Alex Baskin: But once he ended up in the center story, that wasn't great.

Eileen Davidson: PK was looking out for Dorit. I remember having a conversation with him and saying, "You should back off. Dorit is more than capable of handling this." And he said, "No, not now, not this time. Maybe next year. But right now, no, she needs to have me here." And I was like, "Okay, but I don't think this is going to work out so well for you."

Dorit Kemsley: That was a little bit of a struggle for us. We are very codependent. Very. Everything is very intertwined. And this was the first time in our relationship where I was doing something essentially on my own. We both had to adjust to that.

Erika Girardi: You're bound to end up in weird conflicts, that is the nature of the game. You have to roll with the punches.

Dorit Kemsley: That entire story line was a lot of misunderstanding—a few tasteless comments, combined with us being rookies who made some mistakes. There were feelings hurt, but that was never the intention. After that, I really, really wanted to try to work things out with Erika because there was no ill will. Never was.

Erika Girardi: It takes two people that want to move on, and we both did.

Eileen Davidson: Just because you don't like somebody one season doesn't mean that you're not going to be best friends with them the next. Sometimes you have to get along with them because you're on a show.

Also new that season? A "Friend of" with a storied, stylish pedigree.

Jennifer Redinger: Obviously Vidal Sassoon is a huge name and also very synonymous with Los Angeles and Beverly Hills. Eden had some funny stories because she was a dating machine at the time—dating younger guys. I loved that about her because you know what? She's a hot woman and we all love a hot, younger guy.

Eden Sassoon (Friend): Lisa Rinna and I got along really well at first. I loved this woman—like, we just connected in the fun and the healing and the crystals. So she has that side to her, but she also knows how to play the game.

Lisa Rinna: I do come in there and just give it. I leave it on the floor, and leaving it on the floor can get messy.

Eden Sassoon: Rinna put it in my head that Kim was "close to death." So as I was watching Kim—even though I didn't think she was close to death and I didn't witness her drinking—I just saw her behavior. She's a tortured soul, with or without drugs and alcohol. So that got to me.

Chris Cullen: In Mexico, Kyle confronted Lisa Rinna and said, "Did you say my sister is close to death? Did you say I'm an enabler?"

Kyle Richards: I had such bad anxiety after that fight with Kim in the limo in season 1. By the time Eden said this and Rinna repeated it, I was paranoid about any of it coming up again because of what it did to my relationship with my sister.

Lisa Rinna: After the Munchausen year, I had said, "Okay, I'm only going to come back if I can have fun because I'm not having any fun." And they said, "You can have fun this year." And that was going to be my Yoda Lisa Rinna, the nicest fucking Lisa Rinna year. At least that was the plan.

Chris Cullen: Lisa Rinna was caught off guard when Kyle confronted her. And for whatever reason, she said, "No, I didn't say that." Even though I, standing there ten feet away, knew that two weeks earlier she shot a scene with Eden where she said it. It's on camera. So I had to let her live with that for a really long time.

Eden Sassoon: Rinna knows where everything's going, though she plays it really well on camera that she's all over the place. She does an amazing job playing this version of herself.

Chris Cullen: She was getting into more of a hole with the ladies and the ladies were getting frustrated and didn't believe her.

> *Drugs continued to be a fixation throughout the season, and when the women traveled to Hong Kong, things came to a head when Rinna lobbed an unexpected accusation, famously asking Dorit, "Were people doing coke in your bathroom?"*

Dorit Kemsley: When she said that to me, I thought she was the worst human being in the whole entire world. I have two little babies at home, you know? How could you go and do that? Say that?

Andy Cohen: I actually howled when I saw Lisa Rinna say that. I texted her immediately. I didn't see it coming, though it's what you might imagine could happen in Beverly Hills. I just couldn't believe it. I thought it was hilarious.

Lisa Rinna: I wouldn't ask it if I didn't want the answer. I mean, I don't just throw shit out there.

Dorit Kemsley: Lisa is, and has been from the start, one of the controversial characters—she brings it every single time, and she does and says things that might be outrageous. That's part of who she is.

Lisa Rinna: I have spoken to producers since. And, you know, one of the producers did say he walked in on one of the guests doing coke in the bathroom.

Dorit Kemsley: I will say this: I don't believe she makes things up. I don't know if she was told to say that, but Lisa will own the fact that she's made mistakes and then has moved past them. And we certainly were able to move past it.

Lisa Rinna: Any time I open my mouth like that, it takes a while before it comes around to being an iconic moment. Let's put it that way.

Andy Cohen: And that is why Lisa Rinna is a great Housewife.

That same night, another eventually iconic moment went down when Eileen mentioned Erika's grown son, a policeman, sparking a frightening flash of anger.

Eden Sassoon: Eileen, she's harmless in every way, shape, or form.

Eileen Davidson: Something else was going on. I'm really not quite sure what, but Erika explained to me later that I said something that was completely innocuous and it just triggered her.

Erika Girardi: It was an emotional moment and that's it. It came out of nowhere, but it was very real.

Eden Sassoon: Erika was like that the whole trip. She's intense. I mean, she's either sort of laid back and or it's "Don't fuck with me because I will cut your fucking throat." It's all or nothing with that one. I have the chills right now just thinking of it.

Erika Girardi: Every woman who's been on the show will tell you that they've made, not necessarily mistakes, but that they've gotten caught up in the moment.

Eileen Davidson: The next day, right when I saw her, she came up to me and apologized profusely.

Erika Girardi: I knew I'd get raked over the coals for snapping at Eileen.

You really get analyzed for everything. Anything that comes out of your mouth, anything you do, anything that you wear . . .

As the season closed, it was appropriately a twenties-themed party that led to an unexpected roar from Eden, who was no longer willing to play the ladies' games.

Eden Sassoon: This was a buildup after six months of being with those women who just overlooked me and had no respect. The Gatsby Party was when I realized, "I don't know if I can do this." They knew I was on edge. It was all eyes on Eden. What is she gonna do to cause a scene? Then I looked over at Rinna, and it really all clicked for me. I had opened up my heart to her and she put a little dagger in it. I was like, "She's awful." So I went and I sat next to her and of course, she pushed one of my buttons and I just lost my mind. And then the truth just fucking came out of every part of me. It went on for, let's say, a solid three minutes. I mean, if you were in that room, you could literally hear a dime drop. I wouldn't stop.

It was also time to discuss Eileen's future on the show. . . .

Chris Cullen: After three years, she was going back to doing *Days* and *Y&R*. We said, "Look, we've explored all your personal stories. You're important to the group, certainly, but we could see you in a 'Friend of' role." But she didn't want that.

Eileen Davidson: We're sitting there and I looked the other way and he said, "What are you thinking?" And I turned back and said, "I'm relieved."

Douglas Ross: I liked what Eileen did for the group. I liked that she was calm and reasonable and rational. She was a truth-teller.

Lisa Rinna: We were so lucky, weren't we? I was able to get through those years and still have a very honest, pure relationship with Eileen.

Eileen Davidson: I was no saint. I was not proud of every moment that I had on that show. That being said, I don't think I was manipulated—not that I know of, at least.

By the time the season 7 reunion came around, a single tear punctuated a season full of hurt, miscommunication, and animosity. That tear, of course, was for the infamous stuffed bunny that Lisa Rinna gave Kim as a gift for her grandchild.

Lisa Rinna: I gave Kim that bunny as a baby shower gift. Period. End of story. I never thought about it again.

Andy Cohen: I found out early the day of the reunion that Kim was bringing the bunny. And when she brought it out, it was so theatrical the way she did it.

Lisa Rinna: They so got me. I was clueless. It took me off guard, and it was so brilliant the way they filmed it with the crinkling of the paper.

Andy Cohen: I found it to be absolutely delicious for every reason you can think of. I mean, it's just stupid. And my favorite *Housewives* fights are about minutiae. So the idea that she brought the bunny back, I just found it very harmless and absurd. You don't see it, but Kyle and I were actually laughing, until I saw that Rinna had a single tear going down her cheek.

Lisa Rinna: I talked to Harry about it and he's like, "What do you think made you cry like that? What button did it push?" And I said, "I really don't know." I do know that I ended up on the bathroom floor in a fetal position after that night. It really got me. It triggered something in my childhood. It was something deep and dark down there. And I couldn't tell you exactly what.

Andy Cohen: I immediately knew that this bunny was going to become a major artifact in the Bravo lexicon. I immediately said, "I want this for the Clubhouse" for *Watch What Happens Live*.

Lisa Rinna: I mean, the whole thing is really some of the greatest television.

Andy Cohen: It's a real piece of pop culture history now.

In season 8, accountability was put on the agenda as Teddi Mellencamp Arroyave, daughter of famed rocker John Mellencamp, joined the show.

Teddi Mellencamp Arroyave (Housewife): My first season I was bumping into any drama around me. But I had no idea it would be drama. I didn't realize how it worked—that anything you mention, it's out there and it spirals on and on and on.

Alex Baskin: One of the things that we tell all cast members when they're new to the show is, we want you to do something that you don't do in real life—in polite company, you stifle your thoughts or you may whisper them to a friend. On the show, we want you to think out loud, say the thing that's on your mind. If someone does something that annoys you, instead of holding it for a nice private conversation, just say it.

Dorit Kemsley: You can't sit on the sidelines and not do anything. We all have to be team players.

Teddi Mellencamp Arroyave: So one thing about filming is that our timing is very clear—not only do we get a schedule, we also have a car service that picks us up. So one day, Dorit and I were scheduled to meet, and she was late, and I remember sitting there like, "She knows what time we're supposed to meet because we all get the same thing."

Dorit Kemsley: They gave me a different time than they gave Teddi, and they portrayed it that I was an hour late.

Chris Cullen: Production would never give cast members separate call times in the hopes of creating potential drama. Bravo would have my head if I allowed my production team to operate that way. Both Teddi and Dorit were given the same exact call time and the show's talent producer reminded Dorit that she needed to get in the car by 3:15 to make the 4:00 meeting with Teddi. Dorit had another meeting prior to the taping with Teddi. The prior meeting ran long, she was late getting into her car service, and then late meeting Teddi.

Teddi Mellencamp Arroyave: After I finished my first glass of wine, alone, I was like, "Well, I'm not going to order a second glass of wine, this is crazy." I just looked at my producer and said, "Can I go?" And he's like, "What would you do in real life?" And I said, "I'd go." So once she arrived, I said to her in the moment, "Well, this sucks, I've been sitting here," and I left. I made it clear I was not cool with the situation.

Dorit Kemsley: They took a text message and time-stamped it that she sent me a message at four p.m.—but she never did.

Teddi Mellencamp Arroyave: I really didn't know how long to wait and no one was saying anything to me. Her phone was going to voice mail and then when she called, I realized she was still far away, like she had probably just left her house. And listen, my husband is a person that's always late, so I have my tolerance. I was just kind of annoyed, like, your time isn't any more important than my time. I have kids, too, I have a life, too. This isn't cool.

Dorit Kemsley: I got so much shit for it. I can appreciate and accept being late. And I was in a meeting that was running late, but I was given a meeting time thirty minutes later than she was given. They never told her that. They never told me that. I had to try to defend myself in the season without saying that. My words were twisted. But I never sold them down the river.

In season 9, a new household name was added to the cast: actress Denise Richards.

Lisa Rinna: I've known Denise for a really long time and she reached out to me because she saw what the show had done for me and she wanted that.

I sent Andy a text and I said, "You should take a look at Denise." I'll tell you this, I will never do that again. You can't have somebody on that you have history with because it's going to fuck that history up. It's going to fuck it up. It just will.

But most of Season 9 was dominated by a scandal surrounding a puppy who, after being adopted from Vanderpump Dogs, ended up at a shelter. Ultimately the issue of the season was: Who was the source of the Puppygate gossip?

Dorit Kemsley: We had adopted this dog, Lucy Lucy Apple Juice, from Vanderpump Dogs. I did everything to try and make sure she was the right fit because my kids were very young. I was apprehensive to begin with, and she just wasn't the right fit for my children. We were always thinking of the best interests for us and for the dog, and we gave Lucy to a woman we thought wanted her. I told Lisa immediately.

Alex Baskin: Lisa told me about that. She has said many times that she mentioned it because she didn't want it on camera. And that's something the other women would dispute—why would you tell a producer something unless you wanted it to appear on camera?

Erika Girardi: Based on my four years with Lisa Vanderpump, she definitely had a hand in the whole puppy thing playing out how it did.

Alex Baskin: What I recall very clearly is having these conversations with Lisa on the first shoot day of season 9. And, lo and behold, we were supposed to shoot that day at Vanderpump Dogs with Kyle and Teddi. At that point, we were aware of the basics: Teddi was having behind-the-scenes conversations about Dorit's dog with John Blizzard, events coordinator at Vanderpump Dogs, and Teddi thought Lisa wanted her to bring up the dog because she wanted to sink Dorit on the show. She thought Teddi was the perfect person to do that.

Kathleen French: Lisa Vanderpump had a history of bringing the new person under her wing and showing them the ropes. And that season it was Teddi.

Lisa Rinna: Teddi was her new baby bird, as I like to call her: Baby Bird with a Broken Wing.

Teddi Mellencamp Arroyave: At first, you're thinking, "This is an OG, she's coming to me, she's trying to tell me this is a story line. This is what should happen." And I will admit, I didn't like Dorit at first, so I was happy to go along with the plan.

Erika Girardi: Vanderpump gets you on the phone and works you. That's what she was doing to Teddi. For years women would turn around after they had been held responsible for something and Lisa would be standing there with clean hands, like, "It wasn't me. I don't know what you're talking about."

Teddi Mellencamp Arroyave: I didn't really grasp what was happening until it was too late. I made a mistake about that. Because once you hear something spoken about multiple times, it's a story line.

Shari Levine: *Beverly Hills*, more than any other *Housewives* franchise, often gets stuck in a hamster wheel about some story. Munchausen. Puppygate. They start talking about it and chewing on it, and they never stop. It never goes away. It is absolutely maddening.

Dorit Kemsley: It took on a life of its own. And again, what was so frustrating was that the story lingered. I've never mistreated any animal my whole life, but I was getting threats from animal lovers thinking that I took a dog to a kill shelter.

Chris Cullen: At a certain point, Teddi realized, "Oh, Lisa's setting me up to be the only voice on this dog stuff. She pushed it, but it's going to be on me." And then she put the brakes on it.

Teddi Mellencamp Arroyave: When I got to Vanderpump Dogs, I realized what Lisa was doing. I was like, "Holy shit, this is a complete setup. I'm out."

Kathleen French: To have Teddi turn on her hurt Lisa.

Chris Cullen: When Lisa lost the narrative in the show, when she realized that it wasn't going the way she wanted, that's when she leaked the story to the press. She got it out there before we had a chance to show that Lisa wasn't telling the truth.

Teddi Mellencamp Arroyave: There was definitely a pattern where LVP would go to the press in order to get story lines out there, either prior to or during the show airing so that people would look bad and she could continue to look good.

Alex Baskin: Lisa said I should sit the cast down and tell them they needed to believe her. And I said, "Lisa, I can't do that. They don't believe you." She was very unhappy with the group. And frankly, at that point, they did want her off the show.

Dorit Kemsley: It wasn't even so much about the dog. It became about a friendship, and that was an additional sad part of it. Ken and PK and Lisa and I were in each other's lives more off-camera than we were on-camera. But the friendship ended from this.

Douglas Ross: To me it all boils down to the last exchange Lisa had with Dorit.

She said to Dorit, "You need to tell me that you still want to be friends with me, even though you think I lie." And Dorit said, "Yes, I love you. And we all make mistakes." And Lisa said, "If you don't believe me unconditionally, we're not friends." She had to be loved unconditionally. They were all willing to say, "I love you and nobody's perfect. Everybody's done a little white lie. So just admit that and we can go on and be friends." But she couldn't handle that.

Just as Lisa's relationship with Dorit fell apart as a result of Puppygate, so did her showmance with Kyle.

Lisa Rinna: Kyle was the missing link in the real reckoning of Lisa Vanderpump. If you didn't have Kyle, there was not going to be a reckoning. But once Kyle saw it, and finally said it, it was game over.

Kyle Richards: I couldn't sit there on camera and say flat out, "I don't believe she would ever do that" because everybody would say, "You're a fucking liar, Kyle," and I'm not a liar. No one's ever accused me of being a liar, all these years of being on the show. So I went to her to say, "Just so you know, this is what they're saying. And I couldn't say, 'There's no way you would do that.'" I love Lisa but I'm not going to be dishonest when something comes up. I'm not going to "yes" her. She wanted blind loyalty, and people who were going to kiss her ass. I wasn't willing to do that, as much as I love her.

Alex Baskin: Kyle didn't want to be agreeing with the women on one hand, and telling Lisa something else, so that's why she went to her house in that "Goodbye Kyle" scene. The fact that Kyle copped to not believing her, and called her a liar on TV, in the end Lisa felt that was a capital offense.

Kyle Richards: Lisa cannot handle being called out on anything. But it's so obvious what she was doing. It was so blatant. And it was so annoying to me that she wasn't being honest about it. I mean, I've known you all these years. You think I'm stupid?

Lisa Vanderpump: I don't want to be negative about anybody. It's the way it worked out. It's the way the other women wanted it. And that's it. That's all I want to say.

Kathleen French: Lisa was so hurt when she had a fight with Kyle. It really did rock her world in the worst way.

Kyle Richards: That night was so crazy. I even had the crewmembers coming out to check on me. I was shaking so badly, because it felt a lot worse in person to have a man screaming at you like that. At one point he was so close to my face, I was like, "Oh my God." I love Ken but I was literally losing my mind.

Andy Cohen: Lisa felt that the women were pecking away at her too much, and she wanted nothing to do with it anymore.

Of course Vanderpump wasn't going out without a behind-the-scenes fight. Though she waved the pink flag as far as filming with the other ladies, she had other tools.

Kathleen French: The audience always liked Lisa so much. So whatever may or may not have happened, she was in a good position with the viewership.

Andy Cohen: Reading fans' perception of how things are can start to cloud your perception of how things really are.

Brandi Glanville: Every single Housewife is afraid of Lisa Vanderpump's fans because she answers every tweet, every single one. She's obsessed. Like, this is her life.

Lisa Rinna: We had that Vanderpump Army—it was really brutal.

Erika Girardi: They've gone out of their way to call us The Coven. If you could see the hate we get . . .

Dorit Kemsley: Lisa Vanderpump's fans were actually threatening to hurt my children. It was so shocking.

Teddi Mellencamp Arroyave: I was okay with people coming at me, saying that I'm a shit-stirrer or whatever. But the second people start saying "I wish you dead," or "I hope bad things happen to your family," it's just too far.

After weeks of not filming, the Queen of Beverly Hills committed the cardinal sin of refusing to join the reunion.

Kyle Richards: I have gone through so much worse on all my years on *Housewives*, and I've never not shown up to any event, ever, not one time. I've never said I can't go, I've never called in sick. I've never canceled an interview. So when I saw she wasn't coming I was like, "You got to be kidding me."

Dorit Kemsley: I didn't expect her to show up to the reunion. Lisa is a really strong person in a lot of regards, but that would have taken an awful lot of courage. And if you're not being entirely truthful, it's not the easiest position to be in.

Teddi Mellencamp Arroyave: I wish she would have come and just said her piece, like, "You know what, Dorit, I'm not a malicious person, but

I love dogs more than humans. And what was going on really freakin' pissed me off. And I had my minions go to Teddi and go to town."

Lisa Vanderpump: I left at a very low point in my life. It was a sad ending at what could have been an amazing experience.

Andy Cohen: We knew that if she didn't come, that meant for sure she was off the show. That she was deciding to leave the show. I thought—and hoped—that she would come and she'd figure out a way forward with Kyle.

Lisa Vanderpump: I had, a couple of times, tried to leave the show—season 2, season 4, and season 6—because I felt it was just all too much, sitting there at reunions with the whole cast against me. So many times, I was just so tearful. It wasn't something I wanted to be a part of.

Alex Baskin: She had talked about quitting the show so many times that you almost couldn't believe it until it actually happened.

Kyle Richards: It was so hard for me to understand Lisa Vanderpump walking away. I was like, "It's just not that big of a deal. You signed up for a reality show and you act like someone accused you of murder. They're saying they think you could have given a story to the tabloids! Put on your big girl panties and show up!"

Dorit Kemsley: She told the press before she told the network that she wasn't coming. That was a real indication of her relationship with the press. It was a little comical.

Lisa Rinna: It's such a cop-out. It's such a cowardly thing to do. I have a big problem with people signing up to do a job and not finishing it. Big injustice for me.

Lisa Vanderpump: I didn't like it when the show changed and people were like, "It's a job, you have to show up for work." Because I always wanted to be authentic in every story that we told. I wasn't acting for the cameras. The cameras were there to document my reality.

You know, I was on the show for nine and a half years. We had some wonderful experiences, and I'm grateful for Bravo. There'll always be an extraordinary close bond between so many of the people there and at Evolution. And the show changed my life. I became a household name through *Vanderpump Rules* and through *Housewives*. I got to speak at the United Nations and Congress. Got my star on the walk of stars in Palm Springs, and was on *Dancing with the Stars*. I was offered so many opportunities that so many other Housewives weren't. I'm thankful for that. But I'm glad I'm out of it. It was too much. And maybe they're right, it *was* just a job. Because it didn't define who I am.

In season 10 a long-sought-after Housewife with plenty of on-camera experience stepped into the group.

Garcelle Beauvais (Housewife): A few years ago, they came around to see if there was any interest. At the time, my kids were little and I wasn't sure it was the right direction for me. But I believe in timing and the universe and all that stuff. So this time around, I decided to have the conversation. I was single again. I was moving. I was building my house. I thought, "This is the time to do it."

Dawn Stroupe: I've learned over time that, even if people say, "I'm not interested and I'm never going to be interested," you continue to go back after them because you never know what's going to happen in life. They're going to say yes one of these days.

Garcelle Beauvais: Let me tell you, I've been in the industry over twenty years. I've done some cool shit. I've worked with incredible people. I have never gotten more attention than when this announcement came out. And that's when it really hit me: "Oh my God. The first Black woman." Then the pressure started to set in.

Meanwhile, after a freewheeling first season, Denise seemed to pull back her risqué side . . . and judge the other women when they shared theirs.

Teddi Mellencamp Arroyave: Denise's entire thing the year before was, "I have sex with my husband every single day." And then all of a sudden it's like, "Now you won't talk about sex?"

Chris Cullen: It's all they could talk about: "She's going to start playing conservative, modest mom on the show. She's using the show to make us look bad and make her look good."

Erika Girardi: My whole beef started at her barbecue. Why was I the only one she wanted to scold, when two other women, Dorit and Garcelle—you didn't see Dorit's because it was cut—were talking about sex? But I was the only one that she felt that she needed to take to task.

Chris Cullen: Denise was trying to appear different from who she really is.

Just as a big group trip to Rome was on the horizon, a former Housewife offered up some info that sparked a Housewives*-history-making conversation. . . .*

Brandi Glanville: They called me in for the very end of the season. We shot a few times. And then they made it kind of their whole season.

Alex Baskin: We didn't come trolling for Brandi. Brandi brought that story to the group. And it happened very late in our season.

Brandi Glanville: Basically, Denise ghosted me after she had sex with me. She wanted me, she pursued me, she hit it and quit it.

Lisa Rinna: Maybe Denise knew Brandi's reputation and said, "Hey, this is a great person for me to fuck because if it comes out no one will believe her."

Brandi Glanville: What happened with Denise and I happened—it fucking happened. She kept me quiet for seven months. Her entire career was built on being sexual, she is a sex bomb. And now all of a sudden, you're motherfucking Saint Teresa?

Lisa Rinna: I remember them saying, "Okay, we're going to have a party at Kyle's and we're just going to invite everybody and we're going to bring out all the OGs because nothing is going on." And what happened is, Denise found out Brandi was coming to the party and was scared that she would maybe say something to Aaron. And so Denise called Brandi and said, "Whatever you do, don't tell Aaron."

Brandi Glanville: The second Denise knew that I was filming, all of a sudden she was my best friend again. She had disappeared. Literally I saw her when she fucked me and then didn't see her again until Kyle's party.

Lisa Rinna: It pissed her off and hurt her feelings.

Brandi Glanville: It was like, "I'm sorry, but you haven't called me for these past seven months and now all of a sudden I'm your best friend?" She was suddenly keeping me very close. It was some bullshit. Denise does not care about me, clearly. I felt like I was a cheater. And I didn't want to be labeled a cheater. Like, that's my whole brand. So when I told Kim drunkenly after Kyle's party, I knew it was going to be a thing.

Lisa Rinna: My guess is Kim told Kyle and then Kim told production and they called Brandi and that's how it played out.

Chris Cullen: The funny thing is, we did a lot of research this year: Is Brandi credible? Do we have examples of Brandi lying? We went back to all the scenes and we really couldn't find an example where Brandi lied. She told the truth about Adrienne, she told the truth about Lisa Vanderpump. People may not believe her, but she told the truth about Kim being a fucking mess. She might have gotten her drug of choice wrong, but Kim was using again and had fallen off the wagon. All of that was true. So, yes, the critics will say that Brandi is not credible and they will cite examples, but they are incorrect in what they're citing. We don't really have evidence of Brandi ever lying.

Brandi Glanville: So then Kim and I had this giant conversation, and she was like, "She's abusing you, she's an emotional terrorist. You have to fucking talk about this." I said, "I don't want to, let it be my decision." And eventually it was like, "Fuck it, we're on a reality show, right? Let's fucking do this."

After confessing the story to Kim, Brandi told Kyle and Teddi. . . .

Teddi Mellencamp Arroyave: That moment with Brandi was speaking to what we all were feeling with Denise during the season—she was pretending to be somebody she's not. It was less about if she and Brandi actually had sex.

Brandi Glanville: At this point, I figure people are going to believe what they want to believe. But I felt like a weight was lifted off my shoulders.

Alex Baskin: We were off to Rome literally the next day. And then we were done with the season a couple of weeks later. So it all happened very late.

Once the women were in Rome, it was clear several Housewives knew more than they were saying, which led to a very contentious dinner. . . .

Teddi Mellencamp Arroyave: It was brutal. You can see me starting to get more frustrated because I knew that she was lying. I wish with my whole heart that she would have responded differently in the moment. But when she doubled down and was like, "I don't have a relationship with this woman, I don't talk to her," there were just so many inconsistencies.

Lisa Rinna: That's Denise's desperation. Denise is going to double down. And she's never, ever, ever going to admit to anything. Nothing.

Brandi Glanville: Denise is an ultimate victim. She's Lisa Vanderpump in overalls.

Chris Cullen: If she had owned any of her truth, I'm not sure Teddi would have been compelled to reveal the Brandi stuff in such a public way. But when Denise denied all of it and said, "I barely know Brandi" after Teddi and Kyle just sat with Brandi and heard all these intimate details, it was very hard for Teddi to keep her mouth shut.

Erika Girardi: People get mad at Teddi, but she had to bring it up. It was already brought to her. That's what people don't understand. Kyle and Teddi got this information the way they got it. They didn't go looking for it.

Kyle Richards: The audience got mad, but imagine if they saw that scene with Brandi telling Teddi and me, and then we just totally dropped it. They would be furious! You can't have the audience hear that and just be like, "Moving on." So someone unfortunately had the fucking job of bringing it up, and in this case, Teddi answered the call.

Brandi Glanville: Listen, I have no shame in my game. What happened between Denise and me was last season on *Housewives*, so if I was going to talk about it just for a job, I could've done it then. But Denise ghosted me and then all of a sudden she heard I was filming and she's my best friend again. I saw it very clearly. I wouldn't do just anything to get back on the show—but I will tell the truth.

Teddi Mellencamp Arroyave: I felt bad for Denise—what this could mean for her marriage and all of that. But everybody else at the table was pushing me, pushing me, pushing me, pushing me.

Garcelle Beauvais: It's one thing to say, "Oh, she calls me a bitch," or "She said she doesn't like me." And it's another thing to mess with someone where it could affect their marriage and their children. It crossed the line in a lot of ways. That was tough.

Lisa Rinna: I will always say that we work for evil geniuses and it's fucking dirty. I'm fine with saying that. It's just the way that this genre works. And I don't think anybody who's done a *Housewives* show would disagree with me.

Teddi Mellencamp Arroyave: It doesn't matter to me if she does have an open marriage, if she doesn't have an open marriage, if she's bi-curious—I am not judging her in any way about any of that. I want to make that really clear. But her story was constantly changing, and that's the part we had a problem with.

Kyle Richards: It wasn't that she slept with a woman that was shocking. It was that she was a newlywed. Like, "How could this have just happened? Didn't she just get married?" And there's a lot of confusion about that. People are like, "Why are you so shocked it's a girl?" It's not about that! Is cheating not cheating?

Teddi Mellencamp Arroyave: The perfectly prepped speech on her final night in Rome was the straw that broke the camel's back for me. She had said repeatedly, "I don't want to talk about any of this anymore." We all agreed on that the night before. And then she came in with this speech about mean girls and understanding why LVP left this group, and I remembered being at a dinner with her after last season where she was trashing LVP. So that inconsistency was really not sitting well with me.

The conflict peaked when Denise broke the fourth wall, calling "Bravo, Bravo, Bravo" in an attempt to ensure the tape would never air.

Alex Baskin: I know Denise has said she was told that "Bravo, Bravo, Bravo" was the code to get us to stop filming or to make the footage unusable, but I have to say, it wasn't.

Chris Cullen: No one ever calls for a producer—that just never happens.

Alex Baskin: It used to be a joke Kyle and Lisa had in the early days—when they wanted to touch up their makeup, they would say "Bravo, Bravo" or they would make comments about the producers so they could sneak in a moment. But this was Denise's way of trying to end the conversation and take it off camera.

Douglas Ross: It took a while for the network to agree to let us break the fourth wall.

Chris Cullen: We went to the network and were like, "This is what's happening. The ladies are fired up over this."

Erika Girardi: I don't expect any help from anywhere. Ever. I certainly never fell back on "Bravo, Bravo, Bravo!" Because I was never told about "Bravo, Bravo, Bravo."

Chris Cullen: After this all happened in Rome and we came back and we started shooting again, that's when Denise vanished on us. That's when she stopped shooting.

Andy Cohen: The women were pissed toward the end of the season because they were showing up and they were doing the work, but she was not showing up at group events for filming.

Teddi Mellencamp Arroyave: It became, Why did you stop showing up? Why won't you confront Brandi?

Alex Baskin: We encouraged Denise to have a moment with Brandi. We had a whole series of conversations with Denise before Teddi's baby shower at Dorit's Buca di Beppo room where we told her, "Listen, here's your chance to have the moment with Brandi and just be done with it." We did not ambush her. We can't always tell the cast everything, but we don't want to lie to them. And it's like, no shit we'd have Brandi there because what good TV would we be trying to make if we didn't have her there? That's the show. But she worried Brandi was going to try to provoke "a *Jerry Springer* moment"—that's the phrase she kept using. So we talked through all of that, and Denise was advised—poorly, in our view—that she just shouldn't show up. Then she went dark on us on the day of the party.

Chris Cullen: The next day, her lawyers sent a legal letter to Bravo, Evolution, and Brandi. And she vanished.

Brandi Glanville: Denise, seriously, she's the biggest narcissist. For her to stop production, send us all legal letters? Exhausting.

> *For all the ways in which the fourth wall was broken in season 10, there was still more tea to spill—specifically, Denise's denials fell flat with Bravolebrities who went to BravoCon in late 2019 and saw behavior that fit a pattern.*

Lisa Rinna: At BravoCon, we heard that Denise went out with the *RHOC* ladies and asked them to sit on her face. That's what we heard.

Andy Cohen: Why did no one tell me that?! Or mention it at the reunion?!

Teddi Mellencamp Arroyave: Her sex life or her partying or whatever, I would've never brought that up on the show. That would have been bringing something outside of the show into the show to hurt her, and that's not who I am. So to me, what she was doing at BravoCon was off-limits—however you want to live your life off the show, that's fine. But the problem is, once she brought Brandi into the situation, it's no longer off the show.

Lisa Rinna: You can't believe that someone's able to lie this much. She has lied to me, to my face, saying, "I do not have an open relationship. I didn't have an affair with Brandi. I do not do that." It's sickening to me. It's sickening because I don't trust her. She's one of the fakest, phoniest people that I've ever come across, that's what I've realized. I have never had anybody lie to me as deeply as Denise has.

> *Denise's fate hung in the balance as the season came to an end—and a huge part of that centered on the question of whether Brandi would be allowed to tell her side of the story at the reunion.*

Douglas Ross: We were back and forth on that decision for weeks.

Lisa Rinna: At the eleventh hour, as I was sitting down in my chair, they told me, "We're not having Brandi come now."

Erika Girardi: They called me and said, "Brandi's not coming." I said, "Why?" And they said, "Well, we've decided we want Denise there. We're afraid she'll walk off."

Brandi Glanville: I had so much anxiety leading up to when I got that call. There was definitely a feeling of rejection, but at the same time it was like,

"Okay, let them earn their paychecks." I felt played because they'd spun my story into episodes for which I was not getting paid.

Lisa Rinna: And after having to tell the story for five months—it's not even my story—to not have the other side of the story at the reunion? I said, "That's bullshit."

Erika Girardi: I felt like, "You dragged us through all this stuff and Brandi has a right to tell her side of the story. Now you're not going to let her talk to Denise directly? That's what these things are for." Think about how we as a cast felt. This is your star witness, and then all of a sudden you're gonna stop her from testifying? What the fuck are we doing here?

Andy Cohen: Listen, it was frustrating to me. It was frustrating to me, too.

Brandi Glanville: If I had gone on, it would've just been about everyone attacking me. This way, it was still about my story. So I was actually very happy with it. I was relieved.

Andy Cohen: What we should have done was stick with our original plan, which was for me to interview Brandi and then roll it in and have Denise respond to it. We got greedy and decided that we should have her there with the group. Then it became clear that Denise was just going to leave when that happened. And then at the last minute, after talking to Denise and talking to Brandi—who, by the way, was very relieved when we told her she wasn't coming—we thought it was more important that Denise come back to this show than whether Brandi came to the reunion. Ultimately, we didn't get either thing we wanted. Brandi wasn't at the reunion and now Denise isn't coming back to the show. So who's laughing now?

> *The day after season 10 ended, it was revealed that Teddi, like Denise, would not be returning. Soon after, Crystal Kung Minkoff and Sutton Stracke were announced as new additions for season 11, as well as Kyle's sister Kathy Hilton, who would join as a Friend. Just another couple of shake-ups in a cast that never fails to entertain.*

Kyle Richards: My sister Kathy and I, we've gone through so much over the years. We had a falling-out, but we're very close now and I just thought, you know what, this is something for us to do together. Kathy's really fun and funny and people are going to be shocked when they see her because she's so not what anybody would think. It's hilarious. And if there's a problem, I'll deal with it. But I feel like we can handle it, we've been through enough and we don't want to go down that road again. When Kim and I had that fight in the limo, I didn't know production very well. I remember thinking, "Let's just keep us together for a little longer and it'll be over soon"—not realizing I'd be here ten years later.

Erika Girardi: You have to have balance. Oftentimes people are like, "Well, this one's boring. This one doesn't do this." Look, if you had eight maniacs just hurling insults at each other, what does that look like? Go watch something else. People react to the negative, but you never know who you're touching in a positive way. That's why people have their favorite girl. They find things that they identify with, whether it's family, a profession, personality, fashion. The truth is, I'll look at this part of my life forever. I'm forty-nine now. Most women in the industry are tossed aside at this age, but in Beverly Hills, you can become a pop culture phenomenon.

> At the time of writing, season 11 of RHOBH had yet to air, but Erika's sentiments are more timely than ever.

PART VII

"Ocean Views"

The Real Housewives of Miami

PREMIERE DATE: FEBRUARY 22, 2011
ORIGINAL FINALE: NOVEMBER 14, 2013

*It's like when somebody is president of the United States.
They will forever be called president. And a Housewife will
always be a Housewife.*

—ANA QUINCOCES

Matt Anderson (Executive Producer): Lea Black was kind of the unofficial mayor of Miami.

Sheri Maroufkhani (Executive Producer): Even though obviously she's not Latin, she is definitively Miami. She and her husband Roy have the biggest gala in town. They are true influencers—and this was before that word was overused.

Lea Black (Housewife): I am not a girl who does my nails and goes to four-hour luncheons every day. But I looked at it as an opportunity to showcase my charity and my business.

Sheri Maroufkhani: She was like, "I will have parties at my house. We will create excitement and fabulousness. And, of course, the drama will follow." I knew in my gut she was going to bring it every step of the way.

> *Next in was Brazilian art dealer and single mother Adriana de Moura, who instantly won over the team with her fiery, passionate personality.*

Adriana de Moura (Housewife): Lea suggested me. I was eager, willing, and clueless.

Sheri Maroufkhani: Adriana was outrageous. In her initial interview, she was flirting with both my PA and my DP. I loved her for that! Like, look at her. She's a knockout. And here she is flirting with dudes like ten, twelve years her junior, and they were so flustered—as they should be!

It wouldn't be Miami without a Cuban Housewife, the first of which was publicist Marysol Patton. While it wasn't love at first sight for the publicist or the producers, the presence of Marysol's eccentric, outspoken mother, Elsa, proved irresistible—and iconic.

Marysol Patton (Housewife): I remember watching *RHOC* back when it first started and thinking, "I would like to do that." So I went to the audition, and I saw all my friends walking out. They're all loaded—they live in huge, multimillion-dollar mansions, they have personal trainers, they're skinny, they're gorgeous. I'm single, working like a beast, and I have a fucking twisted face because I'd been diagnosed with Bell's palsy.

Sheri Maroufkhani: It was the first thing she pointed out before we even sat down.

Marysol Patton: They were like, "Talk about yourself." I was like, "I don't even know why I'm here. I know my face is fucked up, I just felt like coming. But I know you're never gonna pick me because I don't live in a seven-million-dollar home on the water or have a Rolls-Royce with a driver."

Sheri Maroufkhani: I liked that she was so honest and self-deprecating. I thought Marysol was like Marlo Thomas in *That Girl*, but a Latin version with blond hair.

Marysol Patton: And then in, like, the third scene I filmed, my mom showed up.

Sheri Maroufkhani: Elsa lit up the room. There was something so charismatic about her. And I have to give credit to Andy Cohen because not everyone was on board with Elsa, but when he saw her in the first cut, he was immediately like, "More Elsa—we need her in every episode."

Andy Cohen: You just couldn't take your eyes off her. And she was funny as hell, with no F's to give.

Marysol Patton: She stole every scene. It didn't matter who she filmed with, she had the sound bites.

Sheri Maroufkhani: She was a clairvoyant who was very well known in the community. And the fact that she was an immigrant made it interesting for me. Her voice and her accent and, more importantly, her words, were incredible. She even said some crazy things to my young director of photography, like, "Your girlfriend and you are about to break up, and you're about to go through this whole seven-year odyssey." And it all happened! He went home. He found out she was cheating on him. And you know, I grew up watching *Golden Girls*, so I loved that idea of this older lady with no filter.

If Lea Black was the unofficial mayor of Miami, she had an ally in local politician and businessman Herman Echevarria, whose wife, Alexia, brought modelesque looks and deep connections into the Miami Housewives mix.

Sheri Maroufkhani: Lea called Alexia the Cuban Barbie, and it stuck. That was her energy.

Alexia Echevarria (Housewife): Herman was like, "I would never let you do that. Are you kidding?" Then, right after my interview, I got the call like, "Guess what: You need to tell your husband"—because of course I said in the interview that Herman didn't know I was there. When I got the call that I was selected, Herman was next to me, so I couldn't even say anything. That night I decided to go to dinner so I could get him drunk so he'd be easier to talk to. But that man does not drink, so I was the one that got drunk! We got into a major fight, and the night was over.

Lea Black: He really didn't want her to do the show.

Alexia Echevarria: Eventually Marysol called me, and what helped me convince Herman to let me participate was the fact that she and Lea Black were in it.

Lea Black: I told him, "Look, if I'm going to do it, you know she's going to be fine. I'm not going to let anything bad happen with her."

Rounding out the cast were Cristy Rice and Larsa Pippen, a duo of younger moms who had some experience with the spotlight thanks to their relationships with professional athletes.

Cristy Rice (Housewife): I had already been approached to do *NBA Wives* by Shaunie O'Neal, Shaquille's ex-wife, who was a friend of mine. I was kind of iffy about that because I knew for sure there was going to be fighting, and I was not about that. So instead I signed up for what I was being told was a *Sex and the City*-style show about Miami.

Sheri Maroufkhani: Cristy is the one who brought in Larsa.

Larsa Pippen (Housewife): Her ex, Glen, had played in the NBA with my husband, Scottie, so we were NBA wives together.

Sheri Maroufkhani: The family was still going back and forth between Chicago and Fort Lauderdale. But because Larsa and Cristy's husbands had played basketball together, they were buddies, so we considered them kind of a package deal.

Larsa Pippen: Scottie is super private, so I wanted them to know I was going to respect that.

Lea Black: I will say this, Scottie was a professional basketball player, but he was not one of the players who went around cheating and making a spectacle of himself. He has always been a stand-up guy.

The cast was set and filming began, but like many of the other cities, no one knew they were making a Housewives *show.*

Larsa Pippen: We thought it was going to be something along the lines of, like, *Socialites of Miami.*

Lea Black: They kind of made it into a *Housewives* show along the way, which is the reason the first season wasn't so successful.

Andy Cohen: There's a pattern here. We kept trying to develop other franchises of docusoaps about groups of women so Bravo wasn't going all-in on *Housewives* . . . but would often just fold and say, "It's a *Housewives.*"

Sheri Maroufkhani: Two days before we wrapped principal photography, they said, "It's now *Real Housewives of Miami.*" And it was, like, wow. The whole time we were shooting, we were being directed by the executives: "Don't shoot it like *Housewives.*"

Even if it wasn't shot like a typical Housewives *franchise, there was plenty of drama that first season. It started at Lea's charity gala.*

Cristy Rice: I'd known Lea for a long time and had been invited to her gala previous years but never made it because the timing was always off.

Lea Black: Cristy called me the night before and said, "I'm thinking about coming to the gala." I said, "Cristy, we're sold out of the wait list. I can't let you to come for free. You'll have to buy a ticket." Fast-forward, she shows up with two friends.

Cristy Rice: She was very nice to me when I first saw her. I said hi to everybody, walked around. Everything was fine, great. The night was fine.

Lea Black: She hadn't paid! Everybody at the gala—including me and Roy—paid for our tickets. It's just that simple, it's for charity. So afterward I sent her an invoice. And she didn't pay it. Well, that became part of the show.

Attention also turned to Larsa and the one topic she'd deemed off-limits. . . .

Larsa Pippen: From the very beginning, I said, "I don't want Scottie to be involved in the show." I wanted to stand on my own. But the producers just constantly wanted to make him a part of it, so they basically told Marysol's mom to say stuff about him.

Marysol Patton: My mom told her, "You're worried about a man."

Larsa Pippen: It was out of left field. And I kind of lashed out, like, "Don't talk about Scottie, he's not here to defend himself." I was protective of him and of my marriage.

Cristy Rice: Like, who was her mom to come and tell Larsa all this stuff?

Larsa Pippen: I was willing to do whatever it takes to make the show successful because I don't like to be a part of anything that fails. So here I was, arguing with this girl's mother. And Marysol was just sitting there, listening to her mom rip me and my marriage. It was like, "Stop your mom."

Cristy Rice: I told Marysol, "Your mom is wack." In the first place, I would never in a million years put my mother on television for the world to laugh at her, because they were not laughing with her, they were laughing at her. And then second, she should have stopped her mom, who didn't even know what she was saying.

After filming wrapped, the show's fate hung in the balance as producers scrambled to try to fit the footage into the Housewives *mold.*

Sheri Maroufkhani: It took six months to reshape it, reshoot interviews, and reframe them. We delivered the final masters and they sort of put it on the shelf like, "Okay, we're going to figure out where we're going to slot this in the new year." But then they announced suddenly that the next season of New York wasn't ready so they were going to launch Miami instead. So we only had two weeks' promo time before we hit the air.

Lea Black: They changed the show schedule to a different time every week, which had an effect on the following and ratings.

Sheri Maroufkhani: It was only six and a half episodes ultimately. They didn't even give it a real reunion—it was in the Clubhouse for an hour.

Andy Cohen: That was the first and last time we will ever do a reunion live. What a shit show.

As production looked ahead to season 2, it was clear many changes had to be made, both in front of and behind the camera.

Sheri Maroufkhani: I got a call from Shari Levine in May 2011, and she said, "I respect you, and I thank you for your work on the show. But it was a business decision for us." So they went with the safe bet because they had this overall deal with Matt and Nate at Purveyors of Pop.

Nate Green (Executive Producer): It was sort of Matt's and my thing to come in on newer cities to tweak the casting, improve the storytelling, and improve the look of the show.

Sheri Maroufkhani: It was devastating. I took it personally. I wanted to continue to explore these women's stories.

But those stories would not include Larsa's and Cristy's. . . .

Larsa Pippen: I had no interest in doing season 2.

Cristy Rice: After the show, Larsa became a Kardashian groupie.

Larsa Pippen: When I was on *Housewives*, it opened up my eyes to opportunities. At first I just thought it would be fun, but then I realized, "Hey, I'm growing from this, I learned a lot from it." And I started making money—my own money.

As for Cristy, the same complexities that made her life interesting were also why she had to ultimately exit the show.

Matt Anderson: We liked Cristy, but she wasn't able to shoot with her ex-husband or her kids.

Cristy Rice: Glen made a problem out of everything.

Matt Anderson: So that was the end of that. To be honest, we felt like bringing in some new people would probably create new intrigue and help the show in its second season anyway.

RHOM got a new lease on life after a turbulent, uneven first season, but before the women could get to work, Alexia's life completely changed course when her thirteen-year-old son Frankie was involved in a horrifying car accident.

Alexia Echevarria: We had just come back from Mykonos, from a beautiful trip in Europe, and my son was starting school the next day.

Nate Green: The accident was brutal and so we all agreed that it would be easier for Alexia in that second season to ease into things.

Alexia Echevarria: Of course, I was in a hospital from the day of the accident till six months later.

Matt Anderson: There was always an intention for her to come back to season 2 as a main, but when we talked to her, she was like, "Let me just pull myself together." It was entirely Alexia's decision to go down to a B-character.

Alexia Echevarria: Viewers did see some of what I went through, but probably not even 5 percent. The producers really, really worked with me, and I'm very grateful for that.

With Alexia sidelined and two Miami OGs gone, several new additions were brought in to shuffle the deck. Producers thought jet-setting model Joanna Krupa, who had initially auditioned for season 1, would bring a certain wow factor to the series' reset.

Nate Green: Joanna Krupa was a beautiful model living in Miami part-time. Her story was so different from the others. She was engaged to a very sexy man, who happened to be the owner of one of the coolest, longest-running nightclubs in South Beach, where he'd worked his way up from the bottom. He was half-Brazilian, half-French, and they were both self-made immigrants. They were dramatic, and their relationship wasn't perfect.

Matt Anderson: She was also hosting *Poland's Next Top Model*. So she already had a vibrant TV career, and we thought of her as a get.

Lea Black: Joanna told me they said they were going to make her the breakout star of the show.

Nate Green: We definitely never looked at it like, "Oh, Joanna is going to be the star." But I knew she was going to make a splash.

Also joining the ranks was plastic-perfect real-life housewife Lisa Hochstein, the honey-haired embodiment of a modern American fairy tale.

Nate Green: Lisa Hochstein was a waitress working in Vegas who met this extremely successful plastic surgeon and won the lottery—her life completely changed.

Lisa Hochstein (Housewife): When I did the show, I was very young. I was twenty-seven. I almost felt like I was too young to be a Housewife. But of course I didn't turn it down. It's somewhat of an honor to be chosen to be part of the show—because it's not just about whether I have a rich husband and nice things, it's also your personality that gets you in the door.

Also in the business of beauty, celebrity dentist Karent Sierra joined the cast—but the other wives quickly began to wonder if her relationship with boyfriend Rodolfo Jiménez really had teeth. . . .

Nate Green: We loved that Karent was a successful dentist—she kind of busted the stereotype of what a Housewife was.

382 NOT ALL DIAMONDS AND ROSÉ

Karent Sierra (Housewife): The stigma behind a lot of the women in a lot of the franchises is that they're beautiful but they're bored. Either their husbands are gay and they don't pay attention to them, or they've been married too long and their husbands don't pay attention to them, or they married for money and their husbands don't pay attention to them. I wanted to represent a professional Hispanic woman who stands on her own two feet.

Lea Black: I know for sure that Marysol, Ana, and Adriana wanted to get rid of Karent.

Karent Sierra: They created a Mean Girl Club. They had diva attitudes from the beginning.

Lisa Hochstein: The general consensus was that Karent was fake.

Karent Sierra: I'm always a smiler, and that was something they attacked me on. I was like, "I hope I'm smiling and I have good teeth—I'm a dentist!"

Nate Green: She wasn't married yet, but she was dating this really hot telenovela star, and that became a big topic of conversation.

Alexia Echevarria: Karent lied about her whole story. Rodolfo was my friend, and he had a girlfriend, and Karent knew that, a hundred percent. The producers wanted a Mexican for whatever reason. I said sorry but in Miami, there's really not too many Mexicans. We have Colombians, Venezuelans, Cubans, but the Mexicans stay on the West Coast. So Karent is like, "Oh, guess what? I have a Mexican boyfriend." He was a soap opera actor, and she called him up. "Hey, you want to come on American TV?"

Karent Sierra: I could show pictures where I was with his family. I could show pictures of us kissing. I literally had pictures of him with my parents, pictures of him in my home, the two of us in Mexico. It made no sense that they questioned it.

Alexia Echevarria: I did eventually call out Karent because I had a conversation with Rodolfo, and he was like, "She told me that this was a perfect opportunity. She knew I had a girlfriend." If I hadn't been going through the seriousness that I was going through, there would have been big-time drama.

Ana Quincoces also joined the cast in the second season. With a thriving career as a chef and a legal eagle history, she didn't have any problems mixing it up or making an argument.

Ana Quincoces (Housewife): I'd known Marysol for a long time, but she and I were not friends. She only made an effort to become friendly with me once she knew I was going to be on the show. Marysol's mission was to make Lea look bad, and I was a total pawn in that in season 2.

Adriana de Moura: Lea was starting to attack Marysol, so Marysol wanted to attack back.

Ana Quincoces: Marysol was terrified of Lea, and, of course, I was a perfect mouthpiece. So I fell for that hook, line and sinker. Because I wasn't afraid of Lea in the least. Lea doesn't pay my mortgage. In my world, Lea was meaningless. To them, Lea was somebody because they relied on Lea socially. So I became Marysol's protector.

> While the tension grew between Lea and Ana, another war broke out during, of all things, a charity lingerie party. Though Karent was the intended target, shots were fired—and blows landed—between Adriana and Joanna.

Nate Green: Joanna and Adriana were definitely like oil and water. They did not get along.

Lea Black: They were out for blood from day one.

Adriana de Moura: This is the backstory of that scene: I was filming a movie and I had been on set all day. It was almost nine o'clock at night when I finally got to the party. And when I got there, the producers came to me with this article Karent had done, which was basically calling everyone on the show trashy and fake, and they said, "Did you see this? You need to confront Karent tonight."

Nate Green: Producers are always getting blamed for planting things and telling people to say things. But we never tell anybody what to say or do. There was an article, and I'm sure there were conversations along the lines of, "If you want to talk to her, talk to her about it."

Adriana de Moura: When I confronted Karent, Joanna came into it. I was just rolling my eyes, saying, "Just back off, Joanna, back off. It's not about you. It has nothing to do with you." So I tried to leave, and then she followed me down the hallway.

Matt Anderson: They grabbed a broom from somewhere in the kitchen and wrestled with it. It was sort of a standoff with this broom.

Adriana de Moura: Joanna tried to grab me, and that's when I turned around and hit her. I slapped her on the face.

Matt Anderson: Joanna's head hit the camera.

Lea Black: I was flabbergasted.

Lisa Hochstein: It was almost like *Jersey Shore* drama, like a little too far. If we hadn't been filming, everybody would have been thrown out of my house.

Lea Black: After the slap, I went to lunch with Joanna to convince her to forgive Adriana. I did that to try to get the best for Adriana. What did I get in return? Marysol twisted it and said I was talking with Joanna, so Adriana turned on me.

Adriana de Moura: Even though we had this history of friendship, Lea would side with Joanna and say, "Well, but Joanna was attacked." I was like, "You are my friend, dude. Like, seriously?"

Lea Black: Adriana acted awful. She was so jealous of Joanna. She wanted to be the main person on the show, and she was willing to do anything for that.

Adriana de Moura: Suddenly I became the big bad wolf. I was the bad guy and everybody was out to get me. And the thing is, I don't think Joanna actually had anything against me. If we were just in regular life, we could've been friendly.

Meanwhile, Marysol was also having a hard time, most especially because her marriage was unraveling.

Marysol Patton: Season 2 was very hectic. I was doing a coffee line. I was running a business. I was filming. I had to help my mother film. I was stressed out, and wasn't nice. I didn't have time to be a wife.

Cristy Rice: Everybody knew that marriage wasn't real—Lea called her out on it.

Lea Black: I might've hit a sore spot because the minute filming was over he left.

Marysol Patton: The truth is, he left because I was being a bitch. I wouldn't kiss him. I didn't even want to sit and have a meal with him. He'd come into my office and I'd be like, "Don't you have somewhere to be?" He just was getting on my nerves. So he left, he went to France for a while. Of course, I don't blame him.

Lea Black: She didn't hear from him for months on end.

Marysol Patton: Lea could say whatever she wanted. There was some jealousy there because she always wanted to be a successful businessperson known in the community like I was. But she's got plenty of money, and I would trade places with her in two seconds. People get jealous of the weirdest things.

The season closed with a group vacation that was far from Paradise for the Housewives.

Karent Sierra: You could see in some of the episodes, especially in Bimini, how Alexia and Marysol and Adriana were plotting to embarrass and attack me.

Lea Black: They took me in the bathroom and showed me pictures of Karent's boyfriend kissing some other girl. They were trying to get rid of Karent because Adriana felt that Karent was her big competition.

Karent Sierra: They were so malicious. It was especially cruel how they played that game of saying, "Oh, if we knew something, would you want to know?" It was like mean girls.

Adriana de Moura: The whole story is Adriana did this, and Adriana did that. Adriana didn't do that, didn't say that. And I lied about that. It was always like something, you know? I didn't care if that's what it took, if I'm in a movie, if I'm Angelina Jolie playing Maleficent, you know what I mean? Maleficent is needed for the movie to happen. So that's fine, I'll play that role.

Ana Quincoces: I did feel sorry for her because he used her to get on TV. She's a woman, she was in love, and she was played. It made me sad for her.

Karent Sierra: I was in shock. And I remember even calling him, and he said, "No, honey, that's just a publicity stunt." He denied it all the way.

If anyone was trying to take down Karent, they got what they wanted: she wouldn't be returning for season 3.

Karent Sierra: I was in L.A. filming a Spanish TV show. I met up with one of the executive producers for lunch, and he said, "I just wanted to let you know, we're not inviting you back." I was a little bit taken aback, but I figured they had their reasons.

Lisa Hochstein: I wasn't surprised Karent didn't come back. I thought she had a great presence with me, but I guess there was a feeling she wasn't bringing it as much as she could have.

But before Karent was let go, she had a front-row seat to a nasty reunion battle between Lea and Ana, each of whom was convinced the other woman was out to get her.

Matt Anderson: Ana came in hot, hot, hot for Lea.

Ana Quincoces: I flew to New York with Marysol. She had a really good relationship with the production company, and they told her that Lea was coming after me at the reunion.

Lea Black: That was just not true.

Matt Anderson: We certainly didn't tell Ana that Lea was coming for her at the reunion. But she did come prepared.

Ana Quincoces: I was like, "Coming after me for what?" Look, I'm like Goody Two-shoes on steroids. So I didn't know what she was coming after me for.

Matt Anderson: Ana was close with Marysol, and Marysol made it no secret that there was no love lost between Lea and her. So there was a little of that going on.

Ana Quincoces: So I called my ex-fiancé, who was a former U.S. attorney and didn't like Lea, and I said, "Apparently Lea is coming after me." So he does this deep dive into her charity and all her history, like federal tax liens and everything she's ever done, and he compiles all this stuff. He goes, "Just read through it, have it under your belt. If she comes after you, you have plenty of ammunition."

Lea Black: So she and her lawyer boyfriend did research—but there was nothing there.

Ana Quincoces: I had all this information that didn't make her look good. So I came on set at the reunion and I had this folder in my hand. She looked at the folder and freaked out.

Lea Black: She had this folder that, I was told later, was like 70 percent blank pages. She just wanted to intimidate me. It was stupid. She didn't have anything.

Ana Quincoces: All of a sudden, Lea started going after me. Maybe it was fake, maybe it wasn't. But she attacked me out of nowhere. She said, "Your husband cheated on you. You're so embarrassing. And you're doing his laundry." And I went off.

Lisa Hochstein: The things that Ana said to Lea were super below-the-belt, disgusting. I still remember it to this day when she said, "The best work you did was on your back." I just remember thinking, What kind of person would say something like that to a married woman?

Marysol Patton: I was floored, watching her with my eyes popped open. It was crazy.

Ana Quincoces: And that woman started crying!

Lea Black: I was livid when she started in on the charity. I probably did have tears in my eyes. I was like, How low can you go? I've done nothing to you. I barely know you. I promoted your book. I tried to include your daughters in everything. I've never said one bad word about you on the show. Why are you coming at me about my charity? It infuriated me.

Ana Quincoces: She stormed off set. She hid in her dressing room and would not come out for hours until Roy got on the phone with her.

Lea Black: A stipulation in my contract was that they couldn't talk about Roy's clients. Because at the time he was representing Alex Rodriguez. He had represented Kelsey Grammer, Marv Albert, Rush Limbaugh, a million famous people.

Ana Quincoces: And guess who else Roy represents?

Lea Black: That stipulation also protected the charity.

Ana Quincoces: When that thing aired, it was a shadow of what actually happened.

Andy Cohen: It was not entertaining to watch when it happened, and it wasn't entertaining edited down—that's the reality of the situation. Ana was so great all season long but her reunion performance worked against her.

Lea Black: In Ana's eagerness to bring me down, the audience didn't like her because she came across as nasty. She went too far.

Marysol Patton: She was her own worst enemy. She tried to be too smart, and it wasn't entertaining. And you know what? Producers didn't like her and they took her out.

> *That they did. Ana was downshifted in season 3 as Alexia returned to full Housewife status. But the biggest missing piece of season 3 was Miami's most beloved unofficial Housewife. On the brink of filming, it became clear that Mama Elsa's declining health could no longer be ignored.*

Marysol Patton: She had a stroke, like, the day we were supposed to start filming. But she already had dementia and we didn't know it. The whole world was laughing with, or at, her, but she was actually quite progressed with dementia already. That's where a lot of her behavior came from.

Nate Green: It was really sad to see her health diminish in that last season. Everyone loved her—the cast, the crew. She really had a lot of fun doing it, which is nice to see when somebody is doing this so late in life.

Marysol Patton: When she had the stroke, it progressed at lightning speed. From one day to the next, she just wasn't walking, talking, she didn't know who anybody was. Meanwhile, Andy mentioned to me that people really watched to see my mom. And when she wasn't there anymore, it felt like my story line just fell flat.

Andy Cohen: Mama Elsa was the secret sauce of that show. You really felt her abscence.

Like Ana, Marysol was downgraded to "Friend of" status for season 3. But Elsa's struggle continued long after cameras stopped rolling.

Marysol Patton: For eight years she was in bed with a feeding tube and diapers, and she didn't know who anybody was. It was really hard, but I didn't let anybody know. I didn't want her to be remembered that way.

Matt Anderson: When you take away all the outrageousness, theirs was a really great mother/daughter story to tell. There was something very real and relatable about a mother who wishes her daughter was doing more, wishes she was married, having kids, all of that. And then it was wrapped in this fabulous package of Marysol and Elsa, who were hilarious and funny together.`

Marysol Patton: It's the greatest gift to have those memories of her when she was alive on film.

From start to finish, season 3 was dominated by "I do" as Adriana and Joanna each went full bridezilla, staging over-the-top weddings that got tongues wagging all over Miami.

Lisa Hochstein: Adriana and Joanna had dueling weddings that were set up from the beginning to be competing against each other.

Adriana de Moura: I definitely felt competitive with Joanna—I wanted to have the prettier wedding.

Nate Green: Adriana has exquisite taste. Her wedding was really beautiful, but also outrageous because she's an outrageous person who was late to her own wedding. Not, like, slightly late—very late.

Adriana de Moura: I actually got to the wedding early! But I have ADD. I struggle with time management. I just get so easily distracted. So I was trying to prepare, but then everybody was coming in to get ready in my suite, so that distracted me and I couldn't get myself ready.

Nate Green: I tried to take it with a grain of salt because Adriana was born late.

Adriana de Moura: By the time I really started to get ready, of course, we were very delayed. And on top of that, I felt like I was going to faint because I hadn't eaten anything all day. The stress and the pressure got to me, and my blood pressure went down, so that scene where I lay down was not fake at all. I was like, "Oh my God, I don't know if I can walk to the church."

Nate Green: We definitely told that story, which I don't think she was thrilled about in hindsight because she was so late, many of the guests were annoyed with her.

Adriana de Moura: It became TV gold. It was like a soap opera. I always look for the silver lining and that actually gave season 3 something.

> *Joanna's wedding raised eyebrows as well, since she and her fiancé had spent two seasons chronicling their relationship woes. . . .*

Lisa Hochstein: I don't know if they would have gotten married if it wasn't for the show.

Marysol Patton: Joanna would do anything for production. She knew what she was there for and did what she needed to do.

> *Amid the wedding celebrations, one key friendship continued to fall apart.*

Adriana de Moura: It started after the lingerie party. At that point, Lea started to work against me. I did call her out, like, "Why are you besties with Joanna all of a sudden? You're not my friend like you're supposed to be."

Lea Black: I'll put up with bad behavior for a long time, but if they're rotten to the core or if it's intentional, then I'm kind of done.

Adriana de Moura: Lea expected me to be her mouthpiece. Which I did for years—my fight with Cristy on season 1 was because Lea was annoyed at her. I was getting more uncomfortable attacking people for no reason if I didn't feel they did anything to me, but I did it because she was my friend, she was the one who introduced me to the producers so I was grateful. And loyal. But then behind the scenes, people told me she was really angry at me because I was becoming one of the major protagonists of the show.

Lea Black: I gave her clothes when she didn't have anything to wear. I fixed her up with a guy that had a private plane that flew her to Houston for dinner.

Matt Anderson: Sometimes, doing a show like this forces the women themselves to sort of question or think about things that are bothering them. It's a little bit like therapy—it can lead to breakthroughs.

Adriana de Moura: To me, ending my friendship with Lea due to the stupidity of the show was the biggest loss of this whole thing.

After a bitter, screaming reunion rolled around, there was no love lost between many of the ladies, and ultimately the decision was handed down that it was last call for Real Housewives of Miami.

Lea Black: I knew at the reunion of season 3 the show was not coming back. I saw the look on Andy's face. It was like the light went on. I could just tell he wasn't buying it. We were wrapping up around five thirty or six, and I knew when we walked out the door: The show's not coming back.

Marysol Patton: In hindsight, if we'd all been a little bit smarter and not taken everything so seriously, I think we'd still be there. But you learn as you go along. We literally figured out what we were doing in season 2 and then season 3 we were done.

Adriana de Moura: They said the show was going to be put on hiatus. We never got a big fat no.

Marysol Patton: To this day, they haven't told us it's over.

Lea Black: The other girls would run around trying to get pictures taken everywhere, to look like they were all hanging out together in order to bring the show back. I was cringing. It was so thirsty and so desperate. Everybody in town knows we're not best friends.

Alexia Echevarria: Sometimes you have to keep knocking on that door and show you want something. And I don't know about the other ladies, but I know Lisa, Marysol, and I would love to do it again. We haven't lost hope.

Shari Levine: Our viewers were really vocal about asking for *The Real Housewives of Miami* to return. And now, we had the perfect opportunity to bring it back on Peacock.

Ana Quincoces: From the beginning of time, there's a total of like, 117 Housewives. And—it's kind of a stupid comparison—but it's like when somebody is president of the United States. They will forever be called president. And a Housewife will always be a Housewife. It's a really cool select group that I'm proud to be part of.

PART VIII

"Chesapeake Babes"

The Real Housewives of Potomac

PREMIERE DATE: JANUARY 17, 2016

I always felt that if Bravo ever came to Potomac beating the grass looking for Housewives, my name would come to the top.

—KAREN HUGER

Charrisse Jackson-Jordan (Housewife): Right out of the gate, I knew casting this show would be an uphill battle.

Adrian Wells (Casting Director): The D.C./Maryland/Virginia area is not like New York City, Los Angeles, or Atlanta. People in this world don't want to be on TV.

Andy Cohen: We'd done D.C. already, but when we were presented with this enclave of glamorous, successful women living large in Potomac, it seemed like both a perfect fit and a total left hook that the viewers wouldn't see coming. Who could imagine *Potomac* as our next destination? The women were definitely Real Housewives, though, and they had great pride in their community.

Charrisse Jackson-Jordan: Adrian stressed they weren't looking to duplicate *The Real Housewives of Atlanta* but wanted the Black version of *The Real Housewives of Beverly Hills*. And to be quite honest, we don't flaunt our money like that.

Adrian Wells: The area is very conservative. The women, they're not at all showy about their wealth. They don't throw on a pair of Louboutins and grab their Birkins to run to the grocery store.

Charrisse Jackson-Jordan: I wasn't interested in doing the show at first, because my husband wasn't at all supportive. But I used to be president of the NBA Wives Association, so I have a lot of connections. I figured

I'd help them with casting. One of my first calls was to Gizelle because I knew she would do it.

Gizelle Bryant (Housewife): I'm an independent woman, so I didn't really consult too many people before agreeing to do the show. But I did have a conversation with my girls where I explained to them, "Doing a show like this is going to open me up to all kinds of criticism. There are going to be a lot of people who are going to love me, and also a lot of people who are going to hate me. They're going to say bad things about your mother." And they were like, "Mom, we know who you are and love you no matter what." That made me feel confident moving forward.

Lauren Eskelin: Gizelle is a fascinating woman. She's whip-smart, hilarious, speaks her mind freely, and, when in conflict, will say very biting things without losing her temper or getting out of character. She's also very good at observing other people's worlds and commenting on it, without allowing anyone to comment on hers. And there was something interesting there. She was someone you could keep unraveling, like an onion.

Next up was Karen Huger, who would later become the self-proclaimed Grande Dame of the Potomac Housewives.

Karen Huger (Housewife): I always felt that if Bravo ever came to Potomac beating the grass looking for Housewives, my name would come to the top. I was very confident about that.

Lauren Eskelin: Karen is like a soap opera star. From the day I met her, when she came into the office draped in diamonds and wearing a mink coat, she was a feast for the eyes and so dramatic. The whole office kind of stopped and watched her float by.

Adrian Wells: Karen was just like Gizelle in the sense that you knew she was a star. She had plenty of personality, plenty of story. She was living the life in this big house. Her kids were older, and we loved watching the kind of mother that she was. She was our Lisa Vanderpump.

Not long after Karen joined, a former model and single mother of three named Katie Rost was contacted by casting.

Katie Rost (Housewife): From what I understand, Charrisse was kind of acting as the unofficial casting agent for *Potomac* and suggested me. I wasn't even friends with Charrisse, but she knew I was young, a hot mess, and had some issues in my life that would make a good story.

Adrian Wells: At this point, I had built a mostly Black cast and I wanted to find a group of multidimensional Black women of all ages. Katie reminded me of a lot of Black girls I went to school with, growing up in a suburban area. I liked that she was originally from Potomac, almost like she was the adult version of the children Gizelle, Karen, and Charrisse were raising here.

With openings still to fill, Gizelle passed along the name of one of her best friends, Robyn Dixon—a divorced mother of two still sharing a home (and a bed) with her ex-husband and childhood sweetheart, NBA player Juan Dixon.

Robyn Dixon (Housewife): The way I remember it, both Gizelle and Charrisse contacted me at the same time. They were like, "Bravo's doing a show. We think you should talk to them."

Lauren Eskelin: Aside from being drop-dead gorgeous, Robyn had an undeniably fascinating story. She was living with her ex-husband and sleeping with him in the same bed. That wasn't a story ever told on *Housewives*, let alone reality TV. And she emerged that first season as a fan favorite, because she was the audience proxy who represented what viewers wanted to know. She was very relatable.

By this point, Charrisse had come around and agreed to join the cast. The final addition was Ashley Darby, a spirited twenty-six-year-old former beauty queen married to an Australian real estate developer twenty-nine years her senior.

Katie Rost: They brought Ashley in after we'd been filming for about a month.

Adrian Wells: Ashley felt different. She was younger than all the other women. I liked the big age gap between her and her husband, and she felt like a Housewife. I liked that she was free and open.

Charrisse Jackson-Jordan: I really embraced Ashley from the jump. I thought she was perfect and that she and her husband, Michael, brought a lot to the show.

Gizelle Bryant: It took me maybe half the season before I could appreciate Ashley for who she is. Like, I didn't understand her at all. All I knew was she was this young girl married to this old white man, which didn't make sense because she came off like the antithesis of someone who would be married to a man thirty years older than her. She's so smart and driven, and wanted to own her own business. I was like, "You are not a quintessential gold digger. What are you doing here?"

Ashley Darby (Housewife): I'm no dummy. I have watched *Housewives* shows, I've seen the dynamic. I understand how each person in the franchise brings something different. There's always someone on the quirky side and I was the designated quirky one.

Gizelle Bryant: Ashley is someone who gets under your skin. Either you love her or hate her. I love her. Karen hates her.

Katie Rost: Karen felt nervous because she's the oldest and was already being made fun of behind the scenes for the extremes she was going to in order to look younger; Botox, plastic surgery . . . she used to wear tape under her wig that pulled her face tighter, like *Sunset Boulevard* or something.

Ashley Darby: I'll never forget going shopping with Karen at South Moon Under. She shaded me right from the beginning, because she said her daughter Raven shops there. I was like, "Point being?" I guess it wasn't age appropriate to her, so she had to make it known. And then she gave me a whole lecture about Potomac society and how I needed to have a certain etiquette. It was like, "What? Who made you the president of Potomac? Did I miss the memo?"

> Ashley wouldn't be the only person to get a lesson in etiquette from Karen. As filming began, etiquette became a hot topic among the cast (for better or worse), kicking off a bitter rivalry among Karen, Gizelle, and Charrisse.

Andy Cohen: Part of the reason they didn't shut up about etiquette was because Karen Huger was always carrying on about etiquette and society.

Karen Huger: Well, etiquette still is a part of us, believe it or not. These ladies need to know how to behave and conduct themselves. That's a big part of Potomac. And me being the matriarch, of course, I was the one reading the rules of etiquette, as I still do sometimes.

Ashley Darby: It struck me as odd, Karen's constant schooling. It was a self-appointed authority that felt a little delusional to me.

Gizelle Bryant: I didn't understand it. Karen and I were always cool, but then the cameras started rolling and the whole etiquette thing was thrown in my face.

Karen Huger: Oh my God, Gizelle and I, season 1? Our butting heads was harmless. But it was very real.

Gizelle Bryant: Karen got mad at me right from the get-go. You saw it in that first episode. She told me she was upset about her birthday party, because we went to a restaurant and I sat in the middle. Hello, the producers told me to sit there! They were like, "Gizelle, you sit in the middle." We were basically set up to set her off!

Joshua Brown (Vice President, Current Production, NBCUniversal): I remember filming that first episode and watching from video village with the producers. We were really surprised when Gizelle sat there and didn't offer the seat to Karen.

Karen Huger: She sat in my seat. She needed to get up.

Gizelle Bryant: I was shocked. We were at Charrisse's house and she gave me a gift of this mirror with all these etiquette rules on it. I was like, "This woman is crazy."

Karen Huger: She never did it again, though. . . .

Gizelle Bryant: The Karen that I knew before the show would not have been that bent out of shape over where we were sitting in a booth. The Karen I know now? That's definitely what she would do. She's morphed into the character that she created, no question.

Robyn Dixon: There was definitely some sort of unspoken rivalry between Karen and Gizelle, but Charrisse was in that mix, too. It was like the three of them; the three eldest women competing for this . . . I don't even *know* what it was. But they knew how to push each other's buttons. And they got a kick out of it.

Charrisse Jackson-Jordan: It wasn't me so much, it was Karen and Gizelle. There's a lot of ego at play among those women. All the time. Everybody wants to be in the center of the intro or in the middle of the photo. And they wouldn't fight about it outright, because that's against etiquette, but they would try to position themselves in those places. It's hilarious.

Karen Huger: Relationships grow and Gizelle and I are growing. The viewers get to grow with us. Sometimes it's fun shade, sometimes it's painful shade. We ebb and flow.

Gizelle Bryant: As much as we go at it, with Karen and me, there's a level of respect there. Our history has sustained us.

> *As Karen, Gizelle, and Charrisse tackled etiquette issues, Robyn navigated something much more serious when her financial issues were brought up by Ashley behind her back—a move that led to an off-camera blowup viewers never saw.*

Robyn Dixon: You have to understand, on one of the first phone calls I had with production, I remember being asked, "Is there anything off the table?" And I said, "When it comes to Juan, his personal business, and his financial issues, they're not on the table. He doesn't want to talk about any of that."

Ashley Darby: You can't really do that.

Katie Rost: Ashley and I filmed at a park so she could meet my kids. But before she came over, Ashley was talking to producers for probably thirty, forty minutes—we were there for a very long time.

Katie Rost: While we were on the swing set, Ashley brought up Robyn's finances, claiming she had Googled them.

Ashley Darby: I tried to convey it in a more caring way. Like, "Oh, I didn't know this about Robyn." But in hindsight, no matter how I said it, it was going to look like I was being shady.

Katie Rost: Ashley was like, "Um, why is this Silver Spring, Baltimore, ghetto-ass girl trying to pretend like she has anything?" Her comments were really nasty.

Gizelle Bryant: Later that night, Katie, Robyn, and I were sitting in a car together, waiting to get miked up to film at Charrisse's house. There weren't cameras on us or anything, and out of nowhere, Katie turns and tells Robyn, "Oh by the way, Ashley spilled all your business."

Robyn Dixon: I was livid. I went berserk. Eric, our producer, came into the car to get us miked up, and I flipped.

Katie Rost: She went crazy. I wish they had a camera because this girl got out of the car, went over to Eric, and flipped out on him. She was pointing her finger. She was like, "I told you not to fuck with me like this and not talk about my shit! I trusted you, and you guys are motherfucking liars!"

Robyn Dixon: After that happened, I knew in my mind, "Ashley didn't do this on her own. It had to be producer driven."

Joshua Brown: The cast always wants to think that producers are pulling strings. But it's just not the case. Producers are reactive. They want the women to react to what they are seeing happening in their real lives, not a fabricated one.

Katie Rost: Then she left! She refused to film that night.

Gizelle Bryant: I looked at Katie afterward and she said, "Oh no, was it something I said?" I was like, "I'm going to wring your neck, Katie, because whatever you said sent Robyn to a place that we never want to see again!" Robyn is so sweet, but when you set her off it is over.

Ashley Darby: I had no idea Robyn told production she didn't want to talk about this! I had no clue.

**Lorraine Haughton-Lawson (Executive Producer and Senior Vice Presi-

dent of Programming, Truly Original): Ashley is an interesting House-wife. She's not looking for fame, she just thinks it's a fun thing to do. When you're like that, there's nothing that's not on the table for you because you don't really care. You're not worried about losing your job, you're not worried about keeping your job, you're not catering to a fan base, you're not worried about what your husband might say. That's what makes her so fun to watch; she can do whatever she wants because she's not beholden to anyone.

After filming wrapped on season 1, the debate among producers and the network became what to call the show.

Joshua Brown: We tossed around *Real Housewives of Montgomery County.*

Andy Cohen: We played around with the zip code. We were maybe going to call it *The Real Housewives of* whatever zip code that was.

Lauren Eskelin: We kept coming back to *The Real Housewives of Potomac* because that's where we were and that's what made sense.

Andy Cohen: And they all wouldn't shut up about how great Potomac was, which—pride in one's city is a hallmark of a *Housewives* show.

Joshua Brown: There was a lot of discussion of, "How can you make a *Real Housewives* show about a place that nobody's ever heard of?"

Andy Cohen: I thought it was the most genius curveball to call it *The Real Housewives of Potomac.* It just seemed so weird. And for everyone who thought they knew what the next city was going to be, it was like, "There's no way anyone would have guessed *Potomac.*"

The Real Housewives of Potomac premiered in January 2016, earning strong ratings and immediate comparisons to RHOA.

Joshua Brown: We led it out from *The Real Housewives of Atlanta* and it did really well. In my eyes, any time a show survives its first season, it's a success because it's so hard to launch new series.

Gizelle Bryant: It was great that we were right behind *RHOA.* Obviously, that gave us a big push—even though to this day, I feel like everyone wants to compare us to *RHOA* when there is no comparison. Why do you have to compare the two Black shows?

Katie Rost: We were so different than the Atlanta Housewives and the producers, because they also worked on *RHOA,* didn't understand Potomac at first. They didn't get the culture here, and they were trying to impose

Atlanta culture on Potomac. They didn't understand the nuances of how we shade each other. It took them a bit to get used to us.

Ashley Darby: Production wasn't really too sure about us that first season. They wouldn't even spend money to take us on an international vacation. Other casts go to Greece or South Africa. You take us to Bethany Beach, Delaware?

Charrisse Jackson-Jordan: The *RHOA* Housewives didn't support us either.

Gizelle Bryant: Because we share a production company, they were sent pictures of our franchise with a request of, "Hey, can you post about them and ask people to watch?" And they didn't give us no love.

Lauren Eskelin: We asked the *RHOA* cast to tweet and post about the show. We even sent them the first episode in advance of the premiere. And they all said, "Sure sure sure" and then no one did a thing. It was very icy.

> *In preparation for season 2, casting once again sought out potential House-*
> *wives. A new addition was Monique Samuels, mother of two and wife of NFL*
> *offensive tackle Chris Samuels.*

Monique Samuels (Housewife): I was never a person who thought I would be on reality TV—even though since Chris and I have been dating, all of our friends used to tell us, "Y'all need your own reality show!" because we're very real, we're very open, we have a strong friendship, and we don't hold back. But I just never took that seriously. Like, when they first started airing promos for the show, Chris would tease me, "Oh, that's right down the street . . . we have friends in *RHOP*, you could be on that show!"

Karen Huger: They were a young couple and they had young children. That energy added another dimension to the *Real Housewives of Potomac*, which was a huge asset.

Charrisse Jackson-Jordan: Chris was successful, too. He kept giving me money to gamble with, a hundred dollars a pop, like, "Here you go." I was like, "Oh, I like these people *a lot*! They're *much* better than the others!"

Joshua Brown: We were exploring a circle of athletes within the D.C. area, who all sort of know one another. You had Chris Samuels, who spent his NFL career on the Washington Redskins. And he kind of ran in the same circles as Charrisse's ex-husband Eddie, a retired basketball player who was a former coach of the Washington Wizards. And then Juan Dixon, who played in the NBA for the Washington Wizards as well. There was a natural connection there.

> *Meanwhile, Katie was moved to a guest role in season 2.*

Katie Rost: I was having a lot of personal problems, dealing with my ex-husband. For some reason, my ex-husband thought I was making millions on the show. So he went back to court and was riding my ass every day. Do you know how exhausting that is on your spirit? I couldn't pretend everything was okay anymore.

Joshua Brown: It didn't feel like Katie wanted to share what was going on in her life.

Robyn Dixon: Katie also became very difficult to film with. In season 2, she did her Casino Royale charity event and I remember hearing that her mother was cussing everybody out the entire time, screaming her head off at producers. At some point they just realized, it wasn't worth the trouble.

Monique wasn't exactly welcomed by everyone. Early on, she and Gizelle clashed, a rivalry quickly forming that lasted for years to come.

Monique Samuels: When I first watched the show, I thought I would get along with everyone, including Gizelle. She seemed like a fun, cool chick. I didn't think I was going to have any issues. But if you look back, the only person I didn't meet at Katie's event was Gizelle, and that's because they purposely kept us apart. They knew there would be conflict.

Joshua Brown: Gizelle left the event early that night and production was frustrated she didn't get to meet Monique. There were about two hundred guests there and one of them was a woman who approached Gizelle and claimed they were dating the same guy. Gizelle thought production put the woman up to this, which could not be further from the truth. We were like, "Who is this woman?" That's why Gizelle left.

Gizelle Bryant: Monique and I first met at the Willard Hotel, where we had that infamous high tea.

Monique Samuels: This was my first time talking to Gizelle and she ended up being all shady. We were talking about where I was living and she made the comment, "Oh, you don't have a home?"

Gizelle Bryant: She said, "I'm looking for a home," and my immediate reaction was, "Oh, you don't have one?" That's a logical follow-up question, and I didn't mean anything by that, but they didn't show it that way.

Monique Samuels: I'm from Jersey. I am married to a football player. I've been around football wives who talk trash all the time. When she said it that way, I knew immediately she was throwing shade. And I could have easily just said, "No, I have a home." But I was like, "Nah, forget that. Let me just go ahead and do what I do." So I said, "I have four homes. How 'bout you?" You know, caught that and threw it back!

Gizelle Bryant: That ten seconds, everyone has run with that until the cows have come home. "Oh my God, Gizelle hates Monique!" Today? Yes, I do hate Monique. But I didn't then!

Ashley Darby: I liked Monique when I first met her but I really respected her after the tea party because she stood up for herself without insulting anybody.

Gizelle Bryant: I didn't care anything about her, but for whatever reason it became, "I'm jealous of Monique. I hate her."

Charrisse Jackson-Jordan: That's because Monique, for whatever reason, she thinks everybody is jealous of her or wants something from her. It's like, "No, honey. Nobody wants that life of yours."

Gizelle Bryant: Meanwhile she was at that tea, rapping in the middle of this fancy hotel.

Monique Samuels: They literally begged me to rap for them. I kept saying no, but of course they never showed all of that. Even my producers were like, "Please, just do it."

Gizelle Bryant: Production was not pushing her to rap. She brought that up. We were asking her questions about herself and she said she was a rapper. Somebody said, "Oh, well, then rap!" and I thought she was gonna be like, "Oh, gosh, no, this is not the time or place."

Monique Samuels: They rolled back all of the comments of them saying, "I can't believe she's rapping at the Willard!" I'm like, "What? Y'all begged me to!"

Gizelle Bryant: I felt sorry for her, to be honest with you, because she was really trying so hard. It's like, anybody who tries that hard, maybe they shouldn't really be there?

Tensions between Charrisse and Gizelle were also riding high in season 2, after Gizelle alleged on Watch What Happens Live *that both Charrisse and her now-estranged husband, Eddie, were unfaithful in their marriage.*

Monique Samuels: Charrisse wasn't ready to discuss what was happening between her and Eddie, but that didn't stop Gizelle.

Charrisse Jackson-Jordan: My marriage was in trouble well before Gizelle opened her mouth. Eddie didn't want anything to do with the show from the beginning. I knew he'd be that way and honestly when I first called him and told him they asked me to do the show, I hoped he'd beg me not to do it so that we could focus on our relationship because our marriage was not in a good place. Instead he said, "Well, if you do it, we'll probably get a divorce."

Adrian Wells: Charrisse knew her marriage couldn't be repaired. Doing the show was kind of her way to get out of it.

Charrisse Jackson-Jordan: I did do the show to escape Eddie, but I wasn't allowed to because that's all they would focus on in my edit. I was put in this role of a stressed-out woman dealing with her bad marriage.

Ashley Darby: In hindsight, I'm sure having all her business on international television wasn't easy. She wasn't able to be fully present in the moment and in the experience. And that was really palpable.

Charrisse Jackson-Jordan: For me, that first season was crap. I don't even remember much of it. And then all of a sudden, in season 2, I was getting this divorce and I was like, "Oh shit." Eddie and I were together for twenty-seven years. That's not something you easily walk away from. Add to that Gizelle talking all these lies? It was . . . a lot!

Gizelle Bryant: Charrisse and I have gotten to a wonderful place now because she was able to look back and realize that I was never really trying to hurt her.

Charrisse Jackson-Jordan: The only reason I moved past it with Gizelle was because the production team and the network execs all told me, "You need to make up with her. You gotta let it go."

Gizelle Bryant: I was just calling Charrisse out on her stuff. That's the show! Had she said to me, "Gizelle, chill out. I'm going through a divorce. This isn't helping," there's a whole lot I would not have said.

> *Also in season 2, Robyn reached the end of her rope with Ashley's continued probes into her unconventional relationship. Frustrated, she and Gizelle paid a visit to see Ashley at her since-shuttered Australian-themed restaurant, Oz.*

Robyn Dixon: I didn't anticipate I'd go off on Ashley in that moment. I just wanted to be like, "Look, you need to cut this shit out. I don't know what your obsession is with my family, but you need to leave me alone."

Ashley Darby: Robyn was upset because I was saying she needed to get out of this relationship. She was being a ride or die and the other person in her relationship was not riding for her. And Robyn, she didn't like hearing that.

Robyn Dixon: When we first saw Ashley at the restaurant, she gave us that "Hey, guys!" greeting, all happy and chipper. And it just pissed me off even more. I was like, "This bitch!"

Gizelle Bryant: I knew it would be highly confrontational. But I didn't expect Robyn to get up in Ashley's face like that.

Robyn Dixon: It wasn't my intention to make it some crazy argument, but my emotions took over.

Ashley Darby: I won't lie, I wasn't happy because this was my business, you know? It's a dining environment. Ask me to come outside or go in the back or something!

Gizelle Bryant: It was everything. We rolled in, Robyn explained to Ashley how she felt, and we were out the door. It was epic. I freaking love that scene.

> *Season 3 brought the introduction of Candiace Dillard Bassett, a sassy and savvy former Miss United States, entrepreneur, and aspiring singer/actress engaged to chef Chris Bassett.*

Adrian Wells: Candiace was hilarious! She was very real and honest about her relationship with Chris, her relationship with her mother was interesting, and, most importantly, she was opinionated. She didn't shy away from speaking freely and directly.

Candiace Dillard Bassett (Housewife): You're going to think I'm crazy, but I swear, I got the show because I prayed for it. When the show first started airing, I remember watching and being like, "Why the fuck am I not on this? Where was I when they were casting?" Because I grew up watching *RHOA* and was so excited to see another all-Black *Housewives* ensemble, but as entertaining as the show was, it was also a bit dull and I knew I could spice it up and show another facet of Black women. I have this couch at the foot of my bed where I pray, and I got down on my knees and said, "Lord, if this is something that is an opportunity for me to help accomplish my goals and make my dreams reality, can you make this happen?"

Noah Samton: We had real expectations that Candiace and Ashley were going to be buddy-buddy, since they're both younger and came from that pageant world. But it really didn't play out that way.

Karen Huger: I loved Candiace when we first met. She was fun, bubbly, energetic, articulate, and bright. Immediately, we bonded.

Monique Samuels: Nobody liked Candiace when the show first started. They all thought she was immature and a little girl. They tried to ice her out the same way they did my first season because she's just immature.

Candiace Dillard Bassett: I learned early on, when you're on this show, everybody is given a box, whether you want it or not. You're kind of forced into this space and you have to exist there. There can sometimes be wiggle room—like, if the story makes sense, they'll allow you to shift into a different box. But it's rare that you're allowed to just be a real person. For me, the box was that I'm a spoiled-rotten princess. Everything is centered around me being a brat. Meanwhile, I'm literally the only Housewife on my cast who had all of my businesses *before* I was on the show.

That season, Charrisse was moved to a Friend role and, ultimately, was not asked to return.

Charrisse Jackson-Jordan: I wasn't getting divorced fast enough for them, that was the problem. But that's not how my divorce worked. I had to go to court, there was a trial.

Candiace Dillard Bassett: It would have been different if Eddie filmed, but he would not sign off on filming anything with her. What was she supposed to do? She can't control her husband.

Charrisse Jackson-Jordan: I was trying to get them to tell another story about me, but the producers, they weren't interested in nothing Charrisse. Like, I found out my kids have other siblings that we never knew about, and I wanted them to meet one another for the first time on the show. To me, that was raw, honest, real-life shit.

Andy Cohen: I always liked Charrisse. I thought having her on, she could give Karen a run for her money. But I lost that battle. The viewers didn't really connect with her. She came off kind of snobby and full of herself. And producers and the execs at Bravo felt like we should change things.

Charrisse Jackson-Jordan: There's this perception from the public that I pulled back from the show while I was going through my divorce. I didn't pull back, they pulled me back.

Robyn Dixon: I feel bad for Charrisse, because Charrisse really is the reason why we're all on this show.

Ashley Darby: Charrisse is the president of Potomac. She had the connections, she knew everybody.

Charrisse Jackson-Jordan: I knew I wouldn't be a Housewife that season right from the beginning. They told me they didn't want me to tell anybody, which was weird for me because I was still filming full-time and no one knew. Eventually I started to fill people in. I told Monique, I told Robyn—like, these people were my real friends. It's not like some of the other franchises, like *Atlanta*, where it's a job and you come and film with these people and then go home. Robyn's been my friend for eighteen years. Gizelle's been my friend for, what, fifteen, sixteen years? We have history together.

Gizelle Bryant: I fought to keep Charrisse big time. Unfortunately, in the end, there was nothing I could do.

Charrisse Jackson-Jordan: And I will say, there were some upsides to being a Friend. There's much less pressure to film. That season I went to New York and stopped to see some Bravo executives and they were like, "Aren't you supposed to be at work?" I was like, "I'm a Friend! I'm not on the calendar! I only get two scenes, life is good!"

> *Even without Charrisse, there was plenty of drama in Potomac—including the headline-making news that Karen's husband Ray (a.k.a. "The Black Bill Gates") owed nearly $1.5 million in back taxes on top of the more than $3 million his company owed.*

Joshua Brown: The story about Ray's tax issues was reported in the *Washington Post* before we even started filming. And that was the moment we realized our show was bigger than this little world we were filming in. That's when we saw ourselves crossing over into the pop culture lexicon.

Gizelle Bryant: Karen was trying to keep her financial issues off camera. Her life was falling apart and we were all supposed to act like it's not happening? No, we were going to talk about it. Karen likes to live her life in a fantasy she's created, but I choose not to live on Fantasy Island, I live in reality.

Karen Huger: Everything you've ever witnessed between Ray and me on this platform was trying for us. But all marriages have challenges and we have always taken our challenges head-on. We fight for our marriage, and that's why we're winning.

> *Another season 3 story line involved Monique and an off-camera car accident she got into hours after filming a scene with Ashley.*

Monique Samuels: When the accident happened, we had all been out filming a scene—me, Ashley, and Candiace. When filming wrapped, Ashley and I went to have a drink. I'm a very slow drinker, but over the course of our time there I ordered three drinks, including a Moscow Melon, which I sent back for a martini because I didn't like it.

Candiace Dillard Bassett: I had to leave to film more, but they were done for the day, so they said, "We're going to go to the bar and have a drink." And I wasn't there, I didn't see it, but I've witnessed Monique driving after she's been drinking in the past.

Monique Samuels: I would never get behind the wheel if I was intoxicated. I didn't even feel drunk! But I had been up since four that morning. We just moved into the new house, I didn't have a nanny for the kids, I was managing all the financials of the rental properties, plus starting my business, plus working on the board of a charity—all while filming this reality show. And I had just had a miscarriage weeks earlier. I was exhausted, and as I was driving, the day just hit me and I felt myself start to doze off. I tried to roll down the windows and turn the music up again to keep myself up, but it happened again and when I opened my eyes, I was headed straight for a tree. Luckily, I swerved and wound up in a ditch, but the car still had something like forty thousand dollars in damages and I got whiplash and a mild concussion.

Candiace Dillard Bassett: I believe that she was drunk and I believe that she fell asleep because she had too much to drink.

Monique Samuels: Ashley kept saying I had "four martinis." But any time I'm out drinking and I'm driving, I limit myself.

Candiace Dillard Bassett: Then when we went to Nemacolin—that's when she drank the whole bottle of Camus by herself, if you remember. And Ashley brought it up there.

Monique Samuels: What they didn't show was that when we were at Nemacolin, right before Ashley started lying about how many drinks I had, I told the group about my miscarriage. I'm not a vulnerable person and I actually allowed myself to be vulnerable with them. And in that moment what did they do? They disregarded what I said and started bashing me from left to right. "Oh, you had four drinks." "Oh, you crashed your car because you were drunk." I was like, "Are you kidding me?"

Robyn Dixon: Monique was totally fine with Ashley and the discussion about her drinking when it was brought up in Nemacolin. That night, we were in a hot tub up all night chitchatting and smoking cigars and having fun. But then, we're back home, and she comes to Karen's perfume event all pissed off. I was looking at her like, "What the fuck is your problem? Why are you mad all of a sudden?"

Monique Samuels: I actually didn't want to go to Karen's scent event because I was very hot with Ashley. But I wanted to celebrate my girl Karen. So I said to myself, "Imma go and not say anything. This will be the quietest Monique they'll ever witness, because I don't want to be pushed off the cliff. I don't want to go over the edge." And that's how it was until everyone started coming for me.

Ashley Darby: She got upset. She started saying things about me, I started saying things about her. And the whole situation just spun so far out of control.

Robyn Dixon: Her anger to me was hilarious. If Monique was really mad, she should have said something in the moment. But she wasn't. She was just worried about the perception the audience would have about her drinking and driving. That's why I was laughing—it was all a performance. By the time we were on the street, I was really cracking up.

Candiace Dillard Bassett: Next thing we knew, Monique was choking Robyn out with an umbrella.

Monique Samuels: I tried to walk away, but Robyn and Gizelle were instigating, arguing back at me and doing what they do, talking trash. I called them Pinky and the Brain. And then Robyn got upset and got into my face. I was like, "You better back up out of my face before I hit you with an umbrella."

Robyn Dixon: I wasn't worried she was going to do anything. I knew she was all talk.

Monique Samuels: Ashley later gave me an apology—a real one—but not until she went through something similar with Candiace. . . .

> *Monique is referring to Ashley's feud with Candiace in season 4, which began when Candiace began questioning Ashley's drinking amid her attempts to get pregnant again after a miscarriage.*

Candiace Dillard Bassett: She told me in that scene at Oz that she was not going to drink because she was trying to get pregnant. But then every time I looked, she was throwing back a Corona Light. That, to me, says that you're not trying to get pregnant and have a baby.

Ashley Darby: Say anything you want about my relationship, my marriage, me, my finances—that's par for the course, in my eyes. But when Candiace started being so vocal and attacking my pregnancy journey, that for me was a line.

Robyn Dixon: Talking about my finances was a line, but Ashley didn't mind that.

Ashley Darby: But money is something a person will not have today and may have tomorrow. Losing a child and going through a miscarriage? I'm not going to get that baby back. That's a permanent loss I have to deal with. Don't make a mockery of it.

Candiace Dillard Bassett: Ashley was doing her job by making a big deal out of something that she honestly just didn't care about. She was yelling, she was loud, and I looked like the villain—even though I was making the same statement to her face that everybody was making behind her back.

Gizelle Bryant: Candiace really wanted to be BFFs with Ashley off camera, and when Ashley was like, "I'm not really feeling you like that," it hurt Candiace. They are two little pageant girls. Candiace is over it now, clearly, but that was the source of their issues.

> *The feud between Ashley and Candiace spilled over to Candiace's house, where a dinner party Candiace's husband, Chris, was throwing turned into one of the most jaw-dropping scenes in* Potomac *history.*

Robyn Dixon: That whole party went left fast. We were supposed to be talking about the fact that Michael had said one night while we were out drinking, "Yeah, I would suck Juan's dick." That was the real elephant in the room we needed to discuss. But Ashley immediately brought up the comments Candiace made about her miscarriage.

Candiace Dillard Bassett: We had been at Monique's rainbow baby shower and Ashley and Michael were once again putting on a whole performance. So I let them know.

Ashley Darby: Candiace crossed a line.

Candiace Dillard Bassett: Of course, Ashley had to tell me, "I'm in yo' mama's house"—because once again, it was all about painting me as this spoiled brat. But that set me off because it was like, "Bitch, your entire life is a dumpster fire and it's on display for everybody to see, so leave me and my privileged, Black American princess ass alone!"

Robyn Dixon: Then it was like, boom—here comes Candiace, slamming a butter knife on the table and kicking Ashley out of the house.

Candiace Dillard Bassett: I had been drinking red wine all day, and I had zero inhibitions about climbing on top of the table and telling this bitch to get the fuck out of my house. Period.

Monique Samuels: This is when I started to feel unsafe around Candiace. If she would wave a knife in somebody's face to the point where she literally could've cut her . . . ?

Candiace Dillard Bassett: I was never going to stab anyone with that butter knife. Nor did anyone think I was, by the way. If they had been truly frightened by my actions, you would've seen it on their faces. They wouldn't have been sitting there calmly looking at me.

Monique Samuels: I didn't say much then because I couldn't believe what I was seeing. I've never seen a grown person acting like that. Kicking and screaming? Having this outburst? That's crazy behavior.

Ashley Darby: There is a pressure for more explosive interactions as you go on in the seasons. And in that moment, Candiace was really trying to instigate a physical fight with me. That's why she threw the butter knife at me.

Candiace Dillard Bassett: My plan was to take Ashley's purse to the door and throw it outside, like over the steps into the street to get her to leave. But Chris was like, "You need to calm down." He was sitting on me, pulling me away. So launching the knife was my way of saying, "Okay, I'm not going to get back over there and really cuss her out, so let me just throw this in frustration and make her leave."

Monique Samuels: It was way, way worse than what they showed. Her husband was literally sitting on top of her to restrain her, and she was punching him and mushing him with her elbow, trying to get to Ashley.

Gizelle Bryant: By the way, you're welcome for the butter knife scene.

Candiace Dillard Bassett: Gizelle likes to think she produced that whole damn thing. . . .

Gizelle Bryant: I push the story down the road. I want the truth and I know how to get it.

Ashley Darby: Gizelle thinks she should be in the credits, to be honest! She gives herself a lot of credit for orchestrating things—and you know, to be fair, she does.

Gizelle Bryant: I don't want it to be boring. Nobody wants to watch that.

Lauren Eskelin: Gizelle will not leave without getting the information she wants. And in that sense, she's a great producer of other people's stories. It's when it comes to her own story that she clams up.

Gizelle Bryant: In this case, when Ashley got thrown out, I knew I had to bring her back in because, guess what? We were supposed to be talking about Michael and what he said about the penis that he wanted to suck. That had not happened yet!

Candiace Dillard Bassett: I had to ask Ashley to leave repeatedly. Meanwhile, everyone paints me as the angry, out-of-control Black woman who wants to stab people with knives? Get outta my house! You were asked to get out!

> *Troubles between Candiace and Ashley wound up affecting Candiace and Monique's friendship, too. When Monique stood up for Ashley, it led to a massive argument during a country hoedown, and Monique's now infamous threat to "drag" Candiace, "pregnant and all."*

Candiace Dillard Bassett: Monique and I, we had a friendship off camera. And when we hung out, she would talk all sorts of smack about Ashley and Michael. The general consensus among us and the rest of the group is that Ashley and Michael's relationship is a ruse. Ashley's in it for money and Michael's in it for a trophy wife. Monique would be like, "Ashley's gon' get this baby and she's gonna get the hell out. That's what I think." So then to see Monique, out of the clear blue sky, vehemently defending Ashley to me, like Ashley paid her taxes for her? Like she saved her baby off a burning cliff? It just did not make sense.

Monique Samuels: That's an absolute lie. I'm not a person who would just sit and trash-talk somebody. I like to keep my mind positive.

Candiace Dillard Bassett: When Monique was threatening to drag me at that hoedown, I never thought she would because I thought there was a line that everyone knew not to cross.

Monique Samuels: I wanted to throw that bottle at her head, during that whole "I'll drag you, pregnant and all." I had to restrain myself.

Candiace Dillard Bassett: She's lucky I'm not someone else because if you threaten the wrong person, saying you're going to hit them in the head with a glass bottle, and that person doesn't give a fuck about your life or the life of your unborn baby? Let's just say, it could have been a much worse situation.

Monique Samuels: I'm a zero-to-a-hundred type of person. I can snap at somebody, but I can very easily and quickly apologize in that moment. So I walked over and I said, "You know what, I'm sorry for threatening you with the bottle. I'ma be a woman and apologize right now because that was out of line."

Candiace Dillard Bassett: Looking back, I still don't understand why Monique chose Ashley's side. Ashley screwed her within an inch of her life the year before, with real defamatory, damaging information, saying she was drunk driving in a community where she claimed to have so much clout. You're threatening to become physical with me but you let that slide and "forgave" Ashley? That's fishy.

> Amid all the drama was an allegation that catapulted The Real Housewives of Potomac back into the headlines. Three days after the filming of Monique's rainbow baby shower, a cameraman claimed in court documents that Michael had "grabbed and groped" his butt. The allegation led Michael to be charged with felony assault, as well as misdemeanor improper sexual contact.

Ashley Darby: Michael and I had just gotten back together after being separated. You know, doing this show can be hard on a couple because Housewives, we're meant to share it all. So when the show first started, stuff we normally would keep private I was bringing up on national television. That, plus the fact that we were working together on the business, had us interacting with one another in a totally different way than we had in the past. But now we were back together, stronger than ever. And then this happened. . . .

Candiace Dillard Bassett: It all happened at Monique's rainbow shower, but we didn't hear about it until later into filming, when the TMZ story broke.

Andy Cohen: I couldn't get over that. I was stunned when it came out. And then I was stunned when Michael reminded me on the reunion that he had grabbed my ass. I mean, I had truly forgotten that.

Gizelle Bryant: Michael had been grabbing ass since season 1.

Candiace Dillard Bassett: Two of our other producers had their butts patted or grabbed by Michael. That's why we weren't surprised.

Lorraine Haughton-Lawson: We had heard, off the record, that Michael had grabbed the asses of a lot of the gay men on the producing team.

Gizelle Bryant: Michael likes to squeeze men's buttocks and they don't like it. This cameraman, he took it and responded like any other straight man would in the moment. But there was no doubt in my mind that Michael squeezed the wrong ass.

Monique Samuels: I felt awful that Ashley was going through all that. Like, what if it's true? This is what your husband's doing to you? But also, what if it's not true? Now you're both being dragged through the mud in the media—all while trying to have a baby after you just lost one.

Ashley Darby: It wasn't until this experience that I realized that Monique was really a true friend. Because when Michael was going through his stuff in season 4, the way Monique had our backs and really helped us show the truth—it wasn't just for cameras. She could have taken joy in it and used it as an opportunity to have a story line or a funny sound bite, but she realized the severity of the situation and was really supportive.

Candiace Dillard Bassett: The only reason Monique stood by Ashley's side after the butt tap was because it looked good for her on the show. She needed to be a contrarian and hold a specific position to garner more camera time. That was an unpopular position, and it was a vacant position, and she filled it.

Ultimately, the charges against Michael were dismissed by a Montgomery County court due to insufficient evidence.

Joshua Brown: Ashley and Michael, for all the things they've been through, are actually incredibly open about what's going on in their personal lives and with their marriage.

Ashley Darby: I was not surprised my marriage would be a topic of discussion on the show. We are as polar opposite as you can get; we're from different continents, different races, different ages. There's so much for people to dissect. That's not new to me. So thankfully, I already had pretty strong armor against that.

Andy Cohen: Michael's someone who—not unlike Simon van Kempen, another Australian—really has a love-hate relationship with the camera. There's something he really must enjoy about whatever being on the show brings him. But on the other hand, he gets caught up in a lot of mess season after season.

Gizelle Bryant: Don't get me wrong, I like Michael. He is a wild card. When he's around, you do not know what's going to happen. You cannot predict it. The producer in me knows that's good TV.

As season 5 began, a new cast member joined the show: Dr. Wendy Osefo, a Nigerian-born professor, political analyst, entrepreneur, and married mother of three with four degrees and a penchant to speak her mind.

Wendy Osefo (Housewife): A friend of mine knew one of the executive producers and recommended me.

Joshua Brown: We always look for women who have some sort of organic connection to the group. Wendy and Candiace had worked together on a charity, and they'd both run in political circles. And Wendy had met Karen at a charity event.

Candiace Dillard Bassett: I love Wendy. I was so excited when she was cast. I was like, "Yes, we have a beautiful, dark-skinned woman who is degreed down!"

Karen Huger: The first time I sat down with Wendy for more than five minutes was on the show. And as I said on the show, I wasn't impressed.

Gizelle Bryant: My first scene with Wendy, she screamed at me about something and in my mind I was like, "I know she's just trying to find her footing, so I'm going to give her some slack here." After about a month or so, I could see her feeling more comfortable and being herself. And I really think Wendy is a great addition. It is extremely difficult to come into this cast, especially five seasons in, and meld with the group, but Wendy did just that.

Candiace Dillard Bassett: One of the big pieces of advice I gave Wendy when we first met was about the importance of "having a moment."

Wendy Osefo: That advice really changed the game for me. Candiace gave it to me right before I went on my first trip, the local one at Monique's house in Newburg. She said, "This is where things get hot. Just be prepared. And you haven't had your moment yet. This would be a good time to do that." And I said, "What are you talking about? I've spoken up." She goes, "Yeah, you've said your opinion, but you haven't had a *moment*; something where we all can say, 'That was Wendy's moment.' You need a moment." It was from that conversation that "Dr. Wendy, address me correctly" was born.

> *Season 5 ended up being a breakthrough season for* The Real Housewives of Potomac, *the series garnering its highest ratings yet. But it was a bittersweet success, considering the season also included a horrific physical altercation between Monique and Candiace.*

Robyn Dixon: In the beginning of the season, Candiace was on thin ice with a lot of us.

Candiace Dillard Bassett: I spent the whole first quarter of that season trying to make up with everyone. I was fighting with Gizelle, fighting with Robyn, fighting with Monique. At every turn, I said I was sorry.

Monique Samuels: Candiace kept trying to have conversations with me, but I was not going to do it one-on-one. I wanted witnesses around. And every single time, she didn't want to talk.

All of a sudden, we were at the winery, and she gets this liquid confidence to finally talk. She was trying to start an argument, and I was just laughing.

Candiace Dillard Bassett: It was all light stuff. I teased her about faking like she was asleep when I was leaving her log cabin in the woods. Then she was like, "You're not a mother"—you know, shaming me for not having a child. It just kept escalating from there.

Monique Samuels: She got her hand right in my face, just like she did with Ashley and the butter knife. Her hand was so close to my chin that it could have touched me. And I don't do hands in the face. I don't play.

Candiace Dillard Bassett: My hand was barely in her face. We weren't fighting, remember!

Monique Samuels: So I told her, "You need to back up." And she said, "What are you gon' do? You gon' drag me?" And that just took me over the edge, because I literally gave you the warning and now you're pushing me.

Candiace Dillard Bassett: That's when she flicked my hair and I flicked her vest.

Monique Samuels: She swung over with a wineglass and hit me in my face. When I was hit with the glass, I pulled her head down to the table and started punching her in the back of her head.

Candiace Dillard Bassett: The glass did not leave my hand until after I was pulled down onto the table. I remember everyone screaming, "Monique! Let go of her!" But she wouldn't. All I was thinking was, "I cannot let my wig come off on this camera. I cannot live in infamy on the Internet as a Black woman whose wig has been ripped off and I'm fighting in my cornrows." So I was holding on to my wig.

Robyn Dixon: Yes, Candiace is annoying as shit. Sometimes her mouth is too much. But nothing Candiace did or said warranted any type of physical attack.

Monique Samuels: They eventually led me to a back room, but my adrenaline was pumping. The force from the glass hitting my face caused my tooth to bust my lip on the inside. It was deep. And now I *really* wanted to beat her tail.

Candiace Dillard Bassett: I was a mess. Our co-EP was holding me like I was his child.

Monique Samuels: They were trying to calm me down and I could hear her calling me names and saying, "She's fired! She's fired." I was like, "Wow, she's still talking? If I'm going to be off the show for fighting, I'm about to whoop her ass."

Candiace Dillard Bassett: All of a sudden our co-EP was like, "I need you to get in a car. Please, please. You have to go." I come to find out later, it was because Monique—who had been sequestered in the stairwell—found a way out of the barn and was running to get me.

Monique Samuels: By the time I got there, she was already gone.

> *It didn't take long for the higher-ups at Truly Original and Bravo to get involved.*

Lorraine Haughton-Lawson: I spoke to both Monique and Candiace the night of the altercation. Monique was going crazy about how Candiace deserved it and she finally got what she wanted. Candiace, on the other hand, was a puddle of mush, and really has been ever since. She vacillates between cascading emotions and her anger toward Monique, but also pain because this was someone she thought was a close friend. It was a much deeper situation than just some girl she got in a fight with.

Andy Cohen: We don't like when shit like this happens. It's a bad look for the series. It's not why we created this series. The show is not meant to be *The Bad Girls Club*. It's not meant to be *Love & Hip Hop*.

Monique Samuels: Andy was really there for me when all this stuff was going down. I didn't feel like I was getting support from anybody and I wanted an unbiased ear; someone who had been around so much of this who could give me some advice.

Candiace Dillard Bassett: Do you know Andy never, ever reached out to me, ever? Not until the airing of the season when I was on *Watch What Happens Live*. And I have so many qualms with it, especially when I heard that he had spoken to Monique.

Andy Cohen: I never reached out to Monique, she reached out to me and asked if I was available and said she wanted to speak with me. That's how that conversation happened. She wanted to plead her case and tell me her side of things. She wanted to prove to me that Candiace provoked her.

Monique Samuels: Andy and I had a great talk. Andy listened. He did not try to justify anything. He just said, "Sometimes cameras catch things and sometimes cameras don't catch things. If this is what you feel played out, stay true to what you feel happened. Maintain that. We'll sort it out when we get to see the footage and when we get to the reunion."

Candiace Dillard Bassett: I even reached out to Andy's assistant and asked for him to call me. Nothing. That's fucked up. I know he has well over a hundred Housewives, all texting and calling him all the time. But how many of them were physically attacked on camera by their costar? The fact that he couldn't even schedule ten minutes to reach out to me? You don't give a fuck. You are making money off of our backs and feeding your son with it, and you just don't give a fuck about us and you can't tell me that you do. And when I saw him, I did say it to his face.

Andy Cohen: I knew Candiace was in constant communication with Josh and production, but if she'd left word with my office I absolutely would've called her back. Also, if she'd told me to my face that I didn't give a fuck about her, I would certainly remember that. I don't. I do remember her being upset that I'd spoken to Monique.

Joshua Brown: I am not aware of who Andy calls and doesn't call. I personally spoke to Candiace many times and I hope she feels like the network was and is very supportive of her because we've had a lot of thoughtful and emotional conversations about what happened.

Candiace Dillard Bassett: Bravo didn't give a fuck about me and how traumatic and horrible this situation has been for me. Yes, I have been reached out to and approached and checked on more times than I can count. But in my eyes, they're just doing it to avoid legalities.

Monique Samuels: Andy also told me something I really held on to. He said, "Look. Not saying that anything is right, but there's a thing called cause and effect. If you keep poking a bear, the bear is going to bite back." He wasn't condoning violence or taking sides; I still owned my part in it. But he said, "Just do what you can."

Andy Cohen: My point of view on this stuff has totally been skewed by what happened with Kenya and Porsha because I was the only person in the room that day who didn't understand that Kenya was provoking Porsha and that it was about to escalate. That's why I kind of started looking at, "What was Candiace's role in this?" That's unusual for me because with any case of physical aggression, the person who gets physical is the one who is punished.

Gizelle Bryant: But this was so different. Even as provoking as Kenya was, Porsha apologized profusely immediately! She apologized to Andy Cohen, she apologized to Shari Levine, she apologized to everybody. She didn't then go on social media and try to lie about what happened. She didn't try to vilify her castmates. We to this day have not seen Monique grow from this experience.

Andy Cohen: The irony is that I ultimately pushed Monique on her lack of apologies at the reunion and got crucified for it by the viewers.

> *As discussions happened behind the scenes, news of the fight almost immediately made its way to the blogs and social media.*

Robyn Dixon: Monique leaked the story to her fans in the press right away, and we knew it was her because the details of the fight were totally skewed against Candiace.

Monique Samuels: I never leaked the story to bloggers. I told my family, and a friend. I know who leaked it, but it wasn't me.

Lorraine Haughton-Lawson: Monique is intoxicated by the fame. Like, intoxicated. But at the same time, she would deny, deny, deny, deny that she had anything to do with leaking this story. She'll tell you, "I only told two people." Okay, well then, Monique, they told the blogs! You know what you're doing!

Candiace Dillard Bassett: I was attacked on social media for nearly a year before the show came out.

Robyn Dixon: It was really bad. They were saying Candiace deserved it. "That's what you get for asking to be dragged." I felt terrible for her.

> *Days after the fight, the entire cast (sans Candiace) met at Karen's house.*

Monique Samuels: I asked production for an all-cast scene without Candiace so I could apologize for putting them in harm's way.

Karen Huger: I hosted a meeting for Monique to help her get through it. I offered Candiace the same opportunity, which she declined.

Wendy Osefo: It was at that meeting that Monique admitted she was not remorseful.

Robyn Dixon: That was a problem for me. Monique could have been apologetic, but instead she put down this "tough girl, always right" act—when, in this situation, there's nothing right about what she did.

Gizelle Bryant: If the next day, Monique woke up and was like, "Oh my gosh, I totally screwed up. Let me make this up to Candiace and the ladies"—we would have been able to get on board. Instead, she doubled down.

Robyn Dixon: That was the last time Monique was around the entire group, until the reunion.

Another topic that came up in that meeting had to do with how Black women were represented on television.

Monique Samuels: Some of the women who started the show, the OGs, put themselves on a pedestal. They wanted *RHOP* to be the Black show that didn't act Black. I do not go with that whole campaign. The problem with that is that, number one, we should welcome who we are. Number two, everybody acts out of character, no matter what race you are. Everybody acts the fool.

Robyn Dixon: There's not that much representation of Black women on reality television, or on television, period. And the representation that was already out there—whether it's *Love & Hip Hop* or *Basketball Wives* or even *Real Housewives of Atlanta*—there's been instances where you've seen these women get physical and "ratchet" or whatever.

Candiace Dillard Bassett: There's only a stigma attached to our behavior because we're Black. Because when they're crackin' glasses on the edge of tables in *RHOBH*, smacking camera down in *RHOD*, throwing wine in people's faces in *RHOC*, or flipping tables and pulling ponytails in *RHONJ*, nobody says, "Wow, these white women are ghetto! They're dangerous!" It's not talked about as it is when Black women are being human and doing the same thing.

Gizelle Bryant: Being a Black woman in this country is tough. We've already got every obstacle blocking our success. For you to come on this platform as a Black woman and decide it's okay to physically harm your castmate? That is a problem I can't get past. That's not how I was raised. That's not who I am. If I have an issue with you, I have a brain. I know how to talk.

Ashley Darby: All the women are basically saying that Monique is a disgrace to Black people because she made a mistake. That's not fair.

Gizelle Bryant: There's just a different standard for Black women, and especially for Housewives. Sonja gets drunk and pees in a cornfield. That's hilarious, but we could never do that.

Robyn Dixon: For four seasons, we prided ourselves on, "Yeah, we can call one another out but we always know how to defuse the situation in a classy way." And the fact, in that moment, Monique went to that level, we felt like she tore down everything we represented.

As the Potomac Housewives were working through these feelings, Candiace was working through her own traumas from the fight, and ultimately filed a complaint with the District Court of Montgomery County in Maryland, which charged Monique with second-degree assault. Monique shot back by filing parallel charges.

Candiace Dillard Bassett: I was a mess. It was the lowest place I can recall being in recent years. It got to the point where I could not get through an hour without having a mini panic attack.

Monique Samuels: About ten days after the fight, I started to feel remorseful. I had a conversation with one of my producers and said, "I really want to have a talk with Candiace one-on-one, or perhaps with our husbands." And then that day, I got an email from her attorney, threatening legal action. And I took a screengrab and sent it to my producer saying, "Never mind."

Candiace Dillard Bassett: I didn't file anything for almost two weeks. I didn't plan to. But watching the lie after lie after lie that she was putting out there, I was like, "You want to go to jail. You want to be publicly embarrassed and flogged because you're fucking trying me."

Monique Samuels: Candiace filed a complaint against me knowing what it could do to my family. I have three kids! And she had no guilt about it, no remorse, knowing fully well that she hit me with that glass.

Candiace Dillard Bassett: About a week later, Monique filed counter-charges. And there will never be words to describe how vile, low, and disgusting Monique is for doing that. She is the lowest end of the totem pole of humanity.

Monique Samuels: The whole thing ended up getting dropped. After the state's attorney reviewed the footage, they realized, "Okay, this was a mutual fight" and dismissed it.

As Candiace and Monique's clash worked its way through the legal system, the network and Monique came to an agreement about her role for the rest of the season.

Monique Samuels: I told Bravo's legal department I would finish out the remainder of the season with the cast members who I felt comfortable filming with and who felt comfortable filming with me, so long as I didn't have to go on the cast trip or go to the finale.

Candiace Dillard Bassett: I was told that she was not given a choice to film with us anymore.

Monique Samuels: The network did not penalize me at all. Not a financial demotion, nothing.

Noah Samton: Monique was put at arm's length from the rest of the House-wives, which means she wasn't as much of a part of the show. And that's obviously a form of punishment in terms of the amount of episodes she ends up in and her relationship with the rest of the women. There are repercussions in a lot of different ways.

> *Leading into the premiere of season 5, troubles between Monique and her castmates only got worse on social media.*

Gizelle Bryant: The coronavirus pandemic pushed our premiere back a month. And the day they told us they were pushing the show back, we were on a call with Bravo and they asked us if we could have a unified response on social media. They said, "We'll send you a picture and give you a comment about what to say." We were all in agreement, and then Monique chose to post the photo with our faces scratched out.

Robyn Dixon: Then, we decided to do the "Don't Rush" TikTok challenge video with the whole cast to assure the fans that we'd be back. Monique was super excited to participate, but the day before the videos were due, she texted me and was like, "I'm not going to get the video done because I'm so busy." And then when the video came out and every-one was asking, "Where's Monique?" she was like, "I didn't want to be involved in that fakery." All of a sudden, we had all these people com-ing after us, calling us mean girls because Monique wasn't in the video.

Gizelle Bryant: Then she released a song, boasting about dragging Candi-ace.

Candiace Dillard Bassett: I'm not talking about that piece of trash song. Next question.

Gizelle Bryant: I recognized Monique was good for the show. But, I am going to be honest with you, I couldn't get past all this. She would have to do a lot of apologizing. At this point, you're scratching my face out of pictures. And the song, and the TikTok. Now you have to apologize to me. Because we've all said, "Don't worry about us, Monique. Just apolo-gize to Candiace. We could get past this if you just own it." But now? Now you've got to apologize to me.

> *When the show did finally premiere, Bravo execs and producers had a deci-sion to make: How much of the fight would they show?*

Andy Cohen: We wound up showing more of what happened than we ever have in the past. And that was really Frances Berwick's call. We have gotten so much blowback over the years about cutting away from stuff. So she said, "Why don't you show what really happened? Let people decide what they think." And that's what we did.

Joshua Brown: I hope viewers will appreciate that it gets portrayed in a very documentary way. There's no music. There are no interview bites. You're just seeing the event. The viewer can make their judgment about what happened.

Lorraine Haughton-Lawson: Of course, by the time of the reunion, Monique was in the hot seat. It was the first time she'd seen everyone since the fight and there was a lot to explore.

Andy Cohen: Our question was, "Are you really repentant? Do you really feel bad about this?" Because when you're releasing a song about dragging someone, it's hard. . . .

Lorraine Haughton-Lawson: We offered Monique a chance to return for season 6. I likened it to the situation with Phaedra and Kandi in season 9. After Phaedra got fired, a lot of viewers felt like they were robbed of an ending to that story. So we wanted fans to go on a journey with Monique and Candiace, allowing them to see what could happen next. Would they be able to make up? Would they be able to coexist? We were excited to explore that.

Andy Cohen: I would have never imagined that we would consider bringing Monique back but when you look at public opinion about this, it wasn't as cut-and-dried.

Candiace Dillard Bassett: I was never ever going to film with her again. And I was really struggling as to whether I even wanted to come back to the show. But in the end, I decided I was not going to let this gutter trash brat fuck with my money.

Monique Samuels: There was no way I was moving forward with Candiace. I tried to move forward with her at the last reunion, and no sooner than we started filming again did she start being shady.

Karen Huger: A great deal of humility and accountability would have been required for them to move on. I know they could do it, but it would be hard.

Monique Samuels: There are always going to be people who think I was wrong in this situation. There's nothing I can do to change that. Do I wish that the whole thing never happened? Absolutely. Do I wish that I just would have walked away? Absolutely. I did not realize in the moment that it would escalate the way it did. But, you know, we just gotta live and move on and hope that we learn from our past.

Of course, Real Housewives of Potomac*'s legacy goes far beyond its season 5 battle.*

Andy Cohen: It's been a dream—when you have a great cast like this—to stick with them and watch them grow. The *Potomac* women, they're still friends. Their relationships have not gotten all fucked up by the show and the stuff happening outside the show. That's really the goal.

Gizelle Bryant: I would love there to be another all-Black *Housewives* show. There should be a *Black Housewives* out of Chicago. It would be a hit!

PART IX

"Cowgirl Country"

The Real Housewives of Dallas

PREMIERE DATE: APRIL 11, 2016

The tone was much lighter. It was freeing. They had a lot of fun.
There were hilarious antics and light hijinks, which I loved.
That's classic Dallas.

—RICH BYE

Rich Bye (Founder and President, Goodbye Pictures): We started to get tapped into Dallas society and the world of charity galas and how all of that works. The working title for the series when we sold it that got greenlit was *How to Make It in Dallas*. And one of the underlying narratives, themes that we all began with creatively, was how the women on that first season maintain and kind of boost their social standing within that social milieu of Dallas society, which is pretty much governed by charity galas. And so that was really our focus in season 1.

Andy Cohen: We'd cast in Dallas once before for a potential *Housewives* installment. We also cast in Houston. Neither of them felt right, but when this show came in, it felt like something special. We were going to call the show Charity Wives or something—not *Real Housewives*—and decided while shooting or shortly after it wrapped to call it *Real Housewives*, so we were stuck with all this charity talk, which the viewers hated.

Rich Bye: LeeAnne Locken was our first cast member. She sold herself as the gatekeeper to the charity galas that elite circles of the social strata in Dallas occupied.

LeeAnne Locken (Housewife): I was active in at least sixty charities in the city. And of those sixty charities, they all would have a kickoff party, a patron party, and the check presentation. So that's 240 events, out of 365 days in a year. It was my life.

Rich Bye: LeeAnne also let us know that she was the keeper of a treasure trove of scandalous secrets that belong to the who's who of Dallas society.

Andy Cohen: LeeAnne was a dominating personality, there's no doubt about that. She commanded your attention, in a way that some people loved and some people hated. I also, personally, was obsessed with the fact that LeeAnne was a carnic. I thought it was brilliant.

Once LeeAnne—a former pageant queen and actress—was brought on, she recruited one of her friends: Tiffany Hendra, a married Texas-born actress and Asian American spitfire she knew from their modeling days.

Andy Cohen: Tiffany was married to this Australian rocker, Aaron Hendra. And he looked just like Keith Urban. I don't know who dubbed him it first but he quickly earned the nickname among fans as "Keith Suburban."

Rich Bye: Tiffany had experience with the entertainment industry in L.A., which involved some drug abuse and wild living. But she had picked herself up, dusted herself off, and relocated to Dallas, where one of her closest friends, LeeAnne, could help guide her through the world of high society. There was something very compelling about that.

Tiffany Hendra (Housewife): The whole thing felt like this beautiful dream unfolding in front of my eyes. I left Hollywood, only to book my biggest game.

LeeAnne and Tiffany weren't the only pair of pals cast in season 1. Brandi Redmond and Stephanie Hollman were also close friends—two married mothers who had met through their husbands.

Stephanie Hollman (Housewife): Brandi and I actually auditioned for a Bravo show years prior, when our kids were babies. It was supposed to be about a group of friends and couples. We were actually told we were going to get contracts, but they couldn't find a great mix of girls, so the show turned into *Most Eligible Dallas*, which was all about singles.

Rich Bye: Brandi and Stephanie didn't come as a package; we interviewed them separately, just like LeeAnne and Tiffany. But in their separate casting interviews, they each spoke at great length about their friendship and their history together. There's a bit of a Thelma and Louise quality to their relationship.

Andy Cohen: Brandi was a former Cowboys cheerleader, which I just loved. And she's a ginger, which always gets high marks in my book. But the thing I loved the most about her was that she had this crazy sense of humor. She just was fun.

Rounding out the cast was Cary Deuber, a nurse and mother who was married to a successful plastic surgeon.

Cary Deuber (Housewife): I was the only person on the show who had zero experience in any facet of entertainment—which is funny to me because I'm probably the best at reality TV out of all of them, because I'm most myself and most entertaining.

Andy Cohen: I was *really* into Cary's husband Mark's obsession with her clothes. There was something very Simon van Kempen there. . . .

Before filming started, the cast gathered for lunch to meet for the first time. Tensions emerged immediately between LeeAnne and the team of Brandi and Stephanie.

LeeAnne Locken: I'll be honest, I came off really rude that day. When I go into a situation with new people, I often try to dominate the conversation because I feel comfortable and safe when I'm in control. So that's what I did.

Sezin Cavusoglu: Even in the casting reels, you had a sense of LeeAnne always feeling a little "less than" around the other society women who had money, and a sense of Brandi and Stephanie feeling pooh-poohed by the Dallas charity world because they didn't play by the rules. That was the original source of their conflict.

LeeAnne Locken: After that lunch, I tried to connect with Brandi and Stephanie off camera; they came to a charity event called PositiviTEA, which benefits a program serving women living with HIV/AIDS. But when I saw them at the next filming—a charity gala kickoff party we threw at the home of Marie Reyes, who was a Friend that season—they were laughing about me. Brandi was telling everyone that she does this "impression" of me, which I knew was mean-spirited.

Marie Reyes (Friend): LeeAnne and Brandi, they both have really strong personalities. And they each arrived at my party that night with some kind of preconceived notion about the other.

LeeAnne Locken: Toward the end of the night Brandi came up to me and said, "Can I talk with you about something you said the other day?" And I thought, "Oh my God, this is it! She heard me share my story about being molested as a child at PositiviTEA, and we're going to sit down and have a meaningful conversation!" Yeah, no. Instead she said, "It was really selfish of you to share your story." So after about five minutes of that lecture, I got up and left. Tiffany came over because she knew I was upset, and I was like, "I'm not okay! Brandi's a fucking bitch!"

That was only the first of LeeAnne's explosions that season. Weeks later, cameras rolled as she got into a battle with Tiffany and a passing trolley car.

Cary Deuber: LeeAnne came in real hot that night.

Tiffany Hendra: At that point there was so much stress and division in the group; it was Brandi, Stephanie, and Cary against LeeAnne, and the two groups just weren't talking. Marie was throwing a cocktail party, and LeeAnne and I were off talking with our friends who were there.

LeeAnne Locken: I wasn't going to go anywhere near Brandi and Stephanie and Cary if I didn't have to.

Tiffany Hendra: The problem is, at group events, producers want the cast interacting. So a producer came up to me and said, "This is ridiculous. LeeAnne hasn't even said hello to the girls. Can you bring her over?" And the second I did, Brandi started attacking her. I said to myself, "What the fuck did I just do?"

LeeAnne Locken: I just remember Brandi saying to me, "I'm supposed to address you as 'Miss' since you're older than me?" And I was like, "Oh, we're talking about age now?" That triggered me. And I just lost it. You know, I'm *really* good at losing it.

Tiffany Hendra: It all went downhill after that.

LeeAnne Locken: You have to remember, and this is not an excuse, but I was very drunk that night. I was drinking champagne nonstop, I probably had twelve glasses. I call those "art." A.R.T. Alcohol Related Trage-dies. I paint a lot of art in my life.

Sezin Cavusoglu: That's why you saw LeeAnne curb her drinking the rest of her time on the show. Because that particular incident was not helped by alcohol.

Tiffany Hendra: When LeeAnne stormed out, I was yelling after her, but she would not stop.

LeeAnne Locken: I didn't want to fight on camera, that's why I left. So I flipped her off.

Tiffany Hendra: You don't get to flip me off when I'm the one person who has defended your ass since the day I stepped foot on Dallas soil.

LeeAnne Locken: I said to her, "Thanks for having my back"—which I knew would piss her off, but I was really tired of being the pissed-off bitch all season long!

Tiffany Hendra: She was screaming, "It's your fault!" You know, blaming me. And I was simmering, like, "What the fuck?"

LeeAnne Locken: At some point, she pushed me. Which I don't really even remember.

Tiffany Hendra: That was very hard to watch. I literally couldn't believe it when I saw it back. I've always been a spitfire but you have to push me far to get like that.

LeeAnne Locken: I was more upset about the camera. Which is why finally I yelled, "Stop filming me" and pushed the camera. I had already asked them not to film me. In my world, if I tell you to stop filming me, that is your warning. You get one.

Tiffany Hendra: When she screamed, "Leave me alone"—and took her shoes off, hit that trolley, and walked across the street—I knew she needed to be left alone so she could cool off.

LeeAnne Locken: Here's the thing about Tiffany and me: we know how the other one works. You have a fucking blowup and you separate, you give yourself a twenty-four-hour cooling-down period, then you give yourself some time to process how you really feel. Then you have a text or a conversation about getting together. Then you have a get-together. Fight on Friday, break on Saturday, process on Sunday, Sunday night communicate, Monday lunch.

Tiffany Hendra: To this day, we're still best friends.

> *The same can't be said of LeeAnne and Marie, who were also close friends before filming began. The two had a massive falling-out toward the end of season 1. It was one of the most talked-about battles in the show's history, especially because most of it happened off camera, while on the cast trip to Austin.*

Andy Cohen: The amount of talk surrounding poop on *RHOD* is unparalleled and odd.

Sezin Cavusoglu: I really can't believe we're talking about this. But, okay. This story had been circulating that LeeAnne pooped her pants one time. It was her birthday and she wanted to look skinny, so she took laxatives. But then she drank a lot and had an accident and couldn't make it to the bathroom.

The cast members all heard it, and on the bus ride to Austin, Brandi and Stephanie brought it up.

Tiffany Hendra: It was a way to poke at LeeAnne and upset her. They wanted her to get mad.

Sezin Cavusoglu: LeeAnne shrugged it off, but she really held Marie responsible because she thought Marie was the one spreading that story.

Marie Reyes: It's funny, I didn't pick up that LeeAnne was upset with me. I had no clue what she was pissed about.

Sezin Cavusoglu: That night, LeeAnne confronted Marie.

Marie Reyes: I went down to the kitchen to get some water. As I was reaching into the fridge, LeeAnne came behind me and started screaming— and I mean, this was a blood-curdling scream.

LeeAnne Locken: I wasn't screaming. I was just talking really loud. But I was pissed as fuck!

Sezin Cavusoglu: Everybody else had gone to bed, so it was just the two of them. And LeeAnne kind of lost her mind on Marie.

LeeAnne Locken: I was hurt. And when I feel hurt, I use my words to hurt people back.

Marie Reyes: She threatened to kill me. She was screaming, "I'm going to kill you! How could you tell them!"

LeeAnne Locken: I told Marie, "I'm going to fucking kill you!" but I didn't mean that literally. For me that means, "You're dead to me. You don't exist."

Marie Reyes: LeeAnne felt like someone betrayed her. She felt like someone went to the enemy with this humiliating story. And she immediately thought it was me because I was the one who was nice to them.

LeeAnne Locken: The only people who knew that story were me, Tiffany, and Marie. I know Tiffany didn't say anything, I know I didn't say anything. The only person left was Marie.

Marie Reyes: Meanwhile, as LeeAnne is yelling at me, she's also charging at me. I dodged her at first and went in the other direction, with the island between us—we were basically running around the kitchen island, me being chased and her pursuing.

LeeAnne Locken: I was trying to have a conversation with her.

Marie Reyes: There was a large crystal bowl on the island that she picked up and slammed at me. She actually threw it at my chest, but she missed and it hit the edge of the island and shattered on the floor. I don't know how long the whole thing lasted. It felt like five minutes but it was probably more like ninety seconds!

Cary Deuber: I was upstairs and heard screaming, so I ran to the top of the stairs to see what was going on. I immediately thought, "Production is going to be so pissed they're not here." So that's why I whipped out my iPhone and started filming. Everyone else had their heads in their asses, but I'm a hard worker and knew they'd want this for the show. If only I knew anything about holding the phone horizontally at that time, instead of shooting it vertically!

Rich Bye: Cary didn't capture all of it so it wasn't conclusive as to what exactly had been said. The allegation was that LeeAnne, at one point, had picked up a shard of glass and held it across the kitchen island from Marie and threatened to slit her throat—which LeeAnne ended up denying.

LeeAnne Locken: Everyone was like, "We have you on tape telling Marie, 'I'm going to gut you, carnie-style.'" First of all, they didn't have it on tape or else they would have played it. And second of all, I have never in my life threatened to gut someone, let alone like a carnie. What does that even mean?

Cary Deuber: I don't know if LeeAnne was just wasted, but that definitely scared the absolute shit out of me.

Stephanie Hollman: There were no cameras and no producers there, which made it even scarier because you didn't know what could happen.

Cary Deuber: It's probably what prevented us from being friends that year and in season 2, too. I was like, "There's no way in hell I can be friends with someone who behaves that way."

LeeAnne Locken: I did apologize to Marie the next day.

Marie Reyes: LeeAnne apologized because production made her.

Rich Bye: The whole story line revolving around LeeAnne allegedly threatening Marie's life was a bit much for a *Housewives* franchise. It was too extreme. Even the motivation for that to happen—you know, LeeAnne shitting herself at a charity event—was totally beneath *Housewives*. It was too lowbrow.

> *Season 1 of* The Real Housewives of Dallas *premiered on Bravo on April 11, 2016. The eleven-episode season delivered big drama, but fans were highly critical of two major elements in the show's DNA.*

Sezin Cavusoglu: We got so much negative feedback about the charity element. Every episode had a charity event, and that was too much. There needed to be other reasons for these women to gather and spend time together.

Andy Cohen: It really turned off viewers. They just hated it.

Cary Deuber: I hated it, too! I love giving money to charities, but the charity gala scene, I don't find that super fulfilling. It's always the same twenty people.

LeeAnne Locken: We burned so many bridges in the charity scene that first season anyway, I don't think we *could* have spent much more time on it unless we all started our own charities. And that's all thanks to Brandi and Stephanie.

Tiffany Hendra: Brandi and Stephanie love talking about farting and shit.

Cary Deuber: They have a very juvenile sense of humor.

Stephanie Hollman: All that poop talk and fart jokes we were making, that was stuff I figured would never see the light of day. Yes, Brandi and I are playful people, but we were really just trying to make the cameramen laugh and annoy the producers. Why would they use stuff where we were being stupid and making poo jokes?

Marie Reyes: I remember people going, "Why are they always talking about charity and poop?" I mean, it was in every episode.

LeeAnne Locken: It was disgusting. And because of them and their prank at Mad Hatter's, my reputation in the charity world was ruined.

Sezin Cavusoglu: Oh my God. Yes. The Mad Hatter's Tea.

LeeAnne Locken: You have to understand, Mad Hatter's is the best charity event. It's an afternoon tea luncheon, but it's also a fashion show and a hat contest. Every year there's a theme and eight or nine categories you can compete in. It's just so fun. And it's attended by the who's who of Dallas.

Sezin Cavusoglu: That was a charity event that we were so proud to have gotten into. When we started filming the show, a lot of places shut us out. They did not want us to bring our cameras and our mess—their words, not mine. There were really big events in the Dallas charity calendar we couldn't shoot. So when we got permission to film at Mad Hatter's? We were ecstatic. That was a very big deal.

Shari Levine: We were over the moon. It epitomized Dallas society. Everyone of note was there. All dressed in their charity tea best, wearing crazy hats. You had to watch, and you had to smile. Perfect definition of a Housewife event.

Stephanie Hollman: Brandi and I wanted to make a little bit of a mockery of the event because it is really ridiculous that women spend so much money to go to an event where they wear these crazy hats and give themselves prizes. So Brandi joked, "I'm just gonna wear a shit hat."

LeeAnne Locken: I didn't even notice Brandi's hat when I saw it. When you looked at it in person, you didn't see the turds she had glued on it. I was like, "You look gorgeous" and kept going. The problem was, Brandi's turds started falling off her hat and she thought it would be funny to go to the bathroom and leave them on the sink where the other women were washing their hands. And women of a certain age in a certain generation do not find shit humor funny.

Sezin Cavusoglu: Brandi Redmond is a joker who always wants to say "Fuck you" to tradition, for lack of a better term. Her poop hat was a giant middle finger to Dallas society. But Brandi also knew the hat would get LeeAnne's ire. That's why she wore it, and why she then started putting the fake poop on LeeAnne's chair.

LeeAnne Locken: I still pay for it, even now. Women see me at Mad Hatter's, turn their back, and walk away. These are the same women who used to embrace me and say hello. Now, Brandi's response to that would be, "Who gives a fuck? They weren't your real friends." And maybe she's right. But you know what I used to have in Dallas? Respect. Her dog shit ruined that. And it's not just me, it's everyone. No one on our show is respected by anybody in Dallas anymore.

Stephanie Hollman: The city of Dallas hated us because of moments like that. Everybody here felt like we were going to make them look bad. But we're not on the show to represent all of Texas. We're just here for entertainment.

Rich Bye: We've since moved away from the potty humor and have encouraged Brandi and Stephanie to do practical jokes and find other ways to express their sense of humor.

Andy Cohen: Making those changes after season 1—dropping the charity element, changing up the humor—helped the show improve. It's rare you strike lightning on the first try. In *Dallas*'s case, it needed time to find its way.

The show also needed some new blood, and another casting search brought producers a few options, though none stood out as much as Kameron Westcott. The mother of two was married into one of Dallas's most prestigious families, though it was her love of all things pink that caught the eyes of producers.

Andy Cohen: Kameron was like a living, breathing Barbie doll.

Kameron Westcott (Housewife): The call from casting came and my heart kind of dropped because *Housewives* was my favorite TV show on the planet. I swear, I've watched every city. So it felt surreal to think they wanted *me* to be a part of it.

Stephanie Hollman: When Kameron joined the show I was like, "This girl is a walking *Saturday Night Live* skit." Because she would do these crazy facial expressions and she would get mad at the craziest things. I didn't know if she was pretending or if she was for real.

Kameron Westcott: People wrote me off as a dumb blonde in the beginning, but they don't realize that I'm actually laughing at myself. The producers misunderstood that in my first season. That's changed as they've gotten to know me and realized that I am, in fact, someone who is a lot more savvy than she seems.

> *The show also added D'Andra Simmons, who had already gone through casting for season 1. Back then it hadn't worked out, but this time around was a fit.*

Sezin Cavusoglu: Bringing in D'Andra and Kameron felt like no-brainers to us. They were grounded in Dallas in a way the other women weren't.

D'Andra Simmons (Housewife): I'm the only person on the cast who was actually born and raised in Dallas. I'm sixth generation. I'm old-school Dallas. I did have reservations about joining, but at the same time, I had to sit down with my husband and my mother and we'd kind of like weigh the pros and the cons. I know Andy loves my mother.

Andy Cohen: Who doesn't love Mama Dee?

Rich Bye: D'Andra's affluent, she swims in these high society circles. She's got a sharp tongue, and this unique relationship with her mother. Oh, and Bravo had seen her a year earlier, so I knew there was interest there. She kind of checked all the boxes.

Sezin Cavusoglu: We had looked at a lot of interesting other women before D'Andra, but it was important that there was an organic connection to the cast and D'Andra had that. She was connected to all the women in some way, and was good friends with LeeAnne.

LeeAnne Locken: I was really thrilled at the idea of D'Andra joining because I felt like, "Good, I'm going to have an ally."

D'Andra Simmons: It shocked people out of their seats when they found out I was going to do the show because they thought, "Why is D'Andra Simmons doing a *Real Housewives* show? She has standing in Dallas society. This show is controversial. Why would she do this?" But for me, it was a business decision. I had concerns, but I weighed the pros and cons and realized it would be good in the long run.

LeeAnne Locken: Oh please, there were no concerns. D'Andra was so excited to be a Housewife. She showed up at a party in one of our friends' backyard wearing a T-shirt that said HOUSEWIVES. That was before we even started filming!

There was one other casting decision made ahead of season 2. Though she was a founding Dallas Housewife, Tiffany wasn't asked to return.

Tiffany Hendra: I don't like the word "fired" because it implies I did something wrong, when I didn't do anything wrong.

Rich Bye: She didn't. Tiffany is such a sweet woman. But when we looked at our cast as a whole, it felt like we could move on without her.

LeeAnne Locken: I was really surprised when they said Tiffany wasn't coming back. I really thought after season 1 that they weren't going to ask *me* back because I was "dangerous."

Stephanie Hollman: I will say, to this day, Tiffany's always been very supportive. When she shows up at filming events, she's the biggest cheerleader. That doesn't always happen when people leave. Some people are very bitter, but she's never been that person. I really like her.

Though LeeAnne lost an ally when Tiffany left, she gained an unexpected one around the same time: before filming season 2, LeeAnne and Brandi buried the hatchet and formed a friendship—just as Brandi and Stephanie's bond fell apart.

LeeAnne Locken: After our first season was done airing, I ran into Brandi at the Hotel ZaZa one night; I guess she does a staycation there every year. She saw me and jumped in my lap screaming, "LeeAnne! I love you!" And all the bullshit between us just didn't seem to matter anymore. It never even got brought up! She was drunk, I was drunk, and we just laughed and had fun.

Stephanie Hollman: When season 1 came out, it was really hard for me. I did not know how to handle it. I internalized the negative reception in Dallas and didn't want to go out; didn't want to go to people's homes. And Brandi took it as if I was shutting her out and not wanting to be her friend.

LeeAnne Locken: Brandi befriended me after that. She started texting me and that's when she told me she and Stephanie weren't speaking.

Stephanie Hollman: I'm not exaggerating when I say that one day, Brandi just stopped talking to me. She would not answer my calls. It was the strangest thing.

Shari Levine: It always bothers me to watch friendships of convenience on *Housewives*. Nobody wants that in their own life, why would they want that on a TV show? I also think it's one reason why people become obsessed with the series. Trying to suss out the manipulations from the genuine. When people see something genuine, they just love it. It makes them love those people.

Kameron Westcott: I'll never forget, the first group filming I went to—it was Mark Deuber's birthday—and Brandi came in very upset, eyeing Stephanie down the whole time. There was a lot of awkwardness and we were all in the middle of this friendship storm.

Cary Deuber: At the same time LeeAnne and Brandi were getting close, I was really there for Stephanie. One day, when we weren't filming, I went to her house—which at the time was all the way out in fucking Irving; it took me forever to get there—and I brought her flowers and sat there while she cried to me about Brandi.

LeeAnne Locken: I really tried my best not to get involved. I had my own issues with Stephanie but wanted to be there for Brandi as a friend. Remember when we went to Cary's sushi party, and Stephanie told Brandi, "I really want to talk to you" and I was like, "Call her, that's what phones are for"? That was because Brandi told me, "I don't want to talk to Stephanie tonight. Please don't make me talk to her." I was sticking up for Brandi, as I would for any friend. You tell me you don't like tomatoes, trust me, there will never be a tomato on your plate. I'll pick them off for you. That's just who I am.

Cary Deuber: Was their friendship ever at risk of actually being lost, though? I mean, LeeAnne and I *thought* Brandi and Stephanie were really in a fight. But looking back on it now, I really believe there was no fight. They orchestrated it to have a story line, which is just sad.

LeeAnne Locken: Yeah . . . back then, I really believed my friendship with Brandi was real. Now I realize she was just trying to get me to attack Stephanie. I was being played.

Stephanie Hollman: It really wasn't put on for the show. We were having problems.

Andy Cohen: Brandi and Stephanie's friendship falling apart was a bummer for us because we love their friendship. It resonated as deeply as Bethenny and Jill for viewers, and was one of the foundations of the show. I was none too pleased to hear they weren't speaking.

Sezin Cavusoglu: If we weren't around, Brandi and Stephanie could have dragged their fight out for much, much longer. They wanted to reconcile, they just didn't know how to go about it. Us being there almost facilitated that. I was very proud of them for how fast they put it behind them.

These things can really drag on and it just brings the show down; you don't want to continue watching the same fight over and over again.

Stephanie Hollman: Looking back now, our fight was a good thing, because our friendship was based on hanging out with our husbands, drinking, and going on vacations. We'd never fought because there was never a situation where we would quarrel or disagree. And in season 1, we blindly agreed with everything the other said. That's what we thought friendship should be. We have a much healthier relationship now. Our disagreement in season 2 released us from that feeling that loyalty meant you always agree on stuff.

Kameron Westcott: But . . . Stephanie does always agree with Brandi. I mean, they are a package deal.

D'Andra Simmons: That's true. They protect each other. They only kind of went against each other with this fight; they've remained close since then.

LeeAnne Locken: Once they made up, Brandi wanted nothing to do with me. She realized she needed Stephanie for the show and she turned on me.

Ultimately, Kameron, D'Andra, and LeeAnne formed a tight threesome in season 2, and Kameron found herself in a battle against Brandi and Stephanie once the two were back together.

Kameron Westcott: I did have a preconceived notion about Brandi going into the show, but I really tried with her that first season. I was hoping we could be friends. But from the moment I met her, she was totally cold. I tried to talk to her and she gave me this smirk and brushed me off. It got to a point where I had to tell her, in Mexico, "I'm not okay with you burping in my face. I'm not okay with you putting your feet in my dish. I'm not okay with all this other gross stuff you've been doing." But she and Stephanie just laughed at me. They looked at me like, "You're the new girl. You'll go quick."

Stephanie Hollman: Kameron and I just rubbed each other the wrong way. I've always been the kind of person who hates rules and society, and she loves rules and society. I like being goofy and inappropriate, she doesn't. And Kameron, she felt like my attitude was a big slap in the face to everything she stood for. She felt attacked.

Kameron Westcott: Felt attacked? I *was* attacked. They literally chased me around with a dildo.

LeeAnne Locken: Brandi and Stephanie always find someone to pick on. They make a game out of it, that's just what they do.

Kameron Westcott: I was actually upset about the dildo thing, and uncomfortable. I've never been around behavior like that in my whole life. Not even in college. I grew up sheltered, and my girlfriends and I don't talk about that stuff. It was not something I wanted to be seen with on national television.

LeeAnne Locken: I remember being on the boat saying to Brandi and Stephanie, "Listen, you know she doesn't like this dildo. I get that Brandi is drinking and thinks this is funny, but then Stephanie, you need to be sober enough to tell your best friend to stop." But as I was trying to have that conversation, they started playing tug-of-war with the fucking dildo.

Kameron Westcott: I literally was crying to a producer, saying, "I can't be around this. Those girls are trashy." I was such a diva. And I didn't know the cameras were there, which was my fault. But Brandi was hanging off the boat swinging around a dildo. I mean, it *was* trashy!

Perhaps no one had a tougher time that season than Cary, who fought against insidious claims about her marriage and her husband's sexuality.

Cary Deuber: In season 1, when questions about Mark's sexuality came up, he was like, "This is so stupid. Are you joking me?" He laughed it off at first—like, "Yeah, I'm well dressed and I look good. Fuck off!" And it didn't bother me, because I love him, I love that he's stylish, he looks good, and he fucks me every single day, so it's not like I was concerned.

Mark Deuber (Househusband): I'm very confident in my sexuality and my love of fashion. The gay jokes, they don't bother me because I know they're not true.

Cary Deuber: But it took a turn when it started negatively affecting our kids, who were in high school at the time. They got bullied and taunted. So Mark came on the season 1 reunion to defend himself. He was like, "This is a 1970s stereotype that we have to get over." He turned it into a teachable moment. But once my costars realized we weren't really upset about the gay rumors, the story became, "Well, how did Mark and Cary *really* get together?" And Mark and I were very honest. We worked together prior to dating. There was no cheating, we didn't have an affair. We were friends. I was dating guys like Lance Armstrong and Derek Jeter, and after Mark's marriage ended, we fell in love. That's the truth. But all of a sudden I was being called a homewrecker.

LeeAnne Locken: Several people told me that. I only brought it up because Cary agitated me. She had a tendency to talk down to me, and I just cut her off at her ankles.

Cary Deuber: LeeAnne didn't seem to like me from the jump. The first season, I got close to Brandi and Stephanie instead. I cared about them. I thought they cared about me. But I've since come to find out they didn't.

LeeAnne Locken: They didn't, because Brandi—in season 2, while she was acting like *my* friend—was talking major shit about Cary and doing everything she could to get me to go against her. And that's how the whole "they're just hands" things came out. . . .

LeeAnne is referring to one of the Real Housewives of Dallas's *most infamous scenes, in which LeeAnne told Brandi that Mark had been involved in sexual activities with men at a local gay bar called the Round-Up—and then compared her hands to knives.*

LeeAnne Locken: Oh Lord. Okay . . . here's what happened. I was getting my boobs done and Rich couldn't drive me to the surgery. That's why Brandi "took" me. And in retrospect, I should never have agreed to that. Because if Brandi wasn't there, I never would have had that monologue. You see, the doctors told me to take a diazepam at home so that when I got to the surgery center, I would be calm and relaxed. Well, I did that, but during the car ride, Brandi brought up all this shit Cary had been saying to discredit my doctor. She agitated me the whole time, so by the time I arrived, they said, "You're going to have to take another one." And that just put me over the edge. I was gone by that point.

Rich Bye: LeeAnne had been given the goofy juice.

LeeAnne Locken: I wasn't just goofy, I was *gone*! On Valium, I would have done anything. You could have convinced me to fuck a donkey. I mean, I was out of it. By the time I was doing that soliloquy, I was not even present. I saw the footage and I was like, "Oh my God, did I fucking say that?"

Rich Bye: That audio is the fucking best. That moment behind the closed door at her plastic surgeon's office? "I don't need knives, I've got my hands." That is insane.

LeeAnne Locken: Never in my life have I ever said, "They're not knives, they're just hands." What fucking normal human says that? No normal human! I don't even remember saying it, I was on two diazepam. And I don't do drugs. I've never done illegal drugs.

Andy Cohen: She did say it. And it was iconic.

Rich Bye: Honestly, it was like listening to a serial killer. There was a cold detachment in the tenor and tone of what she said, in addition to the words themselves, that literally put chills up my spine.

LeeAnne Locken: Mine too! It was freaky!

Cary Deuber: Later, Brandi called and proceeded to tell me that LeeAnne had threatened to kill me, and she told me the stuff she said about Mark at the Round-Up.

LeeAnne Locken: I was never planning on saying anything about the Round-Up on the show. I had heard the rumor, but it wasn't something I was going to repeat.

Cary Deuber: She has apologized profusely. And I've forgiven her.

Mark Deuber: We both have.

LeeAnne Locken: And that means everything to me. I apologized to them both and prayed every night that they'd forgive me and that we could move forward. I never brushed it off. I never told either of them to just "get over it." I've always listened and told them every time, "What I did was horrible. I'm sorry."

Cary Deuber: And the thing is, at the time, I thought Brandi was looking out for me by calling and telling me what LeeAnne had done. But looking back on it, it's clear Brandi provoked LeeAnne. She was just as much a part of that conversation, if not more so, because LeeAnne was on something.

Kameron Westcott: Oh, it was a total setup put upon by Brandi. Watch it back, it all seemed to come out of nowhere, completely.

LeeAnne Locken: A producer told me that Brandi walked out of that room and went right up to them and said, "Please tell me you got all that." She knew exactly what she was doing.

Cary Deuber: Do I think LeeAnne's innocent? No. Those words, "The hands and knives" shit, that was her. LeeAnne doesn't sugarcoat stuff and when she feels a certain way, she'll tell you. But I know damn well that Brandi's not innocent, either.

Kameron Westcott: I feel bad for LeeAnne, because after that, those girls were like, "LeeAnne's too dangerous to film with, she wanted to kill Cary." When that's not what was happening at all.

LeeAnne Locken: Brandi plays innocent, like I'm fully responsible for trying to hurt Cary, but if you remember, she was the one who said that Cary was the nanny to Mark's children before they started dating. That wasn't me.

Cary Deuber: That's when Brandi crossed the line for me. She came over to my house the night the first season of *Potomac* premiered. While she was there, she talked to my stepdaughter, who was probably fifteen at the time, and asked her how long she'd known me. My stepdaughter said, "A long time. She used to babysit when she worked for my dad." That was all true, but Brandi completely warped it into this story that I was the nanny when I started dating Mark. It was not true, and my stepdaughter was absolutely wrecked about that. She's gone to therapy for it, and Brandi's never apologized, not once.

To help clear things up, Mark once again returned to the reunion stage— though his appearance this time around was a surprise to the entire cast.

Mark Deuber: I was highly reluctant to show up at the season 2 reunion. But I got a whole mess of phone calls from a whole lot of people at the production company and executive level, all encouraging me to be there.

Kameron Westcott: None of us knew Mark was coming. When he showed up, that was just a total shock.

Mark Deuber: One of my requirements, if I were to show up, was that no one could know about it. I said, "You're going to make it a surprise. If I catch wind that anyone knows I'm there, that's the end of it; I'm not going to step foot on that stage."

Cary Deuber: Yup. We were sick of losing. They would all plot and plan, and we didn't want anyone to plan.

Mark found redemption at the reunion, but LeeAnne wasn't as lucky. Her "they're just hands" comments once again led the women into a discussion about whether LeeAnne was threatening her costars with violence. Smashing a glass during a heated exchange at Brandi's winter white party didn't help, either. . . .

LeeAnne Locken: Did you ever ask yourself how I got that glass in the first place? Because the Brandi Land party, if you remember, was a "no glass allowed" event. We were all given plastic drinkware.

Rich Bye: You know, LeeAnne says that a producer gave that glass to her and told her to throw it. I don't know if that's true or not. It could be. But It did lead to one of the funniest lines of that whole season, or of any season, when Kameron turns to Brandi and says, "Oh, this is why you have plastic."

LeeAnne Locken: Of course, it blew up in my face. It became, "LeeAnne's crazy! LeeAnne's dangerous!"

Kameron Westcott: The whole thing was so incredibly ridiculous. Later, Brandi, Stephanie, and Cary confronted LeeAnne, saying they were scared of her.

D'Andra Simmons: They were all talking about LeeAnne being a dangerous person. And at first, I supported LeeAnne, but then her acting out was getting more and more concerning. I remember saying, "I'm so sorry, guys. I was friends with this person and she never acted like this, all the years I knew her." She became a completely different person.

Cary Deuber: I bought into the "LeeAnne is dangerous" narrative for a while but after the season 2 reunion, I was kind of like, "You know what? Something stinks with this and I don't think it's necessarily all LeeAnne." If LeeAnne was going to kill me, she would have. It wasn't adding up.

D'Andra Simmons: LeeAnne would try to one-up the last extreme situation with another extreme situation. And at some point you're going to run out of extreme situations. And then what's next? Physical violence. That's why they were scared of her.

LeeAnne Locken: The whole thing was bullshit. I was never going to hurt anyone. They all decided to come together and say they were afraid of me because they thought that would get me off the show.

Rich Bye: Were they scared of her or were they just trying to get rid of her? If I'm being honest, it was a combination.

> *In season 3—big surprise—LeeAnne was once again in the hot seat, this time with a surprising adversary: D'Andra.*

Kameron Westcott: LeeAnne and D'Andra, in season 2, were inseparable. They were best friends. I followed them around like a third wheel— which I was okay with because I loved their friendship. I thought it was so special.

Stephanie Hollman: D'Andra would always tell LeeAnne how it was, which I did appreciate. She held her feet to the fire.

Kameron Westcott: It made me really sad when they became enemies, but there was something different about D'Andra that third season. I don't know if she was going through some personal stuff, but she kept getting really upset and emotional over the smallest things.

Stephanie Hollman: D'Andra and LeeAnne, they're both alphas. There was always a bit of competition between them. And after D'Andra's first season, she wanted to stand out more. She didn't want to be LeeAnne's sidekick.

D'Andra Simmons: Our friendship started unraveling because LeeAnne thought I was going to be a doormat and she would be my protector.

LeeAnne Locken: D'Andra was insanely jealous of me. Her mother used to tell her all the time, "LeeAnne is the star of that show. You'll never be the star of that show." She'd say that in front of me!

Cary Deuber: Oh please, they all were in a fight for the crown. Every one of them on the show. Except me, honestly. I was the only one not fighting.

The alleged cold war between LeeAnne and D'Andra turned into a behind-the-scenes battle that fans never got to see. It happened during the girls' trip to Kameron's family vacation home in Beaver Creek, Colorado, well after the cameras went down for the evening.

Kameron Westcott: It was, like, two a.m. and we were all sitting in front of the fire, drinking and laughing together in our pajamas.

LeeAnne Locken: This was the conversation that Brandi claimed was about who was the "queen bee." But that's not at all what we were talking about. D'Andra said, "The show didn't qualify to be a *Housewives* show until I joined the cast." Like Cary, Brandi, Stephanie, and I weren't enough. And the second she said that, I said, "Really, bitch? How do you think you even got to be on the show?" That's what we really fought about.

Cary Deuber: It was a nasty fight.

There was another argument between LeeAnne and D'Andra that traced back to the Beaver Creek trip. It had to do with a shopping trip D'Andra and Brandi went on together. . . .

Kameron Westcott: A lot of stores give us free gifts if we film there. So in this case, D'Andra and Brandi went shopping, and when they rang it up D'Andra's bill was like, three thousand dollars or something. And she was like, "Oh God, I didn't know I was going to actually buy stuff."

D'Andra Simmons: My mother had made some bad decisions and I had been funding her company with my own money. I was having to live on a very small amount of money to keep the business going. So I was watching my spending, and when we got home I said to LeeAnne, "I had to put it on my business card because I literally have two hundred dollars in my bank account until I get paid"—which was like, three days from then. And LeeAnne went and told Cary, who she didn't even like and who she wasn't even getting along with, what I said.

LeeAnne Locken: It was spun like I was making fun of D'Andra for what she had in the bank. And I blame Brandi for that whole thing because Brandi told me D'Andra was *crying* after they went shopping. Brandi said she had to go back into the store and return all the stuff for D'Andra.

D'Andra Simmons: That two-hundred-dollar thing was humiliating to me. And that's not because I was embarrassed to have two hundred dollars in my bank account—plenty of people have that amount in theirs. It was just, having been a socialite, having raised a lot of money, having lived in the nicest part of Dallas, and having always had the means, I didn't want people in Dallas to know the situation I was in.

> In the wake of the two-hundred-dollar controversy, D'Andra made a shocking allegation against LeeAnne and her now husband Rich, insinuating he might be having an affair.

D'Andra Simmons: I swear, I was not getting LeeAnne back about the two-hundred-dollar comment at all. What happened was, production and Bravo somehow knew that Rich had been unfaithful to LeeAnne.

Rich Bye: We "somehow knew" because D'Andra told one of our producers about Rich's infidelity on an open mic and at that point it was "out there." D'Andra then chose to bring it into the show because she truly believed it was a big factor behind LeeAnne's stalled wedding plans and she wanted to make sure LeeAnne was making the best life choice. It was not a petty payback for LeeAnne's assertion that D'Andra only had two hundred dollars in her bank account.

LeeAnne Locken: First of all, Rich was never unfaithful to me, point blank, period. And second of all, even if production told her that, no one put a gun to her head to go on television and lie about me.

D'Andra Simmons: I was filming with Brandi, and producers wanted us to talk about why LeeAnne's wedding wasn't happening. So I said, "I am not going to talk about the fact that Rich has been having affairs for ten years and he has lots of girlfriends."

Rich Bye: Once D'Andra brought that allegation in front of the cameras, that was it for LeeAnne. And regardless of what D'Andra said or did from that point on, LeeAnne was done.

To the surprise of no one, things between LeeAnne and D'Andra didn't get better in season 4.

LeeAnne Locken: Brandi and Stephanie tried to stage an "Friendtervention" at the top of the season to get D'Andra and me back on track, and the whole time, D'Andra talked down to me.

D'Andra Simmons: LeeAnne was never going to ever be friends with me again. And she 100 percent tried to get me kicked off the show by not inviting me to any wedding events. She thought if she didn't invite me then I would be irrelevant and I wouldn't be asked back.

LeeAnne Locken: Why would I invite her to my wedding? She was still going around saying that Rich cheats! And if I invited her to a single party leading up to my wedding, I would have had to invite her to my wedding. And I wasn't going to do that. "Come to my bachelorette party! Come to my bridal shower! But don't come to my wedding"?

D'Andra Simmons: By the way, I wasn't pissed about not being involved in her wedding. In fact, I was so thrilled I didn't have to go. I was like, "I do not want any part of this shit show at all."

Season 4 was also where the decision was made to move Cary to a Friend role. In her place, Kary Brittingham, a married mother of four originally from Guadalajara, Mexico, wound up being the show's first Mexican cast member.

Rich Bye: With Kary, we had a desire to add more fun to the show. Many of Kary's good friends are women in their twenties, so she parties like a twenty-year-old. We thought she could inject some levity into the series.

Sezin Cavusoglu: And to finally have a Mexican woman on the show felt important.

Rich Bye: Texas is, I think, 40 percent Hispanic, so it was important to have a Mexican American represented on *The Real Housewives of Dallas*.

Kary was introduced on the show as a friend of D'Andra's. And like D'Andra, she soon found herself at odds with LeeAnne.

LeeAnne Locken: I wasn't open to Kary Brittingham in the beginning because I knew she was D'Andra's friend and wasn't interested in being mine.

Kary Brittingham (Housewife): I came in with a completely open mind about everyone. The only thing I knew was that D'Andra and LeeAnne had a falling-out, but I'm my own person and make up my own opinions.

LeeAnne Locken: D'Andra was pressuring Kary to go against me, and so were the producers. And apparently when we were in Mexico, they asked her to go against me.

Kary Brittingham: That's true. Production wanted me to go talk to her for not wanting to share a room with me, but I didn't because that didn't bother me. Still, while we were there, LeeAnne complained the whole time. "The drive is too long, I don't climb up these stairs because I don't work out, I don't want to do this." I mean, everything was just Debbie Downer.

LeeAnne Locken: The whole time we were in Mexico, I kept waiting for Kary to come for me. And she didn't waste time.

Kary Brittingham: I was trying to have a good time with LeeAnne on that trip but she was constantly separating herself. And then she'd play the victim and say, "You guys are outcasting me." No, you were outcasting yourself!

Kary Brittingham: She was doing it to put herself in the spotlight. Whenever there were any group scenes and we were all talking about something, Lee-Anne would try to make it about LeeAnne. She'd one-up you. I'd say, "I had a tough childhood, my mom was an alcoholic." And then LeeAnne would go, "I understand. My mom wasn't an alcoholic, but I was raped." It was like, "Wow, that's a lot!" And it's not that I don't want to hear about these things and connect with people that way, but LeeAnne always wanted to have a bigger story than you.

Troubles between LeeAnne and Kary only built throughout the season, and racially insensitive language LeeAnne used to describe Kary had RHOD costars and fans alike questioning whether there was prejudice at play.

Rich Bye: Calling Kary a "chirpy Mexican," or that moment in Bangkok where LeeAnne thumped her chest and said, "I'm a big strong Mexican"— these weren't isolated incidents.

Stephanie Hollman: I did not think the times when LeeAnne used that language would air.

Sezin Cavusoglu: LeeAnne had been saying, "They'll cut that out," which is very troubling. The field team, they caught wind of it, and when they saw the bigger picture forming, they saw it was really ugly and felt it needed to be addressed.

Kameron Westcott: I 100 percent thought this would never make it on the show. People have asked, "Is that because LeeAnne did worse things we never saw?" No, that's not it. Everything LeeAnne has ever done, they've aired. This instance just felt like it was so bad, I figured there was no way they would use it—not to protect LeeAnne, but to protect *Kary*.

Kary Brittingham: If she said those things and they protected her by not airing them, that would be worse. That would be protecting a person who is racist.

Rich Bye: Kary wasn't fully aware of what was happening until Kameron told her at the finale.

Kameron Westcott: LeeAnne had said some things to me that I thought, if I didn't say something, people might think I'm okay with that language, and I'm not.

Kary Brittingham: Walking into that finale party, I was thinking, "Oh, this will be funny, we're going to have a toast and say goodbye and maybe next season, me and LeeAnne will get along." And then all of a sudden Kameron was like, "I have to tell you what LeeAnne's been saying about you."

Kameron Westcott: I also grabbed LeeAnne and told her, because I realized, "I have to get this out so she can apologize to Kary."

LeeAnne Locken: Kameron told me what I had said and I was like, "I don't get it." I didn't get what I did wrong. I didn't see that calling her a Mexican was hurtful right away. You have to understand that in Texas, that sort of jargon is commonplace. Someone will say, "Do you have a good cleaning lady?" "Yes, I've got this amazing Mexican housekeeper!" That's part of the culture of the South, to speak like that. But that night at the party, straight to Kary's face, I said, "I'm sorry. I'm sorry. I hope you can accept my apology." And she said, "No, I don't."

Kary Brittingham: It wasn't a sincere apology, in my eyes. LeeAnne had been coming at me all season and I thought the only reason she was saying she was sorry in that moment was because she was caught, not because she really understood what she did.

LeeAnne Locken: What else could I do in that moment? I just walked away.

The season 4 reunion wound up being one of the tensest reunions in Housewives *history, as Kary confronted LeeAnne for her words.*

LeeAnne Locken: We didn't see the final episodes until days before the reunion. That's when I saw that what I said was being presented in edit as if I was racist.

Rich Bye: LeeAnne knew this was going to be in the show. We do confessional interviews after we wrap principal, so knowing this was a story line, we were doing interviews with her where she said she wasn't racist because she sat in Julio Iglesias's lap and had slept with a lot of Latin men. It was like, "Are you kidding me? You know this accusation is going to be in the show and then you're giving interviews saying these kinds of things?"

Sezin Cavusoglu: She did not think it was a big deal.

LeeAnne Locken: In my eyes, Kary had called herself Mexican time and time again. It was something she was really proud of, and I thought, "I'm going to take what you think is the best part of you and use it against you." I thought I was just mimicking her and using her words against her.

Kary Brittingham: I was blindsided when I saw the show. I truly was thinking, "There's no way people are going to be racist about somebody who's Mexican." I didn't think that was really still a thing. And I have no problem with someone saying something like, "You're Mexican, you can drink a lot of tequila." Yes, that's true! But the way she said it, calling me a "yappy Chihuahua" and a "chirpy Mexican," I was shocked.

LeeAnne Locken: It was only after watching the episodes that I understood the gravity of what I had said. And I was heartbroken that I hurt Kary that way. So going into the reunion taping, I knew I would have to address this issue. What I didn't know is that I would spend the entire reunion being attacked for everything I did.

Andy Cohen: She lied a lot during that reunion. The lying is really what stuck out to me.

LeeAnne Locken: Andy fought me on everything I said. He always had a response. I believe that the direction was coming from Sezin and Rich Bye, who were talking in Andy's earpiece, because there were things he said he would have never known. Like, I said, "My mom had a great time at my wedding, she was there the entire time." And Andy was like, "No, she wasn't, she left at such and such time." I should have said, "Let's get my mom on the phone right now and ask her!" Instead, I looked like I was just lying.

Andy Cohen: She's right. There were things she was saying that production knew were untrue, and they told me. It was a wall of lies.

Rich Bye: At a certain point, LeeAnne's lies just got so tiresome. There was a collective feeling in the control room of, "Oh my God, just tell the truth! It would be much easier for you!"

D'Andra Simmons: LeeAnne had gotten away with so much for so long, people were sick of it. That's why Andy kept calling out her lies.

LeeAnne Locken: People thought I wasn't defending myself because I knew I was guilty but the reality was, I knew I wasn't going to win. By the time we got around to the Kary conversation, I was so broken, I knew there was nothing I could say that was going to satisfy anyone. And they just came at me, one by one, calling me a racist.

D'Andra Simmons: At that point, we all knew that she had done something that was probably irreversible and she was going to lose her job, so we had to have strong opinions about it.

LeeAnne Locken: It felt like they were using this as a chance to push me off the show once and for all. It was the culmination of them poking at me for all these years.

Kary Brittingham: That wasn't it for me. I was hurt. When I was at the reunion and I watched all the things she said about me cut together, that really hit me. You have to remember, I didn't see those comments until days before coming to the reunion. It was all very raw.

Stephanie Hollman: I'm still very torn by this whole thing. I feel bad for LeeAnne but at the same time, those were her words.

D'Andra Simmons: LeeAnne had said so many horrible things about so many different groups of people that would qualify as being racist. I've heard them over the years. And whether or not you want to call what she said about Kary racist, it was disrespectful and it was crossing a line.

Kameron Westcott: I would stand by LeeAnne any day. She made a mistake but she's not a racist. I know that. Everyone makes mistakes. This was a horrible one. But I will always love her.

Kary Brittingham: And see, I do think she's racist. And the only reason I still believe that is because even after she apologized to me, I *still* see her on Twitter being like, "Me and Kary are the same race." I have never seen her respond to anybody saying, "I made a mistake. I am so sorry."

LeeAnne Locken: Technically, Kary and I are the same race. We are both Caucasian. Her nationality is Mexican. I did not make fun of her ethnicity. I did not make fun of her nationality. I just repeated the word she said. Regardless, I recognize my words were unacceptable. My behavior was ignorant.

Season 4 wound up being LeeAnne's last as a Housewife.

Rich Bye: Every season leading up to season 4, we discussed doing the show without LeeAnne. Several Bravo executives were not big fans. But Andy and I always argued for bringing her back because she makes great television.

Andy Cohen: She was always on an island, but in the past I had wanted her to stay. I thought she was good on the show. There was something a bit menacing about her. She reminded me of Danielle Staub, in the sense that she had a rough life and had been through some really dark, unthinkable hardships.

Sezin Cavusoglu: But at the end of season 4, it felt like it all got to a really unpleasant place.

Andy Cohen: There was no remorse there. She did a very poor job falling on her sword about the Mexican comments or even understanding any of it.

LeeAnne Locken: The truth is, there was no way I could do another season with that cast. The trust was completely gone with all of us.

Andy Cohen: This is what no one knows: she said during the reunion that she had been suicidal during production. When she said that, I was like, "She should not be on the show." That really closed the door for me. I just thought, it would be irresponsible of us to put her in this environment, if it is a challenge to her mental health and will do her harm.

LeeAnne Locken: I agree! It had gotten incredibly difficult for me, especially that last season. I really struggled, anyone could see it.

Stephanie Hollman: It's hard to be a part of this franchise. As much as it was fun for her at first, I don't think it was the healthiest for her.

Kary Brittingham: To be honest with you, I didn't want LeeAnne to get fired. I thought she could have learned from her mistakes and that she deserved a chance to show people she had grown.

Rich Bye: I will say, we owe LeeAnne a lot. She was incredibly important to this franchise.

Stephanie Hollman: I will never take away LeeAnne's legacy on the show. LeeAnne honestly made *Dallas* a lot of what it is today. I even told this to Andy Cohen; she made moments that are so memorable and iconic.

LeeAnne Locken: Andy said that, too, on his radio show—which meant a lot considering he had said on *Watch What Happens Live* at one point that I was vile and disgusting. When I heard him saying all these nice things about me after my exit I was like, "That actually makes me feel good."

Amid LeeAnne's exit, a video from Brandi's past resurfaced that found the now reality star mocking Asians. The clip, and the public outrage that resulted from it, put Brandi's position on the show in question.

Sezin Cavusoglu: Brandi had posted this video on her Instagram Story three years earlier. And it was on her social media for a very short time;

I hadn't seen it. Our press team hadn't even seen it! But basically, Brandi was being made fun of for having squinty eyes and she made this video, making fun of that by mimicking an Asian accent.

D'Andra Simmons: When it came up again, Brandi had been answering people on social media and arguing with them, telling them it was funny. It just got her into more trouble.

Rich Bye: To my knowledge, there were never any discussions about whether Brandi's video would impact her role. Remember, Brandi styles herself a comedian. She's always doing impressions. In this particular instance, she was doing an impression of one of the comedians from *In Living Color* and made a very misguided and unthoughtful attempt to be funny by indulging in racial and cultural stereotypes. But her intention was not to hurt, it was just a very bad, uninformed, unenlightened decision.

Sezin Cavusoglu: This was also a stand-alone incident, whereas LeeAnne had repeated her words multiple times.

> In the end, Brandi kept her spot on the show, and she was joined by a new Housewife. Dr. Tiffany Moon—an anesthesiologist, wife, and mother to twin girls—stepped into LeeAnne's spot as a full-time Housewife.

Sezin Cavusoglu: Tiffany is incredibly accomplished. She graduated from Cornell when she was nineteen, went on to get her medical degree, and is now a very in-demand anesthesiologist at UT Southwest. When we were casting her, we obviously had no idea she was going to be a frontline worker during the biggest health crisis of our time. So I was really proud we had her point of view on our show.

D'Andra Simmons: She's also fabulously stylish and is a *really* good fighter. She's very articulate, makes great points, and has a tone that will slice you up and lay down. She wasn't going to take any bullshit from anyone!

> Of course, there was something else that had a major impact on season 5: the coronavirus pandemic.

Sezin Cavusoglu: We put together protocols so that everyone could do their jobs safely, following the lead of the CDC, the governors, the mayors, and NBC's own guidelines. And the cast and crew were really vigilant about following those.

Stephanie Hollman: Bravo tried to keep us very safe, which I appreciated. We were tested constantly, we had to wear a mask constantly, we had to social distance—which felt really stupid because once we'd get to the restaurant, we'd take our masks off and would be right beside each other anyway.

Sezin Cavusoglu: It was certainly a different season. You don't see them eating out a lot. Instead, there were a lot of pool parties. We had to gather in places they could have exclusively to themselves, like private dining rooms or places that offered private tours.

Stephanie Hollman: I have to be honest, I didn't hate it. There was something freeing about it. Part of *Housewives* is getting glammed up to go to these big events or extravagant trips, and in this case, we really got to let our hair down and spend time with each other.

Rich Bye: Season 5 wound up being much looser. The tone was much lighter. It was freeing. They had a lot of fun. There were hilarious antics and light hijinks, which I loved. That's classic *Dallas*.

The Tagline Catalog

REAL HOUSEWIVES OF ATLANTA

Cynthia Bailey
"I know how to work it, and be seen." (Seasons 3 and 4)
"Beauty fades, class is forever." (Season 5)
"My business is beauty, and I'm the boss." (Season 6)
"Life is about choices—and I choose Cynthia." (Season 7)
"Seasons may change, but Cynthia Bailey never goes out of style." (Season 8)
"Life is a runway, and Cynthia Bailey is ready to walk it alone." (Season 9)
"Age is just a number, but these cheekbones are timeless!" (Season 10)
"I age like fine wine, and now, I am ready to chill." (Season 11)
"The only time that I look back is to see how far I've come." (Season 12)

Kandi Burruss
"I have fame and fortune, and I've earned it." (Seasons 3 and 4)
"I may be small, but my empire keeps on growing." (Season 5)
"Music may be my passion, but family is forever." (Season 6)
"I'm not about the drama. Don't start none, won't be none." (Season 7)
"I'm a hitmaker, and this year I will reveal the best one." (Season 8)
"Now that I've got my ace, I have a full house." (Season 9)
"Don't mess with the boss, 'cause you might get fired!" (Season 10)
"I count my blessings—and my checks!" (Season 11)
"Don't check for me unless you got a check for me." (Season 12)

Shamari DeVoe
"I may be an open book, but that does not mean I am easily read." (Season 11)

Kim Fields
"Faith, family, and career—those are the facts of my life." (Season 8)

Claudia Jordan
"Don't hate me because I'm beautiful. Hate me because I'm here to stay." (Season 7)

NeNe Leakes
"I don't keep up with the Joneses. I am the Joneses." (Seasons 1 and 2)
"When I walk into the room, I own it." (Seasons 3 and 4)
"I have arrived, and the spotlight is on me, honey." (Season 5)
"Success is in my DNA. When one door closes, another one opens." (Season 6)

"Why be so nasty and so rude—when I can be so fierce and so successful?" (Season 7)

"Ten years in the game, and I'm still the tastiest peach in Atlanta!" (Season 10)

"I am the glue for my wig and my family!" (Season 11)

"I'm on a spiritual journey and still traveling first class." (Season 12)

Eva Marcille

"I live a model life, now I'm ready to be a top wife." (Season 11)

"I'm living my dreams, not above my means." (Season 12)

Kenya Moore

"I won Miss USA, not Miss Congeniality." (Season 5)

"People may think they have me figured out, but I am always the wild card." (Season 6)

"People get exhausted trying to figure me out. And I just let them." (Season 7)

"Don't come for me, unless I twirl for you." (Season 8)

"I give the people what they want, and they always want more." (Season 9)

"While some were saying 'I can't,' I was saying 'I do!'" (Season 10)

Phaedra Parks

"I'm the ultimate Southern belle. I get what I want." (Seasons 3 and 4)

"I'm a Southern belle. Brains, booty, and all business." (Season 5)

"A true Southern belle knows her worth, and I am priceless." (Season 6)

"When it comes to my family, I'm the judge and the jury." (Season 7)

"Only God can judge me, and he seems quite impressed." (Season 8)

"You can't always get what you want, but I can." (Season 9)

DeShawn Snow

"I always knew I was destined for greatness." (Season 1)

Shereé Whitfield

"People are intimidated by my success." (Seasons 1 and 2)

"I like things that are elegant and sophisticated, just like me." (Seasons 3 and 4)

"Don't call it a comeback . . . call it a takeover." (Season 9)

"Call me a bad server, because I always spill the tea!" (Season 10)

Porsha Williams

"People say I have a picture-perfect life, and I do." (Season 5)

"I am still standing, and I am making my own rules." (Season 6)

"I'm about to give you life, so stay out of my way!" (Season 8)

"I'm too blessed to be stressed and too sexy to be thirsty." (Season 9)

"Friends come and go, but family is forever." (Season 10)

"I took a left turn, but now, things are just right." (Season 11)

"This phoenix has risen and I'm saying bye, ashes!" (Season 12)

Lisa Wu

"If it doesn't make me money, I don't do it." (Seasons 1 and 2)

Kim Zolciak-Biermann

"In Atlanta, money and class do give you power." (Seasons 1 and 2)

"People call me a gold digger, but they just want what I have." (Seasons 3 and 4)
"I asked, believed, and I received." (Season 5)

THE REAL HOUSEWIVES OF BEVERLY HILLS

Taylor Armstrong
"It may look like I have it all, but I want more." (Season 1)
"I finally found my voice, and I'm not afraid to use it." (Season 2)
"I fought too hard for this zip code to go home now." (Season 3)

Garcelle Beauvais
"Life is an audition and, honey, I am getting that part." (Season 10)

Eileen Davidson
"I'm not a bitch, but I've played one on TV." (Season 5)
"I may be an actress, but that doesn't mean I'll stick to your script." (Season 6)
"I speak no evil, but I see and hear everything." (Season 7)

Kathryn Edwards
"My advice: speak your mind and carry a good handbag." (Season 6)

Carlton Gebbia
"In my world, money doesn't talk, it swears." (Season 4)

Erika Girardi
"I'm an enigma, wrapped in a riddle, and cash." (Season 6)
"I may be two people, but I'm not two-faced." (Season 7)
"Some people call me cold, but that's not ice—it's diamonds." (Season 8)
"Most people talk about their fantasies; I'm living mine." (Season 9)
"Break a leg? Not in these heels, honey." (Season 10)

Joyce Giraud de Ohoven
"You can never be too young, too thin, or too honest." (Season 4)

Brandi Glanville
"Money doesn't give you class, it just gives you money." (Season 3)
"In Beverly Hills, the higher you climb, the farther you fall." (Season 4)
"I'd rather spend my life kicking ass than kissing it." (Season 5)

Camille Grammer
"It's time for me to come out of my husband's shadow and shine." (Season 1)
"Diamonds aren't a girl's best friend—freedom is." (Season 2)

Yolanda Hadid
"I like to have fun, but I don't play games." (Season 3)
"Don't tell me you're my friend, act like one." (Season 4)
"Character isn't what you have, it's who you are." (Season 5)
"Fake friends believe rumors, real friends believe in you." (Season 6)

Dorit Kemsley
"When you've traveled the world, you can speak in any accent you want."
(Season 7)

"I believe in an excess of everything, except moderation." (Season 8)

"In business and in life, I wear many hats—and hairstyles." (Season 9)

"I won't settle for anything less than everything." (Season 10)

Adrienne Maloof

"Money is what I have, not who I am." (Season 1)

"Having it all is easy, if you're willing to work for it." (Season 2)

"Know your friends, show your enemies the door." (Season 3)

Teddi Mellencamp Arroyave

"Having the best isn't important to me, but being my best is." (Season 8)

"I'm not afraid of hard work, but I'll never do your dirty work." (Season 9)

"You never know what to expect when I'm expecting." (Season 10)

Denise Richards

"My problem with the tabloids? My real life is so much juicier." (Season 9)

"My life may not be a fairy tale, but I'll always get a happy ending." (Season 10)

Kim Richards

"I was a child star, but now my most important role is being a mother." (Season 1)

"People try to figure me out, but I'm one of a kind." (Season 2)

"Life is a journey, and I'm finding myself every day." (Season 3)

"Everybody loves a comeback story, especially starring me." (Season 4)

"I've been rich and I've been famous, but happiness beats them both." (Season 5)

Kyle Richards

"In a town full of phonies, I'm not afraid to be me." (Season 1)

"I'm not the richest girl in Beverly Hills, but I am the luckiest." (Season 2)

"I'm born and raised in Beverly Hills. This is my town." (Season 3)

"I'm from this town. I know what's real and I know what's fake." (Season 4)

"Planes and yachts are nice, but my happiness starts at home." (Season 5)

"In Beverly Hills you can be anything, but it's most important to be yourself." (Season 6)

"I'm an expert on luxury, and I can always spot a fake." (Season 7)

"In this town, fame and money come and go, but friends should not." (Season 8)

"In Beverly Hills, the truth always has a way of rising to the top." (Season 9)

"Around here, there's more than just dresses in everyone's closet." (Season 10)

Lisa Rinna

"You've heard a lot about me, but it's only true when it comes from my lips." (Season 5)

"My lips were made for talkin' and that's just what they'll do." (Season 6)

"My advice to you: don't hustle the hustler." (Season 7)

"I don't have to buy it, because I already own it." (Season 8)

"In the game of life, it's Rinna take all." (Season 9)

"The secret to life? Dance like everyone is watching." (Season 10)

Lisa Vanderpump

"In Beverly Hills it's who you know, and I know everyone." (Season 1)
"Life in Beverly Hills is a game, and I make the rules." (Season 2)
"Life isn't all diamonds and rosé, but it should be." (Season 3)
"Life is a sexy little dance, and I like to take the lead." (Season 4)
"Throw me to the wolves and I shall return leading the pack." (Season 5)
"I'm passionate about dogs, just not crazy about bitches." (Season 6)
"The crown is heavy, darlings. So just leave it where it belongs." (Season 7)
"The Queen of Diamonds always has an ace up her sleeve." (Season 8)
"You can stab me in the back, but whilst you're there, kiss my ass." (Season 9)

REAL HOUSEWIVES OF D.C.

Mary Schmidt Amons

"I don't make money, I spend money."

Lynda Erkiletian

"I give people enough rope to hang themselves, and the smart people don't."

Catherine Ommanney

"I'm here for a good time, not a long time."

Michaele Salahi

"People have a hard time saying no to me and that's just been my blessing."

Stacie Scott Turner

"D.C. is my town and I thrive in it."

REAL HOUSEWIVES OF DALLAS

Kary Brittingham

"I'm bilingual, but I don't speak B.S." (Season 4)
"If you take a shot at me, it better be tequila." (Season 5)

Cary Deuber

"I'm not a trophy wife! I'm a lifetime achievement award." (Season 1)
"Every girl has skeletons in her closet, mine are next to my Birkins." (Season 2)
"When life gets messy, just build a bigger closet." (Season 3)

Tiffany Hendra

"I came home to Dallas to shine my light, not to fight." (Season 1)

Stephanie Hollman

"I'm the girl next door, if you live in a big ol' mansion." (Season 1)
"I married into money, but family is my fortune." (Season 2)
"Investing in drama is not in my budget." (Season 3)
"I never carry a grudge; it won't match my shoes." (Season 4)
"I don't need your approval, I need you to get out of my way." (Season 5)

LeeAnne Locken

"I grew up a carnie kid. Play games with me, and you're gonna pay." (Season 1)

"I'm a true Texan, no bull, but all horns." (Season 2)

"You don't mess with Texas, and you don't mess with me." (Season 3)

Tiffany Moon

"I can save your life, but not your reputation." (Season 5)

Brandi Redmond

"I was a Cowboys cheerleader, but in Dallas I'm never on the sidelines." (Season 1)

"I cheered for the Cowboys, so I never get played." (Season 2)

"This isn't my first rodeo, so I'm not taking your bull." (Season 3)

"When you mess with a ginger, expect some spice." (Season 4)

"Take it from me: a sinner is just a saint who keeps on trying." (Season 5)

D'Andra Simmons

"I started from a Dallas dynasty, but I'll finish with my own empire." (Season 2)

"Running a family business is a job for one tough mother." (Season 3)

"I'm minding my business, so start minding yours." (Season 4)

"Dallas girls are sugar and spice . . . but I'm still working on nice." (Season 5)

Kameron Westcott

"Dumb blondes get noticed, smart blondes get everything." (Season 2)

"I have heels that are higher than your standards." (Season 3)

"Just because I look like Barbie, doesn't mean you can play me." (Season 4)

"I love to be pampered, but I'm nobody's pet." (Season 5)

REAL HOUSEWIVES OF MIAMI

Lea Black

"I care about a lot of things; what others think of me isn't one of them." (Season 1)

"I can deal with a lot, but I can't deal with stupid." (Season 2)

"I live my life like everything matters because I think it does." (Season 3)

Adriana de Moura

"I speak five languages, but I can get a man with no words." (Season 1)

"I may speak five languages, but my true language is independence." (Season 2)

"Some people say I have secrets, but I say I am full of surprises." (Season 3)

Alexia Echevarria

"Beauty is power, if you know how to use it." (Season 1)

"This Cuban doll is back on the scene and living the dream." (Season 3)

Lisa Hochstein

"My husband's a top plastic surgeon in this town, and I am his best creation." (Season 2)

"Everyone loves to underestimate me, and I love to prove everyone wrong."
(Season 3)

Joanna Krupa

"I'm a model, but not always a model citizen." (Season 2)

"Don't hate me because I have it all, hate me because I'm beautiful." (Season 3)

Marysol Patton

"I put others in the spotlight, but somehow it keeps finding me." (Season 1)

"My job is about making fast decisions, but my personal life I leave up to destiny." (Season 2)

Larsa Pippen

"My husband's got moves, but I run the game." (Season 1)

Ana Quincoces

"Whether in the courtroom or the kitchen, I bring the heat." (Season 2)

Cristy Rice

"In my world, attitude is everything. I'm keeping it real." (Season 1)

Karent Sierra

"If you don't like my smile, then don't look my way." (Season 2)

REAL HOUSEWIVES OF NEW JERSEY

Jennifer Aydin

"I'm obsessed with family, traditions, and Chanel." (Season 9)

"As I always say, 'plastic makes perfect.'" (Season 10)

Dolores Catania

"I was raised Jersey strong. Nothing can shake me." (Season 7)

"Look loyalty up in the dictionary, and you'll find my face." (Season 8)

"I may put up a tough front, but I'll never leave you behind." (Season 9)

"Behind every strong man is a stronger Jersey girl." (Season 10)

Siggy Flicker

"Some people think I'm too much. . . . They're absolutely right." (Season 7)

"My motto is 'know your worth; leave the rest to your plastic surgeon.'" (Season 8)

Teresa Giudice

"People make fun of Jersey girls, but I think they're just jealous." (Seasons 1 and 2)

"I'm a Jersey girl, no one can knock me down." (Season 3)

"When times get tough, you learn who your real friends are." (Season 4)

"Haters are gonna hate, but I just love, love, love." (Season 5)

"You never know how strong you are until it's the only choice you have." (Season 6)

"I used to flip tables, now I'm turning them." (Season 7)

"If you're not about the namaste, get the hell out of my way." (Season 8)

"These days, I don't throw punches. I roll with them." (Season 9)

"If you rub me the wrong way, there will be no more namaste." (Season 10)

Jackie Goldschneider

"I have four kids, two degrees, and one kick-ass life." (Season 9)

"Don't let the minivan fool you. This mom won't roll over for anyone." (Season 10)

Melissa Gorga

"I live a life that most girls only dream of." (Season 3)

"I never throw the first punch, but I'm always a knockout." (Season 4)

"Sexy life, loyal wife, take a page from my book." (Season 5)

"I've learned to forgive and never regret." (Season 6)

"I always act like a lady, but now I think like a boss." (Season 7)

"The only life I envy is my own." (Season 8)

"Don't try to bully me, because I'm a boss." (Season 9)

"Mirror, mirror on the wall, I don't think I look forty at all." (Season 10)

Margaret Josephs

"I bring the power, the pigtails, and the party." (Season 8)

"I can make you laugh or make you cry. Your choice!" (Season 9)

"If you can't take the truth, sue me." (Season 10)

Jacqueline Laurita

"Everyone likes to have nice things, but I'm not one to brag about it." (Seasons 1 and 2)

"I can hold my own. I am my own person." (Season 3)

"I am a Vegas girl; I will call your bluff." (Season 4)

"I've faced my share of challenges, but I'm tougher than I look." (Season 5)

"Fool me once, shame on me. Fool me twice, you better run." (Season 7)

Caroline Manzo

"If you're gonna mess with my family, you're messing with me." (Seasons 1 and 2)

"Life is about change; sometimes you just have to roll with the punches." (Season 3)

"Life is short. I have no time for drama." (Season 4)

"Love me or hate me, I always speak the truth." (Season 5)

Dina Manzo

"If you think I'm a bitch, then bring it on." (Seasons 1 and 2)

"I'm back to bring the Zen. Namaste, bitches!" (Season 6)

Amber Marchese

"I'm a survivor. No one is bringing me down." (Season 6)

Nicole Napolitano & Teresa Aprea

"You're not seeing double, you're seeing trouble!" (Season 6)

Danielle Staub

"You're either gonna love me or hate me. There is no in between with me." (Seasons 1 and 2)

Kathy Wakile

"People say that I'm sweet, but I'm tough, so don't cross me." (Season 3)

"We're old school; we believe in respect." (Season 4)

"If you can't take the heat, get out of my kitchen." (Season 5)

REAL HOUSEWIVES OF NEW YORK CITY

Cindy Barshop

"I have everything I've ever wanted, and it's all on my own terms." (Season 4)

Kelly Killoren Bensimon

"I've created a great life, and I love living it." (Seasons 2 and 3)

"I'm living the American Dream, one mistake at a time." (Season 4)

LuAnn de Lesseps

"I never feel guilty about being privileged." (Seasons 1, 2, and 3)

"I thought I had it good before, but I'm just getting started." (Season 4)

"To some people, living elegantly just comes naturally." (Season 5)

"One should know . . . never count out the countess." (Season 7)

"If you can't be cool, you can't be with the countess." (Season 8)

"The only title I'd trade countess for is wife." (Season 9)

"The most interesting people make the best headlines." (Season 10)

"I plead guilty to being fabulous." (Season 11)

"Raise the curtain, lower the lights, I'm taking center stage in my life." (Season 12, Part 1)

"I rise above the drama and won't settle for the lower level." (Season 12, Part 2)

Aviva Drescher

"Never underestimate a woman born and raised in New York City." (Season 5)

"When people tell me I'm fake, I know they're just pulling my leg." (Season 6)

Bethenny Frankel

"New York City is my playground." (Seasons 1, 2, and 3)

"I'm not a Housewife, but I am real." (Season 7)

"If you can't handle the truth, you can't handle me." (Season 8)

"If you're gonna take a shot at this B, you better not miss." (Season 9)

"It's great to be successful. But it's even better to B Strong." (Season 10)

"When life gives me limes, I make margaritas." (Season 11)

Alex McCord

"To a certain group of people in New York, status is everything." (Seasons 1, 2, and 3)

"I've always had opinions, but now people know it." (Season 4)

Leah McSweeney

"I may float like a butterfly, but I sting like a bitch." (Season 12, Part 1)

"I'll say sorry for what I've done but never for who I am." (Season 12, Part 2)

Dorinda Medley

"I give Uptown a whole new attitude." (Season 7)

"Diamonds aren't a girl's best friend, martinis are!" (Season 8)

"I tell it how it is, but I always keep it nice." (Season 9)

"I have a big heart, but little patience." (Season 10)

"If you've got a problem with me, it's your problem." (Season 11)

"I'm not always right, but I'm never wrong." (Season 12, Part 1)

"Like a mint in my mouth, I can be a bit fresh." (Season 12, Part 2)

Sonja Morgan

"I have a taste for luxury, and luxury has a taste for me." (Seasons 3 and 4)

"A little Sonja will spice up any party." (Season 5)

"Sometimes Sonja has to go commando. What can I say?" (Season 6)

"My yacht may have sailed, but my ship is comin' in." (Season 7)

"If being Sonja is so wrong, why does it feel so right?" (Season 8)

"There's nothing gray about my gardens." (Season 9)

"I'm not just a last name. I'm a legacy." (Season 10)

"People call me over-the-top, but lately I prefer being a bottom." (Season 11)

"I'm no one's accessory. I'm the whole lifestyle brand." (Season 12, Part 1)

"I'm no one's arm candy. I'm the whole bowl of sugar." (Season 12, Part 2)

Tinsley Mortimer

"A good set of lashes can fix anything . . . even a mug shot." (Season 9)

"Come on, why cook when I can order room service?!" (Season 10)

"Game, set, now I need a match." (Season 11)

"Life isn't a fairy tale, but I'm hoping mine's the exception." (Season 12)

Carole Radziwill

"I may be a princess, but I'm definitely not a drama queen." (Season 5)

"If you're going to talk about me behind my back, at least check out my great ass." (Season 6)

"All play and no work makes me a happy girl." (Season 7)

"I plan for the future, but live in the moment." (Season 8)

"In the politics of friendship, I win the popular vote." (Season 9)

"In the marathon of life, loyalty is everything." (Season 10)

Ramona Singer

"I like making my own money, I find that an aphrodisiac." (Seasons 1, 2, and 3)

"If people can't handle the truth, it's really not my problem." (Season 4)

"I'm not afraid to say what everyone else is thinking." (Season 5)

"Get the pinot ready, because it's Turtle Time!" (Season 6)

"I know I'm a piece of work, but now I'm a work in progress." (Season 7)

"Like a fine wine, I just get better with time." (Season 8)

"I'm an acquired taste. If you don't like me, acquire some taste!" (Season 9)

"Age is an issue of mind over matter: if you don't mind, it doesn't matter!" (Season 10)

"The only thing I'll settle for is more." (Season 11)

"I don't need to find love. I love myself." (Season 12, Part 1)

"So what if I'm self-involved? Who else should I be involved with?" (Season 12, Part 2)

Kristen Taekman

"I may not be the sharpest tool in the shed, but I'm pretty!" (Season 6)

"Pretty is smarter than you think." (Season 7)

Heather Thomson

"My success is built on making women look and feel their best. Holla!" (Season 5)

"A true New Yorker never backs down, and I'm no exception. Holla!" (Season 6)

"I'm stronger than anything in my way. Holla!" (Season 7)

Jules Wainstein

"A Jew and an Asian walked into a bar, then they had me!" (Season 8)

Jill Zarin

"I run with a fabulous circle of people." (Seasons 1, 2, and 3)

"Good or bad, I know who I am and I own it." (Season 4)

REAL HOUSEWIVES OF ORANGE COUNTY

Shannon Beador

"The OC is full of secrets, but I have nothing to hide." (Season 9)

"When life gives you lemons, put nine in a bowl!" (Season 10)

"Karma's a bitch, so I don't have to be one." (Season 11)

"The truth is organic, but lies are just artificial." (Season 12)

"Some people say I'm too much to handle. I say I'm just getting started." (Season 13)

"The tables have turned. And this time, I'm dancing on them." (Season 14)

"I've closed the old Bea-door and opened a new one." (Season 15)

Alexis Bellino

"Am I high maintenance? Of course I am, look at me." (Season 5)

"God is my savior, my husband is my king, and my body? It's sinful." (Season 6)

"I thank God every day for my life, and you would, too." (Season 7)

"I don't need to prove anything. I know who I am and God does, too." (Season 8)

Kimberly Bryant

"Eighty-five percent of the women around here have had breast implants." (Season 1)

Lynne Curtin

"I'm just your typical Orange County housewife. I am obsessed with being young." (Season 4)

"It's not about how much money you have, it's about how good you look spending it." (Season 5)

Jo De La Rosa

"He's pretty much keeping me." (Season 1)

"I deserve only the best. . . . I'm worth it!" (Season 2)

Kelly Dodd

"I don't throw parties, I am the party." (Season 11)

"If I want your opinion, I'll give it to you." (Season 12)

"Call animal control, 'cause there's a cougar on the loose in the OC." (Season 13)

"If you don't want me to cross the line, don't draw one." (Season 14)

"Don't judge me by what I do. In fact, just don't judge me at all." (Season 15)

Heather Dubrow

"I may be married to a plastic surgeon, but I'm 98 percent real." (Season 7)

"Whoever said blondes have more fun hasn't met me." (Season 8)

"You may think I have it all, but I'm just getting started." (Season 9)

"No one's life is perfect, but mine is pretty close." (Season 10)

"If at first you don't succeed, try it my way." (Season 11)

Quinn Fry

"I love having a younger man in my life." (Season 3)

Vicki Gunvalson

"I don't wanna get old." (Season 1)

"Here's to not being fake." (Season 2)

"Everything's got to be huge, large, and grand." (Season 3)

"I want the power and the money, and I want them both." (Season 4)

"I love my family, I love my work, I love my life." (Season 5)

"I make my own money, and I make my own rules." (Season 6)

"My tank is full and I'm driving into my future." (Season 7)

"I'm my own boss and it's time for a raise." (Season 8)

"I make my own rules, so don't expect me to follow yours." (Season 9)

"I am the OG of the OC; everyone else is just a copy." (Season 10)

"Before you judge me, you better be perfect." (Season 11)

"I go big or I go home, and I'm not going home." (Season 12)

"The fun bus is leaving, and this time *I'm* in the driver's seat." (Season 13)

Tamra Judge

"I'm the hottest housewife in Orange County." (Season 3)

"I'm not the new girl anymore, so watch out." (Season 4)

"Housewives come younger, but they don't come hotter." (Season 5)

"I'm done being a trophy wife; freedom only makes me hotter." (Season 6)

"I call the shots in my life now, and I have good aim." (Season 7)

"The best thing about starting over is never looking back." (Season 8)

"I'm not getting older, I'm just getting bolder." (Season 9)

"Boldness comes at a cost, and I'm willing to pay." (Season 10)

"My faith is strong, and my ass isn't bad, either." (Season 11)

"I'm pint-sized, baptized, and highly prized." (Season 12)

"I'm still the hottest Housewife in Orange County, and the toughest, too." (Season 13)

"These days faith, family, and fitness are the only F's I give." (Season 14)

Jeana Keough

"It's just money; you can't take it with you." (Season 1)

"I have always wanted things. I crave money." (Season 2)

"I love money and now I'm loving life." (Season 3)

"It doesn't matter what happens in life. I do it my way." (Season 4)

"Money is a girl's best friend, and I love friends." (Season 5)

Meghan King

"Now that I'm in the OC, it's a whole new ball game." (Season 10)

"In the game of life, I choose my team wisely." (Season 11)

"I can handle a baby, and women who act like one!" (Season 12)

Gina Kirschenheiter

"I speak the truth . . . even if it sounds funny when I say it." (Season 13)

"I've made mistakes in Orange County, but I'll fix them in a New York minute." (Season 14)

"Those who live in small houses should definitely throw stones." (Season 15)

Tammy Knickerbocker

"I don't let my kids or my exes drive me crazy." (Season 2)

"No matter how much money you have, you can always rely on others." (Season 3)

Lydia McLaughlin

"You only live once, but if you work it right, once is enough." (Season 8)

"If you can't take my sparkle, stay off my rainbow." (Season 12)

Lauri Peterson

"Are the police involved?" (Season 1)

"I was poor, I was rich, I was poor again, and you know what? Having money is easier." (Season 2)

"You know what, I'm living the OC lifestyle again. I feel like royalty." (Season 3)

"I still get pampered. I still get treated like a princess. I deserve it." (Season 4)

Gretchen Rossi

"I love the bling, I love the jewelry, I love it all." (Season 4)

"I'm smart, I'm sexy, and I'm confident. Of course people are gonna talk about me." (Season 5)

"Happiness means never having to apologize for being me." (Season 6)

"Don't call me a princess; call me the boss." (Season 7)

"When the going gets tough, I just get stronger and stronger." (Season 8)

Lizzie Rovsek

"Standing out is much more fun than fitting in." (Season 9)

Emily Simpson

"When you come from humble beginnings, you count your blessings . . . one diamond at a time." (Season 13)

"In a town full of blondes, I'm legally brunette." (Season 14)

"Life is full of beautiful curves and so am I." (Season 15)

Peggy Sulahian

"I'm living the American dream, one sports car at a time." (Season 12)

Peggy Tanous

"Soccer moms drive minivans, but this girl drives a Bentley." (Season 6)

Elizabeth Lyn Vargas

"I earned my money the old-fashioned way: marrying it, then making more." (Season 15)

Braunwyn Windham-Burke

"I manage to wrangle a family of nine and still look like a ten." (Season 14)

"Cheers to bad choices . . . then making better ones." (Season 15)

REAL HOUSEWIVES OF POTOMAC

Gizelle Bryant

"The word on the street is that I'm the word on the street." (Season 1)

"Word on the street is . . . I'm still the word on the street." (Season 2)

"If you can't handle me being the word on the street, then stop listening." (Season 3)

"I'm the baddest thing walking *and* the smartest one talking." (Season 4)

"I'm still the baddest thing walking and the most anointed one talking." (Season 5)

Ashley Darby

"Throw this spring chicken into the cougar's den and let the games begin." (Season 1)

"I've played by Potomac rules, but now it's time to play by my own." (Season 2)

"You may say I cause trouble, but I say I keep things interesting." (Season 3)

"Karma is a bitch, but luckily, I'm on her good side." (Season 4)

"Now that I have my baby, that's the only crap I take!" (Season 5)

Candiace Dillard Bassett

"Life is a pageant and I'm in it to win it." (Season 3)

"Now that I'm marrying my prince, this sleeping beauty is woke!" (Season 4)

"Reading is fundamental and honey, I own the library." (Season 5)

Robyn Dixon

"I don't have a cookie-cutter life and I'm not apologizing for it." (Season 1)

"Don't let the green eyes fool you, I'm as real as they come." (Season 2)

"Life has its ups and downs, but my game is on the rebound." (Season 3)

"The shorter my hair, the shorter my patience." (Season 4)

"I live in a house full of ballers, but I never get played." (Season 5)

Karen Huger

"In Potomac, it's not about who you know, it's who you are. And I'm everything." (Season 1)

"Potomac put me on a pedestal, and the view is spectacular." (Season 2)

"Baby, don't believe what you hear. The Grande Dame still holds center court." (Season 3)

"You can try to tear me down, but the Grande Dame never crumbles." (Season 4)

"Honey, the Grande Dame doesn't repeat history. She makes it." (Season 5)

Charrisse Jackson-Jordan

"If I don't know who you are, then you're not worth knowing." (Season 1)

"Why cry over spilled milk when you can laugh over champagne?" (Season 2)

Wendy Osefo

"The professor has arrived and class is officially in session." (Season 5)

Katie Rost

"I'm a ball and gala girl. It's my legacy and my calling." (Season 1)

Monique Samuels

"I may be rough around the edges, but baby, so are diamonds." (Season 2)

"You'll never put me in a box because I'm the whole darn package." (Season 3)

"I've traded in my umbrella. It's all gold at the end of this rainbow." (Season 4)

"Maybe if you tried a little harder, you wouldn't have to try me." (Season 5)

Author's Note

The responsibility of chronicling the history of the *Real Housewives* franchise is something that is not lost on this Bravo superfan, and I'm grateful to all of the incredible individuals who trusted me to tell their truths throughout this process.

This book was put together after interviewing more than 175 people connected to the show—from Housewives and Friends of, to producers, network executives, casting directors, and more. Over five hundred hours of conversations were collected, all conducted between June 2020 and July 2021.

Of course, books have page limits, and therefore, there was no way to truly "mention it all" (though, damn, I tried!). To set parameters, it was decided to chronicle the action from the franchise's premiere in March 2006 through November 2020.

While every effort was made to speak with all show stars, past and present, the following Bravolebrities chose not to participate: Brooks Ayers, Kimberly Bryant, Michael Darby, Allison Dubois, Dwight Eubanks, Kim Fields, Bethenny Frankel, Joyce Giraud, Joe Gorga, Danielle Gregorio, Joanna Krupa, NeNe Leakes, Erika Martin, Alex McCord, Demetria McKinney, Tiffany Moon, Tinsley Mortimer, Shamea Morton, Phaedra Parks, Lauri Peterson, Brandi Redmond, Faye Resnick, Denise Richards, Kim Richards, Gretchen Rossi, Michaele Salahi, Stacie Scott Turner, Slade Smiley, Simon van Kempen, Porsha Williams, Sarah Winchester, Lisa Wu, Marisa Zanuck, and Kim Zolciak-Biermann.

And regretfully, the following individuals' interviews did not make the final book: Lynda Erkiletian, Jennifer Gilbert, Katie Hamilton, Elaine Lancaster, Eli Lehrer, Robyn Levy, Cedric Martinez, Ben Medina, Cat Ommanney, Fernanda Rocha, Edwina Rogers, Amanda Sanders, Elyse Slaine, Lisa Spies, Paul Warton, and Dana Wilkey.

Acknowledgments

As Aviva Drescher famously once said, "It takes a village to write a book." And in this case, I had a whole city of people behind me.

None of this would have been possible without Barry Rosenberg, who believed in me from the beginning when I didn't even believe in myself. Thank you, Barry, for seeing my potential and being a constant champion. I'm so grateful for your friendship.

The incomparable Rachel Bertsche offered so many brilliant edits along the way, as well as invaluable encouragement at critical times of need. Lanford Beard, my dear friend and trusted colleague, graciously stepped in while I was drowning and helped me sift through hours of transcripts with ease. And James Melia, my talented editor, steered the ship and miraculously remained enthusiastic, even when I kept pushing back on deadlines. All three of you were paramount in getting this project over the finish line and I hope our paths cross again one day soon.

I am so blessed to have David Doerrer as my agent and confidant. Thank you for always having my back. And my lawyer, Jenn Hoffman, who provided such guidance.

To Jenn Geisser, Rebecca Boswell, Julia Nietsch, Chloe Elders, Sandra Lajoie, Imani Ellis, Toni Tonge, Axie Hulse, and the team at Bravo PR (past and present): thank you for all the support in scheduling. And to Kim McDade, one of a few people who truly understand the difficulty in juggling all these personalities. You're the best.

When I hit emotional roadblocks working on this book, I sought out advice from my brother, Danny Quinn, and my family of dear friends, like Dorothy McGoldrick, Paul Wontorek, Erica Reitman, Gage Edward, Kate Chastain, Amanda Long, Jackie Fields, Alicia Brady, K. C. Baker, Camille Beckles, Ben Liebman, Jen Abidor Eisenberg, Sara Wiesenfeld, and RJ & Kelly Friedman. I adore you all.

Kelly, Sara, and Jen all also generously logged in hours helping me transcribe interviews in my time of need, as did a bevy of kind individuals, listed here alphabetically: Jared Alexander, Michael Ampler, Ross Baron, Laura Berke Mottel, Joel Brady, Ashley Broder, David Carliner, Cindy Cee, Brian Connors, Meg Crane, Maddy Farkas, Clara Gainer, Heather Gershonowitz, Amanda Glodowski, Gina Gross, June Hong, Sue Irving, Grace Johnson, Max Marcus, Maira McDermott, Karen Ok, Amber Osterbrink, Billy Procida, Avery Richardson, Benno Rosenwald, Amanda Sabin, Sam Thor, Ben Vanhoose, and Matt Viera. Many, many thanks.

Two more things. First, I have to thank Andy Cohen for trusting me and allowing me this once-in-a-lifetime opportunity. Andy, I admire you so much and will forever be appreciative of the kindness and respect you have shown me. Thank you for changing my life. If you ever want to take a reunion off, I got you.

And lastly, to my man, Gus Constantellis: thank you for always being by my side, making me laugh, and offering me unconditional love, especially during times of unimaginable sadness. I love you, almost as much as you love Peanut.

This book is dedicated to Stella and Peanut, my angels above.

Photograph Credits

About the Author

An entertainment journalist and lifelong Bravo fan since back in the *Queer Eye for the Straight Guy* days, Dave Quinn has covered the Housewives for outlets like *People* and *Entertainment Weekly*. In addition to reviewing reality TV, much of Dave's career has been spent writing about theater—which, when combined with the Housewives, makes him an expert in drama. He lives in Park Slope, Brooklyn, with his boyfriend and the only thing worth putting in his will: a ginormous TV.

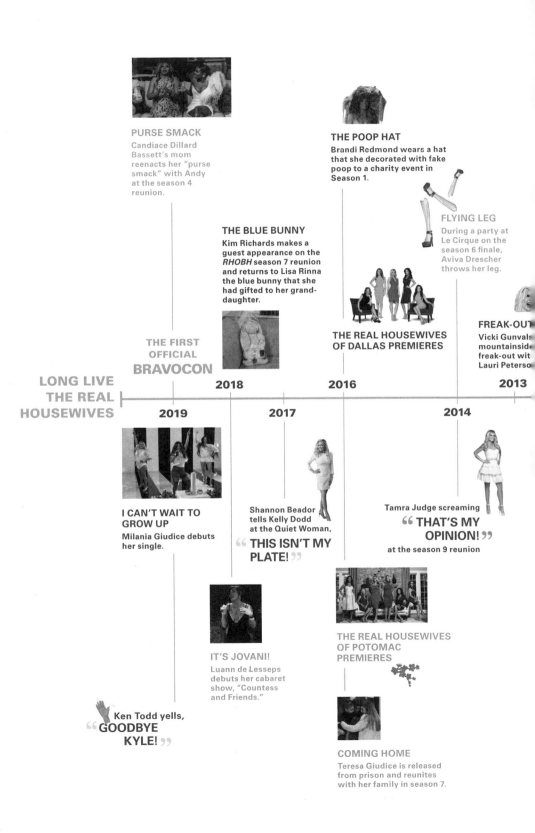

PURSE SMACK
Candiace Dillard
Bassett's mom
reenacts her "purse
smack" with Andy
at the season 4
reunion.

THE POOP HAT
Brandi Redmond wears a hat
that she decorated with fake
poop to a charity event in
Season 1.

FLYING LEG
During a party at
Le Cirque on the
season 6 finale,
Aviva Drescher
throws her leg.

THE BLUE BUNNY
Kim Richards makes a
guest appearance on the
RHOBH season 7 reunion
and returns to Lisa Rinna
the blue bunny that she
had gifted to her grand-
daughter.

**THE FIRST
OFFICIAL
BRAVOCON**

**THE REAL HOUSEWIVES
OF DALLAS PREMIERES**

FREAK-OU
Vicki Gunvals
mountainsid
freak-out wit
Lauri Peterso

**LONG LIVE
THE REAL
HOUSEWIVES**

2018   2016   2013

2019   2017   2014

**I CAN'T WAIT TO
GROW UP**
Milania Giudice debuts
her single.

Shannon Beador
tells Kelly Dodd
at the Quiet Woman,
" **THIS ISN'T MY
PLATE!** "

Tamra Judge screaming
" **THAT'S MY
OPINION!** "
at the season 9 reunion

IT'S JOVANI!
Luann de Lesseps
debuts her cabaret
show, "Countess
and Friends."

**THE REAL HOUSEWIVES
OF POTOMAC
PREMIERES**

Ken Todd yells,
" **GOODBYE
KYLE!** "

COMING HOME
Teresa Giudice is released
from prison and reunites
with her family in season 7.